The World
ATLAS OF WINE

FIRESIDE

The World
ATLAS
A Complete Guide to the Wines & Spir

OF WINE

of the World/Hugh Johnson

A Fireside Book
Published by
Simon and Schuster

The help of innumerable institutions and individuals has been vital to the completeness and authority of this book. Among them the publishers particularly wish to thank:

The Office International de la Vigne et du Vin, Paris

Institut National des Appellations d'Origine des Vins et Eaux-de-Vie, Paris

Ministerium für Landwirtschaft, Weinbau und Forsten, Mainz

The Staatsdomänen of Hessen, Mosel-Saar-Ruwer, Nahe

The Istituto Nazionale per il Commercio Estero, Rome

Casa do Douro, Régua

Sindicato Nacional de la Vid, Madrid

Consejo Regulador de Denominación de Origen Jerez, Jerez de la Frontera

The Wine Institute, San Francisco

The Madeira Wines Bureau, London

The South Australian Department of Agriculture, Adelaide

The Scotch Whisky Association, London

The Bourbon Institute, New York

The Institut Technique du Vin, Paris

The regional Comités Interprofessionnels in France, Weinbauämter in Germany, Consorzi in Italy, Consejos Reguladores in Spain, the Commercial Counsellors of the London Embassies of all wine-growing countries; University Departments in France, Germany, California, Australia, and scores of wine-growers and wine-shippers all over the world.

A more complete list of sources appears on page 256

Every effort has been made to make the maps in this atlas as complete and up-to-date as possible. In order that future editions may be kept up to this standard the publishers will be very grateful for any information about errors, or changes of boundaries or names, which should be recorded

The World Atlas of Wine copyright © Mitchell Beazley Limited 1971
Text copyright © Hugh Johnson 1971
Maps and graphics copyright © Mitchell Beazley Limited 1971
The World Atlas of Wine was prepared and designed under the direction and control of
Mitchell Beazley Limited
14–15 Manette Street, London W1V 5LB
A Fireside Book
Published in the United States by Simon and Schuster
A Gulf+Western Company
Rockefeller Center, 630 Fifth Avenue
New York, New York 10020

ISBN 0–671–21109–9
ISBN 0–671–22417–4 pbk.
Library of Congress Catalog
Card Number 71–163481
Cartography by Fairey Surveys Limited
Reform Road, Maidenhead, Berkshire
Typesetting by Yendall & Co Limited, London
Printed and bound in America
by Banta Division
George Banta Company, Inc.

1|2|3|4|5|6|7|8|9|10

Contents

Le Directeur

PARIS (8e)
138, CHAMPS-ÉLYSÉES
TÉL. 225.54.75

C'est avec un grand plaisir qu'en ma qualité de Directeur de l'INSTITUT NATIONAL DES APPELLATIONS D'ORIGINE DES VINS ET EAUX-DE-VIE DE FRANCE, je présente au lecteur "L'ATLAS DES VINS DU MONDE", édité par Mitchell BEAZLEY.

En premier, parce qu'un jeune écrivain anglais, Mr Hugh JOHNSON, qui avait déjà montré son talent dans un précédent ouvrage consacré à la vigne et au vin, a eu l'ambition et le courage d'entreprendre une oeuvre qui pouvait faire hésiter les écrivains les plus avertis en ce domaine. Et je suis fier de l'en féliciter.

En second, parce que depuis plus de trente ans la politique constante de l'Institut National des Appellations d'Origine a été de défendre que la qualité et le caractère d'un vin dépendent du terroir et de l'homme: du terroir par la nature du sol et du sous-sol, de l'exposition et de l'altitude; de l'homme par les choix qu'il a su faire des cépages, des méthodes de culture et de vinification, des soins qu'il apporte à son vin jusqu'à la mise en bouteille. Et il m'est agréable d'avoir la preuve aujourd'hui, dans un Atlas, que la route suivie était la bonne et restera la bonne.

Cet ATLAS DES VINS DU MONDE est d'une précision remarquable et le soin apporté à la réalisation de l'ouvrage lui donne une valeur internationale permanente.

Il pourra figurer en bonne place dans les bibliothèques des amateurs et de ceux qui ont profession de produire et de vendre le vin, les uns comme les autres y trouvant la satisfaction de mieux comprendre cette admirable géographie de la vigne, étroitement liée au cours des siècles à l'histoire des civilisations.

L'I.N.A.O. a été associé au tracé des cartes françaises, tout comme les services officiels de chaque pays ont contribué à aider l'auteur dans ses patientes et minutieuses recherches.

Nous sommes certains que les talents de l'écrivain sauront présenter les cartes avec objectivité, et il est permis de considérer ce livre comme un évènement majeur de la littérature vinicole.-

Jean PERRACHON
Ingénieur général du Génie rural,
des Eaux et des Forêts.

7

Introduction

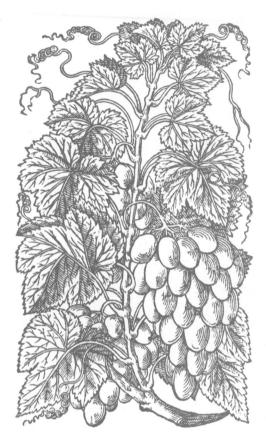

Opposite page: bread and wine, since ancient times the staples of life. This picture is a detail from Caravaggio's *Supper at Emmaus*, painted about 1602 in Rome, now in the National Gallery, London

MAPS, to me, since first I started on the happily absorbing study of wine, have been the vital, logical ally. Even the roughest sketch-map has always helped me, as a framework for organizing memories and impressions. With a map, distinctions and relationships become clear. Things fall into place.

This is how this atlas came into being. Bit by bit it dawned on me that maps on a large enough scale are more than aids to navigation: they are pictures of the ground and what goes on on it. That it was possible, as it were, to take a reader up into a high mountain and show him all the vineyards of the earth.

The relation between maps and wine is a very intimate one. Wine is, after all, the unique agricultural product whose price depends entirely on where it comes from. The better the wine, the more exactly it locates its origin—down, eventually, to one diminutive field in a simple village lying under what Stendhal described as 'an ugly dried-up little hill': named Romanée-Conti.

We have only to see how eerily accurate classifications of quality can remain for over a century to realize that it is the exact spot of earth which is the governing factor. Men change; techniques and fashions change; owners, machines, even the climate changes. What does not change is the soil, the elevation, the exposure. The trial and error of centuries has established where they are best—yet strange to say they have never been comprehensively mapped.

There is one classic wine atlas, Louis Larmat's *Atlas de la France Vinicole*. It was published with the help of the French wine authorities in the 1940s. It is incomplete, even of France, but some of its maps are masterpieces which will not be surpassed. They are, however, out of print.

Of Germany there is nothing comparable. Nor of Italy, nor Spain, nor Portugal, nor any of the wine-growing countries of the New World. Such maps as exist tend to be preoccupied with legal boundaries rather than with topography and viticultural detail.

The emphasis of this atlas is on the consumer's point of view. Faced with the impossibility of mapping all vineyards in the same detail, I had to find a scale of priorities. The scale I have used is more or less that of one of the great wine merchants of London, New York, San Francisco or Bristol—the places in the world where the widest range of good wines is to be found. Only outside wine-growing Europe do such all-embracing, balanced selections exist: a great Moselle wine is not to be found in Paris—still less in Bordeaux.

There was no question of finding one style or one set of criteria to apply to every map. For the very fact which is most enthralling about wine is that no two regions have the same standards, or place emphasis on the same things. In Burgundy there is the most complex grading of fields ever attempted: each field, and even parts of fields, being classified in a hierarchy which is cut-and-dried. In parts of Bordeaux there is a formal grading of properties; not directly related to the land but to the estates on it. In Germany there is no land classification at all, but an ingenious hierarchy of ripeness. In Champagne whole villages are classed, in Jerez soils of certain kinds, in Italy some traditional wine zones, but not others.

Yet behind all this tangle of nomenclature and classification lies the physical fact of the hills and valleys where the vine grows. In each case I have tried to make it plain, so far as I have been able to discover, not only which corner of the countryside gives the best wine, but why; what happy accident of nature has led (in many cases) to the development of a classic taste which has become familiar to half the world.

If the maps succeed in portraying wine-country clearly and appealingly, as I believe they do, it is largely due to the care and vision of Harold Fullard, the cartographer, to whom I and the publishers are deeply indebted.

There are reproductions of paintings; music has scores; poems are printed; architecture can be drawn—but wine is a fleeting moment. One cannot write about wine, and stumble among the borrowed words and phrases which have to serve to describe it, without wanting to put a glass in the reader's hand and say 'Taste this'. For it is not every Nuits-St-Georges which answers the glowing terms of a general description—the corner shops of the world are awash with wine which bears little relation to the true character of the land.

This is the object of giving the most direct form of reference available: the labels of 900 producers whose wines and spirits truly represent the subject-matter of the atlas. Among the many thousands who qualify in every way to be included, the choice of which to use was almost impossible. As it stands it is partly personal, as anything to do with taste must be, and partly arbitrary, as the limitations of space ruthlessly cut out firm favourites. In the case of one or two countries, notably Russia, it was also hampered by the magnificent glue used to attach the labels to bottles.

No book like this could be attempted without the generous help of authorities in all the countries it deals with. Their enthusiasm and painstaking care have made it possible. On pages 4 and 256 there are lists of government and local offices, and some of the hundreds of others, growers, merchants and scholars, who have so kindly helped, and to whom I owe the great volume of information embodied both in the maps and the text. The facts are theirs; unless I quote a source, on the other hand, I must be held responsible for the opinions.

There is only room here to thank by name the Director, the Chef Technique Pierre Bréjoux, and the staff of the Institut National des Appellations d'Origine des Vins et Eaux-de-Vie in Paris who checked all the French maps; Dr Renz and his assistant Dr Hämmerling of the Statistisches Landesamt Rheinland-Pfalz who guided me through the shoals of the new German wine laws, and Peter Hasslacher, of Deinhard's, who accompanied me on numerous trips to Germany while the laws were in preparation; the Wine Institute in San Francisco and the KWV in South Africa who undertook extensive original map research for the atlas; and my diplomatic, patient, gay and indefatigable assistant, Colette Lebreton.

9

The World of Wine

The distribution of the world's vineyards by countries, in thousands of hectares

Wine growing is mainly confined to the temperate zones (shaded on map)

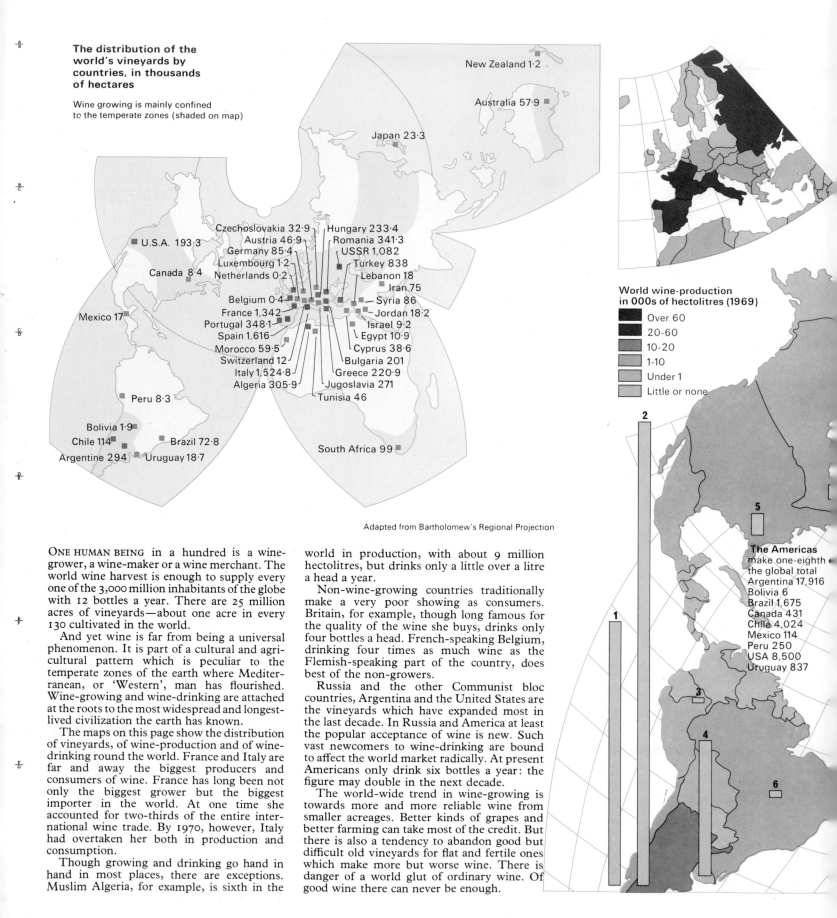

New Zealand 1·2
Australia 57·9
Japan 23·3

U.S.A. 193·3
Canada 8·4
Mexico 17
Peru 8·3
Bolivia 1·9
Chile 114
Argentine 294
Uruguay 18·7
Brazil 72·8

Czechoslovakia 32·9
Austria 46·9
Germany 85·4
Luxembourg 1·2
Netherlands 0·2
Belgium 0·4
France 1,342
Portugal 348·1
Spain 1,616
Morocco 59·5
Switzerland 12
Italy 1,524·8
Algeria 305·9

Hungary 233·4
Romania 341·3
USSR 1,082
Turkey 838
Lebanon 18
Iran 75
Syria 86
Jordan 18·2
Israel 9·2
Egypt 10·9
Cyprus 38·6
Bulgaria 201
Greece 220·9
Jugoslavia 271
Tunisia 46

South Africa 99

Adapted from Bartholomew's Regional Projection

World wine-production in 000s of hectolitres (1969)

- Over 60
- 20-60
- 10-20
- 1-10
- Under 1
- Little or none

The Americas make one-eighth the global total
Argentina 17,916
Bolivia 6
Brazil 1,675
Canada 431
Chile 4,024
Mexico 114
Peru 250
USA 8,500
Uruguay 837

ONE HUMAN BEING in a hundred is a wine-grower, a wine-maker or a wine merchant. The world wine harvest is enough to supply every one of the 3,000 million inhabitants of the globe with 12 bottles a year. There are 25 million acres of vineyards—about one acre in every 130 cultivated in the world.

And yet wine is far from being a universal phenomenon. It is part of a cultural and agricultural pattern which is peculiar to the temperate zones of the earth where Mediterranean, or 'Western', man has flourished. Wine-growing and wine-drinking are attached at the roots to the most widespread and longest-lived civilization the earth has known.

The maps on this page show the distribution of vineyards, of wine-production and of wine-drinking round the world. France and Italy are far and away the biggest producers and consumers of wine. France has long been not only the biggest grower but the biggest importer in the world. At one time she accounted for two-thirds of the entire international wine trade. By 1970, however, Italy had overtaken her both in production and consumption.

Though growing and drinking go hand in hand in most places, there are exceptions. Muslim Algeria, for example, is sixth in the world in production, with about 9 million hectolitres, but drinks only a little over a litre a head a year.

Non-wine-growing countries traditionally make a very poor showing as consumers. Britain, for example, though long famous for the quality of the wine she buys, drinks only four bottles a head. French-speaking Belgium, drinking four times as much wine as the Flemish-speaking part of the country, does best of the non-growers.

Russia and the other Communist bloc countries, Argentina and the United States are the vineyards which have expanded most in the last decade. In Russia and America at least the popular acceptance of wine is new. Such vast newcomers to wine-drinking are bound to affect the world market radically. At present Americans only drink six bottles a year: the figure may double in the next decade.

The world-wide trend in wine-growing is towards more and more reliable wine from smaller acreages. Better kinds of grapes and better farming can take most of the credit. But there is also a tendency to abandon good but difficult old vineyards for flat and fertile ones which make more but worse wine. There is danger of a world glut of ordinary wine. Of good wine there can never be enough.

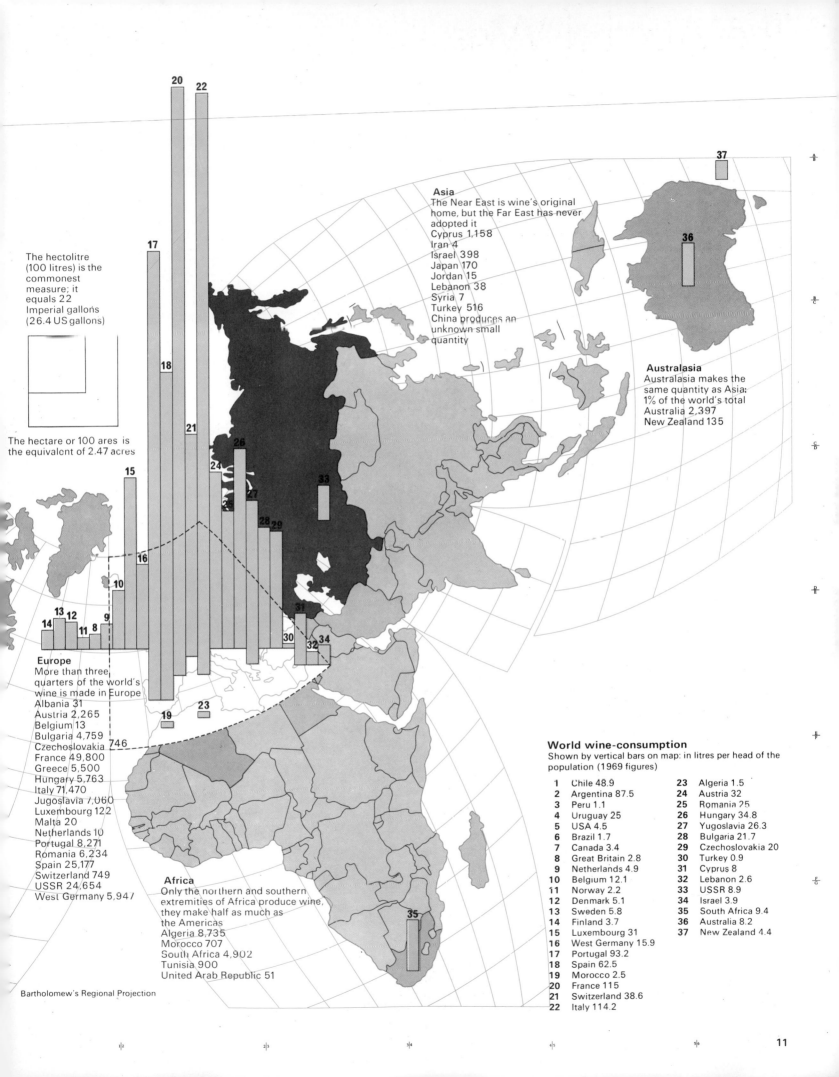

The hectolitre (100 litres) is the commonest measure; it equals 22 Imperial gallons (26.4 US gallons)

The hectare or 100 ares is the equivalent of 2.47 acres

Asia
The Near East is wine's original home, but the Far East has never adopted it
Cyprus 1,158
Iran 4
Israel 398
Japan 170
Jordan 15
Lebanon 38
Syria 7
Turkey 516
China produces an unknown small quantity

Australasia
Australasia makes the same quantity as Asia: 1% of the world's total
Australia 2,397
New Zealand 135

Europe
More than three quarters of the world's wine is made in Europe
Albania 31
Austria 2,265
Belgium 13
Bulgaria 4,759
Czechoslovakia 746
France 49,800
Greece 5,500
Hungary 5,763
Italy 71,470
Jugoslavia 7,060
Luxembourg 122
Malta 20
Netherlands 10
Portugal 8,271
Romania 6,234
Spain 25,177
Switzerland 749
USSR 24,654
West Germany 5,947

Africa
Only the northern and southern extremities of Africa produce wine, they make half as much as the Americas
Algeria 8,735
Morocco 707
South Africa 4,902
Tunisia 900
United Arab Republic 51

World wine-consumption
Shown by vertical bars on map: in litres per head of the population (1969 figures)

1	Chile 48.9	23	Algeria 1.5
2	Argentina 87.5	24	Austria 32
3	Peru 1.1	25	Romania 25
4	Uruguay 25	26	Hungary 34.8
5	USA 4.5	27	Yugoslavia 26.3
6	Brazil 1.7	28	Bulgaria 21.7
7	Canada 3.4	29	Czechoslovakia 20
8	Great Britain 2.8	30	Turkey 0.9
9	Netherlands 4.9	31	Cyprus 8
10	Belgium 12.1	32	Lebanon 2.6
11	Norway 2.2	33	USSR 8.9
12	Denmark 5.1	34	Israel 3.9
13	Sweden 5.8	35	South Africa 9.4
14	Finland 3.7	36	Australia 8.2
15	Luxembourg 31	37	New Zealand 4.4
16	West Germany 15.9		
17	Portugal 93.2		
18	Spain 62.5		
19	Morocco 2.5		
20	France 115		
21	Switzerland 38.6		
22	Italy 114.2		

Bartholomew's Regional Projection

The Ancient World

The history of wine runs back before our knowledge. It emerges with civilization itself from the east. The evidence from tablets and papyri and tombs can—and does—fill volumes. Man as we know him, working and worrying man, comes on the scene with the support of a jug of wine.

Historical evidence gets closer to our experience with the expansion of the Greek empire, starting a thousand years before Christ. It was then that wine first met the countries it was to make its real home: Italy and France. The Greeks called Italy the Land of Vines, just as the Vikings called America Vinland from the profusion of its native vines 2,000 years later. It seems probable that North Africa, Andalusia, Provence, Sicily and the Italian mainland had their first vineyards in the time of the Greek empire.

The wines of Greece herself, no great matter today, were lavishly praised and generously documented by her poets. There was even a fashionable after-dinner game in Athens which consisted of throwing the last inch or so of wine in your cup into the air, to hit a delicately-balanced dish on a pole. Smart young things took coaching in the finer points of 'kottabos'. But such treatment of the wine, and the knowledge that jugs of hot water for diluting it were on every table, makes it seem improbable that the wine was very good. What would have been nectar to Homer, or even to Jove, would probably seem to us like an oversweet vin rosé, possibly with a flavour of muscat, possibly

tasting of resin, and possibly concentrated by cooking, and needing dilution before drinking.

So much was written about wine and wine-making in ancient Rome that it is possible to make a rough map (right) of the wines of the early Roman empire. The greatest writers, even Virgil, wrote instructions to wine-growers. One sentence of his—'Vines love an open hill'—might be called the best single piece of advice which can be given to a wine-grower.

There has been much speculation about the quality of Roman wine. It apparently had extraordinary powers of keeping, which in itself suggests that it was good. The great vintages were discussed and even drunk for longer than seems possible; the famous Opimian—from the year of the consulship of Opimius, 121 BC—was being drunk even when it was 125 years old.

Certainly the Romans had all that is necessary for aging wine. They were not limited to earthenware amphoras like the Greeks—although they too used them. They had barrels just like modern barrels and bottles not unlike modern bottles. It is reasonable to suppose that most Italians of 2,000 years ago drank wine very like their descendants' today; young, rather roughly made, sharp or strong according to the summer weather. The Roman method of cultivation of the vine on trees, in the festoons which became the friezes on classical buildings, is still practised, particularly in the south of Italy and northern Portugal.

But the move of most consequence for history

Above right: this Egyptian painting of treaders under an arbour of vines comes from the tomb of Nakht, a Theban official who died in the 15th century BC
Below: feast scenes are one of the favourite motifs of Greek vase-painting. On a wine-vase of about 480 BC (in the British Museum) the left-hand guest is playing the fashionable after-dinner game of kottabos, which consisted of throwing the last of the wine in the cup at a special mark, a dish balanced on a pole

Left: the early movements of the vine. Starting in Caucasia or Mesopotamia 1 in perhaps 6000 BC it was cultivated in Egypt and Phoenicia 2 in about 3000 BC. By 2000 BC it was in Greece 3 and by 1000 BC it was in Italy, Sicily and North Africa 4. In the next 500 years it reached at least Spain, Portugal, and the south of France 5, and probably southern Russia as well. Finally (see map on opposite page) it spread with the Romans into northern Europe 6, getting as far as Britain

Below: the wines the Romans drank; a reconstruction of wine-growing Italy in AD 100. Names of modern cities are given in italics; wine names in Roman type

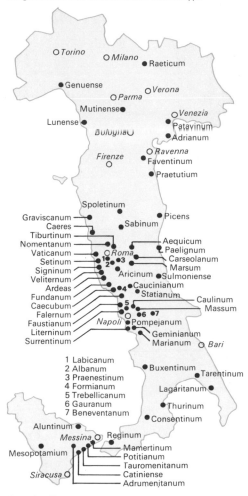

- Torino
- Milano
- Raeticum
- Genuense
- Verona
- Parma
- Mutinense
- Venezia
- Lunense
- Patavinum
- Bologna
- Adrianum
- Ravenna
- Firenze
- Faventinum
- Praetutium
- Spoletinum
- Picens
- Graviscanum
- Sabinum
- Caeres
- Tiburtinum
- Nomentanum
- Aequicum
- Vaticanum
- Paelignum
- Roma
- Carseolanum
- Setinum
- Marsum
- Signinum
- Aricinum
- Sulmoniense
- Veliternum
- Caucinianum
- Ardeas
- Statianum
- Fundanum
- Caulinum
- Caecubum
- Massum
- Falernum
- Faustianum
- Pompejanum
- Literninum
- Napoli
- Surrentinum
- Geminianum
- Marianum
- Bari

1 Labicanum
2 Albanum
3 Praenestinum
4 Formianum
5 Trebellicanum
6 Gauranum
7 Beneventanum

- Buxentinum
- Tarentinum
- Lagaritanum
- Thurinum
- Consentinum
- Aluntinum
- Messina
- Reginum
- Mesopotamium
- Mamertinum
- Potitianum
- Tauromenitanum
- Siracusa
- Catiniense
- Adrumenjtanum

that the Romans made with their vines was to take them to Gaul. By the time they withdrew from what is now France in the fifth century they had laid the foundations for almost all the greatest vineyards of the modern world.

Starting in Provence, which had had vineyards already for centuries, they moved up the Rhône valley, and across (or by sea?) to Bordeaux in the time of Caesar. All the early developments were in the river valleys, the natural lines of communication, which the Romans cleared of forest and cultivated. They found that vineyards had a settling and civilizing effect on the population. Besides, boats were the only way of moving anything so heavy as wine. But they must also have found, as we still do, what a beneficent effect a nearby river has on vines.

By the second century they had vines in Burgundy; by the third on the Loire; and by the fourth at Paris (not such a good idea), in Champagne, and on the Moselle and the Rhine. Languedoc and the Auvergne also had vineyards. It seems that Alsace is the only major French wine region not to have Roman origins at least in part. It had to wait until about the ninth century.

Above: the Romans interpreted the graceful Greek wine god Dionysus as a more fleshly creature; in a mosaic from Pompeii, now in the Museo Nazionale, Naples, he rides his traditional mount, a lion, but boozes from a monstrous pot
Left and below: barrels were used by the Romans. These were found being used as the linings of wells at Silchester in southern England, and are now in Reading Museum

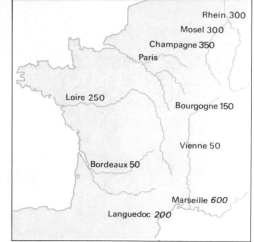

- Rhein 300
- Mosel 300
- Champagne 350
- Paris
- Loire 250
- Bourgogne 150
- Vienne 50
- Bordeaux 50
- Marseille 600
- Languedoc 200

Above: the vineyards of France and Germany at the fall of the Roman Empire. The dates of their founding are mainly conjectural. Vineyards in the Languedoc and Marseille (BC dates in italics) were founded by the Greeks; the rest by the Romans in the heyday of Roman Gaul. The history of all these vineyards has been continuous; Alsace—which does not appear here—was probably founded in about AD 800

The Middle Ages

UT OF the Dark Ages which followed the fall of the Roman Empire we emerge into the illumination of the mediaeval period, to see in its lovely painted pages an entirely familiar scene; one which was not to change in its essentials until this century. The Church had been the repository of the skills of civilization in the Dark Ages. As expansionist monasteries cleared hillsides and walled round fields of cuttings, as dying wine-growers bequeathed it their land, the Church came to be identified with wine—not only as the Blood of Christ, but as luxury and comfort in this world. For centuries it owned many of the greatest vineyards of Europe. Within this stable framework, in which tools and terms and techniques seemed to stand still, the styles of wine familiar to us now slowly came into being.

Above: tying up the vines; see opposite page
Below: in the Bayeux tapestry, Bishop Odo blesses wine before the invasion of England

Above: wine had an important place in mediaeval life as part of both Jewish and Christian observance. This picture of a Jewish Passover comes from an early 14th-century haggadah from northern Spain or Provence

The illuminated capital at the top of this page is from a Northern French manuscript of about 1320

Left: picking the grapes. The crisp and expressive little woodcuts which illustrated the 1493 Speyer edition of Piero Crescentio's *Opus Ruralium Commodorum* have been reprinted constantly ever since (this and opposite page)

Below: in 1497 the Royal Exchequer of England laid down that eight gallons make one Winchester bushel; and 'too pottelys maketh one gallon'. The Winchester bushel is still a legal measure in the USA

Left: a late 15th-century tapestry in the Musée de Cluny in Paris shows the court happily obstructing the vintagers in their work on the banks of the Loire

Right: English wine measures of 1497 included a hogshead (63 gallons), a pipe (two hogsheads) and a tonne (two pipes). The size of ships was measured by the number of tonnes they could carry

Above: the most sumptuous of all the famous prayer-books of the Middle Ages was the Très Riches Heures painted for Jean, Duc de Berry by Pol Limbourg and his brothers about 1416. The month of September is represented by the homely scene of the vintage, under the splendid battlements of Saumur

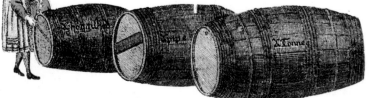

The Evolution of Modern Wine

IT IS POSSIBLE to piece together, from the first enthusiastic mentions of particular growths in the 17th century, the rise of reputations and the evolution of our modern wines. For none of the familiar types sprang fully-grown from the head of Bacchus. Nor is their evolution complete today: change continues. Burgundy, within the last 15 years, has seen a swing to much lighter wines, paler, with less depth of flavour and less able to mature—and the start of a swing back to the old style of dark and deep.

It is hard to have confidence in the descriptions of wine which survive from before about 1700. With the exception of Shakespeare's graphic tasting notes: 'a marvellous searching wine, and it perfumes the blood ere one can say "What's this?"', they tend to refer to royal recommendations or miraculous cures rather than to taste and characteristics.

Burgundy comes into focus in the 18th century: white wines 'spirity, faintly bubbly, fine and clear as spring water'; 'delicate pink wine' from Savigny. Nuits is 'wine to keep for the following year', in contrast to all the others, which were wines to drink as soon as the winter weather had cleared them. There was no call for strong, firm burgundy to lay down. Nobody knew what marvellous searching stuff it could be. Among the *vins de primeur* the first choice was Volnay.

But by the early 19th century there had been a complete revolution. Suddenly the vin rosés went out of fashion; the demand was for long-fermented, dark-coloured wine. In the Côte de Beaune, whose wines are naturally light, prices dropped. Demand moved to the Côte de Nuits, whose wines are naturally *vins de garde*—wines to keep and mature.

The explanation of the change was the discovery of the effect on wine of storing it in bottles. Since Roman times it had spent all its life in a barrel. If bottles were used they were simply carafes for serving at table. But late in the 17th century someone discovered the cork. Bit by bit it became clear that wine kept in a

A famous but anonymous English print of 1778 is the first known illustration of the corkscrew, the instrument which with the bottle and the cork brought in the age of great long-matured wines in the 18th century

tightly-corked bottle lasted much longer than wine kept in a barrel, which was likely to go off at any time after the barrel was broached. It also aged in a different way; acquiring what is known as a 'bouquet'.

The wine that benefited most from this treatment was the fiery port the English had started to drink in the late 17th century. They had doubts about it at first, but as the century, and their bottles, grew older, their opinion of it rose sharply.

The trend is graphically illustrated by the way the port bottle changed shape from a carafe within a hundred years. The old model would not lie down, so its cork dried out. The slimmer bottle is easy to 'bin' horizontally in heaps.

Before long the benefits of bottle-age were beginning to change the style of all the best wines of Europe.

In 1866 A. Jullien published the figures for the alcoholic strengths of recent vintages. By today's standards the burgundies are formidable: Corton 1858, 15.6%; Montrachet 1858, 14.3%; Clos de Bèze 1858, 14.3%; Volnay 1859, 14.9%; Richebourg 1859, 14.3%. In contrast the wines of Bordeaux in the same two years ranged from 11.3% (St-Emilion Supérieur) to 8.9% (Château Lafite).

The low natural strength of the Bordeaux wines explains what seems today a curious habit of the old wine trade. Up to the mid-century the Bordeaux wines for England—which was most of the best of them—were subjected to what was known as *le travail à l'anglaise*. The recipe called for 30 litres of Spanish wine (Alicante or Benicarlo), 2 litres of unfermented white must and a bottle of brandy to each barrel of claret. The summer after the vintage the wine was set to ferment again with these additives, then treated as other wines and kept several years in wood before shipping. The result was strong wine with a good flavour, but 'heady and not suitable for all stomachs'. It fetched more than natural wine.

Today's preoccupation with authenticity, even at the expense of quality, makes these practices seem abusive. But it is rather as though someone revealed as a shocking instance of fraud the fact that brandy is added to port. We like Douro wine with brandy in it; our ancestors liked Lafite with Alicante in it.

German wines of the last century would be scarcely more familiar to us. It is doubtful whether any of today's pale, rather sweet, intensely perfumed wines were made. Grapes picked earlier gave more acid wine which needed longer to mature in cask. People liked the flavour of oak—or even the flavour of oxidization from too much contact with the air. 'Old brown hock' was a recommendation, whereas today it would be as rude a

Below: the evolution of the port bottle in the century from 1708 when it was a carafe to 1812 when it had reached its modern proportions is the vivid record of the emergence of vintage wine. As it was discovered that bottled and corked wine improved immeasurably with keeping, bottles began to be designed to be 'laid down' on their sides. This collection of bottles is at Berry Bros & Rudd, the London wine merchants

1708   1719   1739   1741   1753

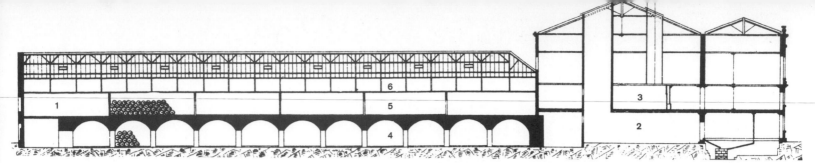

Above and right: the late 18th century saw Bordeaux rebuilt as a magnificent city in classical stone. The big wine shippers established spacious cellars along the quays. These engravings show the plan of a shipping house in the last century. **1** is the entrance hall and offices; **2** are the bottle cellars; **3** is the packing room where bottles are wrapped and cased; **4** is the barrel cellar or *chai*; **5** and **6** are two more floors of barrels; **7** is the cooperage for making barrels; **8** is the covered yard
Below: great estates like Château Beychevelle, built in 1757 in St-Julien, were arising at the same time

remark as you could write on a tasting card.

Champagne too was fuller in colour and flavour—though otherwise very like it is today. Port and sherry had both been perfected. There was much more strong sweet wine from the Mediterranean to be seen: Malaga and Marsala were in their heydays. Madeira, Constantia and Tokay were all as highly regarded as the Trockenbeerenausleses of modern Germany.

The wine trade was booming. In the wine-growing countries an unhealthy amount of the economy rested on wine: in Italy in 1880 it was calculated that no less than 80% of the population more or less relied on wine for a living. This was the world phylloxera struck like a plague.

The methods of this little bug are described on pages 18–19. At the time, when he had succeeded in destroying or causing the pulling up of almost every vine in Europe, it seemed like the end of the world of wine.

The last 80 years have seen wine's Industrial Revolution. More particularly in the last 20 years, the scientific background to wine-making has become so much clearer that many things which were thought impossible before have become easy. Thoroughly bad wine anywhere is now almost a rarity. The New World has wine as good as any but the best of the old.

At the same time have come temptations to lower the standards of the best, to make more wine at the expense of quality.

But worse by far is the insidious trend towards making neutral, safe wine, without character, to please every taste. Wine growers are anxious for a new market, and technology has shown them how to control what they make. It is essential for wine-drinkers at this point in history to demand unblended, individual wines with all their local character intact. It is up to us to see that the most enthralling thing about wine—its endless variety—survives.

1793   1807   1812

Right: it is interesting to compare A. Jullien's classification of the Great Wines of the World a hundred years ago, in 1866, with the wines of today. His list in *Topographie de Tous les Vignobles Connus* (in its original spelling) ran:
Red
A Châteaux Margaux, Laffitte, Latour, Haut-Brion, Rauzan, Lascombes, Léoville, Larose-Balguerie, Gorce (Cantenac), Branne-Mouton, Pichon-Longueville
B Romanée-Conti, Chambertin, Richebourg, Clos Vougeot, Romanée-St-Vivant, La Tâche, Clos St-Georges, Le Corton, Clos de Prémeaux, Musigny, Clos de Tart, Bonnes-Mares, Clos de la Roche, Les Véroilles, Clos Morjot, Clos St-Jean, La Perrière

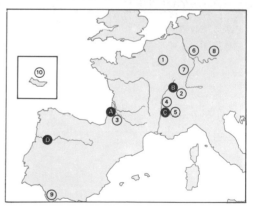

C (Hermitage) Méal, Gréfieux, Beaume, Raucoule, Muret, Guoignière, Les Bessas, Les Burges, Les Lauds
D High Douro
White
1 Sillery, Ay, Mareuil, Dizy, Hautvillers, Pierry, Le Clozet
2 Mont Rachet
3 First growths of Barsac, Preignac, Sauternes,

Bommes; dry wine of Villenave-d'Ornon
4 Château Grillet
5 Hermitage Blanc
6 Schloss Johannisberg, Rüdesheim, Steinberg, Graffenberg, Hochheim, Kiedrich
7 Liebfraumilch
8 Leist, Stein
9 Sherry 'from the white soil', Paxarete
10 Sercial

The Vine

As early as the beginning of April in northern Europe (or September in the southern hemisphere) the gnarled wood of the vine sports tender shoots

Within ten days of budding the stalk, leaves and tendrils are all obvious — and also vulnerable to nights of frost, which can come in late May

In late May or early June the vine forms its flower buds; looking like tiny bunches of grapes in the place where the grapes will eventually be

Early in June comes the vital flowering, which must go on for ten to 14 days for good grapes to form. Heavy rain now is fatal to the vintage

If the flowers escape rain and frost, their place is taken by baby grapes in June. In August the grapes 'set': turn colour from green to red or

translucent yellow; at this point the ripening process begins. From flowering to harvest in September or October is about 100 days (see the chart on page 28)

WINE IS the juice of grapes. Every drop of wine is rain recovered from the ground by the mechanism of the grape-bearing plant, the vine. For the first four or five years of its life the vine is too busy creating a root-system and building a strong woody stalk to bear a crop of grapes. Thereafter, left to nature, it would rampage away, bearing fruit but spending much more of its energy on making new shoots and putting out long wandering branches of leafy wood, until it covered as much as an acre of ground, with new root-systems forming wherever the branches lay along the ground.

This natural form, known as *provignage*, was used as a vineyard in ancient times. To prevent the grapes rotting or the mice getting them, since they lay on the ground, little props were pushed under the stem to support each bunch. If the vine grew near trees, it used its tendrils to climb them to dizzy heights. The Romans planted elms specially for the purpose.

In modern vineyards, however, the vine is not allowed to waste its precious sap on making long branches. Better-quality grapes grow on a vine which is regularly cut back almost to its main stem. The annual pruning is done in mid-winter when the vine is empty of sap.

Vines like most other plants will reproduce from seed. Sowing grape pips would be much the easiest and cheapest way of getting new vines. But like many highly-bred plants its seeds rarely turn out like their parents. Pips are used for experimenting with new crosses between different varieties. For planting a new vineyard, though, every vine has to be a cutting —either planted to take root on its own or grafted to a rooted cutting of another species.

Great care is taken to see that the parent vine is healthy before cuttings are taken. The little 'slips' are put in sand in a nursery for a season until they form roots. They then go out into rows, in traditional vineyards one metre apart but often today one and a half, two or even three metres apart. Oddly enough experiments have found that the total yield of the vineyard in wine remains the same with half as many vines exploiting the same volume of soil.

As a vine grows older its roots penetrate

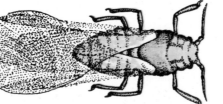
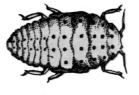

Pests which threaten the vine include, top left, the grub of the cochylis moth, seen here eating the flower buds; top right, the tiny red spider, which sucks the sap from the undersides of leaves; lower left, mildew, which attacks anything green. Mildewed grapes never ripen properly and have a peculiar taste. Copper sulphate sprays are effective against it. Lower right: oidium, or powdery mildew, is often more serious; its attack on Madeira in 1852, just before phylloxera hit the island, began the decline in madeira's fortunes. It rots the stalks, shrivels the leaves and splits the grapes, ruining the wine and finally killing the vine

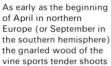

Left and below: the vine's deadliest enemy, Phylloxera vastatrix, in its root-eating form and its flying form. Below right: larvae and eggs. A century ago this American bug almost destroyed the vineyards of Europe Right: every European vine is now grafted on to American roots, which resist its attack. There used to be fierce debate as to whether European wine has suffered, but few now remember 'pre-phylloxera' wine

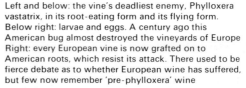
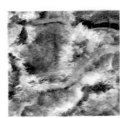
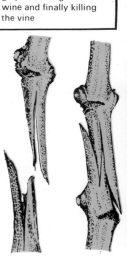

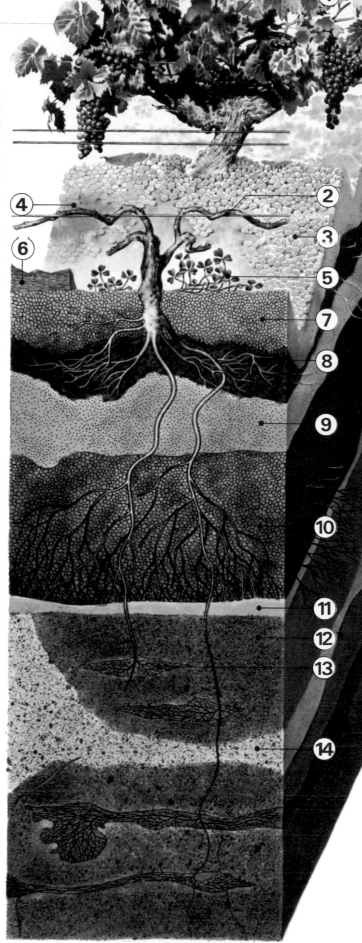

deeper into the earth. While it is young and they are near the surface they are quickly affected by drought or floods or the spreading of manure (which put on the land too liberally can affect the taste of the wine); the vine has little stability; its wine will never be first-class. But if the soil near the surface does not provide enough food it will send its roots down and down. This optimism, or curiosity, often results in its discovering valuable resources far from the surface (see right).

Unfortunately, being a pampered plant, the vine is subject to all manner of diseases. Some varieties fall sick of one particular disease (e.g. oidium or mildew) so readily that they are gradually being abandoned altogether. The best combine reasonable hardiness with fine fruit (though rarely with a very generous yield).

One insect pest is disastrous; the phylloxera. This little creature lives on the roots of the vine and kills it. In the seventies of the last century it almost destroyed the entire European vineyard, until it was discovered that the roots of the native American vine (phylloxera came from America) are immune. Virtually every vine in Europe had to be pulled up and replaced with a European cutting grafted on to a rooted cutting from an American vine.

Red spiders, the grubs of the cochylis and eudemis moths, various sorts of beetles, bugs and mites all feed on the upper works of the vine. Most of them however are taken care of by the sulphur sprays to which the vine is subjected summer-long, or by DDT.

Various moulds attack the vine as well. Oidium and mildew are the two worst in Europe; white, black and grey rot are among the others. All have to be prevented or at least treated by regular sprayings with a copper sulphate solution (known as Bordeaux mixture) and sulphur powder for as long as the vine has leaves and green wood which they can attack.

Below: the map plots the progress through France of phylloxera, starting in the département of Gard in the south in 1864 and not finishing its destruction for 30 years. France regained her production by 1920, but never her pre-phylloxera vineyard area

☐ by 1869		▨ 1880–89	
▨ 1870–79		▨ after 1889	

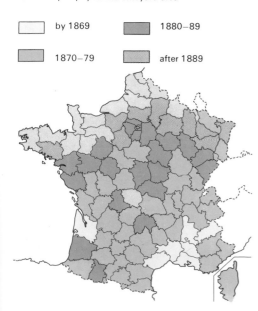

Wine has its origin as water in the soil. This cross-section of the vineyard of a riverside château in St-Julien in the Médoc shows how a vine finds enough moisture and food in poor soil by exploiting a deep and wide area. Gravel and sand are here plus-factors for quality. They make the ground permeable to a great depth, let the rain run through, and encourage the vine to go deep. In the background a 60-year old Cabernet vine 1, trained on wires, bears fruit. In the foreground a 20-year-old vine 2 is in its winter state; pruned and with the earth banked up round it for protection. Pebbles 3 on the surface are stained with copper sulphate 4: so much is sprayed on the vines that traces of copper are analysable in the soil. Clover 5 or other crops are often ploughed in as fertilizer. Pressed skins 6 (marc—see page 20) are also spread on the ground.

The top 12 inches 7 is pebbly and sandy with few roots. Then comes a layer of marl 8 brought from elsewhere and spread by hand years ago; possibly when the vines were planted. Roots and rootlets spread horizontally in it. The next foot 9 is sandy but compacted hard and has nothing to offer. There are no feeding rootlets but only main roots descending to another thicker layer 10 like the surface, gravelly and sandy, but slightly richer in organic matter (possibly from manuring years ago) where roots abound. These roots are again brought up short by a compacted layer 11 of sand at 4 feet deep. Below this different colours of sand, rusty 12 and yellow 14, lie in clearly defined layers, with odd horizontal patches of grey sand 13 among them. The grey is evidently where the water drains; it is filled with rootlets, which are nowhere else in the area. A 50-year-old vine still has roots an inch thick here, going down to deeper layers of grey sand and gravel. Roots can only find so much of the minerals they seek in a form they can use (i.e. in solution). The more grapes a vine bears, therefore, the less of these flavouring elements there will be per grape; the argument for restricting the crop to achieve maximum intensity of flavour. In St-Julien one vine produces enough juice for only half a bottle of wine

Based on investigations by Gérard Seguin published in his *Etude de Quelques Profils de Sols du Vignoble Bordelais* (Bordeaux 1965)

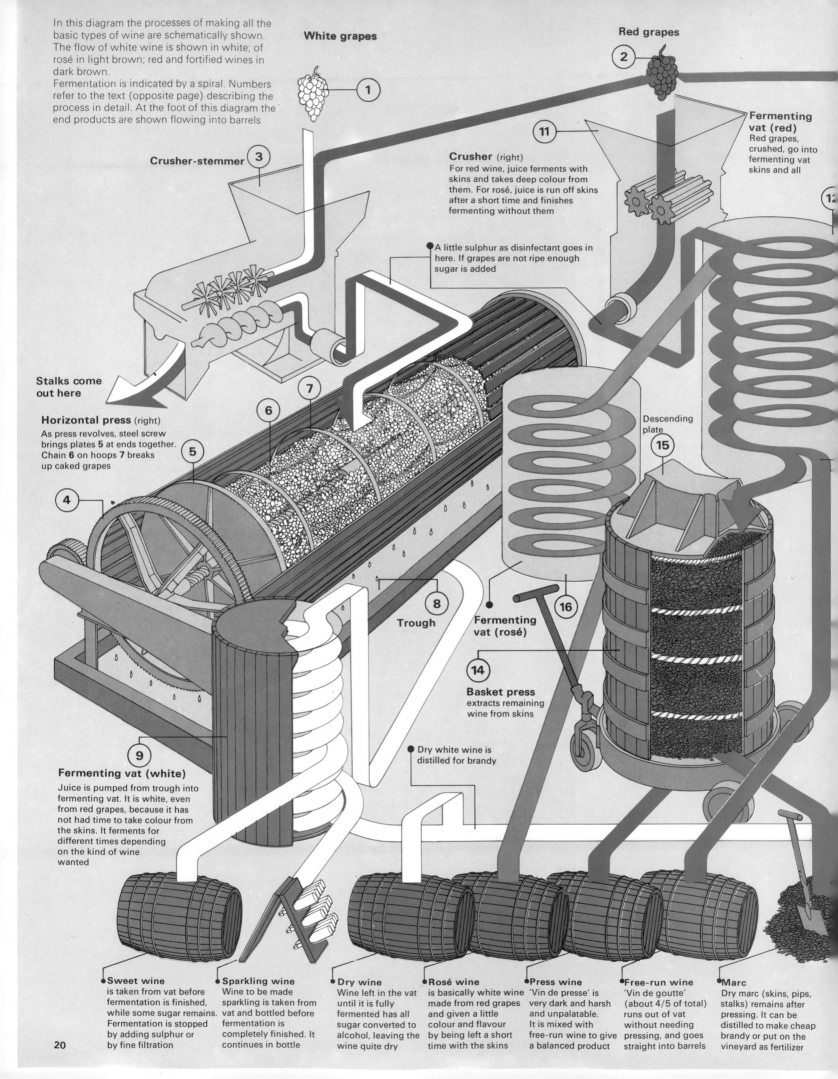

In this diagram the processes of making all the basic types of wine are schematically shown. The flow of white wine is shown in white; of rosé in light brown; red and fortified wines in dark brown.
Fermentation is indicated by a spiral. Numbers refer to the text (opposite page) describing the process in detail. At the foot of this diagram the end products are shown flowing into barrels

White grapes

1

Red grapes

2

Crusher-stemmer

3

11

Crusher (right)
For red wine, juice ferments with skins and takes deep colour from them. For rosé, juice is run off skins after a short time and finishes fermenting without them

Fermenting vat (red)
Red grapes, crushed, go into fermenting vat skins and all

12

A little sulphur as disinfectant goes in here. If grapes are not ripe enough sugar is added

Stalks come out here

Horizontal press (right)
As press revolves, steel screw brings plates **5** at ends together. Chain **6** on hoops **7** breaks up caked grapes

7

6

5

4

8

Trough

Descending plate

15

16

Fermenting vat (rosé)

14

Basket press
extracts remaining wine from skins

9

Fermenting vat (white)
Juice is pumped from trough into fermenting vat. It is white, even from red grapes, because it has not had time to take colour from the skins. It ferments for different times depending on the kind of wine wanted

Dry white wine is distilled for brandy

• **Sweet wine**
is taken from vat before fermentation is finished, while some sugar remains. Fermentation is stopped by adding sulphur or by fine filtration

• **Sparkling wine**
Wine to be made sparkling is taken from vat and bottled before fermentation is completely finished. It continues in bottle

• **Dry wine**
Wine left in the vat until it is fully fermented has all sugar converted to alcohol, leaving the wine quite dry

• **Rosé wine**
is basically white wine made from red grapes and given a little colour and flavour by being left a short time with the skins

• **Press wine**
'Vin de presse' is very dark and harsh and unpalatable. It is mixed with free-run wine to give a balanced product

• **Free-run wine**
'Vin de goutte' (about 4/5 of total) runs out of vat without needing pressing, and goes straight into barrels

• **Marc**
Dry marc (skins, pips, stalks) remains after pressing. It can be distilled to make cheap brandy or put on the vineyard as fertilizer

How Wine is Made

Treading trough (17)
Grapes for port are trodden to extract colour from skins

Fermenting vat (port) (18)
Juice ferments until half its sugar is alcohol

(13)
ee-run wine mes out ithout essing

Brandy is added to stun the yeast and stop fermentation

(10)

Brandy
The product of distilling (see page 240) wine is brandy. If grape skins (marc) are distilled the product is called marc

Port
and most fortified wines and 'vins doux naturels' have their fermentation arrested with alcohol. They need aging to 'marry' their different elements

Above: an ingenious 17th-century project for the mechanization of wine-making on a massive scale foreshadows the modern developments of the industry

ALL that is needed to turn grape juice into wine is the simple, entirely natural process of fermentation. Fermentation is the chemical change of sugar into alcohol and carbon dioxide gas brought about by yeasts—micro-organisms which live (among other places) on grape skins. They need only to have the grape skin broken to go to work on the sugar which comprises about 30% of the pulp. And in an instant there is wine.

Under normal conditions the yeast will go on working until all the sugar in the grapes is converted into alcohol, or until the alcohol level in the wine reaches about 15% of the volume—on the rare occasions when the grapes are so sweet that this happens naturally the yeast is overcome and fermentation stops.

Left to nature, therefore, almost all wine would be dry.

But it is possible to stop the fermentation before all the sugar is used up; either by adding alcohol to raise the level up to 15%, or by adding sulphur—both these anaesthetize the yeast, or by filtering the wine through a very fine filter to take the yeast out. These are the

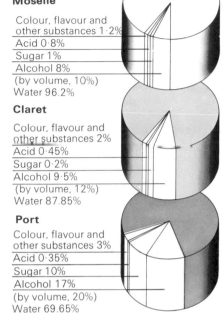

Moselle

Colour, flavour and other substances 1·2%
Acid 0·8%
Sugar 1%
Alcohol 8% (by volume, 10%)
Water 96.2%

Claret

Colour, flavour and other substances 2%
Acid 0·45%
Sugar 0·2%
Alcohol 9·5% (by volume, 12%)
Water 87.85%

Port

Colour, flavour and other substances 3%
Acid 0·35%
Sugar 10%
Alcohol 17% (by volume, 20%)
Water 69.65%

Above: these three diagrams show the proportions of constituents in wines of three different types. The Moselle is an almost-dry white wine; a little sugar has been kept in it, probably by filtering the yeast out. The claret is a totally natural red wine. The brandy added to the port has increased its strength to 17°. Analytical strengths are measured by weight. The % of alcohol by volume (the normal measure) is given in brackets

methods which are used to make sweet wine.

One wine differs from another first and foremost because of differences in the raw material, the grapes.

But various ways of arranging the fermentation can produce all the other differences; between red, white, rosé, sweet, dry or sparkling. The diagram opposite shows how, starting with one basic material—red grapes—six quite distinct kinds of wine can be made.

White
Either white **1** or red **2** grapes are fed into a crusher-stemmer (or égrappoir) **3** which tears off the stalks and pumps the broken grapes into a horizontal press **4**. The press revolves as the steel screw brings the plates **5** at the ends together. Chains **6** and hoops **7** break up the caked grapes. The skins (marc) are left behind as the must (fresh juice) falls into a trough **8** from which it is pumped into a fermenting vat **9**, after which several courses are open to it. It may be made into sweet wine by having its fermentation stopped while it still contains sugar, or bottled before fermentation is finished, to make sparkling wine. Or it may

be fermented until all its sugar is used up, to make dry wine. And finally, the dry wine may be distilled **10** to make brandy

Red
Red grapes **2** are fed through a crusher **11** (or often a crusher-stemmer) and pumped into a vat **12** where they ferment with their skins. Traditionally the stalks go in too but they are usually removed today. The wine gradually draws out the colour and tannin from the skin. Fermentation is allowed to go on until all sugar is gone (up to 14 days). Then the tap is opened and the 'free-run' wine **13** is run off. For lighter, quicker-maturing wine the modern practice is to take the wine off the skins

after a few days to finish fermenting separately. The skins are pressed in a hydraulic basket press **14** by a descending plate **15** which forces the juice out through slatted sides. Layers of matting help juice run out. This press wine, deeply coloured and tannic, is usually mixed with the free-run wine. The 'marc' left in the press is used as fertilizer or distilled to make cheap brandy

Rosé
Red grapes **2** are fed through a crusher **11** and straight into a vat **12** complete with their skins to begin fermentation. The juice for rosé wine takes a light pink colour from the skins but almost immediately it is run off

into another vat **16** to ferment without them. Normally it is allowed to finish fermentation naturally, and is thus completely dry

Port
(the process is similar for other fortified wines) Red grapes **2** are put in a stone trough **17** where they are continuously trodden with bare feet for 12 hours to make the juice take the colour of the skins. The juice is run into a vat **18** to ferment until half its sugar is converted to alcohol, when it is mixed with brandy from the still **10** to raise the alcohol level to above 15%. This stuns the yeast and stops fermentation, so the wine is both strong and sweet

The Choice of a Grape

THE WINE VINE is only one species of one genus of a vast family of plants, which ranges from a huge decorative Japanese climber to the familiar Virginia creeper.

Its name is Vitis vinifera. Its varieties can be numbered in thousands—as many as 5,000 are named. Those which concern a wine-lover, however, are probably not many more than about 50, of which we only show ten here, and in addition a few grape varieties from two or three other related species of vitis which produce the characteristic American wine.

All over the Old World of wine-growing, the natural selection of the variety which does best, and gives the best quality combined with reasonable quantity and a reasonable resistance to disease, has taken place gradually over centuries. In many places (the port country, for example, Chianti, Bordeaux, Châteauneuf-du-Pape) no one grape provides exactly what is needed: the tradition is either to grow a number together, or grow them separately and blend the resulting wines.

It is not the traditional practice in the main wine districts of Europe even to mention the kind of grape which goes into a wine. For one thing the choice is so old it can be assumed: for another modern laws normally make the traditional variety a condition of using the traditional wine name. White burgundy, for example, to be called white burgundy must be made entirely of Chardonnay grapes.

Thus there are very many important grapes few people have ever heard of: the Palomino and the Pedro Ximénez of sherry; the Tintas of port; the Furmint of Tokay; the Syrah of the Rhône or the brilliant white Viognier; the splendid Nebbiolo of northern Italy; the Schiava of the Adige and the Sangiovese of Chianti; the Gamay of Beaujolais; the Melon of Muscadet; the Folle Blanche and Ugni Blanc of Cognac; the Chasselas of Switzerland; the Merlot and Malbec and Petit Verdot of Bordeaux; the Savagnin of the Jura; the Arinto of Portugal.

On the other hand, there are some, like the Sercial and Verdelho of Madeira, the Barbera of Piemonte or the Gewürztraminer of Alsace, which have become the names of their wines.

Ampelography—the study of grapes—is one of the most delicate and difficult studies connected with wine. Experts often disagree about the identities of grapes: their relationships remain far beyond lay comment. There are traditions that certain well-known grapes are 'really' something else: for example that Spain's Pedro Ximénez came from Germany and is really a Riesling.

Today many new hybrids are made, seeking to combine the best qualities of different species of the vine, but none has yet achieved the quality of the old vinifera varieties.

In the New World of wine-growing the choice of grapes is not a question of tradition but of judgement: a realistic balance of quality, quantity and hardiness. Hence the best wines of the New World use the grape names to specify the character of the wine. And hence the curious fact that to an ordinary Californian the words Cabernet Sauvignon are more familiar than they are to a Parisian gourmet.

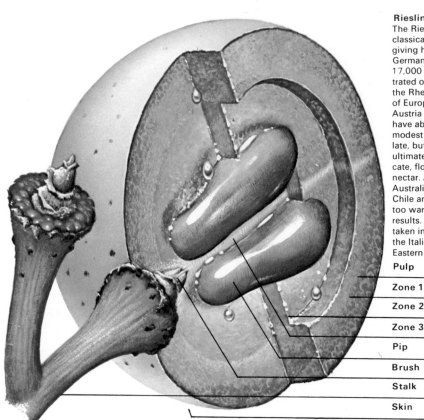

Riesling
The Riesling, left, is the classical German grape, giving her best wine. Germany has about 17,000 hectares, concentrated on the Mosel and the Rheingau; about 80% of Europe's plantation. Austria and Alsace each have about 1,000. It is a modest bearer and ripens late, but can make the ultimate honeyed, delicate, flower-scented nectar. Also planted in Australia, South Africa, Chile and California, all too warm for the greatest results. Its name is widely taken in vain; chiefly by the Italian Riesling in Eastern Europe

Pulp	
Zone 1	
Zone 2	
Zone 3	
Pip	
Brush	
Stalk	
Skin	

Above: an enlargement of a Riesling grape one month before the vintage. It is still green, and about half its final size. Ripening, it grows translucent gold with distinctive dark speckles on the skin (see the photograph of ripe Rieslings on page 103)

The stalk is normally torn off before the grapes are pressed in modern wine-making. Formerly they were left on, but they made the wine watery and could make it bitter. In red wine they also absorbed valuable colouring matter

The pulp divides naturally into three zones. Zone 2 gives up its juice in the press first, before the two zones in contact with pips and skin. The first juice from the press has long been held to make the best wine; perhaps for this reason

The pips should come through the press unscathed. If they are crushed they make the wine bitter. The skin is removed from the juice as quickly as possible for white wine; for red wine it is left in until the juice has taken its colour

The distribution of ten important grape varieties in France

Red		White	
Cabernet Sauvignon	● Gamay	Chardonnay	● Chenin Blanc
● Carignan	● Grenache	● Sauvignon Blanc	● Riesling
	● Pinot Noir		● Ugni Blanc

Gamay

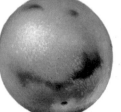

Only makes first-class wine on the granite hills of Beaujolais; in the rest of Burgundy an inferior variety and elsewhere dull (except perhaps in California for rosé). At its best incomparably light and fruity and gulpable, though often over-sugared in Beaujolais today, with the result that it is too strong and dry

Chardonnay

The grape of white burgundy (Chablis, Montrachet, Meursault, Pouilly-Fuissé) and champagne.
Gives firm, full, strong wine with scent and character, on chalky soils becoming almost luscious without being sweet. Ages well. Also used in Bulgaria, and very successful in northern California

Muscat

Easy to recognize by its taste and smell, like a hothouse table grape's. Can be black or white. Some of France's first vineyards were muscat, planted by the Greeks. It spread from the Aegean with civilization, to the Crimea, Sicily, Italy and southern Spain. All muscat wine, except in Alsace and Bulgaria, is sweet—often intensely sweet. The best in France comes from Beaumes de Venise near Avignon. Muscat wines or muscatels are made all over the world. They once included South Africa's Constantia. Portugal's Setúbal is another great one which is dying out

Semillon

This grape has the great gift, shared with the Riesling, of rotting nobly. Under certain conditions of warmth and humidity a normally undesirable fungus softens the skin and lets the juice evaporate, concentrating the sugar and flavouring elements and producing luscious, creamy wine. The great golden wines of Sauternes are made like this, with a proportion of Sauvignon, not so subject to 'Pourriture noble'. Semillon is extensively used in Australia to make white wines which can be labelled anything from Riesling to Chablis

Cabernet Sauvignon

Small tough-skinned grape which gives the distinction to the red wines of Bordeaux, though always blended with Merlot and sometimes Malbec. The best Médoc vineyards have up to 80% Cabernet, but in St-Emilion and Pomerol the Cabernet's slightly lesser cousin, the Cabernet Franc, is used. Cabernet Sauvignon is widely planted in Australia, where its wine is tough and black until a great age, in Chile where it is excellent, like a light Bordeaux, in South Africa and in California, where it is dull to very fine. All Cabernet wines gain by age in bottle as well as wood

Sauvignon Blanc

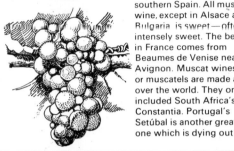

The chief white Bordeaux grape, used with Semillon and a little Muscadelle to make dry Graves and sweet Sauternes. Makes interesting, clean, lighter wine on its own elsewhere: at Pouilly and Sancerre on the upper Loire (though one authority believes the Pouilly Fumé grape to be the Savagnin of the Jura, not the Sauvignon); in the Dordogne; near Chablis; in Chile; and in the Livermore and Santa Clara valleys of California, where its wine is dry, gold and of great character

Chenin Blanc

The white grape of Anjou and Touraine on the Loire. Gives nervy, intense wine, honey-like when very ripe but always with high acidity, so it ages well. Its finest wines are Vouvray, Coteaux du Layon, Savennières; at Vouvray it also makes sparkling wine. Often called Pineau de la Loire and in California (where it is successful), mistakenly, White Pinot

Pinot Noir

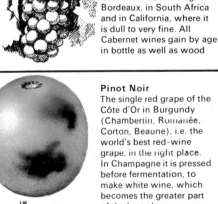

The single red grape of the Côte d'Or in Burgundy (Chambertin, Romanée, Corton, Beaune), i.e. the world's best red-wine grape, in the right place. In Champagne it is pressed before fermentation, to make white wine, which becomes the greater part of the best champagnes. At its best the scent, flavour, body, texture of its wine are all profound pleasures. It transplants from France less well than the Cabernet, makes light wines in Germany and Eastern Europe, where it goes by various names, and, with exceptions, not very exciting wines in California

Grenache

A sweet grape with character but not much colour, used in a blend to make Châteauneuf-du-Pape and on its own to make Tavel, the best rosé of the Rhône. Known as Garnacha in Rioja, where it is the most important red variety. Used for dessert wines at Banyuls near the Franco-Spanish frontier. In Australia and California it makes the best rosés, which usually bear its name

Anatomy of a Château

THE VINTAGE is the climax of the wine-maker's year. Every district has its own way of doing things, yet somehow Bordeaux, with its completely natural and straightforward way of making wine, seems to sum it all up. The grapes are simply picked, destalked, crushed; the rest is nature . . . but nature kept under a careful watch.

In a typical small château such as the one shown (Château Malescasse in the Médoc), the wine is made in oak *cuves* in the *cuvier*. It ferments for about ten days before it is run off the skins and the skins are pressed. If the weather is hot and the fermentation generates too much heat it must be cooled by hosing down the *cuves* with water, or even packing blocks of ice round them.

From the *cuvier* the wine is pumped into a cement tank for two weeks before it is *débourbé* —pumped off its heaviest sediment into another tank. In this it spends the winter, going through its gentle secondary or malolactic fermentation which rids it of malic acid, making it less harsh. Traditionally secondary fermentation does not start till March, when the sap rises in the vines, but modern practice brings it forward. In February the wine is pumped into *barriques* (hogsheads) in the first-year *chai*.

It stays here for a year, being constantly topped up and occasionally 'racked' into a fresh barrel; in some years going on fermenting slightly through the summer.

In the following year it is moved into the second-year *chai*, where it is bunged tight and

left to mature until, after two years, it is ready for bottling. Some bottling is done here with a hand machine; some casks are sold for bottling by merchants. But the bottle cellar has an important role as well: for no good red Bordeaux is ready to drink before it has been in bottle for at least two years.

Château Malescasse at Lamarque is a typical small Cru Bourgeois; a modest specialized farm. Its methods (on which the drawing is broadly based) are up-to-date without being unusually modern. The château was built in about 1830. Like many in the Médoc it was given an air of importance above its station as an ordinary family house

In the kitchen a midday meal of pot au feu or cassoulet is cooked for the pickers. Their breakfast consisted of sardines, bread and red wine

The proprietor's office: on the wall hang large-scale plans of the château and the vineyard which show every barrel and vine

The first-year *chai*. New wine is pumped into oak hogsheads, and stoppered with loose glass bungs. At some châteaux wine goes straight into barrels; here it waits till the following February

Cement *cuves* hold the new wine over the winter while it undergoes secondary fermentation and rids itself of heavy sediment

Hydraulic press will press the skins to extract remaining one-fifth of the wine after the rest has been run off (see pages 20–21). The deeply-coloured vin de presse is mixed with the rest

Remontage. Every morning and evening the fermenting wine is pumped up and sprayed over the floating 'cap' of skins. In fine years it is pumped via an open tub for aeration

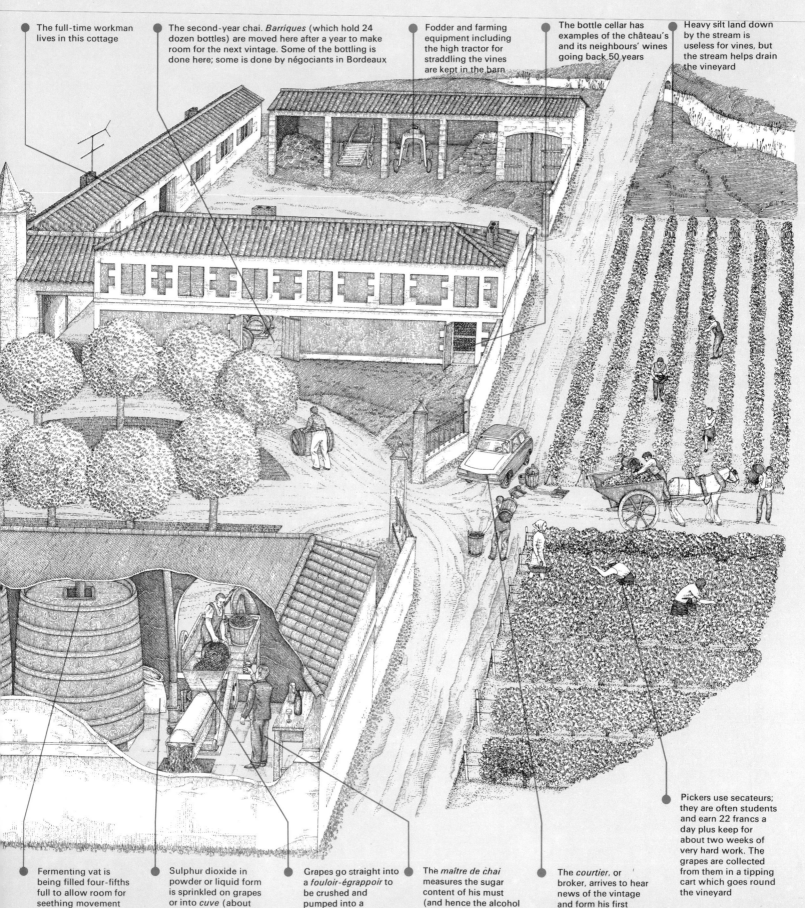

The full-time workman lives in this cottage

The second-year chai. *Barriques* (which hold 24 dozen bottles) are moved here after a year to make room for the next vintage. Some of the bottling is done here; some is done by négociants in Bordeaux

Fodder and farming equipment including the high tractor for straddling the vines are kept in the barn

The bottle cellar has examples of the château's and its neighbours' wines going back 50 years

Heavy silt land down by the stream is useless for vines, but the stream helps drain the vineyard

Fermenting vat is being filled four-fifths full to allow room for seething movement

Sulphur dioxide in powder or liquid form is sprinkled on grapes or into *cuve* (about 10 grammes per 100 litres) as disinfectant

Grapes go straight into a *fouloir-égrappoir* to be crushed and pumped into a fermenting vat. Stalks are ripped off and emerge separately

The *maître de chai* measures the sugar content of his must (and hence the alcohol content of his wine) with a hydrometer

The *courtier*, or broker, arrives to hear news of the vintage and form his first impression of its likely quality

Pickers use secateurs; they are often students and earn 22 francs a day plus keep for about two weeks of very hard work. The grapes are collected from them in a tipping cart which goes round the vineyard

A Wine-Maker's Calendar

There is a job indoors in the cellar, and a job outdoors in the vines, for every day of a wine-maker's year. Every district has different methods, and a different time-table, besides modern innovations. But this is the life of a typical traditional vigneron, somewhere in the heart of France . . .

JANUARY

Pruning. Traditionally pruning started on St Vincent's Day, January 22nd. Nowadays it starts in December. If there is no snow the ground is often frozen. Vines will survive temperatures down to about −18°C

Barrels of new wine must be kept full to the top and their bungs wiped every other day with a solution of sulphur dioxide. In fine dry weather bottling of older wine can be done. Labelling and packing in boxes for shipment

FEBRUARY

Finish pruning and take cuttings for grafting. Make grafts on to root-stock and put them in sand indoors. Prepare machines for the outdoor work of the new season. Remember to order copper sulphate for spraying

Racking. In fine weather with a new moon and a north wind (i.e. when there is high atmospheric pressure), start 'racking' the new wine into clean barrels to clear it. 'Assemble' the new wine in a vat to equalize the casks

MARCH

Ploughing. About mid-month the vine begins to emerge from dormancy; sap begins to rise; brown sheaths on buds fall off. Finish pruning. First working of the soil, deeply, to aerate it and uncover the bases of the vines

Finish first racking before the end of the month. Some mysterious sympathy between vine and wine is supposed to start the second fermentation when the sap rises. Keep the casks topped up. Finish bottling

JULY

Spray the vines regularly with 'Bordeaux mixture' (copper sulphate, slaked lime and water) Third cultivation of the soil against weeds. Trim long shoots so that vines spend their energy on making fruit

No shipping in hot weather. All efforts to keep cellar cool. In heat-waves, when close weather makes it necessary to shut doors at night, burn a sulphur candle. Vine-growth slows down; bottling can start again

AUGUST

Keep the vineyards weeded and the vines trimmed. Black grapes turn colour. General upkeep and preparation of gear which will be needed for the vintage

Inspect and clean vats and casks to be used for the vintage. Vine-growth (and fermentation) starts again about mid-month so bottling must stop. Low-strength wine (being less stable) can turn in warm weather, so it must be carefully watched

SEPTEMBER

Vintage. Keep small boys and birds out of the vineyard. Keep vines trimmed, pray for sunshine. About the third week the grapes are ripe; the vintage begins

Before the vintage, scour out the cuvier where the wine will be made. Put anti-rust varnish on all metal parts of presses etc. Fill fermenting vats with water to swell the wood

APRIL

finish ploughing. Clear up vineyard, burning any remaining prunings and replacing any rotten stakes. Plant one-year-old cuttings from the nursery. Pray for late vegetation, as frosts are frequent and hail possible

Topping up must still go on. There must never be any ullage (empty space) in the cask. Five per cent of the wine evaporates through the wooden sides of the barrel every year

MAY

Frost danger at its height. On clear nights stoves may be needed among the vines, which means sitting up to fuel them. Second working of the soil to kill weeds. Spray against oidium and mildew. Every ten days remove any suckers to encourage the sap to rise in the vines

Send off orders to customers. Towards the end of May, just before vines flower, begin the second racking off the lees into clean barrels

JUNE

The vines flower at the beginning of June when the temperature reaches 18–20°C. Weather is critical; the warmer and calmer the better. After flowering, thin the shoots, tying the best ones to the wires. Spray for oidium with powdered sulphur

Finish second racking of new wine and rack all old wines in the cellar. Evaporation is naturally accelerated by the warm weather; check all the casks for any weeping

OCTOBER

The vintage continues (see page 24) for perhaps two weeks. When it is over, spread manure (pressed grape skins are good) and fertilizer on the vineyard. Deep-plough the land for new plantations

The new wine is fermenting. Year-old wine should be given a final racking, the barrels banged tightly and rolled a quarter-turn so the bung is at the side. Move barrels to second year cellar to make room for new wine

NOVEMBER

Cut off long vine shoots and collect them for fuel. Finish manuring. Plough the vineyard to move soil over the bases of the vines to protect them from frost

Bottling. Rack and 'fine' (filter by pouring in whisked egg-white which sinks to the bottom) wine to be bottled. In rich and ripe vintages rack new wine now; in poor ones leave it on the lees another month

DECEMBER

If soil has been washed down slopes by rain it must be carried back up and redistributed. Pruning the vines can start before Christmas, on about December 15th

Casks must be topped up frequently. More bottling of older wine can be done. Start tasting the new wine with old friends

Wine and the Weather

THE WEATHER is the great variable in wine-growing. Every other major influence is more or less constant, and known in advance. But in the end it is the weather which makes or breaks a vintage—so it receives constant study and analysis.

The vine is dormant from November to March in the northern hemisphere. Only an abnormally deep frost can harm it then. From the time it buds to the vintage in September or October, however, every drop of rain, hour of sunshine and degree of heat has its eventual effect on the quality and character of the crop.

The fine wines of northern Europe are those most affected by irregular weather. In the south and in the New World, vintages tend to be much more consistent. On these pages we look at some of the factors affecting France.

The chart at the bottom of this page shows the chief events in a vine's life cycle over 19 years in Burgundy. There is a 35-day maximum variation in the starting and finishing of this cycle, and infinite variations in between, as the weather hurries it on or holds it back.

On the opposite page are isopleth graphs showing the average rainfall, temperature and sunshine for four wine regions of France. They prove nothing; but they provide a fascinating field of speculation into just what weather in what moment in a vine's cycle will result in a good or great vintage.

A thorough study of this question in Burgundy was done by Rolande Gadille in her great book *Le Vignoble de la Côte Bourguignonne*, to which this atlas owes a considerable debt. The two lower graphs opposite show her plotting of the difference in reality over 17 years between good vintages, mediocre vintages and the average; just where the weather changed to the benefit or detriment of the wine.

Frost in late spring and hail at any time are the grower's nightmares. Hail tends to be localized; one reason why growers like to have little holdings scattered all over the parish. A bad storm can not only wreck a vintage, but bruise the wood so as to affect next year's wine.

The determining factor for the quality of a northern vintage (in Burgundy for instance) is the ripeness of the grapes. As a grape ripens its acidity decreases and its sugar increases. The primitive way of judging when to pick was to crush grapes in your hands; if they were sticky it was time. In the past the danger of a change in the weather (September rain bringing mildew) made growers often pick too soon, whereas today with chemicals and knowledge the vintage gets later and later.

It almost goes without saying that dry years are normally best. But the exact balance of importance between rain, sun, temperature and humidity has never been determined. What gives character to each individual vintage is the interaction between them: bright sunlight causing early ripening; overcast skies slowing growth but sometimes enriching the grapes with minerals which give the wine long life and complexity; high temperatures reducing acidity.

Even given exactly the same ripeness at picking, grapes reflect the year they have been through: scorching by sun or wind; too much vegetation (leaves and stems) or too little;

Below: frost on young shoots can cripple the vine for the year. Protective measures include little stoves, smoke-screens, big fans which keep the air moving on cold nights. Sprays which coat the vine with protecting ice in early spring are the latest method: shown above

Below: there is no protection against hail. It can destroy a whole vintage. Insurance against it is costly: a German broker quotes 16.30 DM per 1,000 marks insured. 10,000 DM a hectare would be modest for a good vineyard; it all adds to the cost of the wine

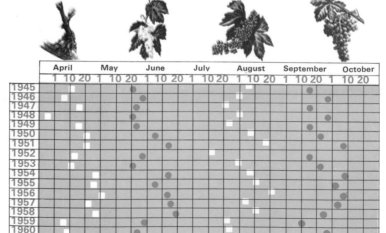

Left: the chart shows the dates of the main events in the annual life cycle of a Burgundy Pinot Noir vine over a 19-year period. In April the buds break; in late May or early June the flowers form; about the beginning of August the grapes 'set'; change from green to be either translucent or red. A hundred days after flowering the grapes should be ripe. Flowering should take about two weeks. But the chart shows how widely the dates can vary
Of the years shown, 1945, 1947, '52, '53 and '61, all early flowering years, produced outstandingly good vintages. 1951, '54, '56, '58 and '63, mostly late, were bad

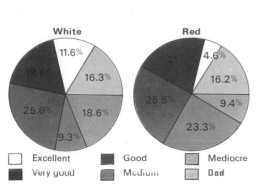

White	Red
11.6%	4.6%
16.3%	16.2%
18.5%	21%
25.6%	9.4%
9.3%	23.3%
18.6%	25.5%

☐ Excellent   ■ Good   ▨ Mediocre
■ Very good   ▨ Medium   ▨ Bad

Above: white burgundy seems less affected by weather than red. Out of 43 vintages the white wines were outstandingly good or bad in only half; the reds divided almost equally into outstandingly good, bad or medium

mould resulting from damp ground or bruises from hail all eventually have a bearing on the wine. No two years are ever the same.

A grower can give a fair guess at vintage time at what the quality of his wine will be, weighing its ripeness against past experience. But there is always a good chance that weather factors he is unaware of have played a part. Two or three times in ten the spring after the vintage will bring him a surprise.

Below: the temperature and sunshine month by month in Burgundy are shown in relation to good, average and bad vintages. The important differences seem to be in midsummer temperature and spring sunshine. Bad vintages suffer cold at flowering time and never catch up

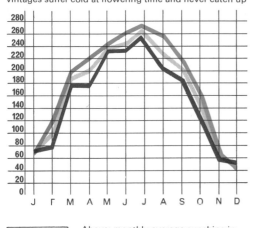

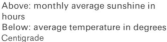

■ Good
■ Medium
■ Bad

Above: monthly average sunshine in hours
Below: average temperature in degrees Centigrade

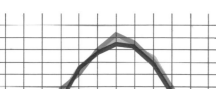

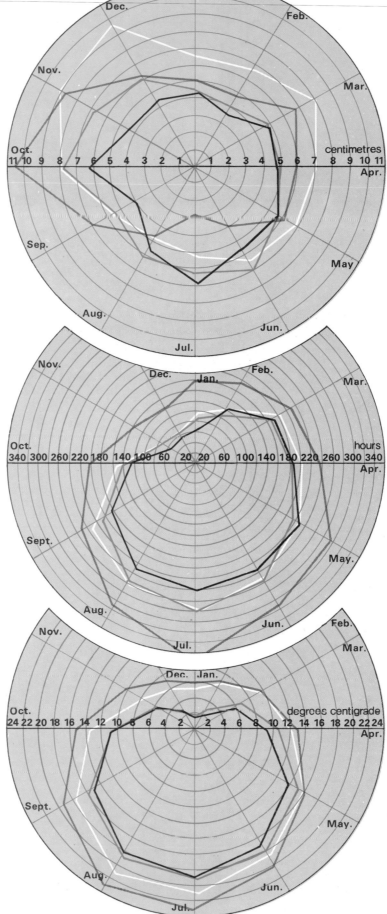

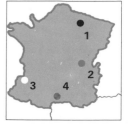

1 Champagne
2 Burgundy
3 Bordeaux
4 Montpellier

Left: isopleth graphs show the year's weather as a continuous process in the four French wine regions marked on the map above

Rainfall (top graph)
Sunshine and temperature come to a peak everywhere in midsummer; rainfall comes and goes more unpredictably. Bordeaux has a very wet winter, a comparatively rainy spring (flowering is in late May), but a long dry summer, growing wetter again, unfortunately for the vintage, in late September. Burgundy is dry in spring, wetter in summer but as dry as Bordeaux in early September. Champagne is wet in July but dry at vintage time

Sunshine (left)
The graph shows that all the regions get their maximum sunshine in July: the south by far the most all the year round. Bordeaux and Burgundy have curiously similar summer patterns from May to August, then Bordeaux has a distinctly sunnier end of season. Champagne has a good May, which is useful for the flowering of the vines

Temperature (left)
Latitude is clearly the chief factor in deciding temperature. Only in June is Burgundy as warm as Bordeaux. By September it is getting cool in Champagne; by November both Burgundy and Champagne are really cold. Bordeaux stays almost as mild as the south all the winter. Regional temperature averages are the least accurate for any particular vineyard, since local conditions of altitude and exposure make wide variations, known as 'micro-climates'

Wine and Time

Above: Louis Pasteur, born in Dôle in the Jura in 1822, was the first scientist to turn his mind to wine. He discovered that yeast causes fermentation, as well as other facts of enormous importance to wine-makers

In these hand-coloured illustrations from his *Etudes sur le Vin*, Pasteur recorded the effect of time and oxygen on red and white wine

Far left: Pasteur found that red wine without air did not change colour
Left: with air it faded

Left: white wine without air was unchanged
Right: with air it grew brown

SOME WINES are ready to drink as soon as they are made. Others improve immeasurably by being kept for even as much as 50 years. As a general rule these *vins de garde* are the better. But why? And why is it that such a mystique attaches to an old bottle of wine?

Most white wines, rosé wines and such light reds as Beaujolais and Valpolicella are at their best young. The pleasure in them is a matter of grapiness and freshness. We want them to be close to fresh fruit; direct in scent and flavour.

The great white wines and most of the best reds, however, are grown to be as full of their own particular character, extracted from their particular soil, as possible. There resides in them when young an unresolved complex of principles: of acids and sugars, minerals and pigments, esters and aldehydes and tannins. Good wines have more of these things than ordinary wines, and great wines than good wines. Which is why, in the end, they have more flavour.

But it takes time for these elements to resolve themselves into a harmonious whole and for the distinct scent of maturity, called (by analogy with flowers) the bouquet, to form. Time, and oxygen.

It was not till Louis Pasteur was asked by Napoleon III in 1863 to find out why so much wine went bad on its way to the consumer, to the great harm of French trade, that the role of oxygen was discovered. Pasteur established that too much contact with the air allows the growth of vinegar bacteria. On the other hand he found that it was very slight amounts of oxygen that makes wine mature; that the oxygen's action is not 'brusque', but gradual, and that there is enough of it dissolved in a bottle of wine to account for an aging process lasting for years.

He showed, by sealing up wine in test-tubes, alternately full and half-full, that the oxygen in the air of the half-full tube caused the same

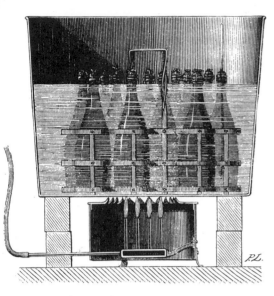

Above: Pasteur's original diagram of his method of
'pasteurizing' wine by heating it in hot water
Right: A Roman bottle of Roman wine, now in Speyer
museum. Air is kept from the wine by a layer of oil on top

deposit in a few weeks as is found in very old
bottles, that it faded red wine and darkened
white wine, affecting their colour in exactly
the same way as extreme old age.

In fact he immensely speeded up the process
that happens in a bottle: the oxygen in the
wine acts on its constituents to mature them,
but beyond the period of maturity it continues
to act; from then on the wine deteriorates.

Pasteur found that even wine which is carefully kept from the air has opportunities to
absorb oxygen: when it is being racked from
one barrel to another; even through the staves
of the barrel (so that their thickness, whether or
not they are encrusted with tartrate crystals,
the capacity of the barrel, whether it stood in a
draught, all become relevant). He told the story
of a painted cask at the Clos de Vougeot whose
wine always tasted a year or two younger than
the others which were unpainted.

If wine in barrels is more subject to the action
of oxygen it also has the wood itself as an agent
for change. It picks up certain characteristics—
extra tannin, and vanillin, which gives a vanilla
flavour, particularly to spirits—from the oak.
Oxygen and oak together age wine far faster
than it will age in bottle.

Left too long in a barrel a light wine fades
rapidly; its colour goes; its fruitiness disap-
pears; it starts to taste dry, flat and insipid. The
same wine bottled after a year or less will keep
the colour, the fruit and the acidity, and last
(and perhaps improve) for several more years.

Every wine and every vintage has its own
time-scale. The riper the grapes, the more
flavouring matter and strength there will be in
the wine. Given the right amount of acidity,
to prevent it becoming soft and flat, wine of
good years with plenty of 'fruit' repays keeping
far more than wine of average ones.

The vintage charts on pages 45–48 are some
degree of guide as to how long the wines of
recent vintages will benefit by being kept.

The Price of Wine

WHEN THE brokers of Bordeaux set out to establish the famous 1855 classification of the Médoc they took as their guide the prices fetched by the different châteaux over the previous hundred or so years. They were safe in assuming that something for which the world is consistently prepared to pay more for so long must be better.

It is impossible to establish any true worldwide picture of the values put on different wines in this way. Particularly today, fashion plays a large part. For example sweet wines, with the exception of German ones, are undervalued today; port and Sauternes are 'better', in terms of absolute quality, than their present price suggests. The best sherry is another underpriced wine, in relation to, say, white burgundy. On the other hand Sancerre and Pouilly Fumé, both in fashion, often cost more than they are worth in the same comparison; and some smart California wines get away with murder on the flood-tide of winemanship in the United States.

Spain, Portugal and Italy all hold real bargains. Chile almost gives away wine of a quality which would cost several times as much in Bordeaux.

Information about the price of wine is scattered in relevant places throughout the atlas. On this page are some examples of the fluctuations of wine prices over recent years.

The graphs plot the retail prices of ten representative wines over the last 17 years at one of the world's most famous wine retailers —Berry Bros & Rudd of St James's Street, London. Customs duties, the only factors which would make them different from prices in comparable shops anywhere in the world, have been subtracted. One can see in them the influence of fashion and the quality of vintages, as well as the movement of inflation. Most revealing of all is to compare them with the British retail prices index; the last graph. It can be seen that in relation to most other goods the prices of several wines have actually come down in the last few years.

The first-growth Bordeaux (Château Lafite) and the first white burgundy (either a Chablis Grand Cru or Corton-Charlemagne) are the only two which are château- (or domaine-) bottled. Both prices have leapt off the tables completely; Lafite after the 1961 vintage, the burgundy more recently. The second-growth Bordeaux, London-bottled, has climbed. The second white burgundy, Meursault, has hardly moved. The red burgundy, London-bottled Corton, has had its ups and downs but remains in the region where it started. The port, always of the latest vintage, sold for laying down, started so low that it was bound to climb.

Champagne (a non-vintage famous brand) has had one of the biggest increases. Alsace (Riesling) has finished with a 30% rise. But most surprising of all are the two German wines, a modest standard Rhine and Moselle, both bottled in London but of steady quality. There are of course German original bottlings whose graphs would be more like that of Château Lafite. But who would have suspected the steadiness of price of good everyday German wine? Or, indeed, of Scotch whisky, in the second graph from the end.

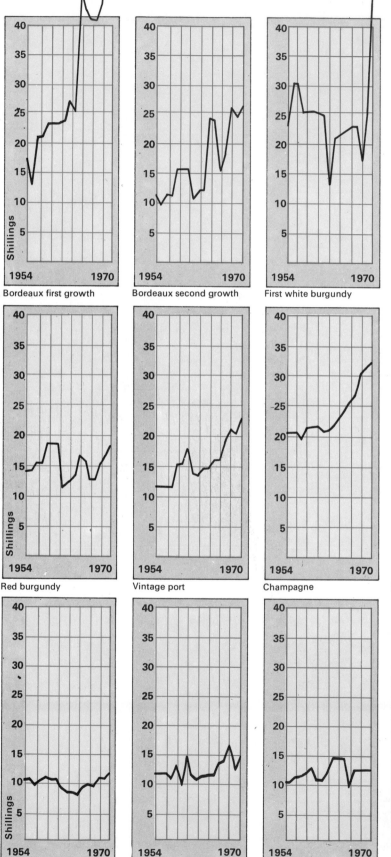

Bordeaux first growth

Bordeaux second growth

First white burgundy

Second white burgundy

Red burgundy

Vintage port

Champagne

Moselle

Rhine

Alsace

Scotch whisky

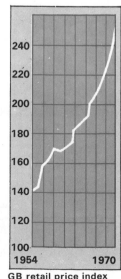

GB retail price index

Prices per bottle without customs duties
1 shilling=5 new pennies=US$0.12 (on February 15th 1971)

Prices at 17th June 1947=100

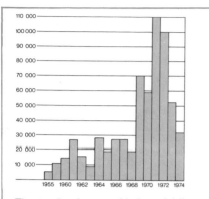

The graphs above and below vividly illustrate the boom in Bordeaux prices in the late 1960s and the reaction that followed. Above are the prices at the château (given in francs per tonneau: four hogsheads or about 1150 bottles) for the first-growth Château Lafite. Below are the prices for a first-class Cru Bourgeois (the Cru Exceptionnel Château d'Angludet at Cantenac in the Médoc). The price of Lafite in 1955 was 5,000 francs. By 1959 it had doubled. The small and excellent 1961 vintage was the first real landmark— the price leapt to 27,000 francs, a level it held remarkably steadily through the later 1960s, until the failure of the 1968s and the small size of the 1969 vintage coincided with growing American demand. In 1970, the economics of scarcity took over. Lafite demanded and got 70,000 francs for the mediocre 1969s. There was so much of the superb 1970 that the price fell back to 59,000 francs at first, but the wine-investment boom had started and 1970s were changing hands later at twice the château price. The boom reached a peak with the small 1971 vintage and the plentiful 1972, poor though it was. Then in 1973 came the October war. Suddenly everyone wondered who was actually going to drink all this wine which was leaving the château at £10 a bottle. The prices of the big vintages of 1973 and 1974 tell their own story.

In contrast, Cru Bourgeois prices (below) have found and held a realistic level. In 1955 Angludet was a quarter of the price of Lafite. At the height of the boom it was one-fourteenth. In 1975 it is back to one-fifth.

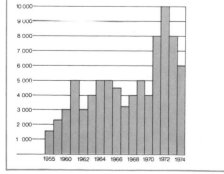

Right: a 19th-century Burgundian merchant's premises show the workings of the traditional wine-shipping trade; here is the entrance hall with offices and the cooperage (barrel workshop) behind

On the first cellar floor barrels are ranged four-high for aging. A négociant-éleveur will keep wine for up to three years in cask before bottling it or selling it

In the vault below, bottling is done with a simple hand machine (as it often still is today) and the bottles are either packed into wooden cases for shipment or binned in the bottle cellar (left) for further aging

Above and right: wine merchants of the old school whose customers rely on them for choosing all their wine are very rare today. One is Berry Bros & Rudd of London, whose list is analysed on the opposite page. In their 17th-century premises there are scales on which customers since King George IV have weighed themselves

The Literature of Wine

Books on wine and wine-growing have been appearing since Roman times. A gentleman farmer in the days of the Empire would have had wine books in his library by several of the greatest writers, including Virgil, Horace, Cato, Varro and Martial.

The first known farming manual was written by Mago of Carthage (in modern Tunisia) at the end of the fourth century BC. Columella, who was born in Cadiz in the sherry country, wrote his classic *De Re Rustica* in about AD 65. Both these books treated wine-growing as an important part of general agriculture, and showed that long study had already been given to factors governing the quality of wine, as well as the economics of vine husbandry . . . largely in those days a matter of how hard you could drive your slaves.

Since the 18th century a great library of technical works has accumulated. In France, particularly, some of them are treated with reverence as classics, so that modern writers still quote what Lavalle, Rodier, Roupnel, Guyot had to say about the character of a certain wine, like 18th-century parliamentarians solemnly quoting Thucydides.

Some of these books have as much value today as they ever did. The place of others has been taken by fresh works. The list which follows is a personal selection of current wine-books, along with a few irreplaceable classics.

General

H. Warner Allen
A History of Wine (London, 1961)

Maynard A. Amerine and Vernon L. Singleton
Wine, An Introduction for Americans (Berkeley & Los Angeles, 1965)

J. M. Broadbent
Wine Tasting (London, 1968)

Maurice Healy
Stay me with Flagons (London, 1963)

Ernest Hornickel
Die Spitzenweine Europas (Stuttgart, 1963)

Edward Hyams
Dionysus, A Social History of the Wine Vine (London, 1965)

A. Jullien
Topographie de Tous les Vignobles Connus (Paris, 1866)

Alexis Lichine
Encyclopaedia of Wines and Spirits (London, 1967)

Salvatore P. Lucia
A History of Wine as Therapy (Philadelphia, 1963)

L. W. Marrison
Wines and Spirits (London, 1957)

Lenz Moser
Un Nouveau Vignoble (Translated from the German, Cadillac-sur-Garonne, 1960)

Louis Pasteur
Etudes sur le Vin (Paris, 1866)

George Saintsbury
Notes on a Cellarbook (London, 1920)

Frank Schoonmaker
Encyclopaedia of Wine (London, 1967)

G. Siloret
Encyclopédie des Connaissances Agricoles: Le Vin (Paris, 1963)

André L. Simon
Bottlescrew Days (London, 1926)

Harry Waugh
The changing face of Wine (London, 1968)
Pick of the Bunch (London, 1970)

Harry Waugh
Diary of a Wine-taster (New York, 1972)

Albert J. Winkler
General Viticulture (Berkeley & Los Angeles, 1962)

William Younger
Gods, Men & Wine (London, 1966)

France

Pierre Bréjoux
Les Vins de la Loire (Paris, 1956)

Cocks et Féret
Bordeaux et ses Vins (Bordeaux, 1970 : 12th edition)

Paul de Cassagnac
French Wines (Translated by Guy Knowles, London, 1930)

Patrick Forbes
Champagne (London, 1969)

Rolande Gadille
Le Vignoble de la Côte Bourguignonne (Paris, 1967)

Cyril Ray
Cognac (London, 1973)

Jean Hugel
Riquewihr, Son Vignoble et ses Vins à travers les ages (Colmar, 1968)

George H. Jackson
The Medicinal Value of French Brandy (Montreal, 1928)

Louis Jacquelin and René Poulain
The Wines and Vineyards of France (Translated by T. A. Layton, London, 1962)

Louis Larmat
Les Vins des Côtes du Rhône (Paris, 1943)
Les Vins de Bordeaux (1944)
Les Vins de Champagne (1944)
Les Vins des Coteaux de la Loire; Touraine et Centre (1946)
Le Cognac (1947)
Les Vins de Bourgogne (1953)

Louis Orizet
Mon Beaujolais (Villefranche, 1959)

Edmund Penning-Rowsell
The Wine and Food Society's Guide to the Wines of Bordeaux (London, 1969)

Pierre Poupon and Pierre Forgeot
Les Vins de Bourgogne (Paris, 1969 : revised edition)

Charles Higounet (editor)
Le Seigneurie et La Vignoble de Chateau Latour (Bordeaux, 1974)

Camille Rodier
Le Vin de Bourgogne (Dijon, 1948)

V. R. Roger
The Wines of Bordeaux (London, 1960)

Gérard Seguin
Etude de Quelques Profils de Sols du Vignoble Bordelais (Bordeaux, 1965)
Les Sols des Vignobles du Haut (Médoc. Influences sur l'Alimentation en Eau de la Vigne et sur la Maturation du Raisin (Bordeaux, 1970)

P. Morton Shand
A Book of French Wines (London, 1928)

Allan Sichel
The Penguin Book of Wines (London, 1965)

H. W. Yoxall
The Wines of Burgundy (London, 1968)

Germany

Hans Ambrosi
Deutscher Wein-Atlas (Bielefeld, 1973)

S. F. Hallgarten
Rhineland Wineland (London, 1951)

Frank Schoonmaker
The Wines of Germany (New York, 1956, 1969)

Heinrich Zakosek and others
Die Standortkartierung der Hessischen Weinbaugebiete (Wiesbaden, 1967)

Australia

Max Lake
Classic Wines of Australia (Brisbane, 1967)

André L. Simon
The Wines, Vineyards and Vignerons of Australia (Melbourne, 1966)

Hungary

R. E. H. Gunyon
The Wines of Central and South-eastern Europe (London, 1971)

Italy

Charles G. Bode
Wines of Italy (London, New York, 1956)

Lamberto Paronetto
Il Magnifico Chianti (Verona, 1967)

Cyril Ray
The Wines of Italy (London, 1966)

Guido Rossati
Descriptive Account of the Wine Industry of Italy (1890)

Luigi Veronelli
The Wines of Italy (Rome, 1966)

Morocco

Michèle Mathez
L'Arboriculture et Viticulture au Maroc (Rabat, 1968)

Portugal

Raymond Postgate
Portuguese Wine (London, 1969)

Dan Stanislawski
Landscapes of Bacchus (Austin, Texas, 1970)

Scotland

Sir Robert Bruce Lockhart
Scotch (London, 1959)

R. J. S. McDowall
The Whiskies of Scotland (London, 1967)

South Africa

Gordon Bagnall
Wine of South Africa (Paarl, 1961)

The K.W.V.
Wines of Origin (Atlas-Calendar) (Paarl, 1974)

Spain

Enrique de Isasi
Con una Copa de Jerez (Madrid, 1970)

Julian Jeffs
Sherry (London, 1961)

George Rainbird
Sherry and the Wines of Spain (London, 1966)

Jan Read
The Wines of Spain and Portugal (London, 1973)

Switzerland

Editions Générales (publishers)
Les Vins Suisses (Geneva, 1968)

USA (California)

Leon D. Adams
The Wines of America (Boston, 1973)

Bob Thompson
California Wine Country (Menlo Park, 1968)

Choosing and Serving Wine

A Burgundy wine grower tastes from the barrel; 'thief' in one hand, silver 'tastevin' in the other

Tasting and Talking about Wine

MOST GOOD, even most great wine is wasted. It flows over tongues and down throats of people who are not attuned to it; not receptive of what it has to offer. They are preoccupied or deep in conversation; they have just drunk strong spirits which numb the sense of taste, or taken a mouthful of vinegary salad which overwhelms it; they have a cold; or they are simply unaware of where the difference between plain wine and great wine lies. Nothing the winemaker can do dispenses with the need for a sensitive and interested drinker.

If the sense of taste were located in the mouth (where our impulses tell us it is), anyone swallowing a mouthful of wine would get all the sensations it has to offer. But as this model of Bacchus shows, the nerves which receive anything more distinctive than the basic sensations of sweet, sour, salt and bitter are higher in the head and deeper in the brain.

In fact we smell tastes, rather than tasting them with our lips and tongues and palates. The real organ of discrimination is in the upper nasal cavity, where in normal breathing the air never goes. And the only sensations that can reach it are the vapours of volatile substances. To reach the brain the vapours of wine need to be inhaled (either through nose or mouth) into the upper part of the nasal cavity where they are dissolved in moisture. From the moisture long thin nerve processes (vacilli) take the sensations to the olfactory bulb, above the nasal cavity and right in the brain.

It is often remarked how smells stir memories more rapidly and vividly than other sensations. From the position of the olfactory bulb, nearest neighbour to the temporal lobe where memories are stored, it seems that smell, the most primitive of our senses, has a privileged position of instant access to the memory-bank. Experienced tasters often rely on the immediate reaction of their memory to the first sniff of a wine. If they cannot relate it straight away to wines they have tasted in the past they must fall back on their powers of analysis, located in the parietal lobe. In the frontal lobe their judgement of the wine is formed (to be stored in turn in the temporal lobe for future reference).

The range of reference available is the great difference between an experienced taster and a beginner. There is little meaning in an isolated sensation—though it may be very pleasant. Where the real pleasures of wine-tasting lie are in the cross-references, the stirring of memories, the comparisons between similar and yet subtly different products of the same or neighbouring ground.

Wines differ from one another in colour, texture, strength and 'body', as well as smell or 'taste'. A taster takes all these into account. His approach is shown in the pictures opposite.

What is much harder than appreciating wine is communicating its sensations. There is no notation of taste, as there is of sound or colour; apart from the words sweet, salt, sour and bitter every word in the language of taste is borrowed from the other senses. And yet words by giving an identity to sensations help to clarify them. Some of the most helpful of the many words tasters use are listed opposite.

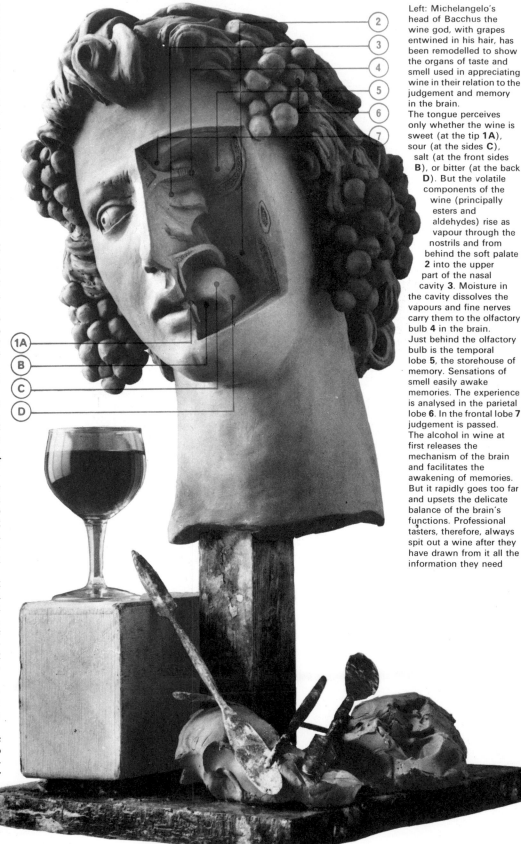

Left: Michelangelo's head of Bacchus the wine god, with grapes entwined in his hair, has been remodelled to show the organs of taste and smell used in appreciating wine in their relation to the judgement and memory in the brain.

The tongue perceives only whether the wine is sweet (at the tip **1A**), sour (at the sides **C**), salt (at the front sides **B**), or bitter (at the back **D**). But the volatile components of the wine (principally esters and aldehydes) rise as vapour through the nostrils and from behind the soft palate **2** into the upper part of the nasal cavity **3**. Moisture in the cavity dissolves the vapours and fine nerves carry them to the olfactory bulb **4** in the brain. Just behind the olfactory bulb is the temporal lobe **5**, the storehouse of memory. Sensations of smell easily awake memories. The experience is analysed in the parietal lobe **6**. In the frontal lobe **7** judgement is passed. The alcohol in wine at first releases the mechanism of the brain and facilitates the awakening of memories. But it rapidly goes too far and upsets the delicate balance of the brain's functions. Professional tasters, therefore, always spit out a wine after they have drawn from it all the information they need

The colour of the wine at the rim of the glass, tipped against a white background, gives the taster his first information. Is it clear? Is red purplish (young) or turning to brick with age? Great wines have strikingly deep and fresh colour. Is white very light and touched with youthful green (chlorophyll) or turning to gold?

The wine's appearance

Blackish—young red, perhaps very tannic, will take a long time to mature
Brick-red—colour of mature claret
Brilliant—completely clear
Brown—except in sherry or madeira brown wine is too old
Cloudy—something is wrong; all wine should be bright
Gris—very pale rosé, the speciality of some parts of France
Intense—a useful but undefinable word for colour
Maderized—brown or going brown with the effect of oxygen and age
Pelure d'oignon—'onion skin'; the tawny-pink of Provençal rosés or the signs of browning in an aging wine
Perlant—'pearling' (or *pétillant*); wine with natural fine bubbles which stick to the glass
Purple—a young colour; translucent in young Beaujolais; deep in red wine which will take time to mature
Rosé—pink; neither red nor white; a term of abuse for red wine
Ruby (of port in particular)—the full red of young wine
Tawny (of port in particular)—the faded dark amber of old wine

The smell of wine

Acetic—wine which is 'pricked' or gone irredeemably sour through contact with the air smells of acetic acid or vinegar
Aroma—the simple grape-smell of young wine
Bouquet—the complex smell arising with maturity in good wine
Complex—the scents-within-scents; suggestions of many different analogies with fruits, flowers etc
Corky—the smell of the (very rare) bottle which has had a mouldy cork

Foxy—the characteristic smell of the native American grape; not like foxes
Heady—attractively high in alcohol
Lively—an indefinable good sign; a fresh, frank, good smell from wine which is young and will last
Musty—unpleasant smell, probably from a barrel with a rotten stave
Rancio—the smell of oxidized fortified wine, the speciality of south-west France and Catalonia
Sappy—translation of the French 'sève'; the lively forthright style of a fine young wine, especially burgundy
Sulphury—the hot and nose-tickling smell often given by cheap white wine in which sulphur is used as a preservative. It will go off if the wine gets enough air
Yeasty—the smell of yeast can be attractive in young wine, though it usually means it has been fermenting slightly in the bottle and is unstable

Describing wine

Many words are borrowed to describe the qualities of their originals; flavours which can be conveyed in no other way, appearing in wine in traces of the same chemical constituents as the fruit (or whatever) in question. Such are:
Apples—malic acid is common in good young wine. In Moselles it is very apparent

Almost everything about a wine is revealed by its scent. The taster inhales deeply. The first impression is the most telling. Is there any 'foreign' or 'wrong' smell? Does it smell of fresh grapes or have a complex 'bouquet' from age in barrel and bottle? Is the grape identifiable (as Riesling, Pinot, Muscat, Cabernet)?

Blackcurrants—smell and flavour in many red wines
Earthy—a virtue or fault depending on the context. A common quality of Italian wines
Flowery—used generally for an attractive and forthcoming scent
Grapy—a great wine has more than grapiness, but a fresh-grape smell is always a good sign

Gun-flint—scent of flint-sparks in some white wine—e.g. Pouilly Fumé
Honey—associated particularly with 'noble rot' in great sweet wines
Nuts—nuttiness is usually found in well-aged wines. It is very marked in good old sherry

The taste in the mouth confirms the information given by the nose. The taster takes a good mouthful, not a sip, and lets it reach every part of his mouth. The body or wininess now makes its impact. Is it generous or meagre? Is it harsh with tannin as young reds should be? Is it soft and flat or well-balanced with acidity?

Oak—the character given to wine by the barrel, important and attractive as it is, should not be obvious enough to be identified as oak
Peaches—associated with a certain fruity acidity, e.g. in some Loire wines
Raspberries—a common flavour in very good red wine, particularly of Bordeaux and the Rhône valley
Smoke—smokiness is claimed for many white wines
Spice—very pronounced in the Traminer and Gewürztraminer grapes
Stalks—a green-wood smell which can arise in an under-ripe vintage
Truffles—the most elusive of all scents, found by Burgundians in Burgundy, Barolans in Barolo, hermits in Hermitage
Vanilla—scent given to wine and (much more) brandy by a component of the oak of the cask
Violets—another elusive scent found by people in their favourite wine

The list could be much extended; many tasters play the free-association game and jot down 'rubber', 'pear-drops', 'wool', etc on their tasting cards

General terms of appreciation

Baked—flavour resulting from very hot sun on grapes
Big—strong, round and satisfying
Body—the 'volume' of a wine, partly due to alcoholic strength

Breed—balance of qualities in good wine due to grapes, soil and skill
Clean—refreshing; free from defects
Coarse—tasting crudely-made
Complete—mature, balanced and satisfying
Distinctive—having its own character
Dry—the opposite of sweet
Dumb—not offering its full quality (wine is too young or too cold)
Elegant—as of a woman; indefinable
Fat—as of a man; well-fleshed. Not a desirable characteristic in itself
Fiery—a good quality, in moderation
Finesse—literally, fine-ness
Finish—aftertaste; in great wine the exact flavour remains in the mouth for a considerable period after swallowing
Firm—young with a decisive style
Flat—the opposite of firm
Fruity—ripe-tasting
Hard—tannin makes young reds hard
Long—what the finish should be
Nervy—vigorous and fine; good in wine as in horses
Noble—the ultimate combination of breed, body, maturity; use with care
Old—by itself often means too old
Racy—from French *race*, meaning breed; or vital and exciting
Rough—poor, cheap, badly-made
Séché—'dried up'—too-old red wine
Short—what the finish should not be
Silky—accurate word for a certain texture (found in good Beaujolais)
Stiff—similar to dumb
Stuffing—the body and character of certain red wines (Côte de Nuits, St-Emilion)
Supple—opposite of hard, but not pejorative as soft would be
Unresolved—not old enough for components to have harmonized
Vigorous—young and lively

Holding the wine in his mouth the taster draws air between his lips. The warmth of his mouth helps to volatilize the wine; a more positive impression of the taste materializes at the very back of the mouth as vapours rise to the nasal cavity from behind. After swallowing (or spitting) is the flavour short-lived or lingering?

Looking after Wine

To buy good wine and not to look after it properly is like hanging a masterpiece in a dark corner, or not exercising a race-horse, or not polishing your Rolls-Royce. If good wine was ever worth paying extra for it is worth keeping, and above all serving, in good condition.

There is nothing mysterious or difficult about handling wine. But doing it well can add vastly to the pleasure of drinking it—and doing it badly can make the best bottle taste frankly ordinary.

Wine only asks for two things: to be kept lying quietly in a dark cool place, and to be served generously, not hurriedly, with plenty of time and room to breathe the air.

Storage is a problem to almost everyone. Cellars like the one opposite, the perfect place for keeping a collection of wine, are no longer built. Most people have to make shift with a cupboard. But even a cupboard can have the simple requirements of darkness, freedom from vibration, and—if not the ideal coolness—at least an even temperature. Wine is not over-fussy about temperature. Anything from 45 to about 70°F will do. What matters more is that it stays the same. No wine will stand alternate boiling and freezing. In high temperatures it tends to age quicker—and there is the danger of it seeping round the cork—but if coolness is impracticable, steady warmth will do.

No special equipment is needed in cellar or cupboard. Bottles are always kept lying down to prevent the cork from drying and shrinking and letting in air. They can be stacked in a pile if they are all the same; but if they are all different it is better to keep them in a rack so that bottles can easily be taken from the bottom. Failing a wooden or metal rack, cardboard delivery boxes on their sides are satisfactory until they sag—which in a damp cellar does not take long.

Given the space, there is every argument for buying wine young, at its opening price, and

The bell, book and candle of a wine-collector's cellar: some of the elegant extras which accumulate where there is good wine. Wine with a very heavy sediment, such as vintage port or old Hermitage, is sometimes filtered into a decanter through a fine muslin cloth placed over a funnel made of glass or silver

'laying it down' in cellar or cupboard until it reaches perfect maturity. Wine merchants are not slow to point out that it appreciates in monetary, as well as gastronomic, value out of all proportion to the outlay. While at the top end of the market with château- or domaine-bottled wines this can mean making a fortune, at the bottom it can mean that even cheap red wines become very pleasant after six months or a year longer in bottles than the shop gives them. The probable ages of maturity of recent vintages are given in charts on pages 45 to 48.

It was Pasteur who discovered (see pages 30–31) the effects on wine of exposing it to the air. The same effects lie behind the custom of decanting, or pouring wine from its original bottle into another—more often a glass carafe —before serving it. Decanting is little understood and not much practised today . . . strangely, because there is no better way of getting the most out of wine.

There is a mistaken idea that it is something you only do to ancient bottles with lots of sediment—a sort of precautionary measure to get a clean glass of wine. In reality it is young wines which benefit most. The oxygen they contain has had little chance to take effect. But the air in the decanter works rapidly and effectively. In a matter of a few hours it produces the full flowering of what was only in bud. This can mean literally twice as much of the scent and flavour that you paid for. Some strong young wines can benefit by even as much as 24 hours in a decanter. An hour makes all the difference to others. The more full-bodied the wine the longer it needs.

The technique of decanting is illustrated below. The only essential equipment is a carafe (or decanter) and a corkscrew. But a basket is a good way of keeping the bottle in almost the same position as in the rack where it was lying —so that any sediment remains along the lower side. And a corkscrew which pulls against the rim of the bottle—either a double-screw or the lever-type—makes it easy to avoid jerking.

Cut the lead capsule and take it off completely. Take the cork out gently. Wipe the lip of the bottle. Hold the bottle (with or without the basket) in one hand and the decanter in the other, and pour steadily until you see the sediment (if any) moving into the shoulder of the bottle. Then stop. Having a light—a candle-flame is ideal—behind or below the neck of the bottle makes it easier to see when the dregs start to move—besides adding to what should be a pleasantly sensuous ritual.

A wine basket should never appear on the table, but using one is the best means of keeping a bottle on its side and steady while the cork is drawn

A double-action corkscrew, with counter-revolving screws, draws the cork steadily and gently without disturbing the wine's sediment

A candle below the neck of the bottle makes it easier to see when the sediment in the wine comes to the neck: the time to stop pouring

A small private wine cellar, beneath a house, has a brick floor and brick 'bins' where the wine is laid, either on the floor or on a shelf. In the bins in this cellar, which can contain about 500 bottles, are, top row, left to right: white burgundies and German Ausleses laid down for maturing; bottles in racks (red, white and champagne) where they can easily be removed without disturbing others. These are ready for drinking. Then two more bins of red wines laid down for maturing, labels uppermost and capsules (with their names) facing out.

Bottom row: claret stored in original cases from the château. Magnums of red burgundy and Bordeaux. Vintage port binned for long aging. Red burgundy newly bought and not yet laid down. The table with candles and a funnel is for opening bottles and decanting

Another decanting technique to avoid disturbing the wine: a silver funnel with the bottom curved to make the wine run down the side of the decanter

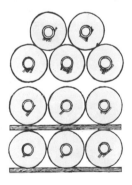

Left: professional cellarmen 'bin' bottles as much as 40 deep; by placing laths between rows they can take one bottle from the bottom of the pile. A simpler method (top) is to lay them directly on top of each other

Right: racks are most convenient for small collections, whether kept in a cupboard or cellar

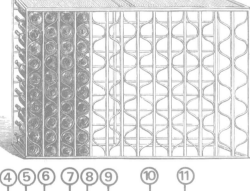

Right: a personal cellarbook is a wine-collector's essential record of prices, judgements, and stock. The one shown has entries for: 1 name of wine; 2 name of shippers; 3 where and when bought; 4 vintage; 5 quantity bought; 6 price; 7 date of drinking; 8 number of bottles left; 9 comments on the wine; 10 the food; 11 the guests

Choosing Wine

THE FRENCH have an inimitable way of expressing the character of a wine in terms of the perfect dish to accompany it. '. . . sur un foie gras' they say with relish: one immediately has a useful idea of the kind of wine and its appropriate place at table. With the thousands of wines in this atlas such an approach is impossible. Here we put forward some suggestions for the choosing of wine by the sort of occasion when it will be drunk, with the object of guiding the reader who is looking for (for example) an after-dinner wine, a wine to order for everyday use or an attractive wine to take on a picnic. Each suggestion is followed by the number of the atlas page where a major reference to it will be found.

Aperitifs

National tastes are most marked in the choice of aperitifs: the Italian with his vermouth or bitters; the American with his highball or dry martini; the Frenchman with his Dubonnet, or 'porto', or Scotch; the Englishman with his sherry or his gin and tonic . . .

The ideal aperitif stimulates the appetite as well as the wits. It is brisk and dry, with either a sparkle (there are many other sparkling wines besides champagne) or a tang (like the bitter vermouths). Dry sherry and many natural dry white wines make perfect drinks for before dinner. Strong cocktails leave the palate unable to appreciate good wine at the table.

All aperitifs should be served thoroughly chilled, with (at least) dry biscuits, olives or crumbled cheese as an accompaniment.

Sparkling wines Champagne, see page *98*; Anjou-Samur, *108*; Vouvray, *110*; St-Péray or Die, *112*; burgundy, *52*; Savoie or the Jura, *117*; Blanquette de Limoux, *118*; Sekt, *125*; Asti Spumante, *151*; Neuchâtel, *184*; Spanish, *162*; Californian, *214*; New York, *222*; Australian, *224*.

Fortified wines Sherry, *164*; Sercial madeira, *172*; white port, *178*; Marsala, *161*; vermouth, *148*.

Natural wines Mâcon blanc, *66*; dry white Graves, *86*; Alsace Sylvaner or Riesling, *102*; Muscadet, *106*; Anjou, *108*; Sancerre or Pouilly, *111*; vin jaune or Apremont, *117*; Luxembourg Moselle, *132*; German Kabinett wines, *124*; Hungarian Riesling, *190*, *192*, Tokay Szamarodni, *191*; Jugoslav Riesling. *194*; Romanian Cotnari or Riesling, *196*; Bulgarian Riesling, *198*; vinho verde, *177*; Alella, *170*; Soave, *155*; Frascati, *156*; Californian Johannisberg Riesling, *214*; Chinese dry white, *210*.

Cups (ideal in summer) Vin blanc cassis (dry white wine and blackcurrant syrup); hock and seltzer (sweeter wine with soda water); Buck's fizz (sparkling wine and orange juice); Pimm's patent cups.

Everyday wine

Wine for everyday, for meals in the kitchen, can be plain vin ordinaire—or something a little more interesting: the wine of a specific region.

Red Coteaux du Languedoc, *118*; Fronsac, *94*; Bourg, Blaye, *96*; Bordeaux Supérieur, *73*; Mâcon rouge, *66*; Côtes du Rhône, *112*; commune Bordeaux wines, *73*; Algerian, Tunisian, Moroccan, *206*; Corvo red, *161*; Sardinian, *156*; Klevner, *185*; Valdepeñas, *162*; Rioja Clarete, *168*; Dão Tinto, *177*; Portuguese branded wine, *174*; Argentine red, *234*; Gamza, *198*; Demestica, *202*; South African Hermitage, *232*; Kadarka, *190*; Australian Claret, *224*; Cyprus red, *205*; Californian Burgundy, *214*.

White Alsace Zwicker, *102*; Gros Plant du Pays Nantais, *106*; Clairette de Bellegarde or Languedoc, *118*; Entre-Deux-Mers, *73*; Hungarian or Jugoslav Riesling, *190* or *194*; Austrian Schluck, *189*; German Tafelwein, *124*; Bulgarian Chardonnay, *198*; Verdicchio, *156*; Lacrima Christi, *161*; Capri, *161*; Gallo or Italian Swiss Colony 'Chablis' or many wineries' 'mountain white', *214*.

Alfresco wine

The wine for a picnic or a meal in the garden should be something lighter, better and with more character than your everyday wine. The ideal has been said to be champagne, taken to the picnic spot the day before and buried under a turf in the cool ground. A stream or, more prosaically, damp newspaper is usually effective in cooling a bottle.

Red Beaujolais-Villages, *68*; Chinon, Bourgueil, *109*; Cabernet d'Anjou, *108*; Bergerac, *97*; local VDQS red, *122*; Chianti in fiaschi, *158*; Barbera or Dolcetto, *150*; Lago di Caldaro, *154*; Valpolicella, *155*; Valdepeñas, *162*; Zinfandel, *214*; Dôle, *182*.

Rosé Marsannay, *65*; Cabernet rosé d'Anjou, *108*; Provençal, *116*; Jura vin gris, *117*; Chiaretto del Garda, *152*; Ravello, *161*; California Grenache, *214*.

White Bourgogne Aligoté, *52*; Alsace Sylvaner or Traminer, *102*; Muscadet, *106*; dry Vouvray, *110*; vinho verde, *177*; Grüner Veltliner, *186*; Bernkasteler Riesling, *134*; Steinwein, *145*; retsina, *202*; Californian Riesling, *214*; Steen or Riesling, *230*; English white, *236*.

Family meals

This big category includes the good but not the great wines of the world, perfect for leisurely but not grand meals, Sunday lunch with the family or entertaining friends. These wines have real character and quality; they are worth taking note of and discussing, without demanding attention and respect. For most formal occasions as well such wines as these are the perfect choice. Unless the company has gathered to discuss wine it is a pity to serve anything which is terribly expensive, rare and irreplaceable.

Red Côte d'Or commune wines and some Premier Crus of Santenay, Volnay, Pommard, Nuits etc, *56*; Grand Cru Beaujolais, *68*; good Cru Bourgeois and lesser classed growths of the Médoc, *76–84*; similar wines from Graves, Pomerol and St-Emilion, *86*, *90*, *92*; Châteauneuf-du-Pape, *115*; Cahors, *120*; Chinon, Bourgueil, *109*; Bandol, *116*; Barolo, Barbaresco, *150*; Chianti Riserva, *158*; Alto Adige Cabernet. *154*; Lambrusco, *152*; Rioja Reserva, *168*; Colares, *176*; Dão Reserva, *177*; Australian Private Bin type clarets from Hunter, Coonawarra etc, *224*; Californian Cabernet Sauvignon or Pinot Noir, *214*; Chilean Cabernet, *234*.

Rosé Tavel, *112*; Marsannay, *65*; Cabernet Rosé d'Anjou, *108*; Chiaretto del Garda, *152*.

White Graves Crus Classés, *86*; Chablis Premier Cru, *70*; Côte de Beaune commune wines, *57*; estate-bottled Muscadet, *106*; Vouvray, *110*, Sancerre, Pouilly Fumé, *111*; Pouilly-Fuissé, *66*; Mâcon Viré, *66*; Côte Chalonnaise, *67*; Alsace Riesling, Traminer, *102*; Middle Mosel, *132*; Nahe, *136*; Rheingau, *138*; Rheinpfalz, *142*; Rheinhessen, *144*; Franconian and Baden Kabinett wines, *145*, *146*, and Spätleses of lighter vintages from these German areas; Soave, *155*, Frascati, *156*; Alvarinho, *177*; Fendant de Sion and Dorin of Vaud, *182*; Rheinriesling from Burgenland and Wachau, *186*, *189*; Balatoni Szürkebarát and Kéknyelü, *192*; Californian Chardonnay or Johannisberg Riesling *214*; Barossa Riesling, *228*.

Great wines

The great wines should never be served except to wine-lovers under ideal conditions—when there is time to appreciate their qualities, to compare them with lesser wines or their own peers, and when they can be partnered with well-chosen and well-prepared, not too highly-seasoned, dishes. They should have the best glasses, and candlelight –a certain formality enhances their enjoyment. Uninhibited discussion of their qualities is essential— or they are wasted.

The qualities of a great wine stand out much more sharply if it is compared with another of the same family—perhaps a neighbour or a lesser vintage of the same vineyard. The lesser wine may well be fine in its own right; the great wine will be all the more memorable coming after it and capping its qualities. Too many magnificent wines served on one occasion, on the other hand, tend to cancel each other out so that none remains a distinct and vivid memory.

The greatest German wines are best drunk without (or after) food; all are sweet, but complete in themselves so that any sweet dish only detracts from them. They need not be thought of in conjunction with a meal at all; their low alcohol-content makes them a perfect drink at any time of day when there is time to give them the attention they deserve. They are never better than when served in a garden.

Red Grands Crus and outstanding Premiers Crus of the Côte d'Or, *56*; the best classed growths of the Médoc, *76–84*; Graves, *86*; Pomerol, *90*; St-Emilion, *92*; Côte Rôtie, *113*; Hermitage, *114*.

White The Montrachets, *57*; outstanding Premier Cru Meursaults, *58*; Grand Cru Chablis, *70*; Corton-Charlemagne, *60*; exceptional Alsace Rieslings or Gewürztraminers, *104*; exceptional Vouvrays, *110*; Quarts de Chaume, Savennières, *108*; Château Grillet, *113*; Spätleses and Ausleses of the Saar, *128*, Ruwer, *130*, Middle Mosel, *132*, Nahe, *136*, Rheingau, *138*, Rheinpfalz, *142*.

The end of the meal

Natural (or sparkling) sweet wines go admirably with a sweet course at the end of the meal– though there are certain dishes, particularly chocolate ones or those containing citrus fruits, which do not agree with them—or equally well as after-dinner drinks on their own. Their sugar and their velvety texture make them soothing and satisfying; they have the opposite effect to aperitifs, leading to contemplation rather than action. Few people drink them in any but small quantities; one glass of Sauternes goes as far as two or three of white burgundy. It is worth remembering the port-merchant's rule-of-thumb in choosing after-dinner wine. He 'buys on an apple and sells on cheese'—knowing that cheese is kind to wine, making it taste better than it is, while fruit is the opposite—only very good wine comes through the ordeal.

The strong dessert wines containing brandy (port, madeira, Tokay and the rest) go well with cheese, apples (if they are good) or nuts, but less well with sweet dishes, except quite plain and cake like ones.

The world's great spirits find their place after dinner, when they can be drunk undiluted in small sips and there is time to enjoy their perfume.

Natural wines Sauternes, *88*; exceptional Vouvrays, *110*; Quarts de Chaume, etc, *108*; Monbazillac, *97*; Jurançon, *120*; German Ausleses, Beerenausleses and Trockenbeerenausleses, *124*; sweet muscat wines–Beaumes de Venise, *112*; Setúbal, *174*; Sicilian, *161*; Russian, *200*.

Sparkling wines Sweet champagne, *100*; Asti Spumante, *151*.

Dessert wines Port, *178*; Tokay, *191*; Malmsey or Bual madeira, *172*; cream sherry, *166*; Commandaria, *204*; vin santo, *148*; Marsala, *161*; Tarragona, *170*; Malaga, *162*.

Spirits Cognac, *242*; Armagnac, *244*; alcools blancs, *254*; Calvados, *255*; marc, *20*; malt or the finest blends of whisky, *246*, *248*, rum, *250*, etc.

Serving Wine

THE CARE we take in serving wine and the little customs and courtesies of the table cannot do much to change its virtues or vices. But they can add tenfold to its enjoyment. If there are different glasses, decanters, even rituals for different wines it is not out of any physical necessity, but as an expression of the varying sensuous pleasures they give. In helping to emphasise the different characters of wine—and reminding us of their origins—they add to the experience and make it memorable.

These pages show a number of the more practical, as well as pretty, forms of glass which have been evolved to put each kind of wine in its best light. Some of the attentions paid to wine are frivolous. Others (notably decanting, for which see page 38) can make all the difference between mere satisfaction and real delight. One aspect of serving it is essential, come what may: seeing that it is at the right temperature. There is little pleasure in stone-cold red wine, or lukewarm white.

There are good reasons why this should be so. Our sense of smell is only susceptible to vapours (see page 36). And red wine has a higher molecular weight—and is thus less volatile—than white. The object of serving red wine at room temperature, or 'chambré', is to warm it to the point where its aromatic elements begin to vaporize—which is at a progressively higher temperature for more substantial and solid wines. A light Beaujolais can be treated as a white wine; even cold its volatility is almost overwhelming. But a Chambertin needs the warmth of the room, of the cupped hand round the glass, and of the mouth itself to volatilize its massive constituents.

The ideal red wine temperature is about 65°F; if you warm it any more than this it will

The champagne 'flûte': the traditional and most beautiful sparkling-wine glass. Slow to fill, as the bubbles rise like a rocket. 'Tulips' are also good for champagne: flat, shallow glasses are not

A spirit decanter; heavy cut crystal made in Poland. There is no practical reason for using a decanter for spirits. They neither improve nor deteriorate for several weeks after opening the bottle. But as an elegant extra, decanting makes whisky, brandy, gin or rum or any spirit look its best

Many wine regions have their own style of wine-glass, designed to show off the local wine. The vintners of Anjou on the Loire use this original design for their fresh white wine. The long stem to hold prevents hands from warming the bowl. The clear glass allows the colour to be seen and the sloping sides concentrate the bouquet

The sherry copita: one of the world's best-designed tasting glasses, funnelling the scent of the wine to the nostrils; also the perfect size for drinking sherry, filled half-full

A wine decanter. Apart from looking magnificent on the table in a decanter, any good red wine benefits from the air (see page 38). This Georgian magnum holds a double bottle but is perfect for allowing a single one plenty of air

A Burgundian silver tastevin. Professional tasters in Burgundy keep one in their pockets. Its gleam through the wine in a dark cellar is a surer judge of colour and clarity than a glass would be; and it is unbreakable. This one is 200 years old

The traditional white-wine glass of Alsace is designed on the same principles as that of Anjou. The green stem reflects a pretty green gleam into the wine

be the alcohol which will start to vaporize, and which you will smell. Better to give the wine more time and air at a moderate temperature than to try to hurry it with heat.

White or rosé wine is much easier to serve perfectly; an hour in a refrigerator is usually all it needs. Quicker still is to put the bottle in a bucket of cold water and ice. In a warm room or in a hot garden it is a good idea to keep the bottle in the bucket. But as soon as the wine begins to feel at all icy it should be taken out. The ideal temperature for good white wine (so that its scent emerges but it is still piquant and refreshing) is about 45 to 50°F; the better the wine the less cold it should be. None except the cheapest wine needs chilling beyond coolness.

Any good wine benefits by comparison with another. It is no affectation, but simply making the most of something good, to serve more than one wine at a meal. A young wine served first shows off an older one; a light wine a massive one; a dry wine a sweet one. Conversely a really good wine puts in the shade a lesser wine served after it, and the same thing happens to a dry white wine served after a red.

The question of how much to serve is more difficult. There are six good glasses of wine (which means big glasses filled half-full, not small ones filled to the brim) in a normal bottle. At a quick lunch one glass a person might be enough, whereas at a long dinner five or six might not be too much. A total of half a bottle a person (perhaps one glass of white wine and two of red) is a reasonable average allowance for most people and occasions—but the circumstances and mood of the meal, and above all how long it goes on, are the deciding factors. There is a golden rule for hosts; be generous, but never pressing

Champagne or any white wine is at its best thoroughly cooled. The ideal way is in a deep ice-bucket full of cold water, with ice-cubes in the water. This more elegant but less conventional ice-bucket is an English silver punch-bowl engraved with the royal arms of George III. Ideally it should be deeper. Most ice buckets are too shallow, so it is necessary to stand the bottle on its head in them for a few minutes to cool the top of the bottle as well as the bottom

An 18th-century cordial glass is perfect for vodka, which is served filled to the brim, but useless for any wine, which should never more than half-fill a glass

A useful glass for port, sherry or madeira; not a classical design but well-balanced and good for tasting

The traditional Rhine-wine or hock glass has a stout knobbed stem of brown glass; again to reflect the desired colour into the wine. Although today the fashion is for pale wine its use continues

A 'tulip' glass filled with red Bordeaux. One of the perfect all-purpose glasses—ideal for champagne or any white wine as well as red. The in-turned rim helps to collect the scent

Decanter for sherry, port or madeira. For vintage port decanting is necessary, for the rest a luxury

The pretty engraved Trier or Treviris glass for Mosel. Even small cafés on the Mosel use this graceful glass to make their pale delicate white wine catch the light and seem more inviting than ever

Silver or gold labels for decanters are a practical old custom which is being revived. A London firm made the reproductions of famous examples used in the picture. They are suitable for any wine or spirit which is served or kept in a decanter

Stands for decanters or bottles to prevent them from making rings on the table are known as 'coasters'. They used to be made of silver or gold, or wood, or papier mâché. Another adjunct to the serving of wine which should be revived

A red wine glass ideal for burgundy or Bordeaux, known as a Paris goblet. Big enough to be filled only one-third full—the perfect amount for appreciating the wine

A cognac glass from the great Baccarat factory. Designed for cupping in the hand to warm the spirit; the vapour is caught and held in the bowl. Monster balloon glasses are never used by experts in Cognac

The Piemontese bottle of Barolo and Barbera, superficially Burgundian but a little heavier with lower shoulders. Made of brown glass

The splendidly embossed Châteauneuf-du-Pape bottle is a slightly heavier and bolder design than Burgundy's

Sherry has no standard bottle shape, but this long-necked and broad-shouldered design is typical

The Loire bottle: a slightly more tapering variant of the Burgundy shape, often in paler green glass

The thick powerful champagne bottle (here a magnum, holding twice as much as a bottle), which must resist repeated handling and a pressure of four to five atmospheres, sometimes for decades

The claret or red Bordeaux bottle, of green glass: a simple shape adopted by all the world. Very easy to stack for laying wine down

The *fiasco* for the sweet white wines of Orvieto in Umbria, like a truncated version of the more famous Chianti *fiasco* with its hand-made straw case

Red and white burgundy both come in slope-shouldered green bottles. Red-wine bottles are usually dark green; white sometimes a more olive colour

The Beaujolais 'pot' is a traditional idea rather than a classical shape. Different merchants have their own interpretations. It holds the same amount as an ordinary bottle

The vintage port bottle, traditionally without a label. The name appears on the capsule and the cork itself. White paint indicates the side to keep uppermost when it is taken out for decanting

The clavelin, reserved in France for the 'yellow' wines of the Jura

The world-wide symbol of Italian restaurants: the Chianti *fiasco*, holding a litre. Bordeaux-style bottles are used for the best Chianti; the straw-plaited flask is for the everyday wine of Tuscany

The classical German bottle. It is always brown for Rhine wine and green for Mosel. It used to be blue for occasional Mosel wines —a beautiful bottle very rare today

The Bocksbeutel, reserved in Germany for Franconia's wine, is seemingly descended from an old flagon or drinking gourd

The Alsace flute is slightly longer than the German model (holding the same amount) and made of green glass like the Mosel bottle

The plainest wine bottle is used, in clear glass, for white Bordeaux: Graves and Sauternes

Recent Vintages

LOCAL weather conditions (and growers' reactions to them) vary so much that any vintage chart is only a broad generalization. Moreover vintages vary not only in quality but in style; there are years of big tender wines and years of firm wines full of tannin and lasting-power; the difference between them lies more in how long they will take to be at their best than how good they will ultimately be – which is after all partly a matter of taste.

Thus in the following vintage charts the following information is given:

1 The size of the vintage. This affects the price, and hence the value-for-money, of the wine. It is worth remembering that the greatest vintages are almost always small ones. The fewer grapes there are on the vine the more flavour there is in each grape, because each gets a larger share of the soil's minerals.

2 The general standard and particular style of the wine in each area for each year.

3 Dates when the wine will probably be ready for drinking; the first date for the lightest – which would normally be the cheapest – wine and the second for the best of the area and year. The second date is impossible to calculate with precision, since the development of wine in bottle often produces surprises. These forecasts are approximate.

Other factors which affect the aging of wine should also be taken into account. Half-bottles age quicker than bottles, and bottles than magnums. Wine brought slowly to its maturity in a magnum is as good as it can be. Distance from the vineyard also makes a difference; a transatlantic journey may have the effect of making a wine seem a year or two older than it would if it remained in the grower's cellar. Warm cellars sometimes seem to age wine faster than cold ones.

Germany

Mosel/Saar/Ruwer

Mosels (including Saar and Ruwer wines) are so attractive young that their keeping qualities are not often explored, and wines older than seven years are unusual. But well-made wines of Kabinett class gain from at least a year in bottle, Spätleses by a little longer, and Ausleses by even as much as 15 years.

Rhine

Even the best wines can be drunk with pleasure after two or three years, but Spätleses and better wines of good vintages gain enormously in character and complexity by keeping for five or six years. Rheingau wines tend to be the longest-lived, often improving for ten years or more: Rheinhessen wines mature sooner; the best Palatinate and Nahe wines are comparable with the Rheingau. None the less bottles older than six or seven years are unusual.

Year	Size	Middle Mosel	To drink
1975	●●●	An extremely good year	Now-'88
1974	●●	Some useful light wines	Now
1973	●●●	Run-of-the-mill with few a exceptions	Now-'79
1972	●●●	Poor, with few exceptions	Now
1971	●●●	A great vintage	Now-'85
1970	●●●	Supple and pretty; few Ausleses	Now
1969	●●	Very fine; some great wines	Now-'80
1968	●●	Very poor	Now
1967	●●	Excellent	Now
1966	●●	Very good; light	Now

Year	Size	Rheingau	To drink
1975	●●	Very good	Now-'85
1974	●	Adequate and enjoyable – not more	Now-'80
1973	●●●	Good average; some Spätleses	Now-'79
1972	●●●	Moderate to good	Now-'79
1971	●●	Superb spicy	Now-'85
1970	●●	Good and attractive; not outstanding	Now-'77
1969	●●●	Very good; not great	Now-'79
1968	●●	Very poor	Now
1967	●●	Very good, elegant, complete	Now-'79
1966	●●	Excellent, fruity and balanced	Now

Year	Size	Palatinate	To drink
1975	●●	Best year since '71	Now-'84
1974	●●	Similar to '73	Now-'78
1973	●●●	Very useful easy wines	Now-'78
1972	●●●	Good, not exceptional	Now-'79
1971	●●	A great vintage	Now-'85
1970	●●●	Good, attractive, not outstanding	Now-'77
1969	●●	Excellent	Now-'79
1968	●●	A few good light wines	Now
1967	●●	Excellent; long and spicy	Now
1966	●●	Very good	Now

Year	Size	Saar/Ruwer	To drink
1975	●●●	Comparable with 1971	Now-'88
1974	●●	Few unsugared wines	Now
1973	●●●	Rather shaky average	Now-'78
1972	●●●	Bad	Never
1971	●●●	A very great vintage	Now-'85
1970	●●●	Fair to good	Now
1969	●●	Excellent, even great	Now-'80
1968	●●	Bad	Never
1967	●●	Very good	Now
1966	●●	Good	Now

Older fine vintages: '64, '59, '53, '49, '45

Year	Size	Rheinhessen	To drink
1975	●●	Very good	Now-'82
1974	●	Similar to 1973	Now-'79
1973	●●●	Good average; a few Spätleses	Now-'78
1972	●●●	Moderate	Now-'78
1971	●●	A great vintage	Now-'80
1970	●●●	Good, attractive, not outstanding	Now
1969	●●	Very good	Now
1968	●●	Very poor	Now
1967	●●	Excellent, fruity and fine	Now
1966	●	Very good	Now

Older fine vintages: '64, '59, '57, '53, '49, '45

Year	Size	Nahe	To drink
1975	●	Good to very good	Now-'84
1974	●●	Some enjoyable wines	Now-'79
1973	●●●	Average; nothing outstanding	Now-'78
1972	●●●	Some excellent light wines	Now
1971	●●	A great vintage	Now-'84
1970	●●	Good	Now-'77
1969	●●	Great; big and elegant	Now-'80
1968	●	Very poor	Now
1967	●	Exceptional	Now
1966	●	Excellent	Now

Older fine vintages: same as Rheingau and Rheinhessen

Size of vintage: ●●● notably copious   ●● average   ● small

Recent Vintages: France

Red Bordeaux

Médoc, red Graves Five years should be the absolute minimum age for a good Médoc. Few decline before ten years. Great wines can live for 50 years or more.

Pomerol/St-Emilion Tend to mature slightly faster than Médocs, but the wines of good vintages will improve for 20 years or more in bottle.

Year	Size	Médoc/red Graves	To drink
1975	●●	Splendid summer : possibly excellent	From 1980
1974	●●●	Rain at vintage : hollow, astringent wine	'78-'83
1973	●●●	A light vintage ; charm without depth	'77-'80
1972	●●	Unripe, few good wines	Now-'80
1971	●	A good, sometimes very good, vintage	Now-'88
1970	●●●	Superb, elegant and easy	Now-'90
1969	●●	Inconsistent, light, mostly poor	Now-'80
1968	●	Very poor	Never
1967	●●●	Good, particularly Graves ; rather light	Now-'79
1966	●●	Excellent, consistent, full	Now-'84
1965	●●	Bad, a few passable wines	Now, if at all
1964	●●	Good but patchy ; many disappointments	Now-'78
1963	●●	Very poor ; a few pleasant wines	Now
1962	●●	Very good middleweights	Now-'77
1961	●	Magnificent ; one of the best vintages ever	Now-'85

Older fine vintages : '59, '57, '55, '53, '52, '49, '47, '45, '29, '28

Year	Size	Pomerol/St-Emilion	To drink
1975	●●	Perhaps less successful than the Médoc	From '79
1974	●●●	Average to poor quality	'77-'80
1973	●●●	Light, attractive ; not for keeping	Now-'79
1972	●	Rather better than the Médoc	Now-'80
1971	●	Very good ; Pomerol especially	Now-'85
1970	●●	Excellent	Now-'84
1969	●	Adequate or better	Now-'79
1968	●	Very poor	Never
1967	●●●	Very good ; Pomerol especially	Now-'80
1966	●●●	Excellent ; round and full	Now-'78
1965	●●	Bad	Never
1964	●●●	Excellent	Now-'78
1963	●	Bad	Never
1962	●●●	Fair ; unreliable	Now
1961	●	Superb	Now-'80

Older fine vintages : same as Médoc/Graves

White Burgundy

Côte de Beaune The best wines of well-balanced vintages with plenty of acidity as well as fruit improve for as long as ten years. But in most vintages some light wines are made which are ready for drinking almost immediately.

Chablis of very ripe vintages rarely improve very much after two or three years. More acidic wines are often more worth keeping. The ideal Chablis is at its best after about ten years.

Year	Size	Côte de Beaune	To drink
1975	●●	Ripe, fruity, alcoholic wines ; excellent promise	'77-'85
1974	●●	Similar to '73, some finer and better	Now-'83
1973	●●●	Fine, fat, charming : less concentrated than '71	Now-'79
1972	●●	Character and complexity ; some classic wines	Now '83
1971	●	Great power and elegance ; superb	Now-'82
1970	●●	Very good ; fragrant, not very strong	Now-'78
1969	●	Excellent ; full, strong	Now-'78
1968	●●	Poor ; some good but light wines	Now
1967	●	Very good	Now
1966	●●	A great vintage	Now-'77
1965	●	Poor ; some fair	Now
1964	●●●	Very good ; rather soft	Now

The white wines of the Maconnais (Pouilly-Fuissé, St-Veran Mâcon-Villages) follow a similar pattern

Year	Size	Chablis	To drink
1975	●●●	Excellent ; balanced and true to type	'77-'84
1974	●●	High acidity, lively and attractive	Now-'85
1973	●●●	Very good ripe vintage	Now-'80
1972	●●	Poor, thin wines	Now
1971	●	Excellent, classic, well balanced	Now-'80
1970	●●●	Round, flowery	Now
1969	●●	Too heavy, flat	Now
1968	●●	Poor, acid	Now
1967	●●	Good	Now
1966	●●●	Excellent, some great wines	Now
1965	●●	Poor	Now
1964	●●●	Good	Now

Older fine vintages : '61, '59, '57, '55, '53, '49

Red Burgundy

Côte d'Or Earliest drinking dates are for lighter commune wines : Savigny, Volnay, etc. Latest for the biggest wines of the Côte de Nuits : Chambertin, Bonnes-Mares, etc. But different growers make wine of different styles : for longer or shorter maturing.

Beaujolais is made in two ways : 'nouveau' (or de l'année) is for drinking immediately. Beaujolais-Villages and named crus normally gain from one to three years in bottle. Exceptional Moulin-à-Vent vintages improve for as long as eight to ten years.

Year	Size	Côte d'Or	To drink
1975	●	Warm wet vintage caused rot : very few successes	'77-'81
1974	●●	Mostly poor ; even the best light and lean	'77-'82
1973	●●●	Patchy (too much wine) ; the best rich, fruity and showy	Now- 82
1972	●●●	Very fine, deep-coloured, firm and classical	Now-'85
1971	●	Ripe and strong ; some overstrong	Now-'80
1970	●●●	Attractive and fruity ; not very strong	Now-'78
1969	●●	Magnificent ; complete, full	Now-'80
1968	●●	A disaster	Never
1967	●●	Rather light, pale ; elegant	Now-'77
1966	●●	Excellent round strong wines	Now-'78
1965	●	Very bad	Never
1964	●●●	Good, rather light	Now
1963	●●	Very weak ; a few good wines	Now
1962	●●	Very fine, delicate	Now-'78
1961	●	Was magnificent ; now mostly too old	Now-'79

Older fine vintages : '59, '57, '55, '53, '52, '49, '47, '45

Year	Size	Beaujolais
1975	●	Hail damage : plain Beaujolais poor, some excellent Grands Crus
1974	●●	Attractive average vintage : drink soon
1973	●●●	Good for early drinking
1972	●●●	Some Grands Crus have kept well
1971	●●	Very good, but should be drunk now
1970	●●●	Past its best
1969	●●	Excellent, drink soon

Size of vintage : ●●● notably copious   ●● average   ● small

With very few exceptions older Beaujolais is too old

Sweet White Wines

Good vintages of Sauternes/Barsac and the luscious Chenin wines of Anjou (notably Côteaux du Layon) and Touraine (notably Vouvray) are among the longest-lived white wines, improving for up to 25 years. Even moderate vintages are often worth keeping for the added depth of flavour which comes in bottle.

Year	Size	Sauternes/Barsac
1975	●●	Exceptional rich wines
1974	●	Another disaster
1973	●●●	Crop ruined by rain
1972	●	Poor
1971	●	Very good stylish vintage
1970	●●	Rich and splendid wines
1969	●	Good, rather light
1968	●	Very poor
1967	●●	A great year
1966	●●	Some good lightish wines
1965	●●	Very poor
1964	●●	Crop ruined by rain

Older fine vintages : '62, '61, '59, '53, '49, '45, '21

Year	Size	Anjou/Touraine
1975	●	Excellent, especially in Anjou
1974	●●	Well balanced, should turn out well
1973	●●●	Fine ripe wines
1972	●●	Great acidity : a few good sweet wines
1971	●	Good in Anjou, great in Touraine
1970	●●●	Good
1969	●●	Excellent, some great wines
1968	●●●/●	Average
1967	●●	Good ; Anjou better
1966	●●	Poor
1965	●●	Nothing of consequence
1964	●	Rich, balanced, excellent wines

Older fine vintages : '61, '59, '55, '49, '43, '34

Dry White Wines

White Graves and other dry white Bordeaux, the Sauvignon wines of the upper Loire (Sancerre/Pouilly Fumé) and Muscadet are all wines to drink young, though good white Graves can age well up to ten years. Muscadet drinks best the year after the vintage, Sancerre/Pouilly usually the year after that.

Year	Size	Bordeaux
1975	●●	Very good
1974	●●	Adequate, drink soon
1973	●●●	Good, drink soon
1972	●	Good average
1971	●	Good, lasting well
1970	●●	Excellent, maturing well
1969	●	Good, keeping well
1968	●	Bad : avoid
1967	●●	Excellent, now mature

Year	Size	Upper Loire
1975	●	Good, some very good
1974	●●	Excellent
1973	●●●	Ripe, now failing
1972	●●	Unripe : avoid
1971	●	Very good, drink up
1970		Too old
1969		Too old
1968		Too old
1967		Too old

Year	Size	Muscadet
1975	●●	Good
1974	●	Dry, lean
1973	●●●	Lacked acidity, aged quickly
1972	●●	Unripe, too old now
1971	●	Very good, drink up
1970		Too old
1969		Too old
1968		Too old
1967		Too old

Red Rhône

Northern Rhône reds repay keeping longer than southern. Big vintages will keep 20 years at least.

Year	Size	Northern (including Hermitage)	To drink
1975	●	Poor ; rot	'77-'80
1974	●●	Thin, rather short wines	Now-'80
1973	●●●	Light wines, some good cuvées	Now-'80
1972	●●	Very fine indeed	Now-'88
1971	●●	Firm, well balanced, excellent	Now-'87
1970	●●●	Very good, ripe and round	Now-'84
1969	●●	Excellent, powerful	Now-'86
1968	●	Light	Now
1967	●●	Very good	Now-'78
1966	●●●	Very good	Now-'77
1965	●●	Light, some fine	Now
1964	●●	Rich colour and body	Now-'77
1963	●●	Bad	Never
1962	●	Some very good	Now
1961	●	Superb	Now-'80

Year	Size	Southern (including Châteauneuf-du-Pape)	To drink
1975	●	Disappointing	'77-'80
1974	●●	Average : early maturing	Now-'79
1973	●●●	Better, firmer wines	Now-'83
1972	●	Very good	Now-'80
1971	●●	Excellent	Now-'80
1970	●●●	Very good, a bit soft	Now-'80
1969	●●	Very fine	Now-'79
1968	●	Good	Now
1967	●●●	Well balanced, good body	Now
1966	●●	Rather light	Now
1965	●●	Disappointing	Now
1964	●●	Very good	Now
1963	●●	Bad	Never
1962	●●	Hard ; only fair	Now
1961	●	Excellent	Now

Older fine vintages : '59, '55, '54, '53, '52, '50, '49, '47, '45

Alsace

The ordinary cheaper wines need little or no aging. 'Réserves' and 'Grands Vins' of good vintages gain interest and quality in bottle for five or six years.

Year	Size	Alsace	To drink
1975	●●	Very satisfactory	Now-'79
1974	●●	Average to good	Now-'79
1973	●●●	Excellent, fruity and typical	Now-'78
1972	●●	Poor	Now, if at all
1971	●	Glorious	Now-'80
1970	●●●	Plentiful and good ; not great	Now
1969	●●	Excellent	Now
1968	●●	Poor	Now
1967	●●	Very fine	Now
1966	●●	Good average	Now
1965	●●	Bad	Never
1964	●●	A great vintage	Now

Wines before 1964 are likely to be too old

Champagne

Vintages are not sold until about five years old : the best improve for another five. Non-vintage champagne improves for at least a year after shipping.

Year	Size	Champagne
1975	●●	Excellent : vintage quality before rain
1974	●●	Good but non-vintage
1973	●●●	Very good, probably a vintage year
1972	●●●	Average ; useful
1971	●	Very good ; vintage quality
1970	●●●	Very good but very few vintage wines
1969	●●	Beautiful balanced vintage wines ; not heavy ; keeping well
1968	●●	Non-vintage
1967	●●	Good average
1966	●●	Very good ; great finesse ; drink soon
1965	●●	Non-vintage
1964	●●	A popular vintage but a shade heavy ; drink now

Size of vintage ●●● notably copious ●● average ● small

47

Recent Vintages

The detailed analysis which is given to the vintages of France and Germany is not so appropriate to the way the wines of the rest of the world are made and sold. Outstanding years are worth noting everywhere, and particularly in Italy, but the concept of a vintage year is only loosely understood in Portugal, Spain, Greece and the rest of wine-growing Europe, with the exception of the peculiar case of vintage port. In these countries years with particularly good reputations become almost brand names: a bodega may go on selling '1949' because 1949 was a popular wine while it lasted. In many cases it is the practice to blend older and younger wine, not with the idea of misleading the customer but to produce the balanced wine he will like best.

Where vintages printed on labels are most helpful in such cases is in giving an idea of the age of the bottle, which makes it easier to avoid, for example, white wines which are too old.

Italy

Exceptional years in the last decade have been:

Chianti Classico	1968	1971	1975		
Barolo	1964	1968	1969		

Very good years:

Chianti Classico	1962	1964	1967	1969	1970
Barolo	1962	1965			

Port

Long aging in bottle is part of the essential process of making vintage port. Each shipper decides whether his wine each year is worthy of early bottling and 'declaring' as 'vintage' port.

Year	Size	Quality	Characteristics	To drink
1975	●	Harvest very late and small; excellent		
1974	●	Good, may not be vintage quality		
1973	●●●	Not a vintage		
1972	●●	Unlikely to be a great vintage		
1971	●●	Not a vintage		
1970	●●●	Declared by 17 shippers	Excellent	From 1985
1969	●●●	Not a vintage		
1968	●●●	Not a vintage		
1967	●●●	Only declared by five shippers	Flowery	From 1978
1966	●●●	Declared by 17 shippers	Big and fruity	From 1980
1965	●●	Not a vintage		
1964	●●	Not a vintage		
1963	●●	Declared by 20 shippers	Very good, full-bodied and fruity	From 1980
1962	●●	Not a vintage		
1961	●●	Not a vintage		
1960	●●	Declared by 13 shippers	Rather light but good	Now–'85
1959	●●	Not a vintage		
1958	●	Declared by six shippers	A very light vintage	Now
1955	●●	Declared by 21 shippers	Excellent full and strong	1975–'82
1954	●	Not a vintage		
1950	●	Declared by nine shippers	Very good, delicate and fine	Now
1948	●	Declared by seven shippers	Very full and excellent	Now–'78
1945	●	Declared by 20 shippers	A great vintage	Now–'80

The New World: California

In the New World vintages tend to be very much more regular than in Europe. It is not safe to assume, however, that every year has the same qualities. The following notes on recent vintages in California's Napa valley indicate some of the climatic and other factors involved.

Year	California
1975	Wet spring, cool summer, late harvest into autumn rains. Good for whites and early ripening reds, not for Cabernet
1974	Little frost, long cool summer, ideal ripening conditions. A big crop in perfect condition
1973	Record vintage for quantity, quality overall fair to very good
1972	A year of extremes: dry winter, early spring, late frost, hot July, wet harvest. Quality very mixed
1971	Spring was late and September very hot. Quality about average overall
1970	Bad frost year. Crop down possibly 40%. Mild ripening conditions. Good sugars with tremendous acidity. Quality excellent
1969	Very hot weather in August; high sugar and burning in some varieties. Normal crop size. Reds big and heavy. Whites were picked early, but most were still big heavy wines
1968	Much like 1967. Some frost damage. Picking season late, ending the last of October. Some late varieties were rained upon. Whites again better overall than reds
1967	Near-normal growing conditions and yield. Some frost damage. Tremendous white wines; reds varied from heavy to thin
1965	Relatively cool year. Crop size below normal. Wines generally thin but highly aromatic
1965	Tremendous year in all respects: climate, yield and quality for both whites and reds
1964	Severe frost year. Low crop. Cold ripening conditions. Harsh wines

Size of vintage: ●●● notably copious   ●● average   ● small

France

Champagne: in one word the sensuous elegance which is the genius of France

France

Left: France has over 1,200,000 hectares of vineyards. Nurturing and protecting the vines is an unceasing task. Here, in midsummer near Saumur on the Loire, farmers spray with sulphur against the risk of mildew

WHEN the last raindrop has been counted, and no geological stone is left unturned, there will still remain the imponderable question of national character which makes France the undisputed mistress of the vine; the producer of infinitely more and more varied great wines than all the rest of the world.

France is not only sensuous and painstaking; France is methodical. She not only has good vineyards; she defines, classifies and controls them. The listing, in order, of the best sites has been going on for nearly 200 years. In the last 40 or so it has become more and more important, as the world's interest, not only in wine but also in consumer-protection, has grown.

This atlas does not attempt to reproduce the boundaries set by law to every French wine region. It has the wine-drinker rather than the lawyer in mind. There are two classes of wine with which we are concerned. All the best regions have Appellations Contrôlées, which are guarantees not only of origin but of a certain standard, administered by the central Institut National des Appellations d'Origine in Paris and its 'engineers' scattered round France. A second rank, for good wines of chiefly local interest, is called VDQS—Vin Délimité de Qualité Supérieure.

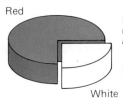

Red

White

France consumes 56 million hectolitres of wine a year: 112 litres per head

9% of the population is employed in wine-growing or the wine trade

Germany 40%
Belgium 12%
Great Britain 10%
Switzerland 8%
USA 7%

Above: France produces 62 million hectolitres of wine a year. 75% is red. 9m is Appellation Contrôlée

The average price for red wine is 70 francs per 100 litres to the grower; to the consumer, 1.53 francs a litre (1969 figures)

Above: France exports about 3.5m hectolitres a year. Germany is by far the biggest customer by volume. By value however she comes second to the USA: $43m to the USA's $47m. Britain pays $31m
Below: France imports 2.5m hectolitres more than she exports. Most imports are blending wine

Exports
Imports

——·—— International boundary

----- Département boundary

○ Chief town of département

● Centre of VDQS area

Vins du Thouarsais VDQS name — a guide to VDQS wines not mapped elsewhere appears on page 122

Appellation Contrôlée areas

☐ Champagne (pages 98 – 99)

☐ Alsace (pages 102–103) and Provence (page 116)

☐ Loire Valley (pages 106 – 107)

☐ Burgundy (page 53)

☐ Jura (page 117)

☐ Côtes du Rhône (page 112) and Jurançon (page 120)

☐ Cognac (page 242 – 243)

☐ Bordeaux (page 72) and Savoie(page 117)

☐ Bergerac (page 97)

☐ Armagnac and Madiran etc. (page 245)

☐ Gaillac (page 121) and Bellet

☐ Languedoc(page 118–119) and Cahors (page 120)

☐ Other wine-growing areas

Proportional Circles

● 44 Area of vineyard per département in thousands of hectares

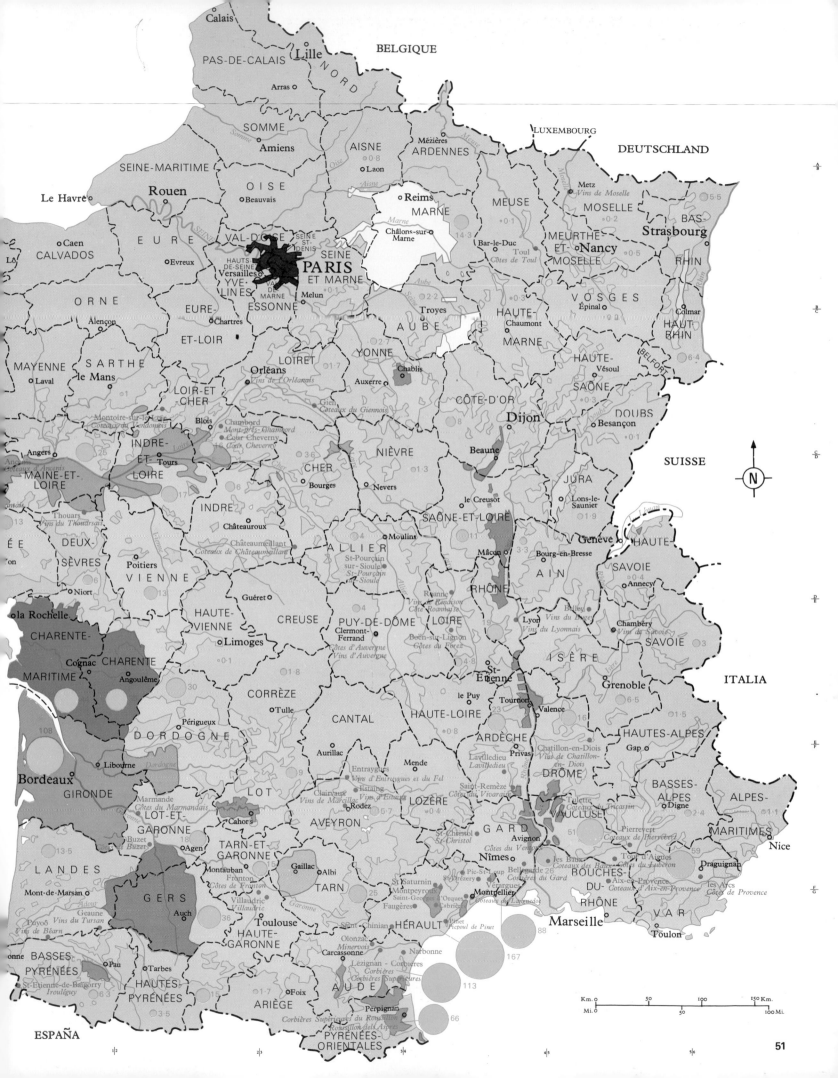

Burgundy

Above: Beaune is the wine capital of Burgundy; many would say of the world. The city's great landmark, the silvery roof of the mediaeval Hospices, gleams through the mist of an autumn evening, seen from the heights of the Montagne de Beaune to the west of the town

THE VERY name of Burgundy has a ring of richness about it. Let Paris be France's head, Champagne her soul, there is no doubt about what Burgundy is: her stomach. It is a land of long meals, well supplied with the best materials (Charolais beef to the west, Bresse chickens to the east). It is the most famous of the ancient duchies of France. But long before either, even before Christianity came to France, it was famous for its wine.

Burgundy is not one big vineyard, but the name of a province which contains at least three of France's best. By far the richest and most important is the Côte d'Or, in the centre, composed of the Côte de Nuits and the Côte de Beaune. But Chablis and Beaujolais and the Mâconnais have old reputations which owe nothing to their elder brother's.

For all her ancient fame and riches Burgundy still seems curiously simple and rustic. There is hardly a grand house from end to end of the Côte d'Or—none of the elegant country estates which stamp, say, the Médoc as a creation of leisure and wealth in the 18th and 19th centuries. Some of the few big holdings of land,

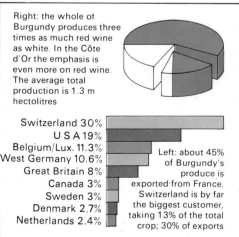

Right: the whole of Burgundy produces three times as much red wine as white. In the Côte d'Or the emphasis is even more on red wine. The average total production is 1.3 m hectolitres

Switzerland 30%	
USA 19%	
Belgium/Lux. 11.3%	
West Germany 10.6%	
Great Britain 8%	
Canada 3%	
Sweden 3%	
Denmark 2.7%	
Netherlands 2.4%	

Left: about 45% of Burgundy's produce is exported from France. Switzerland is by far the biggest customer, taking 13% of the total crop; 30% of exports

those of the church, were broken up by Napoleon. Now, in fact, it is one of the most fragmented of the important wine-growing districts of France.

The fragmentation of Burgundy is the cause of the one great drawback of its wine: its unpredictability. From the geographer's point of view the human factor is unmappable, and in Burgundy, more than in most places, it needs to be given the limelight. For even when you have pinned down a wine to one particular climat (field of vines) in one particular finage (village) in one particular year, it could still, in many cases, have been made by any one of six or seven men who own small parcels of the land, and reared in any one of six or seven cellars. 'Monopoles', or whole vineyards in the hands of one grower, are rare exceptions. Even the smallest grower has parcels of two or three vineyards. Bigger ones may own a total of 40 or 50 acres spread in two- or three-acre lots in a score of vineyards from one end of the Côte to the other. The Clos de Vougeot has over 60 growers in its 124 acres.

For this very reason the great majority of

burgundy is bought in barrel from the grower
when it is new by négociants (or shippers), who
blend it with other wines from the same area to
achieve marketable quantities of a standard
wine. It is offered to the world not as the product
of a specific grower, whose production of that
particular wine may be only a cask or two, but
as the wine of a given district (be it as specific as a vineyard or as vague as a village) élevé—
literally educated—by the shipper.

The reputations of these négociant-éleveurs
(many of whom are also growers themselves)
vary from being the touchstone of the finest
burgundy to something rather more earthy.

What is certain is that all the very finest wine
goes to market, as it does all over the world, with
the most detailed possible description of its
antecedents on its label . . . and these almost
always include the name of the proprietor of
the vineyard and the fact that he bottles the
wine in his own cellars.

The map on this page shows the whole of
wine-growing Burgundy, the relative sizes and
positions of the big southern areas of Beaujolais
and the Mâconnais, Chablis in the north, the
tiny Côte Chalonnaise and the narrow strip of
the Côte d'Or and its little-known hinterland,
the Hautes Côtes de Beaune and the Hautes
Côtes de Nuits. The key is an index to the
large-scale maps of the individual areas which
follow.

There are a hundred or so Appellations Contrôlées in Burgundy. Most of them refer to geographical areas and appear on the next 18 pages.
Built into these geographical appellations is a
classification by quality which is practically a
work of art in itself. It is explained on page 56.
However, the appellations Bourgogne, Bourgogne Aligoté (for white wine), Bourgogne
Passe-Tout-Grains and Bourgogne Grand
Ordinaire can be used for wine made from the
appropriate grapes coming from any part of
Burgundy, including the less good vineyards
within famous communes which have not the
right to the commune name.

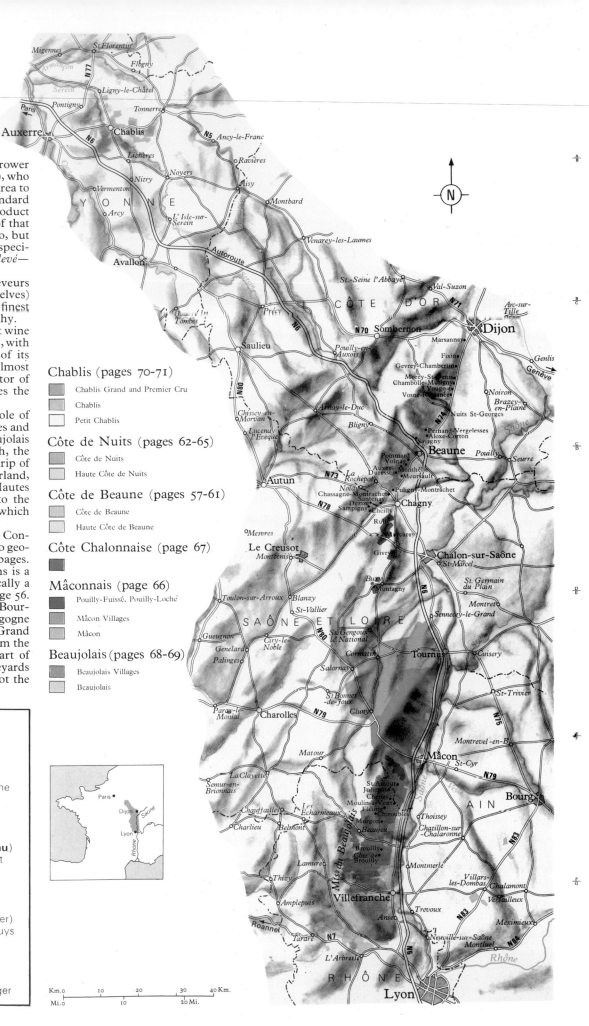

Chablis (pages 70-71)

- Chablis Grand and Premier Cru
- Chablis
- Petit Chablis

Côte de Nuits (pages 62-65)

- Côte de Nuits
- Haute Côte de Nuits

Côte de Beaune (pages 57-61)

- Côte de Beaune
- Haute Côte de Beaune

Côte Chalonnaise (page 67)

Mâconnais (page 66)

- Pouilly-Fuissé, Pouilly-Loché
- Mâcon Villages
- Mâcon

Beaujolais (pages 68-69)

- Beaujolais Villages
- Beaujolais

The Language of the Label

Climat Vineyard (individual field)
Commune or **Finage** Parish
Récolte Vintage
Grand Cru or **Tête de Cuvée** One of the
top growths, with its own Appellation
Contrôlée
Premier Cru The second class of
burgundy vineyard
Mise (or **Mise en bouteilles**) **du** (or **au**)
Domaine (or **à la propriété**) Bottled at
the property where it is made
Mise par le propriétaire Bottled by
the grower
Mise dans nos caves Bottled in our
cellars (not necessarily those of the grower)
Négociant-Eleveur A merchant who buys
wine from the grower in its first year and
'brings it up' in his own cellars
Monopole The whole of the vineyard
named belongs to the same proprietor
Propriétaire-Récoltant Owner-manager

Km.0   10   20   30   40 Km.
Mi.0   10   20 Mi.

Burgundy/the Quality Factor

A BURGUNDIAN understandably feels a certain reverence towards the commonplace-looking ridge of the Côte d'Or, as towards an unknown god. One is bound to wonder at the fact, witnessed by the tongues and palates of generation after generation, that a few small parcels of land on this hill give superlative wine, each with its own positive personality, and that others do not. Surely one can discover the facts which distinguish one parcel from another—giving to some grapes more sugar, thicker skins, a pulp more rich in minerals.

One can. And one cannot. There are millions of facts to collect and collate. Soil and subsoil have been analyzed time and again. Temperature and humidity and wind-direction have been recorded; must examined under the microscope . . . yet the central mystery remains. One can only put down certain physical facts, and place beside them the reputations of the great wines. No one can prove how they are connected.

Burgundy is the nothernmost area in the world which produces great red wine. Its climate pattern in summer is, in fact, curiously like that of Bordeaux—the continental influence making up to some extent for its position further north. Yet total failure of the vintage is a greater problem here. No overriding climatic consideration can explain the excellence of the wine—or even why a vineyard was established here in the first place. There are certain local or micro-climatic advantages: the shelter provided by the hills from wet west winds; the slight elevation above the fogs of the plain; but nothing unique.

Looking further for reasons, one turns to the soil. Here there are more clues. The ridge of the Côte d'Or is the edge of a plateau built up of various sandy limestones. Erosion, by the action of ice in the last periglacial period 18,000 years ago and since then by weather and cultivation, has broken them down into soil. Rubble and soil fall down the slope, which benefits both the nourishment and the drainage of the vine lower down. The more the soil is cultivated the greater the mixture of varied soil-types—helped also by the carting of good earth on to the better vineyards: in 1749 150 wagon-loads of turf were spread on the vine-

yard of Romanée-Conti, and the same sort of earth-moving goes on today.

The Côte de Nuits is a sharper slope than the Côte de Beaune. Along its lower part, generally about a third of the way up the slope, runs a narrow outcrop of marlstone, making limey clay soil. Marl by itself would be too rich a soil for the highest-quality wine, but in combination with the silt and scree washed down from the hard limestone higher up it is perfect. Erosion continues the blend below the actual outcrop. Above the marl, the thin light limestone soil is generally too poor for vines.

In the Côte de Beaune the marly outcrop (Argovien) is wider and higher on the hill; instead of a narrow strip of vineyard under a beetling brow of limestone there is a broad and gentle slope vineyards can climb. The vines almost reach the scrubby peak in places.

On the dramatic isolated hill of Corton the soil formed from the marlstone is the best part of the vineyard, with only a little wood-covered cap of hard limestone above it.

In Meursault the limestone reappearing below the marl on the slope forms a second and

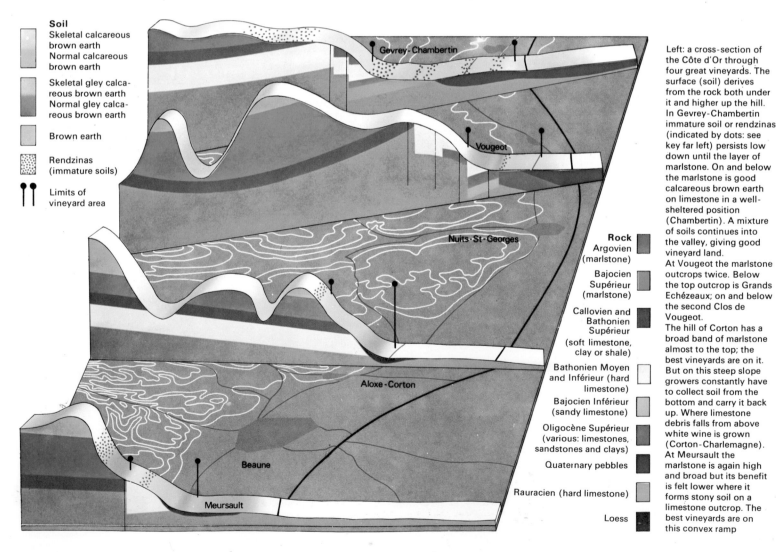

Soil

Skeletal calcareous brown earth
Normal calcareous brown earth

Skeletal gley calcareous brown earth
Normal gley calcareous brown earth

Brown earth

Rendzinas (immature soils)

Limits of vineyard area

Gevrey-Chambertin

Vougeot

Nuits-St-Georges

Aloxe-Corton

Beaune

Meursault

Rock

Argovien (marlstone)

Bajocien Supérieur (marlstone)

Callovien and Bathonien Supérieur (soft limestone, clay or shale)

Bathonien Moyen and Inférieur (hard limestone)

Bajocien Inférieur (sandy limestone)

Oligocène Supérieur (various: limestones, sandstones and clays)

Quaternary pebbles

Rauracien (hard limestone)

Loess

Left: a cross-section of the Côte d'Or through four great vineyards. The surface (soil) derives from the rock both under it and higher up the hill. In Gevrey-Chambertin immature soil or rendzinas (indicated by dots: see key far left) persists low down until the layer of marlstone. On and below the marlstone is good calcareous brown earth on limestone in a well-sheltered position (Chambertin). A mixture of soils continues into the valley, giving good vineyard land. At Vougeot the marlstone outcrops twice. Below the top outcrop is Grands Echézeaux; on and below the second Clos de Vougeot. The hill of Corton has a broad band of marlstone almost to the top; the best vineyards are on it. But on this steep slope growers constantly have to collect soil from the bottom and carry it back up. Where limestone debris falls from above white wine is grown (Corton-Charlemagne). At Meursault the marlstone is again high and broad but its benefit is felt lower where it forms stony soil on a limestone outcrop. The best vineyards are on this convex ramp

lower shoulder to the hill, limey and very stony; excellent for white wine.

Such illustrations are only random examples of the varied structure of the Côtes. And with each change of soil, caused by changes in the parent rock, there comes a change in drainage, the soil's temperature—any one of a hundred factors which will affect the wine.

Probably it is the micro-climate, which, in combination with the physical structure, has the most decisive effect. The best vineyards of the Côtes face due east, or even a shade north of east in places; it is the morning sun they want, to warm the ground gradually all day and let it cool gently in the evening without a sudden lowering of temperature at sunset. They are sheltered from the south-west, the moist rain-bearing wind—but not so sheltered as to be frost pockets on still nights. What other details of their position count in the thousands of hours that the grapes are hanging on the vines, forming the character of the cru and the character of the vintage, it is interesting to speculate—even though it seems unlikely we shall ever have the complete answer.

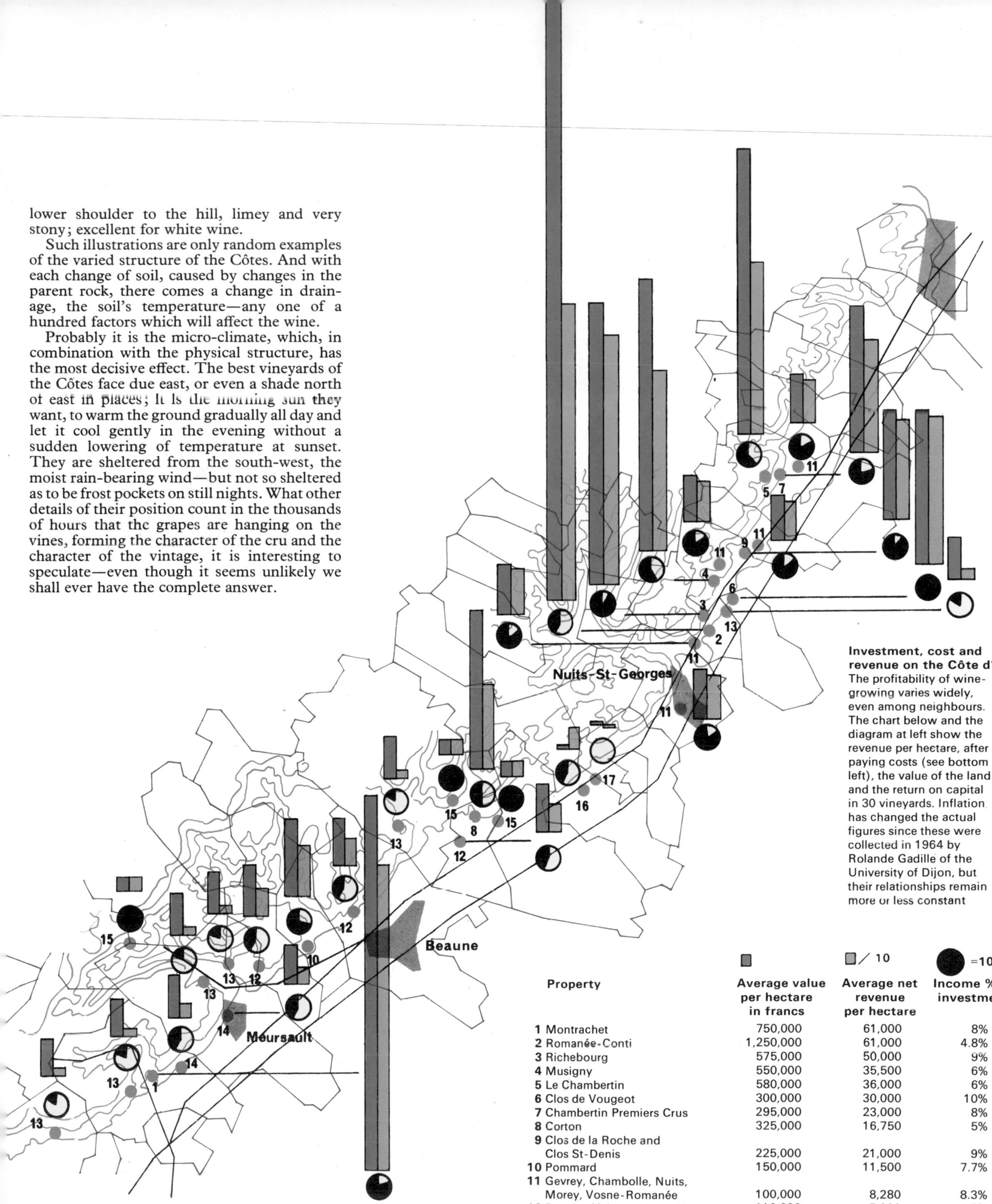

Investment, cost and revenue on the Côte d'Or
The profitability of wine-growing varies widely, even among neighbours. The chart below and the diagram at left show the revenue per hectare, after paying costs (see bottom left), the value of the land and the return on capital in 30 vineyards. Inflation has changed the actual figures since these were collected in 1964 by Rolande Gadille of the University of Dijon, but their relationships remain more or less constant

Right: the costs of these Burgundy estates were reckoned (in 1964) at 8000 francs per hectare per year for estates of over three hectares which employ labour; and at 5250 francs per hectare for two hectares or less where the work is done by the family

Property	Average value per hectare in francs	Average net revenue per hectare	Income % of investment
1 Montrachet	750,000	61,000	8%
2 Romanée-Conti	1,250,000	61,000	4.8%
3 Richebourg	575,000	50,000	9%
4 Musigny	550,000	35,500	6%
5 Le Chambertin	580,000	36,000	6%
6 Clos de Vougeot	300,000	30,000	10%
7 Chambertin Premiers Crus	295,000	23,000	8%
8 Corton	325,000	16,750	5%
9 Clos de la Roche and Clos St-Denis	225,000	21,000	9%
10 Pommard	150,000	11,500	7.7%
11 Gevrey, Chambolle, Nuits, Morey, Vosne-Romanée	100,000	8,280	8.3%
12 Beaune, Volnay, Aloxe-Corton	110,000	5,000	4.5%
13 Vougeot, Monthélie, Auxey, Chassagne, Santenay, Savigny	75,000	1,730	2.6%
14 Meursault, Puligny-Montrachet	80,000	2,830	4.2%
15 Côtes de Beaune-Villages, Ladoix, Pernand-Vergelesses	30,000	2,890	10%
16 Bourgogne	10,000	3,675	3.7%
17 Aligoté	1,500	-675	net loss

Nuits-St-Georges

Beaune

Meursault

The Côte d'Or

THE WHOLE Côte d'Or—the Côte de Beaune and the Côte de Nuits, separated only by a few miles without vines—is an irregular escarpment 30 miles long. Its top is a wooded plateau. Its bottom is the beginning of the flat, plain-like valley of the River Saône. The width of the slope varies from a mile and a half to a few hundred yards—but all the good vineyards are limited to this narrow strip.

The classification of the qualities of the land in this strip is the most elaborate on earth.

As it stands it is the work of the Institut National des Appellations d'Origine, based on classifications going back for over 100 years. It divides the vineyards into four classes, and lays down the law about the labelling of the wine accordingly. Grands Crus (also known as Têtes de Cuvée) are the first class. There are 30 of them. Each has its own appellation. Grands Crus do not normally use the name of their commune on their labels. The single, simple vineyard name: Musigny, Corton, Montrachet or Chambertin, is the patent of Burgundy's highest nobility.

The next rank, Premiers Crus, use the name of their commune followed by the name of their vineyard (or, if the wine comes from more than one Premier Cru vineyard, the commune name followed by the words Premier Cru).

The third rank is known as Appellation Communale; that is, having the right to use the commune name. A vineyard name is permitted —though rarely used—if it is printed in letters much smaller than the name of the commune. A few such vineyards, often called Clos de . . . though not officially Premiers Crus, are in the hands of a single good grower, and can be considered in the same class.

Fourthly there are inferior vineyards, even within some famous communes, which have only the right to call their wine Bourgogne.

The system has only one drawback for the consumer. Elaborate as it seems, there remains a class of vineyards which it does not specifically recognize, but which do distinguish themselves in practice. For only in the Côte de Nuits and three communes of the Côte de Beaune are there any Grands Crus; all the rest of the finest vineyards are Premiers Crus, despite the fact that, particularly in such communes as Pommard and Volnay, some Premiers Crus consistently give better wine than the others.

Besides controlling the use of place names, INAO lays down the regulations which control quality, demanding that only the classical vines be used (Pinot Noir for red wine, Chardonnay for white); that only so much wine (from 30 hectolitres per hectare for the best, to 40 for more ordinary) be made; that it achieve a certain strength (from 12% alcohol for the best white and 11.5 for the best red down to 9% for the most ordinary red).

It remains up to the consumer to remember to make the distinction between the name of a vineyard and of a commune. Many villages (Vosne, Gevrey, Chassagne, etc) have hyphenated their name to that of their best vineyard. The difference between a Chevalier-Montrachet (from one famous vineyard) and a Chassagne-Montrachet (from anywhere in a big commune) is not obvious; but it is vital.

Chancelier Nicolas Rolin & Guigone de Salins son épouse Fondateurs des Hospices de Beaune en 1443

Above and right: Beaune has one of the world's most famous hospitals, built in the mid-15th century and still busily in practice. The Hospices de Beaune was founded by Nicolas Rolin, Chancellor of the Duke of Burgundy, and his third wife Guigone de Salins, in 1443, and endowed with vineyards in the surrounding country. Since then wine growers have continued to bequeath their land to the hospital (or Hôtel-Dieu). The proceeds of the annual sale of its wine maintains it with all modern equipment, tending the sick of Beaune without charge. Above is a Victorian engraving of the founder and his wife. Top right is the splendid main courtyard.

The Hospices vineyards are shown on the maps and their recent prices given on the following pages. Their prices tend to establish the level for the burgundy of that year Right: the new wine in the cellars of the Hospices

The Hospices auction is held every November in Beaune's market hall

In the Grande Salle des Pôvres the beds are the original scarlet cubicles

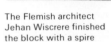

The Flemish architect Jehan Wiscrere finished the block with a spire

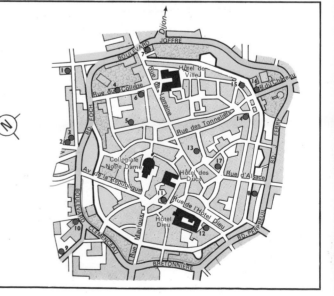

The wine merchants of Beaune

Beaune still keeps its town walls; their turrets are often used as cellars. Many of the best merchants of Burgundy work within the old city

1 Pierre Ponnelle
2 Brocard
3 Cave du Bourgogne
4 Chanson Père & Fils
5 Bouchard Aîné & Fils
6 Patriarche Père & Fils
7 Caves de la Reine Pédauque
8 Calvet
9 Albert Morot
10 Jaffelin Frères
11 Joseph Drouhin
12 Cave des Cordeliers
13 Léon Violland
14 Louis Latour
15 Remoissenet Père & Fils
16 Bouchard Père & Fils
17 Louis Jadot

The Côte de Beaune: Santenay

THE MAPS on this and the following eight pages trace the vineyards of the Côte d'Or from south to north. The orientation of the maps has been turned through approximately 90 degrees so that what appears to be south is east-south-east.

The Côte de Beaune starts without a great explosion of famous names. It leads in gradually, from the villages of Sampigny, Dézize and Cheilly, with the one well-known cru of Les Maranges which they share (all beyond the limits of this map; see page 53), into the commune of Santenay. After the hamlet of Haut-Santenay and the little town (a spa, but not a very gay one) of Santenay, the Côte half-turns to take up its characteristic slope to the east.

This southern end of the Côte de Beaune is the most confused geologically and in many ways is untypical of the Côte as a whole. Complex faults in the structure of the hills make radical changes of soil and subsoil in Santenay. Part of the commune is analogous to parts of the Côte de Nuits, giving a deep red wine with a long life. Other parts give light wine more typical of the Côte de Beaune. Some of the highest vineyards are too stony and have been abandoned altogether.

Les Gravières (the name draws attention to the stony ground, as the name Graves does in Bordeaux) and La Comme are the best climats of Santenay. The well-known Clos de Tavannes is part of Les Gravières. As we move into Chassagne-Montrachet the character of these excellent red wine vineyards is continued. The name of Montrachet is so firmly associated with white wine that few people expect to find red here at all. But almost all the vineyards from the village of Chassagne south grow at least some red wine: Morgeot, La Boudriotte and Clos St-Jean (the last mapped on page 58) are the most famous. Their wines are solid, long-lived and deep-coloured, again unusual for the Côte de Beaune.

Indeed no one really knows why white-wine-growing took over in this district. Thomas Jefferson reported that white-wine growers here had to eat hard rye bread while red-wine men could afford it soft and white. It has been suggested that local growers were trying to ape the success of Le Montrachet (which had been famous for white wine since the 16th century). Also that the Chardonnay is a more accommodating vine in stony soil—which it certainly finds in Meursault. Whatever the answer, Chassagne-Montrachet is known to the world chiefly for its dry but succulent, golden, flower-scented white wine.

The southern end of the Côte de Beaune is known principally for its substantial red wines. Maufoux is a distinguished négociant of Santenay; the remainder are some of the good growers with vineyards on this map

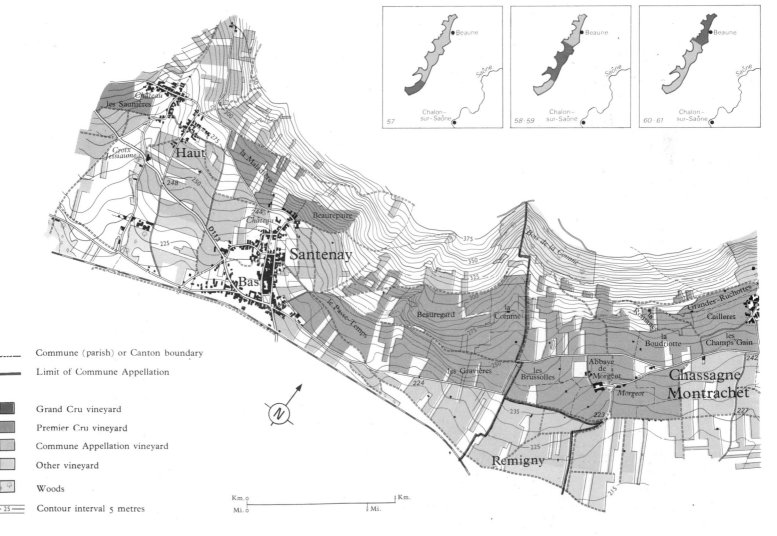

Commune (parish) or Canton boundary

Limit of Commune Appellation

Grand Cru vineyard

Premier Cru vineyard

Commune Appellation vineyard

Other vineyard

Woods

Contour interval 5 metres

The Côte de Beaune: Meursault

A SIDE VALLEY in the hills just north of Chassagne, leading up to the hamlet of Gamay (which gave its name to the Beaujolais grape in the bad old days before the Pinot came into its own), divides the vineyards of the commune in two. South of it there is excellent white wine but the emphasis is on red. North, on the border of Puligny, there is the best white wine in Burgundy, if not the world.

The Grand Cru Montrachet earns its fame by an almost unbelievable concentration of the qualities of white burgundy. It has more scent, a brighter gold, a longer flavour, more succulence and yet more definition; everything about it is intensified—the mark of truly great wine. Perfect exposure to the east, yet an angle which means the sun is still flooding down the rows of vines at nine on a summer evening; a sudden streak of very limey soil, are factors in giving it

Top: Volnay from the east
Above left: Chardonnay grapes at Meursault
Centre left: Comte Lafon in his Meursault caves
Centre right: Pinot Noir grapes at Pommard
Right: Le Montrachet at nine on a summer evening

Average price a cask (228 litres) at the 1970 Hospices de Beaune auction

Commune	Vineyard	Cuvée	francs
Auxey-Duresses	Duresses	Boillot	2,200
Monthélie	Duresses	Lebelin	2,500
Meursault	Charmes	de Bahèzre de Lanlay	4,000
Meursault	Charmes	Albert Grivault	3,500
Meursault	Genevrières	Baudot	2,600
Meursault	Genevrières	Philippe le Bon	3,500
Meursault	Poruzots	Goureau	3,400
Meursault	Poruzots	Jehan Humblot	2,400
Pommard	Epenots & Noizons	Billardet	3,500
Pommard	Epenots & Rugiens	Dames de là Charité	4,000
Volnay	Champans & Taille-Pieds	Blondeau	3,200
Volnay	Santenots	Gauvain	3,500
Volnay	Santenots	Jehan de Massol	3,800
Volnay	Village & Carelle	Général Muteau	3,200

The vineyards in which the Hospices de Beaune owns land are marked with a cross on this and the next map. Above and on page 61 are listed the 'cuvées', vineyards donated by the benefactors named, with the wines' prices in the 1970 sale, an indication of their relative reputations

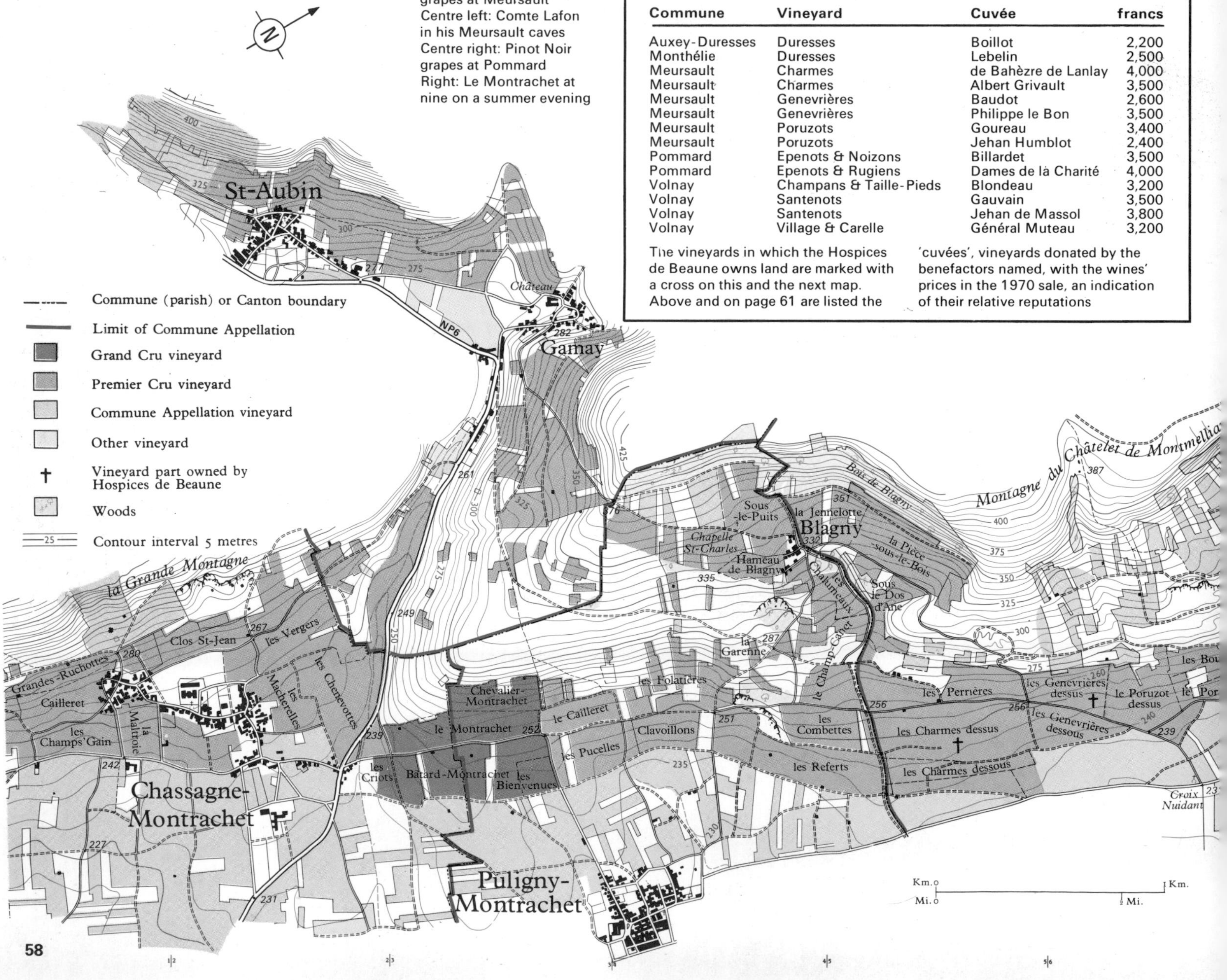

---- Commune (parish) or Canton boundary

── Limit of Commune Appellation

Grand Cru vineyard

Premier Cru vineyard

Commune Appellation vineyard

Other vineyard

✝ Vineyard part owned by Hospices de Beaune

Woods

─25─ Contour interval 5 metres

St-Aubin

Gamay

Blagny

Sous-le-Puits la Jennelotte

Chapelle St-Charles la Pièce sous-le-Bois

Hameau de Blagny

Sous le Dos d'Ane

Montagne du Châtelet de Montmellia

la Grande Montagne

Clos-St-Jean les Vergers

les Macherelles

les Chenevottes

la Garenne

Grandes-Ruchottes les Perrières les Genevrières dessus le Poruzot dessus

Cailleret

Chevalier-Montrachet

le Cailleret les Combettes les Genevrières dessous

les Champs Gain

la Maltroie

le Montrachet

Clavoillons les Charmes dessus

les Pucelles

les Folatières

les Referts les Charmes dessous

les Criots Bâtard-Montrachet les Bienvenues

Croix Nuidant

Chassagne-Montrachet

Puligny-Montrachet

Km. 0   Km.
Mi. 0   Mi.

58

an edge over its neighbours. For the other Grands Crus grouped about it come near but rarely excel it. Chevalier-Montrachet tends to be more delicate (coming from ground so stony that tilling it is barely worthwhile; its good soil is even used for renewing Le Montrachet). Bâtard- lies on richer ground and often—not always—fails to achieve quite the same finesse. Les Criots and Bienvenues belong in the same class—and so very often do the Puligny Premiers Crus Les Pucelles and Le Cailleret.

There is a distinction between Puligny-Montrachet and Meursault, quite clear in the minds of people who know them well, but almost impossible to define—and to account for. The vineyards of the one flow without a break into the other. In fact the hamlet of Blagny—which makes excellent wine high up on stony soil—is in both, with a classically com-plicated appellation: Premier Cru in Meursault, Blagny Premier Cru in Puligny-Montrachet, and only AC Blagny when (which is rare) the wine is red.

Meursault is—to attempt the impossible—a slightly softer, drier, less fruity wine than Puligny-Montrachet. The words 'nutty' and 'mealy' are used of it; whereas Puligny is more a matter of peaches and apricots. On the whole there is less brilliant distinction (and no Grand Cru) in Meursault—but a very high and gener-ally even standard over a large area, making it a reliable and often good-value wine to buy.

The big village lies across another dip in the hills where roads lead up to Auxey-Duresses and Monthélie, both sources of very good red wine which tend to be overlooked be-side Beaune (page 60), Pommard and Volnay.

Meursault's streets are lined with the court-yards and cellars of scores of growers, each of them owning parts of several climats.

Meursault in turn flows into Volnay. A good deal of red wine is grown on this side of the commune, but called Volnay-Santenots rather than Meursault. White Volnay can similarly call itself Meursault.

Volnay and Meursault draw as near together as red and white wines well can without being rosé; both rather soft, delicate, the red some-times rather pale yet with great personality and a long perfumed aftertaste. If Volnay makes the lightest wine of the Côte it can also be the most brilliant. Its life-span is relatively short—per-haps ten years. Caillerets is the great name in Volnay; Champans and Clos des Chênes are similar; the steep little Clos des Ducs, belong-ing to the Marquis d'Angerville, is the best climat on the other side of the village.

Right: a handful of the dozens of famous growers of this part of the Côtes; Le Montrachet has five noted owners: Laguiche, Bouchard Père, Thénard, Calvet and the Domaine de la Romanée-Conti

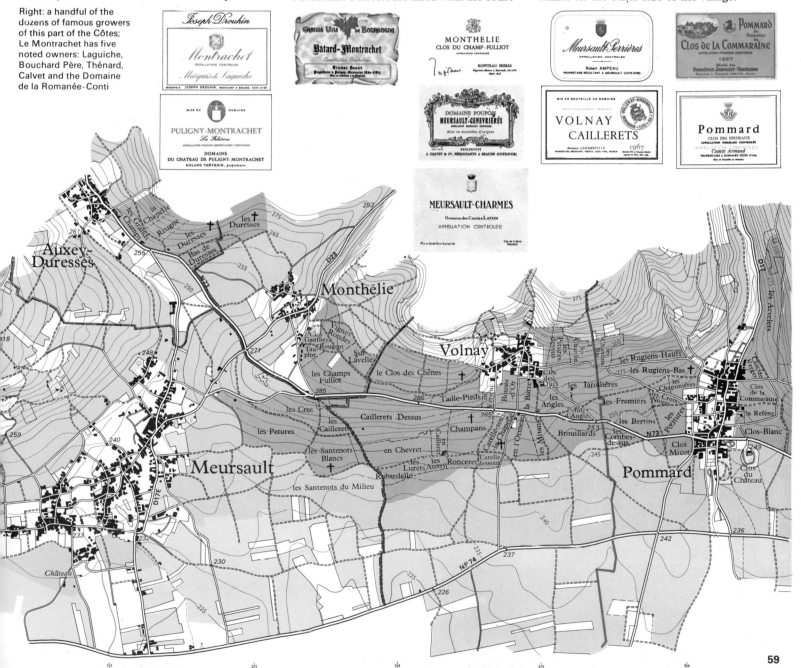

The Côte de Beaune: Beaune

POMMARD (mapped on this and the previous page) is unaccountably the best-known and most sought-after commune of the whole Côte. Unaccountably, because the commune wine is not outstanding, and there is no single vineyard with a world-wide reputation. Most critics of burgundy find Pommard the slight levelling off between the high-points of Volnay and Beaune. But what should not be ignored is the individual growers. In Burgundy the grower counts as much as the vineyard; the saying goes 'there are no great wines; only great bottles of wine'.

Pommard's most prestigious vineyard is the lower part of Les Rugiens (map page 59) above the village. One of the best cuvées of the Hospices de Beaune, Dames de la Charité, is made from Rugiens and Epenots (combined). Clos de la Commaraine is the monopole of the famous firm of Jaboulet-Vercherre. These are among the great Pommards; medium-weight wines but with the lovely savoury character of the best burgundy.

In the line of famous vineyards which occupy what the Burgundians call 'the kidney of the slope' above Beaune, a large proportion belongs to the city's négociants: Drouhin, Jadot, Bouchard Père et Fils, Chanson, Patriarche among

them. The late Maurice Drouhin was the most recent of the centuries-old list of donors to the Hospices de Beaune. His firm's part of the Clos des Mouches is now famous; it makes a rare white Beaune there as well as a superb red one. A part of Grèves, belonging to Bouchard Père et Fils, is known as the Vigne de l'Enfant Jésus, and makes another marvellous wine. No Beaune is a Grand Cru; partly, it is said, because of the sustained high standard of so much land here. Beaune is gentle wine, lasting well but not demanding to be kept ten years or more, like a Romanée or a Chambertin.

After Beaune the road crosses a flat plain and the hills and vineyards retreat. Ahead looms the prow of Corton, the one isolated hill of the whole Côte d'Or, with a dark cap of woods. Corton breaks the spell which prevents the Côte de Beaune from having a red Grand Cru. Its massive smooth slide of hill, vineyard to the top, presents faces to east, south and west; all excellent. Indeed it has not one but two Grand Cru appellations; for white wine and red, covering a large part of the hill. The white, Corton-Charlemagne, is grown on the upper slopes, where debris from the limestone top is washed down, whitening the brown marly soil.

The red, Le Corton, is grown in a broad band all round. The map names are misleading; they record the original sites of Corton and Corton-Charlemagne rather than the present appellations. The appellations cover a much wider area; the narrow strip labelled Corton is of little account, most red Corton comes from Renardes, Clos du Roi, Bressandes and the rest. Similarly the part marked Corton-Charlemagne grows both white wine (above) and red Corton (below). There is a slight Alice in Wonderland air about the legalities, but none whatsoever about the wine; both red and white, forceful, lingering, memorable wines, are among Burgundy's very best.

The most celebrated grower of Corton is Louis Latour, whose fine press-house, known as Château Grancey, stands in an old quarry in Les Perrières. Aloxe-Corton is the appellation of the lesser wines (red or white) grown below the hill, still often excellent.

If Savigny and Pernand are slightly in the background here it is only because the foreground is so imposing. The best growers of both make wines almost up to the Beaune standard. Part of Pernand has the appellations Corton and Corton-Charlemagne.

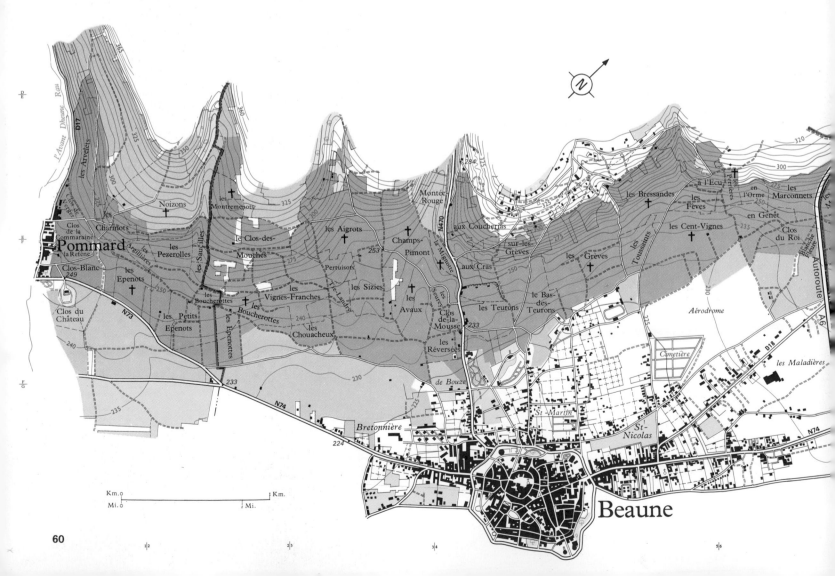

The hill of Corton from the south-east; left is the valley of Pernand-Vergelesses; centre right the village of Aloxe-Corton. High up under the woods Corton-Charlemagne is grown, lower on the right red Corton

Right: the top label is a new design just adopted by the Hospices de Beaune; among the others are some of Beaune's illustrious collection of merchant-growers

Commune	Vineyard	Cuvée	francs
Aloxe-Corton	Corton-Charlemagne (white)	François de Salins	10,200
Aloxe-Corton	Renardes & Bressandes	Charlotte Dumay	5,000
Aloxe-Corton	Bressandes & Clos du Roi	Docteur Peste	3,300
Beaune	Avaux	Clos des Avaux	4,200
Beaune	Grèves & Aigrots	Hugues & Louis Bétault	3,400
Beaune	Bressandes & Mignotte	Brunet	3,000
Beaune	Bressandes & Mignotte	Dames Hospitalières	7,000
Beaune	Avaux, Boucherottes, Champs-Pimont & Grèves	Maurice Drouhin	2,600
Beaune	Cent-Vignes & Grèves	Nicolas Rolin	4,800
Beaune	Cent-Vignes & Montremenots	Rousseau-Deslandes	3,000
Beaune	Bressandes & Champs-Pimont	Guigone de Salins	4,500
Pernand-Vergelesses	Basses Vergelesses	Rameau-Lamarosse	3,200
Savigny-les-Beaune	Vergelesses & Gravains	Fouquerend	2,700
Savigny-les-Beaune	Vergelesses & Gravains	Forneret	3,600
Savigny-les-Beaune	Marconnets	Arthur Girard	3,300

Average price a cask (228 litres) at the 1970 Hospices de Beaune auction

Legend:

- ⎯⎯⎯ Commune (parish) or canton boundary
- ⎯⎯⎯ Limit of Commune Appellation
- Grand Cru vineyard
- Premier Cru vineyard
- Commune Appellation vineyard
- Other vineyard
- † Vineyard part-owned by the Hospices de Beaune
- Woods
- ⎯300⎯ Contour interval 5 metres

The Confrérie des Chevaliers du Tastevin is Burgundy's wine fraternity and the most famous of its kind in the world. It was founded in 1933 and meets regularly for banquets with 600 guests, ceremonial (bottom right) and songs from a choir of growers (left above), the Cadets de Bourgogne. Its headquarters is the old château in the Clos de Vougeot (bottom left); there are branches in many countries and members among wine men all over the world. The Confrérie's own 'Tastevinage' label (detail above) may be used by wines which have been tasted and approved by a special committee

Left: Nuits-St-Georges has a Hospices like a smaller version of the Hospices de Beaune; Château Gris is not strictly a Grand Cru, as it says, but the excellent domaine of a shipper, Lupé-Cholet. Among the others are growers of some of the world's greatest red wines

MORE 'stuffing', longer life, deeper colour are the signs of a Côte de Nuits wine compared with a Volnay or Beaune. Very little white is made; what there is shares the qualities of the red.

The line of Premiers Crus, wriggling its way along the hill, is threaded with clutches of Grands Crus. These are the wines which express with most intensity the inimitable sappy richness of the Pinot Noir. The line follows the outcrop of marlstone below the hard limestone hilltop, but it is where the soil has a mixture of silt and scree over the marl that the quality reaches peaks. Happily this corresponds time and again with the best shelter and most sun.

The wines of Prémeaux (the southernmost commune) go to market under the name Nuits-St-Georges. The two communes between them have over 900 acres of vines. The quality is very high and consistent: they are big strong wines, almost approaching the style of Chambertin at their best. They age well, have a particularly marked scent, and altogether deserve better than their reputation, which has suffered from 'la grande cuisine' of the blending vats. Les St-Georges is one of the best climats of the Côte; its neighbours Vaucrains, Cailles, Porets and Pruliers are comparable.

Nuits has neither hotel nor restaurant to speak of, but it is the headquarters of a number of négociants, some of whom make sparkling

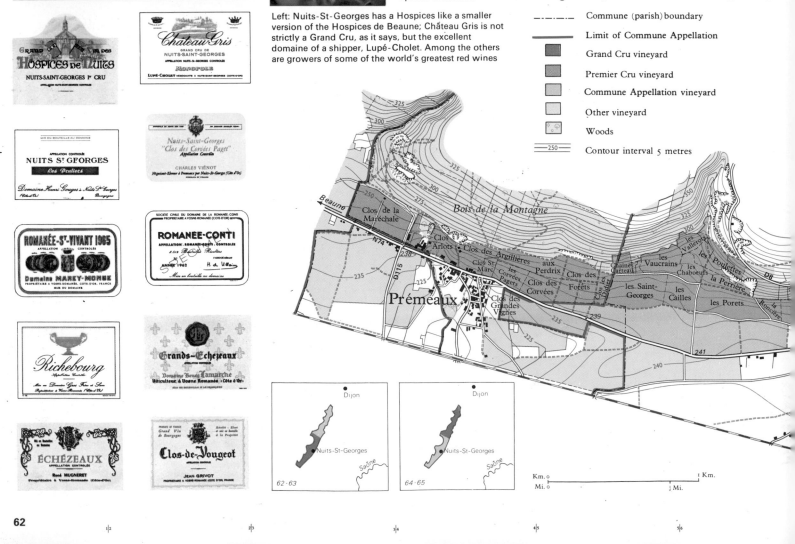

----- · ----- Commune (parish) boundary

————— Limit of Commune Appellation

Grand Cru vineyard

Premier Cru vineyard

Commune Appellation vineyard

Other vineyard

Woods

—250— Contour interval 5 metres

Looking straight up the hill from the track above Romanée-St-Vivant; in the foreground Romanée-Conti with its stony red earth; beyond it La Romanée. This soil gives France's most perfumed, satiny, expensive wine

burgundy out of the year's unsuccessful wine.

Vosne-Romanée is a modest little village. There is nothing to suggest that the world's most expensive wine lies beneath your feet. It stands below a long incline of reddish earth, looking up severely trimmed rows of vines, each ending with a stout post and a taut guy.

Nearest the village is Romanée-St-Vivant. The soil is deep, rich in clay and lime. The mid-slope is Romanée-Conti; poorer, shallower soil. Higher up, La Romanée tilts steeper; it seems drier and less clayey. On the right the big vine-yard of Le Richebourg curves round to face east-north-east. Up the left flank runs the nar-row strip of La Grande Rue, and beside it the long slope of La Tâche. All are among the most highly-prized of all burgundies. Romanée-Conti, La Tâche, Richebourg and Romanée-St-Vivant are all owned or managed wholly or in part by the Domaine de la Romanée-Conti. For the finesse, the velvety warmth combined with a suggestion of spice, the almost oriental opulence of their wines the market will seem-ingly stand any price. Romanée-Conti is con-sidered the most perfect, but the whole group has a family likeness.

Clearly one can look among their neighbours for wines of similar character at less stupendous prices. All the other named vineyards of Vosne-Romanée are superb. One of the textbooks on

Burgundy remarks drily: 'There are no common wines in Vosne.'

The big (79 acres) climat of Echézeaux and the smaller Grands Echézeaux are really in the commune of Flagey, a village over the railway, to the south, but they can use the name Vosne-Romanée for their wine if it does not reach the statutory standards for a Grand Cru. Some very fine growers have property here, and make beautiful, sometimes rather light wines. They are often a bargain—people say because the name looks hard to pronounce. Grands Eché-zeaux has perhaps more regularity, more of the lingering intensity which marks the very great burgundies; certainly higher prices.

One high stone wall surrounds the 125 acres of the Clos de Vougeot; the sure sign of a monastic vineyard. Today it is so subdivided that it is anything but a reliable label on a bottle. But it is the climat *as a whole* which is a Grand Cru. The monks used to blend wine of top, middle and sometimes bottom to make what we must believe was one of the best burgundies of all . . . and one of the most consistent, since in dry years the wine from lower down would have an advantage, in wet years the top slopes. There are wines from near the top—La Perrière in particular (just outside the Clos)—which can be as great as Musigny. The name of the grower must be your guide.

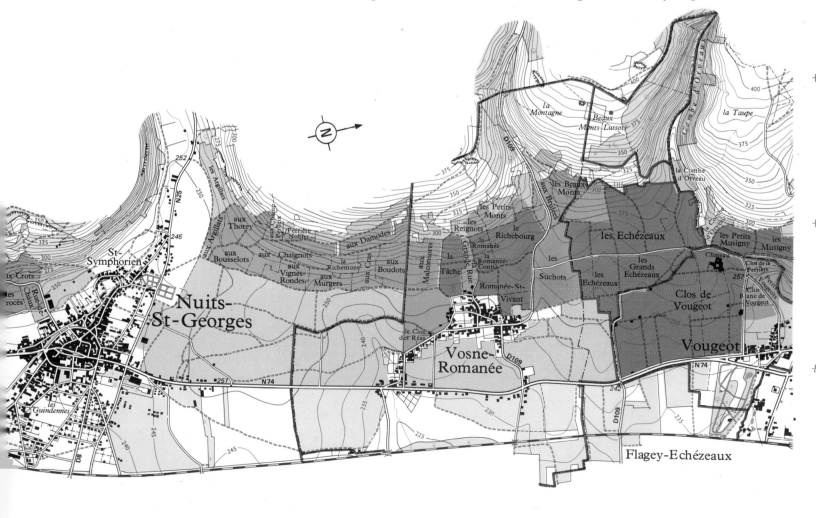

The Côte de Nuits: Gevrey-Chambertin

HERE, at the northern end of the Côte d'Or, the richest, longest-lasting red burgundies are made. Nature here adds rich soil to the perfect combination of shelter and exposure which the hills provide. The narrow marlstone outcrop, lightly overlaid with silt and scree, follows the lower slopes. From it Chambertin and the Grands Crus of Morey and Chambolle draw their power. For they are wines of body and strength, unyielding when they are young, but eventually offering more complexity and depth of flavour than any others.

Musigny, the first of the Grands Crus, stands apart, obviously related to the top of the Clos de Vougeot. There is only just room for it under the barren limestone crest. The slope is steep enough to mean the vignerons carrying the brown limey clay, heavy with pebbles, back up the hill when it collects at the bottom. This and the permeable limestone subsoil allow excellent drainage. Conditions are right for a wine with plenty of 'stuffing'.

The glory of Musigny is that it adds to its undoubted power a lovely haunting delicacy of perfume; a uniquely sensuous savour. A great Musigny makes what is so well described as a 'peacock's tail' in your mouth, opening and be-coming more complex and seductive as you swallow it. It is not so strong as Chambertin, not so spicy as Romanée-Conti—but he must have been a great respecter of women who called it 'feminine'.

Les Bonnes-Mares, at the far side of the village, is the other Grand Cru of Chambolle-Musigny. It leads over into Morey-St-Denis, both geographically and gastronomically, for it starts as a slightly tougher wine than Musigny, and ages perhaps a little slower, but achieves a similar power and tenderness.

Les Amoureuses and Les Charmes—their beautiful names are perfectly expressive of their wine—are both among the best Premiers Crus of Burgundy. Any wine from Chambolle-Musigny, however, is likely to be very good.

The commune of Morey is overshadowed in renown by two of its Grands Crus. Clos de la Roche, with little Clos St-Denis (which gave its name to the village), like Chambertin are wines of great staying-power, strength and solidity, fed by rich soil. Clos de Tart and the neighbouring Clos des Lambrays (which is the proprietor's name for the Premier Cru Les Larreys) have more in common with Bonnes-Mares. Clos de Tart, in fact, the monopole of the house of Mommessin, has been making a remarkable light wine recently; a marvel of delicacy, but not for long laying-down.

In Morey the vineyards climb the hill, finding soil higher up than anywhere else in this area. Les Monts-Luisants, on stonier ground, makes a correspondingly lighter wine than Clos de la Roche.

Gevrey-Chambertin has an amazing amount of good land. The ideal vineyard soil stretches further out from the hill than elsewhere, so that even land beyond the main road has the appellation Gevrey-Chambertin, rather than plain Bourgogne. Its two greatest vineyards, Chambertin and Clos de Bèze, lie under the woods on a mere gentle slope. They were acknowledged Grands Crus at a time when the citizens of Gevrey were quarrelling with the worthies of Beaune who were handing out the honours. Otherwise it is probable that the constellation of vineyards—Mazis, Latricières and the rest—around them would have been Grands Crus in their own right as well. Instead they have an in-between status, with the right to add -Chambertin after their names, but not (like Clos de Bèze) before. French wine law sometimes becomes more subtle than theology.

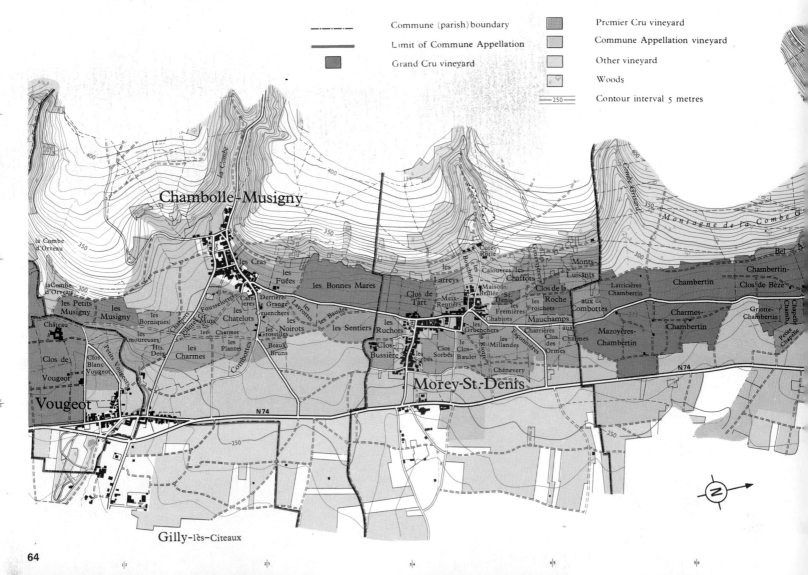

Commune (parish) boundary	Premier Cru vineyard
Limit of Commune Appellation	Commune Appellation vineyard
Grand Cru vineyard	Other vineyard
	Woods
250	Contour interval 5 metres

The commune has another slope with a very good, though rather different, exposure. Here Clos St-Jacques and Les Véroilles are arguably Grands Crus in everything but name.

There are more individual vineyards known all over the world in this village than in any other in Burgundy. To many people the forceful rich wine they make *is* burgundy. Hilaire Belloc told a story about his youth, and ended dreamily: 'I forget the name of the place; I forget the name of the girl; but the wine . . . was Chambertin.'

The slopes to the north used to be known as the Côte de Dijon, and until the last century were considered among the best. But their growers were tempted to use their rich land for bulk wine for the city and planted the 'disloyal plant', the Gamay. Brochon became known as a 'well of wine' from the quantities it made. Today it has no appellation of its own: its southern edge is included in Gevrey-Chambertin; the rest has only the right to the name Côte de Nuits-Villages.

Fixin, however, has a tradition of quality. La Perrière at one time made wine 'comparable to Chambertin'. But Les Hervelets is the best-known vineyard there today.

Above: the end of the year at the end of the Côtes. A grower of Fixin burns the prunings of his vines. North of here is the Côte de Dijon, once famous but now known only for the excellent pale rosé of Marsannay

Below: Gevrey-Chambertin is a big commune with over 1,000 acres of vines, one-fifth of which are Grands Crus. Many famous growers have holdings here. Others include Damoy, Ponsot, Camus, Naigeon-Chauveau

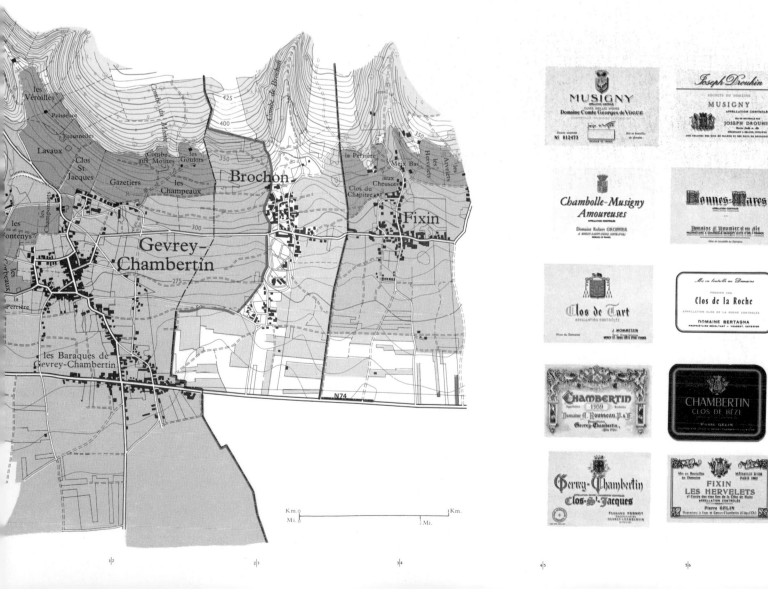

The Mâconnais

THE TOWN of Mâcon on the Saône, 35 miles south of Chalon, gives its name to a wide area which in general has neither the distinction of its neighbour to the north nor of Beaujolais to the south. Mâcon, plain and simple, is a good cut above vin ordinaire. But plain honest wine, red or white, is what it remains.

On the Beaujolais border, however, there is a pocket of white-wine growing with distinction of a different order. The Pouilly-Fuissé district is a sudden tempest of odd wave-shaped lime-stone hills, rich in the chalk the Chardonnay grape loves. The map shows how the five villages of Pouilly-Fuissé—Vergisson, Solutré-Pouilly, Pouilly, Fuissé and Chaintré—shelter in the valleys.

Good Pouilly-Fuissé is a pale, refreshing, often delicate wine for a Chardonnay, without the scent of a Meursault or the style of a Chablis Grand Cru, but in its gentle way exactly what one is often looking for from white burgundy. Domaine-bottled wines from the best vineyards can be really memorable.

Pouilly-Vinzelles and Pouilly-Loché are comparable, but a shade cheaper, not having the right to call themselves -Fuissé. A new appellation, St-Véran, applies to similar white wines from a handful of villages north and south of Pouilly-Fuissé.

Chardonnay elsewhere in the Mâconnais is often sold as what Californians would call a 'varietal'—called Pinot Chardonnay, to distinguish it from the common white wine, from the lesser Aligoté grape. It is often very good value for everyday use.

One other part of the Mâconnais, not mapped here, must be mentioned: the village of Viré, north of Mâcon. The growers' co-operative makes excellent white wine, and the Clos du Chapitre in particular is an outstanding vineyard. To have such a reputation, far from one's peers, argues a long tradition of competent wine-making, as well as a lucky patch of ground.

The fresh and gentle white wines of Pouilly-Fuissé are the Mâconnais' best. The village of Viré is also famous for white Mâcon. Ordinary Mâcon Blanc from a famous shipper is good everyday wine

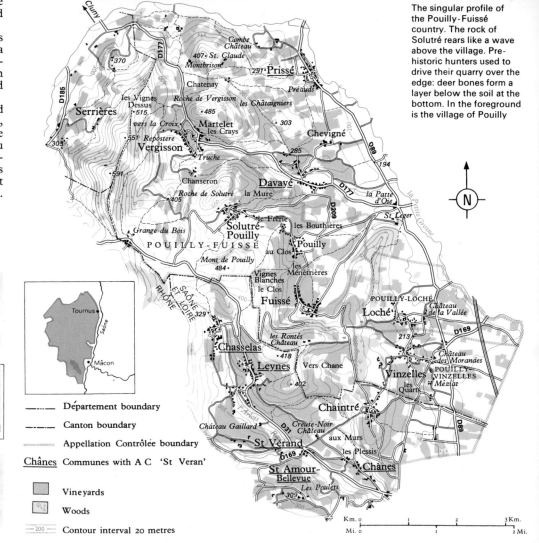

The singular profile of the Pouilly-Fuissé country. The rock of Solutré rears like a wave above the village. Prehistoric hunters used to drive their quarry over the edge: deer bones form a layer below the soil at the bottom. In the foreground is the village of Pouilly

———— Département boundary

—·—·— Canton boundary

∿∿∿∿∿ Appellation Contrôlée boundary

Chânes Communes with A C 'St Veran'

Vineyards

Woods

—200— Contour interval 20 metres

The Chalonnais

As DEMAND and prices play leapfrog in the most famous wine areas of the world, the names of what used to be considered lesser regions inevitably come to the fore. The hills south of Chagny are in many ways a continuation of the Côte de Beaune, though the regular ridge is replaced here by a jumble of hillocks on which vineyards appear among orchards and crops. They take the name of the Côte Chalonnaise from the town of Chalon-sur-Saône which lies to the east.

The best of the Chalonnais wines merit comparing with standard, or better, Côte de Beaune wines. Recently the names of Mercurey (for red wine) and Montagny (for white) have been heard more and more.

The map shows the east-and-south-facing slopes of the Côte Chalonnaise, with the four major communes which have appellations: Rully, Mercurey, Givry and Montagny, and some of their better-known vineyards—though at the moment only a few proprietors' wines carry vineyard names.

Rully has a growing reputation for its dry and sappy white wine, which almost all used to be made into sparkling burgundy. Acidity can be a problem, as this implies.

Mercurey is already famous for its red wines, which are not unlike light-weight Pommards, best drunk quite young. The Cave Co-operative is good, and a number of growers have started domaine-bottling. St-Martin-sous-Montaigu and the other little hamlets to the south share the appellation.

Givry becomes better and better known for both red and white, helped by the fact that an important grower of the Côte de Beaune, Baron Thénard, has vineyards and his cellars there.

And, finally, Montagny (which includes Buxy) has the prestigious aid of the négociant Louis Latour of Beaune, whose white Montagny now fetches a price that a Meursault would not be ashamed of.

Above: a cool tank of trout gleams in the courtyard of a wine grower's house. The light, often slightly sharp white wines of the Côte Chalonnaise are ideal for drinking with delicate fish dishes

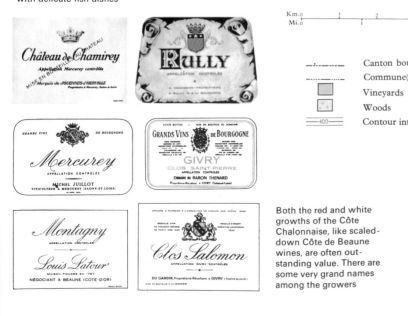

| Km.0 | 1 | 2 | 3 | 4 | 5 Km. |
| Mi.0 | 1 | | 2 | | 3 Mi. |

- Canton boundary
- Commune(parish) boundary
- Vineyards
- Woods
- 400 — Contour interval 20 metres

Both the red and white growths of the Côte Chalonnaise, like scaled-down Côte de Beaune wines, are often outstanding value. There are some very grand names among the growers

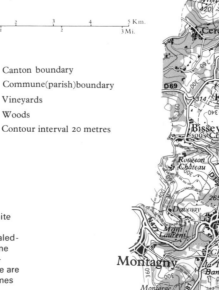

Beaujolais

Above: young Gamay vines are staked along a track leading to the village of Juliénas
Left: the lower hills sloping to south and east are almost unbroken vineyard. The Beaujolais mountains to the west, covered with pine and chestnut, rise to 3,000 feet. Their few primitive villages were immortalized in the story of Clochemerle

IF ONE single name stands for uncomplicated and satisfying red wine it is Beaujolais. The world has adopted it as a model of something deep red, fruity, lightish in body, fairly alcoholic and all too easy to drink. Merchants have never been very fussy about where it really comes from. The area is relatively big and very productive: if samples match up to a reasonable standard few questions are asked.

The Beaujolais region covers a 45-mile-long stretch of mainly granite hills south of Mâcon in south Burgundy. Most of its 60-odd villages remain obscure: the highest their wine can aspire to is the extra degree of alcohol to qualify as Beaujolais Supérieur. From this deep well about 15 million gallons of wine a year are drawn—to be drunk, in the main, before the next vintage.

The northern part of the region, however, has different standards. A group of 35 villages on steep foot-hills leading up to the Beaujolais mountains are classified as Beaujolais-Villages. They are expected to give wine with a shade more strength, and with the extra strength an extra touch of character and style.

Nine of the villages (the larger map) use their own names and are expected to show distinct characteristics of their own. These are the Grands Crus. The group lies just south of the Mâconnais, adjacent to Pouilly-Fuissé. Part of the best Beaujolais cru of all, in fact, Moulin-à-Vent, is actually in the Mâconnais, though to simplify things it is all regarded as Beaujolais.

The Grands Crus villages lie on spurs, outlying knolls and on the Beaujolais mountains themselves. This is much more seriously hilly country than the Côte d'Or. The road climbs and twists and climbs until vines and farms are left behind, woods thicken and upland streams tumble by. Looking behind and below, the broad band of vineyards dwindles and an immense view of the plain of the Saône expands: in clear weather Mont Blanc hangs in the far distance to the east.

The country is owned mostly by small farmers who sell their wine through négociants in Mâcon and Villefranche and Lyon, but there are a few big estates. Their wine is the grandest of Beaujolais and is often nowadays bottled on the property; but this does not change its basic nature of being a delicious easy-going drink rather than a Grand Vin.

Lightest and most luscious of all is Fleurie, with its neighbour Chiroubles. Good young Fleurie seems to epitomize the Beaujolais style: the scent is strong, the wine fruity and silky, brilliantly translucent, a joy to swallow.

'Best' in the most serious sense is Moulin-à-Vent, which now includes some of Chénas and Romanèche-Thorins. In good years this wine has darker colour, more strength and initial toughness and improves with age: not the thing Beaujolais is known for nowadays. Chénas used to be reckoned the best and strongest wine of

Beaujolais; it would be kept in barrel for two or three years and even blended with Moulin-à-Vent (then a smaller area) to lighten it.

Local experts will distinguish between all the other crus, telling you that Morgon lasts for longer, Juliénas has more substance and vigour, St-Amour is lighter, Brouilly is grapy and rich but Côte de Brouilly grapier and richer. It would be wrong to exaggerate the differences, however: what they have in common is more important; the beautiful inviting quality given by the Gamay.

This vine which is virtually outlawed from the Côte d'Or is in its element on the granite-derived soil of Beaujolais. Its plants are almost like people, leading independent lives: after ten years they are no longer trained, but merely tied up in summer with an osier to stand free. A Gamay vine will live as long as a man.

The fashion today is to drink Beaujolais—even Grand Cru Beaujolais—as young as possible, the *vin de l'année* being rushed to the eager world as early as mid-November, a few weeks after the harvest. The idea of the new Beaujolais is romantic, but wine for this purpose is never the best the country can produce. It is very quickly made, mere vin rosé with a purple tinge and a great surging sappy smell. The best Beaujolais has more to it than this; but no wine of real quality was ever made overnight: it takes time in bottle as well as barrel to achieve the miracle.

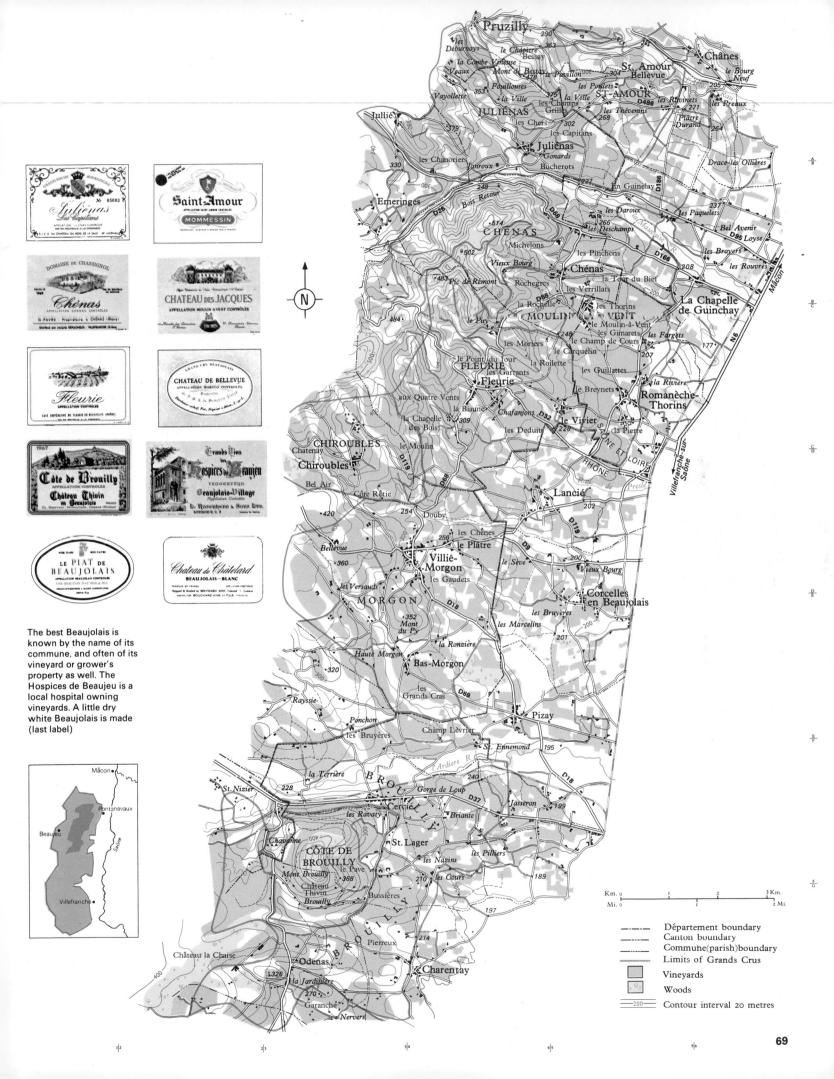

The best Beaujolais is known by the name of its commune, and often of its vineyard or grower's property as well. The Hospices de Beaujeu is a local hospital owning vineyards. A little dry white Beaujolais is made (last label)

Chablis

SLEEPY little Chablis on its reedy river in the valley does not look the part of the world's most famous wine town. There is not a hoarding, not an illumination, not a whisper of the fact that round the world, every day, as much wine is drunk under its name as it often produces in a whole harvest.

While every wine-producing country of the new world, and several of the old, has appropriated the name for any dry (or even sweet) white (or even pink) wine, real Chablis continues to be produced in limited quantities, with real distinction. So distinctive is it, in fact, that it is not to everybody's taste.

Chablis sends one rummaging for descriptive phrases even more desperately than most wines. There is something there one can so nearly put a finger on. It is hard but not harsh, reminds one of stones and minerals, but at the same time of green hay; actually, when it is young, looks green, which many wines are supposed to. Grand Cru Chablis tastes important, strong, almost immortal. And indeed it does last a remarkably long time; a strange and delicious sort of sour taste enters into it at ten years or so, and its golden green eye flashes meaningfully.

Grand Cru Chablis comes only from the seven small vineyards on the hill across the river from the town. As the map shows, it faces south, giving a slight advantage in sunlight, and hence in strength, besides what the chalky soil of this particular slope has to offer. As well as the Grands Crus, the same slope bears the grapes for Chablis Moutonne—a brand name which sounds like a vineyard but is in fact the property of one grower to use as he sees fit. It is normally reckoned to be of a standard approaching the seven Grand Crus, without having their official standing.

There used to be more Premiers Crus, but the names of the better-known have recently been granted to their neighbours as well. Chief ones now are Monts de Milieu, Montée de Tonnerre, Fourchaume, Vaillons, Montmains, Mélinots, Côte de Léchet, Beauroy, Vaucoupin, Vosgros, Vaulorent and Les Fourneaux. A Premier Cru Chablis will be at least half a degree of alcohol weaker than a Grand Cru, and correspondingly less impressive and intense in scent and flavour. None the less it will be a very good wine indeed—all the better if it comes from one of the vineyards designated Premier Cru on the same (north) bank of the river as the Grands.

Chablis, without a vineyard name, is made in about the same quantity as Chablis Premier Cru, from less favoured slopes. Again it is a step down in strength and character.

And finally there is Petit Chablis, rarely seen in bottle or exported, which is the relatively feeble and often rather acid produce of vineyards on the outskirts of the region. In bad years Petit Chablis can even be the best some illustrious vineyards can make: the weather is not kind here; frost in the spring often reduces the crop, and cool weather often prevents it ripening. Prices in the relatively rare great years are accordingly high, and always have been. A great bottle of Chablis has never been cheap, but few people realise just what style and character lie behind the too-famous name.

Above: in the cellars of a Chablis grower, M Simonet, a tasting-glass of wine catches the light
Above left: the Chablis landscape in spring. The vines are beginning to sprout, vulnerable to late frost. A flat vineyard like that on the left will make Chablis but not one of the Grands Crus
Above right: tools in a cooperage, for refitting barrels—one of the recurring tasks of growers

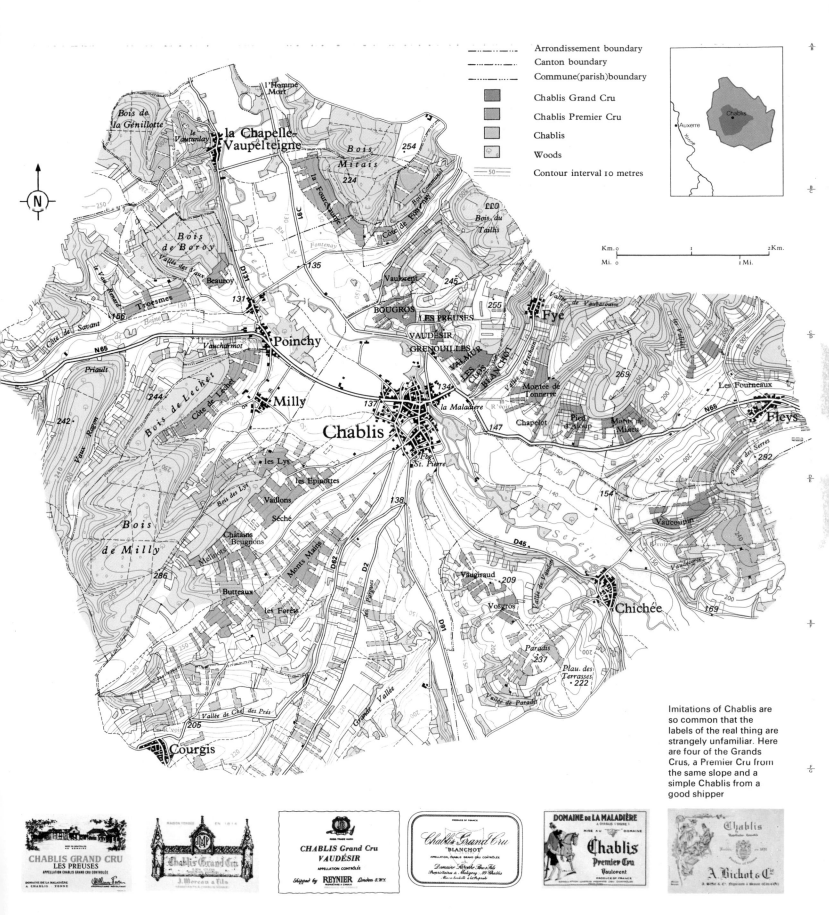

Imitations of Chablis are so common that the labels of the real thing are strangely unfamiliar. Here are four of the Grands Crus, a Premier Cru from the same slope and a simple Chablis from a good shipper

Bordeaux

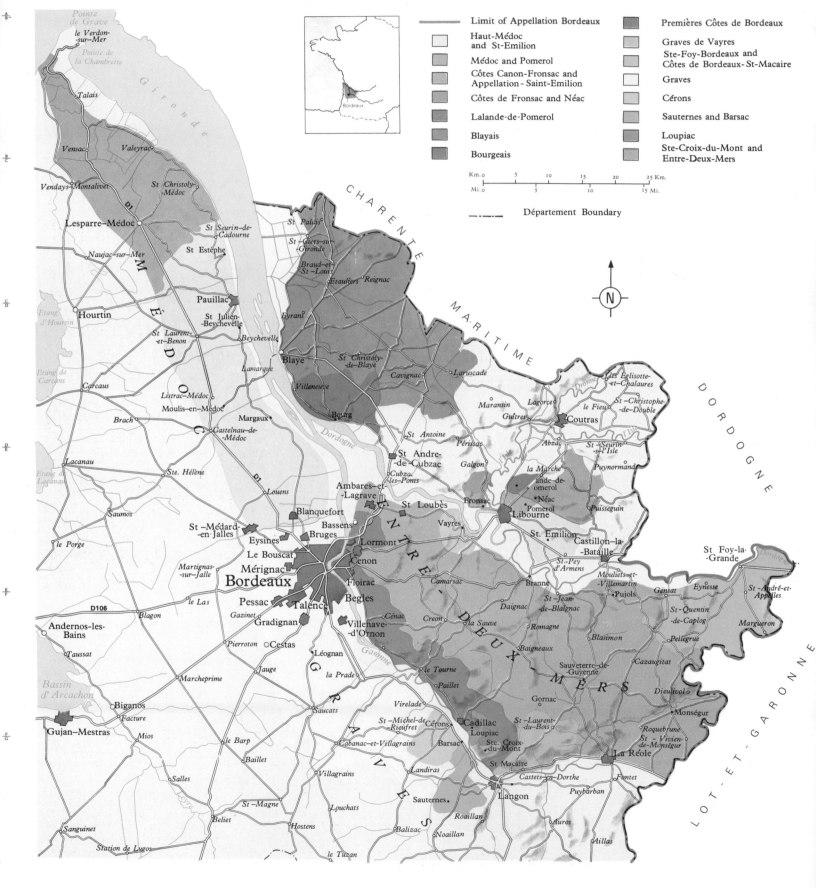

Legend:

- Limit of Appellation Bordeaux
- Haut-Médoc and St-Emilion
- Médoc and Pomerol
- Côtes Canon-Fronsac and Appellation - Saint-Emilion
- Côtes de Fronsac and Néac
- Lalande-de-Pomerol
- Blayais
- Bourgeais
- Premières Côtes de Bordeaux
- Graves de Vayres
- Ste-Foy-Bordeaux and Côtes de Bordeaux-St-Macaire
- Graves
- Cérons
- Sauternes and Barsac
- Loupiac
- Ste-Croix-du-Mont and Entre-Deux-Mers

Km.0   5   10   15   20   25 Km.
Mi.0   5   10   15 Mi.

- - - - Département Boundary

N

IF THE NAME of Burgundy suggests richness and plenty, Bordeaux has more than a hint of elegance about it. In place of the plump prelate who seems to symbolize Burgundy, Bordeaux calls to mind a distinguished figure in a frockcoat. Picture him tasting pale red wine from a crystal glass. He has one thumb tucked into his waistcoat, while through the open door beyond him there is a glimpse of a turreted house, insubstantial in the pearly seaside light. He enters his moderate enthusiasms in a leather pocketbook, observing the progress of beauty across his palate like moves in a game of chess.

Aspects of Bordeaux appeal to the aesthete, as Burgundy appeals to the sensualist. One is the nature of the wine: at its best indescribably delicate in nuance and complexity. Another is the sheer intellectual challenge of so many estates in so many regions and sub-regions that no one has mastered them all.

Bordeaux is the largest fine-wine district on earth. The whole Department of the Gironde, where the waters of the Dordogne and the Garonne unite to flow into the Bay of Biscay, is dedicated to wine-growing. All its wine is Bordeaux. Its production dwarfs that of Burgundy. In 1970 it produced 73,988,068 gallons.

The total is equally divided between red wines and white. The great red wine areas lie to the north: the Médoc; the country immediately south of the city of Bordeaux; the country along the north bank of the Dordogne and facing the Médoc across the Gironde. The country between the two rivers is called Entre-Deux-Mers. Most of its wine is white, except for a fringe of villages which make red wine as well, facing Bordeaux across the Garonne. Premières Côtes de Bordeaux is the name given to their wines. All the bottom third of the map is white-wine country.

But of the white wine of this large area a relatively small proportion is notably fine. Bordeaux's great glories are its range of good to superlative red wines, and the small production of very sweet golden wine of Sauternes.

Compared with Burgundy the system of appellations in Bordeaux is simple. The map opposite shows them all. Within them it is the wine estates or châteaux which look after their own identification problem. On the other hand there is a form of classification by quality built into the system in Burgundy which is missing in Bordeaux. In its place here there are a variety of local classifications, unfortunately without a common standard.

By far the most famous of these is the classification of the châteaux of the Médoc—and one or two others—which was finalized in 1855, based on the prices the wines had fetched over the previous hundred years or more. Its first, second, third, fourth and fifth 'growths', to which were added Crus Exceptionnels, Crus Bourgeois Supérieurs, Crus Bourgeois and later Crus Artisans and Crus Paysans, are the most ambitious grading of the products of the soil ever attempted.

The overriding importance of situation in deciding quality is proved by the accuracy of the old list today. Where present standards depart from it there is usually an explanation: there was a particularly industrious proprietor

Handsome 18th-century architecture and a sensuous approach to the table are Bordeaux in a nutshell. The Allées de Tourny is here reflected in a window of the famous restaurant and food store, Dubern

in 1855, and a lazy one now . . . or vice versa.

None the less more weight is placed today on whether a château is first or fifth growth than the system really justifies. The first growths regularly fetch three times the price of the second growths . . . without necessarily being any better. The relative qualities of different châteaux really need expressing in a more subtle way than by suggesting that one is always 'better' than another. The system adopted on the maps which follow is to distinguish between classed growths and Crus Bourgeois. Many other minor growths are also marked.

Château is the word for a wine estate in Bordeaux. Its overtones of castle or stately home are rarely justified. In most cases the biggest building at the château is the *chai*—the long sheds,

often half underground, where the wine is stored—attached to the *cuvier* where it is made. (A Bordeaux château and its working routine is anatomised on pages 24–25.)

The vineyards of the château sometimes surround it in a neat plot. More often they are scattered and intermingled with their neighbours. They can produce annually anything from eight to 800 barrels of wine, each holding 288 bottles. The best vineyards make a maximum of 4,000 litres from each hectare of vines, the less good ones rather more. A hectare can have anything from 6,500 to 10,000 vines.

The *maître de chai* is an important figure at the château. At little properties it is the owner himself, at big ones an old retainer. It is he who welcomes visitors, and lets them taste the new wine, cold and dark and unpalatable, from the casks in his care. Be knowing rather than enthusiastic; the wine will not be ready to drink for two years after it has been bottled at the very least—and maybe not for twenty.

Bordeaux/the Quality Factor

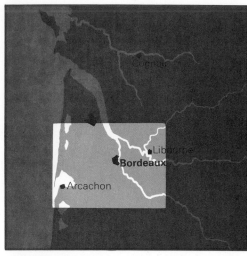

THE ADVANTAGES of the Bordeaux region for wine-growing can be listed quite simply. Its position near the sea and threaded with rivers gives it a moderate and stable climate. Forests on the ocean side protect it from strong salt winds and reduce rainfall. The bed-rock is well-furnished with minerals, yet the topsoil in general is quite poor, and often very deep.

The most earnest studies have been made to decide what it is that makes one piece of land superior to its neighbour. They all start by defining exactly the geological, pedological (i.e. soil) and climatological set-up for a very fine vineyard . . . and then tend to find that exactly the same considerations seem to apply next door, where the wine is not and never has been half so good.

In Bordeaux, however, there are more variables to help explain the differences. Instead of one constant grape variety, like the Pinot Noir for all red wine on the Côte de Nuits, all Bor-

deaux is made from a mixture of three or four varieties; the proportions depending on the taste of the proprietor. To jump to the conclusion that, let us say, the soil of Château Lafite gives lighter wine than that of Château Latour would be rash, unless you have taken into account that Lafite grows a good deal of the Merlot grape while Latour is nearly all Cabernet Sauvignon . . . and Merlot wine is lighter.

Another factor is the status of the vineyard. Success breeds success, meaning more money to spend on expensive care of the land. Differences which were originally marginal can therefore be increased over the years.

Furthermore the soil of the Médoc, to speak of only part of Bordeaux, is said to 'change at every step'. No one has ever been able to isolate the wine made from a vine on one patch and compare it with that from two steps away. So nobody really knows what vines, on what kind of soil, give what kind of wine—except in the

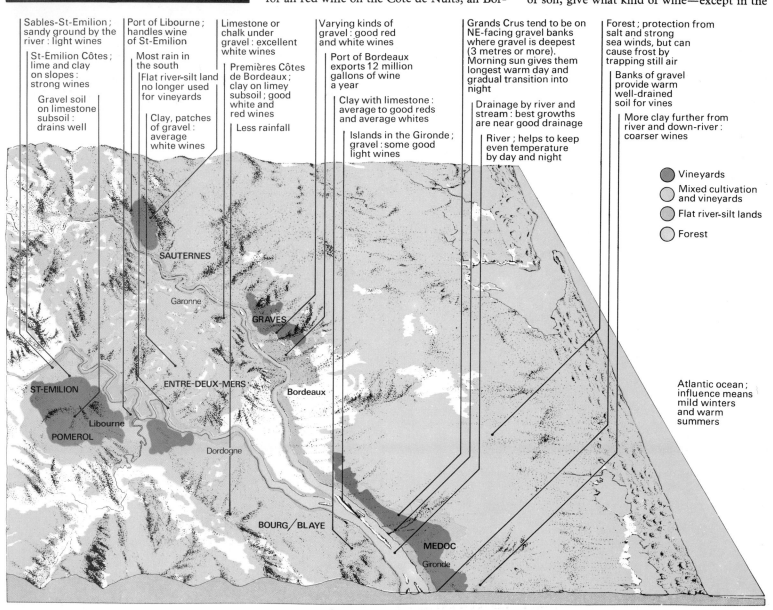

Sables-St-Emilion; sandy ground by the river: light wines

St-Emilion Côtes; lime and clay on slopes: strong wines

Gravel soil on limestone subsoil: drains well

Port of Libourne; handles wine of St-Emilion

Most rain in the south

Flat river-silt land no longer used for vineyards

Clay, patches of gravel: average white wines

Limestone or chalk under gravel: excellent white wines

Premières Côtes de Bordeaux; clay on limey subsoil; good white and red wines

Less rainfall

Varying kinds of gravel: good red and white wines

Port of Bordeaux exports 12 million gallons of wine a year

Clay with limestone: average to good reds and average whites

Islands in the Gironde; gravel: some good light wines

Grands Crus tend to be on NE-facing gravel banks where gravel is deepest (3 metres or more). Morning sun gives them longest warm day and gradual transition into night

Drainage by river and stream: best growths are near good drainage

River; helps to keep even temperature by day and night

Forest; protection from salt and strong sea winds, but can cause frost by trapping still air

Banks of gravel provide warm well-drained soil for vines

More clay further from river and down-river: coarser wines

- ● Vineyards
- ◐ Mixed cultivation and vineyards
- ○ Flat river-silt lands
- ○ Forest

SAUTERNES

Garonne

GRAVES

ST-EMILION

ENTRE-DEUX-MERS

Bordeaux

Libourne

POMEROL

Dordogne

BOURG/BLAYE

MEDOC

Gironde

Atlantic ocean; influence means mild winters and warm summers

most general terms, and even then with many reservations.

You would not expect this to prevent the University of Bordeaux from going on trying, however. The latest theory which finds wide support is that (contrary to traditional belief) geology is scarcely a factor at all in deciding quality, at least in Bordeaux. A vine will find all the nourishment it needs almost anywhere; but the poorer the soil the deeper and wider it will root. Hence the mysterious fact that poor soil is often good for wine. Give a vine rich soil, or spread generous helpings of manure round it, and its roots will stay near the top. But plant it in stony ground, give it only the bare necessities, and it will plunge metres deep to see what it can find. For the deeper the roots go, the more constant is their environment, and the less they are subject to floods on the one hand, drought on the other, and fluctuations of food supply from manuring or lack of manuring on the surface. Then there can be a lake around it, or total drought can parch and crack the ground, and the vine will feed normally. Provided only that the subsoil is well drained, so that the roots do not drown.

Enlarging on this idea, Dr Gérard Seguin of the University of Bordeaux suggests that the nearer a vineyard is to an effective drain, the drier the subsoil will be and the deeper the roots will go. He suggests that the first growths are vineyards nearest the drainage channels, the second growths slightly further from them, and so on. There has always been a saying that 'the vines should look at the river', this theory explains it. It also explains why old vines give the best wine; their roots are deepest. The theory can be examined by studying the streams on the following maps in relation to the classed and other growths.

Hence, this theory continues, it is not the chemical composition of the soil, but its physical make-up which must be taken into account. Heavy clay or sand which drains badly is the worst for wine: gravel and larger stones are best. Add to this the way stones store heat on the surface, and prevent rapid evaporation of moisture from under them, and it is easy to see that they are the best guarantee of stable conditions of temperature and humidity that a vine can have.

In the Médoc it is the deep gravel beds of Margaux and St-Julien and Pauillac which drain best. As you go north the proportion of clay increases, so that in St-Estèphe drainage is much less effective. This does not mean that all Margaux wines are first growth and all St-Estèphe fifth—though there are many more classed growths in Margaux—but it does account for higher acidity, more tannin, colour, and less scent in St-Estèphe wines. It is, after all, not only a question of quality but of the character of the wine.

Left: some of the factors affecting the varying qualities and character of Bordeaux wine are shown in this diagram of the river basin of the Gironde from the south-east. The Gironde is formed by the confluence of the rivers Dordogne (left) and the Garonne (right). Soil and subsoil have a bearing on the wine, but there is doubt about how important they are in determining its quality and character. Such factors as rainfall, and whether the sun reaches the vine in the morning or afternoon, and above all the rapid drainage of the ground, may play just as large a part.
The southern part of the area has most rainfall, the north least. White wine is grown in the south, both red and white in the centre, and more red than white in the north.
No positive link between the two facts can be proved, but it seems likely that the mists of the wetter area have been found helpful to white grapes over the years and have tended to cause rot in the red

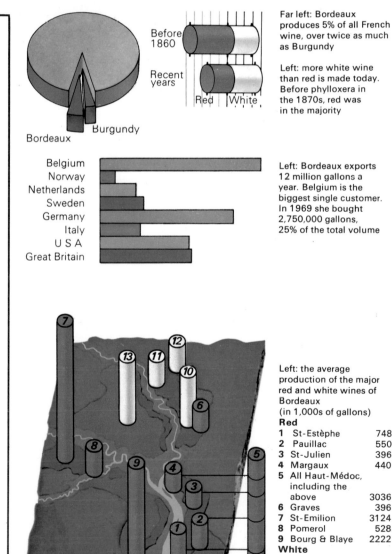

Far left: Bordeaux produces 5% of all French wine, over twice as much as Burgundy

Before 1860
Recent years
Red | White

Left: more white wine than red is made today. Before phylloxera in the 1870s, red was in the majority

Bordeaux — Burgundy

Belgium
Norway
Netherlands
Sweden
Germany
Italy
USA
Great Britain

Left: Bordeaux exports 12 million gallons a year. Belgium is the biggest single customer. In 1969 she bought 2,750,000 gallons, 25% of the total volume

Left: the average production of the major red and white wines of Bordeaux (in 1,000s of gallons)

Red
1 St-Estèphe — 748
2 Pauillac — 550
3 St-Julien — 396
4 Margaux — 440
5 All Haut-Médoc, including the above — 3036
6 Graves — 396
7 St-Emilion — 3124
8 Pomerol — 528
9 Bourg & Blaye — 2222
White
10 Graves — 1100
11 Barsac — 264
12 Sauternes — 528
13 Entre-deux-Mers — 1518

St-Estèphe

Left: Château Calon-Ségur in the north of St-Estèphe has 150 acres of walled vineyard on gently rolling ground, classified in 1855 as a third growth. Its deep red wine is substantial and long-lasting

Above and right: the five Crus Classés of St-Estèphe. Château Phélan-Ségur is an example of the many Crus Bourgeois of outstanding quality in the area

THE GRAVEL banks which give the Médoc and its wines their character and quality, stretching along the shore of the river Gironde, sheltered from the ocean to the west by miles of forest, begin to peter out at St-Estèphe. It is the northernmost of the four famous communes which are the heart of the Médoc. A little *jalle* —the Médoc word for a stream—divides it from Pauillac, draining on the one hand the vineyards of Château Lafite, on the other three of the five classed growths of St-Estèphe, namely Châteaux Cos-d'Estournel, Lafon-Rochet and Cos-Labory.

There is a distinction between the soils of Pauillac and St-Estèphe: as the gravel washed down the Gironde diminishes there is a stronger mixture of clay found in it. Higher up, in Margaux, there is very little. In St-Estèphe it is heavier soil, which drains more slowly. The wines have more acidity, are fuller, solider, often have less perfume, but fairly fill your mouth with flavour. They are sturdy clarets of the kind which the British, in particular, love, and which become with age gentle but still vigorous, unfaded.

Château Cos-d'Estournel is the most spectacular of the classed growths. It is an eccentric Chinese-pagoda'ed mansion, impressively crowning the steep slope up from the Pauillac boundary (with all-too-good a view of the Shell refinery below). Together with Château Montrose, overlooking the river, it makes the biggest and best of St-Estèphes; strong wines with a dark colour and a long life. Montrose is an excellent château to visit to get an idea of a prosperous old-style wine estate. Its rather dark *chai*, heavily beamed, and its magnificent oak fermenting vats prepare you for the deep-coloured, deep-flavoured claret you will taste.

The other two classed growths near Cos, Châteaux Lafon-Rochet and Cos-Labory, had not distinguished themselves in recent years until Lafon-Rochet was bought by M Tesseron, a Cognac merchant, when it gained the distinction of being the first new château to be

A hundred-year-old print from Château Loudenne shows hardly-altered scenes of Médoc château life

built (or rebuilt) in Bordeaux in the 20th century. Its wine is gaining in reputation. Calon-Ségur, north of the village, has always been well-known: perhaps more steady than brilliant. The Comte de Ségur, from whom it takes its name, at one time owned Châteaux Lafite and Latour into the bargain.

Above all, St-Estèphe is known for its Crus Bourgeois. There is an explosion of them on the plateau south and west of the village. Châteaux Phélan-Ségur and de Pez are both outstanding producers of very fine wine, year after year. Château Meyney, like a huge and immaculate farmyard without a farmhouse, belongs to the négociant house of Cordier and makes good

wine. Châteaux Tronquoy-Lalande, Haut-Marbuzet, Les Ormes-de-Pez . . . all the Crus Bourgeois are fountains of full-bodied, reliable, often exceptional claret.

In addition more than 200 small growers, some with named châteaux, some with just small plots of vines, send their grapes to the co-operative, whose good standard wine is sold as 'Marquis de St-Estèphe'. Co-operatives play a large and important part in the life even of such famous communes as this.

To the north of St-Estèphe the gravel bank diminishes to a promontory sticking out of the *palus*—the flat river-silt land on which no wine of quality grows. On top of the promontory the little village of St-Seurin-de-Cadourne has half a dozen Crus Bourgeois. If their wine does not usually have the strength or the distinction of St-Estèphe it is still often admirable, and excellent value for money.

Where St-Seurin ends is the end of the Haut-Médoc: any wine grown beyond that point is only entitled to the appellation Médoc, plain and simple. Anchored just beyond the promontory like a ship just sailed in from Bristol lies one final gravel island in the *palus*: the British-owned Château Loudenne. In the monumental Victorian *chais* of Loudenne, Gilbey's (who bought the château in 1875) hold an imposing stock of wine from all over Bordeaux for shipment overseas. Loudenne's own wine is light, of good medium quality; a typical minor Médoc. There is also a dry white Loudenne, not at all typical of the Médoc; somewhat closer to a very dry Graves.

The country in behind St-Estèphe, further from the river, has a scattering of Crus Bourgeois, none of them very well known. Cissac and Vertheuil lie on rather stronger and less gravelly soil on the edge of the forest. It would be fascinating to spend a day finding a favourite among their châteaux and their wine. Each has character and many have charm—yet hardly anyone except a few local brokers has investigated them in detail.

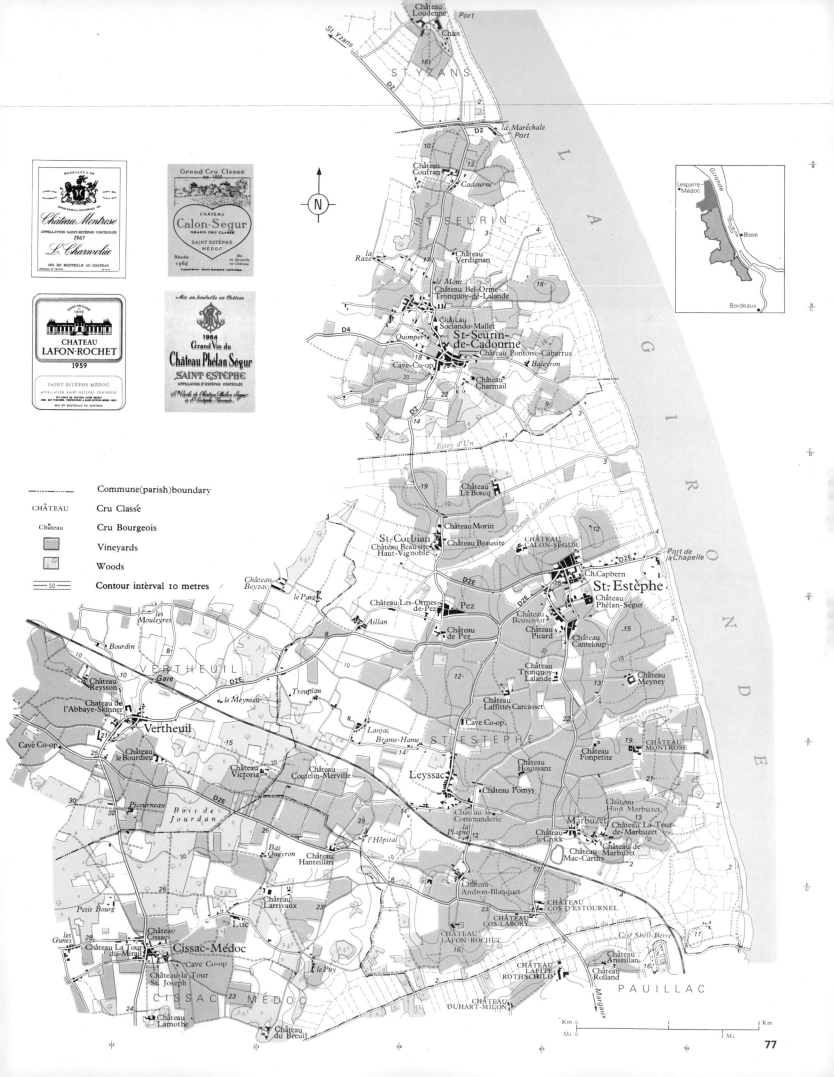

Pauillac

The Crus Classés of Pauillac have a sober approach to labelling. The one tearaway is Mouton-Rothschild, which commissions a different artist every year

IF ONE had to single out one commune of Bordeaux to head the list there would be no argument. It would be Pauillac. Châteaux Lafite, Latour and Mouton-Rothschild, three out of the first five of the Médoc and Graves, are its obvious claim. But many claret-lovers would tell you that the wines of Pauillac have the quintessential flavour they look for in Bordeaux—a combination of fresh soft-fruit, oak, dryness, subtlety combined with substance, a touch of cigar-box, a suggestion of sweetness. Even the lesser growths of Pauillac approach their ideal claret.

At Pauillac the gravel *croupes* of the Médoc get as near as they ever do to being hills. The highest part, with Châteaux Mouton-Rothschild and Pontet-Canet on its summit, reaches 100 feet above the sea—quite an achievement in this coastal area, where a mere swelling of the ground provides a lookout point.

The town of Pauillac is the biggest of the Médoc. Recently it has grown faster than ever before—and for a new reason. For many years it has had an oil refinery at its northern end. Now the refinery has become the centre of an expansion programme which begins to make the most illustrious piece of agricultural landscape in the world look industrial. The town's tree-shaded quay is pleasant, but there is no hotel or restaurant worth the name.

The vineyards of the châteaux of Pauillac are on the whole less subdivided than in most of the Médoc. Whereas in Margaux (for example) the châteaux are bunched together in the town, and their holdings in the country round are inextricably mixed up—a row here, a couple of rows there—in Pauillac whole slopes, mounds and plateaus belong to one proprietor. One would therefore expect greater variations between the different wines.

The three great wines of Pauillac are all very much individuals. Lafite-Rothschild and Latour stand at opposite ends of the parish; the first almost in St-Estèphe, the second almost in St-Julien. Oddly enough, though, their characters tend the opposite way: Lafite more towards the smoothness and finesse of a St-Julien, Latour more towards the strength and firmness of a St-Estèphe.

Lafite, with 200 acres one of the biggest vineyards in the Médoc, makes about 800 barrels of its fabulously expensive wine; a perfumed, polished, gentlemanly production. It also makes a second wine which it sells as Carruades de Château Lafite, after the plateau of Carruades above the château to the west.

The firmer and more solid Latour does not ask quite such high prices, although there are few who would say it was worth less than Lafite. It has the great merit of evenness over uneven vintages, and a superb depth of flavour.

Baron Philippe de Rothschild at Mouton makes a third kind of Pauillac: strong, dark, long-lasting. Given the ten or often even 20 years they need to mature (depending on the quality of the vintage), these wines reach into realms of perfection where they are rarely followed. But millionaires tend to be impatient: too much is drunk far too young.

The undoubted similarity in strength and staying-power of Latour and Mouton can ap-

parently be put down to the unusually high proportion of Cabernet vines in their vineyards: as high as 90% at Mouton.

No visitor to Pauillac should miss the beautiful little museum of works of art connected with wine—old glass, paintings, tapestries—as well as the very fine *chais*, which make Château Mouton-Rothschild the show-place of the whole Médoc.

The two châteaux Pichon-Longueville—Baron and Lalande—face each other across the road south from Pauillac like mad old duchesses in party clothes. Lalande is the bigger half of

Top: châteaux Pichon-Lalande and, left, Grand-Puy-Lacoste have the typical solid dignity of Pauillac
Right: Cabernet grapes, bloom-covered, at Lafite

what was once one huge property—partly in St-Julien, mainly in Pauillac. It usually seems to make the better wine of the two, Baron the 'bigger'—though one thinks of it for reliability rather than sublimity.

The two best-known of the remaining classified growths of Pauillac are Pontet-Canet, with the biggest production of any cru classé (as much as 1,600 barrels a year), the property of the Cruse family, and Lynch-Bages, whose rather full, heavy wine, with a most distinctive scented bouquet, is immensely popular.

Château Duhart-Milon belongs to the Rothschilds of Lafite, and Château Mouton Baron Philippe to the Mouton Rothschilds. Both clearly benefit from the wealth and technical knowledge of their proprietors and managers.

Châteaux Batailley and Haut-Batailley, lying

back in the fringe of the woods, do not spring to mind straight away. They are relatively small (Haut-Batailley has the little Château La Couronne, classified below the crus classés as a Cru Exceptionnel, as neighbour and partner). One does not expect quite the same finesse from them as from the great wines nearer the river. Haut-Batailley is perhaps the finer of the two.

The two châteaux called Grand-Puy-, Lacoste and Ducasse, both have high reputations, although the former is very much the bigger and more important. It is one fine continuous vineyard on high ground, surrounding its château, while Ducasse is scattered in three separate parcels north and west of Pauillac, and its

old château is now the Maison du Vin on the quay in the town itself.

Of the remaining classified growths, Croizet-Bages and Clerc-Milon-Mondon are probably the best, the former being the stronger and less fine of the two from its position to the west. Haut-Bages-Libéral is owned by the Cruse family and made at Pontet-Canet, although its vineyard is, as the map shows, at the other end of the parish. Pédesclaux and Lynch-Moussas are smaller and less well known châteaux.

Pauillac, having so many large estates, is not, like St-Estèphe, a warren of small-to-middling growers. Its one small Cru Exceptionnel, La Couronne, has already been mentioned. The

Crus Bourgeois châteaux Fonbadet, Haut-Bages-Monpelou and Haut-Bages-Avérous, La Fleur-Milon, La Tour-Pibran and Anseillan are all more or less familiar names.

The local co-operative, however, is probably better known than any of them. Under the name La Rose-Pauillac around 180 small growers sell their blended wine—a reliable and distinctive, though a light-weight, product of the famous parish.

The map includes part of the next parish to the west, St-Sauveur. There are no wines of outstanding quality; the Crus Bourgeois marked, however, are respectable and useful. Château Liversan is perhaps the best known.

St-Julien

Top: Château Langoa-Barton, built in 1758, is one of the Medoc's most elegant. Its wine is a typical St-Julien—the epitome of classical claret

Above: pickers at the end of a late September day. The children still seem to have energy, although it is gruelling work and everybody joins in

St-Julien has many of the Médoc's most illustrious Crus Classés, and comparatively few but excellent Crus Bourgeois, of which Château Gloria is best-known

NO OTHER commune in Bordeaux has so high a proportion of classed growths as St-Julien. It is a small commune, with the smallest production of the famous four of the Médoc, but almost all of it is superlative wine-growing land; typical dunes of gravel, not as deep as in Pauillac (a cross-section of a St-Julien vine and its soil is on page 19) but very close to the river and consequently well drained.

There are few Crus Bourgeois, and those there are are very good indeed: one of them, Château Gloria, being easily on a par with the classed growths and sometimes making a wine as good as any in the district. As for spare land, or unknown little holdings to supply the very popular 'St-Julien' of the corner wine-shop, there is practically none.

If Pauillac makes the most striking and brilliant wine of the Médoc, and Margaux the most refined and exquisite, St-Julien forms the transition between the two. With one or two exceptions its châteaux make rather round and gentle wine—gentle, that is, when it is mature: it starts as tough and tannic in a good year as any.

The chief proponents of the typical smooth St-Julien style are Châteaux Gruaud-Larose and Talbot—both belonging to the négociant Cordier. There is drier, and perhaps more exciting wine made at the Italianate mansion of Ducru-Beaucaillou, and lighter, more elegant wine (in keeping with a very beautiful Louis XV château) made at Beychevelle.

The principal glory of the commune is the vast estate of Léoville, once the biggest in the Médoc, now divided into three. It lies on the Pauillac boundary, and it would be a brave man who would say that he could distinguish a Léoville from a Longueville every time (although he certainly should be able to distinguish a Château Latour, which lies equally close).

Château Léoville-Lascases has the biggest vineyard of the three, with 150-odd acres. At the moment Château Léoville-Barton has the best reputation. It belongs, together with the neighbouring Langoa, to the Bartons of Barton & Guestier, one of the best-known négociant

Map labels:

PAUILLAC   Daubos

CHÂTEAU PICHON-LONGUEVILLE-BARON

CHÂTEAU PICHON-LONGUEVILLE-LALANDE

Ch. la Couronne

CHÂTEAU HAUT BATAILLEY

CHÂTEAU LATOUR

Cach

Château Moulin-Riche

CHÂTEAU LÉOVILLE-LASCASES

St.-Julien-Beychevelle

Château Larose-Trintaudon

Château Peymartin

CHÂTEAU LÉOVILLE-POYFERRÉ

ST JULIEN

Perganson

CHÂTEAU TALBOT

CHÂTEAU LANGOA

CHÂTEAU LÉOVILLE-BARTON

la Mouline

le Bouscat   ST. LAURENT

Gare

Château Barateau

St.-Laurent-et-Benon

CHÂTEAU SAINT-PIERRE-BONTEMPS ET SEVAISTRE

Château du Glana

Château Terrey Gros-Caillou

Château Gloria

Beychevelle

CHÂTEAU DUCRU-BEAUCAILLOU

CHÂTEAU BELGRAVE

LA TOUR-CARNET CHÂTEAU

CHÂTEAU CAMÉNSAC

CHÂTEAU LAGRANGE

Château d'Hortevie

CHÂTEAU BRANAIRE-DUCRU

CHÂTEAU GRUAUD-LAROSE

le Bourdieu

CHÂTEAU BEYCHEVELLE

Lamothe

le Graveyron

le Vivey

le Marais de Beychevelle

Château Lanessan

le Cul du Bosc

CUSSAC

Jalle du Nord

Chenal du Milieu

Chenal du Despartins

LA GIRONDE

Inset map: Lesparre-Médoc, Gironde, Blaye, Bordeaux

Legend:

Canton boundary	
Commune (parish) boundary	
CHÂTEAU	Cru Classé
Château	Cru Bourgeois
	Vineyards
	Woods
Contour interval 10 metres	

Km. 0   1   2 Km.
Mi. 0   1 Mi.

---

houses of Bordeaux. Ronald Barton lives in the beautiful 18th-century Château Langoa, and makes his two wines side by side in the same *chai*. Langoa is usually reckoned the slightly lesser wine of the two, being fuller and more tannic, but both are among the finest clarets in a traditional manner. Such wines should be laid down for a good seven years even in lesser vintages; in great ones they will last for a generation or more.

Léoville-Lascases is seen everywhere, and has made very fine wine steadily through the sixties. Léoville-Poyferré one sees less. It sometimes seems to lack the roundness which makes St-Julien so pleasant to drink. Of course it is hard to know how much of such a characteristic is due to the techniques in use and how much to the soil and situation. A different balance of Cabernet and Merlot vines will produce different barrels from the same vineyard. On the other hand people who have tasted the wines of different grape varieties from one vineyard before they have been 'assembled' in one barrel

have often said that even while they tasted of the different grapes, each had the characteristic of the estate.

Château Ducru-Beaucaillou celebrates in its name the 'beautiful pebbles' which fill the vineyards nearest the river. They are not only large and round; they form the greater part of the topsoil. Only about two feet down does the subsoil of finer gravel and curious lumpy deposits of iron-bearing clay begin. Ducru, and Château Gloria next to it, rarely fail to produce some of the best wine of Bordeaux.

Château Beychevelle is even better-known; its wine is supposed to be the height of elegance rather than power; in poor vintages it does not always keep up with some of its rivals. Château Branaire-Ducru next door, though as good or better, remains relatively obscure, respected rather than fashionable, at the moment.

The group of classed growths that stand away from the river, on soil becoming slightly less outrageously stony, include the stablemates Gruaud-Larose and Talbot, which epito-

mise the tender, faintly sweet, easy-to-drink style of St-Julien. In several vintages recently Gruaud-Larose has made one of the best wines of the commune. The united châteaux St-Pierre, Bontemps and Sevaistre, which separate them, are not so well-known. They belong to a Belgian wine merchant.

Château du Glana, the Cru Bourgeois next door, is far bigger, and hence its produce is more often met with. It makes rather a hard wine for a St-Julien.

The last of the classed growths, Château Lagrange, used to be better-known than it is for its good, substantial wine. It lies far back in the country, in a group with three classed growths in St-Laurent. It is doubtful whether in any new classification of the Médoc these would rank above Crus Bourgeois. There is a world of difference between their sleepy hinterland and the exciting air of the riverside châteaux. At Château Larose-Trintaudon, on the other hand, much planting has gone on recently, which is always a healthy sign.

The Central Médoc

THIS is the bridge passage of the Médoc, the mezzo forte between the andante of St-Julien and the allegro of Margaux. Four villages pass without a single classed growth. The gravel dunes rise less proudly above the river; wood and marsh mingle with the vineyards. Many châteaux with fine great *chais* have let their vineyards dwindle to nothing. . . . And yet, as you pick your way through this less spectacular landscape, a surprising number of comfortably familiar names appear.

Rather than dismiss the centre of the Haut-Médoc as being without interest, as so many authors do, it is worth paying attention here. Great wines are rarely made, but there is a steady flow of excellent wine for—what shall we call ourselves? The middle classes?

At the moment Cussac, Lamarque, Arcins are not names which help to sell anything. There is a strong tradition in this region of supplying the richer neighbours to north and south with what they need for topping up, or perhaps for the insatiable public demand for 'Margaux' and 'St-Julien'.

But recently there has been more confidence to be seen, modern vinification methods have appeared, and extremely good light wines are being made. The fine old fortress of the Château de Lamarque is producing a very attractive pale red wine, fruity and ready to drink after a mere year or two. Château Malescasse, also at Lamarque, has been bought by an American-English combine and is replanting an estate which used to be well-known in the Low Countries and Germany. Château Courant at Arcins belongs to Nicolas Barrow, a young Englishman; his 1964 at six years old did not look like a wine from an obscure commune. Château du Cartillon has also made some admirable wine in recent years.

This is not to say that all the central Médoc shares the same obscurity. The St-Julien border boasts the very fine Cru Bourgeois Château Lanessan, which regularly makes wine of classed-growth standard (and has, besides, an entertaining carriage museum housed in the old stables).

Château La Chesnaye-Ste-Gemme stands in the same park and is part of the same estate. Château Caronne-Ste-Gemme is another big growth, rather further inland.

The forests come towards the river for a space here, narrowing the vineyards down to a handful of Crus Bourgeois at Cussac. At Cussac also is the handsome Fort Médoc, down by the river, a 17th-century fortress which is being restored. There are plans to make it into a resort and yacht harbour.

South-west of Lamarque there is a great opening-out of vineyards as the gravel ridges fan out inland to Grand Poujeaux (which lies in the commune of Moulis) and Listrac. Château Chasse-Spleen at Grand Poujeaux is classed as a Cru Exceptionnel (in the class, that is, between Bourgeois and classé). Several others, such as Châteaux La Closerie du Grand Poujeaux, Gressier Grand Poujeaux and Poujeaux-Theil, are well known, and the two châteaux Fourcas at Listrac, -Hostein and -Dupré, have good reputations as solid, firm wines for laying down.

The pattern here seems to be for solider and perhaps harsher wines to come from further west; lighter and easier ones as you get nearer the river. So much depends, however, on the style adopted by the château—of longer or shorter fermentation, when the wine is racked and how it is looked after—that any such observation must be tentative.

Beyond the jalle de Tiqueforte, in the southeast corner of the area, we begin to enter the sphere of Margaux. The big Château Citran and the smaller Villegeorge (off the map; a Cru Exceptionnel) lie in the commune of Avensan. Both are well-known, and approach Margaux in style. Soussans is among the communes whose Appellation Contrôlée is not merely Haut-Médoc but Margaux. Châteaux La Tour-de-Mons here is one of the best-known Crus Bourgeois of Bordeaux, and Château Paveil-de-Luze is also popular. Cocks and Féret's *Bordeaux et Ses Vins* says Soussans wines are 'promptement buvables'—soon ready to drink. Soon in this context means at least four years.

The hand-operated press is obsolete, but an old photograph still perfectly catches the atmosphere of many small châteaux in this part of the Médoc

20 or 30 Crus Bourgeois between St-Julien and Soussans, the beginning of Margaux, are well-known for outstanding value in far-above-average claret

St. Laurent and Cussac · St. Julien, Beychevelle

St. Julien · Beychevelle · St. Laurent · Cussac · Lamarque · Moulis · Listrac

Legend:

Canton boundary
Commune (parish) boundary
CHÂTEAU   Cru Classé
Château   Cru Bourgeois
           Vineyards
           Woods
50   Contour interval 10 metres

Km. 0 — 1 — 2 Km.
Mi. 0 — 1 Mi.

N

Lesparre-
Médoc

Gironde

Blaye

Bordeaux

ST. JULIEN   Pauillac   Beychevelle
CHÂTEAU
GRUAUD-LAROSE
                CHÂTEAU
                BEYCHEVELLE
                        D.101   Port de Beychevelle
        CHÂTEAU
        BRANAIRE-DUCRU
                le Bourdieu
le Marais de Beychevelle
                Château
                Lanessan
        le Cul du Bosc
                        Sainte-Gême
ST. LAURENT
                        Château
                        la Chesnaye-
                        Ste-Gême
Labat
Château
Caronne
Ste-Gemme
        les Valets
le Marais du Merich
                        Château du
                        Moulin Rouge
                                    le Grand Pré Neuf
        le Parc Neuf
                CUSSAC   Gaston
                        Pcylande   Caudot   Château Lamothe-
                                             de-Bergeron
                                                    Bernones
                Cussac   Château
                                            Du Raux
                                                    Fort Médoc
        Château Beaumont   Langa
                Château la Tour-
                du-Haut-Moulin   Château
                                    de Romefort
                Vieux Cussac   les Martins
                        Château   Château
                        Fort-de-Vauban   de Lamarque
                                    Milous   D.5
        Château   Lamarque
        la Bécade   Château
                            du Cartillon
Couhenne   les Calinottes
                Château Lafon   la Planche du Roi
                                            LAMARQUE
                                            Château
                                            Moulin-Rose
Château
Fourcas-Dupré   Maucaillou   Château
le Fourças   Malescasse
                les Marcieux
Château   Château   Château
Saransot-Dupré   Maucaillou   Barreyres
le Tris   Gare
la Potence   Médrac
                        Château
                        Poujeaux-Theil
Château   Grand Poujeaux   Château Gressier
Fourcas-Hosten 39   Grand-Poujeaux   Château
Cave-Co-op   Courant-Barrow
        Château   Château Dutruch-   le Beyan   ARCINS
        Pierre-Bibian Grand-Poujeaux
Listrac-Médoc   Château la Closerie- Château
                     Grand-Poujeaux   Chasse-Spleen
        Peyrelebade   Château   Arcins
                                                 d'Arnauld
                le Bourdieu   Cagnac
LISTRAC-MÉDOC   Château
                Château   Tramont
Berriquet   Guitignan   Queue de Boeuf Château
                                                  d'Arcins
        MOULIS-EN-
        MÉDOC
Château
Sémeillan   Château   Château   SOUSSANS
                Lestage   Brillette
                                            Peyvignau   Grand Soussans
Château   Château la
Fonréaud   Tour-de-Mons
                                        Segnin   Beauriche
        la Tranponnette   Château
        Moulis-en-Médoc   Tayac
                le Petit-Pujeaux   13
Château   Soussans
Moulin-A-Vent   Château
        Château Duplessis-   Château   Haut-Breton
        Hauchecorne   Paveil-de-Luze   Larigaudière
le Maypie   AVENSAN
        Château
        Moulis   Château Citran   Château
                                          Villegeorge   Laudère

Margaux and the Southern Médoc

BY MANY accounts this, the southernmost stretch of the Haut-Médoc, makes the finest wine of all. Margaux has a tight concentration of classed growths, which continue into the hamlets of Issan, Cantenac and Labarde. The map here shows a rather different picture from Pauillac or St-Julien. Instead of the châteaux being spread out evenly over the land they are huddled together in the village. An examination of the almost unliftable volumes of commune maps in the Mairie shows a degree of intermingling of one estate with another which is far greater than in (say) Pauillac. One would therefore look to differences in technique and tradition more than changes of soil to try to explain the differences between one château and another.

In fact the soil of Margaux is the thinnest in the Médoc, with the highest proportion of rough gravel. It has the least to offer the vine in the way of nourishment, but it drains well even in rainy years. The result is wines which start life comparatively 'supple', though in poor years they can turn out thin. In good and great years, however, all the stories about the virtues of gravel are justified: there is a delicacy about good Margaux, and a sweet haunting perfume, which makes it the most exquisite claret of all.

The wines of Château Margaux and Château Palmer next door are the ones which most often reach such heights. Château Margaux is not only a first growth of the Médoc, it is the one which most looks the part: a pediment at the end of an avenue; the air of a mansion, with *chais* to match.

Within the estate of the château there is an outcrop of totally different soil—a patch of chalk in place of the ubiquitous gravel. White wine vines are planted here to make a wine called Pavillon Blanc de Château Margaux. It is good, but not at all comparable to the great red wine, and only allowed the simple appellation Bordeaux.

Château Lascombes (which belongs, like Château Prieuré-Lichine in Cantenac, to the well-known American wine merchant Alexis Lichine) also often makes exceptionally good wine. Of the famous pair which used to be the big Rausan estate, Rausan-Ségla and Rauzan-Gassies, Ségla is bigger and better-known: Gassies has lately made even better wine.

In this immediate area there are no fewer than three marquises named on labels, and looking at the labels together one is struck by the fondness for gold. Margaux somehow seems to be the worldly end of the Médoc, where you are forced to forget the simplicity of the country estates and remember the operations of big business.

In Margaux a château name is often in truth a brand name; several châteaux are paired off under common ownership, with the label of one château apparently being used for the best wine of the property while the other goes on the less successful casks—an obvious manoeuvre where vineyards are so split up and intermingled. In this way a château which was once well known can disappear altogether as a wine-making unit and exist only as the second brand of a neighbour. Château Desmirail is an instance; it is no longer on the map; it is a subsidiary name for Château Palmer.

There are several distinguished pairs of châteaux in Margaux. Brane-Cantenac (a reliable château, making a good light-weight wine even in poor years like 1965) goes with Durfort-Vivens. Malescot-St-Exupéry goes with Marquis-d'Alesme-Becker—the Malescot is the better wine, often miraculously scented and one of the best of Margaux. Prieuré and Ferrière go with Lascombes. Pouget goes with Boyd-Cantenac, neither of them very special. Further down the road, Siran goes with Dauzac.

Château d'Issan, which belongs to the famous négociant family of Cruse (owners of Pontet-Canet in Pauillac), is perhaps the most beautiful house in the Médoc: a 17th-century fortified manor within the complete moat of an old *château-fort*. The admirable gentle slope of its vineyard to the road is one of the best situations in Margaux. It makes a lovely delicate wine.

The Crus Bourgeois include a group on the theme of Labégorce; none is world-famous, but their names stick in the mind like a nursery rhyme. Of the three, Château Labégorce-Zédé is the best-known. None of the other Crus Bourgeois has a great reputation—but this does not mean that they should be ignored.

Our rather erratic path to and fro in Margaux becomes a little simpler as the châteaux thin out in Cantenac and further south. Most of the land in the communes of Cantenac, Labarde and Arsac, as well as Soussans to the north, has been granted the appellation Margaux, making wines of very similar style and quality. If one had to generalize it would be safe to say that Cantenac wines often have more power than Margaux, with correspondingly less fragrance, and that the same applies more markedly the further south one goes.

One hears comparatively little of châteaux Cantenac-Brown and Boyd-Cantenac, which straddle the better-known Brane-Cantenac on its plateau, though Cantenac-Brown at least makes very good, rather full wine. Neither Château Kirwan nor du Tertre seems to be in full flight at the moment either.

There are three more big and famous classed growths before the vineyards come to an end: Giscours, whose tall half-timbered buildings in the graceless style of Deauville or Le Touquet face a most impressive sweep of vines; Cantemerle, a perfect Sleeping Beauty château, approached through a pretty wooded park, and the top-flight Château La Lagune, a neat 18th-century building just off the Bordeaux road (and the nearest classed growth of the Médoc to the city). They have in common a style which is bigger and more solid than a Margaux; Giscours and La Lagune rather soft but full of flavour, Cantemerle a powerful, long-lasting, classical wine.

Dauzac, the fourth classed growth of this southern area, partnered by its neighbour Siran, is said to be entering a period of higher production and better wine than of late; it certainly is a very honourable old name. Château d'Angludet, admirably situated on the banks of a stream for drainage, has been in the hands of the Sichel family for ten years and has consistently made wine of more than Cru Bourgeois quality.

Below: a magnificent concentration of Crus Classés distinguishes Margaux and its area. They emphasize their prestige with more gilded labels than the rest of the Médoc

Graves

Château Haut-Brion in the western suburbs of Bordeaux; the only first-growth château outside the Médoc

Domaine La Solitude at Martillac, like many Graves estates, is a clearing in the middle of the forest

THE CHANGE from the last section of the Médoc is obvious from the map. Here the city reaches out into the pine-woods, which continue (as the Landes) from here to the Basque foot-hills of the Pyrenees. The vineyards are clearings, often isolated from one another in heavily-forested and almost flat country.

The district of Graves takes its name from its gravel-and-sandy soil, which it came by in just the same way as the Médoc—the spoil of the Garonne from inland hills.

Graves as a whole is known chiefly for its white wines; dry to medium sweet, pale yellow, with a peculiar faintly chemical or metallic character. They are rarely very good. Only a small part of the big region reaches distinction; the part near Bordeaux where the majority of the wines are red. They have much in common with the stouter and drier wines of the Médoc. The greatest red Graves are however in their own way the equivalent of the best wines even of Pauillac or Margaux. The fact was recognized by the authorities who classed Château Haut-Brion with three châteaux of the Médoc as a first growth. Today Haut-Brion has challengers. It is the favourite game of the millionaire wine-lover to make it defend its title against Château La Mission-Haut-Brion. La Mission, with La Tour-Haut-Brion and Laville-Haut-Brion, all in Pessac, belongs to a wine-maker of genius, M Henri Woltner. With the most modern techniques of controlled fermentation he makes marvellously fruity, complex, deep-scented wine. Which is not to say that Haut-Brion does not continue to make powerful wine with all the old distinction. The name La Tour-Haut-Brion is used for the second wine of La Mission; Laville-Haut-Brion is white, and one of the best of the white Graves.

Châteaux Pape-Clément and Les Carmes-Haut-Brion are the only other growths which survive in Pessac. The former is one of Bordeaux's oldest vineyards, named after the churchman who brought the papacy to France in the 14th century. Its wine today is as good as ever; usually rather light in comparison with its neighbours.

Several châteaux in the next commune going south have gone out of business. It seems there is no great demand for red Graves as such; few

except the famous classed growths can survive, particularly in an area where the woods make late frosts all too frequent a danger to the crop.

It is the commune of Léognan, well into the forest, which has the next clutch of châteaux. No one would suspect its Domaine de Chevalier, which currently has the highest reputation among them, of being any such thing. It resembles a small industrial building at the end of a flat field of vines surrounded by pine-trees. None the less it succeeds in making exceedingly fine red and white wine year after year. There is something almost Californian about the little winery with its two flavours . . . both of which turn out to be brilliant.

Château Haut-Bailly is the other leading classed growth of Léognan; it is unusual in these parts for making only red wine. Haut-Bailly has always been a respected name but its last few vintages have been particularly good.

Château Carbonnieux is more noted for its white wine, perhaps the best in Graves. Châteaux de Fieuzal and Malartic-Lagravière do not seem to distinguish themselves particularly. Château Olivier is a big vineyard also specializing in white wine. Château La Louvière is another big property, though not among the classed growths. And oddly enough there is yet another Haut-Brion château—Larrivet.

Three other communes, on the Bordeaux-Langon road to the east, have classed growths. In Villenave-d'Ornon there is Château Couhins, a white-wine château which also makes a vin rosé. Part of its vineyard is run separately as Château Cantebau-Couhins, and makes a very good dry white wine. The substantial châteaux Pontac-Monplaisir and Baret are not classed. In Cadaujac there is the well-known Château Bouscaut, where a great deal of money has recently been spent by new American proprietors. And finally in Martillac are the excellent Château Smith-Haut-Lafitte, making only red wine, and La Tour-Martillac, making both red and white. An important minor growth, Château La Garde, makes another good and full-bodied typical red Graves.

Right: Crus Classés of Graves. Seven are included in the classification for both red and white; one, Laville-Haut-Brion, for white only; the rest for red wine

Sauternes and Barsac

ALL THE other districts of Bordeaux mapped here make wines which can be compared with, and preferred to, one another. Sauternes is different. The famous white wine of Sauternes is a speciality which finds its only real rival not in France at all but in Germany. It depends on local conditions and a very unusual wine-making technique. In great years the results can be sublime; a very sweet, rich-textured, flower-scented, glittering golden liquid. In other years it can frankly fail to be Sauternes (properly so-called) at all.

Above all it is only the famous châteaux of Sauternes—and in this we include Barsac—which make such wine. Ordinary Sauternes, whether called Haut or Supérieur makes no difference, is ordinary sweet white wine. Very cold it makes a pleasant drink for serving before or after a meal.

The special technique which only the considerable châteaux can afford to employ is to pick over the vineyard as many as eight or nine times, starting in September and sometimes going on until December. This is to take full advantage of the peculiar form of mould (known as *Botrytis cinerea* to the scientist, or *pourriture noble*—noble rot—to the poet) which forms on the grapes in a mild misty autumn and shrivels the skins to the ugly wizened condition shown in the photograph.

Instead of affecting the blighted grapes with a flavour of rot, this botrytis engineers the escape of a proportion of the water in them, leaving the sugar and the flavouring elements in the juice more concentrated than ever. The result is wine with an intensity of taste and scent and a smooth, almost oil-like, texture which can be made no other way.

But it does mean picking the grapes as they shrivel, berry by berry—and the small proprietors of little-known châteaux have no alternative but to pick at once, and hope for as much botrytis as possible.

Production is very small, since evaporation is actually being encouraged. From each one of its 100 hectares of vineyard Château Yquem, the most famous of Sauternes, makes only about 9 hectolitres (about 1,200 bottles) of wine. A first-class Médoc vineyard would make about three times as much.

Château Yquem, confusingly, calls the wine it makes Château d'Yquem.

The risk element is appalling, since bad weather in October can rob the grower of all chance of making sweet wine, and sometimes any wine at all. Costs are correspondingly high, and the low price of even the finest Sauternes (with the exception of Yquem) makes it one of the least profitable wines to the grower; to the drinker it is one of the great bargains of the wine world.

Sauternes was the only area outside the Médoc to be classed in 1855. Château Yquem was made a First Great Growth—a rank created for it alone in all Bordeaux. Eleven châteaux were made first growths and 12 more were made seconds.

Five communes, including Sauternes itself, are entitled to use the name. Barsac, the biggest of them, has the alternative of calling its wine either Sauternes or Barsac. All five communes have at least one first-growth château. The ones which today seem to make the very best wine, sometimes even on a par with the super-château, Yquem, are Suduiraut in Preignac, Rayne-Vigneau in Bommes, Rieussec in Fargues and Coutet and Climens in Barsac.

Sauternes of this quality is immensely long-lived, and repays keeping more than any other white wine. At first it is so sweet that its subtleties are masked. Gradually it takes on a warmer colour (since its bottles are clear this is easy to see) and the flavour grows deeper and more interesting.

Eventually it will 'maderize'; go brown and lose some of its sugar—but this can be after as long as 40 years.

The days when Russian archdukes would drink nothing but Château Yquem—and ordered it bottled in cut-crystal decanters lettered in gold—are over. For a long time Sauternes has been banished to the end of formal banquets, and the tables of a few connoisseurs who realize that the statement it makes about the grape has no equivalent. In the sixties there was a run of bad vintages. But there is a revival on foot; the Anglo-Saxon world, Germany and Scandinavia have discovered its pleasures. Given sunshine in October before the vintage, the seventies will see Sauternes come back to the height of fashion.

Above: Sauternes labels match the glittering gold of the wine. A few châteaux make a strong dry wine as well as the famous sweet one, particularly in poor vintages
Below: the Semillon grapes to make Sauternes. 'Noble rot' shrivels them, intensifying sweetness and flavour. Pickers select the shrivelled berries and leave the rest for a week before picking again

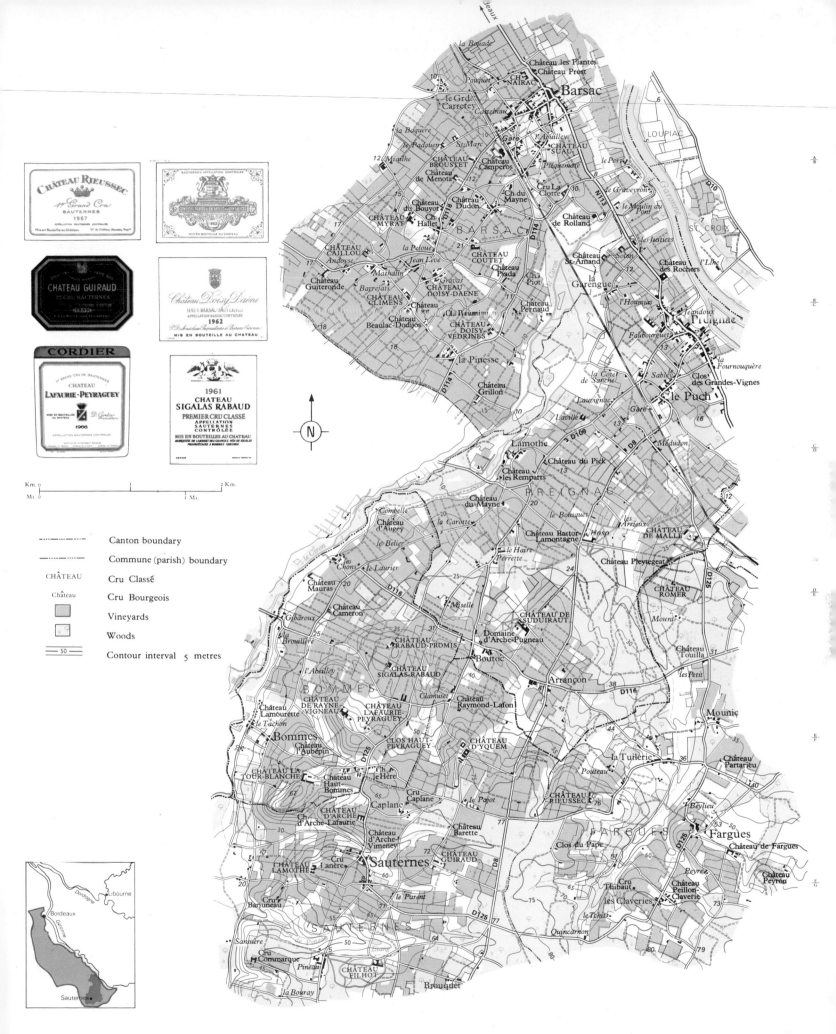

Pomerol

Above: crimson must from Merlot grapes—the variety which gives Pomerol its softness, fruitiness and strength

The grapes are carried from the pickers to the *cuvier* in wooden tubs; each full tub makes a load for two men

Left: Vieux-Château-Certan is one of Pomerol's best vineyards and also one of the few Pomerol châteaux which looks more important than an ordinary modest house. It makes on average about 55,000 bottles a year of wine, fetching a price similar to a very good classed growth of the Médoc

It is curious there should be a new star in such an ancient wine country as Bordeaux. You would think it had all been known for centuries. Yet, although Romans had vineyards in Pomerol, a hundred years ago it was known only for 'good common wine'. Even 30 years ago it was not considered in the top flight. Yet today its best château fetches the same price as the first growths of the Médoc, and an astonishing number of properties, for such a small area, are generally agreed to be among the best in the whole of Bordeaux.

Pomerol is such a curious corner of the world that it is hard to get your bearings. It is a good 25 miles east of Bordeaux along the Dordogne, almost in the suburbs of the sleepy old port of Libourne.

There is no real village centre in Pomerol; every family there makes wine, and every house stands apart among its vines. The landscape is evenly dotted with modest houses—each rejoicing in the name of château. The church stands oddly isolated too, like yet another little wine-estate. And that is Pomerol; there is nothing more to see.

Pomerol is another big gravel bank, or rather plateau, slightly rising and falling but remarkably flat overall. In the western part the soil tends to be sandy; to the east, where it meets St-Emilion, to be enriched with clay. It is entirely planted with vines, to the exclusion of all lesser plants. In the eastern part lie the best growths, so cheek by jowl with St-Emilion and under such identical conditions that it would be surprising to find any constant difference between them.

None the less the consensus is that Pomerols are the gentlest, richest, most instantly appealing clarets. They have deep colour without the acidity and tannin that often goes with it, a comforting ripe smell, and sometimes great concentration of all their qualities: the striking essence of a great wine.

Pomerol is a democracy. It has no official classification, and indeed it would be very hard to devise one. There is no long tradition of steady selling to build on. Châteaux are small family affairs and subject to change as individuals come and go. Furthermore a great number rank together as—to keep everyone happy—'first growths'. Even to the wine merchant this is largely uncharted country. A strong tradition of direct supply to customers in France flourishes. Many orders that go off by train are the odd case to some doctor or lawyer in Amiens or Clermont-Ferrand.

There is a good deal of agreement, however, about which are the outstanding vineyards of Pomerol. Pétrus is allowed by all to come first. Vieux-Château-Certan, next door, is reckoned comparable. Then in a bunch come La Fleur-Pétrus, La Conseillante, La Fleur, L'Evangile, Trotanoy, Petit-Village, Certan-de-May. It would be wrong to distinguish one group from another too clearly. Latour-à-Pomerol, L'Eglise-Clinet, Le Gay, Clos l'Eglise (how confusing the names are), La Croix-de-Gay, Clos René, Nenin and Gazin each have very high standards. On the map we distinguish the growths whose wines usually fetch the highest prices today.

Names sometimes become quite absurd. When, in eagerness to sound like some popular growth, compound names get too exuberant, we find part of the name being a claim that this is the Real and Original Château X: thus Château Vraye-Croix-de-Gay carries a picture of disagreeable neighbours which one hopes is a totally false one.

Before being overwhelmed by the complications of Pomerol (and St-Emilion, where the situation is similar), it is worth knowing that the average standard is very high here. The village has a name for reliability.

Another advantage which has certainly helped Pomerol up the ladder recently is the fact that these wines are ready remarkably soon for Bordeaux. The chief grape variety here is not the tough-skinned Cabernet Sauvignon, whose wine has to live through a tannic youth to give its ultimate finesse: in Pomerol and St-Emilion the Merlot, secondary in the Médoc, is the leading vine. Great growths have about

More typical of the region, Château Moulin-à-Vent in the neighbouring commune of Lalande-de-Pomerol is a neat unit with its *chai* and *cuvier* round a yard. It produces about 40,000 bottles of red wine a year

70 or 80% Merlot, with perhaps 20% of the local Cabernet cousin, the Bouchet. Merlot wine is softer than Cabernet. Helped by rather richer soil than in the Médoc it gives the warmth and gentleness which characterize Pomerol. Even the best Pomerol has produced all its perfume and as much finesse as it will ever achieve in 12 or 15 years, and most are already attractive at five, as against the Médoc's eight or nine.

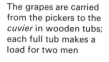

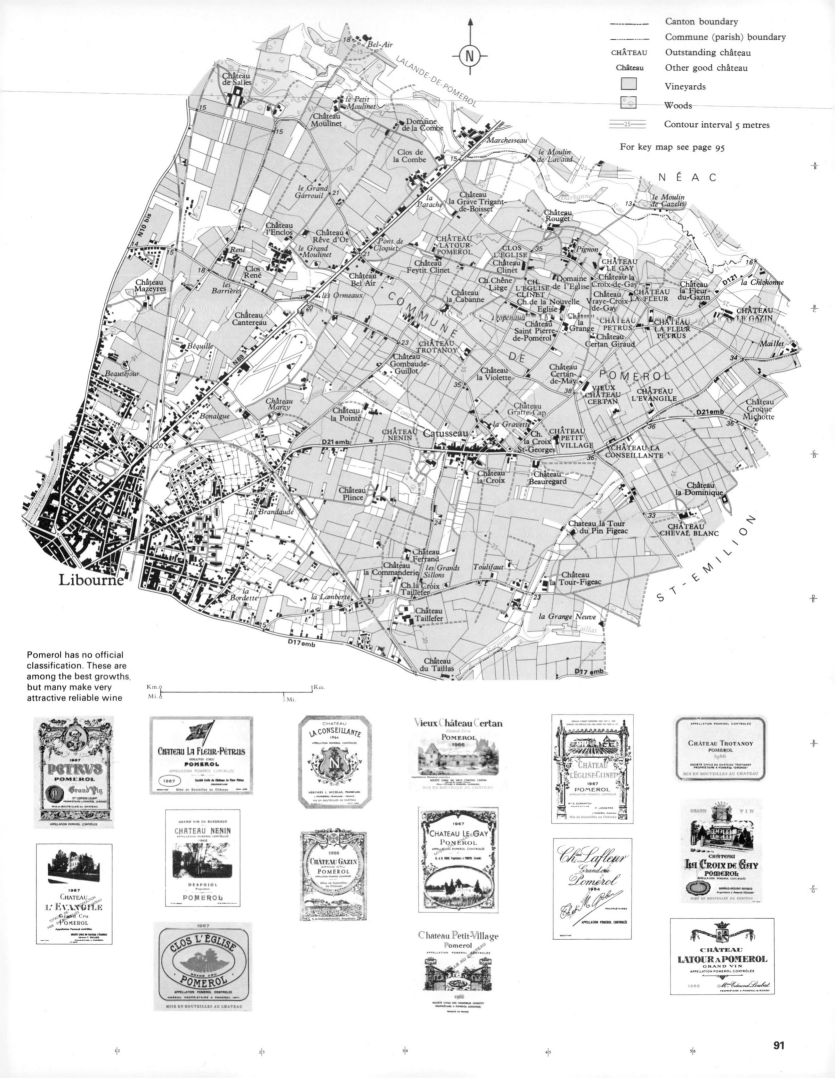

Pomerol has no official classification. These are among the best growths, but many make very attractive reliable wine

St-Emilion

THE OLD town of St-Emilion is propped in the corner of an escarpment above the Dordogne. Behind it on the plateau vines flow steadily on into Pomerol. Beside it along the ridge they swoop down into the plain. It is the little rural gem of the Bordelais—inland and upland in spirit, Roman in origin, hollow with cellars and heady with wine.

Even the church at St-Emilion is a cellar: cut, like them all, out of solid limestone. The excellent restaurant in the town square is actually on the church roof, and you sit beside the belfry to eat your lampreys stewed in red wine à la Bordelaise.

St-Emilion makes rich red wine. Before many people can really come to terms with the dryness and delicacy of Médoc wine they love the solid tastiness of St-Emilion. The best of them in ripe and sunny seasons grow almost sweet as they mature.

On the whole St-Emilion wines take less long to reach perfection than Médoc wines, if a little longer than Pomerols: say four years for the wine of a poor vintage; eight and upwards for a good one.

There are two distinct districts of St-Emilion, not counting the lesser vineyards of the river plain and the parishes to the east and north-east which are allowed to use the name (and which are described and mapped on pages 94–95).

One group of the inner châteaux lies on the border of Pomerol, on the sandy and gravelly plateau. The most famous of this plateau district, and of the whole of St-Emilion, is Château Cheval Blanc, a trim little cream-painted house in a grove of trees which is far from suggesting the splendid red wine, some of the world's most full-blooded, which its vines produce. Like the nearby Château Pétrus in Pomerol it fetches the same colossal prices as the first growths of the Médoc.

Of Cheval Blanc's neighbours, Château Figeac comes nearest to its level, and Châteaux La Tour-du-Pin-Figeac and La Dominique are outstanding.

The other, larger group, the Côtes St-Emilion, occupies the escarpment round the town. At the abrupt edge of the plateau you can see that not very thick soil covers the soft but solid limestone in which the cellars are cut. At Château Ausone, the most famous château of the Côtes, you can walk into a cellar with vines, as it were, on the ground floor above you.

The Côtes wines may not be quite so fruity

Above: the Jurade de St-Emilion, the district's ancient association of wine growers, processes in scarlet robes through the streets of the town
Below: Château Ausone commands a view of the Côtes to the east and of the valley of the Dordogne

as the 'Graves' wines from the plateau (the name Graves is confusingly applied to them because of their gravelly soil), but at their best they are the fullest-flavoured and most 'generous' wines of Bordeaux. They usually have 1% more alcohol than wine from the Médoc. Alkaline (i.e. chalky) soil is supposed to give wine strength; here it has the help of a full south-facing slope and in many places shelter from the west wind as well.

One other advantage the Côtes châteaux have over the Graves is their relative immunity to frost. Around Château Cheval Blanc a slight dip in the ground acts as a sump in which freezing air can collect on cloudless winter nights. On one dreadful night in February 1956 the temperature went down to −24°C. So many vines were killed that it took five or six years for production to pick up again.

Châteaux Canon, Magdelaine, La Gaffelière, Pavie and Clos Fourtet would certainly be on a short short list of the top Côtes wines: but the comfort of St-Emilion to the ordinary wine-lover is the number of other châteaux of moderate fame and extremely high standards providing utterly enjoyable but relatively accessible wine—the equivalent, perhaps, of the Premiers Crus vineyards of Beaune, Pommard and Volnay for value and character.

St-Emilion is not classified as the Médoc is. It merely divided its châteaux (in 1954) into Premiers Grands Crus and Grands Crus. There were 12 of the first, headed by Cheval Blanc and Ausone in a separate category of two, and 73 of the second. Some of the 73 are easily of the Médoc Cru Classé standard; others are the equivalent of Crus Bourgeois . . . but the list is alphabetical, so it is impossible to tell from it which are the best.

For consumers' purposes, if not officially, some further guide is helpful. On the map the 24 Grands Crus which normally fetch the highest prices are indicated as an intermediate category, in bigger type than the others.

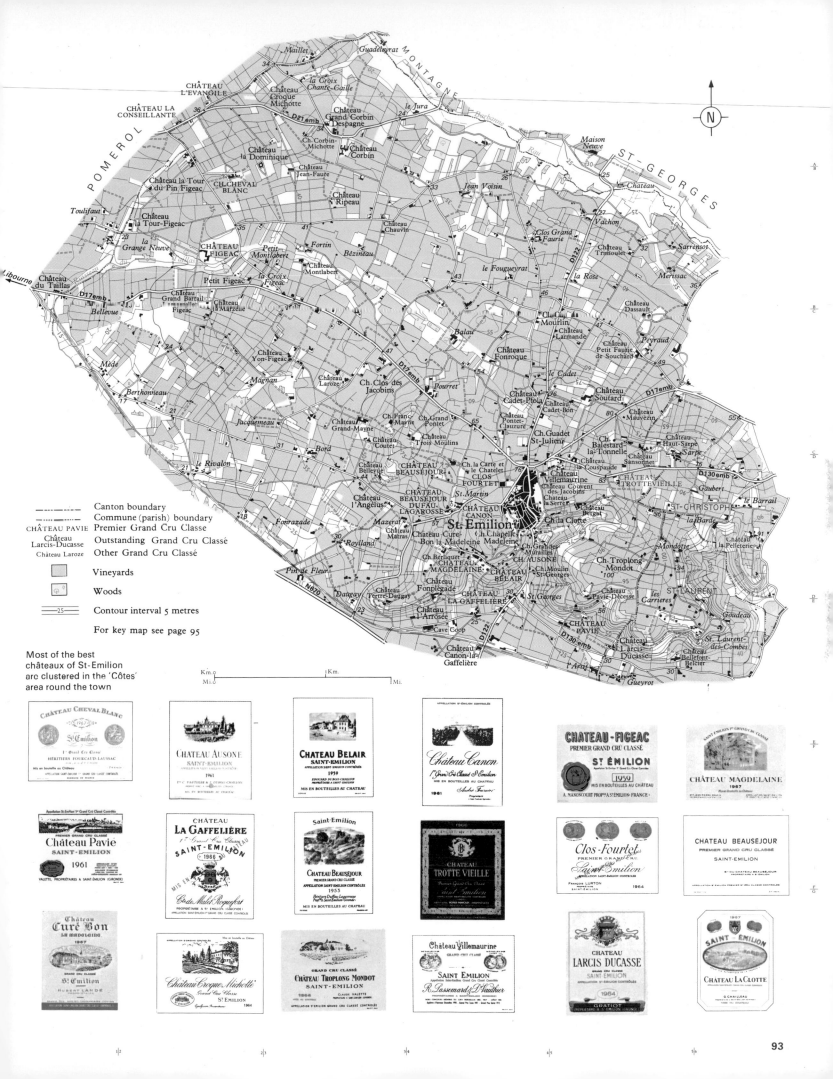

Canton boundary
Commune (parish) boundary
CHÂTEAU PAVIE Premier Grand Cru Classé
Château Larcis-Ducasse Outstanding Grand Cru Classé
Château Laroze Other Grand Cru Classé

Vineyards

Woods

Contour interval 5 metres

For key map see page 95

Most of the best châteaux of St-Emilion are clustered in the 'Côtes' area round the town

Km.0   1Km.
Mi.0   1Mi.

Château St-Georges dominates the plateau of St-Emilion from its hilltop in the neighbouring village of St-Georges. It was built in 1774 by Victor Louis, the architect who designed Bordeaux's theatre, the finest in France

Below: Fronsac may be the next area of Bordeaux to become famous. Its wines have the classical attributes: deep colour, attractive fruitiness and long life

THE ILLUSTRIOUS parishes of Pomerol and St-Emilion are the heart of a much larger and more diffuse wine-district. St-Emilion's name is shared by seven small villages south and east, and a further five to the north-east can add the name of St-Emilion to their own. Pomerol is hemmed in by the communes of Fronsac, Néac and Lalande.

With their mixture of vines and woods and pastures and their little hills and valleys the villages east and north and west are more attractive than the monotonous vineyard of the plateau in the centre.

They are still a little-known wine-country. Even Libourne and Bordeaux négociants tend to take a local broker with them as guide when they penetrate their narrow lanes. It is almost impossible to identify the little châteaux. One wonders how their wine is distributed in a world which likes the reassurance of a famous name. Yet a network of private contacts all over France is well satisfied with their sound and solid red wine, besides what reaches 'le grand négoce' one way or another.

The châteaux shown on this map are most of the bigger and better-known of the hinterland. Fronsac, for example, has many small properties; the 11 on the map are those with more than local reputations. Fronsac as a whole is reputed the coming thing in Bordeaux; one can expect to hear more of it; its wines are splendidly

fruity and full of character, and they are also still (quite) cheap.

Lalande's Château Bel-Air has long been famous. Néac also can produce some wines to compare with Pomerol.

The equivalent back-country châteaux north of St-Emilion are probably slightly less-known, with the exception of the splendid Château St-Georges, which overlooks the whole district from its hill, and makes excellent wine.

The cluster of villages east of St-Emilion, however, are a different matter. In St-Laurent Château Larcis-Ducasse is a Grand Cru and rated among the top 15 or so wines of St-Emilion. Bellefont-Belcier is also well-known. Châteaux Haut-Sarpe (another Grand Cru) and Fombrauge in St-Christophe, Châteaux de Ferrand and Capet-Guillier in St-Hippolyte, Château Puy-Blanquet in St-Etienne and Château Monbousquet in St-Sulpice to the south command prices comparable to St-Emilion Grands Crus.

There is also a minor wine-district between St-Emilion and Libourne on the river-flats, known after its soil as Sables (sand)-St-Emilion. Only Château Martinet here is well-known for wine, but the splendid residence of Libourne's biggest négociant, M Jean-Pierre Moueix, Château Videlot, is a place of pilgrimage for wine-lovers who know him, as one of the most cultured and beautiful houses in the Bordelais.

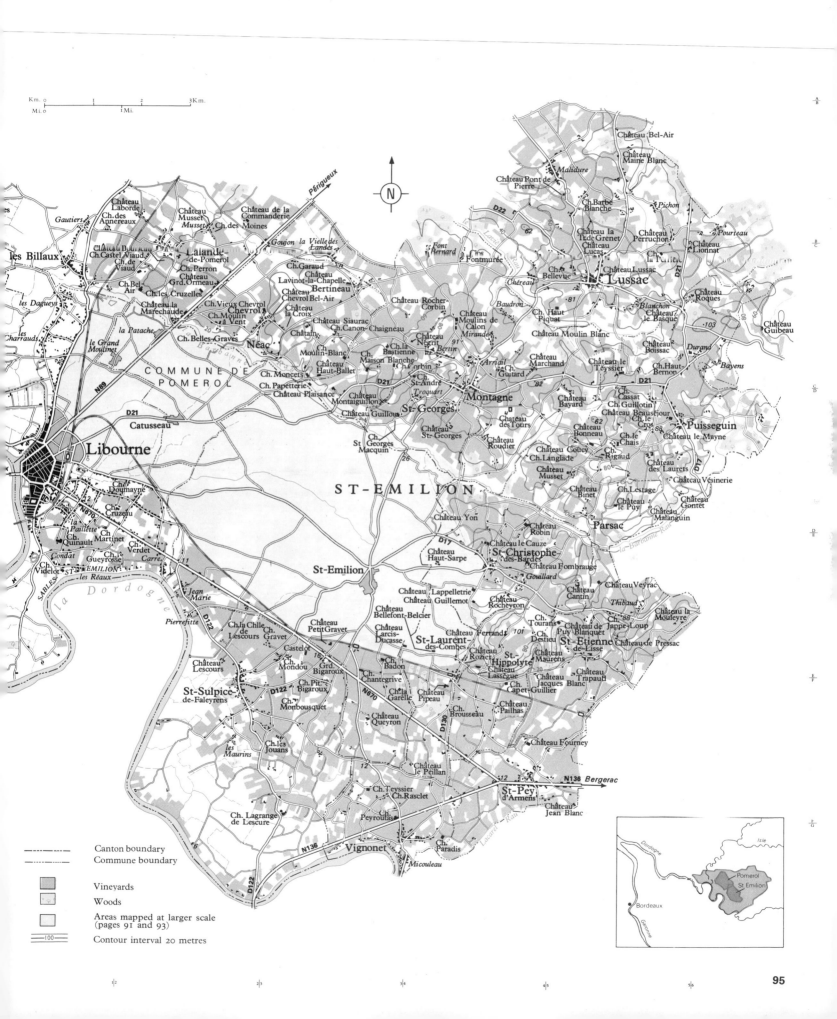

Bourg and Blaye

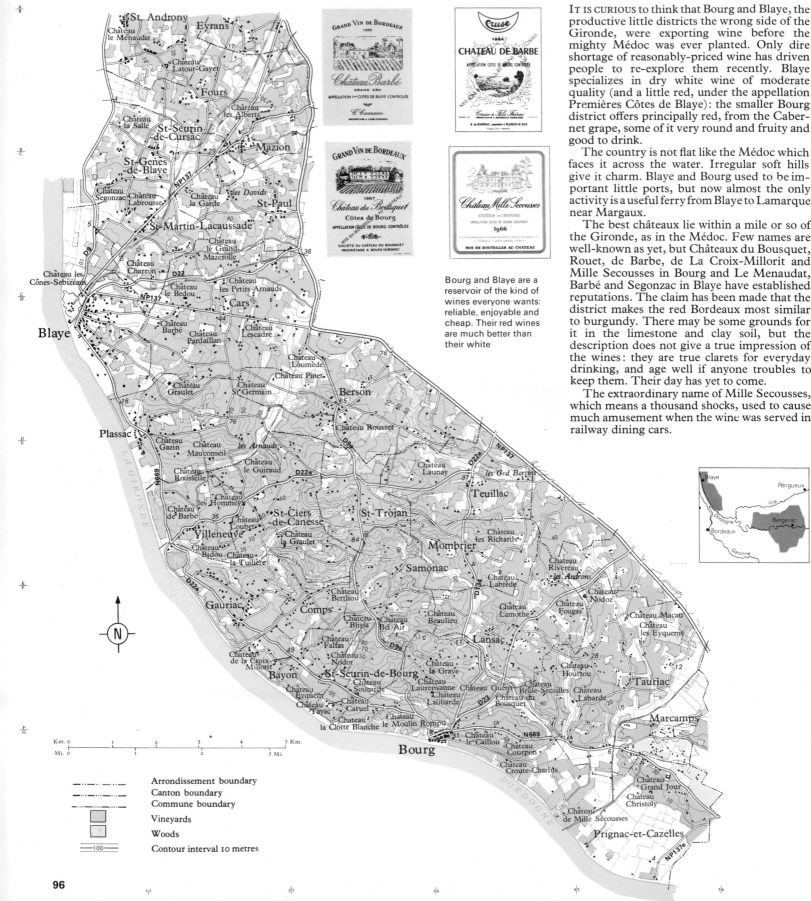

It is curious to think that Bourg and Blaye, the productive little districts the wrong side of the Gironde, were exporting wine before the mighty Médoc was ever planted. Only dire shortage of reasonably-priced wine has driven people to re-explore them recently. Blaye specializes in dry white wine of moderate quality (and a little red, under the appellation Premières Côtes de Blaye): the smaller Bourg district offers principally red, from the Cabernet grape, some of it very round and fruity and good to drink.

The country is not flat like the Médoc which faces it across the water. Irregular soft hills give it charm. Blaye and Bourg used to be important little ports, but now almost the only activity is a useful ferry from Blaye to Lamarque near Margaux.

The best châteaux lie within a mile or so of the Gironde, as in the Médoc. Few names are well-known as yet, but Châteaux du Bousquet, Rouet, de Barbe, de La Croix-Millorit and Mille Secousses in Bourg and Le Menaudat, Barbé and Segonzac in Blaye have established reputations. The claim has been made that the district makes the red Bordeaux most similar to burgundy. There may be some grounds for it in the limestone and clay soil, but the description does not give a true impression of the wines: they are true clarets for everyday drinking, and age well if anyone troubles to keep them. Their day has yet to come.

The extraordinary name of Mille Secousses, which means a thousand shocks, used to cause much amusement when the wine was served in railway dining cars.

Bourg and Blaye are a reservoir of the kind of wines everyone wants: reliable, enjoyable and cheap. Their red wines are much better than their white

Legend

- —·— Arrondissement boundary
- ——— Canton boundary
- ——— Commune boundary
- Vineyards
- Woods
- —100— Contour interval 10 metres

Bergerac

BORDEAUX'S beautiful hinterland, the Dordogne, leading back into the maze of succulent valleys cut in the stony upland of Périgord, makes simple country wine compared with Bordeaux. Yet Périgord's restaurants are famous, and their wine is the local wine. The driest and the sweetest white wines of Bergerac are very good, the red is excellent *vin de carafe*. If the district has a fault, it is a tendency to produce white wine which is neither dry nor sweet.

Monbazillac is the best of the appellations within Bergerac. At one time it was a rival to Sauternes; old Château Monbazillac is supremely rich-textured, golden and intense. Now it is a co-operative and its wine, though good, is no longer made in the same laborious way. Pécharmant has the best red wine; Rosette and the Montravels better-than-average white.

Monbazillac's vineyards slope towards the north— an unusual situation. Château Monbazillac is a shade left of the centre of the skyline in this picture

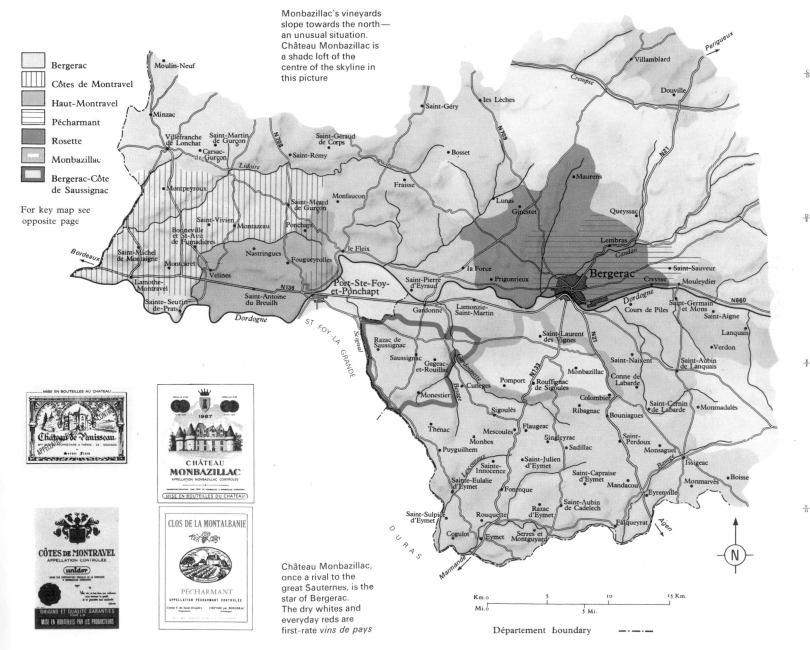

Key

- Bergerac
- Côtes de Montravel
- Haut-Montravel
- Pécharmant
- Rosette
- Monbazillac
- Bergerac-Côte de Saussignac

For key map see opposite page

Château Monbazillac, once a rival to the great Sauternes, is the star of Bergerac. The dry whites and everyday reds are first-rate *vins de pays*

Km.0   5   10   15 Km.
Mi.0   5 Mi.

Département boundary   ─ · ─ · ─

The Champagne Country

Immense rollers of vines stalk Champagne like the evidence of a far-off hurricane. At vintage time a gilded chill falls on the landscape; the coal-miners and their families who come to pick cannot animate the drowsy hillsides. The leaves go furiously red, and fall, and a frosty wind drives everyone indoors

THE NAME OF champagne is limited not only to a defined area, like the appellations of Bordeaux, but to a process, through which every drop of wine must go before it can claim the name. Some countries outside Europe, indeed, use the name as though it only meant the process. But it is the special qualities of this northernmost of France's great wine regions which make champagne unique.

It would be claiming too much to say that all champagne is better than any other sparkling wine in the world. There are champagnes and champagnes. But good champagne has a combination of freshness, delicacy, richness and raciness, and a gently stimulating power, which no other wine has ever quite attained.

The region whose soil and climate have so much to offer is only 90 miles north-east of Paris, its biggest customer. It centres round a small range of hills rising from a plain of chalk, and carved in two by the wanderings of the River Marne. Within this area, unlike in Burgundy, the names of villages do not directly concern the consumer, for the essence of champagne is that it is a blended, branded wine; and as such known by the name of the maker, not the vineyard.

There are 55,000 acres in Champagne, with 16,250 proprietors. Only 14% belongs to the famous firms who make and sell the wine. The country is owned not by great landowners but by thousands of local, almost amateur, growers,

many of whom have other jobs as well. It has been estimated that out of 18,000 men who work in the vineyards 15,500 own at least some vines: only 2,500 are employees with no vines of their own. There are 8,000 holdings of only one acre.

What the map here shows is the heart of the region, where the grapes which the best houses buy for their best champagne are grown. Outlying districts (the small map) are still legally Champagne, but their wine is acid in comparison with the best growths. There are three distinct zones here; some of the character of the wine of each is essential to the classical champagne blend.

The Montagne de Reims is planted with Pinot Noir vines, whose black grapes have to be pressed very rapidly to give white wine without a trace of colour. No one has quite explained how in this most northern vineyard a north slope, which some of the best of the Montagne is, can give good wine. The theory is that the air heats up on the plain below, and flows encouragingly up through the vines. . . . Montagne wines contribute to the bouquet, the headiness and what the French call the 'carpentry'—the framework, or backbone perhaps —of the blend.

The Vallée de la Marne, the next area, has south and south-east slopes which trap the sun and make these the fullest, roundest and ripest wines, with plenty of bouquet. These are largely

Pinot Noir vineyards as well. Bouzy in fact makes the small quantity of still red wine which the Champenois jealously keep for themselves. It can be like a rather faint but exquisite burgundy.

The east-facing slope south of Epernay is the Côte des Blancs, planted with the white Chardonnay grapes which give freshness and finesse to the blend. Wine from here is sometimes sold as Blanc de Blancs, without the traditional proportion of black-grape wine. It is a question of taste, but most experienced champagne-lovers find Côte des Blancs wine on its own lacks the perfect balance—is too light. If you see any village name on champagne it will probably be Cramant (long famous, confusingly, for its *crémant*, or half-sparkling, wine) or Avize.

Since it is not the growers in Champagne who make and sell the wine there is an unusual pricing system for grapes which expresses the quality of the different areas. At the start of the harvest, one price (per kilo of grapes) is decided on by a committee of growers and merchants. Growers in the best communes, or Grands Crus, are paid 100%, the full price. Premiers Crus receive between 90 and 99%, and so on down to 50% for some of the outlying areas.

On the map the leading communes are indicated in larger type. The greater part of the wine in all first-class brands comes from these villages. If they use any from the Champagne outskirts it would be in their sweeter blends.

Reims

Tinqueux

Janvry   Gueux

Ormes

Cité
Charbonneaux

Cormontreuil

Bouleuse   Méry-   Coulommes   N 380
            Prémecy   la Montagne   Tassy

St. Euphraise
et Clairizet   Pargny-   Bezannes
Aubilly   les-Reims   Jouy-
Sarcy   les-Reims   LES   TROIS   SILLERY
                                          MESNEUX   PUITS   PUISIEUX
          Bouilly   VILLE-   Villers-   Mont de
    Bligny   DOMMANGE   aux Noeuds   Champfleury   la Cuche

                                     SACY   MONTBRE   BEAUMONT-
Chambrecy   N 380   ÉCUEIL   SUR-VESLE
        136   le Bois de   Mont
    Chaumuzy   la Fosse   Trouilly
                        244   267   Chamery   Rilly   VERZENAY
        Marfaux   148   149   CHIGNY-   MAILLY   VERZY
                                                            LES ROSES   283
Chambrecy   les Pâtis d'Écueil   151
    Champlat et   Pourcy   268   VILLERS-   Ludes   Chemin de la Barbarie   N 44
    Boujacourt   Bois de   ALLERAND   265   128
Jonquery   Reims   les Battis   VILLERS-
    Bois de   182   Le Bois de St. Remy   les Battis   279   MARMERY
    la Cohette   260
Cuchery   Nanteuil   FORÊT DE LA MONTAGNE DE REIMS
        Belval-   la Fosse   Bois de   271   TRÉPAIL
    sous-Châtillon   Bois de   St. Quentin   Ville-   260   Mont Tournant
                        Bois de   Nanteuil   Bois de Notre Dame   en Selve   257   Bois des Dames   208
Bois de la   Bois de Fleury   263   Germaine   LOUVOIS   VAUDEMANGES
Rodemat   Cormoyeux   St. Imoges   Bois du   112
Bois du Roi   Gouffre   Mont Hurlet   TAUXIÈRES-   Mt.   BOUZY   120
    Villers-   Fleury-   234   MUTRY   Écouve
    sous-Châtillon   la Rivière   Romery   FORÊT DE LA MONTAGNE DE REIMS   Fontaine   99   AMBONNAY
Reuil   154   sur Ay   98
    Venteuil   Bois de   HAUTVILLERS   Mt
                    St. Marc   CHAMPILLON   des Plantes
        CUMIÈRES   Bois de
            67   Charlefontaine   AVENAY
Damery   69   VAL D'OR   Mont Charlier   TOURS-
    Boursault   DIZY   MUTIGNY   BISSEUIL   SUR-   Condé-
Mardeuil   N3   MAGENTA   MAREUIL-SUR-AY   MARNE   sur-
    Vauciennes   AŸ   Marne
        91   Épernay   69
Vinay   Moussy   CHOUILLY
            PIERRY   106   178
        Chavot
                CUIS
Monthelon   Butte
        Mancy   de
                    Saran
Morangis   128
    Moslins   Grauves   CRAMANT
                        AVIZE   108
            B. d'Avize
                    OGER
        Forêt d'Oger   239
            Forêt du Mesnil   116
229   245   LE MESNIL-
            SUR-OGER
        Gionges   123
    203   232
VERTUS

        Bois de
        Cormont
        226

Km. 0   1   2   3   4   5   6 Km.
Mi. 0   1   2   3   4 Mi.

--- · --- · ---   Arrondissement boundary
--- ·· --- ·· ---   Canton boundary
MAILLY   Grand Cru commune
VERZY   Premier Cru commune
▨   Vineyards
▢   Woods
═200═   Contour interval 20 metres

99

The Champagne Towns

Above: in 1858, bottles of champagne were (right to left) disgorged, topped up, had the cork hammered home and tied on with string
Right: today's dégorgeur uses precisely the same technique. The essential process has not changed

WHAT HAPPENS in the towns of Champagne concerns us just as much as what happens in the country. The process of champagne-making has only just begun when the grapes are picked and pressed. Without delay the murky must is taken to the shipper's 'maison' in Reims or Epernay or Ay. There it will spend at least the next two years.

It ferments busily at first, but as the fermentation dies down the doors and windows are thrown open to let in the wintry air. In the cold the fermentation stops. The wine will spend a chilly winter, still with the potential of more fermentation latent in it.

So it used to be shipped. England in the 17th century was an eager customer for barrels of this delicate, rather sharp wine. According to Patrick Forbes, the historian of champagne, the English bottled it on arrival; and found that they had created a sparkling wine.

Whether or not it was the English who did it first, early bottling is the vital stage in the historical process which changed the *vin du pays* of northern France into the prima donna of the world.

For the wine continued to ferment in the bottle and the gas given off by the fermentation dissolved in the wine. If the natural effect was given a little encouragement—a little more sugar, a little more yeast—what had been a slight, though very attractive, wine was found to improve immeasurably, gaining strength and character over a period of two years or more. Above all the inexhaustible bubbles gave it a miraculous liveliness.

Dom Pérignon, cellar-master of the Abbey of Hautvillers at the end of the 17th century, is credited with the next round of developments; the cork tied down with string, the stronger bottles (though still not strong enough; he lost half his wine through bottles bursting), and above all the art of blending wines from different parts of the district to achieve the best possible flavour.

The chief difference between the brands of champagne lies in this making of the cuvée, as the blending is called. All depends on the skill of the director tasting the raw young wines and peering into their future—and on how much his firm is prepared to spend on its raw materials; for the more top-quality wine goes

into the cuvée the better it will be. Each firm has a tradition of the kind of wine it makes; no difference should be noticeable in its non-vintage wine from year to year. One might instance Krug, Bollinger, Veuve Clicquot and Pol Roger as typical of the old style, making full-flavoured, mature-tasting champagne. Some firms follow a modern trend towards lighter, younger-tasting wine.

Another fashion today, started by Moët et Chandon with their 'Dom Pérignon', is to make a super-luxury wine, relegating (in theory) even the best vintages to second place. Dom Ruinart, Heidsieck Diamant Bleu, Roederer Cristal and Taittinger's Comtes de Champagne are all in this bracket.

The widow Clicquot made her contribution to champagne in the early years of the 19th century. She devised a method of removing the sediment which resulted from bottle fermentation without removing the bubbles at the same time. Briefly what she invented was a desk of wood in which the mature bottles of wine could be stuck in holes upside down (*sur point*). Her cellarmen gave each bottle a gentle shake and twist (*remuage*) every day until all the sediment had dislodged from the glass and settled on the

cork. Then they took out the cork with the bottle still upside down, let the eggcupful of wine containing the sediment escape (*dégorgement*), topped up the bottle with wine from another of the same and put in a new cork.

The process which thousands of visitors go to Reims and Epernay to see remains essentially the same. Not the least spectacular thing is the immense cellars where it is done. Some of them are Roman chalk pits under the city. One firm uses trains in its 15 miles of tunnel.

Every trace of sugar in champagne is used up when it is re-fermented in its bottle: it becomes totally dry—what is known as Brut. Only the best wines have the gentleness to be perfect without any 'dosage'. Most people prefer it sweeter, so when it is *dégorgé* a dose of sugar-sweetened wine is added: as little as 1% of the total for Extra Dry; but as much as 10% for a sweet champagne, designed for drinking at the end of a meal.

The full flavour of champagne is lost if it is served very cold. Ideally it should be thoroughly cool but not at all icy.

Most important of all it should be mature. Very young champagne makes enemies. Time finds in it inimitable glorious flavours.

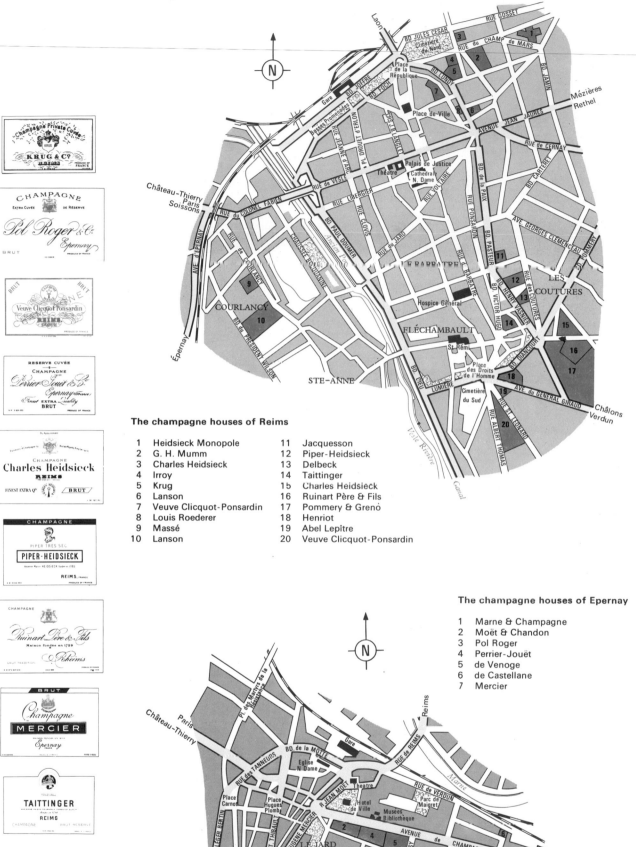

The champagne houses of Reims

1	Heidsieck Monopole	11	Jacquesson
2	G. H. Mumm	12	Piper-Heidsieck
3	Charles Heidsieck	13	Delbeck
4	Irroy	14	Taittinger
5	Krug	15	Charles Heidsieck
6	Lanson	16	Ruinart Père & Fils
7	Veuve Clicquot-Ponsardin	17	Pommery & Grenò
8	Louis Roederer	18	Henriot
9	Massé	19	Abel Lepître
10	Lanson	20	Veuve Clicquot-Ponsardin

The champagne houses of Epernay

1 Marne & Champagne
2 Moët & Chandon
3 Pol Roger
4 Perrier-Jouët
5 de Venoge
6 de Castellane
7 Mercier

Some of the most famous names of Champagne. The bottom labels are a white 'champagne nature' (still wine) and the rare still red of Bouzy, made from Pinot Noir grapes—like a very delicate burgundy

101

Alsace

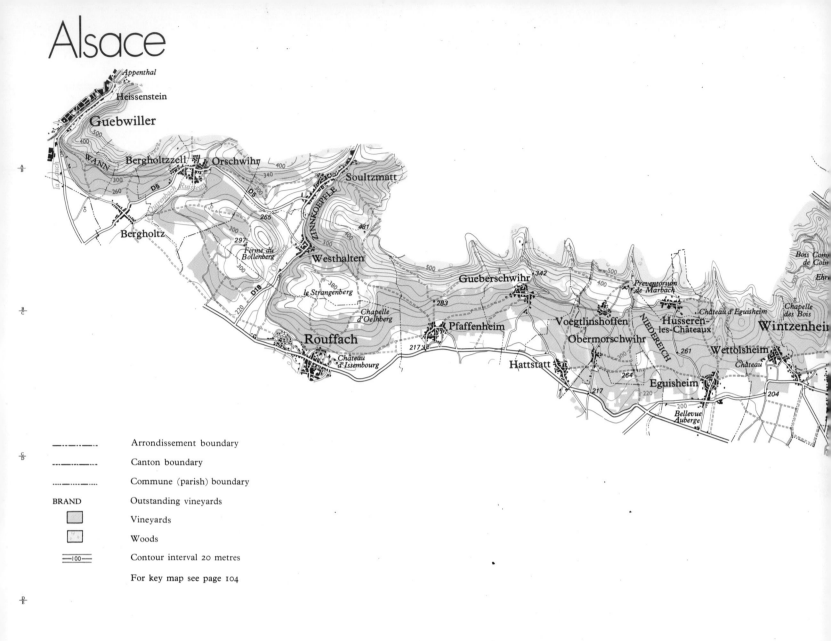

THE WINE of Alsace reflects the curious situation of a border province. A traveller at the time of the French Revolution found it incredible that this land, so clearly intended by nature to be part of Germany, was actually annexed to France.

Today the Alsatians, although they still speak a sort of German, feel very differently. What has not changed is the physical barrier between them and the rest of France; for it is the Vosges, not the Rhine, which makes the great change in landscape, architecture, climate—and not least in wine.

Alsace makes Germanic wine in the French way. The tone is set by the climate, the soil and the choice of grape varieties: all comparable with the vineyards of slightly further north, slightly further down the Rhine valley, which are in Germany. What differs is the interpretation put on these things—because today German and Alsatian wine growers hold opposite points of view of what they want their wine to do and be.

To put the difference in a nutshell, the Germans look for sweetness, the Alsatians for strength. German wine at its best is not for the table, but the drawing-room, or the garden. Alsatian wine is the great adjunct to one of France's most splendid cuisines.

Alsace gives the flowery-scented grapes of Germany the body and authority of such table

The Confrérie St-Etienne is Alsace's red-robed wine growers' and shippers' association

Alsace vines are trained tall. On the wooded Vosges Eguisheim's three ruined châteaux are a landmark

wines as white burgundy, proper accompaniments to strong and savoury food.

Instead of grape-sugar lingering delicately in the wine, the grower likes a dry, firm, clean flavour. He ferments every ounce of the sugar which the long dry summers of Alsace give him, concentrating the essences of his highly-perfumed German-style grapes into a sometimes astonishingly spicy fragrance.

The Vosges Mountains are the secret of the success of these east-facing vineyards, which lie along their flank at an altitude of between 600 and 1,200 feet, in a ribbon rarely more than a mile wide. The higher the mountains are, the drier the land which they shelter from the mois-

ture of the west. In the north where they are lower their influence is less marked; the wines of Bas-Rhin tend to be the weaker in strength and savour. In the centre and the south of the vineyard, where the best wine villages are found, the mountains can keep the sky clear of cloud for weeks on end.

Alsace, like Champagne, is an exception to the usual French pattern of a complex structure of Appellations Contrôlées, pinning every wine down to the exact district of its birth. Its map, therefore, is not so much a guide to buying the wines of Alsace as to the reasons for their exceptional character and qualities. What is mapped here is the central and southern part of the

The finest of Alsace's many grapes, the Riesling of the Rhine is recognizably speckled when it is ripe

The heart of Colmar, the wine capital of Alsace, is a typical superb survival from the 16th century

60-mile-long Alsace vineyard; the part which gives all the best wines.

Local variations of sun and soil notwithstanding, Alsace has only one Appellation Contrôlée. No distinction is officially made between commune and commune, or slope and slope.

The trade is based on the activities of merchant houses, most of whom are growers, but who can buy wine up and down the country for their branded blends. Instead of place names they market grape names. Alsace is the one part of France where you order 'a bottle of Riesling' or 'a bottle of Sylvaner', instead of specifying a vineyard, village or regional name.

The wines of the different merchants and growers, however, do tend to reflect the style and quality of the part of Alsace they come from. Barr, for example, is perhaps the best commune of the Bas-Rhin, in the north, but its wines have more acidity, are less substantial than those of Riquewihr. The region of Riquewihr, centrally placed with good south-facing slopes standing out from the Vosges, seems to have the ideal situation. At the far southern end of the region, at Guebwiller, the perfectly-sheltered vineyards give distinctly softer and richer wine.

Between these three each village has some style and some speciality of its own, known to few and to virtually no one outside the area. Some ten or a dozen have a particularly good vineyard whose reputation has spread. Where they are owned by négociants their names are sometimes used as a sort of brand name. Some of these appear on the map on these pages: it is easy to see why these particular slopes are favoured—all have south and east exposure.

A signposted Route des Vins takes visitors on a meandering course the whole length of the Alsace wine country. It calls on the way at some of the prettiest wine towns in the world. The richest possible operatic Gothick is standard architecture here: overhanging gables and flowery courtyards and well-heads and cobbles and leaded lights and carved beams survive en masse in many of the villages. Riquewihr and Kaysersberg are the most beautiful. Colmar, the capital of Alsace wine, has a magnificent collection of timber-frame houses from the 15th century on. Other towns, notably Ammerschwihr, were totally destroyed in 1945 and have been rebuilt in the heavy modern mid-European mountain style.

Between them the high-trained vines block out the view along narrow lanes, until you reach a ridge and suddenly see the gleaming green sea rolling against the mountains before and behind, disappearing in a haze in the distance, with neither sound nor movement but the bump of a supersonic fighter patrolling the border, over the Rhine.

The Wines of Alsace

THE GRAPES which give their names and special qualities to the wines of Alsace are the Riesling of the Rhine—responsible here and in Germany for the best wine—the Sylvaner, Muscat, Pinot Gris, the lesser Chasselas and Knipperlé, and the unique and fragrant Traminer or Gewürztraminer.

The Gewürztraminer is the perfect introduction to Alsace. You would not think that so fruity a scent could come from any wine so clean and dry. Gewürz means spice in German; the spice is there all the way down, and stays on your palate for two or three minutes after you have swallowed.

To the initiated a wine with so marked a character becomes dull after a while. It has its place with some of the richest of the very rich Alsatian dishes; goose or pork. But Alsatians consider the Riesling their true Grand Vin. It offers something much more elusive; a balance of hard and gentle, flowery and strong, which leads you on and never surfeits.

These two, and two more less generally known, the Pinot Gris (or Tokay d'Alsace) and the Muscat, are classed as the Noble Wines of Alsace. Recently there has been renewed interest in the Tokay d'Alsace (no connection with Hungarian Tokay), which makes the fullest bodied but least perfumed wine of the region; it has obvious uses at table as an alternative to a 'big', and therefore more expensive, white burgundy. The Muscat surprises everyone who knows the wine the muscat grape makes anywhere else in the world, which is always sweet. Here it keeps all its characteristic grapy scent but makes a dry wine as clean as a whistle, a very good aperitif.

In a class above the common wines of the region, but not quite reckoned noble, comes the Sylvaner, the maid-of-all-work of the German vineyards. Alsace Sylvaner is light and sometimes nicely tart. Without the tartness it can be a little dull and coarse in flavour. It is often used as the first wine at an Alsatian dinner, to build up to the wine which will build up to the main wine, the Riesling.

The lesser grapes, the Chasselas and the Knipperlé (there are others, too), are not usually identified on the bottle—or indeed very often bottled at all. They are the open wines of cafés and restaurants. Very young, particularly in the summer after a good vintage, they are so good that visitors should not miss them by insisting on bottled wine. Zwicker is the word used for a blend of the commoner grapes, Edelzwicker (Edel means noble) for a blend made from the grander grape varieties.

What all these wines have in common is the Alsatian style of wine-making, which is almost fanatically concerned with naturalness. To hear an Alsatian grower talking about German wines you would think they were all made by white-coated chemists on a laboratory bench. 'Once you let a chemist in your house he will make himself indispensable by frightening you with all the diseases your wine might catch', they say. They scorn refinements of fining, or anything which involves additions to the wine of any kind. They keep it undisturbed in huge wooden casks, racking and filtering as little as possible. They even take precautions to fill the

bottle as full as possible and to use a specially long cork—all to protect the wine from the air. They achieve a remarkable balance of strength and freshness, fruit and acidity by their pains.

None the less when a really fine autumn comes on the heels of a good summer, and they find grapes ripening beautifully with no threat of bad weather, not even an Alsatian, dedicated as he is to clean dry table wines, can resist doing as the Germans do and getting the last drop of sugar out of his vines.

These late-pickings are even sometimes labelled with the German words Auslese and Beerenauslese, although the phrase Vendange Tardive is more in keeping with Alsatian feelings. They reach heights of lusciousness not far removed from the rarest and most expensive of all German wines. A late-picked Gewürztraminer or Muscat has perhaps the most exotic smell of any wine in the world, and can at the same time keep a remarkable cleanness and finesse of flavour.

At less exalted levels, the words Grand Vin, or Réserve Exceptionnelle, or any combination with the words Grand or Réserve, appearing on a bottle of Alsace wine means that it is 11% alcohol—a shade more than most fine German wines and the same as a good white burgundy. These are the best standard wines which most growers or négociants market.

A little red wine is made from the Pinot Noir, but it rarely gets a deeper colour than a rosé, and never a very marked or distinguished flavour. Rouge d'Alsace, and sometimes vin gris, or very pale pink wine, will be found in *brasseries* (the word for a restaurant serving Alsatian food, traditionally to go with beer) in Paris and elsewhere.

Alsace itself has two of the best restaurants in France: Gaertner's Aux Armes de France at Ammerschwihr and Haeberlin's Auberge de l'Ill at Illhaeusern. Foie gras frais (whole goose liver, as opposed to pâté de foie gras) is one of the dishes worth travelling for. In general, Alsace cooking demonstrates what a French artist can do with German ideas. Sauerkraut becomes choucroute, and suddenly delicious. Dishes which look as though they are going to be heavy turn out to be rich but light. Quiches and onion tart are almost miraculously edible. In Alsace no one looks beyond the range of white wines of the country to accompany this profusion of dishes.

Alsace labels usually feature the grape variety in type as big as the producer's name. Where producers have their own vineyards their names are sometimes used—'Clos St-Landelin', 'Clos Gaensbroennel'—on their better wine. But vineyards in Alsace are not classified or controlled as they are in Burgundy

The Language of the Label

Cépage Grape variety (e.g. Riesling)
Cuvée Blend (normal practice in Alsace)
Grand Vin Wine with over 11% alcohol
Grand Cru The same
Réserve Exceptionnelle The same
Grande Réserve The same
Vendange Tardive Late-picked wine, implying more strength and/or sweetness
Spätlese, Beerenauslese, etc These German terms are sometimes used
Le Sigille de la Confrérie St-Etienne A red seal awarded to particularly good wines by the growers' promotional body

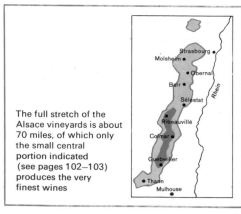

The full stretch of the Alsace vineyards is about 70 miles, of which only the small central portion indicated (see pages 102–103) produces the very finest wines

Most famous and
unspoilt little mediaeval
wine town in France,
Riquewihr huddles in
its wall below the
Schoenenberg in
H. Bacher's wood engraving

The Loire Valley and Muscadet

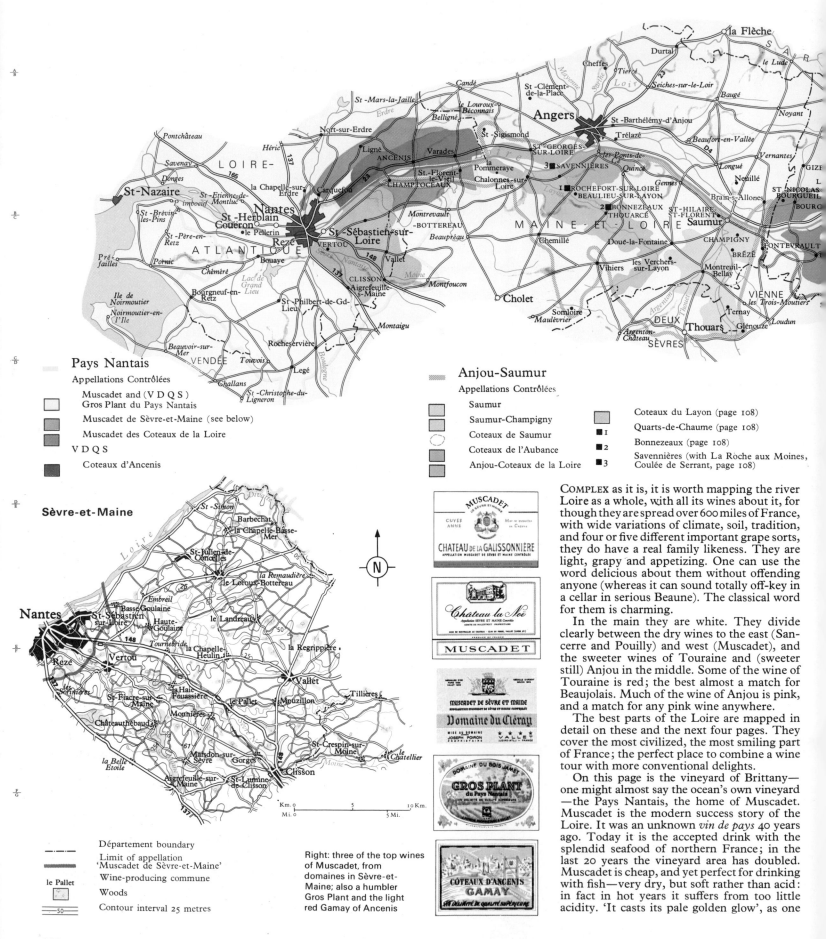

Pays Nantais

Appellations Contrôlées

Muscadet and (V D Q S)
Gros Plant du Pays Nantais

Muscadet de Sèvre-et-Maine (see below)

Muscadet des Coteaux de la Loire

V D Q S

Coteaux d'Ancenis

Anjou-Saumur

Appellations Contrôlées

Saumur

Saumur-Champigny

Coteaux de Saumur

Coteaux de l'Aubance

Anjou-Coteaux de la Loire

Coteaux du Layon (page 108)

Quarts-de-Chaume (page 108)

Bonnezeaux (page 108)

Savennières (with La Roche aux Moines,
Coulée de Serrant, page 108)

Sèvre-et-Maine

Département boundary

Limit of appellation
'Muscadet de Sèvre-et-Maine'

Wine-producing commune

Woods

Contour interval 25 metres

Right: three of the top wines
of Muscadet, from
domaines in Sèvre-et-
Maine; also a humbler
Gros Plant and the light
red Gamay of Ancenis

COMPLEX as it is, it is worth mapping the river Loire as a whole, with all its wines about it, for though they are spread over 600 miles of France, with wide variations of climate, soil, tradition, and four or five different important grape sorts, they do have a real family likeness. They are light, grapy and appetizing. One can use the word delicious about them without offending anyone (whereas it can sound totally off-key in a cellar in serious Beaune). The classical word for them is charming.

In the main they are white. They divide clearly between the dry wines to the east (Sancerre and Pouilly) and west (Muscadet), and the sweeter wines of Touraine and (sweeter still) Anjou in the middle. Some of the wine of Touraine is red; the best almost a match for Beaujolais. Much of the wine of Anjou is pink, and a match for any pink wine anywhere.

The best parts of the Loire are mapped in detail on these and the next four pages. They cover the most civilized, the most smiling part of France; the perfect place to combine a wine tour with more conventional delights.

On this page is the vineyard of Brittany—one might almost say the ocean's own vineyard—the Pays Nantais, the home of Muscadet. Muscadet is the modern success story of the Loire. It was an unknown *vin de pays* 40 years ago. Today it is the accepted drink with the splendid seafood of northern France; in the last 20 years the vineyard area has doubled. Muscadet is cheap, and yet perfect for drinking with fish—very dry, but soft rather than acid: in fact in hot years it suffers from too little acidity. 'It casts its pale golden glow', as one

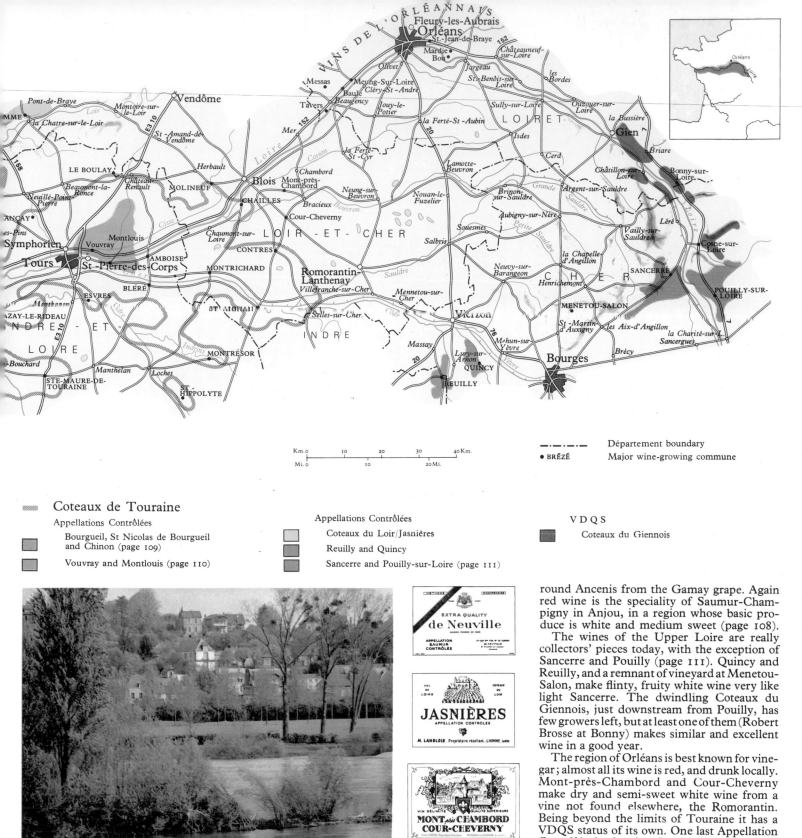

Coteaux de Touraine

Appellations Contrôlées

Bourgueil, St Nicolas de Bourgueil and Chinon (page 109)

Vouvray and Montlouis (page 110)

Appellations Contrôlées

Coteaux du Loir/Jasnières

Reuilly and Quincy

Sancerre and Pouilly-sur-Loire (page 111)

VDQS

Coteaux du Giennois

---- ·---- ·---- Département boundary

● BRÉZÉ   Major wine-growing commune

Km.0   10   20   30   40 Km.
Mi. 0   10   20 Mi.

French critic has said, 'over the purple of lobsters and the pearl of oysters, the pink of shrimps and the red of mullet.'

Muscadet is the name of the vine, not of a place. The region of Sèvre-et-Maine, at far left, is the heart of the vineyard, giving the softest wines; most scented, soonest ready. Within three months of the vintage they are sold 'sur lie'—straight from the barrel, unracked. The other important area, the Coteaux de la Loire, gives better wine in hot years, with more lasting properties. The second wine of the region, Gros Plant, is also good—a minor Muscadet with more acidity. Some pleasant red wine is made

The soft watery landscape of the Loire perfectly suggests the gentle spring-like quality of its wine. Here, near Saumur in Anjou, white, pink and red wines are all light and refreshing

Right: sparkling Saumur, sweet Jasnières, obscure Mont-près-Chambord and flinty Reuilly and Quincy are among the wide variety of Loire wines

round Ancenis from the Gamay grape. Again red wine is the speciality of Saumur-Champigny in Anjou, in a region whose basic produce is white and medium sweet (page 108).

The wines of the Upper Loire are really collectors' pieces today, with the exception of Sancerre and Pouilly (page 111). Quincy and Reuilly, and a remnant of vineyard at Menetou-Salon, make flinty, fruity white wine very like light Sancerre. The dwindling Coteaux du Giennois, just downstream from Pouilly, has few growers left, but at least one of them (Robert Brosse at Bonny) makes similar and excellent wine in a good year.

The region of Orléans is best known for vinegar; almost all its wine is red, and drunk locally. Mont-près-Chambord and Cour-Cheverny make dry and semi-sweet white wine from a vine not found elsewhere, the Romorantin. Being beyond the limits of Touraine it has a VDQS status of its own. One last Appellation Contrôlée is the tiny Jasnières, on the little River Loir north of Vouvray. Its wine is very like those of Vouvray.

Irregular quality is the curse of wine-growing so far north. Many Loire growths vary so widely from one year to another that they seem hardly the same wine. A fine autumn makes it possible to gather grapes dried almost to raisins and make intensely sweet wine, but a wet one means (as in Germany) a very acid product. Hence the importance of the sparkling wine industry in Touraine and Anjou. The comparative failures of Vouvray or Saumur, fruity but acid, are ideal for transforming into sparkling wine, using the champagne method.

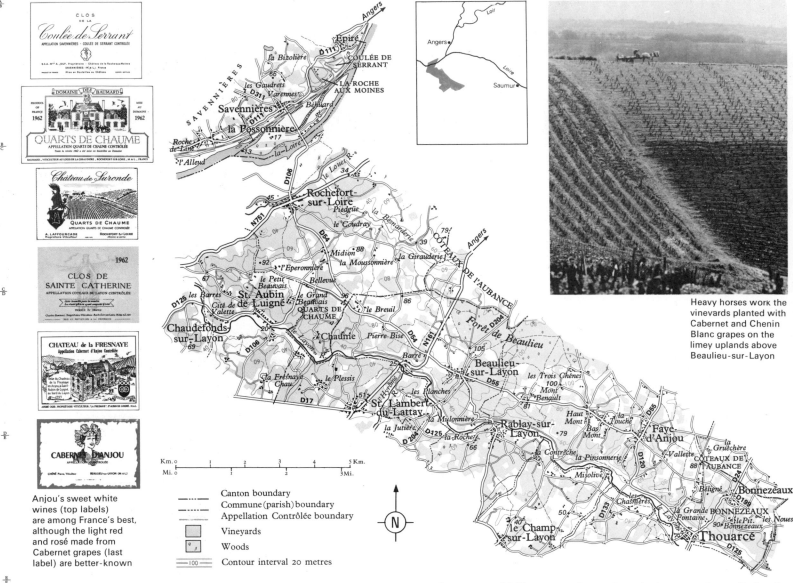

Heavy horses work the vinevards planted with Cabernet and Chenin Blanc grapes on the limey uplands above Beaulieu-sur-Layon

Anjou's sweet white wines (top labels) are among France's best, although the light red and rosé made from Cabernet grapes (last label) are better-known

Legend:
- Canton boundary
- Commune (parish) boundary
- Appellation Contrôlée boundary
- Vineyards
- Woods
- Contour interval 20 metres

THE WHITE wines of Anjou and Touraine have this in common with those of Germany: the better they are the sweeter they are. At their very best they are dessert wines of velvet texture, smooth with glycerine, richly and yet freshly scented, tasting of grapes, peaches, apricots, hazel-nuts, but with an underlying elusive flintiness which prevents them cloying. This is after a long warm autumn. Such wines go on improving for many years. But even in medium years they often have the balance of good German wines in which fruit and acid seem perfectly matched; the secret of making you want to sip and go on sipping.

The grape that gives us all this is the Chenin Blanc, called locally Pineau de la Loire. The area mapped on this page is where it reaches its ripest; several geographical circumstances combine to give it the dry open slopes, sheltered from north and east, which it needs. The River Layon, heading north-west to join the Loire, has cut a deep enough gulley to provide per-

fectly exposed but sheltered corners of hill.

A large part of its course has the appellation Coteaux du Layon, providing on average sweet wines notably above the general Anjou standard. But Quarts de Chaume (only 120 acres) and Bonnezeaux (about double) are outstanding enough to have appellations of their own, like Grands Crus in Burgundy. Beaulieu, Rablay, Rochefort and St-Aubin are communes with particularly good wines; Rochefort is the centre for the district.

The River Aubance, parallel with the Layon to the north, makes similar wines; both also grow the red Cabernet to make good light red wine, the famous delicate Cabernet Rosé d'Anjou, and, paler still, vin gris, barely more than a blushing white.

Just south of Angers, and facing Rochefort, the north bank of the Loire has a series of small appellations which are locally important. Again it is the Chenin Blanc, though here—to confound all generalization—the wine at its best is

dry. Savennières is the general appellation for this small region (which comes within the bigger one of the Coteaux de la Loire). Within Savennières there are two Grands Crus—La Roche aux Moines (about the same size as Quarts de Chaume) and the mere 12 acres of La Coulée de Serrant.

Coulée de Serrant epitomizes the exceptional situation which makes outstanding wine: it faces south-west in a side-valley even more sheltered than the main river bank. Its old stone press-house has an ecclesiastical air. The view over the Loire with its wooded and flowery islands is like the background to one of the mediaeval tapestries of Angers.

Savennières wine has a honey-and-flowers smell which makes its dryness surprising at first. It is a 'big' wine which improves for two or three years in bottle. Salmon is said to be its perfect partner, but there is such pleasure in its lingering flavour that it is a pity not to drink it on its own before a meal.

Chinon and Bourgueil

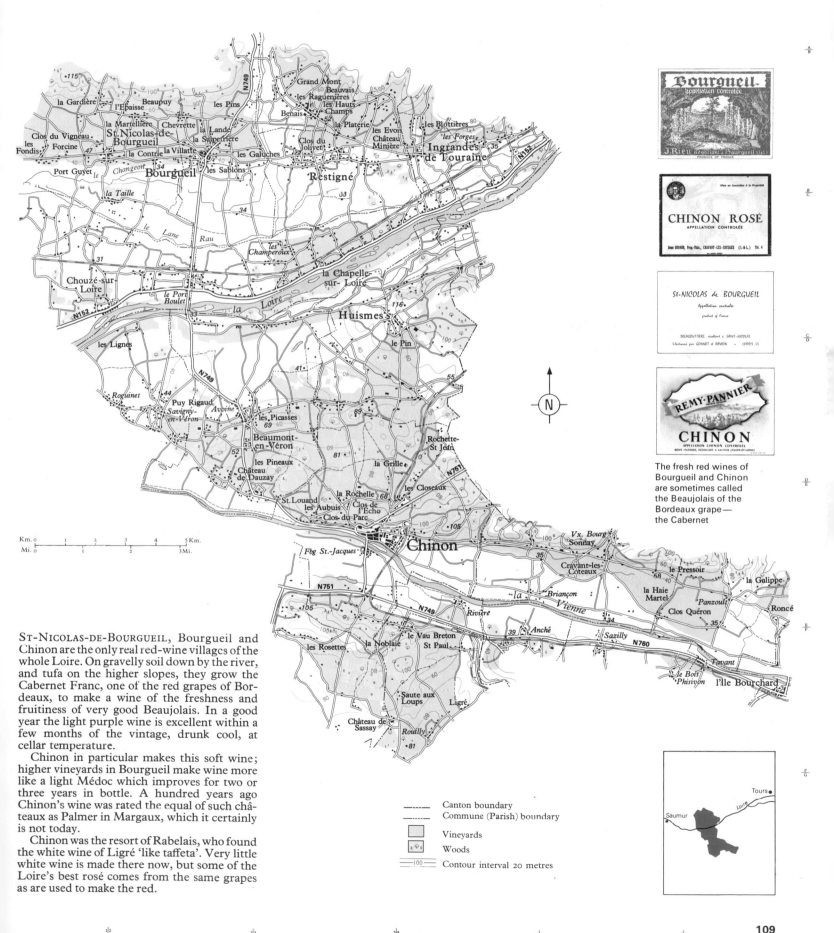

The fresh red wines of Bourgueil and Chinon are sometimes called the Beaujolais of the Bordeaux grape— the Cabernet

ST-NICOLAS-DE-BOURGUEIL, Bourgueil and Chinon are the only real red-wine villages of the whole Loire. On gravelly soil down by the river, and tufa on the higher slopes, they grow the Cabernet Franc, one of the red grapes of Bordeaux, to make a wine of the freshness and fruitiness of very good Beaujolais. In a good year the light purple wine is excellent within a few months of the vintage, drunk cool, at cellar temperature.

Chinon in particular makes this soft wine; higher vineyards in Bourgueil make wine more like a light Médoc which improves for two or three years in bottle. A hundred years ago Chinon's wine was rated the equal of such châteaux as Palmer in Margaux, which it certainly is not today.

Chinon was the resort of Rabelais, who found the white wine of Ligré 'like taffeta'. Very little white wine is made there now, but some of the Loire's best rosé comes from the same grapes as are used to make the red.

Km. 0   1   2   3   4   5 Km.
Mi. 0   1   2   3 Mi.

----- Canton boundary
------- Commune (Parish) boundary
Vineyards
Woods
—100— Contour interval 20 metres

Vouvray

Canton boundary
Commune (parish) boundary
Vineyards
Woods
Contour interval 20 metres

JUST AS Savennières stands almost at the gates of Angers, Vouvray and Montlouis lie just outside Tours on the way to Amboise. Everything royal and romantic about France is summed up in this countryside of great châteaux and ancient towns along the gently flowing river.

Low hills of chalk flank the stream along the reach from Noizay to Rochecorbon. For centuries they have provided both cellars and dwellings in caves to the wine growers of the district. Above the cellars, which are often great caverns extending to two acres or more, the Chenin Blanc grows in chalky soil. Its wine here, though often drier than in Anjou, at its best is honey-like and sweet. What distinguishes it more than anything, however, is its long life. For a comparatively light wine its longevity is astonishing. You may expect madeira to live for half a century, but in a pale, firm, rather delicate wine the ability to improve and go on improving for so long in bottle is very rare.

Most Vouvray today is handled by négociants, who blend the produce of one clos with another. The once-famous names of the individual sites are not often heard today. More important is the need to know whether any given bottle is dry, semi-sweet, sweet or for that matter *pétillant* or fully sparkling: Vouvray alters character radically from vintage to vintage, and its natural tendency to re-ferment in the bottle has led to an industry in converting less successful vintages into very good sparkling wine. None the less growers do triumphantly bottle their best produce and keep it for a small band of connoisseurs. To them names like Vallée Coquette are a rallying call.

Montlouis has very similar soil and conditions to Vouvray, without the perfect situation of the first rank of Vouvray's vineyards along the Loire. Montlouis tends to be slightly softer and more gently sweet, but it takes a native to tell the difference.

A dwindling number of small growers still make the great sweet wines of the Vouvray area. Another (label not shown) is Gaston Huet of Le Haut Lieu in Vouvray. Much modern Vouvray is made sparkling, either sweet or dry, using the champagne method

Pouilly and Sancerre

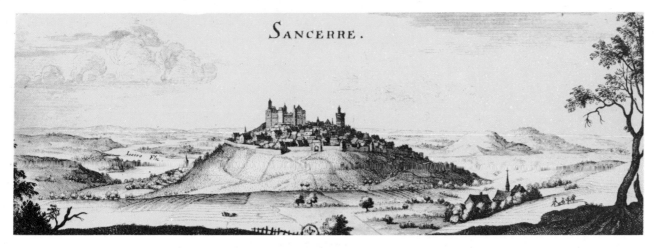

THE WINES of Pouilly and Sancerre on the upper Loire are perhaps the easiest to recognize in France. On these chalky hills, cut by the river, the Sauvignon grape gives a smell to the wine which is called gun-flint; it is slightly smoky, slightly green, slightly spicy and appeals to most people intensely at first. Compared with the Chenin Blanc of the middle Loire, however, the Sauvignon lacks interest after a while. Sancerre and Pouilly Fumé have strong immediate appeal as good with food, particularly shellfish. But it is only exceptional vintages which add subtlety and intriguing nuances to these wines. They are rarely wines to linger over for themselves.

Pouilly-sur-Loire is the town; its wine is only called Pouilly Fumé when made from the Sauvignon. Its second wine, from the Chasselas and often excellent in its own way, is called Pouilly-sur-Loire. Neither have anything to do with Pouilly-Fuissé, the white wine of Mâcon.

There is not much to choose between Pouilly Fumé and Sancerre. The best of each are on the same level; the Sancerre perhaps slightly ripertasting. In bad vintages however they can be very acid; their smell has been compared to wet wool. A year or two in bottle brings out the qualities of a good one, but they are not wines to lay down, like Vouvrays.

There is a growing fashion for Sauvignon wine, and vineyard names are more and more in evidence. Les Monts Damnés in Chavignol and Clos du Chêne Marchand in Bué are the two best-known vineyards of Sancerre; the Château du Nozet and Château de Tracy the biggest and best-known estates in Pouilly.

Above: Sancerre is still the walled town with the Loire winding by shown in this early print

Right: the best Sancerres come from Chavignol and Bué. Two big châteaux, du Nozet and de Tracy, dominate Pouilly. Only the best Pouillys are known as Fumé. The lesser (Chasselas) wines are called Pouilly-sur-Loire

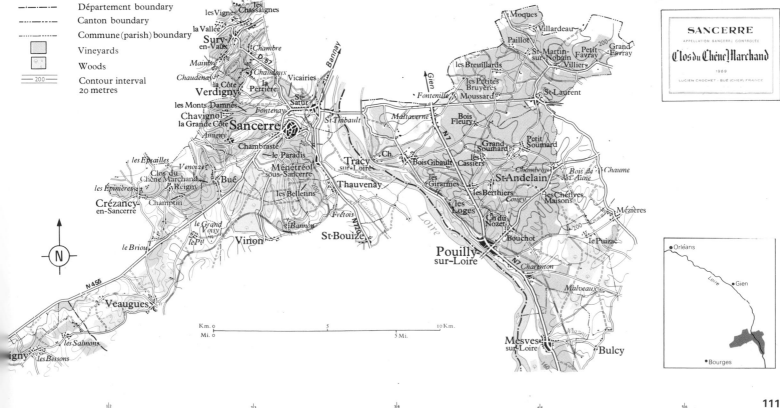

	Département boundary
	Canton boundary
	Commune (parish) boundary
	Vineyards
	Woods
200	Contour interval 20 metres

The Rhône Valley

THE VALLEY of the Loire and the valley of the Rhône are two sides of the same coin. They contain respectively the best of northern and the best of southern French viticulture. Most Loire wine is white, most Rhône red. In each case there is a wide variety of styles of wine but a distinct family feeling.

Rhône red wines develop from blackness and bitterness to roundness and warmth, to a heady smell, to great softness and depth of flavour. In the north they are comparatively delicate, in the south sometimes downright enormous; but they conform to a certain pattern. Similarly the white wines are all full gold in colour and much headier than (say) white burgundy.

One characteristic of almost all Rhône wines is that they need time—much more than they are usually given. Few wines add so much to their intrinsic value by laying down as good Rhône reds. Darkness and strength become depth and warmth: undreamt-of subtleties appear . . . but it takes ten years, not the two or three they often get.

In the course of the Rhône the country changes from oak forest, where the vine shares the fields with peach-trees and nut-trees, to the herbal scrub and olive groves of Provence. In the north the vine perches on terraced cliffs of crumbling granite wherever the best view of the sun can be found. In the south it lies baking in flat fields of smooth round stones where the sun is everywhere.

Rhône wines are not as a rule made from one grape variety on its own, as burgundy is, but from a blend of anything from two to 13. It is common practice to add a little of a white variety to the very dark wine of the Syrah, the classic red-wine grape of Côte Rôtie and Hermitage. Châteauneuf-du-Pape, like Chianti, is made from a whole roll-call of vines, including both red and white.

The vineyards round the Rhône fall naturally into two groups; northern and southern. The appellation Côtes du Rhône is a general one for the wine of 120-odd communes, red, white or rosé. Côtes du Rhône-Villages is applied only to 14 specific (and superior) communes in the southern part. Fifteen areas have their own separate appellations, of which all except Die are shown on the map.

On the following pages the three best areas of the Rhône are mapped in detail. Around them lie regions of strong local character: St-Joseph and Cornas with excellent and undervalued red wines; St-Péray with an unusual strong and deep-gold sparkling wine; Die (on the River Drôme to the east) with its pale and sparkling Clairette; Tavel and Lirac with their famous and excellent, strong and orange-pink rosés. Finally Rasteau and Beaumes de Venise to the east make dessert wine—the latter the best sweet muscat wine in France; amber, soft and only gently fortified. Drunk young and fresh it is a sheer delight.

At present the great Rhône wines like Hermitage are absurdly cheap in comparison to many inferior burgundies. Their vineyards (with the exception of Châteauneuf-du-Pape and Tavel) are small and their price will rise sharply when they come back into fashion—as they undoubtedly will in the next few years.

The four top labels are from co-operatives in the widely varying Rhône areas of Die (sparkling wine), Gigondas (red), Beaumes de Venise (sweet muscat) and Chusclan (vin rosé)

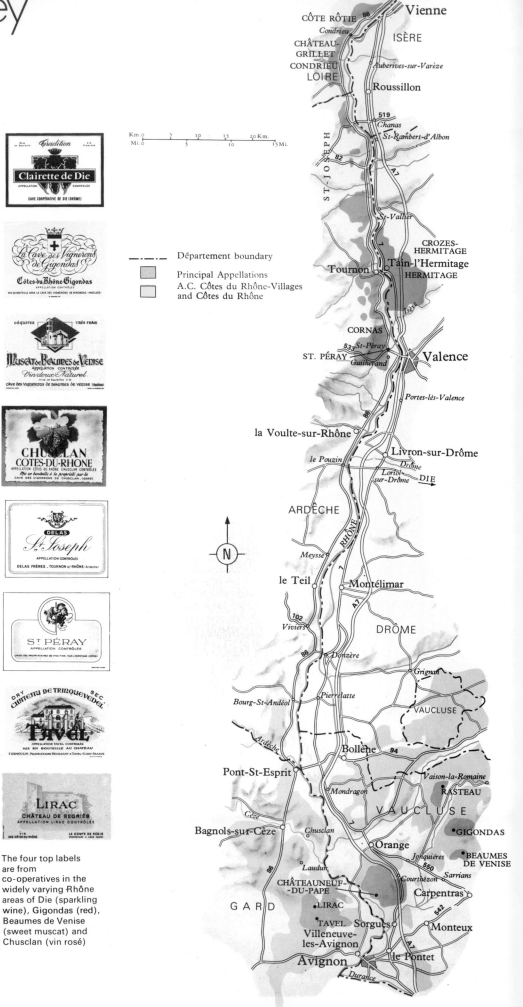

Département boundary

Principal Appellations

A.C. Côtes du Rhône-Villages and Côtes du Rhône

Côte Rôtie and Condrieu

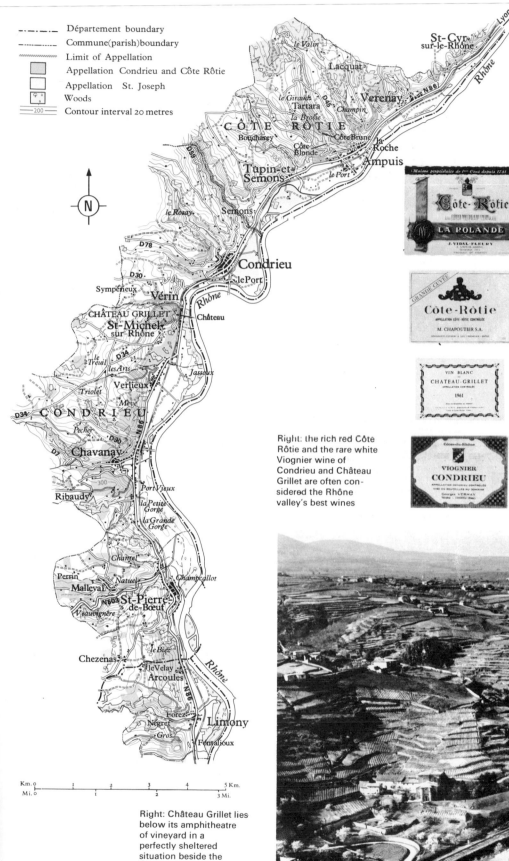

Legend:
- ·—··—·· Département boundary
- ·———·——· Commune (parish) boundary
- ∾∾∾∾∾ Limit of Appellation
- ▢ Appellation Condrieu and Côte Rôtie
- ▢ Appellation St. Joseph
- ▢ Woods
- —200— Contour interval 20 metres

Km. 0 — 1 — 2 — 3 — 4 — 5 Km.
Mi. 0 — 1 — 2 — 3 Mi.

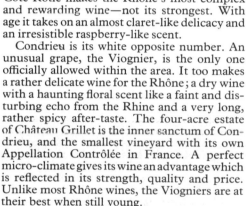

Right: the rich red Côte Rôtie and the rare white Viognier wine of Condrieu and Château Grillet are often considered the Rhône valley's best wines

CÔTE RÔTIE and Condrieu, in the northern group of vineyards round the Rhône, have nothing like the fame of Châteauneuf-du-Pape in the south. They are bound to remain collectors' wines because their vineyards are so tiny. But there is no doubt that Côte Rôtie is one of the best, if not the very best of the Rhône red wines. Those who have tasted Condrieu at the famous restaurant Pyramide at Vienne feel equally strongly about the white.

The right-hand bend of the river after Vienne provides a short stretch of very steep hill perfectly aligned for the sun. The soil varies even within the few miles of the vineyard, and there are three distinct appellations.

The northern part is called Côte Rôtie—literally 'roasted hill'—and is itself divided—though not legally—into Côte Brune and Côte Blonde; slopes with darker and lighter soil. The wines of the two are normally blended together. Côte Rôtie makes the Rhône's most complex and rewarding wine—not its strongest. With age it takes on an almost claret-like delicacy and an irresistible raspberry-like scent.

Condrieu is its white opposite number. An unusual grape, the Viognier, is the only one officially allowed within the area. It too makes a rather delicate wine for the Rhône; a dry wine with a haunting floral scent like a faint and disturbing echo from the Rhine and a very long, rather spicy after-taste. The four-acre estate of Château Grillet is the inner sanctum of Condrieu, and the smallest vineyard with its own Appellation Contrôlée in France. A perfect micro-climate gives its wine an advantage which is reflected in its strength, quality and price. Unlike most Rhône wines, the Viogniers are at their best when still young.

Right: Château Grillet lies below its amphitheatre of vineyard in a perfectly sheltered situation beside the Rhône. This is the smallest vineyard with its own Appellation Contrôlée in France

Hermitage

THE BLUE TRAIN snakes by under the stacked terraces of the hill of Hermitage, making the vineyard's magnificent stance looking down the Rhône familiar to millions.

The Romans grew wine here. A hundred years ago its 'mas'—the local name for the individual vineyards—were named beside Château Lafite and Romanée-Conti as among the best red wines of the world. A. Jullien listed them in order of merit: Méal, Gréfieux, Beaume, Raucoule, Muret, Guoignière, Bessas, Burges and Lauds. Spellings have changed: the mas remain—but today few of their names are heard, and never in the same breath as Château Lafite.

The adjective 'manly' has stuck to Hermitage ever since it was first applied to it. It has almost the qualities of port without the brandy. Like port it throws a heavy sediment in the bottle (it needs decanting) and improves for many years until its scent and flavour are almost overwhelming. Sadly, however, it is rarely kept long enough for more than its darkness and strength to become apparent.

The hill is famous for its white wine too. 'Raucoule' was named as the best by Jullien. Today Chante-Alouette is the best-known. Besides being a mas, it is the trade-mark of the house of Chapoutier. The wine is golden, dry and full with a remarkably delicate and interesting flavour, and lasts, like the red Hermitage, for years.

Crozes-Hermitage is a wider appellation surrounding Hermitage—good but without the same distinction.

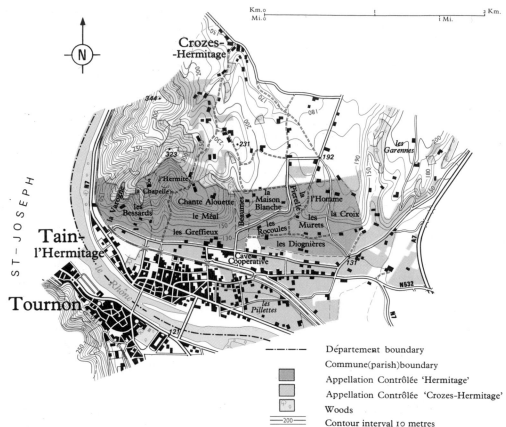

Km.o ———————————————— 1 ———————————————— 2 Km.
Mi.o ———————————————————————— 1 Mi.

- - - - - - -   Département boundary
———————   Commune(parish)boundary
Appellation Contrôlée 'Hermitage'
Appellation Contrôlée 'Crozes-Hermitage'
Woods
——200——   Contour interval 10 metres
For location see map on page 112

The hill of Hermitage, its granite terraced from top to bottom, rises above a bend of the Rhône at Tain-l'Hermitage. A hundred years ago Hermitage red wines were reckoned among the best in the world

Right: Chante-Alouette is the best-known white Hermitage. Crozes-Hermitage is the appellation of the vineyards not on the Hermitage hill itself

Châteauneuf-du-Pape

CHÂTEAUNEUF-DU-PAPE lies in the centre of the biggest concentration of Rhône vineyards, on hills dominated by the ruined papal summer palace. Its vines are widely-spaced; low bushes in a sea of smooth stones with no earth to be seen. The deep red wine of Châteauneuf has the distinction not only of having the highest minimum strength of any French wine (12.5% alcohol) but of being the first to be so regulated. Its most famous grower, the late Baron Le Roy, initiated here what has become the national system of Appellations Contrôlées. Part of his original proposal, made in 1923, was that suitable land for fine Châteauneuf vines (there are 13 varieties) should be identified by the conjunction of lavender and thyme growing there. In addition, grape sorts, pruning, quantity and strength were to be controlled.

His foresight has been rewarded by Châteauneuf-du-Pape emerging from obscurity to become one of the world's most famous wines.

Well over a million gallons of wine a year are made here; 99% of it red. Most of it is good average; made relatively light (though not in alcohol) by increasing the proportion of Grenache grapes so that it can be drunk after a mere year or two. The neighbouring Gigondas (recently granted an appellation of its own) makes similar wine. A number of big estates, like Bordeaux châteaux, are the producers of the classical, blackish, slow-maturing Châteauneuf-du-Pape. In seven or eight years it grows soft-flavoured and almost gentle, with a powerful soft-fruit scent—ideal winter-weight wine, sometimes overpowering in Provençal heat.

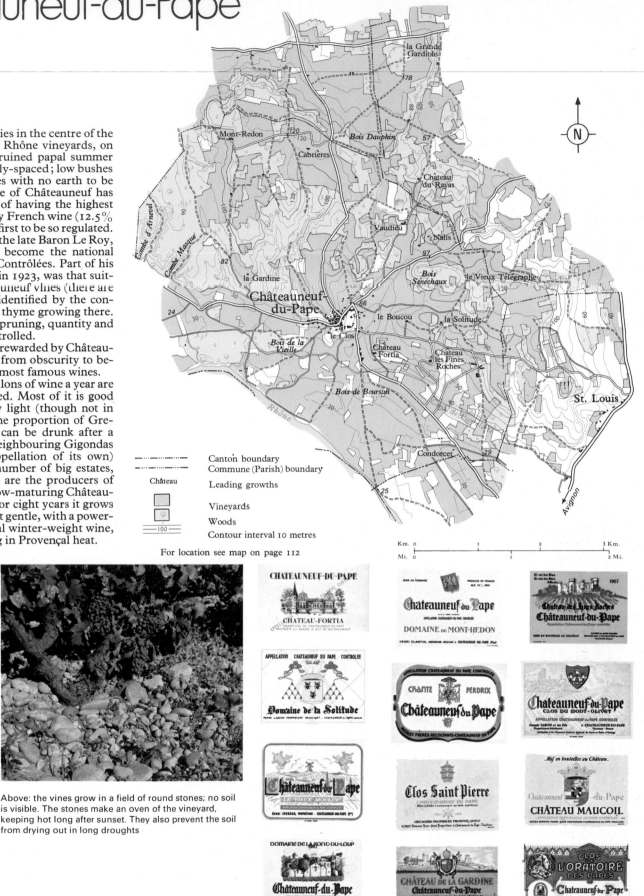

Canton boundary
Commune (Parish) boundary

Château

Leading growths

Vineyards

Woods

Contour interval 10 metres

For location see map on page 112

Km. 0   1   2   3 Km.
Mi. 0   1   2 Mi.

Above: the vines grow in a field of round stones; no soil is visible. The stones make an oven of the vineyard, keeping hot long after sunset. They also prevent the soil from drying out in long droughts

Left: Château des Fines-Roches, one of the top estates of Châteauneuf-du-Pape which cover the bare-looking ridge south-east of the little town

Châteauneuf-du-Pape has large estates comparable to the châteaux of Bordeaux. Their impressive labels are in keeping with their strong and big-scale wine

115

Provence

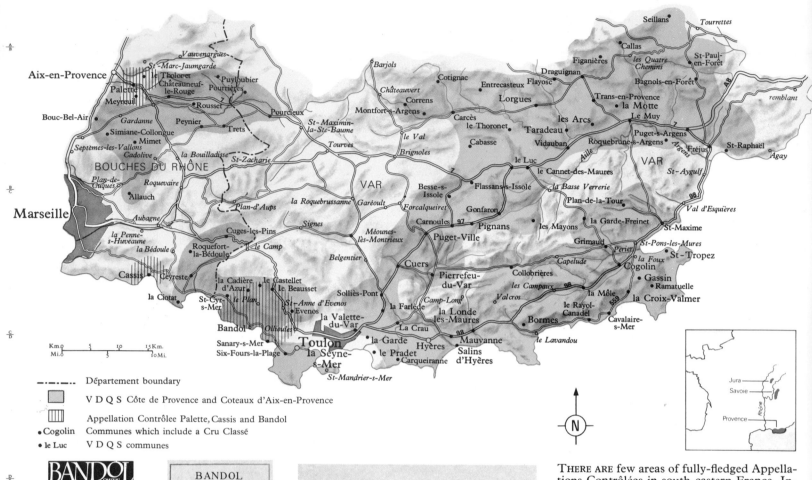

N

Bandol and Palette are Provence's best red-wine areas. Other estates from Aix to St-Tropez make good wine, particularly a strong rosé

Les Baux, west of Aix, is a typical rocky Provençal hill town. It has Provence's best restaurant, the famous L'Oustaou de la Baumanière

THERE ARE few areas of fully-fledged Appellations Contrôlées in south-eastern France. Instead it is the homeland of the VDQS—the noteworthy local wine with aspirations. A whole series of VDQS areas spread from the southern Rhône east and south: Côtes du Ventoux, Côtes du Luberon, Haut-Comtat, Coteaux de Pierrevert, Côtes du Vivarais, Coteaux du Tricastin. This page shows the most famous of them (partly because it surrounds the Mediterranean resorts)—the Côtes de Provence, with the Coteaux d'Aix and three small appellations: Palette, Bandol and Cassis.

An optimistic description of Provence wines always mentions the sun-baked pines, thyme, lavender and claims that the wine takes its character from them. This is true of some of the best of them—notably the wine of Palette, Château Simone. Others get by on a pretty colour and a good deal of alcohol. 'Tarpaulin edged with lace' is a realistic summing-up of one of the better ones. The whites are dry and can lack the acidity to be refreshing; the reds are straightforward, strong and a trifle dull; it is usually the rosés, often orange-tinted, which have most appeal. A number of the better estates are known as 'Crus Classés'.

Cassis and Bandol distinguish themselves for their white and red wines respectively. Cassis (no relation of the blackcurrant syrup, though they go excellently together) is altogether livelier than the run of Provençal white wine, and Bandol leads the red in much the same way.

Another small appellation for red, white and rosé wines, Bellet, just inland from Nice to the east, does not come within the area of the map.

Savoie and the Jura

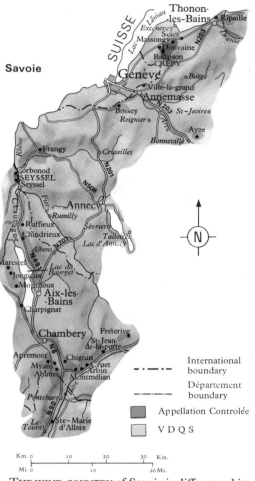

International boundary
— — — Département boundary
■ Appellation Contrôlée
▨ VDQS

Km. 0 ... 10 ... 20 ... 30 Km.
Mi. 0 ... 10 ... 20 Mi.

THE WINE-COUNTRY of Savoie is diffuse and its produce little known. In many ways it epitomizes the 'little local wine' which travels only in legend: its cleanness and freshness are at one with the mountain air, the lakes and streams. Savoie wine is nearly all white—as water. There is a dry softness about it like a sort of ethereal Muscadet.

The sparkling version is better-known than the still: it too has this pale, elusive quality. The best is drier and more delicate than any other sparkling wine—an intriguing alternative to champagne as an aperitif.

There are two Appellations Contrôlées in Haute-Savoie: Crépy and Seyssel. Crépy is just across the border to Switzerland, its grape is the Chasselas of Switzerland and its whole nature is more Swiss than French.

Seyssel is commonly made sparkling, but sparkling or still has delicacy and charm. Several white wines made of the predominant local vine, the Jacquère, have recently become VDQS, and are considered extremely successful recruits to the label. Of these Ayze is the best-known for sparkling wine, and Apremont and Abymes for still. A dwindling traditional white grape, the Altesse, makes wine which is sold as Roussette de Savoie, and sometimes by such place names as Monterminod, Frangy and Marestel.

The chief local red grape is the Mondeuse. Arbin, Montmélian and St-Jean-de-la-Porte are its best-known crus. At Chautagne the grape is the Gamay of Beaujolais. It makes a pleasant light wine—but the reds of Savoie are not in the same class as the white.

Most Savoie wine is white and very dry and light. Crépy and Seyssel are Appellations Contrôlées; Varichon & Clerc make excellent sparkling wine; Chautagne is a pleasant light red

The Jura range is wider: yellow, red, white, 'grey', and 'mad' (fou)—sparkling wine

A LITTLE enclave of only 1,500 acres of vines scattered among pretty woodland and meadow in what seem like France's remotest hills. . . . The Jura's production is a fraction of its old total; yet its wines are varied, good and totally original. Its three superior appellations, Arbois, Château-Chalon (a village) and L'Etoile, all count for something.

Jura wine is not only red, white and rosé, but yellow and grey. The best of it is 'yellow'; firm, strong white wine from the little-known Savagnin grape which is kept for a minimum of six years in cask while it undergoes a transformation like that of sherry. The appellation Château-Chalon is limited to this odd but excellent wine, but good 'vin jaune' is also made at L'Etoile and Arbois. A special squat bottle, the clavelin, is used only for vin jaune.

The grey wine is simply very pale rosé, rather sharp and sometimes extremely appetising. The best Jura vin rosé, from Arbois, by contrast is more like pale red wine, unusually silky. Some of the white is made from the Chardonnay and compares well with minor Côte de Beaune wine. The red is perhaps the least interesting, though even this can be soft, smooth and enjoyable with the good local game.

In addition to all these from such a small area, Arbois is famous for its 'vin fou', pleasant cheap sparkling wine.

A large proportion of the Jura's production is controlled by one firm, Henri Maire; but one or two small growers of real quality exist.

Jura

Km. 0 ... 1 ... 6 Km.
Mi. 0 ... 5 Mi.

——— Appellation Contrôlée boundary
▨ Vineyards
▨ Woods
══100══ Contour interval 20 metres

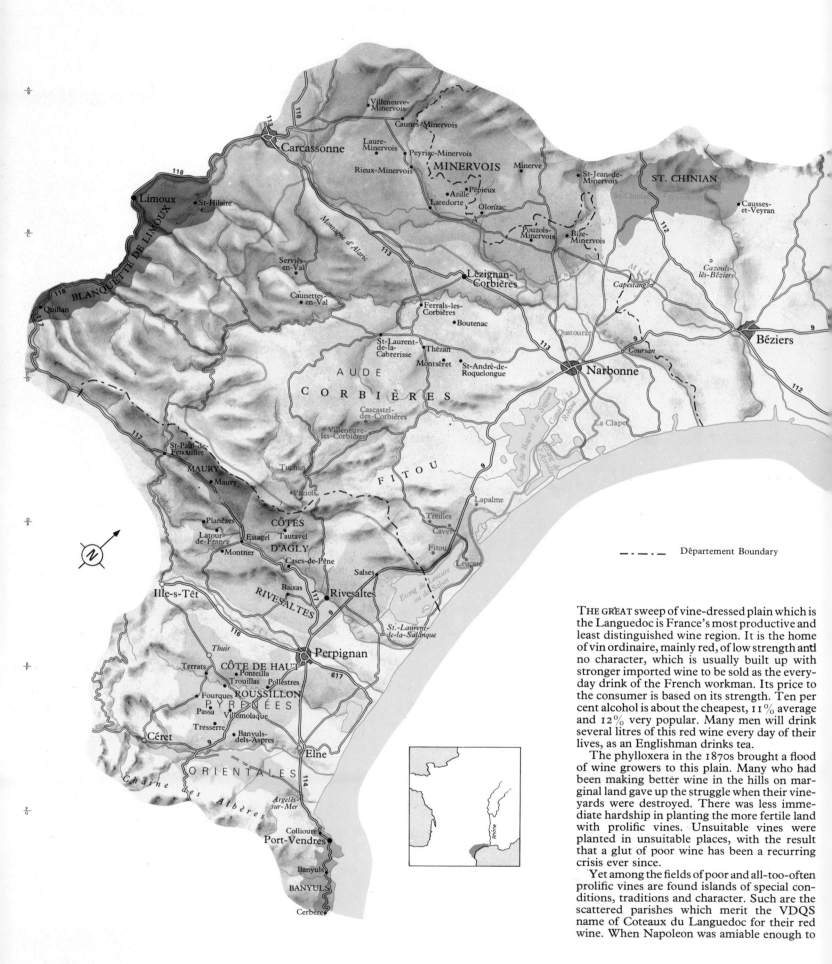

- · - · - Département Boundary

THE GREAT sweep of vine-dressed plain which is the Languedoc is France's most productive and least distinguished wine region. It is the home of vin ordinaire, mainly red, of low strength and no character, which is usually built up with stronger imported wine to be sold as the everyday drink of the French workman. Its price to the consumer is based on its strength. Ten per cent alcohol is about the cheapest, 11% average and 12% very popular. Many men will drink several litres of this red wine every day of their lives, as an Englishman drinks tea.

The phylloxera in the 1870s brought a flood of wine growers to this plain. Many who had been making better wine in the hills on marginal land gave up the struggle when their vineyards were destroyed. There was less immediate hardship in planting the more fertile land with prolific vines. Unsuitable vines were planted in unsuitable places, with the result that a glut of poor wine has been a recurring crisis ever since.

Yet among the fields of poor and all-too-often prolific vines are found islands of special conditions, traditions and character. Such are the scattered parishes which merit the VDQS name of Coteaux du Languedoc for their red wine. When Napoleon was amiable enough to

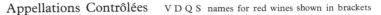

▮	Banyuls		▮	St-Jean-de-Minervois
▮	Rivesaltes (Corbières du Roussillon) includes Côtes de Haut Roussillon (Rousillon dels Aspres) and Côtes d'Agly (Corbières du Roussillon)		▮	Clairette du Languedoc
			▮	Muscat de Frontignan
			▮	Muscat de Mireval
▮	Maury (Corbières du Roussillon)		▮	Lunel
▮	Blanquette-de-Limoux		▮	Clairette de Bellegarde

V D Q S

• Langlade – Commune having the right to the name Coteaux du Languedoc

▯	Corbières			
▮	Minervois		▮	St-Chinian
▮	Picpoul de Pinet		▮	Costières du Gard

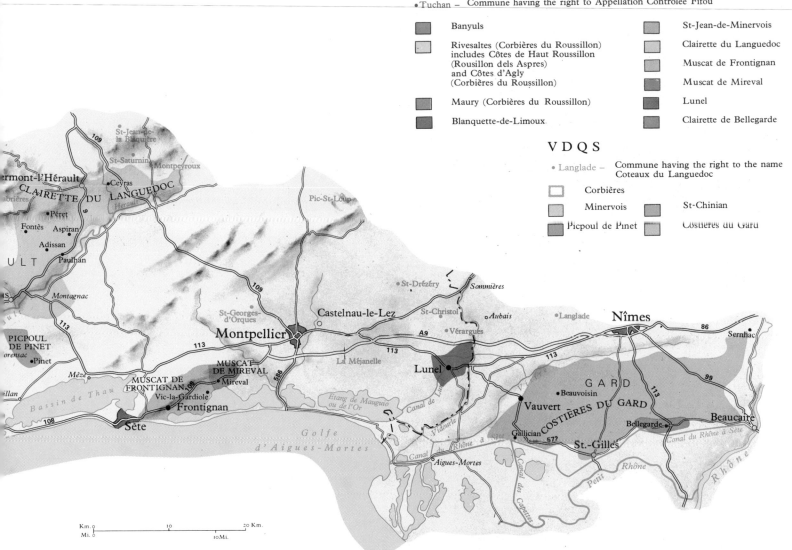

intern British residents in the South of France at Montpellier they took a particular liking to the wine of St-Georges-d'Orques nearby. The larger areas whose plain dry white wine is known as Clairette du Languedoc and Clairette de Bellegarde are other exceptions, and so are the districts that specialize in sweet muscat wine: Lunel, Mireval and Frontignan.

Further west things get better as they get hillier. Minervois and St-Chinian are huge areas of VDQS quality which make light red wine, some rosé and a little white. St-Jean-de-Minervois is a little pocket of muscat-growing. To the south of them the vast viticultural zone of Corbières-Roussillon leads a double life, as producer both of medium-quality red wines and of a true speciality, their 'vins doux naturels'—sweet dessert wines (which are not as natural as their name makes out, being fortified with alcohol like port). Their red wines have only VDQS status, but their sweet wines are Appellation Contrôlée and command a vast supermarket sale in France, packed in screw-top bottles. One district, Fitou, has an AC red wine—a better-than-ordinary ordinary. Another district, higher in the hills to the west, has an AC for its very dry white, much of which is made into sparkling Blanquette de Limoux.

Red ordinaire and strong sweet (often muscat) 'vin doux naturel' are the specialities of Languedoc-Roussillon. The Clairettes, Picpoul and sparkling Blanquette de Limoux are the exceptions: white wine of some character, though tending to be too heavy and flat

FRANCE has a way of producing, even in corners which have little contact with the outside world, wines which are better than any but the best from any other country. She is intensely aware of her 'little' wines, and through the corps of inspectors of her admirably-organized Institut National des Appellations d'Origine, is constantly taking their temperature, rather like a coach keeping an eye on the colts team.

It is up to the industry and assiduity of local growers to advance from mere *vin de pays* status to that of VDQS, and then, if things go well, to Appellation Contrôlée.

Cahors has just been made AC, after years when none were promoted. For many years Cahors was known as the senior VDQS wine of France. In Cahors they would tell you how, centuries ago, it was their wine, not meagre Médocs, which was most in demand among foreign buyers in the port of Bordeaux itself.

The name given to Cahors' sturdy red wine was 'black'—and with reason. The local grapes and climate, together with old-fashioned methods of wine-making, give it more tannin than it knows what to do with, a black-tinged 'robe' and a way of not being ready to drink for 12 or 15 years. On the other hand when it does come round there is far more distinction there than its merely local reputation suggests. The best Cahors, that from the slopes of reddish soil leading down to the River Lot, is notably soft-scented, smooth-textured, full-flavoured and worth discussing. Such wines can sometimes be identified by a reference to '*pentes*' (slopes) on the label.

In 1971 justice was done. Cahors was promoted to be an AC. It is bound to widen its horizons, and probably to make its wine less black for a wider and less patient market.

There is a big co-operative, Les Caves d'Olt, at Parnac. It handles about half the production of the area, making rosé and white wines as well as Vin de Cahors, which is always red. Jouffreau and Tesseydre are other very good growers who bottle their own wine. Leygues near Puy-l'Evêque, Prayssac and Luzech are important centres for the best wines. Mercuès, north-west of the town of Cahors, is principally famous for its hilltop château, now one of the most luxurious country hotels in France.

JURANÇON remains a name to conjure with, though very few people have ever tasted the reason why. These steep Pyrenean foot-hills, with Pau as their market-place, used to make a substantial amount of what was one of France's very best sweet wines, seriously comparable to the best Sauternes or the rarities of the Loire. Descriptions of it, even moderate ones, make mention of peaches and carnations.

The region is Appellation Contrôlée, though today production is a fraction of what it was, and the high risk of picking grapes as late as November, necessary for *vin liquoreux*, has led most growers to make dry wine without particular merit.

Essentially Jurançon is a historical curiosity. What is so intriguing to consider, however, is that even in such backwaters of France the potential for making superb wines exists.

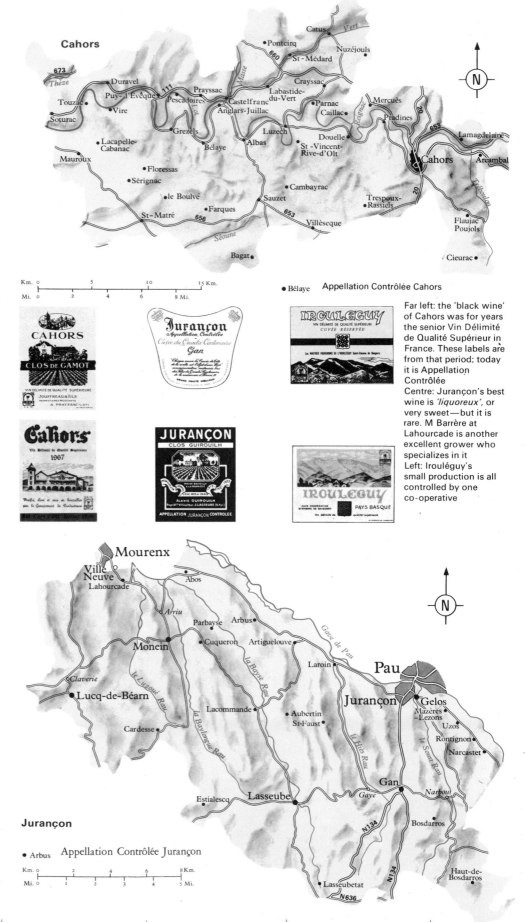

Cahors

● Bélaye   Appellation Contrôlée Cahors

Far left: the 'black wine' of Cahors was for years the senior Vin Délimité de Qualité Supérieur in France. These labels are from that period: today it is Appellation Contrôlée
Centre: Jurançon's best wine is *'liquoreux'*, or very sweet—but it is rare. M Barrère at Lahourcade is another excellent grower who specializes in it
Left: Irouléguy's small production is all controlled by one co-operative

Jurançon

● Arbus   Appellation Contrôlée Jurançon

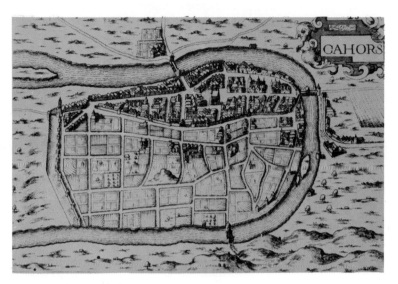

Modern Cahors is recognizable in this 17th-century print. The famous embattled bridge on the right, though much restored by the architect Viollet-le-Duc, still crosses the tree-lined River Lot

Irouléguy

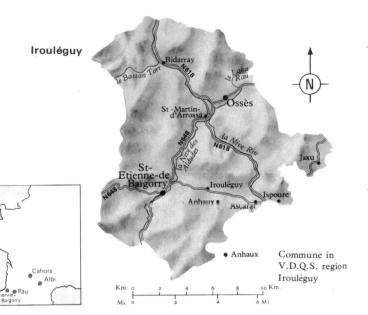

• Anhaux   Commune in V.D.Q.S. region Irouléguy

Km. 0   2   4   6   8   10 Km.
Mi. 0   2   4   6 Mi

THE TINY VDQS area of Irouléguy, with only 100 acres of vines, is typical of the sort of local tradition which goes doggedly on in country corners from the Belgian border to this Basque extremity of France. It makes red and rosé wine in the main, chiefly from a rather difficult grape, the Tannat of Béarn, which gives a sour twist to its wine unless something soothing is added . . . in this case some of the lesser Bordeaux grape varieties.

The whole production of Irouléguy is made by the co-operative cellar. It goes to Biarritz and St-Jean-de-Luz to irrigate Basque dishes.

On the label of the rosé is found the Basque message Hotx Hotxa Edan, which is not, sad to say, as stirring or original as it sounds. (It means simply 'Chill before serving'.)

• Vieux   Appellation Contrôlée Gaillac
• BROZE   Appellation Contrôlée Premières Côtes de Gaillac

Km. 0   2   4   6   10 Km.
Mi. 0   2   4   6 Mi.

Gaillac

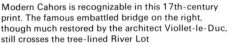

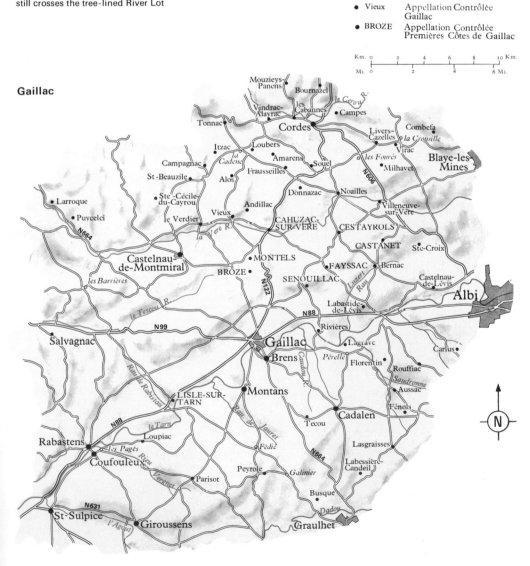

IN CONTRAST to some of the VDQS areas, which have forged ahead since they were given their status (Provence and Savoie are the most notable examples), there are a few areas of France which are Appellation Contrôlée but which hardly make the wine they must once have made to earn the title. Gaillac is the biggest of these.

The hills round the River Tarn just below Albi, and below the magnificent gorge the river makes in the Cevennes mountains, are still lovely country with beautiful towns and villages. Seventy-three of them are contained within the appellation Gaillac, which is thus a very general name for any wine, red, white or rosé, made from a mixture of a fairly wide choice of grapes (including the Sauternes varieties and one with the charming name of Len de l'El for white; and stressing the Rhône-type grapes rather than the Bordeaux ones for red).

Any white or rosé from this area which is 'champagnized'—and a little is—can be called Gaillac Mousseux.

The classical Gaillac, however, was always sweet white wine, and the inner appellation for a mere eight communes (which do not include Gaillac), Gaillac Premières Côtes, is for sweet white only. The wine is not normally sweet enough, however, to attract much attention.

Corsica

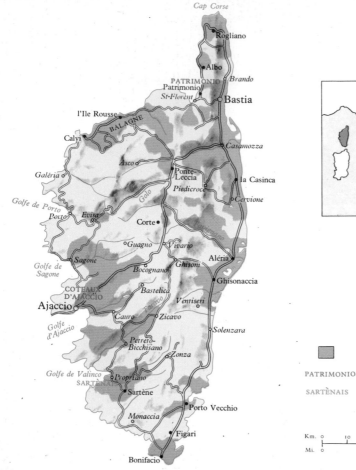

Wine-producing areas

PATRIMONIO   Appellation Contrôlée

SARTÈNAIS   V D Q S

Km. 0   10   20   30   40   50 Km.
Mi. 0   10   20   30 Mi.

CORSICA has only come on to the world wine map in the last 15 years. The maquis, the famous scrub-covered, bandit-haunted mountains, are scarcely suitable for wine-growing. The plains were malaria-infested. A general air of mayhem ruled. France was ready enough to forget about her largest island. But then came the split with Algeria.

In a few years the island's old total of about 8,000 hectares of rather desultory vineyards, more like the Italian variety than the French, grew to 30,000 or more. The malaria was beaten and the plains were invaded by wine growers who had had to leave Algeria. The most modern methods rapidly made Corsica a major producer of blending wines for the French market, while improvements to the old vineyards have brought Patrimonio and the Coteaux d'Ajaccio up to the standard of Appellations Contrôlées, and the Sartène vineyards one rank lower, to be VDQS.

There are five districts of Corsica today with reputations of their own. Patrimonio chiefly for its vin rosé made with Grenache grapes, although the appellation extends to its red and white wines as well. Ajaccio's hillside vineyards for red and rosé. Sartène chiefly for strong red wine. Cap Corse for dessert wine (and for a fortified aperitif which bears its name). La Balagne for good fruity ordinaire.

In many ways Corsican wine can be compared with Provençal. The rosé in both cases is commonly the best. In both it tends to be overstrong. Both have found huge new markets waiting for their wines, eager to find in them the elusive smell of the hot herbs of the maquis.

Precipitous traditional terraced vineyards on the fringe of the Corsican maquis near Ajaccio. The massive new planting has nothing in common with this. It uses the easily-worked plains on the east coast

VDQS

Some of France's Vins Délimités de Qualité Supérieure appear on the foregoing maps of districts of France. Others, however, are remote from areas of real wine-growing importance. Those which appear on the map of France on page 51 but not elsewhere are listed here, with their principal types of wine

Lorraine
Côtes de Toul and Vin de Moselle: very pale vin gris and rather acid red. The grapes used to be sold for making champagne

Savoie-Bugey
Vin du Bugey: Roussette white, similar to Crépy etc. Ordinary light red

Loire Valley and Central France
Côtes d'Auvergne: fresh Gamay red (Chanturgues) and rosé (Corent)
Châteaumeillant: Gamay red, vins gris
Côtes du Forez. Gamay red
Renaison, Côte Roannaise: light red
St-Pourçain-sur-Sioule. dry white, adequate rosé
Vins du Thouarsais: sweetish white, light red and rosé

South-East
Chatillon-en-Diois: Gamay red, light
Coteaux des Baux-en-Provence: the red is best
Vins du Lyonnais: Gamay and Syrah, light and fruity
Coteaux de Pierrevert: expanding district; Provençal-type wines
Coteaux du Tricastin: similar, mainly red
Côtes du Luberon: mainly white, rosé and even sparkling
Côtes du Ventoux: 'café' red wines, lively and good
Côtes du Vivarais: ordinary reds and rosé
Haut-Comtat: similar, mainly red

Languedoc-Roussillon
Cabrières: rosé
Coteaux de St-Christol: red and rosé
Coteaux de Vérargues: similar, ordinary
Fougères: fruity red wine
Montpeyroux: run-of-the-mill red
Pic-St-Loup: strongish red

South-West
Béarn: dry white and rosé (Roussellet)
Côtes de Buzet: good ordinary from a big co-operative cellar
Côtes du Marmandais: similar wines
Vins d'Estaing: good reds and dry white
Vins d'Entraygues et du Fel: very small area; light red and rosé, little white
Côtes de Fronton: very small area; red wine
Lavilledieu: also tiny; ordinary red
Vins de Marcillac: also tiny; light red
Tursan: red; white and (best) rosé
Villaudric: small area; red

In addition, two small AC areas, Madiran and Pacherenc du Vic Bilh, are mapped on page 245 with Armagnac

Germany

The Riesling vine in its element: the vineyards of Bernkastel on the Mosel

The Wines of Germany

GERMANY'S best vineyards lie as far north as grapes can be persuaded to ripen. They lie on land unfit for normal agriculture: if they were not there, forest and bare mountain would take their place. All in all their chances of giving the world's best white wine look slim. And yet on occasion they do, and stamp it with a style which no one, anywhere, can imitate.

Their secret is the balance of sugar against acidity. Sugar without acid would be flat; acid without sugar would be sharp. In good years, when the equation works out right, the two are so finely counterpoised that they have the inevitability of great art. They provide a stage for a mingling of essences from the grape and the ground, an ensemble customarily described in the single word 'breed'. It is all the more apparent in German wines because they are low in alcohol; there is less body in the background; nuances of flavour are brilliantly distinct; more often than not there is a great canopy of bouquet.

The best such wines are so full of character and charm, and if the word does not sound too pedantic, interest, that they are best enjoyed, unlike French wines, alone rather than with food. A bottle of a Spätlese or Auslese from the Mosel or Rheingau is a complete experience from which food, however good it may be, can only detract.

Knowing how passionately wine-lovers will follow his successes and failures, sensing vividly the drama in his battle to get the best from his grapes and from the ground he works, a German grower will treat his different barrels, from one year and one vineyard, as different wines. 'Best barrel' is not empty sales talk; cask numbers are matters for emotion. In France even Château Yquem 'equalizes' all the barrels of one year to make one standard wine—even if standard is hardly the word for it.

This is one side of the picture; the connoisseur's side. In Germany he is catered for as nowhere else in the world. On the other hand, 95% of German wine is blended if necessary, and gives uncomplicated pleasure.

Germany's vineyards lie along the river Rhine and its tributaries. They are scant in the extreme south and thickest near the French border in Rheinland-Pfalz. All the important areas are mapped on the following pages.

In addition to place names and (for the best wines) vineyards and wine qualities which appear on German labels, they often name the grape from which the wine is made.

The Riesling (see page 22) is the great grape of Germany; virtually all the best German wines are made from it and it is planted to the exclusion of almost everything else in the Mosel, Saar, Ruwer and Rheingau, and in the best sites of the lesser areas.

The price of quality, however, is quantity. The Riesling gives only half as much wine per plant as the commoner Sylvaner, which forms the majority of the vineyards of Rheinhessen, the Nahe, the Palatinate (Pfalz) and Franconia (Franken—small map). In its best sites, notably in Franconia, the Sylvaner gives very good wine, but it very rarely has the breed and balance of a good Riesling.

A new vine, called Müller-Thurgau after its propagator, has been produced by crossing the

The Great Tun of Heidelberg, built in 1663, held 37,500 gallons or 19,000 dozen bottles of wine

Sylvaner and the Riesling. It has most success in the Palatinate.

Pinot Noir (known as Spätburgunder—the late Burgundy) and the commoner Portugieser are the main sources of red wine. The valley of the Ahr near Bonn is the only district that specializes in red wine: it rarely reaches the standards of German white.

Wine Law 1971

German wine laws do not classify vineyards as the French do. Any vineyard in Germany can in theory produce top-class wine. Instead they specify exactly what degree of sugar the must (crushed grapes) should contain to qualify for each classification.

New laws made in 1971 lay down three basic grades of quality, wherever in Germany the wine comes from. They are:
Tafelwein The most ordinary, which need not attain any particular strength or come from any particular place or grape. It is not allowed to use a vineyard name.
Qualitätswein Must come from a particular region (*Gebiet*), from certain grape varieties, attain a certain must-weight* (60, which would give 7½% natural alcohol before adding sugar), and carry a test number.
Qualitätswein mit Prädikat The grade for the traditional top wines which do not use sugar—and thus in practice can only be made in good years when the grapes are really ripe. Their must-weight has to be 73 (the equivalent of 9½% alcohol), their grapes of certain varieties; they must come from a particular area (*Bereich*), carry a test number and may not be sugared.

Within the last grade the traditional classifications by sweetness of the top wines are given exact meanings. They are:
Kabinett: minimum must-weight of 73 (or 70 in certain cold areas like the Mosel)
Spätlese: minimum must-weight 85 (Mosel 76) *Auslese:* minimum must-weight about 90 *Beerenauslese:* minimum about 120 *Trockenbeerenauslese:* minimum about 150. (Weights vary by area and grape variety).

At the same time the new law reduced the number of individual vineyards in Germany from the 30,000 in the old land register to a considerably more manageable number: those shown on the maps in this atlas. The process of doing so caused a vast upheaval in the German wine world, for in addition to forgetting many favourite old names and learning (admittedly fewer) new ones, wine-lovers will have to become more or less familar with the concepts of *Gebiet*, *Bereich* and *Grosslage*.
A Gebiet is imply a wine-growing region —e.g. Nahe, Rheinplalz.
A Bereich is a smaller district within a *Gebiet* (see map opposite).
The third sub-division is a *Grosslage*: an area formed by a number of neighbouring vineyards (whether in the same village or not) and called by the name of the best-known of them. It is important to distinguish this from a 'site' (*Einzellage*); one individual vineyard. Site names will continue to be carried by all the top-class wines from the best growers. They are the subject of the maps in this atlas.

*The number of grammes by which one litre of must is heavier than one litre of distilled water

Left: Germany's wine production is only one-tenth of that of France

Left: the United States and Great Britain are her biggest export customers

Below: imports of wine exceed exports by almost 20 to 1

Exports
Imports

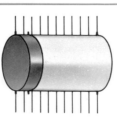

Germany consumes 9½ million hectolitres of wine a year: 16½ litres per head of the population

1·6% of the population is employed in wine-growing and the wine trade

Above: 85% of German wine is white. Red wine is only grown for local consumption and is often blended with imported wine

The average price for wine received by the grower is 121 DM per 100 litres

The average price of wine to the consumer of a bottle (0·7 litre) of white wine is 2·42 DM (1969 figures)

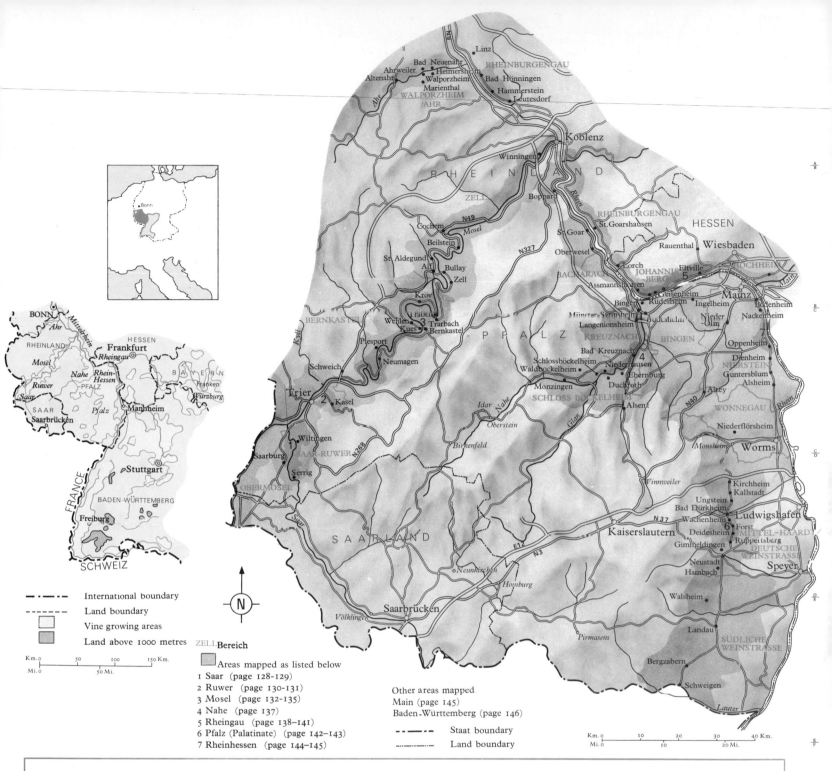

Km. 0 50 100 150 Km.
Mi. 0   50 Mi.

International boundary
Land boundary
Vine growing areas
Land above 1000 metres

ZELL Bereich
Areas mapped as listed below
1 Saar (page 128–129)
2 Ruwer (page 130–131)
3 Mosel (page 132–135)
4 Nahe (page 137)
5 Rheingau (page 138–141)
6 Pfalz (Palatinate) (page 142–143)
7 Rheinhessen (page 144–145)

Other areas mapped
Main (page 145)
Baden-Württemberg (page 146)

Staat boundary
Land boundary

Km. 0 10 20 30 40 Km.
Mi. 0   10   20 Mi.

The Language of the Label

The labels on the following pages incorporate the old phrasing, which will be phased out from 1971 onwards. The estate names and designs will not change, but future labels will incorporate the following words and phrases:

Tafelwein Ordinary table wine
Qualitätswein Superior table wine subject to certain controls
Qualitätswein mit Prädikat Strictly controlled top-quality wine
Kabinett The basic grade of Qualitätswein mit Prädikat
Spätlese Wine made from late-gathered and therefore riper grapes; better than Kabinett

Auslese Spätlese from which all unripe grapes have been rejected
Beerenauslese Made from only the ripest grapes
Trockenbeerenauslese Made from grapes which have shrivelled, either from very late gathering or 'noble rot'
Weisswein White wine
Rotwein Red wine
Roseewein or **Weissherbst** Pink wine made from red grapes
Rotling Pink wine made from red and white grapes mixed
Schillerwein The same (from Württemberg)
Perlwein Slightly sparkling wine
Schaumwein Sparkling wine
Sekt Sparkling wine made in Germany

Prädikat Sekt The same made from at least 60% German wine
Eiswein Wine made of grapes which were frozen during the harvest and pressing; rare and usually very sweet
Trocken Dry (with not more than 4 grammes per litre of unfermented sugar)
Aus eigenem Lesegut or **Erzeuger Abfüllung** From the producer's own estate
Eigene Abfüllung Bottled by the producer
Weinkellerei Wine cellar
Winzergenossenschaft Wine growers' co-operative
Winzerverein The same
Prüf.-Nr. (followed by figures) The wine's test number

125

Germany/the Quality Factor

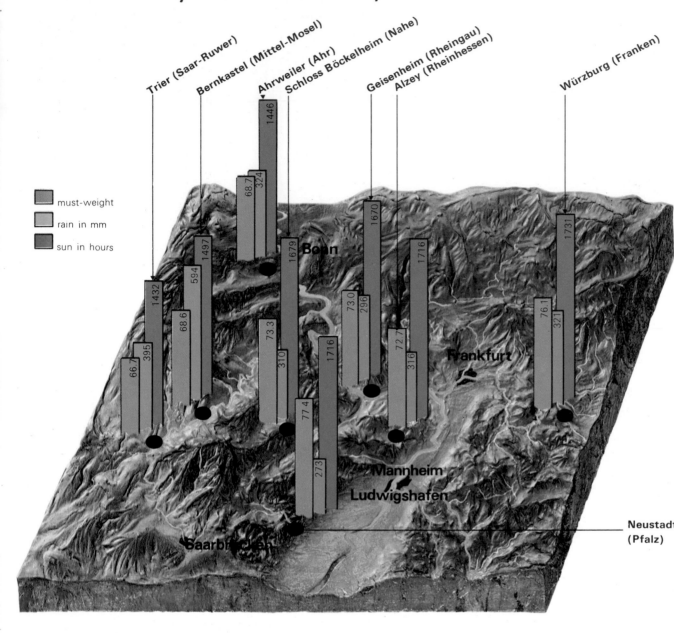

Trier (Saar-Ruwer)
Bernkastel (Mittel-Mosel)
Ahrweiler (Ahr)
Schloss Böckelheim (Nahe)
Geisenheim (Rheingau)
Alzey (Rheinhessen)
Würzburg (Franken)

■ must-weight
■ rain in mm
■ sun in hours

Bonn
Frankfurt
Mannheim
Ludwigshafen
Saarbrücken
Neustadt (Pfalz)

Left: the weather is the biggest single quality factor in Germany. This map shows the hours of sunshine and millimetres of rainfall from May to October, region by region, with the resulting ripeness of the grapes, averaged over ten years. Ripeness is measured by 'must-weight': the higher the figure the more sugar in the must

Right: Germany's greatest wine area analysed: the Rheingau's soil, sunshine, frost, and wind, all major factors affecting the quality of the wine, are recorded in these maps prepared by the Hessische Landesamt für Bodenforschung, Wiesbaden. They are reproduced with their kind permission. The significance of the maps is discussed below. The bottom map is the first attempt at classifying German wine-growing land, based on the findings in the maps above

IF IN BURGUNDY the emphasis for the study of quality is on the soil and the micro-climate, and in Bordeaux on the physical make-up of the soil affecting drainage, in Germany it centres on the weather. Every conceivable aspect of weather is examined for its possible effect on the specific gravity of the grape juice, or 'must-weight': in other words on the amount of sugar in the grapes.

The map above shows sunshine, and rainfall in the growing season for the principal wine regions of Germany. On the page opposite are some of the findings of perhaps the most elaborate investigation ever mounted into wine quality. The government of Hesse spent vast sums and many years studying the Rheingau—the state's best wine region and probably the best in Germany.

They recorded the soil type (which changes abruptly and often) in great detail, and then the amounts of sunshine, wind, late frost (in May; which can interfere with flowering) and early frost (in September; which can kill the leaves and stop the grapes ripening: map not shown) that every spot of ground could expect. Finally, with a daring all too rare among scientists, they

plotted the areas where the wine *should* be best (the last map).

Certain sites do emerge with a distinctive tint in almost every map. The Rüdesheimer Berg at the western end of the Rheingau is the only one which achieves 'excellent' in the aptitude test (map 5). But a consistent string of vineyards at a certain altitude is noticeable on each map. They happen to include most of the highest-priced of the Rheingau. The Rüdesheimer Berg, Schloss Johannisberg, Schloss Vollrads, Steinberg, the southern slopes of Kiedrich and Rauenthal are among them. And curiously the most consistently noticeable down by the river is also a very expensive vineyard—Markobrunn, between Hattenheim and Erbach. A great deal can be gleaned from these maps used in conjunction with the detailed maps of the Rheingau on pages 139–141.

On the other hand no sooner was the wind map (for example) published than meteorologists at the famous Wine School at Geisenheim were shaking their heads and saying that it's all very well showing wind speed; what is really needed is a wind-direction map. The reason is that vines are planted in rows. An east wind

blowing along a row of vines can make a difference to the temperature of the grapes. In fact they advise growers to plant on a north-south axis to keep the east wind from blowing warm air out of the vineyard.

Rainfall is comparatively light in the Rheingau. Drainage is not a big quality factor—indeed there are places (Rüdesheim is one) which suffer from drought in dry years. Since winter rain sinks right in and summer showers run off quickly the vines tend to root near the surface, and thus are particularly vulnerable to rain just before picking, water which the vine immediately pumps into the grapes. The must-weight can easily be lowered by 10° by one downpour at the last moment.

If frost and rain hold off long enough and Edelfäule (noble rot) takes a hold, the grapes go on sweetening until enormous must-weights of as much as double the normal are recorded.

As a last resort, if the grapes do freeze on the vine, which is not uncommon, the growers can pick and press them frozen. The Eiswein (ice wine) he makes will not be as good as a Trockenbeerenauslese would have been. But there are worse risks in wine-growing.

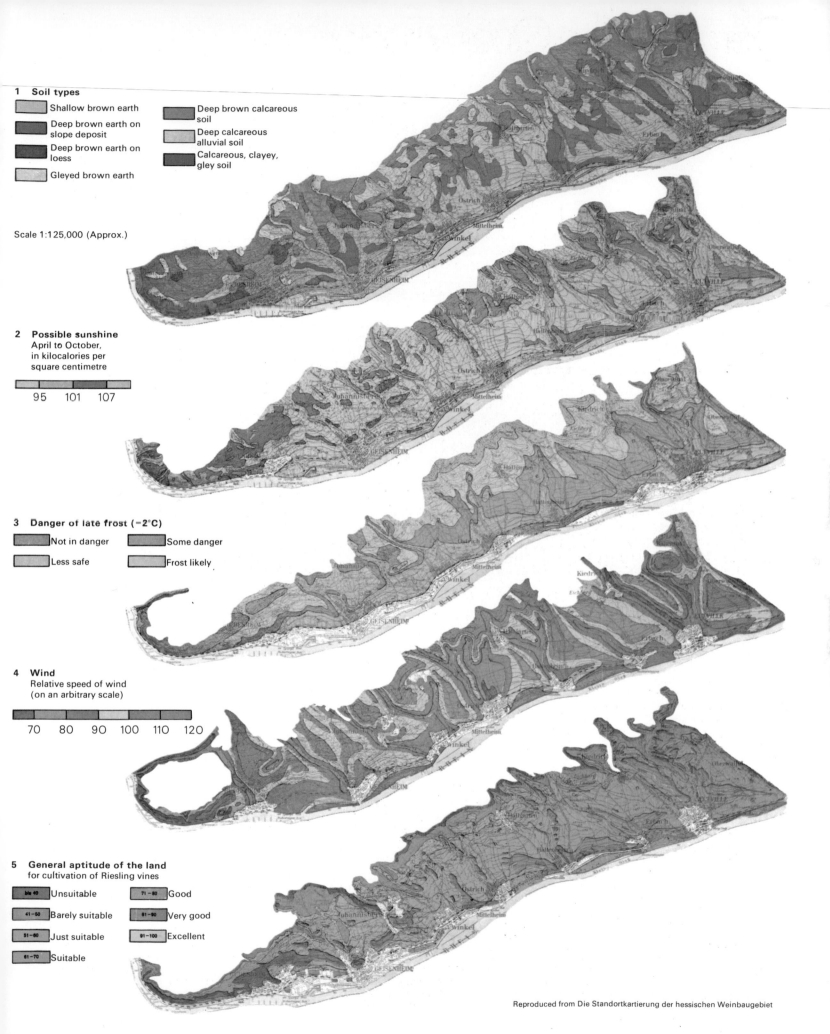

1 Soil types

- Shallow brown earth
- Deep brown earth on slope deposit
- Deep brown earth on loess
- Gleyed brown earth
- Deep brown calcareous soil
- Deep calcareous alluvial soil
- Calcareous, clayey, gley soil

Scale 1:125,000 (Approx.)

2 Possible sunshine
April to October, in kilocalories per square centimetre

95   101   107

3 Danger of late frost (−2°C)

- Not in danger
- Less safe
- Some danger
- Frost likely

4 Wind
Relative speed of wind (on an arbitrary scale)

70   80   90   100   110   120

5 General aptitude of the land
for cultivation of Riesling vines

- bis 40 — Unsuitable
- 41–50 — Barely suitable
- 51–60 — Just suitable
- 61–70 — Suitable
- 71–80 — Good
- 81–90 — Very good
- 91–100 — Excellent

Reproduced from Die Standortkartierung der hessischen Weinbaugebiet

The Saar

GERMAN wine with its problems and its triumphs is epitomized nowhere better than in the valley of the Mosel's tributary, the Saar. The battle for sugar in the grapes rages fiercest in this cold corner of the country. It is only won perhaps three or four years in ten. Yet those years give one of the world's superlative white wines; every mouthful a cause for rejoicing and wonder.

A mere 1,500 acres of vines share the valley with orchard and pasture. It is calm open agricultural country; impossible to believe that only just upstream the blast-furnaces of the industrial Saar are at work, so that even here the river is poisonous with their pollution.

The map shows clearer than any other the way south slopes—here nearly all on banks of hill sidling up to the river—offer the wine grower his chance of enough sunshine.

As in the best part of the Mosel the soil is slate and the grape the Riesling. The qualities of Mosel wine: apple-like freshness and bite, a marvellous mingling of honey in the scent and steel in the finish, can find their apogee in Saar wine. If anything the emphasis here (again a question of weather) is more on the steel than the honey.

Unsuccessful vintages are so spectacularly unsuccessful that even the best growers can only sell their wine to the makers of sparkling Sekt, who are looking for something really acid to work on.

But when the sun shines and the Riesling ripens and goes on ripening far into October the great bosomy smell of flowers and honey which it generates would be too lush without the apply emphasis of acidity. Then the Saar comes into its own. It makes sweet wine which you can never tire of. The balance and depth make you sniff and sip and sniff again.

Some sites are better than others. Most are in the hands of rich and ancient estates which can afford to wait for good years and make the most of them. The labels of the principal ones

—themselves austere compared with the flowery creations of some parts of Germany— are on this page. One of the finest of the state domains operates here, with its headquarters in the nearby old Roman wine-city of Trier. Its holdings in Ockfen (the Domäne house in the vines can be seen on the map) and in Serrig are celebrated. That at Serrig is unusual in having been created by the State from virgin woodland at the turn of the century: an optimistic move since Serrig has even more uncertain weather than the rest of the Saar. It takes a fantastic autumn . . . but then it justifies everything.

The most famous estate of the Saar is that of Egon Müller, whose house appears on the map as Scharzhof at the foot of the Scharzhofberg in Wiltingen. Among the other owners of parts of the Scharzhofberg is the cathedral of Trier ('Hohe Domkirche') which adds the word Dom before the names of its vineyards. Egon Müller also manages the Le Gallais estate, with the famous Braune Kupp vineyard at the other end of Wiltingen. Ayler Kupp and Herrenberger, Ockfener Bockstein and Herrenberg, Wawerner Ritterpfad and the Niedermennig vineyard of Falkensteiner Hofberg are all renowned . . . for their good vintages. The new Grosslage names for the Saar are Wiltinger Scharzberg for the northern half down to Ayl, and Saarburger Schlossberg for the south.

Many of the vineyards of the Mosel, and particularly the Saar, belong to a group of religious and charitable bodies in Trier. The Friedrich Wilhelm Gymnasium (Karl Marx's old school); the Bischöfliches Konvikt (a Catholic boarding-school); the Bischöfliches Priesterseminar (a college for priests); the Vereinigte Hospitien (an almshouse) besides the cathedral are all important wine growers. The two Bischöfliches and the cathedral operate together as the Vereinigte Bischöfliches Weingut. In their broad, dark, damp cellars in the city one has the feeling that wine is itself an act of charity rather than mere vulgar trade.

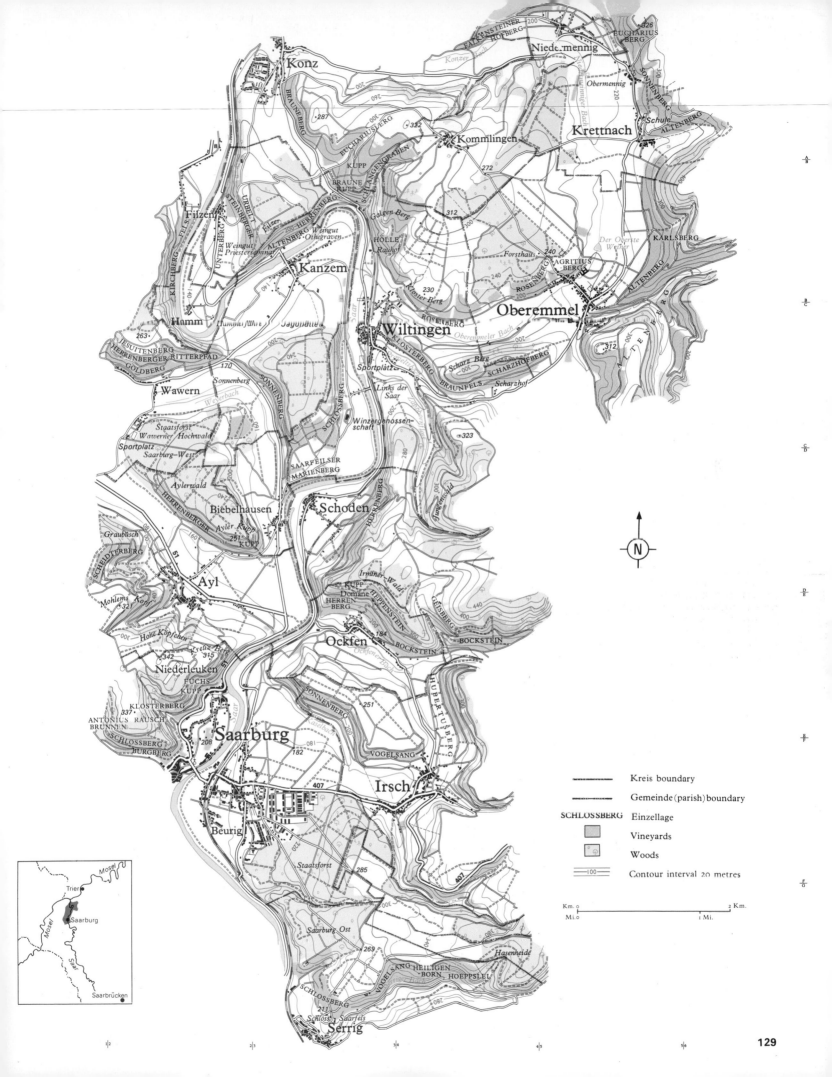

The Ruwer

THE RUWER is a mere stream. Its vineyards add up to about half the acreage of one Côte d'Or commune. In many years its wine is unsatisfactory; faint and sharp. Yet like the Saar when conditions are right it performs a miracle. Its wines are Germany's most delicate; gentle yet infinitely fine and full of subtlety.

Waldrach, the first wine village, makes good light wine but rarely more. Kasel is more important. The famous von Kesselstatt estate and the Bischöfliches Weingut of Trier have holdings here. There are great Kaselers in hot years.

Mertesdorf and Eitelsbach could not be called famous names; but each has one supreme vineyard, wholly owned by one of the world's best wine-growers. Mertesdorf's Maximin Grünhaus stands obliquely to the left bank of the river, with the manor-house, formerly monastic property, at its foot. The greater part of its hill of vines is called Herrenberg; the top part Abtsberg (for the abbot) and the less-well-sited part Bruderberg (for the brothers).

Across the stream Karthäuserhofberg echoes its situation, again with an old monastic building, now the manor-house, in a green garden below. The divisions of this big vineyard are shown on the map.

The town of Trier lies five miles away up the Mosel. Within the city there is one good vineyard, the Tiergarten. On the way there lies an isolated clearing belonging to the state domain and Trier cathedral; the hill of Avelsbach. Its wine is like that of the Ruwer; particularly perfumed and forthcoming.

Above: the beautiful old-fashioned label and (below) the manor of Maximin Grünhaus from its vineyard. In the background is Kasel and beyond, Waldrach

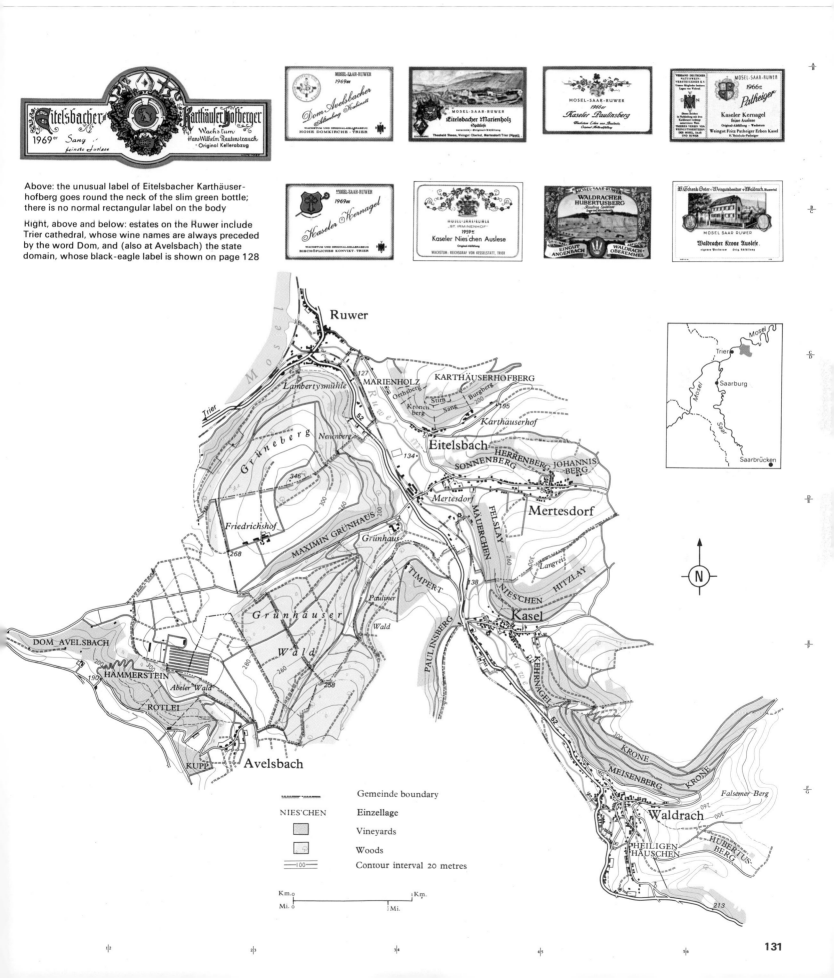

Above: the unusual label of Eitelsbacher Karthäuserhofberg goes round the neck of the slim green bottle; there is no normal rectangular label on the body

Right, above and below: estates on the Ruwer include Trier cathedral, whose wine names are always preceded by the word Dom, and (also at Avelsbach) the state domain, whose black-eagle label is shown on page 128

Gemeinde boundary

NIES'CHEN   Einzellage

Vineyards

Woods

Contour interval 20 metres

Km. 0   1 Km.
Mi. 0   ½ Mi.

Left: the really famous estates of the Mosel start down-river from Dhron. Dünweg and Milz, both in Neumagen, are two of the better-known growers of the upper stretch. The Sonnenuhr slope in Neumagen was made part of Rosengärtchen by the 1971 wine law

THE RIVER Mosel is acquainted with the reflections of vines all the way from its rising in the Vosges mountains to its union with the Rhine at Koblenz. Light wines of little consequence grow on the French Moselle; in Luxembourg larger quantities are made, attractive but still very slight. Only in the central part of the German Mosel do the spectacular river-walls of slate, rising sometimes to 700 feet above its course, provide the perfect conditions for the Riesling vine. In the central 40 miles of the river's snake-like meandering, which only take it 18 miles as the crow flies, the Mosel's great wine is made.

The wines of the river vary along the banks even more than, say, the vines of Burgundy vary along the Côte d'Or. Given south, south-east or south-west exposure, the steeper the bank the better the wine. It is only because the thin soil here is pure slate, through which rain runs as if through a sieve, that any soil stays in place on near-precipices. The coincidence of quickly-drying stable soil in vineyards which are held up to the sun like toast to a fire is the Mosel's secret.

There is no formal agreement on what constitutes the Middle Mosel. In the maps on these pages we have extended it beyond the central and most famous villages to include several whose wine is often underrated.

The first that we come to is Klüsserath. Bruderschaft, its best-known vineyard in the past, is now the permitted name for all the wine from its principal slope.

The long tongue of land which ends in Trittenheim is almost a cliff where the village of Leiwen jumps the river to claim the vineyard of Laurentiuslay and only a gradual slope by the village of Trittenheim. At least 20 names have been telescoped into those of Apotheke and Altärchen; Apotheke being steeper and

Above, left and right: dark grey slate and golden Riesling grapes are the elements which give Middle Mosel wine its quality. Each vine is staked independently on the vertiginous south-facing slopes above the river

with rather better exposure. These are the first vineyards of the Mosel which make wine of real breed. It is always delicate and slight, but not soft or faint. In such a year as 1964, when the wines of the Saar and Ruwer were Germany's best, Trittenheimers come into their own.

The town of Neumagen, a Roman landing place, keeps in its little leafy square a remarkable Roman carving of a Mosel wine ship, laden with barrels and weary galley-slaves.

The wine of Dhron is better-known. The best of it comes from the tributary valley of the Dhron. Dhroner Hofberger is partly owned by the Bischöfliches Weingut of Trier. The name Roterde has been liberally given to both good and not so good vineyards on both sides of the Mosel by the new laws.

Piesport has a standing far above its neighbours. It is the ideal site: an amphitheatre two miles long and 500 feet high, facing due south. The world-famous name Goldtröpfchen, once only the centre part just above the village, has now been given to virtually the entire magnificent vineyard. Piesporters are round and gently sweet wines, not with great power but with real fragrance and breed. The vast new plantation across the river known as Piesporter Gunterslay does not share Goldtröpfchen's distinction.

Minheim, Wintrich and Kesten are all minor producers. There are no perfectly aligned slopes in this stretch, except for the beginning of the great ramp which rises to its full height opposite the village of Brauneberg. In Kesten it is called Paulinshofberg. In Brauneberg it is the Juffer; 100 years ago reckoned the greatest wine of the Mosel, perfectly satisfying the taste of those days for full-bodied golden wine.

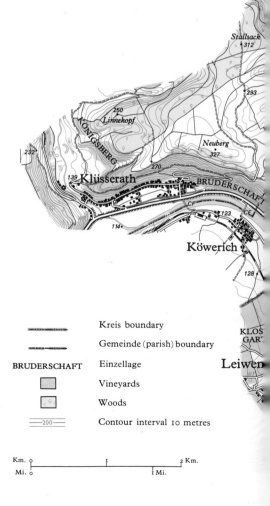

▓▓▓▓▓	Kreis boundary
─────	Gemeinde (parish) boundary
BRUDERSCHAFT	Einzellage
▨	Vineyards
▨	Woods
—200—	Contour interval 10 metres

Km. 0 ———————— 2 Km.
Mi. 0 ———————— 1 Mi.

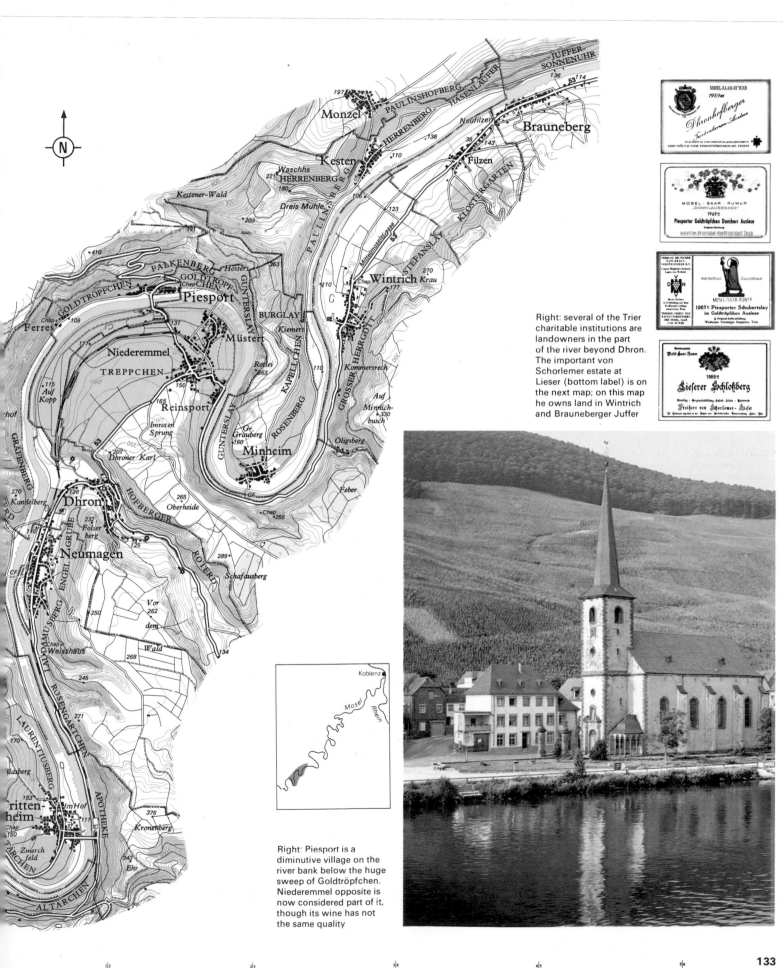

N

JUFFER-SONNENUHR

Monzel
PAULINSHOFBERG
HERRENBERG
HASENLÄUFER
Neufilzen
Brauneberg

Kesten
Filzen

Waschhs
HERRENBERG
KLOSTERGARTEN

Kestener-Wald

Dreis Muhle

PAULINSBERG

STEFANSLAY

Wintrich
Krau

FALKENBERG
Hostert
GOLDTROPFCHEN
Chap CHEN
GUNTERSLAY

GOLDTRÖPFCHEN
Ferres

Piesport

BURGLAY

Müstert
Kiemert

Niederemmel

GROSER HERRGOTT

TREPPCHEN

Auf
Kopp

Rotlei

Kommersrech

Reinsport
KAPELLCHEN
ROSENBERG
GUNTERSLAY

Imroten
Sprung

Gr.
Grauberg

Auf
Minnich-
busch

Dhroner Karl

Minheim

Oligsberg

Feber

Dhron

HOFBERGER

Oberheide

Chap

Neumagen

ROTERD

Schafausberg

ENGEL

ROSENGARTCHEN

Vor
dem
Wald

LAURENTIUSBERG

Chap
Weisshaus

Koblenz

Mosel

Rhein

rittenheim
UmHof

Chap

APOTHEKE

Kronenberg

Zmerch
feld

Ehr

ALTARCHEN

Right: several of the Trier charitable institutions are landowners in the part of the river beyond Dhron. The important von Schorlemer estate at Lieser (bottom label) is on the next map; on this map he owns land in Wintrich and Brauneberger Juffer

Right: Piesport is a diminutive village on the river bank below the huge sweep of Goldtröpfchen. Niederemmel opposite is now considered part of it, though its wine has not the same quality

THE VIEW north from the bridge at Bernkastel is of a green wall of vines 700 feet high and five miles long. Only perhaps the Douro in the whole gazetteer of rivers to which the vine is wedded has any comparable sight.

From Brauneberg to Bernkastel's suburb of Kues the hills are relatively gentle. The Kirchberg in Veldenz (the village is just off the map) is one of those marginal vineyards which, like the Trittenheimers, makes beautiful wine after a hot summer. Lieser is perhaps best-known for the grim great mansion of the von Schorlemers, one of the biggest estate-owners of the district. Niederberg has a slight edge on Schlossberg. Kues, though united with Bernkastel, has none of its distinction.

The Mosel's greatest vineyard starts abruptly, rising almost sheer above the gables of Bernkastel; dark slate frowning at slate. The butt of the hill, its one straight south elevation, is the Bernkasteler Doktor—perhaps the most famous vineyard in Germany. From its flank the proudest names of the Mosel follow one after another. Comparison of Bernkasteler with Graacher and Wehlener, often with wines from the same growers in each place, is a fascinating game, but to place them in order is impossible. It matters more who grew the wine and when.

The least of these wines should be something of very obvious personality; almost water-white with a gleam of green and with 40 or 50 little bubbles in the bottom of the glass, smelling almost aggressively of grapes, filling and seeming to coat your mouth with sharpness, sweetness and scent. The greatest of them—long-lived, pale gold, piquant, profound as honey, frivolous as flowers—are wines that beg to be discussed in an evening garden in

Above: the town of Bernkastel and the bridge to Kues seen from the Doktor vineyard high above. Imaginative tasters detect the smoke from Bernkastel's chimneys in the flavour of Doktor, often the most expensive Mosel

Below: a charity hospital (top left) and the parish church (top right) are among famous Bernkastel growers. In Wehlen the outstanding name is Prüm; four branches of the family are all among the artists of German wine

shameless comparisons with music and poetry.

The name of Bernkastel, for these very reasons, is used for ten times as much wine as the place grows. And amazingly enough, under the German system (see page 124) the law allows it. What it does not allow is the use of the Einzellage names shown on the map, except for their genuine produce. They and only they are a guarantee of the real thing. Under the new law Bernkastel has two Grosslage names: Bernkasteler Schwanen (the permissive one, including vineyards as far away as Brauneberg and Wintrich) and Badstube, for a much smaller and more distinguished area.

Zeltingen brings the Great Wall to an end. It is the Mosel's biggest wine commune, and certainly among the best.

At Ürzig, across the river, reddish clay mixed with slate, in rocky pockets instead of a smooth bank, gives the wines of the Würzgarten ('spice garden') a different flavour, more penetrating and 'racy' than Zeltingers.

Erden at its best is in the same rank as Ürzig. The rest of the river does not contain the concentrated quality of this stretch. Lösnich and Kinheim begin a decline. Kröv fills cafés with tourists giggling over the label of Nacktarsch, which shows a little boy with a bare bottom. It remains to be seen how the market in such a popular wine will be hampered by its becoming an Einzellage under the new law.

Traben-Tarbach is one community; Trarbach wines from steep side-valleys to the south are well-known. Enkirch, a lovely old village, should be much better-known than it is. In its ancient inn there is round, light, slightly spicy wine with all the delicate complexity that the Middle Mosel is famous for.

Below: old-fashioned hydraulic presses like these are used alongside modern ones by Deinhard's in their Kues cellars. The latest model contains a long balloon which squeezes the grapes against the sides as it inflates

	Regierungsbezirk boundary
	Kreis boundary
	Gemeinde (parish) boundary
BURGLAY	Einzellage
	Vineyards
	Woods
—100—	Contour interval 20 metres

Km. 0   2 Km.
Mi. 0   1 Mi.

The Nahe

THE RIVER Nahe, flowing north out of the Hunsrück hills to join the Rhine at Bingen, is surrounded by scattered outbreaks of wine-growing. But at one point a sandstone barrier impedes the river's flow, a range of hills rears up along the north bank; and suddenly there are all the makings of a great vineyard.

Its wine seems to capture all the qualities one loves best in German wine. It is very clean and grapy, with all the intensity of the Riesling, like a good Mosel or Saar wine. At the same time it has some of the full flavour which in the Rheingau makes one think of the alchemist's shop; as though rare minerals were dissolved in it; possibly gold itself. The word complexity, at a pinch, might do.

Bad Kreuznach is the wine capital of the Nahe. It is a pleasant spa, beneath hanging woods, with a casino and rows of strange brushwood erections like two-dimensional barns down which salt water is poured to produce ozone for the benefit of convalescents.

Bad Kreuznach itself has some of the Nahe's best vineyards and the premises of most of the best growers. The Kauzenberg and Brückes sites, nearest to be the river, often make exceptional wine. Across the river to the east, just off the map, Lerchensang, Höllenbrand, Feuerberg, Tilgesbrunnen and Rosenberg are the new Einzellage names.

The fireworks really begin upstream at the Bad Münster bend. A red precipice, the Roten-fels, said to be the highest cliff in Europe north of the Alps, blocks the river's path. At the cliff-foot there is a bare hundred feet of fallen rubble, a short ramp of red earth. The vines are planted thick in the cramped space. They have ideal soil and a complete suntrap. This is the Rotenfelser Bastei.

The amount of spice and fire in a Rotenfelser of a good year is exceptional for such a northerly vineyard. It can remind one of great Palatinate wine, with some of the freshness and finesse of the Saar thrown in.

From this bend on upstream there is a succession of fine slopes, through the villages of Norheim and Niederhausen, to the Nahe's most illustrious vineyard of all; the Kupfer-grube ('copper mine') on the eastern limit of the village of Schlossböckelheim.

The cellars where wine-making is brought to its highest peak here, if not in the whole of Germany, face the Kupfergrube from the last slope of Niederhausen. The Nahe state domain has holdings in several Niederhäusen vineyards, including the excellent Hermanns-höhle and Hermannsberg, and planted the Kupfergrube on the site of old copper-diggings. Photographs still exist of the steep hill facing the cellars when it had no vines: it is easy to picture the director observing the daylong sun on the mine workings, and forming his plan.

Many find in this domain everything they look for in white wine. The wines it makes are clean-tasting and fresh, fruity, racy and well-balanced; very pale, with almost as much scent as a Bernkasteler and a long, lingering flavour in which sweetness and acidity are perfectly matched; the sign that, though the wine is so attractive new, it will take on yet more fascinating nuances as it ages.

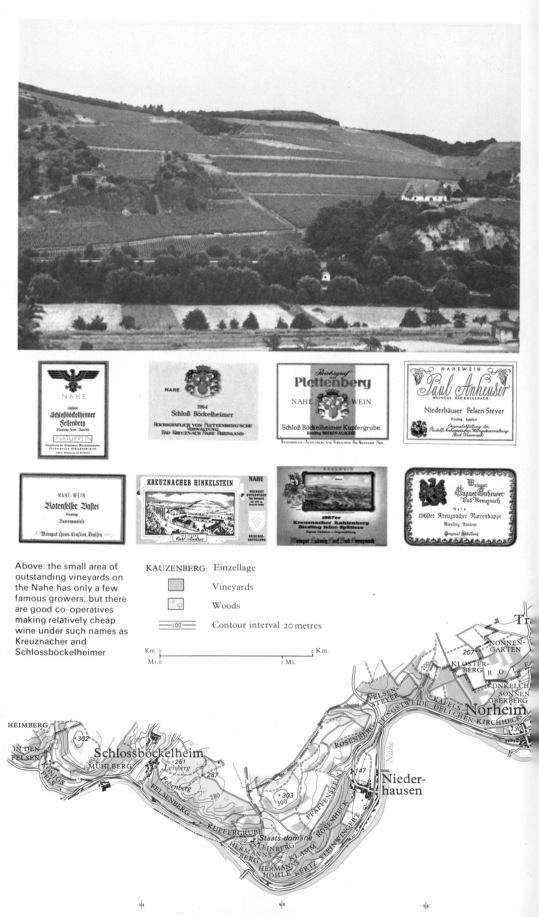

Above: the small area of outstanding vineyards on the Nahe has only a few famous growers; but there are good co-operatives making relatively cheap wine under such names as Kreuznacher and Schlossböckelheimer

KAUZENBERG Einzellage

☐ Vineyards

☐ Woods

══100══ Contour interval 20 metres

Km. 0 ———— 2 Km.
Mi. 0 ———— 1 Mi.

Left: the white building of the state domain on the end
of the Hermannsberg at Niederhausen looks across a
narrow defile (see map) to the most famous vineyard of,
the Nahe, Schlossböckelheimer Kupfergrube (in the
centre in the picture). In the foreground is the little
river Nahe

Right: the Rotenfels, or red mountain, on the Nahe's
bend at Bad Münster, is said to be the highest cliff in
Europe north of the Alps. At the foot of its 600 feet is
the six-acre strip of the Rotenfelser Bastei, admirably
sheltered and facing south or south-west

——————— Staat boundary

——————— Kreis boundary

——————— Gemeinde(parish)boundary

The Rheingau: Rüdesheim

THE RHEINGAU is the climax of the wine-growing Rhine. For almost all its length the river flows steadily north-west, except for the point just below Mainz where the high forested Taunus mountains stand in its way. It turns south-west for only 20 miles, until it reaches the Rüdesheimer Berg. There with a flurry of rocks and rapids it forces a passage northwards again. But the influence of its broad waters in that space gives Germany its most magnificent vineyard.

The best part of the Rheingau is mapped on the page opposite and the following two pages. Opposite is the downstream end, where the Rüdesheimer Berg Schlossberg is practically a terraced cliff. This is the only part of the Rheingau which is so steep. Most of it consists of stiff slopes but no more.

The Riesling is the grape of the Rheingau, as it is of the middle Mosel, but not of any except the best sites in the rest of the Rhine. The soil, which is exactly described on page 127, is a great mixture, but it comes nearer in type to the soil of Burgundy than of Germany's other Riesling areas. The climate is comparatively dry and sunny, and the river's presence makes for equable temperatures, the mists which encourage the 'noble rot' as the grapes ripen, and, they say, extra sunlight by reflection off its surface. It is half a mile wide here, a throbbing highway for slow strings of barges.

The Rheingau style of wine, at its best, is the noblest in Germany. It unites the flowery scent of the Riesling with a greater and more golden depth of flavour than the Mosel. There is a strong sense of maturity about it; with maturity comes complexity and, in a strong character (the human parallel is irresistible), balance. Soft and charming are words you should never hear in the Rheingau.

The westernmost town which is mapped opposite is Assmannshausen, round the corner from the main Rheingau and an exception to all its rules, being famous only for its red wine. The grape is the Pinot Noir; its wine is very pale here and without the power it should have, but (among others) the state domain makes much-sought-after sweet pink wine by late-gathering the grapes. Dry red Assmannshausen is Germany's most famous red wine.

The Rheingau is considered Germany's finest wine land, and the distinction of having owned the same Rheingau vineyard for as much as (in one case) 600 years is as great a patent of nobility as any in Europe. Among the big estates are the three shown here, and Prince Frederick of Prussia's at Erbach, Count Eltz and Baron Langwerth von Simmern at Eltville, Count von Schönborn at Hattenheim, Baron Ritter zu Groenesteyn at Rüdesheim, the Landgraf of Hessen at Johannisberg and Prince Löwenstein in Hallgarten. The biggest estates outside this aristocratic circle are the 50-acre Wegeler property which belongs to Deinhard's, the Koblenz shippers, and the 45 acres of

Above: the magnificent 12th-century church of Kloster Eberbach in Hattenheim is the symbolic headquarters of the German state domain, which has 300-odd acres in the Rheingau, including the great Steinberg, left

the Geisenheim wine school. Some Rheingau growers, particularly the three here, distinguish between their grades of wine with a complex code of different labels, and as many as 12 different coloured lead capsules over the cork. The labels here are for their higher grade wines

Left and below: Schloss Vollrads at Winkel has been the home of the Counts Greiffenclau since the 14th century. Eighty acres produce some of Germany's most noble wines

Left and below: Schloss Johannisberg was granted to Prince Metternich by the Austrian Emperor in 1816. The present Fürst von Metternich consistently makes good wine from its 66-acre slope to the Rhine

The Rüdesheimer Berg is distinguished from the rest of the parish by having the word Berg before each separate vineyard name. At their best (which is not always in the hottest years, since the drainage is too good at times) these are superlative wines, full of fruit and strength and yet delicate in nuance. In hotter years the vineyards behind the town come into their own.

Among the growers of the big parish is the wine-school of Geisenheim, one of the most famous centres of wine-learning in the world.

The new wine laws have radically simplified the vineyard names of the Rheingau. They are bound to make the few remaining names better-known than the many old ones were. Geisenheim makes excellent wine, but it had a dozen Lagen, and none with a great reputation. Rothenberg, considered the best, has now swallowed its very good neighbours; we can expect to hear its name more often.

Left: growers in the big commune of Rüdesheim include, top, the famous Geisenheim wine school. The two lower labels are from estates on the Rüdesheimer Berg

Right: looking towards the Rhine from the slope of Schloss Johannisberg in winter. There is a story that Charlemagne noticed the snow melted first on this slope

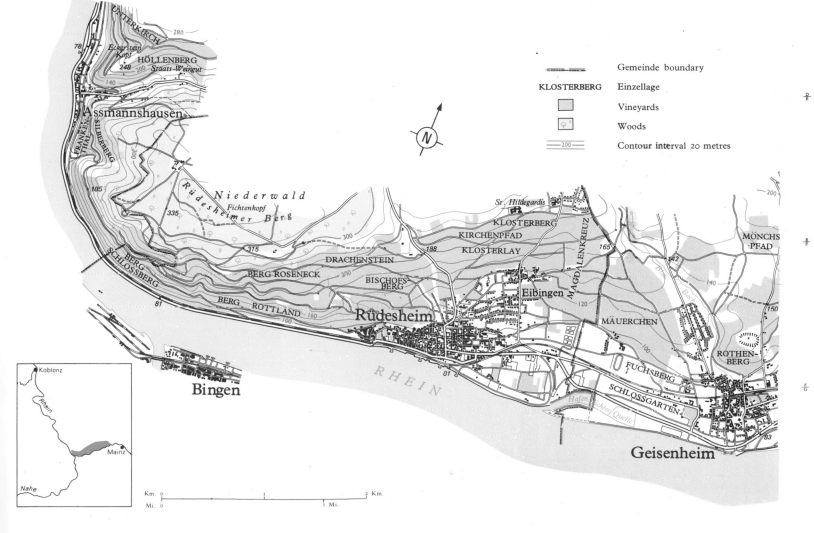

Gemeinde boundary	
KLOSTERBERG	Einzellage
	Vineyards
	Woods
200	Contour interval 20 metres

UNTERKIRCH

Eckerstein Kopf

HÖLLENBERG
Staats-Weingut

Assmannshausen

FRANKEN-THAL

SILBERBERG

Niederwald
Fichtenkopf
Rüdesheimer Berg

BERG SCHLOSSBERG

BERG ROSENECK

DRACHENSTEIN

BISCHOFS BERG

BERG ROTTLAND

Rüdesheim

St. Hildegardis

KLOSTERBERG

KIRCHENPFAD

KLOSTERLAY

MAGDALENKREUZ

MÖNCHS PFAD

Eibingen

MÄUERCHEN

ROTHEN BERG

FUCHSBERG

SCHLOSSGARTEN

Hafen

Bingen

R H E I N

Geisenheim

Koblenz

Rhein

Mainz

Nahe

Km. 0 ..... 1 ..... 2 Km.
Mi. 0 ..... 1 Mi.

The Rheingau: Eltville

SCHLOSS JOHANNISBERG, standing above a great apron of vines, dominates everything between Geisenheim and Winkel. The enormous prestige of its production, for which the wine-taster's favourite term, 'elegant', might have been invented, tends to overshadow the excellent vineyards of the rest of Johannisberg. About a third of the whole belongs to the Schloss (see page 138).

Schloss Vollrads (see page 138) stands over a mile back from Winkel and leaves the name of the town off its labels—unfortunately for Winkel, whose name would otherwise be better known than it is. Even its second-best vineyard, Hasensprung (which means hare-leap) is capable of producing superlative wine with the endless nuances which put the Rheingau in a class by itself.

Mittelheim has little identity as distinct from the more important Winkel and Oestrich. Its name does not appear on any wine of special note. There are those who say the same about Oestrich. Oestrichers have been criticized for lack of 'breed'. But character and lusciousness they certainly have. Doosberg and Lenchen are not names to be dismissed.

In Hallgarten the Rheingau vineyards reach their highest point. The Hendelberg is 1,000 feet above sea level. There is less mist and less frost up here. In the Würzgarten and Schönhell there is marly soil which gives strong wines of great lasting-power and magnificent bouquet. No single vineyard makes the village name world-famous—though the fact that an excellent shipper has the same name makes it familiar.

The boundaries of Hattenheim stretch straight back into the hills to include the most illustrious of all the vineyards of the German state: the high ridge of the Steinberg, walled like the Clos de Vougeot with a Cistercian wall.

Below in a wooded hollow stands the old monastery which might fairly be called the head-quarters of German wine, Kloster Eberbach (see page 138). The place, the astonishing wine and the implications of continuous industry and devotion to one idea of beauty going back 600 years make any comment seem trivial. To any wine-lover the hill behind Hattenheim is a true place of pilgrimage.

Like Hallgarten, Hattenheim has marl in the soil. On its border with Erbach is the only vineyard which makes great wine right down by the river; in a situation which looks as though the drainage would be far from perfect. The vineyard is Markobrunn, or Marcobrunn, partly in Hattenheim but mainly in Erbach. Marco-brunner (or Erbacher Markobrunn) wine is very full flavoured, often rich, fruity and spicy. Its owners include Count Schönborn and Baron Langwerth von Simmern on the Hatten-

Above: substantial private estates make the most celebrated Rheingau wine. Some of the growers' co-operatives, as that at Erbach for example, also have excellent reputations. No outstanding wine is sold under any but a grower's label today

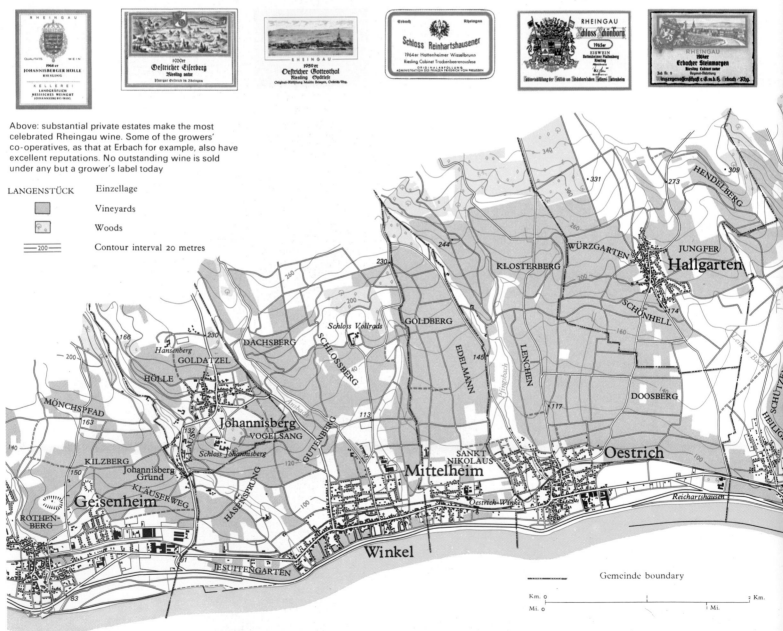

LANGENSTÜCK — Einzellage

Vineyards

Woods

200 — Contour interval 20 metres

Gemeinde boundary

Km. 0 ... 1 ... 2 Km.
Mi. 0 ... 1 Mi.

heim side, and the state domain and Prince Frederick of Prussia's estate in Erbach.

Again in Erbach the town's land goes back into the hills in a long narrow strip. These are good vineyards, but not the best. Steinmorgen, by the town, gives more powerful and memorable wine than Michelmark and Hönigberg.

Kiedrich's beautiful gothic church is the next landmark. The vineyards of the village make exceptionally well-balanced and delicately spicy wine. Dr Weil is the biggest Kiedrich-based grower. Gräfenberg is reckoned the best part of the vineyard, although Wasseros and Sandgrub are almost equally renowned.

Superlatives become tiring in an account of the Rheingau. Yet if the qualities of great white wine mean anything to you the peculiar sort of wine these growers make offers more to taste, consider and discuss than any other in the world. The wines which fetch the high prices, and by which the vineyards are ultimately judged, are always the late-picked, sweet and intense ones which demand to be drunk with conscious attention, and on their own rather than with food. There are better wines for any meal in other parts of Germany—and far better in Burgundy. The Rheingau's raison d'être must be understood. It is wine for wine's sake. And it does, without exaggeration, give rise to such scents and flavours that only superlatives will do.

Thus Rauenthal, the last of the hill villages and the furthest from the river, makes a different kind of superlative wine: the most expensive. Rauenthalers are the Germans' German wine. The Ausleses of the state domain and of the two lordly growers of Eltville, Baron Langwerth von Simmern and Count Eltz, as well as those of smaller growers on the Rauenthaler Berg, are prized for the combination of power and delicacy in their flowery scent and in their spicy aftertaste.

Eltville makes bigger quantities of wine without the supreme cachet. It is the headquarters of the state domain (see page 138) as well as having the beautiful old mansions of the Eltz and von Simmern families, in a group of buildings of white plaster and rosy stone, draped with vines and roses, beside the river.

Without sharing the fame of their neighbours the united Nieder- and Ober-Walluf and Martinsthal share much of their quality.

Fifteen miles further east the Rheingau has an unexpected outpost; Hochheim. The Hochheim vineyards (which gave us the word hock) lie on gently sloping land just north of the river Main, isolated in country which has no other vines. Good Hochheimers (three labels are shown here) are on a level with the better, not the best, wines of the Rheingau.

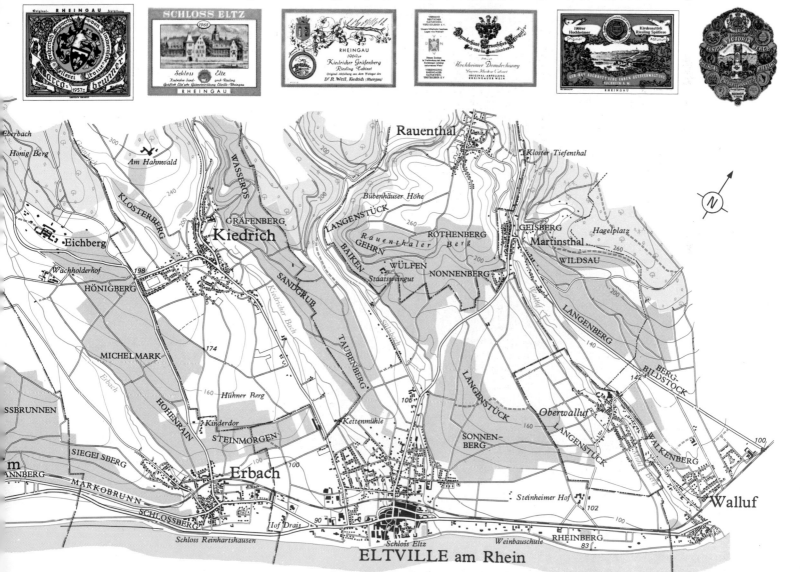

Rheinpfalz: the Middle Haardt

Above: morning mist at vintage time in the Middle Haardt
Above right: Ungstein; the lie of the land is curiously like Burgundy's Côte d'Or
Right: Deidesheim; substantial houses with arches into stone courtyards are typical of the Middle Haardt
Far right: orchards surround wine-making villages along the route of the German Weinstrasse

THE PALATINATE (German Pfalz) is Germany's biggest vineyard; a 50-mile stretch just north of Alsace, under the lee of the German continuation of the Vosges mountains—the Haardt.

Like Alsace, it is the sunniest and driest part of its country, and has the never-failing charm of half-timbered villages among orchards, seeming part of a better, sunlit, half fairy-tale world. A labyrinthine road, the Deutsche Weinstrasse, like the Alsatian Route du Vin, starts at the gates of Germany (literally; there is a massive gateway called the Weintor at Schweigen on the border) and winds northwards through more vines and villages than you ever hope to see. Almost all their production is café wine, handsomely served in thick-trunked glasses called *Pokale* but not bottled (unless in some such blend as Liebfraumilch). The Muscat, Traminer, Tokayer, Sylvaner and almost everything except Riesling are grown. When it is young and rather sweet the wine is often enjoyable, though usually heavy. But it can be disagreeable, coarse and headachey.

North of Neustadt, however, you are in a different world. In the Mittel-Haardt, the name of the short string of villages mapped opposite, the wine suddenly achieves the unmistakable quality of breed. Here Riesling jumps from 3% to 70% of the plantation.

Ruppertsberg is the first of these villages. Hoheburg and Geisböhl, small vineyards by the village, are considered the *Spitzen*, or peak sites. The latter belongs entirely, and the former largely, to one of the district's three most famous producers; Bürklin-Wolf.

Dr Albert Bürklin-Wolf and the estates of von Bassermann-Jordan and von Buhl (the biggest private estate in Germany) between them own the most substantial part of the best land in the Mittel-Haardt. In the next village, Deidesheim, generally reckoned the best of the whole area, besides being one of the prettiest in Germany, von Bassermann-Jordan and von Buhl have their cellars. The number of Lage names has been greatly reduced here by the new wine laws. Kieselberg, Kalkofen, Grain-

hübel and Leinhöhle however are all top Lagen which remain more or less as they were, and Hohenmorgen, perhaps the best of all, jointly owned by Bassermann-Jordan and Bürklin-Wolf, has been kept intact.

Forst has a unique reputation, as the source of Germany's sweetest wine (not in mere sugar, but in style and character). A black basalt outcrop above the village provides dark soil, rich in potassium, which is not found elsewhere—though it is quarried and spread on other vineyards, notably in Deidesheim. Basalt here, as on Lake Balaton in Hungary, holds the heat and keeps the temperature up at night. Forst's one street is the main road. The Jesuitengarten, its most famous vineyard, and the equally fine Kirchenstück lie just behind the church. These and Freundstück (largely the property of von Buhl) remained little altered by the new laws.

The village of Wachenheim marks the end of the best part of the Mittel-Haardt with a cluster of small vineyards which were famous enough

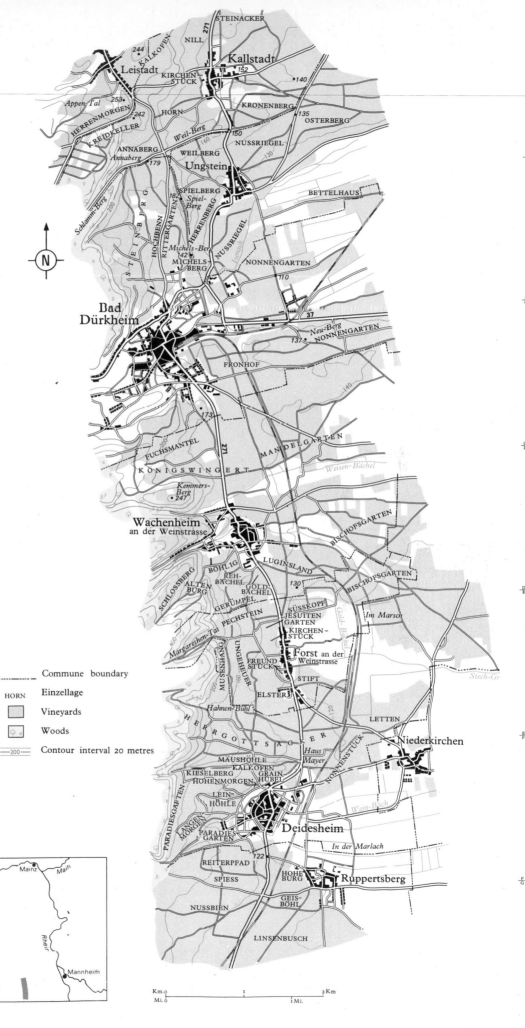

Above: the first three labels are among the most famous designs in Germany, appearing on the cream of Palatinate wine. Senator von Buhl's estate is the biggest private wine property in the country. The growers' co-operatives of Forst (right, second from top) and Bad Dürkheim (bottom left) are represented among other good growers. The village of Gimmeldingen (right, third from top) is just off the map to the south

to survive the levelling of the new laws. A large part of them belongs to Bürklin-Wolf, whose headquarters are at the southern boundary of the village. Rechbächel, Goldbächel, Gerümpel and Böhlig are the top names here. Richness is not such a marked characteristic of Wachenheim; its great quality is finesse; finely-poised sweetness and purity of flavour.

Bad Dürkheim is the biggest wine commune in Germany, with 2,000 vineyard acres. A Wurstmarkt, or Sausage Fair, is held here before the vintage. There is a red Dürkheimer to drink with the sausages as well as white; the Riesling is in the minority except in the top vineyards of Hochbenn and Michelsberg.

From here north the quality which distinguishes the Mittel-Haardt is not found, but certain Lagen have very good reputations. Annaberg, south-west of Kallstadt, is one. Its wine from the Scheurebe, a Riesling-Sylvaner cross, is especially rich and distinctive. Kallstadt's most famous old Lage, Kobnert, is now the Grosslage name for the whole village.

Commune boundary

HORN Einzellage

Vineyards

Woods

—200— Contour interval 20 metres

143

Rheinhessen

The Liebfrauenstift vineyard, origin of the name of Liebfraumilch (though long since divorced from it) lies round the Liebfrauenkirche in the city of Worms, 20 miles south of Nierstein. Nylon protects it from birds

Left and far right:
Nierstein has as many as 300 sizable wine estates. Those of Guntrum, Balbach and Franz Karl Schmitt are the biggest. Baron Heyl zu Herrnsheim is another excellent grower. Rehbach (second label left) used to be the southern end of Pettenthal before the new law. The last label, right, is of the most important estate at Bingen to the west

RHEINHESSEN lies in the crook of the Rhine, hemmed in by the river and the wine regions of the Palatinate and the Nahe. Its 150-odd villages, spaced out in an area 20 miles by 30, grow wine as part or all of their livelihood. It is dull, rolling, fertile country, without exceptional character except where the Rhine flows by. The bulk of its wine, made from Sylvaner vines, is equally unexceptional; light, soft, sometimes sweetish, sometimes earthy, rarely alive enough to claim attention. It finds its outlet as Liebfraumilch, a name with no legal connotations which can be used for any wine, but normally applies to mild semi-sweet blends.

The short stretch of Rhine-front shown on the map is the exception. The town of Nierstein has become, partly through its size and the number (about 300) of its growers, partly because its name is widely and shamelessly borrowed (usually with the make-believe vineyard name Domthal attached), but mainly because of its superb vineyards, as famous as Bernkastel. The two towns which flank it, Oppenheim and Nackenheim, have vineyards as good as most of Nierstein, but none better than the sand-red roll of hill going north with the river at its foot. Hipping, Pettenthal and Rothenberg (which is in Nackenheim) make Riesling wine as fragrant and full of character as the Rheingau, and thought by some to be a shade softer and more luxuriant.

Any true Niersteiner will use one of the Einzellage names on this map. The best also specify that they are made from the Riesling.

Outside the area of the map the best villages of Rheinhessen are just north (Bodenheim) and south (Guntersblum and Alsheim) along the river, and on the far side of the district where Bingen faces Rüdesheim across the Rhine. Bingen's big Scharlachberg gives very distinguished wine.

Franconia

Above: flask-shaped Franconian wine bottles have round or oval labels. Bottom right is a blank from the famous Veitshöchheim wine-growers' school before overprinting with the name of the vineyard and vintage

Right: Würzburg is the great marriage of the vine and the baroque. Vine rows are the only straight lines in this exuberant city. Below Marienberg Castle the Leiste vineyard runs down to the river Main

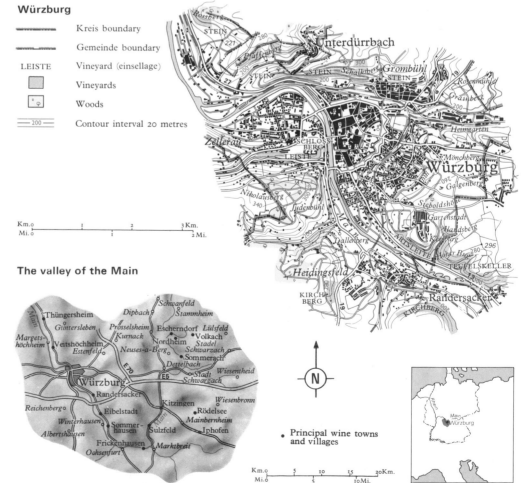

FRANCONIA (Franken) is out of the mainstream of German wine both geographically and by its quite separate traditions. It makes the only German wine not to come in flute bottles; the only great wine made of the Sylvaner instead of the Riesling. And in savour and strength it draws away from the delicate sweetness of most German and nearer to some French wines, making it one of the best of German wines to drink with food.

The name Steinwein is often used for all Franconian wine. Stein is in fact the name of one of the two famous vineyards of the city of Würzburg on the Main, the capital of the district. The other is Leiste. Both distinguished themselves in the past by making wines which lasted incredibly long periods. A 16th-century Stein wine (of the great vintage of 1540) was still just drinkable only seven years ago, and the Pfalz wine museum at Speyer has bottles of early 17th-century Leisten with late 19th-century labels from the royal house of Bavaria.

Such wines were Beerenauslesen at least: immensely sweet. Franconia makes few of such rarities today. The bulk of the wine in the pretty flask-shaped Bocksbeutel is decidedly dry by German standards, with something more like the size and strength of white burgundy.

Ten or twelve villages along the bends of the Main above and just below Würzburg are the producers. The most famous are Iphofen (15 miles south-east of the city), Randersacker and Escherndorf. Among the best growers are two charities, the Juliusspital and the Bürgerspital zum Heiligen Geist, with magnificent cellars in Würzburg. Vineyards occupy sites right inside the city itself, making it, together with its baroque buildings (the Residenz, built for the Prince Bishop by Balthasar Neumann in 1720, is the finest 18th-century palace in Germany), one of wine's most splendid outposts.

Würzburg

	Kreis boundary
	Gemeinde boundary
LEISTE	Vineyard (einsellage)
	Vineyards
	Woods
200	Contour interval 20 metres

Km.0   1   2   3 Km.
Mi.0   1   2 Mi.

The valley of the Main

N

• Principal wine towns and villages

Km.0   5   10   15   20 Km.
Mi.0   5   10 Mi.

Baden-Württemberg

YOU WOULD expect southern Germany to make more wine than the north. A hundred years ago it did. Baden was Germany's biggest producer. But the peculiar conditions of soil and climate which make wine-growing worthwhile in apparently unlikely spots on the Mosel and Rhine are not matched by anything in the huge state of Baden-Württemberg. The best of the wine is very good, but in tiny quantities, scattered here and there and made from a surprising number of different grapes.

The 'Seewein' (lake wine) of the southern-most area, round Meersburg on the Bodensee, is traditionally pink-tinted Weissherbst, white wine pressed from red Spätburgunder grapes —it makes good holiday drinking.

Markgräflerland has the same grape as Switzerland; the Chasselas (here the Gutedel). It makes adequate Swiss-style wine.

The best vineyards of Baden are on a volcanic outcrop in the Rhine valley, detached from the Black Forest massif: the Kaiserstuhl. The Ruländer (or Pinot Gris) here makes fruity white wine and the Pinot Noir light red.

The Ortenau has three lordly estates, those of the Margrave of Baden (Schloss Staufenberg), Baron von Neveu and Count Wolff Metternich, whose Ruländer and Klingelberger (the local name for Riesling) are famous. Neuweier is the centre for growing the Riesling 'Mauerwein', the excellent carafe wine of Baden-Baden's luxurious spa. North again, the Kraichgau has few vineyards left today. Over the river Neckar in Hessen the Bergstrasse makes better-known wine; the Rheingau state domain has vineyards here.

Württemberg grows more red wine than white, and some pale pink. The white is best. Its climate is much harsher and good sites are rare. Most are on the river Neckar. Big co-operatives handle the bulk of the production and the City of Stuttgart is a major producer.

Fine wine estates are widely scattered in Baden-Württemberg. Below are the labels of six of the most famous: four lordly houses—Graf Adelmann, of Württemberg, calls his wine 'Brussels Lace'—and the City of Stuttgart and the state domain of Meersburg

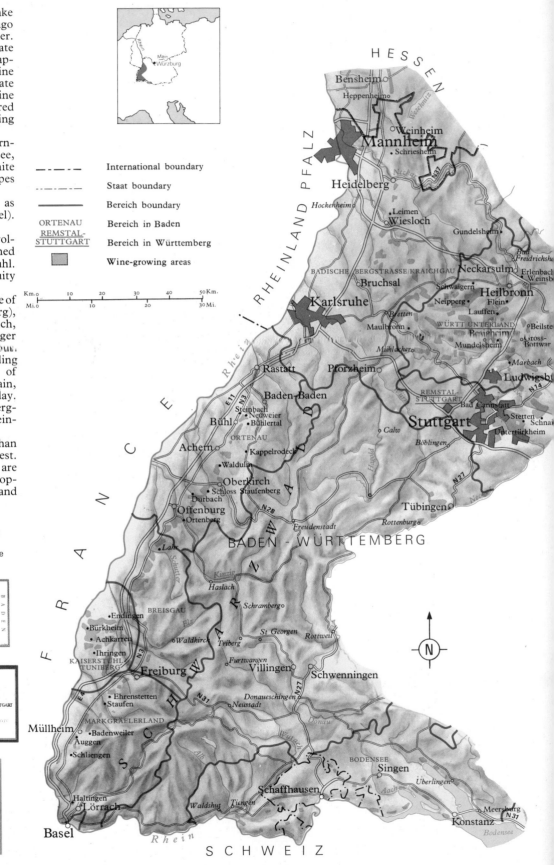

International boundary
Staat boundary
Bereich boundary
ORTENAU
REMSTAL-STUTTGART — Bereich in Baden
Bereich in Württemberg
Wine-growing areas

Km.0 10 20 30 40 50 Km.
Mi.0   10   20   30 Mi.

Southern and Eastern Europe
and the Mediterranean

Vintage-time at Colares on the coast of Portugal near Lisbon

Italian Wine

THE GREEKS called Italy Oenotria—the land of wine. The map reminds us that there is little of Italy which is not more or less wine country. Her annual production is now easily the biggest in the world. Yet what is at the same time amiable and maddening about her is her age-old insouciance about it all. With a few important exceptions, Italian wine has always been, with its delights and disappointments, enough to drive any tidy-minded wine merchant to drink.

To start with, the orderly identifying of wine by its place of origin, the method used in France and Germany, is only one of Italy's. By and large Italian wines have *names*, which may be that of the grape, or a place, or both, or pure fantasy, or pure poetry, or a historical reference, or a brand. It is not unusual for the same name to refer to red and white, sweet and dry wines equally, though they may bear no resemblance to one another.

Reference books in the past have had to be content with listing as many names as possible, and pinning them down as far as they could to where such wine is found. The limiting of a name to a definite area, in line with international practice, is a new idea in Italy. Without it control is impossible; exports were getting nowhere; something had to be done.

The Italian government entered the fray in 1963, with a well-conceived system of control based on the laws of Appellation Contrôlée

(see *Wine Law* below). It had as a foundation a number of voluntary consorzi, or associations, which had been formed by growers in the more organized regions. Chianti, for example, already had an embryo wine law, which the government could learn from and adapt.

The maps on the following pages show the limits of the wine areas which have been settled. Other wine districts are shown without limits: the old practice.

In the long run the result of the present legislation will be more reliable Italian wine for everyone. Already it is helping exports and putting up the price of wines which are Denominazione Controllata.

One should not forget, however, that the best producers have been making reliable wine for a long time, and that standards in some parts of Italy (notably Piemonte, Chianti, Verona and the Alto Adige, the four mapped in detail in this atlas) are high.

In general in Italy the red wines are best. If they never reach the heights of a great Bordeaux or burgundy they have qualities of their own which range from the silky and fragile to the purple and potent. Above all their qualities, and the qualities of all Italian wine, must be seen in the context of the incredibly varied, simple, sensuous Italian table. The true genius of Italy lies in spreading a feast. In the Italian feast wine plays the chief supporting role.

Wine Law

The Italian wine law of 1963 lays down three standards of control. The first is:

Denominazione Semplice. It is equivalent, more or less, to the German Tafelwein; only a simple statement of the region of production is allowed; there are no set standards.

Denominazione di Origine Controllata is the next rank. A body of wine growers may apply to have their wine registered as DOC. They must suggest limits to where it can be produced and standards of quality which it must reach. A committee in Rome decides whether or not the wine merits DOC standing and confirms the specifications. DOC wines are subject to testing and must wear a DOC label, in addition to their own.

Denominazione Controllata e Garantita, the top rank, is awarded only to certain wines from certain producers, rather than whole regions. To be controllata e garantita a wine must be bottled and sealed with a government seal by the producer or someone who takes full responsibility for it. Eventually all the best wines of Italy will be controllata e garantita; at present the scheme is only in embryo.

This atlas maps the delimited areas of all DOC wines declared up to 1971. The fact of their acceptance by this date does not prove their importance, however; it is easier for some small regions with few producers to apply early. Some important regions will be very late in being delimited, and the full working of the scheme lies in the unknown future.

Below: Cinzano, Martini, Carpano, Campari, all household words for aperitifs, have their cellars round Turin. Beyond central Piemonte, however, wine districts are small and reputations mainly local. Frecciarossa, Spanna and Dolceacqua are exceptions

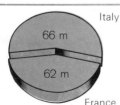

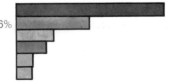

Italy consumes 62 million hectolitres of wine a year: 118 litres per head of the population. 7·5% of the population is employed in wine-growing and the wine trade.
The average price for wine received by the grower is 8,600 lire per 100 litres (1968 figures)

Above: Italy is the world's biggest wine-grower (66 million hectolitres on average to France's 62)

Germany 52%
Switzerland 16%
USA 7%
Britain 5%
France 4%
Austria 3%

Above: Germany takes half the wine Italy exports. Switzerland is her next biggest market (1969 figures)
Below: Italy's exports exceed imports by 30 to 1. They almost doubled in 1970, to 5½ m hl; one of the results of quality being stabilized by her new wine laws

Imports

Exports

The North-West

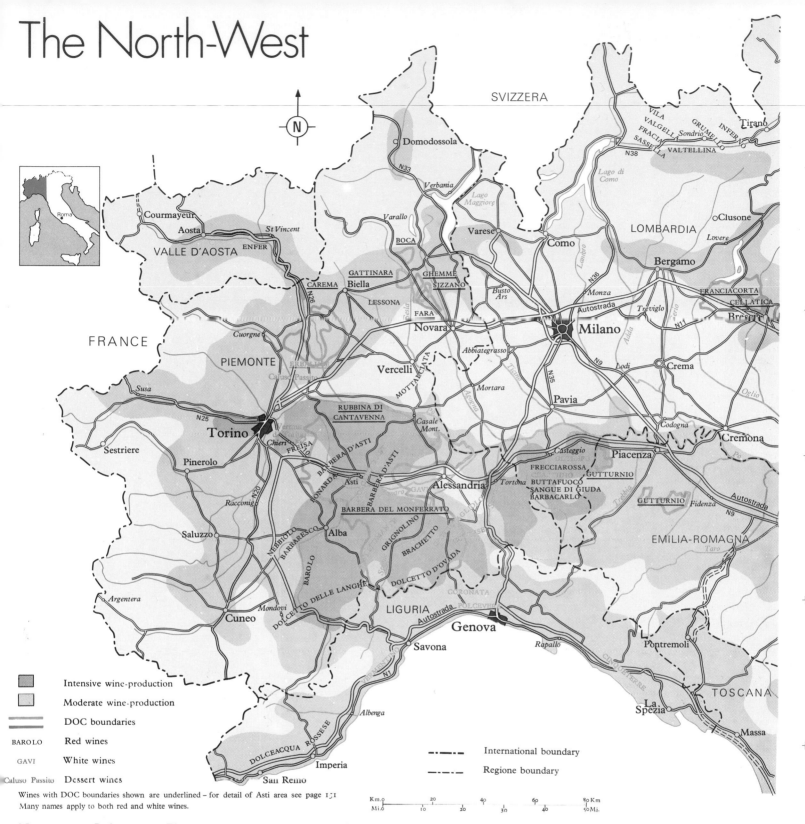

SVIZZERA

LOMBARDIA

FRANCE

PIEMONTE

VALLE D'AOSTA

FRANCIACORTA CELLATICA

EMILIA-ROMAGNA

LIGURIA

TOSCANA

Intensive wine-production

Moderate wine-production

DOC boundaries

BAROLO   Red wines

GAVI   White wines

Caluso Passito   Dessert wines

– · – · –   International boundary

– – – –   Regione boundary

Wines with DOC boundaries shown are underlined – for detail of Asti area see page 151
Many names apply to both red and white wines.

NORTH-WEST Italy means Piemonte to any
wine-lover. In its bitter-sweet vermouths, its
grapy spumantes, its pungent purple wines for
dishes and game and cheese, it epitomizes the
sensuality of gastronomic Italy. On the next
two pages its heart is shown in detail.

The rest of north-western Italy has good
wines, but the production is small and only
locally famous. The French-speaking Valle
d'Aosta has a substantial red, Carema, and a
lighter one, Enfer. Turin converts much of the
Piemontese wine into the world's most famous
brands of vermouth. Its southern outskirts—
notably Chieri—have their pleasant red Freisa
—pleasant, that is, until it is made into sweet
sparkling wine, which happens all too often.

A group of towns between Novara and Lake
Maggiore grow the excellent Nebbiolo grape
(though they call it the Spanna) and make wine
like the famous Barolo; often less good but
sometimes, particularly at Gattinara and
Ghemme, even better. Boca, Fara, Sizzano,
Lessona, Mottalciata are all local names for
this wine, which scarcely varies enough to
justify so many—whereas under a single name,
say Spanna, it might well become famous.

The wines of Liguria are better-known by
name, although the genuine article is rarely
seen outside the region. Cinqueterre, the very
good sweet and unusual dry white wine of five
small villages on the coast north of La Spezia,
is almost legendary. Polcevera and Coronata,

Genoa's white wines, made of the Vermen-
tino (among other grapes) go well with fish.
Dolceacqua and Rossese are the red wines of
the Italian Riviera; they are pleasant but plain.

Lombardy's main wine districts fall within
this map: the Oltrepo Pavese (or Pavia beyond
the Po), and Brescia and the Valtellina
(described on page 152). Casteggio is the main
centre of the Oltrepo Pavese; its wines are
Clastidio (red or white), red Buttafuoco,
Sangue di Giuda and Barbacarlo. The best of
them, Frecciarossa, is the brand name of one
particularly good grower.

The neighbouring region of Gutturnio,
which produces a good light red wine for
drinking young, is in Emilia-Romagna.

149

Piemonte

Left: Fontanafredda, under a ridge of Nebbiolo vines, is one of the finest estates of Barolo

Below: dark red wines, full of character, and sweet sparkling white wines, delicate and grapy, are the specialities of Piemonte

Pâté of cream cheese and white truffles
Pâté of tunny fish and butter
Raw San Daniele ham
Cold spinach pancakes
Mushroom salad
Chick-pea and pork soup
Fonduta (melted cheese and eggs) with white truffles
Bollito misto (boiled salame, calf's head, pork) with green sauce
Chocolate, chestnut and lemon ice creams
Menu in a traditional restaurant in Asti

PIEMONTESE food and wine, like those of Burgundy, are inseparable. They are strong, rich, individual, mature, somehow autumnal. One

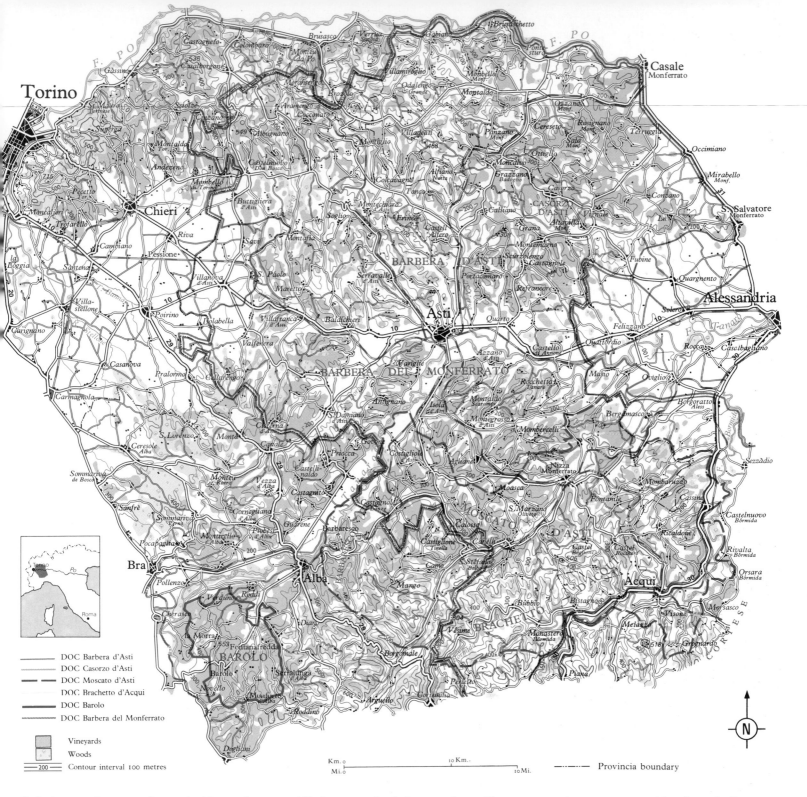

Torino

Casale
Monferrato

Chieri

Alessandria

BARBERA D'ASTI

Asti

BARBERA DEL MONFERRATO

S. Salvatore
Monferrato

Acqui

Bra

Alba

BAROLO

DOC Barbera d'Asti
DOC Casorzo d'Asti
DOC Moscato d'Asti
DOC Brachetto d'Acqui
DOC Barolo
DOC Barbera del Monferrato

Vineyards
Woods
200 Contour interval 100 metres

Km. 0   10 Km.
Mi. 0   10 Mi.

- - - - - Provincia boundary

N

feels it must be more than coincidence that
this is the Italian province nearest to France.

Piemonte means at the foot of the mountains;
the Alps. But it is on the substantial range of
the Monferrato hills that the great Piemontese wines are grown. None the less the Alps
have their effect, encircling the region and
giving it a climate of its own, with a very hot
growing season and a misty autumn.

At vintage time in Barolo the hills are half
hidden. Ramps of copper and gold vines, dotted
with hazel- and peach-trees, lead down to the
valley of the Tanaro, lost in the fog. It is a
magical experience to visit Serralunga or La
Morra and see the dark grapes coming in, and
smell the fermentation, a compound of wood
and cheese and fruit, promising comfort.

The two best red wines of Piemonte, Barolo

and Barbaresco, take their names from villages.
The rest have the names of their grapes—
Barbera, Dolcetto, Grignolino, Freisa. If to the
grape they add a district name (e.g. Barbera
d'Asti) it means they come from a limited and
theoretically superior area. The map shows the
zones of central Piemonte—including that of
the famous Moscato d'Asti spumante. The
still dry white Cortese (Gavi and Casteltagliolo
are local variants) is grown to the south-east.

Barolo is a wine on the scale of Châteauneuf-du-Pape. Its minimum strength is 12°_0:
going up to 15. It often throws a heavy sediment in its bottle, even after a minimum of
three years in cask and often longer, so Barolo
bottles are traditionally kept standing up, unlike all other red wines.

The flavour of Barolo, and above all its scent,

are the most memorable of any Italian wine.
The Nebbiolo grape gives it a suggestion of
truffles, a touch of tar, a positive note of rasp-
berry. Barbaresco only differs from Barolo in
coming from lower down, where fog affects the
vineyard sooner, making a slightly drier, less
fully-ripened wine.

Barbera is dark, tannic, often rather plummy
and acidic; excellent with rich food. Freisa, the
speciality of Chieri, can be similar—or sweet
and sparkling. Dolcetto is light, faintly bitter,
the carafe wine of the region. Grignolino is also
a light-weight but has rather more character.

Some of the bigger firms make all these
wines; family businesses tend to make one or
two, in which the characters of the grapes are
likely to be more pronounced. These individual wines are worth looking for.

North-East Italy

Left: vineyards in the north-east of Italy frequently see snow, as here at Denno near Trento
Above: the wine produced is correspondingly northern and well-balanced in character

NORTH-EASTERN Italy owes less to tradition and more to modern development that the rest of the country. Whether it is the realism of the Venetians, the pressure of Austrian influence, the moderate climate, or all these and more, more wine is exported from the north-east than from elsewhere, more different grapes are grown and experimented with, and a more prosperous and professional air pervades the vineyards.

Verona and its wines—Valpolicella, Soave; Bardolino and the southern Lake Garda wines; the Alto Adige with its Lago di Caldaro and Santa Maddalena are mapped and discussed in detail on pages 154–155. The other biggest concentrations of wine-growing are due north of Venice round Conegliano, on the Jugoslav border in Friuli and in the Trentino, north of Lake Garda.

For some reason little is seen of any Lombardy wines abroad. Some are excellent. The best of all are the red wines of the Valtellina, coming from a narrow strip of vineyard which hugs the north bank of the River Adda (map on page 149). They go by the names Inferno, Grumello and Sassella, though it is hard to find anyone who knows the difference between the three. Their grape is the Nebbiolo, but they are harder and less splendidly pungent wines than Barolo and the Piemontese Nebbiolos, needing several years in barrel followed by several in bottle before they reach maturity. There is real delicacy for anyone with the patience to wait.

Few of these wines have controlled areas for the moment—perhaps because tradition plays a relatively small part and wine-growers' interests are diffused among many kinds of wine. One of the few is the Prosecco of Conegliano-Valdobbiadene; white wine, sweeter or drier, still or sparkling, made of the Prosecco grape but not otherwise easily to be distinguished

from many others. Wine simply known as Colli di Conegliano or Valdobbiadene is partly Prosecco and more likely to be dry. Raboso is the local red. There is more interest in the less traditional vines: Merlot for its gentle red wine and Sylvaner for its white equivalent. Verdiso is very light white, at its best a touch sharp.

There is a similar mixture of old grape types with imports from Germany and notably France in Friuli. Collio Goriziano is the only DOC so far, but does not claim to be the region's best wine; simply a standard light dry white. The pride of the region is the rare white dessert wine Piccolit, the medium-sweet Verduzzo, and the dry white Tocai—which is a local grape, and nothing to do with the Hungarian Tokay.

The Sauvignon (of white Bordeaux) and the Riesling (Italian version, not the Rhine Riesling) are widespread, but perhaps less successful than the other import, the red Merlot, which makes the region's best wine, superseding, to a large extent, the traditional Refosco.

The Merlot is found over the border in Jugoslavia, and all the way across northern Italy to Italian Switzerland. But none can remotely compare with the Merlot's masterpiece, the great wines of Pomerol and St-Emilion.

The DOC Breganze is not likely to make headlines. There are red and white wines of average quality. In the southern Veneto the Colli Euganei are nearly all white, and certainly get as far as Venice. For red wine in the region there is the light Friularo and for sweet wine a Moscato.

The Vicenzan Colli Berici wines (red and white, sometimes called Barbarano or Costozza or other village names) are not great travellers. Nor is Torcolato, Vicenza's dessert wine. Gambellara, neighbour to the famous Soave and not distant in quality (though again sometimes

sweet and sometimes even red, to make sweeping statements impossible), is better-known.

Only one name from the flat Po valley is famous—the sparkling red Lambrusco from Sorbara near Modena. There is something appetizing about this vivid, grapy wine, despite the red bubbles, which goes well with rich Bolognese food. The white Scandiano of the region is not in the same class.

Of the Lombardy wines on this map, the Garda-side wines are very close to the Veronese Garda wines in character. There is little to choose between Chiaretto from the Riviera del Garda (of which the best part is south of Salo, particularly round Moniga del Garda) and Bardolino. Both are reds so light as to be rosé, or rosés so dark as to be red, with a gentle flavour, soft-textured and faintly sweet, made all the more appetizing by the hint of bitterness, like almonds, in the taste which is common to all the best red wines of this part of Italy. They should be drunk very young.

Red Botticino, Cellatica and Franciacorta are all light, too—though not often as attractive as Chiaretto. White Lugana, from the south end of Lake Garda, is good, dry, but rare.

Trentino wine is exported less than Alto Adige wine but is similar in many ways. The vertical-sided Adige valley is in places a vineyard from wall to wall, with the vine everywhere on pergolas, carpeting the crinkling valley floor. Red wine is in the majority, and most of the red, of quality varying from ordinary to very good, is called Teroldego. Marzemino and Valdadige are also standard red wines; Sorni and Casteller are light reds from the local Schiava grape; Negrara and Vallagarina are stronger.

The Merlot, too, gives a good wine here. Riesling and Traminer are grown as well as traditional Vernaccia among white, and some good dry sparkling wine is made in Trento.

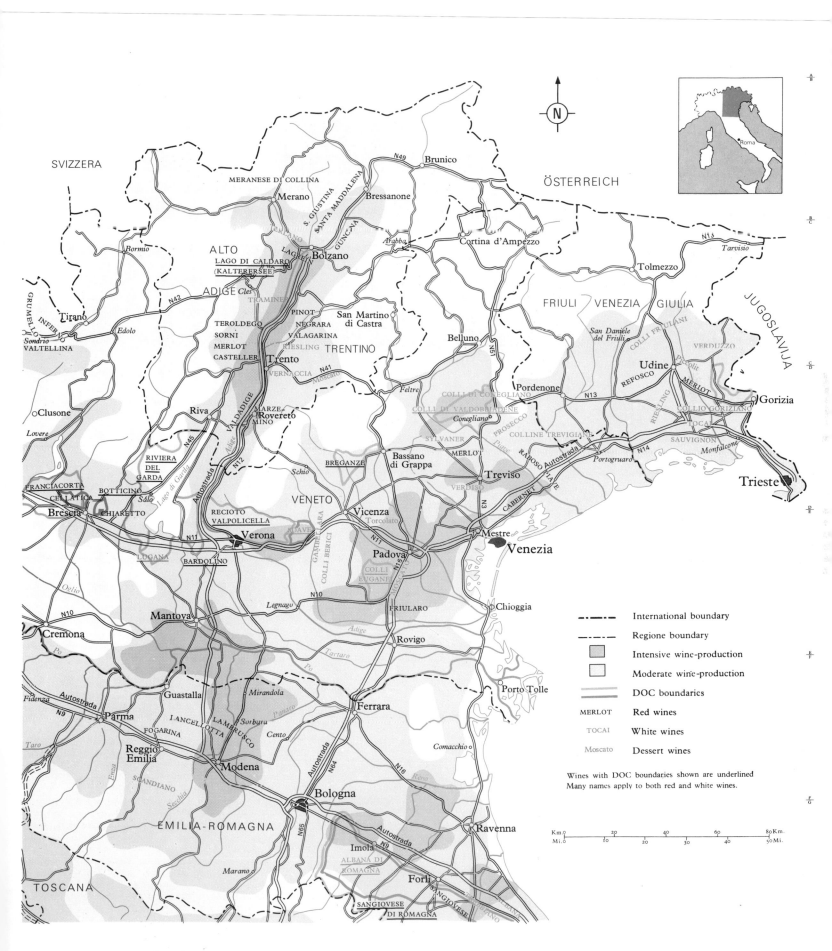

SVIZZERA

ÖSTERREICH

N

MERANESE DI COLLINA

Brunico

Merano

Bressanone

S. GIUSTINA
SANTA MADDALENA

GUNCINA

Cortina d'Ampezzo

Arabba

FRIULI VENEZIA GIULIA

Tolmezzo

Tarvisio

JUGOSLAVIJA

Bormio

ALTO

LAGO DI CALDARO
(KALTERERSEE)

LAGREIN

Bolzano

ADIGE Cles

TRAMINER

PINOT

San Martino
di Castra

San Daniele
del Friuli

COLLI FRIULANI

VERDUZZO

GRUMELLO
INFERNO

Tirano

Edolo

N42

TEROLDEGO
SORNI
MERLOT
CASTELLER

NEGRARA
VALAGARINA
RIESLING

TRENTINO

Belluno

Udine

Picolit

Gorizia

Sondrio
VALTELLINA

VERNACCIA

N41

Moscato

Feltre

Pordenone

REFOSCO

MERLOT

N13

Trento

COLLI DI CONEGLIANO

RIESLING

COLLIO GORIZIANO

Clusone

Riva

MARZE-
MINO

Rovereto

COLLI DI VALDOBBIADENE

TOCAI

Lovere

N45

Conegliano

PROSECCO

SAUVIGNON

Monfalcone

RIVIERA
DEL
GARDA

N12

Schio

BREGANZE

Bassano
di Grappa

SYLVANER

MERLOT

COLLINE TREVIGIANE

Piave

Trieste

FRANCIACORTA

Autostrada

Treviso

RABOSO Autostrada

Portogruaro

N14

CELLATICA

BOTTICINO

Salò

VENETO

VERDISO

N3

CABERNET

Brescia

CHIARETTO

RECIOTO
VALPOLICELLA

Vicenza

Torcolato

Mestre

Venezia

LUGANA

N11

Verona

SOAVE

GAMBELLARA

COLLI BERICI

Padova

MOSCATO

Chioggia

BARDOLINO

COLLI
EUGANEI

Oglio

Legnago

N10

FRIULARO

Porto Tolle

Mantova

Adige

Rovigo

Cremona

Po

Tartaro

Po

Guastalla

Mirandola

Sorbara

Ferrara

Fidenza

Autostrada

Pànaro

Cento

Parma

N9

LANCELLOTTA

LAMBRUSCO

FOGARINA

Taro

Reggio
Emilia

Modena

N64

Comacchio

Enza

SCANDIANO

Secchia

Bologna

Ravenna

EMILIA-ROMAGNA

N65

Autostrada

Reno

Imola

N9

Marano

ALBANA DI
ROMAGNA

TOSCANA

Forlì

SANGIOVESE
DI ROMAGNA

Roma

————— International boundary

—·—·— Regione boundary

Intensive wine-production

Moderate wine-production

DOC boundaries

MERLOT   Red wines

TOCAI   White wines

Moscato Dessert wines

Wines with DOC boundaries shown are underlined
Many names apply to both red and white wines.

Km. 0   20   40   60   80 Km.
Mi. 0   10   20   30   40   50 Mi.

Alto Adige

Alto Adige labels are usually in German, and Gothic in style. Much of the wine is drunk north of the Alps; to Austria it is 'South Tyrol'. The two bottom labels are from Trentino to the south. Teroldego is red; Ferrari makes sparkling wine

——— Provincial boundary

——— Boundary of DOC area

——— Boundary of Classico area

——— Boundary of Valpantena area

Vineyards

Woods

——500—— Contour interval 100 metres

CANTINA SOCIALE

——— Limit of DOC 'Lago di Caldaro'

Important cellars

Vineyards

Woods

——1000—— Contour interval 200 metres

Provincia boundary

THE ALTO ADIGE, the upper part of the Adige valley, round the city of Bolzano, is a vigorous and exciting region. Its connections with Austria are close and many of its people speak German—which partly explains why this small area supplies half the wine exported from Italy, though it ranks only eleventh for wine production.

A wide range of both red and white wines are made, largely from local grapes, among which is the famous Traminer, native to the village of Tramin (Italian Termeno).

The red wines are soft and well-balanced and tend to have a delicious touch of bitterness. It is most noticeable in the excellent dark rosé made from the Lagrein grape and usually known by its Tyrolean name, Lagrein-Kretzer. The Schiava, the most widespread local red grape, also has it; Lago di Caldaro is the name of the large quantities of Schiava wine from the western side of the valley south of Bolzano, still the only Alto Adige wine to be DOC. In Germany and Austria, where most of it is drunk, it is known as Kalterersee.

Santa Maddalena is a smaller region perched on the mountain above Bolzano. Its wine fetches a higher price than Lago di Caldaro.

A little Pinot Noir and more Merlot are grown; both are successful. Rare but best of all is the Cabernet, comparable at times to a good Napa Valley wine.

White wines are as good as red. Terlano, on the way north to Merano, has some of the best. They include Riesling and Traminer, Pinot Blanc (known as Terlaner) and Sauvignon. On the steep hillsides all ripen well and make excellent fruity and lively wine. A little very dry and good sparkling wine is also made.

Verona

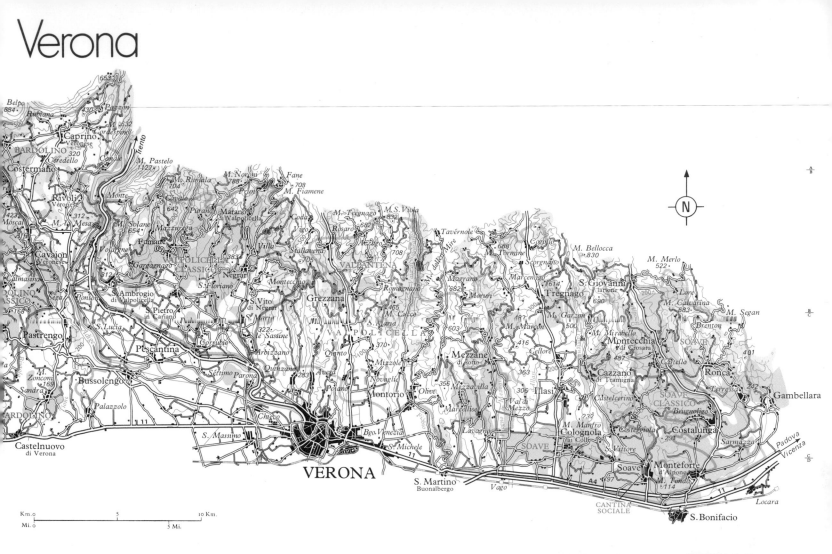

THE LOVINGLY-GARDENED Verona hills, stretching from Soave, east of the city, westwards to Lake Garda, are so fertile that vegetation is uncontrollable; the vine runs riot on terrace and pergola, among villas which are the image of Italian grace.

Their Soave is probably Italy's most famous white wine. The region is tiny, and largely controlled by its cantina sociale, said to be the biggest in Europe. Considering the large-scale standardization which this involves, the wine is astonishingly good. It is relevant to wonder what the result would be if, say, all the wines of Pouilly-Fuissé were to be made together in one vat.

Soave (whether simple Soave or the slightly stronger and more expensive Classico) is a plain, dry, pale white wine. It is hard to characterize it in any more exciting way. And yet it has something—it may be a particularly soft texture—which singles it out and always makes it enjoyable. Its plainness also makes it very versatile. The thing to remember is to drink it young; even three-year-old Soave is no longer so fresh as it should be.

The same is true of the red wine of Valpolicella and its sub-district Valpantena. It has a beautiful cherry colour, a gentle sweet smell, a soft light flavour and a nice trace of bitterness as you swallow—when it is young. The best Valpolicellas (some are even kept in glass rather than wood from the start to stop them aging) come from a few small producers in the Classico heart of the district—the prettiest imaginable hills. You may taste their wine with them, eating their bread and grilled sausage, and think you have never tasted better in the world. They will insist you go on to taste their

Above: cypresses, pale stone and leggy vines in grass like a garden: Castelnuovo di Verona in Bardolino is typical of the gentle Veronese country
Right: Verona and Garda wines are gentle, too; pale and smooth. White Soave and cherry-red Valpolicella are the best. Stronger Recioto is locally esteemed

Recioto (sweet) or Amarone (strong and dry); dark and sometimes fizzy; made of grapes dried in racks in well-ventilated lofts until after Christmas.

Almost every part of Italy makes some of its wine from grapes dried either in this way or in the sun, and prizes it highly. Verona's Reciotos are some of the best.

Bardolino is a paler, more insubstantial wine than Valpolicella—almost a rosé; drinkable as soon as it is made. Chiaretto del Garda, from the opposite side of the lake, is similar.

Central Italy

THE BEST-LOVED Italian wines, best-known to travellers, most drunk in restaurants from Soho to Sydney, are encompassed by the big map opposite. Above all Chianti, whose zone with its Classico heart (see next pages) occupies the better part of Tuscany. Chianti is *the* central Italian wine, and it is red. Curiously enough, though, this is the one part of Italy whose white wines outnumber the red and (Chianti aside) overshadow them in personality.

The island of Elba makes the best-known Tuscan white: Procanico, with plenty of acidity, the natural partner for fish—sometimes, indeed, in a fish-shaped bottle. Tiny Giglio and the Argentario peninsula make Ansonica, which is similar. San Gimignano on the fringe of Chianti makes a good dry Vernaccia. Michelangelo is quoted as saying that it 'kisses, licks, bites, thrusts and stings'—such lively tasting notes are rare.

On the other side of Chianti in the Val di Chiana and round the River Arbia north of Siena delicate white wines are made—more kiss than thrust. And there is Montecarlo, good white (and red) from Montecatini Terme in the north of Tuscany.

Umbria's only famous wine is white—and comes, indeed, from the very borders of Lazio, from Orvieto. It is a sweet wine, but not intended for dessert; not liquorous or lush. Various means are used for keeping Orvieto sweet or abboccato, rather than letting all the sugar ferment away. The classical one is to keep some half-dried grapes to add to the wine when it is nearly ready for bottling, and then to pasteurize it in bottle. A dry version is made, which does not have the very pleasant delicacy of the sweet. Even those who will normally only drink dry white wines are seduced by the fragrant lightness which Orvieto can have, and will sit happily for hours in the restaurant facing the glittering cathedral, drinking it with fish, pasta, meat, cheese. . . .

Orvieto is late in becoming DOC. There are local difficulties about where the district should begin and end. But there are some where it was easier, such as Est! Est! Est! round Lake Bolsena and Pitigliano nearby, whose wine is not nearly so good.

The Roman wines are white too. They tend to be thought of, and referred to, as Frascati whether they really are or whether they come from the more broadly defined Castelli Romani. For Frascati at its best is another of Italy's most exciting wines: strong, fragrant, with a sweet flavour of ripe and golden grape skins and yet finally quite dry. The deep cellars of Frascati date from ancient Rome and hold more than any modern vintage has ever made. It is worth going out from Rome to taste the wine cold in a jug brought from its own cave, and to eat roast pork and bread with it in the open air: an experience to carry a romantic back 2,000 years.

More wine was made down this coast in ancient times than is today (see map on page 13). The DOC Aprilia, for white Trebbiano and red Merlot and Sangiovese, does not correspond with the old Albanum, which grew on the hills further from the sea. Cesanese, the red wine from south of the Castelli Romani, may be a descendant, but the hills behind Gaeta and Formia, some of Rome's most important vineyards then, no longer bear the vine.

The east coast also has its much-loved white; the Verdicchio dei Castelli di Jesi which appears in Italian restaurants all over the world in vase-shaped bottles—one better than fish-shaped bottles, one may think. Verdicchio is pale, full of flavour but not too heavy, and very dry: an admirable all-purpose table wine, without leading to raptures. Its neighbour Bianchello is similar.

The Vernaccia and the Trebbiano, both grapes familiar from other parts of Italy, make their appearance in Marche and the Adriatic end of Emilia-Romagna without special distinction. The white Albana is better; it is the restaurant wine of Bologna to the north, famous for its cooking. You can expect a good clean medium-dry white wine but no more.

DOCs are thick on the ground along the Adriatic coast. Territory has been staked out for the red Sangiovese di Romagna, for Rosso Conero and Rosso Piceno, both made from the Montepulciano grape (Montepulciano is both a grape *and* a town, making the customary Italian confusion still worse), and Montepulciano di Abruzzo. The quality of these red wines declines from north to south.

One lonely little DOC lies in the heart of Umbria—the red Torgiano. It is a much better wine than you would expect to find on its own up in the hills; full and rounded with a good scent and plenty of substance.

Strong and usually sweet wines are the speciality of Sardinia. Cannonau and Oliena, her best-known red wines, are too heavy and sweet for most visitors. The favourites are Vernaccia, a strong dry white which has a distinct affinity with sherry, and Nuragus, a good dry white wine without too much alcohol and with (sometimes) a firmness which makes it really appetizing. Sardinia is to watch, as they say of promising young actors.

Left: 'promiscuous cultivation' is the graphic term for the happy-go-lucky way vines are scattered among trees and crops in central Italy. Little has changed in the 50 years since this photograph was taken
Below: the famous wines of central Italy, apart from Chianti, are white: Frascati, Orvieto, Verdicchio

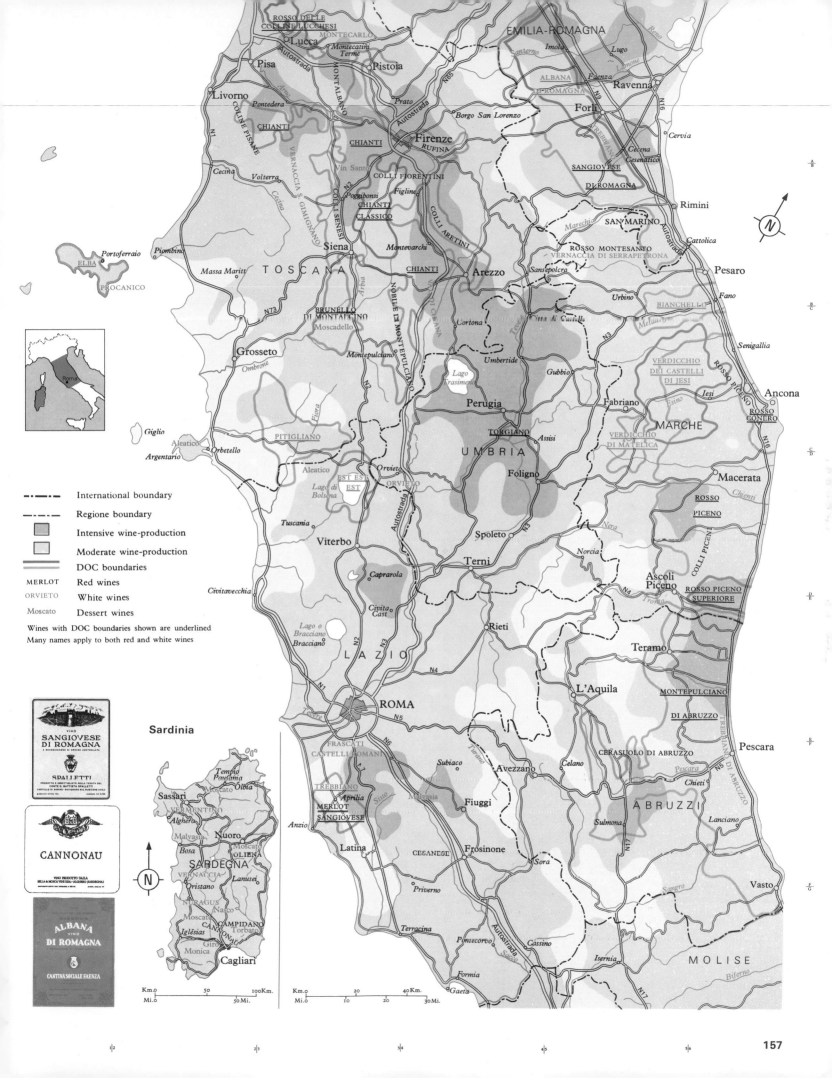

Chianti

THE HILLS between Florence and Siena come as near to the Roman poet's idea of gentlemanly country life as anywhere on earth. The blending of landscape and architecture and agriculture is ancient and profound. The villas, the cypresses, the vines, the rocks and woods compose pictures which could be Roman, Renaissance, Risorgimento . . . there is no way of telling.

In this timeless scene vineyards, in the sense of ranks of disciplined vines, are the only newcomers. Traditionally vines and olive-trees have clothed the dry gritty and sandy slopes together. On a recent agricultural map of Tuscany still not a single piece of vineyard was marked as such: the symbol everywhere was 'vines and olives'. Yet this is Chianti, and the world's entire supply (27 million gallons, of which 3¾ million gallons are Chianti Classico) must come from these apparently primitive plots. It is no surprise that the olives are losing, and files of vines are beginning to march up hill and down dale.

Chianti is more orderly than it seems. It was one of the first Italian wine areas to organize a consorzio of producers and discipline itself. The concept of Chianti Classico, the central and best area (mapped here), among six others with district names (Chianti Rufina, north-east of Florence, being the best of them), was established long before the present law of DOC. Not that it prevented a disgraceful amount of wine from elsewhere in Italy being sold as Chianti.

The wine is made from four grape varieties. A formula was established 100 years ago by the illustrious Baron Ricasoli, sometime Prime Minister of Italy, whose descendants still live in his castle at Brolio and (there and at Meleto) make the same wine. Chianti for current drinking is livened up in an unusual way by the addition of a little unfermented must of dried grapes (a trick known as 'il governo') after it has fermented; the result is a faint prickle which helps to make it refreshing.

The best Chianti, however, is left untreated and aged for longer in oak before being bottled. It is distinguished from the common wine by appearing in Bordeaux bottles instead of the pretty tubby flask which means Chianti, if not Italian wine itself, to all the world.

Both styles of Chianti, the current and the Riserva, are outstandingly good at their best and in their respective ways. In a trattoria in Florence the house wine to drink with the magnificently tender and tasty steaks is sometimes as compulsively drinkable as Beaujolais; faintly sweet, just frizzante, grape-smelling, with a delicious slight edge to it. A ten-year-old bottle of Riserva, on the other hand, sums up the warmth and attractiveness of Italian wine with a delicacy of its own. Its scent is powerful and it remains marvellously lively.

At Siena a unique institution, the Enoteca or Wine Library of Italy, housed in an old Medici fortress, provides an opportunity to taste not only every possible Chianti but most other Italian wines of note, with good food.

The map shows, besides the chaotic hilliness of the Chianti countryside, and the scattering of vines and olives among woods, the cellars of most of the leading producers of Chianti Classico. Two very important firms, Melini and Bertolli, have their premises just beyond the Classico boundary to the west, which does not, of course, prevent them making Chianti Classico from grapes grown within the region. One firm outside the region altogether, Frescobaldi at Nipozzano north-east of Florence, also makes Chianti of the very highest standard.

Southern Italy

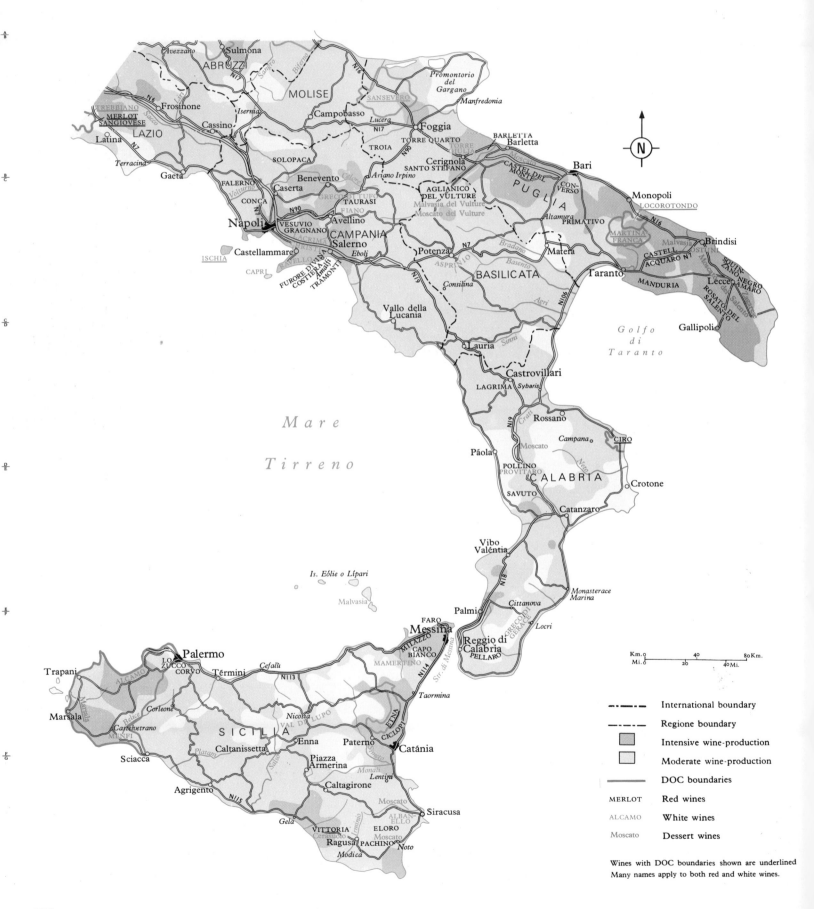

Avezzano Sulmona
ABRUZZI
MOLISE
Biferno
N16
Promontorio del Gargano
Manfredonia
SANSEVERO
N6 Frosinone Isernia Campobasso Lucera
TREBBIANO
MERLOT
SANGIOVESE
LAZIO Cassino N17 TORRE QUARTO Foggia BARLETTA
Latina SOLOPACA TROIA N90 Barletta
Terracina FALERNO Benevento Ariano Irpino Cerignola SANTO STEFANO CASTEL DEL MONTE Bari
Gaeta Caserta Volturno GRECO DI TUFO AGLIANICO DEL VULTURE CON-VERSO
CONCA N90 TAURASI Malvasia del Vulture Monopoli
FIANO Moscato del Vulture LOCOROTONDO
Napoli VESUVIO Avellino Altamura PRIMATIVO MARTINA FRANCA
Castellammare GRAGNANO CAMPANIA Malvasia Brindisi
ISCHIA Salerno Eboli Potenza N7 Matera CASTELL ACQUARO N7 SQUIN-ZANO Lecce
CAPRI RAVELLO Taranto MANDURIA NEGRO AMARO ROSATO DEL SALENTO
FURORE D'UVA COSTIERA Consilina BASILICATA
TRAMONTI Vallo della Lucania Agri N106 Gallipoli
Golfo di Taranto
Lauria Sinni
Mare Castrovillari
Tirreno LAGRIMA Sybaris
Cratι Rossano
POLLINO Campana CIRO
Páola PROVITARO Moscato Neto Crotone
CALABRIA
SAVUTO
Catanzaro
Vibo Valéntia
Is. Eólie o Lípari N18 Monasterace Marina
Malvasia Palmi Cittanova
FARO GRECO DI GERACE Locri
Messina MILAZZO
Palermo CAPO BIANCO Reggio di Calabria
LO ZUCCO MAMERTINO PELLARO
Trapani ALCAMO CORVO Cefalù N114 Str. di Messina
Marsala Corleone TÉRMINI N113 Taormina
Castelvetrano Nicosia ETNA
MENFI VAL DI LUPO CICLOPI
SICILIA Enna Paternò Catánia
Sciacca Caltanissetta Piazza Armerina
Agrigento Caltagirone Lentini
N115 Monati
Platani Moscato
Gela ALBAN-ELLO Siracusa
VITTORIA Cerasuolo ELORO
Ragusa Moscato
Modica PACHINO Noto

Km. 0   40   80 Km.
Mi. 0   20   40 Mi.

—·—·— International boundary
—··—··— Regione boundary
▨ Intensive wine-production
▧ Moderate wine-production
—— DOC boundaries
MERLOT Red wines
ALCAMO White wines
Moscato Dessert wines

Wines with DOC boundaries shown are underlined
Many names apply to both red and white wines.

THERE IS ALWAYS a faint air of unreality about any complete list of Italian wines. There are indeed that many names—but are there that many identities? The question is impossible to answer. It depends on the farmer, or more often today the co-operative. Some proud local traditions, particularly here in the south, go straight into the blending vat every year to emerge as anything from Austrian wine to Beaujolais. Those wines of southern Italy which do appear in public are gaining ground, however. They used to be mere poor relations, selling (if they sold at all) on the power of association—the vine-hung terraces of Amalfi—alone. The climate coupled with old methods usually produced flat wines, deficient in acidity. But modern methods improve them every year, even as they lessen the differences.

In Campania, Ischia was not slow to define the limits of its red and white wines for a DOC. It is easy enough to do with an island. Sicily staked out Marsala for its delicious treacly-dark aperitif wine like a distant (coloured) cousin of sherry, and the foot-hills north, east and south of Mount Etna for their above-average table wines.

Calabria registered Cirò for its dark red, rosé and white wines. Puglia delimited Sansevero, Martinafranca and Locorotondo—largely, it is said, for the quality of neutrality which makes them a useful base wine for vermouth. But this still leaves most of the more interesting wines to be defined.

Most famous of them are the ones tourists meet around Naples. Lacrima Christi has become a brand name for normally inoffensive, sometimes good red and white wines from the area of Mount Vesuvius.

Capri has long been a sort of brand name for white wines; though those of the island itself are said to be much better than most 'Capri'.

Ravello wines, particularly those made by the Caruso family, are well-balanced, fresher than most of the south (the altitude of Ravello and its sea-mists are said to help).

Less known than the wines of the Campanian coast are those inland: Taurasi, the strong dark monarch of the Aglianico family, and the lesser Aglianicos (though you would never suspect it from the name) del Vulture. Of Basilicata the only other known wine is white Asprinio, which the Potenzans manage to make mercifully unpotent compared with most southern whites.

It is strange to think of the ancient city of Sybaris, the byword for luxury, being on the barren east coast of Calabria. Ignorance and poverty have long since made a dust-bowl—here and in Sicily—of what the Greeks considered to be the garden of the Mediterranean.

More than any of the wines of Puglia, except possibly the very good rosé of Castel del Monte and Bari, it is the Sicilian wines which are regaining their reputation today. Marsala has been famous since Nelson's day, when he fortified the Royal Navy with it. But Corvo's good straightforward red and white, the wines of Etna (particularly Ciclopi), Faro red and Val di Lupo white, sweet Mamertino—a survivor, at least in name, from ancient times—and the various moscatos and malvasias of Siracusa and Noto and the islands of Lipari and of Pantelleria (100 miles south-west of Agrigento) are all appearing outside Sicily.

In parts of Sicily every cottage seems to have either grapes for their vino passito or brilliant red bowls of tomato pulp drying and concentrating their sweetness by the door.

If most of the wines of southern Italy are still used for blending or local consumption there is distinct evidence that improvement and export are on the increase. Much more so than, for example, in Spain. The talent is there. For the other great export of southern Italy has been wine-makers. Some of the best of those in the Americas took ship from Naples.

Spain

Left: Spain's one really great wine is sherry, from Andalucia. At a *caserio*, where sherry is made, a mule fetches water from the well in the porous amphoras which keep it cool in the heat

SPAIN has the distinction of having more land under vines than any other country—even Italy. Curiously enough, however, she has only a third of Italy's production of wine. This anomaly is partly due to different ideas of what constitutes a vineyard; mixed planting of vines and other crops in Spain may be included, and in Italy (where it happens almost everywhere) omitted. Partly, though, it reflects the slightly desultory nature of a great deal of Spain's wine industry. With the exception of Jerez, one of the most highly-organized wine regions of the world, and perhaps the Rioja, the wine regions of Spain tend to be casually defined and their activities a touch penumbral.

Individual growers occasionally stand out like good deeds in a naughty world, but in the main Spanish wine is just wine, not so highly regarded by its makers that its blending, or labelling under what we may politely call a pseudonym, causes them any heartache.

The quality wine regions (Jerez and Rioja, Montilla and Catalonia) are separately mapped on subsequent pages. What immediately emerges from the maps opposite is the huge concentration of production on the plains of La Mancha, south-east of Madrid. The town of Valdepeñas gives its name to a large part of this production; chiefly red, strong (about 13%) but light-tasting and not unpleasant vino de pasto which is drunk with little if any aging. Much of it is still made in huge earthenware pots (*tinajas*) like Roman amphorae ten feet high. Less attractively it is often transported in wineskins, the *pellejos* of whole pigs among which Don Quixote wrought such havoc.

The next highest production, though way behind La Mancha, is in Valencia and Utiel-Requeña, and consists of heavier and sweeter red wines (in the main) than those of the inland plain. The whole of this coast is a great reservoir of blending wine. The Jumilla-Denia region (strong reds and strong whites), Alicante and Tarragona (also substantial reds and whites) are the same. The market for a large proportion of all this is the blending vats of France and Germany, where it makes up for the thinness of the cheap local product.

In the scattered inland regions of the north and west, production is smaller. The name Cariñena is commonly applied to the heavy wines of Aragon, red, white or sweet, as Valdepeñas is to the wine of La Mancha. Navarre is a small producer; the best of its red wines, from Las Campanas, is good, though still over-weight. In the Basque north there is a speciality called Chacolí, a thin white with, in contrast, no more alcohol than a moselle—and only worth making into brandy, according to one authority.

Westwards in Castile the wine region of La Nava makes well-balanced red and white wines of moderate strength. Toro is another red heavy-weight.

North-west Spain is largely cider country, but Ribeiro and Pontevedra make 'green' wine like the Portuguese speciality. One area, Valle de Rosal, is famous for its Albariño, the best green-wine grape variety.

More or less common wines are made round Madrid (in the Cebreros area) and in Extremadura (Cáceres and Almendralejo). It is not till the coast of Andalucia at Huelva that very interesting wines are made . . . and these have no reputation, since the best of them have long gone to market as sherry. Most of Huelva's production is white wine, much of it in the sherry class, even if not at the top of it.

Andalucia's other famous name (sherry is discussed on pages 164–167) is Malaga. Malaga—once known as Mountain—is one of the great has-beens of wine. The fashion for such dark sweet wines, unless they have the finesse of port or sherry or madeira, has passed. And yet good Malaga is—good Malaga.

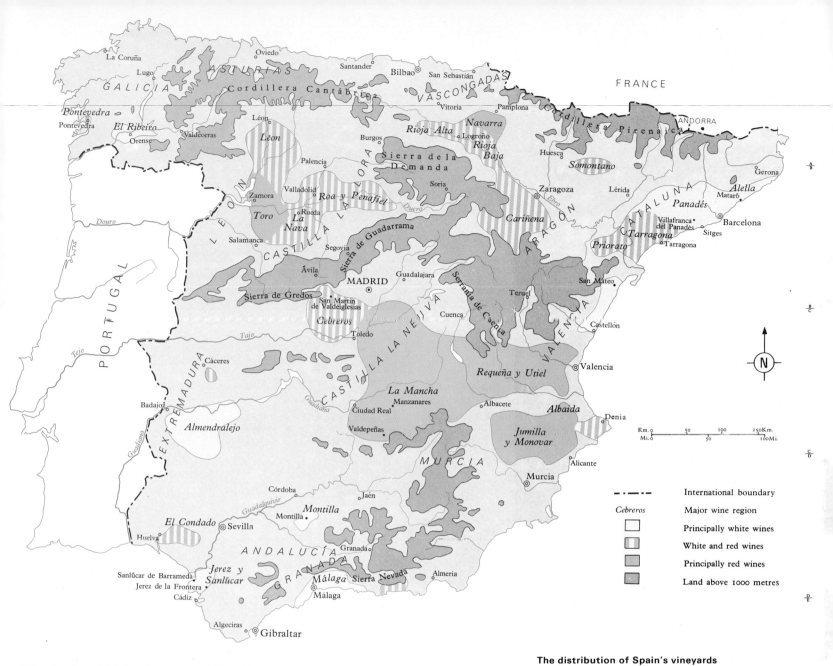

Wine-production map legend:

- — · — · — International boundary
- *Cebreros* Major wine region
- Principally white wines
- White and red wines
- Principally red wines
- Land above 1000 metres

Below: few Spanish labels are known abroad. Most of her table wine which is not drunk locally is blended

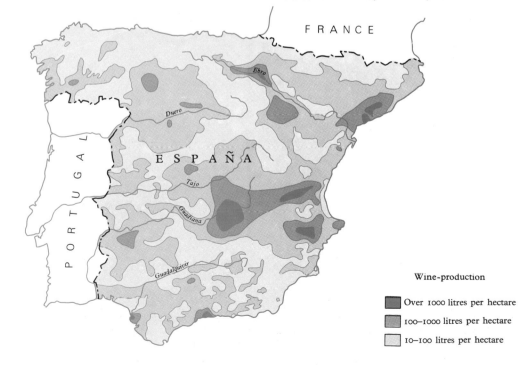

The distribution of Spain's vineyards

Wine-production

- Over 1000 litres per hectare
- 100–1000 litres per hectare
- 10–100 litres per hectare

The Sherry Country

FINESSE—meaning fine-ness in its most literal sense, a combination of strength and delicacy —is not one of the qualities you normally find in scorched-earth wines. Where the sun fairly grills the ground, and the grapes ripen as warm as fruit in a pie, wine sometimes develops wonderful thews and sinews, power and depth. But finesse . . .

This is sherry's great distinction. It is a question of chalk; of the breed of the Palomino grape; of huge investment and long-inherited skill. Not every bottle of sherry, by a very long way, has this quality. But a real fino; the rarely-shipped unstrengthened produce of the bare white chalk dunes of Macharnudo or Sanlúcar de Barrameda, is an expression of wine and wood as vivid and beautiful as any in the world.

One does not think of sherry normally in direct comparison with the other great white wines of the world—but it is, strange to say, the cheapest of them, even bodega-bottled and fully mature, ready to drink.

The sherry country, between the romantic-sounding cities of Cadiz and Seville, is almost a caricature of grandee Spain. Here are the bull ranches, the caballeros, the castles on the sky-line, the patios, the guitars, the night-turned-into-day. Jerez de la Frontera, the town that gives its name to sherry, lives and breathes sherry as Beaune does burgundy and Epernay champagne.

The comparison between sherry and champagne can be carried a long way. Both are white wines with a distinction given them by chalk soil, both needing long traditional treatment

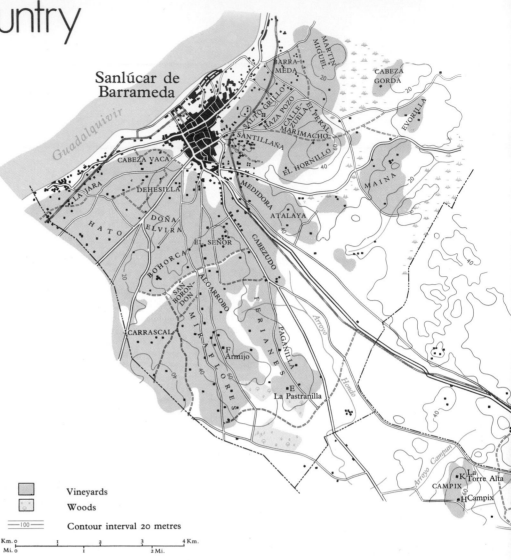

Sanlúcar de Barrameda

Vineyards

Woods

Contour interval 20 metres

Km. 0   1   2   3   4 Km.
Mi. 0   1   2 Mi.

Right and below: there is a strange dazzling light reflected off the chalk in the sherry vineyards. Golden Palomino grapes almost cook in the heat; before they are pressed they are often laid out on esparto mats in the sun to sweeten even more, so that their high sugar content will give strong and stable wine. The miracle is that it is delicate as well

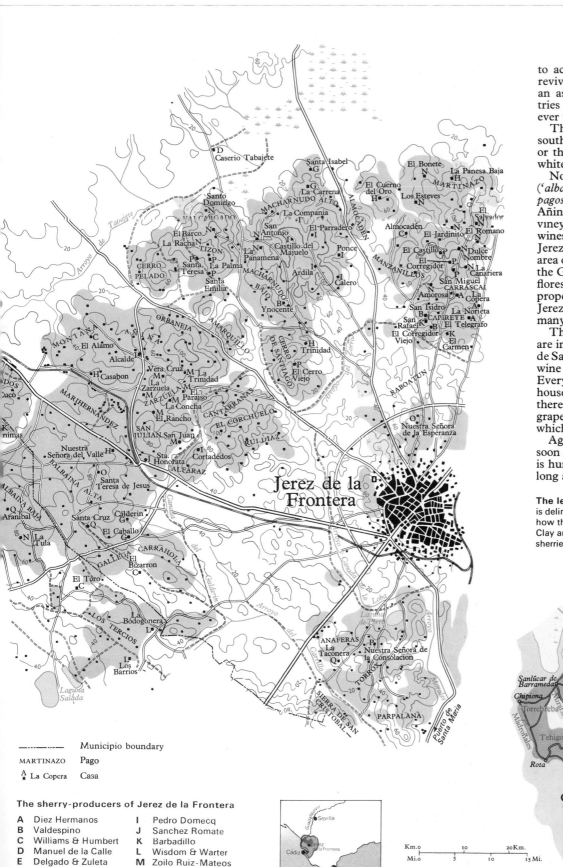

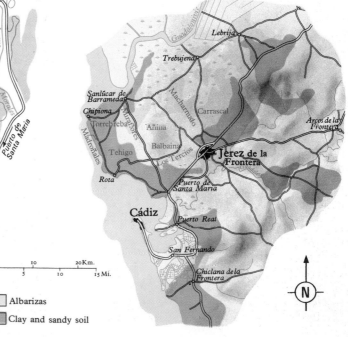

to achieve their special characters. Both are revivifying aperitifs, of which you can drink an astonishing amount in their home countries and only feel more alive than you have ever felt before.

They are the far-northern and the far-southern interpretation of the same equation, or the same poem: the white grape from the white ground.

Not all the ground is white. The chalk areas ('*albarizas*' on the map below) are best; the *pagos* (districts) of Carrascal, Macharnudo, Añina and Balbaina the most famous. Some vineyards are on sand and produce second-rank wines for blending. The main vineyards of Jerez, to the west of the town, and the distinct area of Sanlúcar de Barrameda further west on the Guadalquivir, with its famous *pago*, Miraflores, are enlarged on the big map. The properties of most of the principal owners of Jerez are shown; Sanlúcar is divided among many smaller owners, impracticable to show.

The shippers' headquarters and bodegas are in the towns of Jerez, Sanlúcar and Puerto de Santa Maria. But traditionally they make the wine at their *caserios* among their vineyards. Every hill-top seems to have its low white house. The workers eat and sometimes sleep there at vintage time, and there they tread the grapes in boots with protruding rows of nails which crush the skins but spare the pips.

Again in the same way as in Champagne, as soon as the must is separated from the skins it is hurried into town, to ferment and begin its long and vital processing.

The legal area for sherry
is delimited largely in terms of the soils. This map shows how the best region falls in *albarizas* (or chalk zones) Clay and sandy soil zones make useful blending sherries; never the classical finos

---

Municipio boundary

MARTINAZO   Pago

A̅ La Copera   Casa

The sherry-producers of Jerez de la Frontera

A	Diez Hermanos	I	Pedro Domecq
B	Valdespino	J	Sanchez Romate
C	Williams & Humbert	K	Barbadillo
D	Manuel de la Calle	L	Wisdom & Warter
E	Delgado & Zuleta	M	Zoilo Ruiz-Mateos
F	Gaspar F. Florido Cano	N	Gonzalez Byass
G	Jose de Soto	O	Emilio Lustau
H	Garvey	P	Sandeman
		Q	Fernando A. de Terry

Km.0   10   20Km.
Mi.0   5   10   15 Mi.

☐ Albarizas

▨ Clay and sandy soil

Jerez de la Frontera

THERE ARE little bars in Jerez where the tapas, the morsels of food without which no Jerezano puts glass to mouth, constitute a banquet. From olives and cheese to prawns, to raw ham, to peppery little sausages, to lobster claws, to miniature steaks streaked with amber onions, the path of temptation is broad and long.

Your little copita, a glass no more imposing than an opening tulip, fills and empties with a paler wine, a cooler wine, a more druggingly delicious wine than you have ever tasted. It seems at the same time dry as dust and just teasingly sweet, so that you have to sip again to trace the suggestion of grapes.

It comes in half bottles, kept on ice. A half bottle is reckoned a reasonable drink to spin out over an hour or two among the tapas. And in half bottles it stays as fresh as it was when it left the bodega—for no bottle is left half-full.

The most celebrated sights of Jerez are the bodegas of the shipping houses. Their towering whitewashed aisles, dim-roofed and criss-crossed with sunbeams, are irresistibly cath-edral-like. In them, in ranks of butts sometimes five tiers high, the new wine is put to mature. It will not leave until it has gone through an elaborate blending process which is known as the solera system.

The first job when the new wine has got over its fermentation is to sort it into categories; better or worse, lighter or more full-bodied. Each wine is put into the *criadera*, or nursery, appropriate to its character. Each character, or category, of wine has a traditional name.

From these *criaderas* the shipper tops up a number of soleras, consisting of perhaps 20, perhaps several hundred butts; each wine again going into the solera nearest to its character. As new wine goes into butts at one end of the solera, mature wine for blending is drawn from the other. The solera system is simply a pro-gressive topping up of older barrels from younger of the same style, so that wine is con-tinuously being blended, and hence always emerges tasting the same.

The solera wines are the shipper's paintbox for the blending of his brands, or for brands ordered by other wine merchants for sale under their own names. Most sherry when it is sold is a blend of several, sweetened and strengthened to the public's taste. The few 'straight solera' sherries which are sold tend to be unsweetened and therefore wines for the connoisseur.

The categories into which all young sherry is classified begin with fino. Finos are the best sherries: delicate and distinctive wines which will need a minimum of blending and sweeten-ing. They will age excellently, but they also have the qualities which make them perfect young. Their strong individuality comes from an unusual form of yeast, flor, which forms on their surface. Tasted from the butt, when the *capataz* of the bodega thrusts his long cane-handled *venencia* through the flor into the pale wine to bring out a sample, they have a magical new-bread freshness and vitality; they

The solera system in action: sherry from younger butts, higher in the pile, is siphoned into jugs and poured from a height into an older, lower butt. The pouring allows air to mix with the wine

The sherry bodegas of Jerez de la Frontera

1	Williams & Humbert	6	Garvey
2	Zoilo Ruiz-Mateos	7	Valdespino
3	Gonzalez Byass	8	Pedro Domecq
4	Sandeman	9	La Riva
5	Diez Hermanos	10	Agustin Blazquez

are, beyond question, Spain's finest wine of all.

Amontillado—a softer, darker wine—comes next. The best amontillados are old finos, finos which did not quite have the right freshness to be drunk young, though the name is often used in commerce for middle-character blends of no real distinction. Great amontillado soleras (for only from the solera can you taste the real individuality of the wine) are dry and almost stingingly powerful of flavour, with a dark, fat, rich tang—but words fall short.

Oloroso is the third principal class. Wines which have great possibilities for aging, but which seem a little heavy at first, go into this solera. They are the basis for the best sweet sherries—often known as milk or cream, which suggests their silky fatness.

Sweetening wines and colouring wines for blending are specially made from sun-dried grapes and kept in their own soleras. Lesser wines which go into cheaper blends are known as *rayas*, and a final rare character, something between fino and oloroso, as *palo cortado*.

In addition there are the wines of Sanlúcar de Barrameda, known as manzanillas. Manzanilla finos are some of the most delicate and lovely of all, always with a faintly salty tang which is held to come from the sea. A manzanilla amontillado is rare, but can be exquisite, salty and brown as burnt butter.

No blend, medium-sweet or sweet as most blends are, can compare with these astonishing natural sherries. They are as much collectors' pieces as great domaine-bottled burgundies.

Right: a trade directory lists over 600 brands of sherry. Many of them, including some famous ones, belong to wine merchants who have no establishment in Spain. They order wine to their own specifications, for sale under their own name, from one of the big shipping houses. Most of the best sherries, however, come from bodegas, large or small, who bottle their own style of wine themselves. All have a wide range from dry to sweet; these labels are a representative selection

The most famous fino of all does not mention fino on the label. Extremely dry, fresh and young with real delicacy

Tres Palmas is the conventional sign on the butt for a superlative fino. La Riva bottles some very old sherries as well

Excellent light fino from Valdespino's Ynocente vineyard in Macharnudo; the only sherry vineyard named on a label

A very pale and dry manzanilla, from one of the bigger shippers in Sanlúcar de Barrameda, where big ones are few

The De Terry bodegas are in Puerto de Santa Maria, seven miles south of Jerez on the sea, the second town of the Jerez area

The Garvey family came to Jerez from Ireland originally. They have called their best fino after Ireland's patron saint

Dos Cortados is the sign for very dry oloroso with great distinction. Williams & Humbert's is one of the best sherries sold

Varela is another of the shippers with bodegas in Puerto de Santa Maria. A typical popular, middle-ranking fino

An old, unsweetened (*al natural*) wine from a good small shipper. Amontillado character, though it does not say so

Duff Gordon is the export name of Bodegas Osborne El Cid is their most popular wine. It is a medium-sweet amontillado

A magnificent old dry oloroso from Macharnudo, one of the best wines from one of the biggest and best shippers

No type is mentioned. It is hard to know what to expect from this bottle; in fact the wine is a pungent, dark, dry oloroso

Old oloroso is the basis for good sweet sherries; the cream style is very sweet but should not mask the nuttiness of the base

The most famous of all Creams come from a British firm in Bristol, made to their requirements in Jerez

A firm equally famous for port and sherry. Pemartin is the name of an old bodega, given to one of their sweet wines

Rioja

Left: much of Rioja outside the river valley has a bare highland feeling emphasised by the Sierra de Cantabria in the distance, often snow-covered. Vineyards, crops and pasture alternate on the stony ground. The vines grow as low bushes without posts or wires

RIOJA has long had a virtual monopoly of the wine lists of good restaurants in Spain. They offer local wine, often free, in carafes. But if you want bottled wine, especially red wine, Rioja is the Bordeaux and the Burgundy of Spain. You will get Rioja.

It is partly a question of human geography, as well as the physical kind. Rioja is not far from the French frontier; not far from Bordeaux. When the phylloxera arrived in the 1870s many wine growers took off for Spain. They found in Rioja rather different conditions, but an opportunity to make good wine all the same. Then the phylloxera caught up with them, and they went home. But they left French methods and ideas.

Rioja is distinctly mountainous in atmosphere. It lies in the shelter of the Sierra de Cantabria to the north, but its best vineyards are still 1500 feet above sea level. They get plenty of rain and long springs and autumns, rather than endless parching summers. The wine is correspondingly less hearty and more interesting than other Spanish wine: well-made and at the right age exceedingly delicate and fine, yet with a faintly toasted sweet warmth which seems to proclaim it Spanish.

The area is divided into three by terrain and altitude. The areas further up-river, Rioja Alta and Rioja Alavesa (in the province of Alava, whereas the rest is in Logroño) are cooler and wetter. Rioja Alta (the high Rioja) has the lightest and best wines; Alavesa slightly stronger but still excellent reds. Rioja Baja (the low Rioja) has a more Mediterranean climate. Its wines are more alcoholic and only

used for the cheaper blends of Rioja, or as vino corriente on their own. The division comes around the town of Logroño, one of the two main centres of the wine trade.

The chief wine centre is Haro. The rather insignificant town is dwarfed by its outskirts, which contain 12 large bodegas—half the total of Rioja. The country round is beautiful in an upland way: tall poplars and eucalyptus trees line the roads; orchards cover slopes along with tilting fields of vines, each vine an individual bush without posts or wires. In the rocky valley-bottom the infant river Ebro, draining the Sierra de Cantabria eastwards towards the Mediterranean, is joined by the little Rio Oja, whose shortened name the region has adopted.

There are no wine estates, large or small, in Rioja which grow, make and bottle their own wine. In many matters of technique the Bordelais left their mark, but châteaux and château-bottling are not among them. To qualify for the Certificate of Origin of Rioja a bodega has to be big enough, and the big bodegas operate as sherry houses do, or the wineries of California. They buy grapes from farmers to supplement those they grow themselves, and make a blend of wine of their own house style. Vineyard names appear frequently on Rioja bottles: Viña Tondonia, Zaco, Paceta, Pomal are all well-known. But they have no direct relation to the plot of land in question. They are used as brand names for the better wines by the shippers.

The best Rioja wine is red. It is made from a mixture of grapes, of which only the Garnacha (the pale red Grenache of the Rhône) is familiar.

Bordeaux- and burgundy-shaped bottles are used for, respectively, the drier and the fuller wines. Very pale red is called Clarete.

By and large these wines are made as Bordeaux was in the last century; with the idea that they should be aged for several years in barrels (two or three for ordinary wine; up to ten for Reservas) until their darkness and fruitiness has been tamed and replaced with the almost tawny colour and soft vanilla flavour which comes from oak. In Spain (where most red wine is inky) they are much appreciated light and smooth as a long time in wood makes them. By modern French standards they should be bottled earlier, so they can develop a bouquet in bottle, still with much of their fruitiness in them. It is a question of taste, but certainly many Rioja wines are older than would seem necessary; whereas the French usually err the other way.

Even white Rioja wines are often given four or five years in barrel; when they have grown round, golden and rather flat from oxidization they are reckoned at their prime, whereas earlier, sometimes marvellously stony and up to Rhône white-wine standards, they are considered too young. The dry whites are better than the sweet, which have no *pourriture noble* to concentrate their sugar and tend to be medium rather than honey-sweet.

Vintage years are treated lightly. If a vintage is stated it is a good one, even if there is no guarantee that all the wine in the bottle was made that year. Among white wines look for the youngest, among red wines look for one ten years old or even more.

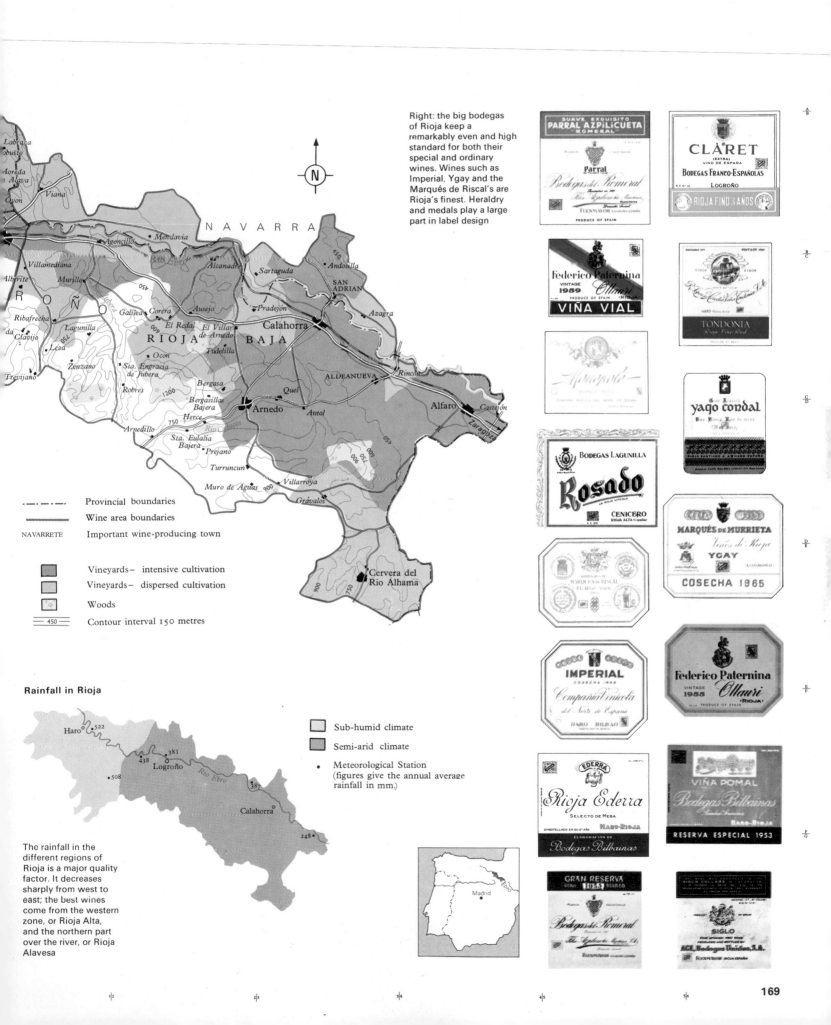

Right: the big bodegas of Rioja keep a remarkably even and high standard for both their special and ordinary wines. Wines such as Imperial, Ygay and the Marqués de Riscal's are Rioja's finest. Heraldry and medals play a large part in label design

Provincial boundaries

Wine area boundaries

NAVARRETE Important wine-producing town

Vineyards– intensive cultivation

Vineyards– dispersed cultivation

Woods

450 Contour interval 150 metres

Rainfall in Rioja

Sub-humid climate

Semi-arid climate

• Meteorological Station (figures give the annual average rainfall in mm.)

The rainfall in the different regions of Rioja is a major quality factor. It decreases sharply from west to east; the best wines come from the western zone, or Rioja Alta, and the northern part over the river, or Rioja Alavesa

Catalonia

ON A COAST whose production is nearly all heavy and dark red wine for the world's blending vats it is a surprise to come across the world's biggest cellars for sparkling wine. But Catalonia is different from the rest of Mediterranean Spain. The Catalans have more vitality; are more demanding, destructive, creative. Several of their denominaciós de origen should be taken more seriously than they are by the world, which at present looks to them merely as a source of cheap wine.

The Panadés sparkling wine (the centre of the industry is San Sadurní de Noya and the big cellars those of Codorníu) is extremely good. The export quality at least is well-matured, clean and very dry—with none of champagne's richness and finesse, it is true. Some of the other white wines of the coast are also remarkably light and well-balanced. Those of Alella labelled Marfil (the word means 'ivory' —a fair image for them) are perhaps the best.

There is however a tendency to go too far in the treatments which make the wine pale and light—some of it is practically colourless, whereas nature gave it a good golden sheen. The most expensive bottles are therefore sometimes not so good as the well-chosen carafe wine of, for example, Barcelona's great fish restaurants. In fishing villages north of Barcelona the white wine put on the table with the bread and included in the cover charge can turn out to have the most difficult thing for a southern wine to achieve; freshness combined with full golden depth.

The name of Tarragona can only be used for sweet fortified wine. Priorato is a small area within it which specializes in strong dry red wine. Sitges in Panadés also has its own denominación for sweet Malvasia and muscat wine.

Above: the best of Catalan wine (which includes good sparkling wine) is surprisingly dry and delicate compared with the heavy sweet produce of Tarragona
Left: Picasso, Barcelona-born, designed a wine jug on the theme of Don Quixote and his mare

Montilla

─ · ─ · ─ · ─ Provincial boundary

─────── Denominación de Origen boundary

SHERRY HAS a shadow in Montilla. The very same chalk that gives rise to the marvellous finos of Jerez and Sanlúcar down on the coast recurs a hundred miles inland near Córdoba. In fact only comparatively recently, with the drawing up of boundaries, has real distinction been made between the wines of the Jerez zone and those of the similar but hotter hill area where Montilla is made.

Montilla is still little heard of abroad, though it is one of the most popular wines in Spain, with a production almost half that of Jerez. Its special attraction lies in its very high natural strength, which allows it to be shipped without fortification, in contrast to sherry, which is nearly always strengthened slightly. It seems strange to speak of delicacy in a wine with a natural strength of 16% alcohol—but this is in fact the characteristic which distinguishes all finos, and in a really good Montilla it is easy to appreciate.

The Montilla grape is the Pedro Ximénez—the one which in Jerez is kept for the sweetest wine. The even hotter inland climate of Montilla gives it an even higher sugar content which ferments rapidly (fermentation is done in open earthenware jars). The flor yeast also comes quickly. Within a year or two the wine is ready, with all the finesse of a fino, but more softness than, for example, a manzanilla, which always has a characteristic bite. Montillas make deceptively perfect aperitifs, slipping down like table wines despite their high strength. People claim to find in them the scent of black olives (which are of course their perfect partners).

Since they are shipped unfortified they have the advantage over most sherries of being exactly the wine which brings back such vivid memories of the south of Spain.

Above: the strong wines of Montilla ferment furiously in open earthenware tinajas which look like the amphoras used in the ancient world

Montilla

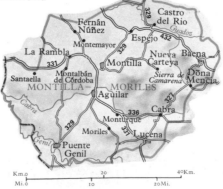

Montilla and Moriles are the two centres of the Montilla trade, still largely confined to Spain. Their most popular wines are their aperitif finos, but like Jerez they also produce old, dark and sweet wines, using the same terms—oloroso, amontillado and the rest

Madeira

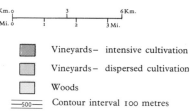

Km. 0   3   6 Km.
Mi. 0   1   2   3 Mi.

◼ Vineyards– intensive cultivation

◼ Vineyards– dispersed cultivation

◻ Woods

—500— Contour interval 100 metres

THE CLUSTER of volcanic islands 400 miles off the coast of Morocco which the ancients knew as the Enchanted Isles are known to us as Madeira, Porto Santo and the Desertas. Madeira is the largest island of the little archipelago and one of the prettiest in the world, as steep as an iceberg and as green as a glade. For over 500 years it has been considered by the Portuguese as part of Portugal.

The story goes that when the Portuguese landed on the island (at Machico in the southeast) they set fire to the dense woods covering the mountain slopes. The fire burned for seven years, leaving the already fertile soil enriched with the ashes of an entire forest.

Certainly it is fertile today. From the water's edge to over half-way up the 6,000-foot peak it is steadily terraced to make room for patches of vines, patches of sugar-cane, little flower gardens. As in northern Portugal the vines are grown above head-height in arbours, making room for yet more cultivation beneath.

Wine has been the principal product of the island for 400 years. Its natural wine, however, is not all that its beautiful vineyards seem to promise. It has a bite of acidity which makes it a taste not easy to acquire. Like port, it had to wait for a blender of genius to make it suitable for export, except as the ballast of sailing ships, to be drunk only in emergencies.

It was brandy (to stop it fermenting and keep it sweet) and travelling as ballast that made madeira. A long sea voyage, including a double crossing of the equator, would finish off any lesser wine, but it was found to hasten madeira's awkwardly long maturing process to a gallop.

Instead of long sea voyages madeira today is subjected to ordeal by fire. A similar effect to the tropical heat is produced by warming the wine over a long period to a temperature of 120°F or more. It stays in the stoves (*estufas*) where this is done for four or five months. When it comes out it has the characteristic caramel tang by which all madeiras can be recognized.

The shippers of Madeira use the solera system of Jerez to blend their wine into consistent brands. Very old soleras are quite common: the date given (i.e. Solera 1853) is when the first wine was put in.

At the peak of their prosperity in the 19th century madeira shippers used to declare vintages, as port shippers still do—but the double disaster of oidium in the 1850s and phylloxera in the 1870s, destroying the island's vines, put an end to the heyday of madeira, when it was

Above left: the breakneck slopes of Madeira are terraced for vineyards from near sea level up to 3,250 feet

Right: most madeira is labelled with the name of the shipper and the grape variety: Sercial Verdelho, Bual or Malmsey, in ascending order of richness and sweetness. The only place name used today is Cama de Lobos, famous for its sweet wines blended from Malmsey and other grapes

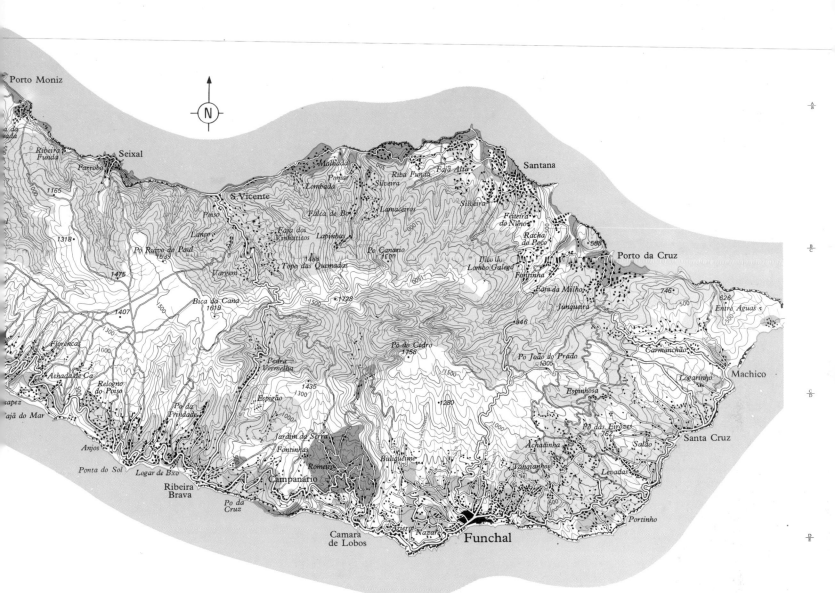

on literally every upper-class table in Britain and America. A few of the madeiras of that period still exist, none the worse for being 100 years old or more.

Today's madeira is known by the principal grape varieties used in its making. There are four, corresponding approximately to degrees of sweetness, though the sweetness is controlled not by the grape but by the amount of brandy and when it is added to the wine.

The sweetest of them all, and probably the best, is Malmsey; dark brown wine, very fragrant and rich, soft-textured and almost fatty, but with the tang of acidity and the slight taste of cooked sugar which all madeiras have. It is as good an after-dinner wine as any but excellent vintage port.

Bual madeira is lighter and slightly less sweet than Malmsey—but still distinctly a dessert wine. A good Bual is about the equivalent of a Bristol Milk-type sherry.

Verdelho is a shade less sweet than Bual; a peculiarly soft and sippable wine; the faint honey and distinct smoke of its flavour make it good either before or after meals. A light Verdelho blend used to be very popular in America under the name Rainwater.

Sercial, the driest wine of Madeira, is grown on the upper vineyards and harvested last. The legend is that the grape is none other than the Riesling of the Rhine. Like the Riesling, it is a late-ripener, not a big cropper, and gives uncommonly good wine. Sercial wine is light, fragrant, slightly sharp—it has all these things in common with Riesling, but with the madeira tang. It is more substantial than a fino sherry, but still a perfect aperitif.

Each of the shippers of madeira sells all of these wines, as brands at various price levels. Neither age nor a specific place name is normally mentioned on the label. Though it is possible that one day early 20th-century vintages will be offered on the market.

Funchal is the biggest wine-growing district, as well as the headquarters of the trade, where the shippers' 'lodges' are. Names which used to occur on labels and which may occasionally still be seen include Camara (or Cama) de Lobos and Campanário; both famous wine villages along the south coast.

Today the market for madeira has shifted from America and Britain to Scandinavia, France and Germany. The French long ago discovered its unique value in cookery; its sharpness makes it the perfect wine in sauces. It is, after all, accustomed to heat.

Portugal

PORTUGAL is the place for wine romantics. Even more than Italy it is the country of groaning ox-carts, of dappled sunlight through arbours of vines, of treading the purple must, of maidens bearing pitchers, of songs handed down for centuries.

Fifteen per cent of the population lives by making or selling wine, and this despite the fact that a good third of the country, south of the Tagus (the Tejo), is almost wineless. In some places it must be more like 50%.

The climate of Portugal is ideal for grapes. The wine-growing northern half of the country has ample rain, except in the high Douro beyond the mountains, and a long, bright rather than blazing summer; Atlantic characteristics which make it rather like a more southerly Bordeaux. The general standard, even of vinho de consumo, is as high as any country's, and if the best wines (apart from port) cannot compete with those of France or even Italy the run-of-the-mill produce is at least as good, and markedly cheaper.

Portugal's best wine is port. It is treated in detail on pages 178–181. Besides the port area the government distinguishes two major table-wine areas and a handful of minor ones in rather the same way as the French Appellations Contrôlées. Indeed the French words have been seen on Portuguese bottles. Wine from these areas bottled in Portugal carry a government seal, *selo de origem*, as witness to their authenticity—a praiseworthy idea; but by no means all Portugal's best wines come from these areas, nor are all their wines very good.

The two biggest and three famous minor areas round Lisbon are mapped overleaf. While exports from the former—Minho and Dão—are booming, little is left of the smaller areas which used to stamp their wine with local character. The importance has shifted to the very good non-regional wines of a number of big firms, who may buy their wine for blending all over the country. The big vineyards which supply them are little-known by name, and not distinguished with seals of origin. They are on the Tagus north of Lisbon, the Ribatejo; between the Tagus and the sea, centred round Torres Vedras and Alcobaça; Bairrada, between Coimbra and Oporto, Lafoes, adjoining the vinho verde country to the south; the upper Douro (famous only for port) and the country both north and south of it. A very large part of northern Portugal, in fact.

The most famous Portuguese table wine of all, Mateus rosé, does not come from a de-limited area, but from Vila Real, on the fringes of both the port and the vinho verde country. Clearly it is the demarcation system, not the wine, which is at fault.

Among the merchants who market good wine from outside the official areas, known by brand names, as well as *selo de origem* wines, are Sogrape, Real Companhia Vinicola do Norte de Portugal, José Maria da Fonseca, Borges & Irmão, Arealva, J. C. Alves, J. F. Pinto Basto. Often it is possible to deduce from the label where the wine comes from – but it is not sold as such; simply as the shipper's brand.

There are two wine regions south of the Tagus, one of real historical importance, the other of rising reputation.

Moscatel de Setúbal is the demarcated zone just south of Lisbon where one of the world's very best muscat dessert wines is made. It is fortified, though not as much as port, and the grape skins, which in muscats contain much of the flavouring elements, are steeped in it to intensify the scent. Unlike the equivalent light muscats of the south of France, of which Beaumes de Venise is the best, Setúbal improves with age. Eventually it becomes the world's most fragrant wine—a rare delight.

Lagoa is quite different—a hot-country wine, profiting by the touristic development of the Algarve to improve its standards.

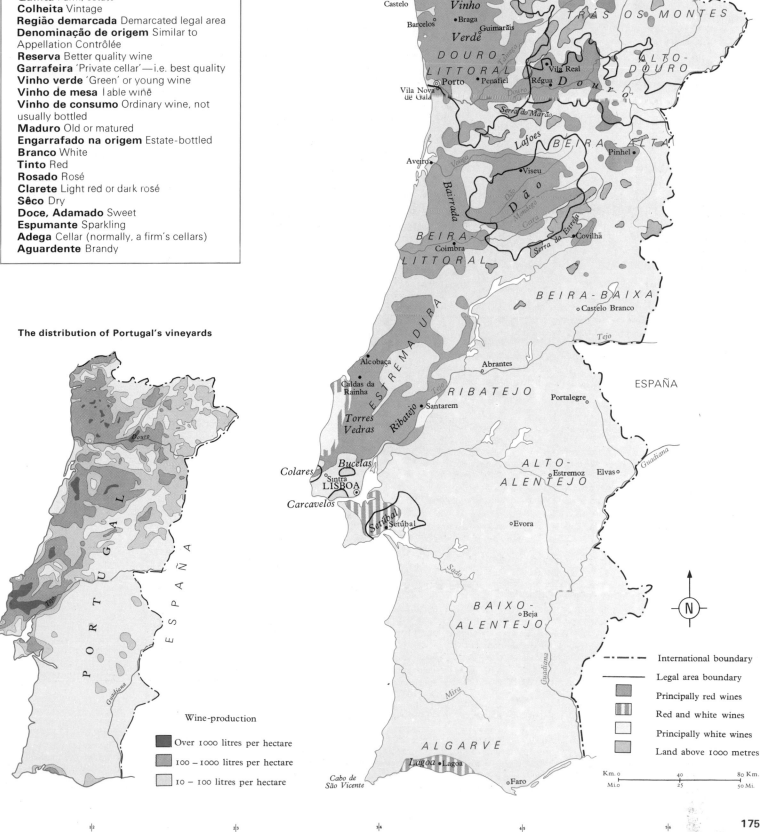

The Language of the Label

Vinha Vineyard
Quinta Farm, estate
Colheita Vintage
Região demarcada Demarcated legal area
Denominação de origem Similar to Appellation Contrôlée
Reserva Better quality wine
Garrafeira 'Private cellar'—i.e. best quality
Vinho verde 'Green' or young wine
Vinho de mesa Table wine
Vinho de consumo Ordinary wine, not usually bottled
Maduro Old or matured
Engarrafado na origem Estate-bottled
Branco White
Tinto Red
Rosado Rosé
Clarete Light red or dark rosé
Sêco Dry
Doce, Adamado Sweet
Espumante Sparkling
Adega Cellar (normally, a firm's cellars)
Aguardente Brandy

The distribution of Portugal's vineyards

ESPAÑA

Valença
Viana do Castelo
MINHO
Lima
Chaves
Bragança
Vinho
Braga
Barcelos
Guimarãis
Verde
TRAS OS MONTES
DOURO
Vila Real
LITTORAL
ALTO-DOURO
Porto
Penafiel
Régua
Douro
Vila Nova de Gaia
Douro
Serra do Marão
Lafões
BEIRA-ALTA
Aveiro
Vouga
Pinhel
Viseu
Barrada
Dão
Dão
Mondego
Ceira
Serra da Estrela
Covilhã
BEIRA-
Coimbra
LITTORAL
BEIRA-BAIXA
Castelo Branco
Tejo
ESTREMADURA
Alcobaça
Abrantes
ESPAÑA
Caldas da Rainha
Tejo
RIBATEJO
Portalegre
Santarem
Ribatejo
Torres Vedras
Ribatejo
ALTO-
Colares
Bucelas
ALENTEJO
Sintra
Estremoz
Elvas
LISBOA
Guadiana
Carcavelos
Setúbal
Setúbal
Sado
Evora
BAIXO-
ALENTEJO
Beja
Guadiana
Mira
ALGARVE
Lagoa
Lagoa
Cabo de São Vicente
Faro

Wine-production

- Over 1000 litres per hectare
- 100 – 1000 litres per hectare
- 10 – 100 litres per hectare

PORTUGAL
Douro
ESPAÑA
Tejo
Guadiana

- – – – International boundary
- ——— Legal area boundary
- Principally red wines
- Red and white wines
- Principally white wines
- Land above 1000 metres

Km. 0   40   80 Km.
Mi. 0   25   50 Mi.

Above: vines trained over a little stream on wires are typical of the lush vinho verde country
Left: the village of Azenhas do Mar, north of Colares

Right and below: Colares deep red and Bucellas (from Bucelas) lively white are the only survivors of the Lisbon wine area. Many consider them Portugal's best red and white wines, but they are hard to find today

IN KEEPING with Portugal's reputation as a maritime nation she brings vines as near as they ever get to the sea. At Colares, on the Atlantic coast, the vines grow on the beach in the sort of place where wind-beaten tamarisk and gorse are usually the only growing things.

The phylloxera cannot live in sand, so the vines are safe from him here. They creep low along the ground, their old limbs like driftwood bearing small bunches of intensely blue grapes. Low stone walls or plaited cane fences for shelter wander among them; one old vine, straggling here and there, may fill a whole little pen of its own, for instead of pruning the growers go in for the old Roman method of layering their vines—making them reroot their long branches in the sand where they will.

The small, dark, thick-skinned Ramisco is the Colares grape. Its wine is correspondingly black and tannic and needs as long to mature as claret needed a hundred years ago. It has always been esteemed Portugal's best red table wine, though little is made today, at least in the sandy soil where it is best, and none is exported.

Carcavelos, another demarcated wine region, has been virtually swamped by Estoril. The remaining vineyards are in neighbouring villages. The wine they make is sweet and amber. During the 18th century there was a vogue for Carcavelos, and the early 20th saw an attempt to revive it, but there are more profitable investments today round Lisbon than vineyards.

Of Lisbon's local wines the one in best shape is probably Bucellas. The wine is pleasant, fresh, white and dry, but not necessarily much better than some of Portugal's branded white wines without a geographical description.

BUCELAS Legal area

Vineyards

Woods

500 Contour interval 100 metres

Km 0   5   10   15   20 Km
Mi 0   5   10 Mi

Minho and Dão

Right: sharp and fizzy vinho verde comes in infinite variety. Good Dãos, the complete contrast, smooth and solid, are made by relatively few producers

PORTUGAL'S MOST distinctive and best contribution in the way of table wines is the speciality of her northern counties; their vinho verde. The name green wine describes its fresh, slightly underripe style, not its colour, which is red (three-quarters of it) or almost water-white.

Partly as a result of land shortage in the Minho, this most densely populated (though still utterly rural) part of the country, the vines are grown high up trees and on pergolas round the little fields. In late summer the sight of the grape-bearing garlands along every road gives almost pagan pleasure.

The grapes are picked early and fermented briefly—the object being wine with a low alcohol content and a decided tartness which continues to ferment gently until it is drunk. The red wines tend to be cloudy as a result, but both they and the whites (which foreigners prefer) have a scintillating little bubble about them which is marvellously refreshing. It is all too easy to swallow them in gulps like beer on a hot day.

Unfortunately, like sherry, they are usually sweetened for export, which hides their true freshness. They are best from the barrel in the spirited little taverns of Monção and Barcelos and Penafiel.

A superior sort of vinho verde is made from the white Alvarinho grape round Monção. It is bottled, and will even keep, developing a freesia-like scent but losing its bubbles. It is almost certainly Portugal's best white wine.

Basto and Amarante are considered the next best areas of the Minho for wine, followed by the more productive Braga and Penafiel. Lima makes a slightly stronger and deeper-coloured red wine than the others. But officially it is all vinho verde, and wines from the different regions are often blended together.

Dão is to Portugal what Rioja is to Spain. It does not have Rioja's tradition or range, or number of distinguished growers and merchants. But well-aged bottles suggest that given the right conditions—above all a demanding and discriminating public—the soil and the climate are right for fine wine.

Dão is granite hill country, where bare rocks show through the sandy soil. It is well inland, with a hotter and drier climate than down on the coast. Vineyards seem to have little part in the landscape, only cropping up here and there in clearings in the sweet-scented pine forests.

There are both red and white Dãos. The white can be rather soft and flat unless it is drunk very young. It makes a good everyday table wine. The red as it is usually sold—a blend from a big merchant perhaps four years old— is a clean, smooth and well-made wine, but hard and without attractive sweetness. On the other hand a Reserva from the same merchant 15 years old had developed a very fine scent like good Bordeaux and was gentle and interesting to drink. Such Reservas are not easy to find, and there are as yet no estate wines.

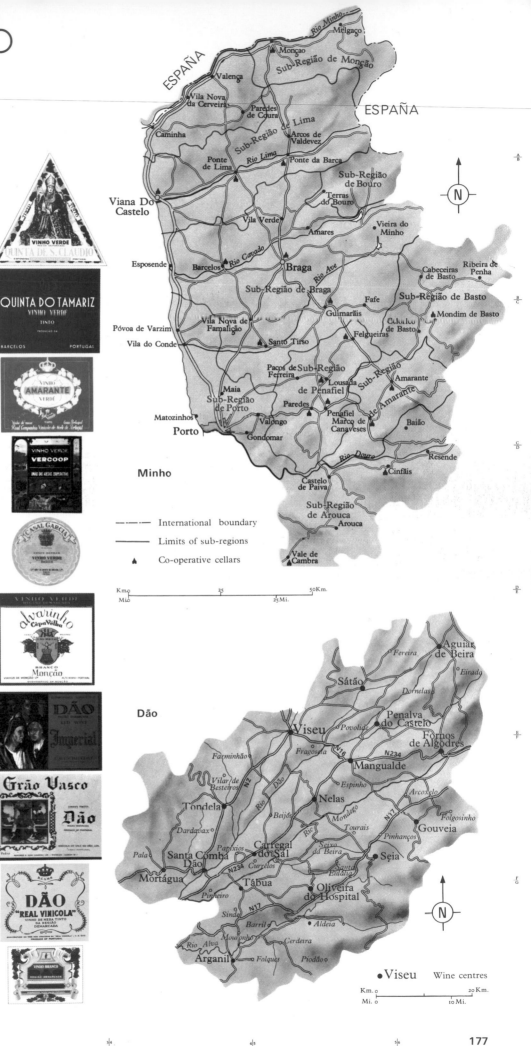

Minho

- · – · – International boundary
- ——— Limits of sub-regions
- ▲ Co-operative cellars

Dão

•Viseu Wine centres

The Alto Douro

The little town of Pinhão is the centre of the best port-growing area. Its main street is on the left of the picture; the little tributary river Pinhão in the centre flows into the Douro in the background. In the foreground a terraced vineyard steps down typically steeply towards the town centre

OF ALL THE PLACES where men have planted vineyards the upper Douro is the most improbable. To begin with there was not even soil: only 60° slopes of slate and granite, flaking and unstable, baked in a 100° sun. It was a land of utter desolation.

The vine, however, is the one useful plant which is not quite deterred by these conditions. The Mediterranean-type climate of this region suits it. What was needed was simply the engineering feat of putting soil on the Douro slopes and keeping it there. Which meant building walls along the mountain-sides, thousands of them, like contour lines, to hold up patches of ground (one could hardly call it soil) where vines could be planted.

Once the ground was stabilized and rainwater no longer ran straight off, it began to form soil, and plants began to add organic matter. Now olives, oranges, cork oaks and pines flourish, and villages are surrounded with vegetable and flower gardens. But before this could happen anywhere men had to blast and chip away at the slate, piling chunks of it into terrace walls often 15 feet high. The Douro terraces today are like the earthworks of a titanic fortress more than 50 miles long.

The Douro reaches Portugal from Spain in a wilderness which is still inaccessible except by mule or canoe. It has carved a canyon 1,500 to 2,000 feet deep through the layered rock uplands of eastern Portugal. This is the port country. The 4,600-foot Serra do Marão to the west prevents the Atlantic rain-clouds of summer from reaching it.

Many of the original terraces dating from the 17th century survive in the mountains above Regua, in the original port-wine zone, given its first official limits (the first such limits ever given to any wine) in 1756. Today it remains the biggest producer, but the search for quality has led further and further up-river. The modern zone is 20 times the size it was in the 18th century, and all the best part is comparatively new. Below the tributary Corgo the wine is reckoned definitely inferior. The best vineyards of all today are those round Pinhão, including the tributary valleys of the Távora, Torto, Pinhão and Tua rivers.

Steps are the nightmare of workers in these

District boundary

Parish boundary

QTA. DA FOZ   Quinta

[ ] Vineyards

[ ] Woods

═══500═══   Contour interval 100 metres

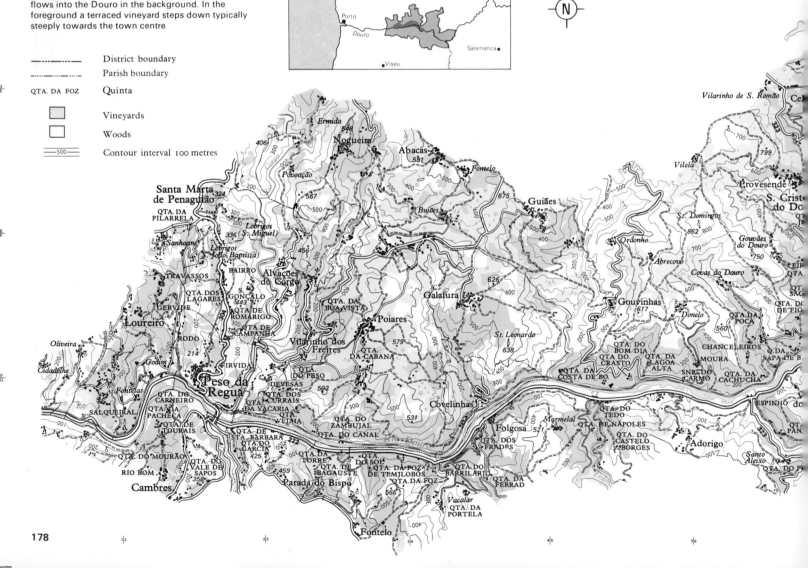

vineyards. Hundreds of little slate staircases link plot with plot. No beast can negotiate them. Every grape must be carried out of the vineyard on the back of a man.

Vintage-time anywhere is the climax of the year, but on the Douro, perhaps because of the hardship of life, it is almost Dionysiac. There is an antique frenzy about the ritual, the songs, the music of drum and pipe, the long nights of treading by the light of hurricane lamps while the women and girls dance together.

The famous shipping firms have their own quintas up in the hills, where they go to supervise the vintage. They are rambling white houses, vine-arboured, tile-floored and cool in a world of dust and glare. Most of the famous quintas are shown on the map on these pages. Quinta names however rarely appear as wine names. Only three or four of the whole valley, of which by far the most famous is Quinta do Noval above Pinhão, sell their wine unblended. For the essence of port, as it is of champagne and sherry, is blending, and the main source of grapes and wine is not big shipper-owned estates but a multitude of small farmers.

Top left: workers carry the grapes out of the port vineyards in baskets on their shoulders
Lower left: new wide and old narrow terraces contrast at the corner of a hill
Above right: graceful *barcos rabelos* are still used for fishing on the Douro, but rarely now for carrying wine

Port/the Quality Factor

Low yield	Altitude	Nature of land	Locality	Training of vines	Grape varieties	Degree of slope	Exposure	Spacing of vines	Type of soil	Age of vines	Shelter
21%	21%	14%	13%	12%	6%	4%	3%	2%	2%	1%	1%

The port vineyards are graded into six classes. The quantity of wine they can sell as port is regulated by their standing. The factors by which they are judged are the same as in Burgundy, say, or Germany, but the emphasis is different. The diagram shows how here small production (as little as 600 litres per 1,000 vines) and the altitude of the vineyard (it should be below 1500 feet) are considered of primary importance (brown) in the marking. Grape varieties are secondary factors (blue) and exposure (north or south) only tertiary (green) —though both those things would be vital in Burgundy

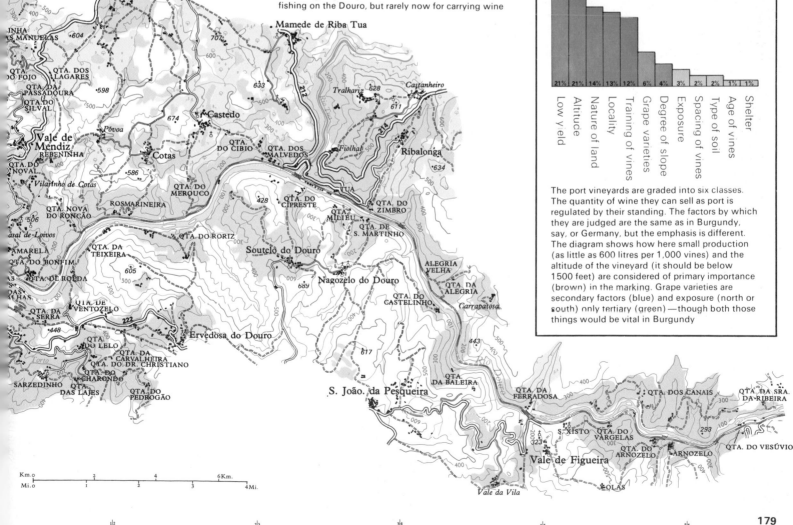

The Port Lodges

A trough made of great granite blocks, set up like a stage beneath the low roof of a farmer's outhouse, is the *lagar* where the grapes for port are trodden. There are girls treading with the men in this picture, taken in the remote village of Ribalonga; a revolutionary innovation in this superstitious country. Huge barrels like the one in the foreground are used for fermentation. The shipper who intends to buy the farmer's wine makes an inspection of every barrel before it is used, in case it is musty or vinegary and could spoil the wine

PORT is made by running off the partially fermented red wine into a barrel a quarter full of brandy, while it still contains at least half of its grape sugar. The brandy stops the fermentation so that the mixture is both strong and sweet.

The wine also needs the pigmentation of the grape skins to colour it, and their tannin to preserve it. In normal wines these are extracted during the course of fermentation. But since with port the fermentation is unnaturally short they have to be procured some other way—which traditionally in the Douro means by treading.

Treading is a means of macerating the grape skins in their juice so as to extract all their essences. The naked foot is the perfect instrument for this, being warm and doing no damage to the pips, which would make the juice bitter if they were crushed. A dozen men for a dozen hours (they work in four-hour shifts), rhythmically stamping thigh-deep in the mixture of juice and skins in a broad stone trough (a *lagar*) are the means of giving port its colour, its grapiness, and its ability to last and improve for many years, instead of being a pale and uninteresting liquid.

A mechanical substitute for treading has been introduced in the more modern quintas. It consists of a closed fermenting vat in which the carbon dioxide pressure makes the juice circulate up a pipe from the bottom to the top where it pours over the 'cap' of floating skins. In several days this continuous churning has the same effect as the more expensive man-hours in the *lagar*. But the majority of port will continue to be trodden for a long time to come. Most port at the moment, being blended, is a mixture of wines made in both ways.

Port which is kept up the Douro is rare. It is said to take on a character known as 'the Douro burn'—a faintly roasted flavour. Virtually all port is taken down the river soon after it is made, to complete its processing in the port suburb of Oporto, Vila Nova de Gaia.

The journey down-river used to be made in high-prowed sailing boats like Viking longships, which had to be controlled through the rapids by eight men working long sweeps in the bows. Now the port is taken by train, for the railway goes where the road gives up in the higher reaches of the river.

The shippers' warehouses in Vila Nova de Gaia are known as lodges. They have much in common with the sherry bodegas. In the lodges the port is kept in pipes, 115-gallon barrels, for anything from two to 50 years.

Perhaps three years out of ten conditions are near perfect for port-making. The wine of these years needs no blending; nothing can be done to improve it except wait. It is bottled at two years just like claret, and labelled simply with its shipper's name and the date. This is vintage port, and there is never enough of it. Eventually, perhaps after 20 years, it will have a fatness and fragrance, richness and delicacy which is incomparable.

A great vintage port is incontestably among the world's very best wines. Other port, from near vintage standard to merely moderate, goes through a blending process, to emerge as an unvarying branded wine of a given character. This wine, aged in wood, matures much faster than vintage port and loses some of its sugar in the process. A very old wood port is comparatively pale and dry, but particularly smooth. This sort of wine is called Tawny from its colour. Expensive tawnies cost as much as vintage port and many people prefer their

mellowness and moderated sweetness to the full, fat and flowery flavour which a good vintage port keeps.

Run-of-the-mill wood ports are not kept for nearly so long, nor would such age find any great qualities in them to reveal. They taste best while they are still fruity with youth, and often fiery too, with perhaps five years as the average age of a blend. France is the great market for these wines. They used to be the staple winter drink in British pubs, where they were kept in a barrel in the bar.

Vintage port has disadvantages. It needs keeping for a very long time. And it needs handling with great care. As the making of the wine does not reach its end until after bottling, the sediment forms a 'crust' on the side of the bottle; a thin, delicate, dirty-looking veil. If the bottle is moved, other than very gingerly, the crust will break and mix with the wine, so that it has to be filtered out again. In any case the wine must be decanted from its bottle before it is served. Which is enough to discourage many people from buying it.

As a compromise between vintage and 'wood' port, shippers now also ship Late-bottled Vintage wines—port from good years (though not always the very best) which is kept unblended but in barrel instead of being bottled at two years. After eight years or so it has rid itself of its crust and matured as far as it would in twice as long in bottle. In many ways it is the modern man's vintage port, being speeded up and cleaned up in this way. Yet there are those who argue that vintage port is not a modern man's drink, and that if you are going to indulge in an old-fashioned pastime you might as well do it properly. Certainly the old method makes the one port which deserves to be called great wine.

The port lodges of Vila Nova de Gaia

1. Fonseca
2. Graham
3. Diez Hermanos
4. Ferreira
5. Companhia Velha
6. Delaforce
7. Nie Poort
8. Martinez Gassiot
9. Cockburn
10. Barros
11. Junta Nacional dos Vinhos
12. Dow
13. Burmester
14. Mackenzie
15. Ramos Pinto
16. Sandeman
17. Hunt Roope
18. Rozés
19. Kopke
20. Wiese & Krohn
21. Gonzalez Byass
22. Rainha Santa
23. Croft
24. Taylor
25. Offley Forrester
26. Warre
27. Noval
28. Borges
29. Calem

Above: the cooperage where barrels are made and repaired is a vital part of a port lodge; most port is kept in wood until it is ready to drink; from three to as many as 50 years. Good oak is the only material which allows its steady development

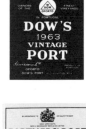

Left: traditionally, vintage port bottles had no labels; a stencilled name in white paint, more durable than paper, is still used by one shipper, Quinta do Noval. Many of the best names in the port trade are British; a reminder that it was the British taste for sweet wine that built up the industry in the 18th century. Today France is the biggest customer

The Language of the Label

Vintage The wine of a single exceptional year bottled early for laying down
Late-bottled vintage Similar wine bottled when mature; lighter than vintage
Crusted Good but not vintage port bottled early for laying down
Vintage character Similar to crusted
Tawny Port kept many years in wood until it fades to a tawny colour; smooth and lighter than any of the foregoing
Ruby Port aged in wood comparatively briefly; darker and rougher
White port From white grapes; often much drier than red and sold as an aperitif

Switzerland–Valais and Vaud

THE STEEP sides of the valley which the young river Rhône has carved through the Alps are followed by gentler slopes where it broadens into Lake Geneva. An almost continuous band of vines hugs the river's north bank all the way.

In the higher valley peculiarly Alpine conditions, dry and sunny, and by the lake the mildness brought about by a great body of water both favour the vine in different ways. The Valais and the Vaud, as the two regions are called, are Switzerland's biggest and best vineyard. Including the production of Geneva's vineyards the Rhône valley gives more than three-quarters of the national total.

Four-fifths of this is white wine. The proportion used to be even higher, but Swiss growers have recently planted the Pinot Noir on a large scale and the Gamay of Beaujolais on an even larger.

The great grape of both the Valais and the Vaud is the white Chasselas. In the Valais it is called Fendant, in the Vaud Dorin. It is not reckoned a fine-wine grape in France, but the best of it in Switzerland is extremely pleasant.

In the Valais the centre of Fendant-growing is Sion and the villages just to the west, Conthey, Vétroz and Ardon. There is little rain (Sierre is the driest place in Switzerland) and endless sun. If the vines escape spring frosts they make a powerful wine with as much as 13% alcohol. Irrigation has to be done by wooden channels called *bisses*, coming breakneck down the mountainside.

The Sylvaner (called Johannisberg), the Marsanne of the French Rhône (called Ermitage), the local Amigne, Arvine and Humagne and the Pinot Gris (called Malvoisie) are the other white Valais grapes which give their names to their wines. All their wine is heady; Malvoisie is sweet; the others can be. The grapes are often dried to make sweet wine.

The best red wine of the Valais is called Dôle. To use the name it must be made of Pinot Noir and Gamay mixed. Inferior Dôle is called Goron. In the Vaud, Dôle-type wine is called Salvagnin. The name Oeil de Perdrix is limited to rosé wine made from Pinot Noir.

Chablais, the district between Valais and Vaud, though part of the Vaud, shares the characteristics of both regions. Aigle and Yvorne and Bex are its best-known villages. Their white wine is also strong, but drier and less full than Valais wine. It is said to have the 'gun-flint' taste.

The central part of the Vaud along the lakeshore between Montreux and Lausanne is confusingly called Lavaux. Switzerland's most appealing wines, dry, gentle and fruity, are grown in the districts of Lutry, Villette, Epesses, St-Saphorin, Chardonne and Vevey. The most famous vineyard, that of Dézaley, belongs to the city of Lausanne.

After Lausanne, La Côte has lighter and less distinguished wines; 40% of the Vaud total. Nyon, its commercial centre, sees more and more Gamay light reds. The same is true of the vineyards round Geneva. In Geneva the Chasselas makes a wine of lower quality, known as Perlan: Crépy, one of the rare French Appellation Contrôlée wines to be made from Chasselas, is just across the border.

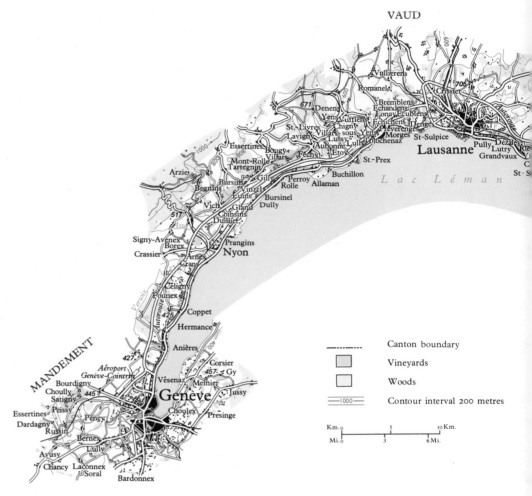

Canton boundary

Vineyards

Woods

Contour interval 200 metres

The castle of Aigle stands out in the Rhône valley where it begins to broaden out to Lake Geneva. The centre and south-facing slopes of the valley are thickly planted with vines; where it faces north they are bare

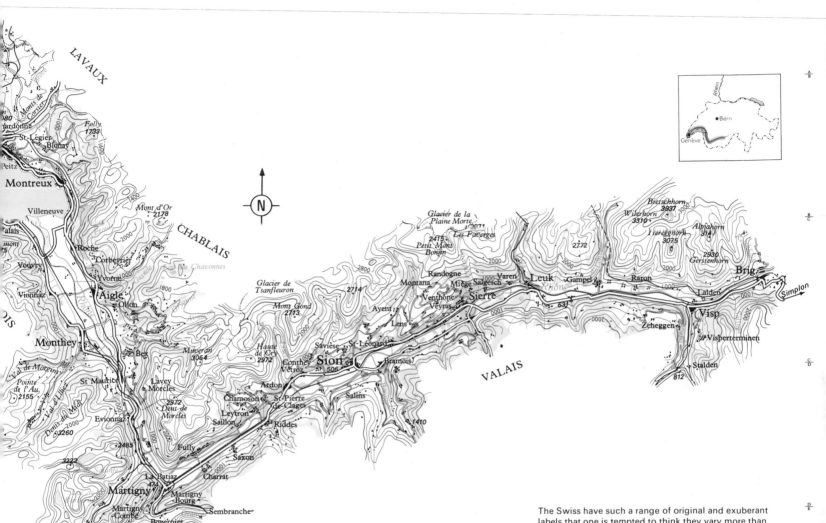

The Swiss have such a range of original and exuberant labels that one is tempted to think they vary more than the wine. Most of the principal producers of the Valais and the Vaud are represented in the selection here

Switzerland

Above: Schloss Werdenberg on the upper Rhine in north-east Switzerland. Most of the wine of German Switzerland is very light red made from the Spätburgunder (Pinot Noir) grape
Left: Europe's highest vineyards are 3700 feet up at Visperterminen, high above the railway which takes skiers and climbers to Zermatt
Below: in Scheuchzeri's *Itinera Alpina* of 1723 the sources of the rivers Ticino (Tesin) and Reuss are represented by angels hovering round Mount St Gotthard pouring water out of pitchers

SWITZERLAND is an intensely wine-conscious, insatiably wine-importing country as well as an important producer. She comes between France, the natural land of wine, and Germany, the land where wine is an extra, worth every bit of effort it demands. The Swiss are loyal to their own local wines, without pretending that better things do not happen in France. They are the world's biggest importers of burgundy; Beaujolais is almost their national drink.

The Swiss wine industry is in evolution, as rising costs make it a problem to many growers whether or not to persevere. The inevitable result is that poor vineyards are abandoned as not paying their way. Studies are made as to how to run the remainder, the better ones, more profitably and with less labour—which often means a change to better varieties of grapes, and more modern ways of training them.

At the same time the long near-monopoly of white wine in Switzerland has been broken. Red wine is in fashion, a development of the last 20 years. There has been an enormous increase in the planting of the Burgundian varieties of red grapes, Pinot Noir and Gamay, in the most important areas: Vaud, Valais and Geneva. The

Ticino has concentrated on the Merlot, introduced from Bordeaux. It remains to be seen whether the fashion comes soon enough to save the dwindling vineyards of German Switzerland, which have long specialised in Blauburgunder or Pinot Noir, without making of it any more than a decent light wine.

Almost every canton in Switzerland makes a little wine. Two areas apart from the Rhône valley and Lake Geneva have important industries: the Ticino and Neuchâtel.

Italian Switzerland, the Ticino, has not long been an exporter of wine. The local tradition is a peasant one, and only 50 years ago hardship was still sending emigrants to America. (The famous Italian Swiss Colony vineyards near Santa Rosa in California are one result.) The typical local red wine, called Nostrano, is no great matter. But the Merlot is growing well there, as it does in north-east Italy and northern Jugoslavia, making a strongish but rather soft red wine. Better Ticino Merlots, attaining 12% alcohol, now use the name Viti to distinguish themselves from the rest.

Neuchâtel is equally famous for its red wine and its white. The north shore of the lake is

International boundary

Principally white wines

White and red wines

Land above 2000 metres

Km.0 10 20 30 40 50 60 Km.
Mi.0 10 20 30 40 Mi.

temperate and well-sheltered by the Jura. The Pinot Noir grows well, giving a pale and light wine, often called Cortaillod after the village which makes a speciality of it.

White Neuchâtel is made from the Chasselas, like Fendant and Dorin wines from Valais and Vaud. It is lighter than either and encouraged to fizz faintly by being bottled *sur lie*—without being separated from its yeasty sediment. In some cases the process is carried further to making fully sparkling wines.

Lake Bienne (the Bieler See) just to the north-east has similar wines.

The wines of other cantons do not travel much. The Herrschaft, a little district on the borders of Austria and Liechtenstein which has the distinction of being the first wine region of the infant Rhine, grows Blauburgunder almost exclusively; the best are dear and are said to be excellent. The Herrschaft also grows the otherwise-unknown Completer, which is picked in November to give a sort of Beerenauslese.

There used to be a romantically named, heroically strong Glacier wine, which legend says was toted to and fro up and down mountains. But today Glacier is only a brand name.

Below: red and white wine labels from Neuchâtel, Merlot from Ticino and Klevner (or Pinot Noir) from north-east Switzerland. The red and white wines of Neuchâtel are both light; the white, which has a tendency to bubbles, is often made fully sparkling. The city of Neuchâtel (first label) is a top grower

Austria

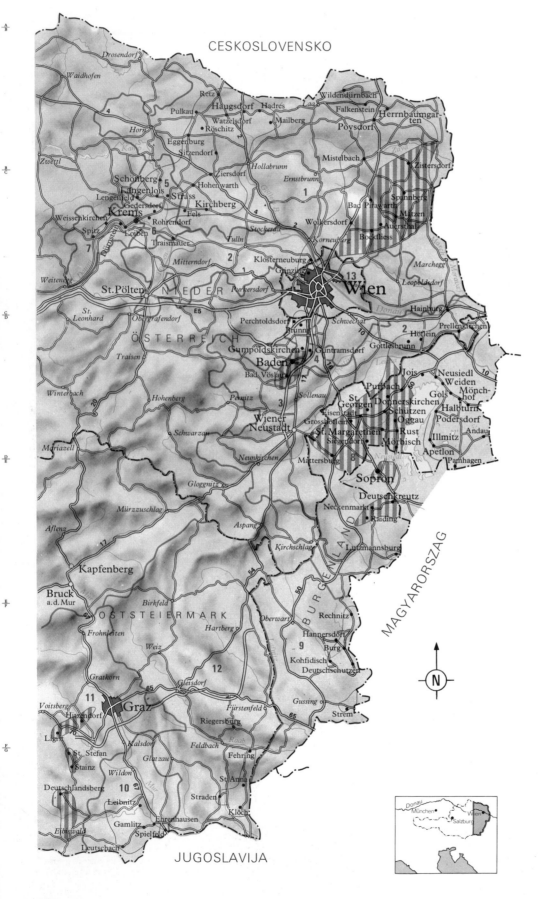

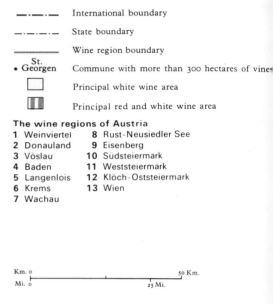

International boundary
State boundary
Wine region boundary
• St. Georgen   Commune with more than 300 hectares of vine
Principal white wine area
Principal red and white wine area

The wine regions of Austria

1 Weinviertel	8 Rust-Neusiedler See
2 Donauland	9 Eisenberg
3 Vöslau	10 Südsteiermark
4 Baden	11 Weststeiermark
5 Langenlois	12 Klöch-Oststeiermark
6 Krems	13 Wien
7 Wachau	

Km. 0   50 Km.
Mi. 0   25 Mi.

IT IS ODD that one should have to say of a 1,000-year-old industry that it is in mid-evolution. But this is true of Austrian wine. Austria has such a flourishing tradition of making light wine for prompt local consumption that it is only now in the process of discovering itself and its own potential as a serious wine country. One result of this is that excellent wines appear from places you have never heard of, in contrast to some fairly ordinary performances from those you have.

Red wine is of no great significance in Austria. All her best wine, like Germany's and Hungary's, is white. Her central position among Europe's northern and eastern vineyards shows in the character of the wine she makes. There is something of the freshness of the Rhine in it—but more of the fieriness and high flavour of the Danube.

Only eastern Austria makes wine. The vineyards are concentrated north and east of Vienna. Styria (Steiermark) in the south, bordering on Jugoslavia's principal vineyard region, Slovenia, is of minor importance. The regions which are flourishing, and of which we are likely to hear more, are the Wachau and Vienna with its Südbahn (both mapped in detail overleaf), Burgenland round the Neusiedler See southeast of the capital, and the Weinviertel in the north-east.

Burgenland lies on the Hungarian border—indeed the Hungarian wine district of Sopron is carved out of it. Like Hungary, it specializes

Top: Heurigen—a word for new wine and the taverns that sell it
Above: the monastery of Gottweig has vineyards by the Danube opposite Krems
Below: labels from Burgenland and (right) Klöch in Styria

in sweet wines. The country is flat and sandy and warm round the lake, and late-picking of grapes is normal.

The most historically famous wine of the area comes from Rust. Ruster Ausbruch (or Auslese) was formerly mentioned in the next breath to Tokay. Today some of the best Ausleses and Beerenausleses come from the other side of the lake. Apetlon has recently produced sweet wines of real distinction, at their best comparable with the full-flavoured Ausleses of the German Palatinate.

The grapes include Rhine Riesling, Italian Riesling, Muskat-Ottonel (one of the many varieties of this ubiquitous grape), the Hungarian Furmint and Gewürztraminer. Where the name Riesling is used alone it means the inferior Italian Riesling; real Riesling in Austria is always called Rheinriesling.

The red wines, made of Pinot Noir (Blauburgunder) and Portugieser, are not up to the standard of the whites.

Sometimes Austrian labels go into full details of village, vineyard, grape and quality; German-style. Sometimes equally good wines, on the other hand, only have a brand name such as Edelfräulein. If you recognize the name of the merchant who made it, well and good.

In contrast to those of Burgenland the wines of the Weinviertel (the name means 'wine quarter') are in the main light and dry. The great grape here is Austria's favourite, the Grüner Veltliner. Veltliner wine when it is well-

made and young is marvellously fresh and fruity, with plenty of acidity and an almost spicy flavour. To compare it with Rhine Riesling is like comparing a wild flower with a finely-bred garden variety in which scent and colour and size and form have been studied and improved for many years.

There are times, when Grüner Veltliner wine is drawn straight from the barrel into a tumbler, frothing and gleaming a piercing greeny gold, when it seems like the quintessence of all that a wine should be. Drink it then, with a sandwich on the terrace. It will never taste like that under any other conditions; certainly not when it has been bottled.

There is a tendency, nurtured in France, to think that bottled wine is always best. Austria is the place to forget it. Only a few big vintners possess the elaborate plant it takes to bottle such wine successfully. Even the most carefully chosen light wines from small growers (those on the list at Vienna's famous Hotel Sacher, for example) tend to turn dry and coarse when put in a bottle.

Another reason for the disappointing quality of some Austrian wines shipped abroad is that they do not come from Austria at all. Austria is free and easy about wine-naming, both of her own and other countries' products. Unfortunately, the practice of using her name on the labels of wine from eastern Europe and Italy is helping to obscure the emerging quality of some of the wine she really makes.

Vienna

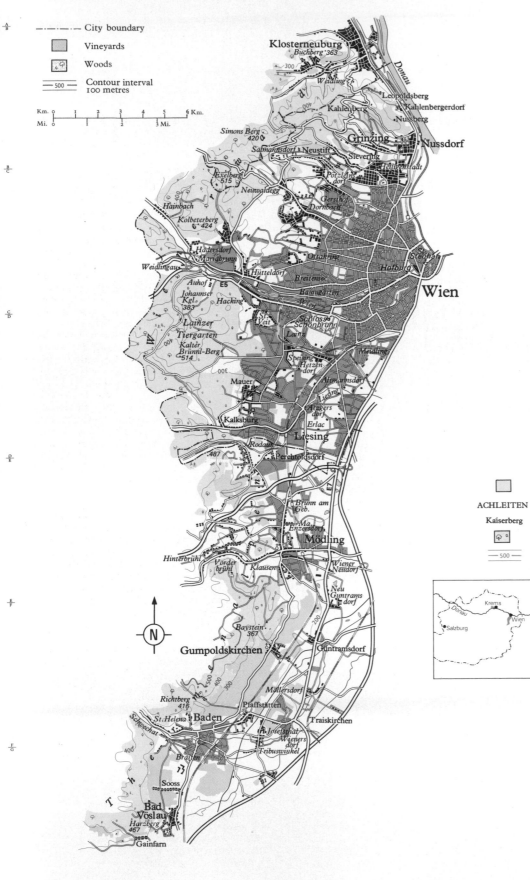

City boundary

Vineyards

Woods

Contour interval
100 metres

Km. 0 1 2 3 4 5 6 Km.
Mi. 0 1 2 3 Mi.

Klosterneuburg
Buchberg 363
300
Weidling
Leopoldsberg
Kahlenberg
Kahlenbergerdorf
Nussberg
Simons Berg 420
Salmannsdorf
Neustift
Grinzing
Nussdorf
Sievering
Heiligenstadt
Exelberg 515
Pötzleinsdorf
Neuwaldegg
Gersthof
Dornbach
Hainbach
Kolbeterberg 424
Hadersdorf
Mariabrunn
Ottakring
Hofburg
St. Stephan
Weidlingau
Hütteldorf
Breitensee
Wien
Auhof
Johannser Kgl. 383
Hacking
Baumgarten
Wien
Schloss
Schönbrunn
Lainz
Lainzer
Tiergarten
Kalter
Brünnl-Berg 514
St. Veit
Meidling
Speising
Hetzendorf
Altmannsdorf
Mauer
Liesing
Kalksburg
Atzgersdorf
Erlaa
Rodaun
Liesing
Perchtoldsdorf
487
Brunn am Geb.
Ma. Enzersdorf
Mödling
Hinterbrühl
Vorderbrühl
Klausen
Wiener Neudorf
Neu Guntramsdorf
Baystein 367
Gumpoldskirchen
Guntramsdorf
Müllersdorf
Richtberg 416
Pfaffstätten
St.Helena
Baden
Traiskirchen
Josefsthal
Wienersdorf
Tribuswinkel
Schwechat
Brauen
Sooss
Bad Vöslau
Harzberg 467
Gainfarn

Krems
Donau
Wien
Salzburg

THERE IS no capital city which is so identified with wine as Vienna. New wine seems to be its life-blood. Vineyards hold their ground within the heart of the residential districts and surge up the side of the surrounding hills into the Vienna woods. North, east and south, where the line of hills circles and protects the city, there are vines. To the south they continue along the Südbahn—the southern railway—flanking the last crinkle of the Alpine foothills facing the Hungarian plain.

Most of their wine is drunk as Heurige, in Heurigen—for this untranslatable word means both the new wine and the tavern where it is drunk. Every vintner seems to be a tavern-keeper as well, and chalks up on a board the wines he has and the (very low) prices he wants for them, by jug or litre bottle, label-less, to be drunk on the spot or carried away. When Heurige is good it is sensational; spirited, sprightly stuff which goes straight to your head. Most of it is Veltliner or Sylvaner, some is Riesling, some is Traminer; the best of the new wines are not too dry.

Viennese connoisseurs know every grower in Neustift, Grinzing, Sievering, Nussdorf and Kahlenberg, the wine villages which are actually in Vienna. The atmosphere varies in their leafy taverns from idyllic to hilarious. In most of them Beethoven wrote at least a concerto.

The Südbahn wines are better known to the outside world. Gumpoldskirchen, above all, for its fine late-gathered white wines made from Veltliner, Riesling, or Gewürztraminer, and a few reds, and Baden and Bad Vöslau more for their reds. The red wine is dark, dry and pleasant, appetizing and heady without having particular character.

Vineyards

ACHLEITEN Vineyard name used by the Wachau Co-operative, Dürnstein

Kaiserberg Traditional vineyard name

Woods

500 Contour interval 100 metres

Tiefental
Schildhütt
Weitenberg
Achleiten 511
Achleiten
Grubbach
ACHLEITEN
Seiberer
Weissenkirchen
Ritzlingbach
St.Lorenzen
Ritzling
Joching
Donau

188

The Wachau

Dürnstein in the Wachau, from a 19th-century drawing by Sir David Wilkie. The castle on the crag, where Richard Coeur de Lion was imprisoned, is a total ruin today; that by the church on the Danube is a first-class hotel called after the captive king

Above: this is almost the only part of Austria with vineyard names known abroad. The co-operative (top) is the biggest bottler

THE WACHAU is Austria's best-known wine area. It lies only 40 miles west of Vienna, at a point where the Danube broaches a range of 1600-foot hills. For a short stretch the craggy north bank of the river, as steep as some of the Mosel slopes, is patchworked with vines on ledges and outcrops, along narrow paths up from the river to the crowning woods.

There are patches of deep soil and others where a mere scratching finds rock, patches with daylong sunlight and others which always seem to be in shade. There is no grand sweep of vines here; no big estates and no unique vine variety. The Wachau is a pattern of small growers with mixed vineyards—who make good wine.

The principal export from the Wachau is the dry wine known as Schluck, made in the main from the Sylvaner. Much of it also comes from the Kamp valley, an important vineyard area running south from Langenlois to Krems. The real character of the region, though, is better seen in its Grüner Veltliner—often a marvellously high-flavoured and fiery performance. Best of all, though rarer, is the Rhine Riesling. In the Wachau it can make great wine.

The whole area is overshadowed by its efficient growers' co-operative. A thousand growers belong to it. It has even rearranged the names of the vineyards to simplify the marketing of its wines. (The map shows the names it uses for the different 'Rieds', or sections of the hills.)

The co-operative is at Dürnstein, the scenic climax of the valley. A very good hotel by the river is named after Richard the Lionheart, who was imprisoned here and found, they say, by his lead guitar, Blondel. The baroque steeple, the ruined castle and the tilting vineyards of Dürnstein are irresistibly pretty and suggestive.

Near-by, to the east of the Wachau, beyond Krems (and off the map), the hills slant away from the Danube to the north-east, are lower and become sandy. Just round this corner is the village of Rohrendorf, where Austria's most famous grower, Lenz Moser, has his cellars.

Lenz Moser is the originator of a method of training vines on wires at twice the usual height which has been adopted by many progressive growers all over the world. He achieves higher yields, better quality and lower labour costs, he says, with his 'high culture' system. Certainly his own wines, made from the produce of his vineyards in several parts of Austria, are a good advertisement for it.

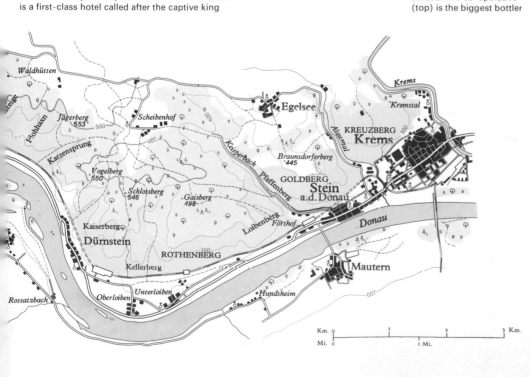

The Language of the Label

Many of the words that used to appear on German labels before the new wine law are still seen on Austrian ones, including.
Naturwein Wine without added sugar
Reinsortig Only this particular type
Originalabfüllung Estate-bottled
Eigenbaugewächs From the maker's own vineyard
Weingarten, Weingut Wine estate
Ried Vineyard (as in French clos)

Hungary

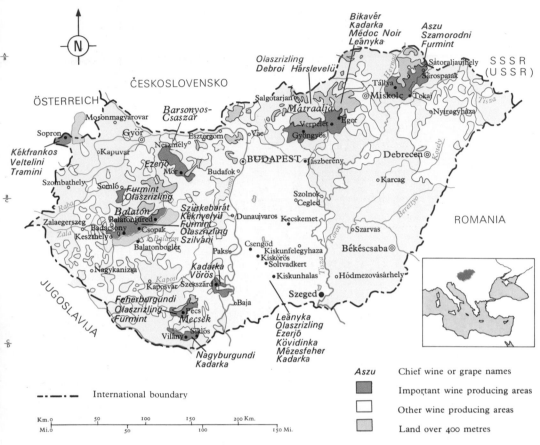

International boundary

Km. 0   50   100   150   200 Km.
Mi. 0   50   100   150 Mi.

Aszu   Chief wine or grape names

Important wine producing areas

Other wine producing areas

Land over 400 metres

The Language of the Label

Hungarian labels tend to have few descriptive phrases, since virtually all bottled wine comes from one or other of the dozens of state cellars round the country, or the principal cellar for export at Budafok near Budapest.

Aszu The equivalent of the German Auslese—overripe grapes collected for the sweetening of Tokay

Szamorodni Literally 'as it comes', i.e. Tokay not specially treated with Aszu, and therefore more or less dry. Also sometimes used for other wines than Tokay

Minösegí bor Best quality wine

Borkülönlegessége szölögazdaságának A speciality from the vineyards of the region named

Asztali bor Table wine

Kímert bor Ordinary wine

Palackozott Bottled

Fehér White

Vörös Red

** Száraz** Dry

Édes Sweet

Habzó Sparkling

Magyar Állami Pincegazdaság Hungarian state cellars

Monimpex The state export monopoly

HARDLY ANY country has a national character so pronounced in its wine—and food—as Hungary. The characteristic Hungarian wine is white—or rather warmly gold. It smells more of a pâtisserie than a greengrocer, if one can so distinguish between ripe yeasty smells and the green ones of fresh fruit. It tastes, if it is a good one, distinctly sweet, but full of fire and even a shade fierce. It is not dessert wine; far from it. It is wine for meals cooked with more spice and pepper and fat than a light wine could stand.

Like Germany, Hungary treasures her sweet wines most. Tokay (opposite page) is her pride and joy. But most of the country makes wine and there are dry ones and good reds as well.

On the map the chief wine types are listed where they grow. They bear the names of their districts followed by those of their grapes.

Over half Hungary's vineyards ($\frac{1}{4}$ million acres) are on the Great Plain of the Danube (Duna) in the southern centre of the country, on sandy soil which is little use for anything but vines. The vine, indeed, has been used for reclaiming sand dunes which used to shift in storms, as they do in the Sahara. Great Plain wine, about half of it red Kadarka, and much of it the white Italian (known as Olasz) Riesling, is light and soft—the vin ordinaire of Hungary.

The other half is scattered among the hills which cross the country from south-west to north-east, culminating in the Tokajhegyelja—Tokay hills. In the south the districts of Szekszárd, Vilány and Mecsek grow both red and white wines, but here the red are coming to the fore. Kadarka is the traditional grape; Pinor Noir the rising star, making fruity lightish wine of good quality.

Round Lake Balaton (see next pages) some of Hungary's best table wines are made. The small isolated hill-districts of Somló to the west, growing Furmint and Riesling, and Mór to the north, growing Ezerjó grapes, also both have very distinct characters: Somló for gentler, Mór for drier and more highly-flavoured wine. Both are among what Hungary calls its 'historical wine regions'.

Sopron, almost on the Austrian border, is a red wine outpost, growing Kékfrankos, a lively wine but hardly a great one. Barsonyos-Császár to the east of Sopron makes dry white wine; unlike the other named 'historical' districts it was formed by law in 1959.

Then along the south of the Mátra range to Eger comes the second biggest of Hungary's vineyards, formed by combining (again in 1959) the old districts of Gyöngyös-Visonta and Debrö. The sweet white Hárslevelü of Debrö (that is the villages of Aldebro, Feldebro and Verpelét) is its best-known wine, but Olasz Riesling and Kadarka, Hungary's commonest grapes, are also grown.

Best-known, perhaps, of all Hungary's table wines is Eger's Bikavér, or Bull's Blood. The fine old town of Eger is one of Hungary's most important wine centres, with huge State cellars, magnificent caverns cut in the soft dark tufa of the hills. Hundreds of time-blackened oak casks, ten feet in diameter and bound with bright red iron hoops, line their galleries.

Not only Bikavér, which ages well and at ten years is not unlike a good old Chianti, but 'Médoc Noir' (or Merlot) is made in the district. Once Eger was a red-wine centre exclusively. Today her Leányka (one of Hungary's lesser grapes, here giving very good light white wine) is thought by some to be her best product.

The place name, ending in 'i' (which is equivalent to the German 'er') is usually followed by the grape variety in Hungary. Most bottled wines come from state cellars

Tokay

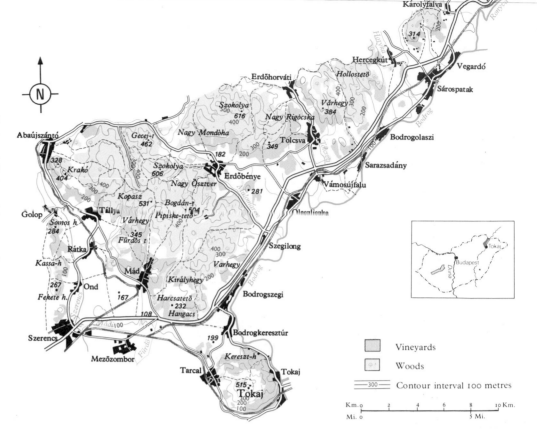

PAINTED yellow four-in-hand gigs overtake grey old wagons of barrels on the road into Tokay. The cobbles are covered in mud and straw. A mist steams up from the Bodrog river, wreathing the coppery vines on the hill. From the door of the Halászcsárda comes a great smell of pike and paprika and bacon and dumplings and sour cream and coffee.

Tokay is like one of the provincial towns in Russian novels which burn themselves into the memory by their very plainness. And indeed Russia is only 40 miles away.

The Tokay hills are ancient volcanoes, lava covered with sandy loam—perfect soil for vines. From the plain to the south come warm summer winds and from the river moisture, while the hills themselves give shelter.

The same grapes as grow in other parts of Hungary, the Furmint and Hárslevelü, ripen perfectly here. Better still, they undergo the same 'noble rot' as the grapes of Sauternes, concentrating their sugar and flavours into quint-essential-grapiness. They ferment slowly but give strong and intensely-flavoured wine.

The Tokay custom is to keep the most nobly-rotten (or 'Aszu') grapes to one side and crush them into a pulp in tubs called puttonyok. A number of seven-gallon puttonyok of pulp is added to barrels of one-year-old wine. Tokay barrels, called Gönci, only hold 35 gallons, so if five puttonyok are added the wine is entirely Aszu—like a German Beerenauslese.

The qualities of Tokay are known by the number of 'putts' in the Gönci barrel. If none have been added the wine is 'Szamorodni'—rather heavy and harsh but not sweet.

The most luxurious Tokay of all is made only from the juice which Aszu berries naturally exude as they are waiting to be crushed. This 'essencia' is as much as 60% sugar and will hardly ferment at all. Its normal use today is for sweetening Aszu wines—but formerly it was very slowly fermented and kept for the death-beds of monarchs, where it was supposed to have miraculous powers. The State cellars at Tállya have only 60 barrels of essencia; none is bottled, but a persuasive visitor might be allowed a taste. Of all the essences of the grape it is the most velvety, peach-like and penetrating. Its flavour stays in the mouth for half an hour. What it is like at 200 years old (some of the great Polish cellars kept it that long) only the Tsars can tell.

Even today Tokay is kept for six or seven years in narrow, pitch-black tunnels cut in the lava. With their single files of small barrels, their thickly moss-covered vaults and the only light from flickering candles, they are some of the world's most romantic cellars.

Modern Tokay is stabilized by pasteuriza-tion, which may account partly for its faintly madeira-like or cooked flavour. Anciently brandy was added instead. The few bottles which survive of wines from the famous old private cellars of Erdöbénye, Sárospatak, Tállya and Tarcal suggest that the old wine was, at its best, finer than today's. But even today an Aszu of four or five puttonyok has a silky texture, a haunting fragrance and flavour of mingled fruit and butter and caramel and the breath of the Bodrog among October vines.

Above: Tokay labels in order of sweetness and quality, culminating in Aszu. The little neck label indicates the number of sweetening puttonyok added (the adjective is puttonyos, or puttonos) Right: the wine market in the village of Tokay on a typical misty autumn day

Lake Balaton

LAKE BALATON, besides being the biggest lake in Europe, has a special significance for Hungarians. In a country with few landmarks and no coast it is the sea and the chief beauty spot. Its shores are thick with summer villas and holiday resorts, fragrant with admirable cooking. It has good weather and a happy social life. These things, rather than anything intrinsically unusual about the lake, are its attractions.

The north shore of Lake Balaton has all the advantages of good exposure and shelter, as well as the air-conditioning effect of a big body of water. It is inevitably a vineyard. In late summer the hot moist air is said to make monster leaves on vines, which in turn hasten the ripening of the grapes.

Its special qualities come not only from the climate, but from the combination of a sandy soil and curious extinct volcano stumps, of which Mount Badacsony is the most famous, dotted around among otherwise flat land. The steep slopes of basalt-rich sand drain well and absorb and hold the heat. Grape vines are in their element.

At one time many of the noble families of the Austro-Hungarian Empire kept vineyards here. The Esterhazy farm, with a modest brick villa, stands in an ideal position half-way up the south side of Mount Badacsony, below that of the poet Kisfaludy, which is now a restaurant. In

BALATONI RIESLING
PRODUCE OF HUNGARY

BALATONI FURMINT
PRODUCE OF HUNGARY

Badacsonyi **KÉKNYELŰ**

Top left: in the vineyards of Balaton, grapes are collected into open tubs where they are crushed with a wooden pestle, then funnelled into a barrel
Left: the commoner Balaton wines are shipped abroad in cask and bear a house label from a foreign merchant. The superior Kéknyelű and Szürkebarát from Badacsony have Monimpex labels

▢ Vineyards
▢ Woods
—250— Contour interval 50 metres

N

its plain cellars, with no equipment dating from later than about 1900, the character of Hungarian wine is easy to grasp. It is strong and simple and fresh, and often has the beauty of things which are young and belong to the country.

Olasz (Italian) Riesling is the common white grape. Its wine is very good when it is only a year old; dry but fresh and clean and not too strong. The real specialities, however, are the grapes which make powerful, honey-scented wine; the Hungarian white varieties Furmint, Szürkebarát and Kéknyelü.

Even at a year old, tasted from the barrel, a Szürkebarát can still be as white as milk and prickly and fierce with fermentation. In two or three years these wines—of which the Kéknyelü is reckoned the 'stiffest' and best—have remarkable presence. They are aromatic and fiery; not exactly dessert wines but very much the wines for the sort of spiced and pungent food the Hungarians love.

The whole north shore of the lake produces them. Csopak, Balatonfüred and Badacsony are the main centres. Normally the ordinary district wine will carry the simple name Balatoni, with the name of the grape. The name Badacsonyi on a label implies a stronger, sweeter, and to the Hungarian way of thinking altogether better wine.

Top right: a 19th-century view of the summer resort of Tihany on a peninsula jutting out from the north shore of Lake Balaton
Right: the coffin shape of Mount Badacsony with the lake behind, from Mount St George (Szt György). The basalt outcrop makes the soil for Hungary's best table wines, light gold, lively and fiery

Jugoslavia

Above: Jerusalem, the best-known vineyard of Ljutomer
Left: barrels are cleaned out with sea water before the vintage on the island of Hvar in Dalmatia

JUGOSLAVIA has its feet in the Balkans, its head in the Alps, and leans towards Italy. The conundrum is not a bad way of visualizing Jugoslav wine, even if it is politically 50 years out of date. The range of Jugoslav wine is exceptionally wide—from relatively northern, light and fruity white wine to profoundly southern, black and bitter red. She is the tenth-biggest producer in the world.

The simplest way to think of the wine regions is as those of the north, Slovenia and parts of Croatia, which are the best; the coast from Rijeka south to Dubrovnik and beyond, which are the least predictable, and the eastern and inland areas—Vojvodina on the Great Plain, the Fruška Gora hills above the Danube (the Dunav), central Serbia, Kosovo and Macedonia, which are the least known.

The map shows the main regions of production with the names of their most widely-grown wines. Many of the wines are called simply by the name of their home town or district followed by the name of the grape variety. Dozens of unheard-of and undistinguished grapes, however, proliferate, and (as in Italy) grape and wine are easily confused.

Some of Jugoslavia's grapes are already familiar. The Riesling she grows is the Italian Riesling (also known here as the Graševina)—not such a temperamental or distinguished a plant as the Rhine Riesling. A little Rajnski Rizling, as they call it, grows in northern Slovenia, round Maribor and Ljutomer, and makes the white wine which is Jugoslavia's most successful export. But even the Rajnski tends to have about $12\frac{1}{2}\%$ alcohol in this climate; too much for its true German delicacy.

The Slovene wines on the whole are lightly disguised versions of wines found in the neighbouring parts of Italy, Austria and Hungary. There is Merlot and Cabernet and Tokay (the Italian grape, not the Hungarian wine); Muscat, Malvasia and Pinot Blanc (here *bijelo*—white); Portugizac (the Austrian red Portugieser), Traminac and Sauvignon. The unfamiliar wines are the good light red Cviček, the white Šipon (which is supposed to be the Furmint of Hungary), sweet Radgonska Ranina

(its name of Tigrovo Mleko means Tiger's Milk) and heavy white Pekrčan.

Other grape names become familiar as one travels the country . . . for few are exported. Žilavka makes its best wine round the pretty old Turkish town of Mostar, north of Dubrovnik. Žilavka is dry and pungent and memorably fruity white wine—very often the best to be found in Jugoslav restaurants. Another is the red Prokupac, whose wine is the standard in southern Serbia and Macedonia. Between Smederevo and Svetozarevo, in Župa and Kruševac and south into Macedonia it forms about 85% of the production. It makes good rosé, firm and with plenty of flavour, and a red wine varying from dark and bitter to pleasantly fruity and drinkable. Often it is blended with the milder Plovdina and given local names (e.g. in Župa, Župsko crno). But it is slowly being ousted by such imported vines as Cabernet and Gamay, planted by co-operatives with their eye on an international market. Germany is a big customer for the red Burgundac of Kosovo, for example, under the name Amselfelder.

The biggest contrast to the massive co-operatives of the north and east is on the Dalmatian coast. A number of wines of strong personality are made on the islands, often from little rocky patches under fig-trees, pressed by an antique press and hoarded as a treasure which is none of the government's business. The dry brown Grk of Korčula, the pale and sometimes even perfumed Bogdanuša of Hvar and the similar Vugava of Vis, the thick sweetish Dingač and Postup of the Pelješac peninsula and the mighty Prošek, which can be like syrup of figs and can (occasionally) make a fair substitute for port, are all the specialities of small communities. Plavina, Plavac and Opol are their lighter reds and Maraština and Pošip their equivalent (though none too light) whites.

After the usual glasses of šljivovica, the oily dry plum spirit which is the national drink, and with Dalmatian food—tiny oysters, raw ham, grilled fish, smoky and oniony kebabs and mounds of sweet grapes—the fire and flavour of such local wines can seem ambrosial.

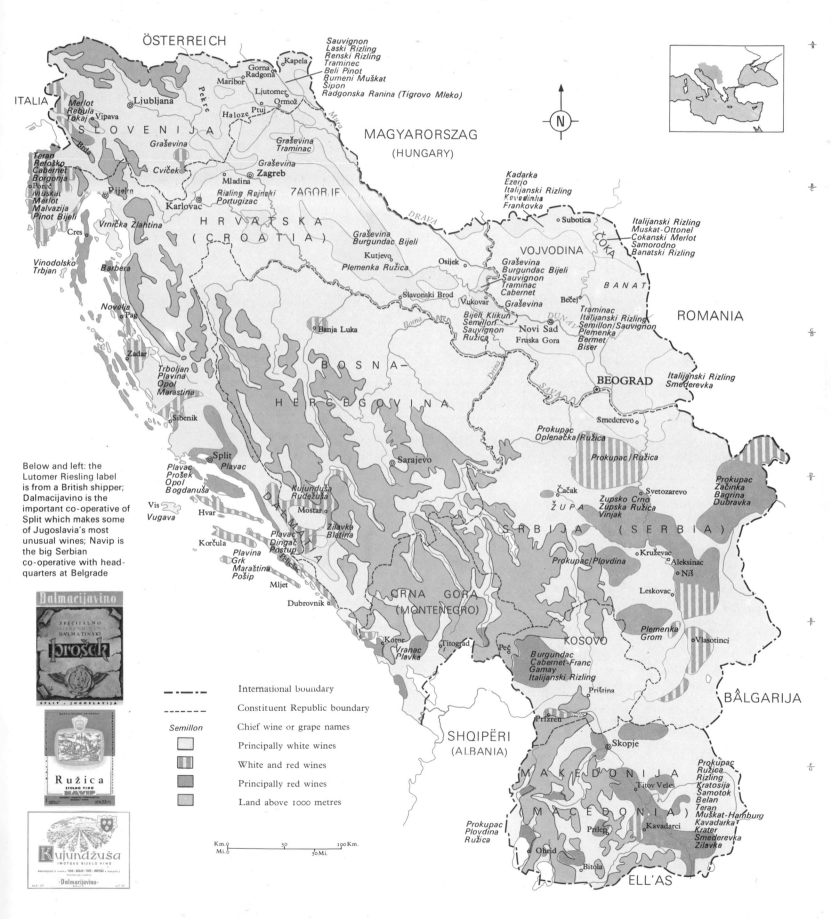

Below and left: the Lutomer Riesling label is from a British shipper; Dalmacijavino is the important co-operative of Split which makes some of Jugoslavia's most unusual wines; Navip is the big Serbian co-operative with head-quarters at Belgrade

International boundary
Constituent Republic boundary
Chief wine or grape names
Principally white wines
White and red wines
Principally red wines
Land above 1000 metres

Semillon

Romania

OF THE rapidly-expanding wine country of the Black Sea and the Balkans, Romania almost certainly has the greatest potential for quality. It is not only a matter of situation—though Romania lies on the same latitude as France—but of temperament. There seems to be a natural affinity for the culture of France in Romania. Romanian wine literature shares the sort of hard-headed lyricism of much of French gastronomic writing. There is a great difference between the Atlantic influence which makes France moist and mild, and the continental influence which gives Romania blazing summers. But it is the more temperate conditions of the coast and the north of the country which give Romania's best wine.

The Carpathian mountains curl like a snail in the middle of Romania. They occupy almost half the country, rising from the surrounding plain to about 8,000 feet at their peaks, and enclosing the Transylvanian plateau, which is still about 2,000 feet above sea level. Across the south of the country the Danube (the Dunărea) flows through a sandy plain. Here, and in the southern and eastern foot-hills of the Carpathians, is Romania's biggest vineyard.

In Romania, as in Russia, though not to the same extent, a great planting programme has increased the national vineyard by 51% in 15 years, making her at present the sixth largest wine-producer in Europe. It is interesting to see, however, that even now only 16% of the land under vines belongs to the state. Fifty per cent belongs to the big local co-operatives and the rest, 34%, is still private property.

Like Hungary, Romania has one wine whose name was once famous all over Europe. But Tokay, though shorn of its imperial glory, soldiers on in the wine-lists of the world, whereas Cotnari, which used to appear in Paris restaurants as 'Perle de la Moldavie', has faded into obscurity. Cotnari is a natural white dessert wine like Tokay, only with rather more delicacy and less intensity. There is no doubt, in tasting it, that one is tasting something of unusual quality and character.

Cotnari comes from the part of Moldavia, in north-east Romania, which was left to the Romanians after Russia had annexed a large slice of the country. The part the Russians took, anciently known as Bessarabia, contained a large proportion of Romania's vineyards. The great concentration of vineyards south of the Carpathians dates from since that time.

All the best of Romania's wine today is white. Both old-fashioned indigenous grape varieties with such names as Fetească, Grasă and Tămîioasă are used, and the international Rieslings and Pinots and Aligotés. The most widely-planted sorts are the Italian Riesling and one called the Fetească regală.

Apart from Cotnari, two areas produce white wines of a quality worth exporting: Tîrnave in Transylvania, which makes an adequate Riesling and a light, slightly sweet local speciality known as Perla, and Murfatlar near the coast on the plateau of Dobrogei. Murfatlar's best-known wine is a sweet pale golden-brown muscat; although Chardonnay and other French grapes are also successfully grown. It is possible that the muscat tradition here goes back to

The Language of the Label

Vie Vine
Viile Vineyard
Strugure Grape
Recolta Vintage
Vin superioare Superior wine
Vin de masă Table wine
Vin uşoare Light wine
GAS (Gospodaniile Agricole de Stat) State agricultural enterprise
IAS (Intreprinderile Agricole de Stat) More up-to-date name for the same
Imbuteliat Bottled
Vin alb White wine
Vin roşu Red wine
Vin rose Rosé
Sec Dry
Dulce Sweet
Spumos Sparkling
Pivniţă (pl pivniţele) Cellar
Ţuica Plum brandy
Fructexport The government exporting agency

ancient times, for the Greeks are supposed to have taken the muscat grape as far north as the Crimea, and where the port of Constanţa now stands stood the ancient city of Tomis.

The biggest wine region of modern Romania is Focşani, east of the Carpathians, including three wine-towns with lilting names: Coteşti, Odobeşti and Nicoreşti. The terrain varies but much of it is sand, which has only recently been mastered, here as in the great plain of Hungary, for vines. The vines have to be planted in pockets dug deep enough for their roots to reach the subsoil; sometimes as much as three metres below the surface. It seems a desperate expedient, especially as it takes the vine some time to grow up to ground level and come into bearing. But in fact good light wines are being made where nothing would grow before, here and in places along the Danube.

The red Băbească of Nicoresti is a good example of the character of the country; it is pleasantly acidic with a clove-like taste; fresh, original and enjoyable.

Following the curve of the Carpathians the next vineyard is Dealul Mare, where Romania's biggest state experimental vineyard, Valea Călugărească, lies in the foot-hills. The Cabernet is grown here with great pride, but with not always fortunate results. Like many Romanian red wines it can be sweet, heavy and without grace: possibly the result of the very hot late summer on these south-facing slopes.

Further west the vineyards continue with both red and white wines round Piteşti and Drăgăşani. From the south on the plain near the Danube Segarcea Cabernet and Sadova rosé are exported. Both suffer from the customary sweetness. One wonders whether it is entirely traditional or whether it is in the belief that the foreign market demands it.

In the western corner of Romania the Hungarian influence makes itself felt; many of the red wines of Banat are made from the Kadarka (here spelt Cadarca) of the Hungarian plain.

Below: Cotnari is Romania's most distinguished white wine; a strong, dryish natural dessert wine based on the Grasă grape, which is subject like the Semillon (see page 23) to 'noble rot'. Most Romanian labels name the grape variety first and foremost; the whites (Riesling, Fetească, Furmint etc) are best. Perla is a white wine; a speciality of Transylvania; gently sweet and pleasant. French is commonly used as the label language: German names are also adopted (last label) for wines designed for the German export market

Above: the massive maturing and bottling works of the Romanian state wine and spirit monopoly (formerly known as Romagricola, now as Fructexport) are in the capital city of Bucharest
Right: vineyards near the delta of the Danube, on sandy soil, produce Romania's traditional type of light and fruity red wine from such grapes as the Băbească. Niculitel is the best-known wine centre of this region

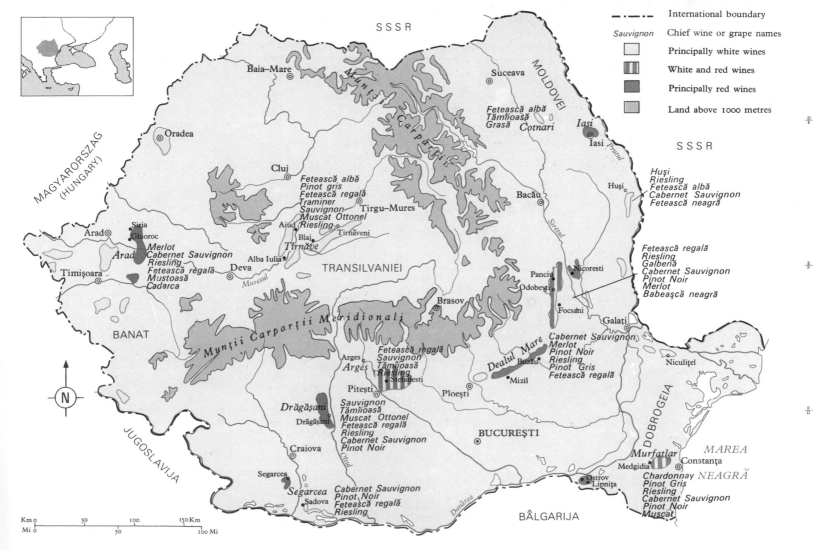

Sauvignon Chief wine or grape names
Principally white wines
White and red wines
Principally red wines
Land above 1000 metres
International boundary

SSSR

MAGYARORSZAG (HUNGARY)

Baia–Mare

Oradea

Cluj

Suceava

MOLDOVEI

Fetească albă
Tămîioasă
Grasă Cotnari

Iasi

Iasi

SSSR

Huşi
Riesling
Fetească albă
Cabernet Sauvignon
Fetească neagră

Huşi

Fetească albă
Pinot gris
Fetească regală
Traminer
Sauvignon
Muscat Ottonel
Riesling

Tirgu–Mures

Bacău

Siria
Ghioroc

Arad

Aiud
Blaj
Tîrnave Tirnaveni

Merlot
Cabernet Sauvignon
Riesling
Fetească regală
Mustoasă
Cadarca

Alba Iulia

Deva

TRANSILVANIEI

Muresul

Panciu Nicoresti

Odobesti

Fetească regală
Riesling
Galbenă
Cabernet Sauvignon
Pinot Noir
Merlot
Babeaşcă neagră

Timişoara

Brasov

Focsani

Galaţi

BANAT

Munţii Carparţii Meridionali

Fetească regală
Sauvignon
Tămîioasă
Riesling

Dealul Mare

Cabernet Sauvignon
Merlot
Pinot Noir
Riesling
Pinot Gris
Fetească regală

Buzău

Mizil

Niculiţel

Arges

Arges

Pitesti

Stefanesti

Ploeşti

Drăgăşani

Sauvignon
Tămîioasă
Muscat Ottonel
Fetească regală
Riesling
Cabernet Sauvignon
Pinot Noir

BUCUREŞTI

DOBROGEIA

Drăgăşani

Craiova

Oltul

Murfatlar Constanţa

Medgidia

MAREA

Segarcea

Cabernet Sauvignon
Pinot Noir
Fetească regală
Riesling

Ostrov
Lipnita

Chardonnay
Pinot Gris
Riesling
Cabernet Sauvignon
Pinot Noir
Muscat

NEAGRĂ

Segarcea
Sadova

Dunărea

BÂLGARIJA

JUGOSLAVIJA

N

Km 0   50   100   150 Km
Mi 0   50   100 Mi

Bulgaria

Above: Bulgaria was under Turkish influence until the end of the last century; the mosque at Karnobat is a reminder that wine is a newcomer

Right: highly industrialized methods of treating the huge flat vineyards have led to a relatively consistent standard of wine and to high exports

The Language of the Label

Лозова пръчка (Lozova prachka) Vine or variety of vine
Лоза (Lozia) Vineyards
Винопроизводител (Vinoproizvoditel) Wine-producer
Бутилирам (Butiliram) To bottle
Натурално (Naturalno) Natural
Бяло вино (Bjalo vino) White wine
Червено вино (Cherveno vino) Red wine
Сухо вино (Suho vino) Dry wine
Сладко вино (Sladko vino) Sweet wine
Искрящо вино (Iskriashto vino) Sparkling wine
Коняк (Koniak) Brandy
С остатъчна захар (S ostatachna zahar) With residual sugar—in other words semi-sweet or sweet
Vinimpex Bulgaria's 'State Commercial Enterprise for Export and Import of Wines and Spirits', a monopoly, controls the entire wine export trade

Bulgaria produces more and more Cabernet, Chardonnay, Riesling and other internationally famous grapes. These are the labels of her own sorts: Gamza, Kadarka (from Hungary), Melnik and Mavrud are red table wines; Trakia and Dimiat dry or medium white wines; Hemus sweet white, Tirnovo a sweet red and Iskra Bulgaria's semi-dry sparkling wine

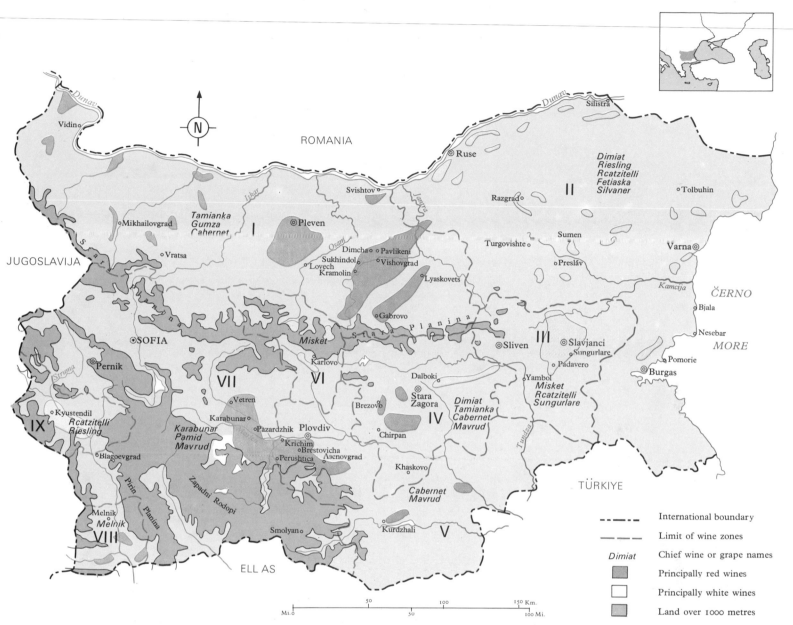

ROMANIA

Dunav

Vidin

Mikhailovgrad

Vratsa

Tamianka
Gumza
Cabernet

I

Pleven

II

Dimiat
Riesling
Rcatzitelli
Fetiaska
Silvaner

Silistra

Ruse

Svishtov

Razgrad

Tolbuhin

JUGOSLAVIJA

SOFIA

Pernik

Misket

Karlovo

VII

VI

Dimcha
Sukhindol
Lovech
Kramolin

Pavlikeni
Vishovgrad

Lyaskovets

Gabrovo

Stara Planina

Turgovishte

Sumen

Preslav

Varna

ČERNO

Kamcija

Bjala

Nesebar

MORE

Sliven

III

Slavjanci
Sungurlare

Pádavero

Dalboki

Brezovo

Stara
Zagora

IV

Dimiat
Tamianka
Cabernet
Mavrud

Yambol

Misket
Rcatzitelli
Sungurlare

Pomorie

Burgas

Kyustendil

Rcatzitelli
Riesling

IX

Vetren

Karabunar

Karabunar
Pamid
Mavrud

Pazardzhik

Krichim
Perushtica

Brestovicha

Plovdiv

Asenovgrad

Chirpan

Khaskovo

TÜRKIYE

Blagoevgrad

Pirin Planina

Zapadni Rodopi

Cabernet
Mavrud

Melnik
Melnik

VIII

Smolyan

Kurdzhali

V

ELLAS

International boundary

Limit of wine zones

Dimiat   Chief wine or grape names

Principally red wines

Principally white wines

Land over 1000 metres

50   100   150 Km.
Mi. 0   50   100 Mi.

PERHAPS because it is in most ways a less civilized and sophisticated country than Romania, Bulgaria, once it had made up its mind to modernise its wine industry, forged ahead with complete state control at a remarkable rate. Modernization only began in 1949, and yet by 1966 Bulgaria had become the sixth largest wine exporter in the world, following after the much older-established wine countries of Algeria, France, Italy, Spain and Portugal. Eighty per cent of the crop is exported now, mainly to Iron Curtain countries and Germany. The wine industry, in fact, is looked on as a currency-earner first and foremost.

Vineyards in Bulgaria are huge blocks of flat land which can be cultivated entirely by machinery. Wine-processing plant is modern and Bulgarian wine—at least exported wine—tends to be more stable and arrive in better condition than that of Romania. There is very little in the way of a peasant wine-making tradition, for a historical reason: the architecture, the traditional costumes and the food of the country all bear the marks of the Turkish domination, with its Muslim rules against drinking wine, which ended less than a hundred years ago.

As in Romania, the white wine is better than the red. There is a Chardonnay made which is outstanding and would be perfectly acceptable in the south of Burgundy.

The country is divided into nine wine regions, varying widely in size: one north of the Balkan mountains which makes mainly red wine; one to the east on the coast of the Black Sea which makes most of the best white, and the remainder in the south and west making red and heavy or sweet white, with the exception of a pleasantly scented muscat, known as Misket—which unlike all the other muscats of Eastern Europe and Russia is fully fermented to be quite a dry wine, not unlike the muscat of Alsace, though rather heavier and less elegant. It is the speciality of Karlovo, in the valley which grows musk roses as a crop for making attar of roses, and also at Sungurlare nearer the coast.

The red wines range from a quickly-fermented light vin ordinaire called Pamid to a darkly plummy Mavrud and a strong 'Alicante-style' Melnik in the south-west. At least some of the Cabernet is as sweet as in Romania. The Gamza (or Gumza), which seems to be the

same grape as the Hungarian Kadarka, on the other hand, in the north, makes a pleasant dry red wine of a rather brown colour and without much body. It carries the name of its district—Pleven, Sukhindol, Pavlikeni or Kramolin.

Eastern Bulgaria, from Ruse on the Danube (the Dunav) to Burgas, grows most of the country's very drinkable dry white wines. Dimiat is the most widespread variety; the white opposite number of the Gamza, and like the Gamza attributed to a district—Varna, Preslav or Pomorie. The Riesling is the Italian version; its produce is comparable with the wine it makes in Hungary. Rcatzitelli is a grape which appears all round the Black Sea making strong white wine—in Russia it is often made sweet as well.

For the important German market, Vinimpex, the export organization, devises names like Sonnenküste for the Rcatzitelli, Klosterkeller for the full-bodied dry Sylvaner and Donau Perle for the rather neutral dry Fetiaska. The very popular white Hemus is medium-sweet, and Tamianka very sweet; these and numerous other dessert wines are made mainly in the south.

The Soviet Union

THE SOVIET UNION officially decided in favour of wine—at the expense of vodka—in the fifties. In 1950 she had one million acres of vineyards. No less than 4½ million acres were ordained to be planted by 1965. In reality 1966 came with something over 2½ million actually planted—but this is certainly the biggest and fastest extension of the world's wine-growing capacity there has ever been.

The Soviet wine belt sweeps east round the north of the Black Sea from Moldavia—which was formerly in Romania—to Armenia on the border of Turkey. Two areas, the Crimean peninsula, and Georgia on the southern slopes of the Caucasus, have been famous since ancient times for good wine and remain the best today. The Russian taste is for sweet wine; the names of port, madeira and sherry are widely taken in vain. Many of the specialities named on the map are dessert wines of between 16% and 19% alcohol and more or less sweet.

The Moldavian vineyards grow the traditional Romanian varieties alongside newcomers like Cabernet and Aligoté. The Fetjaska makes fresh dry white; Negru de Purkar is the traditional dry but fruity red. Romanesti is made with a Bordeaux-like blend of Cabernet,

Merlot and Malbec. But Chumai is Cabernet made into a dessert wine. Trifesti (Pinot—or Pineau—Gris) and Gratiesti (the local Rcatzitelli) are white dessert wines.

Of Ukrainian wines from anywhere except the Crimea, only the names have come to light. In the Crimea, the name of the best-known estate, Massandra, the former property of Prince Woronzow, is widely used on dessert wines, which are the speciality of the south coast. Massandra muscat is full and brown; like Frontignan from the south of France. Of the others listed on the map, Kokur Niznegorsky and Silvaner Feodosiisky are dry but full-bodied white wines. Alushta (from the valley behind the port) is reckoned the best red, Solnechnaya Dolina and Chorny Doktor are respectively white and red dessert wines and the Pinot Gris of Ai Danil is sweet, like Moldavian Trifesti.

The Don basin round Rostov specializes in sparkling wine. The red, sweet and sparkling Tsimlyanskoye is highly regarded. South of Krasnodar, the only Russian Riesling exported is grown at Anapa. Chyorniye Glaza ('Black Eyes') is the 'port' of the Russian republic.

Several of Georgia's traditional types have made a modest name for themselves in the

world, as good dry everyday wines. In fact Tsinandali and Gurdzhaani, which are white, are comparable with good Spanish or Portuguese white wines; better than the heavy red Mukuzani, and lighter Saperavi and Napareuli.

Armenia, Azerbaijan and the area along the Caspian up to Machackala are dessert-wine country. All the types listed are sweet and strong, red, brown or white, some cooked like madeira. The Matrasa and Sadilly of Baku, red and white table wines, are the only exceptions.

The Language of the Label

Винозавод (Vinozavod) Wine factory
Столовое вино (Stolovoe vino) Table wine
Белое вино (Beloe vino) White wine
Красное вино (Krasnoe vino) Red wine
Розовое вино (Rozovoe vino) Rosé
Сухое вино (Sukhoe vino) Dry wine
Дессертное вино (Desertnoe vino) Dessert wine
Шампанское (Shampanskoe) 'Champagne'
Грузинское вино (Gruzinskoe vino) Georgian wine

Above: labels from Georgia (top); the Russian republic (second row); Georgian 'champagne' and dessert wine from Azerbaijan (third); Moldavia and Crimea (bottom)
Left: a state farm in Azerbaijan where sweet grape types are developed for making dessert wines
Right: near Tbilisi (Tiflis) in Georgia a winery bottles 'champagne' under pressure

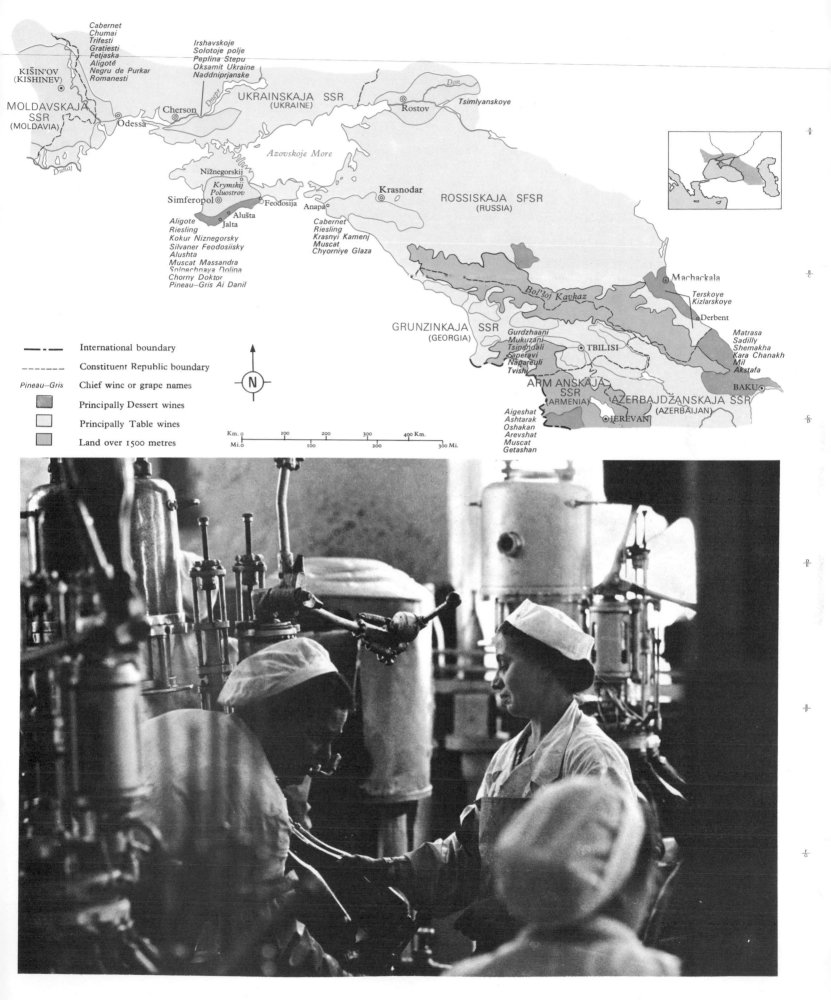

Cabernet
Chumai
Trifesti
Gratiesti
Fetjaska
Aligoté
Negru de Purkar
Romanesti

KIŠIN'OV
(KISHINEV)

MOLDAVSKAJA
SSR
(MOLDAVIA)

Odessa

Cherson

Dnepr

Irshavskoje
Solotoje polje
Peplina Stepu
Oksamit Ukraine
Naddniprjanske

UKRAINSKAJA SSR
(UKRAINE)

Don

Rostov

Tsimlyanskoye

Azovskoje More

Nižnegorskij

Krymskij
Poluostrov

Simferopol

Alušta
Jalta

Feodosija

Anapa

Krasnodar

ROSSISKAJA SFSR
(RUSSIA)

Machackala

Aligote
Riesling
Kokur Niznegorsky
Silvaner Feodosiisky
Alushta
Muscat Massandra
Solnechnaya Dolina
Chorny Doktor
Pineau–Gris Ai Danil

Cabernet
Riesling
Krasnyi Kamenj
Muscat
Chyorniye Glaza

Bol'šoj Kavkaz

Terskoye
Kizlarskoye

Derbent

GRUNZINKAJA SSR
(GEORGIA)

Gurdzhaani
Mukuzani
Tsinandali
Saperavi
Napareuli
Tvishi

TBILISI

Matrasa
Sadilly
Shemakha
Kara Chanakh
Mil
Akstafa

BAKU

ARM ANSKAJA
SSR
(ARMENIA)

AZERBAJDŽANSKAJA SSR
(AZERBAIJAN)

Aigeshat
Ashtarak
Oshakan
Arevshat
Muscat
Getashan

JEREVAN

International boundary

Constituent Republic boundary

Pineau–Gris   Chief wine or grape names

Principally Dessert wines

Principally Table wines

Land over 1500 metres

N

Km. 0   100   200   300   400 Km.

Mi. 0   100   200   300 Mi.

A/B

B/C

C/D

D/E

E/F

F/G

Greece

Above: the temple of Zeus near Nemea in the Peloponnese stands among vines for Nemean red wine
Right: Sifnos is typical of the rocky Aegean islands where the vine is grown casually on the hot slopes

Right: Greek labels appear in Greek, English, French, German or mixtures. From left: a dry white wine from Marmarion at the southern tip of Euboea; a good standard red from Attica; the red of Naoussa in Macedonia; the 'Romaic' red of Crete; the best-known unresinated brand of table wine; the sweet Malvasia or Malmsey which is the speciality of Rhodes; a dark rosé from Nemea in the Peloponnese; perhaps the best branded red table wine; a strong rosé from Crete; a famous brand of retsina; the sweet red of Patras; the famous sweet muscat of Samos

ANCIENT and modern Greece are divided by a gulf with few bridges. The taste for resinated wine or retsina is one; perhaps the only characteristic habit of Greece which goes straight back 3,000 years and beyond, to the time when gods walked on earth.

The god of wine, Dionysus, was Zeus' son by Semele, daughter of the King of Thebes. His mother having been destroyed by Olympian intrigue, Dionysus was brought up by the nymphs of Nysa in Thrace. His tutor was the Rabelaisian old satyr Silenus, who taught him to make wine. From Thrace Dionysus set out to take the knowledge of wine to the world . . . both in legend and in fact; as the Greek Empire spread, it took the vine with it.

Traces of pine resin have been found in wine amphorae from earliest times. It is usually assumed that it was used to preserve the wine. But resinated wine does not age well. The real reason is surely that Greek wine is much improved by the fresh, sappy, turpentine-like flavour which resin gives if added during the fermentation. Half the wine made in Greece is so treated, and the result is one of the most individual and appetizing drinks of the world. Where peasant food is always oily (and often musty) it is also particularly effective in cancelling the flavour of a doubtful mouthful.

Attica, the region of Athens, is the home of retsina. Most of it is white, from the Savatiano grape, but some rosé or kokkineli is also made.

More than a third of the vineyards of Greece are in the Peloponnese. Both the major firms in the wine trade, Achaia-Clauss and Andrew Cambas, now have their headquarters here. The traditional speciality of the Peloponnese is sweet wine; from Monemvasia come the names Malmsey, Malvasia and Malvoisie.

Mavrodaphne, a sweetish red wine rather in the manner of Italian Recioto, dark and strong, is reckoned the best of the region.

Mavro is the general word for red wines; its literal meaning of black is often justified; the Mavro of Naoussa in Macedonia, Nemea in the Peloponnese, Crete (where it is sometimes called Mavro Romeiko), Páros, Límnos (Kalpaki), Lefkás, Delphi's Mavroudi and Corfu's Ropa are all recognized. Few, with the exception of brands like Castel Danielis for which you pay a premium, have much appeal, but they are useful for blending, being very dark.

Dry white Greek wine is not usually remarkable. One or two brands, such as Santa Laura, Hymettus and Demestica, are pleasant; the Rombola of Cephalonia, the Verdea from Zákynthos, the Thíra of Santorin and Lindos of Rhodes are said to be above average. The sweet white muscat of Samos is, at its best, something much more individual.

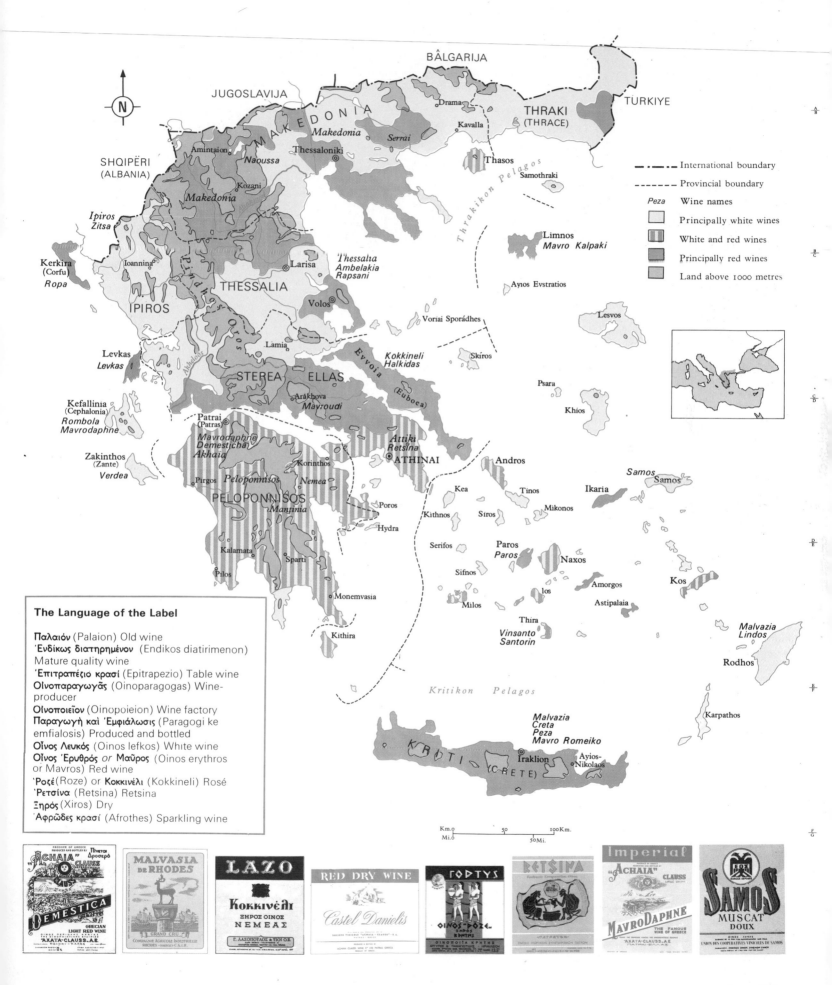

BÂLGARIJA

JUGOSLAVIJA

MAKEDONIA

THRAKI (THRACE)

TÜRKIYE

Drama
Kavalla

Makedonia
Serrai

Amintaion
Thessaloniki
Makedonia

SHQIPËRI (ALBANIA)

Naoussa
Kozani

Thasos

Thrakikon Pelagos

Samothraki

Ipiros
Zitsa

Limnos
Mavro Kalpaki

Peza — Wine names

Kerkira (Corfu)
Ropa

Ioannina

Larisa

Thessalia
Ambelakia
Rapsani

Ayios Evstratios

Principally white wines

White and red wines

Principally red wines

Land above 1000 metres

THESSALIA

IPIROS

Volos

Lesvos

Levkas
Levkas

Lamia

Kokkineli
Halkidas

Voriai Sporádhes

Skiros

Psara

Kefallinia (Cephalonia)
Rombola
Mavrodaphne

STEREA ELLAS

Arákhova
Mavroudi

Evvoia (Euboea)

Khios

Patrai (Patras)

Mavrodaphne
Demesticha
Akhaïa

Korinthos

Attiki
Retsina
ATHINAI

Andros

Samos
Samos

Zakinthos (Zante)
Verdea

Peloponnisos

Nemea

Poros

Kea

Tinos

Ikaria

Pirgos

PELOPONNISOS

Mantinia

Hydra

Kithnos

Siros

Mikonos

Kalamata

Sparti

Serifos

Paros
Paros

Naxos

Pilos

Sifnos

Milos

Ios

Amorgos

Kos

Monemvasia

Astipalaia

Thira

Malvazia
Lindos

Kithira

Vinsanto
Santorin

Rodhos

Kritikon Pelagos

Malvazia
Creta
Peza
Mavro Romeiko

Karpathos

KRITI (CRETE)

Iraklion

Ayios-Nikolaos

International boundary

Provincial boundary

The Language of the Label

Παλαιόν (Palaion) Old wine
Ἐνδίκως διατηρημένον (Endikos diatirimenon) Mature quality wine
Ἐπιτραπέζιο κρασί (Epitrapezio) Table wine
Οἰνοπαραγωγᾶς (Oinoparagogas) Wine-producer
Οἰνοποιεῖον (Oinopoieion) Wine factory
Παραγωγὴ καὶ Ἐμφιάλωσις (Paragogi ke emfialosis) Produced and bottled
Οἶνος Λευκός (Oinos lefkos) White wine
Οἶνος Ἐρυθρός or Μαῦρος (Oinos erythros or Mavros) Red wine
Ροζέ (Roze) or Κοκκινέλι (Kokkineli) Rosé
Ρετσίνα (Retsina) Retsina
Ξηρός (Xiros) Dry
Ἀφρώδες κρασί (Afrothes) Sparkling wine

Km.0   50   100 Km.
Mi.0   50 Mi.

Cyprus

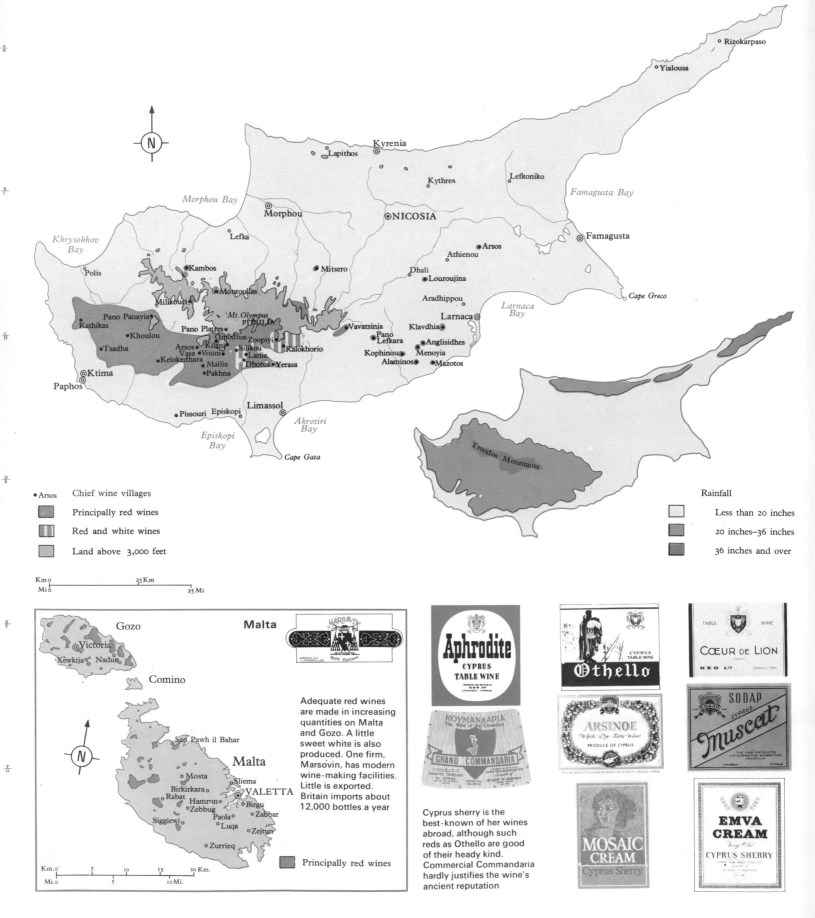

Rizokarpaso

Yialousa

Kyrenia

Lapithos

Kythrea

Lefkoniko

Famagusta Bay

Morphou Bay

Morphou

⊙NICOSIA

Famagusta

Khrysokhov Bay

Lefka

Arsos

Athienou

Polis

Kambos

Mitsero

Dhali

Louroujina

Cape Greco

Moutoullas

Aradhippou

Larnaca Bay

Milikouri

Mt. Olympus

PITSILIA

Larnaca

Pano Panayia

Pano Platres

Vavatsinia

Klavdhia

Kathikas

Omodhos Zoopiyi

Pano Lefkara

Anglisidhes

Khoulou

Arsos Kilani

Silikou

Kophinou

Menoyia

Tsadha

Vasa Vouni

Lania

Kalokhorio

Alaminos

Mazotos

Kelokedhara

Mallia

Dhoros Yerasa

Ktima

Pakhna

Paphos

Pissouri

Episkopi

Limassol

Akrotiri Bay

Episkopi Bay

Cape Gata

Troodos Mountains

Legend

- Arsos — Chief wine villages
- Principally red wines
- Red and white wines
- Land above 3,000 feet

Rainfall
- Less than 20 inches
- 20 inches–36 inches
- 36 inches and over

Km 0 ... 25 Km
Mi 0 ... 25 Mi

Malta

Gozo

Victoria
Xewkija Nadur

Comino

Malta

San Pawh il Bahar

Mosta
Sliema
Birkirkara
VALETTA
Rabat Hamrun
Birgu
Zebbug
Zabbar
Paola
Siggiewi
Luqa
Zejtun
Zurrieq

Principally red wines

Km. 0 ... 5 ... 10 ... 15 ... 20 Km.
Mi. 0 ... 5 ... 10 Mi.

Adequate red wines are made in increasing quantities on Malta and Gozo. A little sweet white is also produced. One firm, Marsovin, has modern wine-making facilities. Little is exported. Britain imports about 12,000 bottles a year

Cyprus sherry is the best-known of her wines abroad, although such reds as Othello are good of their heady kind. Commercial Commandaria hardly justifies the wine's ancient reputation

MARSOVIN

Aphrodite
CYPRUS TABLE WINE

Othello
CYPRUS TABLE WINE

Coeur de Lion
KEO L^D

KOYMANAΔPIA
The Wine of the Crusaders
GRAND COMMANDARIA

ARSINOE
White Dry Table Wine
PRODUCE OF CYPRUS

SODAP
CYPRUS
Muscat

MOSAIC CREAM
Cyprus Sherry

EMVA CREAM
Very Old
CYPRUS SHERRY

KOYTI

In the Troodos mountains, under silver olive-trees, mules carry grapes to the press-house. Heat and drought are what give Cyprus wine its strength. Only in the Troodos, which occasionally get rain, can the vine flourish

CYPRUS not only has one of the oldest wine-growing traditions in the world. It is by far the most developed and successful of the wine countries of the eastern Mediterranean; the first (during her period of British rule starting in 1878) to restore wine to a prime place in her economy, from which Islam had toppled it.

In the last 15 years an enlightened and en-quiring approach to wine-making has opened a huge export market for Cyprus wine. Her 'sherry' has made the running so far, but there is every chance that her table wine will follow. They will never be better than good ordinary wine, but they have plenty of strength and character which careful wine-making can turn into an ideal drink for rough peasanty food. Excellent Cypriot restaurants all over the world serve it already as a matter of course. The more authentic their cooking the better the dark red wine tastes with it.

The Troodos mountains, attracting rain, make viticulture possible in Cyprus. The vine-yards lie where the rain falls, up to nearly three thousand feet into the hills. The whole

south-facing Troodos is possible wine country. Limassol, the port on the south coast, is the entrepôt and headquarters of the three big wine firms; Keo, Sodap and Haggipavlu.

The most individual of Cyprus wines is the almost liqueur-like Commandaria which is made of dried grapes, both red and white, in the villages of Kalokhorio, Zoopiyi, Yerasa and four or five others on the lower slopes of the Troodos. Commandaria has been made at least since the crusading Knights Templar es-tablished themselves in their Grande Com-manderie on the island at the end of the 12th century. Its intense sweetness (it can have four times as much sugar as port) harks back in fact far further than records go; there are references in Greek literature to such wines, which were invariably drunk diluted with water.

Commandaria is now made both as a straight commercial dessert wine of moderate age, cheap

and pleasant but without interest, and by a few traditionalists as the quite alarming concentra-ted wine of legend. The taste and texture of an old true Commandaria are more than treacly; they have a remarkable haunting wininess.

The range of grapes grown on Cyprus is much less eclectic than in most of the develop-ing wine countries. The island has never had phylloxera, and rather than risk it by importing new stock, growers have kept to the three tra-ditional island grapes, the black Mavron, the white Xynisteri and the muscat of Alexandria. Platres is said to make the best red wine, and the region round about the best kokkineli; heavy alcoholic rosé. The white wine centre is round Paphos, with Pitsilia the best-known village for Xynisteri.

White wines represent only a quarter of the total. They are hard to prevent from oxidizing; until recently Cyprus sherry was in fact just fortified and sweetened oxidized white wine. Experiments have been made, however, with Spanish sherry methods, and the recent boom in exports has been partly the result.

North Africa

Above vineyards were almost unknown in North Africa before the beginning of French influence in the last century. Between 1860 and 1880 Algeria's total went up from 4600 to 22,720 hectares. Later it reached 400,000 hectares

THE NORMAL SITUATION in which the countries who grow the most wine are also those which drink most is reversed in North Africa. In the rest of the world, on an average, exports only account for 10% of wine-production; the home market for 90%. But Algeria, Morocco and Tunisia, which together grew about 10% of the world's wine, in the early fifties accounted for no less than 2/3 of the entire international wine trade. In other words they were alone in growing specifically for export—and, unfortunately for them, specifically for one market; France. Muslim prohibition meant that their home market was practically limited to the European population.

The main appeal of North African wines was to wine-growers and blenders in France, rather than consumers. Light sandy soil and a very hot summer gives them very little acidity—the preservative of northern wines. They age quickly, and naturally help to bring into balance over-acid wine. They are also between 12 and 15% alcohol, which made them vital raw material for transforming the poor under-strength wine of the Midi, often as low as 9%, into the 11% vin ordinaire which is the French workman's staple diet.

However in 1962 Algeria, by far the biggest producer in North Africa, became independent. And at about the same time measures taken in France to improve the wine of the Midi began to take effect. There was much bargaining, but the upshot was that France bought a fraction of her old total from Algeria. With the French population also greatly reduced, Algeria had far more wine than she could sell; most of it only suitable for blending.

All this is politics, but it deeply affects the

Above: Moroccan labels tend to be reticent. The second down is that of vin gris, the pale pink speciality of Boulaoune
Left: Algeria's best vineyards are all on the hills. Today their future is uncertain because of the loss of the French market

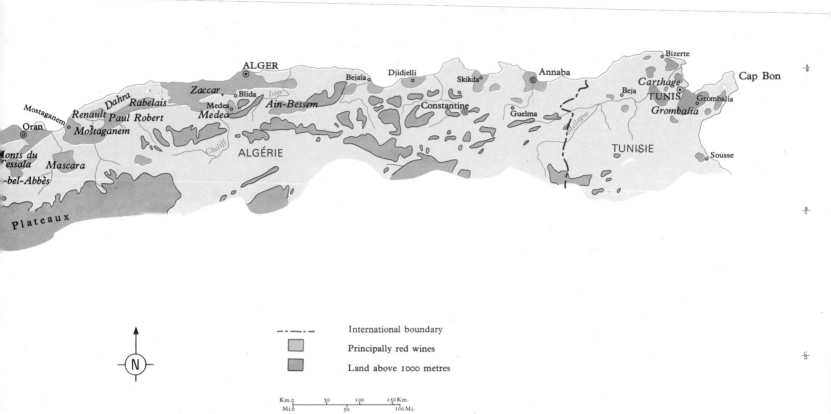

International boundary

Principally red wines

Land above 1000 metres

Km.0   50   100   150 Km.
Mi.0   50   100 Mi.

N

future of North African wine. There are new markets: Germany and Russia are now customers, and the franc zone countries of Africa—Madagascar, Senegal, the Ivory Coast, Chad—now buy from North Africa rather than from their old supplier, France. But a world glut of vin ordinaire is an extreme danger, if not a fact already. The only sensible course is to abandon massive plains-plantations and concentrate on making better wine in the hills.

Being the butt of endless stories about clandestine tanker-loads to Beaune, North African wines are rarely even thought of as existing in their own right. Visitors to North Africa, particularly Morocco, are invariably surprised at how good the local wine is. The fat soft red wines taste delicious with the grilled meat and the young rosés—Morocco's speciality is a very pale 'vin gris', remarkably hard, dry and refreshing—go well with the shellfish. Visitors soon learn not to try the white wines.

Morocco is the newest wine country of the three. Not until after the second world war were modern vineyards planted in place of the traditional sparse scattering of vines among trees. Her new vineyards are concentrated south and east of Rabat, the capital, stretching inland along the plain (where Sidi Larbi and Dar bel Amri make her best-known red wines) south of Meknès to Fès. Some of these vineyards are in the foot-hills of the Atlas mountains but most are on the plain. South of Casablanca, where the map shows them continuing from Boulaouane almost to Essaouira, they are much more scattered, and largely traditional in style: though Boulaouane has a modern winery.

The French planted the vineyards of Algeria in the second half of the last century. So

Above: Tunisian wine harks back to the great days of Carthage. She makes good red ordinaire and muscat
Left-hand column: during the French regime a dozen Algerian wines were rated Vins Délimités de Qualité Supérieure. The technical problems of making good red wine in the African climate were largely overcome. These labels are from some of the better estates which may continue

thoroughly did they carpet the bare red hills with vines that almost 40% of the country's work force at one time were vineyard workers. Now the Algerian hill vineyards are particularly beautiful: low green bushes in endless files against the red soil over long waves of rocky hills. In the dry air the light is clear.

Until 1962, twelve of the Algerian hill wine regions were ranked in France as Vins Délimités de Qualité Supérieure. The best-known of them are in the hills of Tlemcen (the domaines of Lismara and Mansourah, 800 metres up and facing north-west); in the Haut-Dahra hills (the three villages with the memorable names of Rabelais, Renault and Paul Robert make red wine which is often said to be Algeria's best); Mascara (particularly the Clos de l'Emir); the hills of Zaccar west of Algiers (Château Romain) and the Domaine de la Trappe Staouëli south-east of the capital.

Seventy-two per cent of Algeria's vineyards are in the province of Oran in the west, mainly on flat land. Oran makes strong, dark-coloured, under-acid, good blending wine. Twenty-three per cent are in the province of Algiers; as they go east, the produce has less strength and character. The names on the map are those of regions of above-average quality.

Tunisia was known for its wine in ancient times; indeed Mago, the first author of a classic manual for wine-growers (and other farmers) was a native of Carthage in the fourth century BC. The muscat grape is a speciality—under the French there was an Appellation Contrôlée Muscat de Tunisie. The best of her red table wine is on a par with the best of Algeria's but the present lack of a market is causing the pulling-up of much of the Tunisian vineyard.

The Eastern Mediterranean

BÅLGARJA
(BULGARIA)

ELL'AS
(GREECE)

Kirklareli

Uzunköprü

III

Tekirdağ

Istanbul

Çanakkale

Erdek

Marmara
Denizi

Balikesir

Bursa

İzmit

Adapazari

Zonguldak

VII

Karabük

Bafra

Samsun

Sakarya

Kızıl

Çorum

Amasya

Tokat

I

Çubuk

Kalecik

ANKARA

Keskin

Sivas

VIII

VI

Eskişehir

Kütahya

Porsuk

TÜRKİYE

Simav

Akhisar

Uşak

Afyonkarahişar

Kayseri

Malatya

Elâziğ

Bornova
İzmir

II

Tire

Akşehir

Ürgüp
Nevşehir

Söke

Konya

IX

Niğde

Denizlio

Burdur

Isparta

Ereğli

IV

Maraş

Euphrates
(Firat)

Antalya

Karaman

Seyhan

Ceyhan

V

Toros

Dağlari

Adana

Mersin

Gaziantep

Goksu

İskenderun

Kilis

Antakya

Halab
(Aleppo)

Al-Lādiqīyah
(Latakia)

KIPROS
(CYPRUS)

AS–SŪRĪYAH
(SYRIA)

Hamah

Tarābulus
(Tripoli)

Hims
(Homs)

Bekaa

Ba'labakk
(Baalbek)

BAYRUT
(BEIRUT)

Ksarā

AL-LUBNAN
(LEBANON)

DIMASHQ
(DAMASCUS)

Hefa
(Haifa)

Zichron-Jacob

Irbid

YISRA'EL

Tel Aviv-Yafo
Richon-le-Zion

Ram
Allah

Az-Zarqa
(Zarqua)

AMMAN

Nahr al-Urdunn

YERUSHALAYIM
(JERUSALEM)

Bayt Lahm
(Bethlehem)

Al-Iskandariyah
(Alexandria)

Būr Sa'id
(Port Said)

Gazzah

AL-URDUNN
(JORDAN)

Abū Hummus

Nahr an-Nil

Be'er Sheva

AL-JUMHURIYAH AL'ARABIYAH
AL-MUTTAHIDAH
(UNITED ARAB REPUBLIC)

Legend

- – ‒ · International boundary
- – – – Limit of wine zones
- Red and white wines
- Principally white wines
- Land over 1500 metres

N

Km. 0   100   200   300 Km.

Mi. 0   100   200 Mi.

Above: the top two labels are those of Turkey's two best-known wines, both red. Below them are two of Turkey's prettiest. Below them are, left, two Israeli and, right, Lebanese and Egyptian labels
Right: vineyards in the valley of Bekaa in the Lebanon

IT IS A sobering thought that some spot on this map may be the very place where man first tasted wine. Whether it was in Persia or Egypt that the first wine was made, there is no doubt that the Middle East is its home country. Noah, Naboth, Christ, St Paul, the great Roman temple at Baalbek are all evidence that the eastern Mediterranean was the France of the ancient world. And so it continued until the eighth century, until the advent of Islam.

The Prophet forbade the use of wine. How effective his teaching was has often been discussed. Some wine-growing went on, but it was not until the end of the last century that wine began to come back to its homeland in earnest. As phylloxera destroyed Europe's vineyards Asia leapt into the breach. In 1857 the Jesuits founded the cellars of Ksara in the Lebanon, still the biggest winery in the Middle East. In the 1880s a Rothschild established wine-growing once more in Israel. Turkey exported nearly 15 million gallons in one year in the 90s. In 1903 Nestor Gianaclis planted the first vines of a new Egyptian wine industry, near Alexandria, whose wine in Roman times was famous.

Turkey is the biggest producer and exporter of the eastern Mediterranean. She has the fifth largest vineyard acreage in the world, but only 3% of her grapes are made into wine. The rest

are eaten. The wine industry is held back by lack of a domestic market, for 99% of the population remains Muslim. Kemal Atatürk himself built a winery in 1925 in the hope of persuading Turks of the rightness of wine-drinking, but progress is slow.

The country is divided into nine ecological zones. Zones II and III, the Aegean coast and Thrace/Marmara, are by far the biggest wine-producers, making three-fifths of the total. They are followed by zone I, Ankara, and then, much smaller, IV and IX, south-east Anatolia and south-central Anatolia. The state monopoly has 17 wineries and accounts for most exports of Turkish wine. High-strength blending wine is most in demand, though the names of Trakya and Buzbağ, its lighter and darker red wines (from Thrace and south-east Anatolia, in that order) are familiar. There is also a white Trakya, made of the Semillon grape.

Of the private firms, Doluca and Kavaklidere are probably the best, and Aral the biggest. Wineries on the whole do not own their vineyards but buy their grapes from farmers. Phylloxera is now a problem; many farmers have yet to learn about grafting vines to overcome it.

Ksara's big installation is the centre of Lebanese wine-growing. Its red wines, made from French ordinaire grapes—Cinsault, Cari-

gnan, Aramon—are its best. Small farmers still use biblical methods of vinification and keep their wine in amphoras, or distil it themselves to make the aniseed-flavoured arack which is the national drink.

The considerable wineries at Richon-le-Zion and Zichron-Jacob were a gift to Israel from Baron Edmond de Rothschild. They make three-quarters of Israel's wine. Most of the 13,000 acres of wine-grape vineyard is planted with the common French red grapes (41% is Carignan and 32% Alicante-Grenache); the white grapes are Muscat, Semillon and Clairette, also familiar from the Languedoc. Despite the hot dry climate, modern equipment allows the making of a wide range, including a good sparkling wine, 'The President's'. Seventy per cent of Israel's wine exports (which are only 14% of her production) go to the United States. There is a substantial market for Kosher wine.

The Gianaclis vineyards still operate in Egypt, north-west of the Nile delta at Abu Hummus. Four times more white grapes than red are grown, but three-quarters of the white wine is distilled. The best-known whites are Cru des Ptolemées and Reine Cléopatre. One of the red wines, Omar Khayyam, is smooth and well-made, with what seems an intriguing faint flavour of dates.

THE VINE travelled west from its earliest home, conquered the Mediterranean, and has ever since given its best performance in western Europe. But it also travelled east, across India into China. The vine was known to gardeners in China—who called one variety 'vegetable dragon pearls'. They knew how to make wine with it, and did so. Why then did it not become part of their way of life, as it has in every western country where it will grow successfully?

Mr Edward Hyams, who has studied the references to wine in oriental literature, concludes that it simply does not suit the Asiatic temperament. It clearly brings out the best in Mediterranean man—but for the Chinese it does nothing. The East is not averse to alcohol. It makes what it calls wine from rice. But wine from grapes, with its soothing, inspiring effect, has never 'taken'.

This being said, there is wine being made in modern China, and a little being exported—and it is very good. The white wine of Tsingtao (or Shantung) province—on about the latitude of Gibraltar—can be compared with a natural sherry with rather more pronounced acidity. It makes a very pleasant aperitif. Clearly there is no reason why fine wines should not grow on Chinese soil . . . yet it somehow seems unlikely that the Chinese will suddenly take to viticulture at this stage in their history.

Japan is another matter. Until the end of the last century she went even further than China in rejecting the ways of the West. But her reaction has been a wholesale trying out of western notions. Wine has taken its turn. At first it was American varieties, not the true wine grape Vitis vinifera, which were tried. There is Concord and Delaware wine made (see page 223). But only recently have true wine grapes, particularly Semillon and Cabernet, been planted with any success.

The damp climate and heavy rainfall of Japan have led to a great deal of disease, and most people who have tried their wine speak of it rather pityingly. A French wine official, however, who has tasted a Cabernet from Kofu, says that it was a perfectly respectable wine. And it is hard to believe that if the Japanese feel the inclination to grow wine in quantity, as they have felt the need to make whisky, they will not make a similar success of it.

At the moment almost all of Japan's production of about 100,000 gallons a year is made at Kofu and Katsunuma in Yamanashi province, west of Tokyo. A little wine is also made in Osaka and Yamagata provinces. Mann's Wine Co and Sanraku Occan are the biggest producers and a grape called Koshu (which is said to have come from Europe many years ago) and the muscat Baily A (an American hybrid) are the main grape sorts.

Above left: grape vines appear in Chinese art from 200 BC. In this 18th-century ink painting by Hsü Lan, in the British Museum, the five little animals in the vine symbolize the success of the patron's five sons in the Imperial examinations
Left: Japanese wine labels bear such phrases as Premier Grand Cru Classé and Mis en Bouteille au Château; and even pictures of the château itself.
The label second from right is a good dry white wine from the Shantung province in northern China

Working a corking machine for 'sparkling burgundy' in the early days of a California winery

The New World

THE VINE was there at the foundation of the New World as it was at the emergence of the old. First in the haversacks of mission fathers, to make wine for the sacrament. Then with the governors of new colonies, to help establish European civilization on the tip of Africa or in the unpromising land round Botany Bay.

The Americas had had their first vintage by the mid-16th century. South Africa was making wine by a hundred years later. But it was not until the 19th century that the real development of the new wine countries began.

The 1840s and 50s saw wine-growing firmly established in Australia, Argentina, California. It was tentative and imitative to begin with; the wine-maker's chief aim was to make a local version of the familiar wines of Europe. It was natural to use their names for wines which he hoped would resemble them. Each wine-maker tried to make wine of all the classical kinds: red, white, sweet, dry, sparkling, in the same vineyard—and even from the same grapes.

So a tradition grew up which was to have unfortunate consequences. The names of Chablis, Sauternes, Burgundy, Champagne—all names of parts of France—became so imbedded in the wine industries of far-off countries that it began to seem as though they could not move without them.

So long as viticultural knowledge and technique was limited to adapting Old World methods this was the best the wine-makers of the New World could do.

But the last 20 years have seen a revolution which may turn out to be the most important event in the history of wine. Study in universities, followed up by experiments in the fields, has so far improved the selection and cultivation of vines and the techniques of making wine, that good light table wines can be made from bulk-cropping grapes grown in country which is virtually a desert.

Above all refrigeration has come to the aid of the wine-maker. Grapes ripening late in a north-European October ferment in cold sheds gently. But in (for example) March in South Africa the run-away boiling of the must is enough to drive off all the acids and essences that go to make its character. Flat, overstrong wines tended to result.

The introduction of temperature control has meant that, for the first time, light, scented, refreshing wines can be made in the hot countries where they are wanted. Proud of making excellent wine, the vintner has taken to calling it by the name of its grape rather than a borrowed name.

The wine industries of Australia, California and South Africa at least are still only in their infancies. The years 1971–1974 saw unprecedented expansion of the acreage of the best wine grapes in California especially. As these start producing the amount of excellent wine available is bound to spread the wine-drinking habit faster than ever. Australia and South Africa present similar pictures. It seems possible, to say the least, that one day wine will be the everyday drink of the inhabitants of the New World.

Right: there are places, as here in north California, where the New World promise comes true, and a homestead clearing in the forest turns into a fruitful vineyard

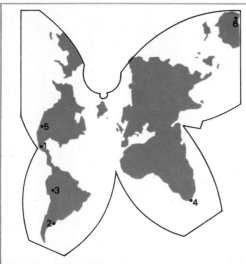

The vine moved to the New World with the early missionaries: around 1520 to Mexico **1**; 1560 to Argentina **2**; Peru **3** before the end of the century. In southern Africa, the first vines were planted by the Dutch at the Cape **4** in 1655. In 1769 missionaries had planted in California **5**. The Antipodes were the last to get vineyards: vines were brought to Australia **6** by settlers in 1788 and wine-growing was established by the first 20 years of the 19th century

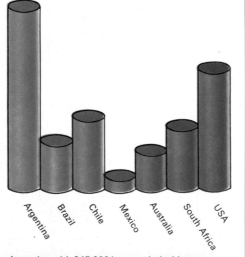

Argentina with 345,000 hectares is the biggest vineyard of the New World, and the fifth biggest in existence (in the future she may well become one of the important sources of vin ordinaire for the world). The United States comes next with 301,000 hectares (of which 85% are in California), then Chile with 130,000, South Africa with 110,000, Australia with 72,000, Brazil with 63,000, Mexico with 33,000 and New Zealand (not on the diagram) with 2,000. Modern methods have recently made such a profound difference to the quality of their wines that the years of fame for New World vineyards are only just about to begin.

California

WHAT GIVES California pre-eminence among the wine countries of the New World is largely its climatic but partly also its social conditions. France and Germany proved long ago how advanced civilizations demand and promote the improvement of viticulture. Today northern California is one of the world's great cultural centres. The concentration of intelligent demand, interest and discussion is a constant challenge to wine-makers to experiment with and to improve their wine.

The best of California's wines today are among the world's best. But more important, California has discovered how to make *good* ordinary wine cheaply and consistently. With both top-level and everyday wine outstanding in any comparison, and a rapidly growing market, California is destined to be one of the great wine countries of the future.

Her production is growing apace. Today it is already a third of that of Spain and almost a fifth of that of Italy or France. New plantings are just bearing fruit, whole new valleys just making wine for the first time.

The wine country divides very broadly into its coastal and inland parts. Inland it is very hot. Common wines used to be the whole production until new methods improved things. The coastal vineyards vary widely. An early study of the influential Viticulture and Enology Department of the University of California was to zone the state by a method known as heat-summation, adding up the number of degrees over 50°F achieved during the annual growing period of the vine. Five zones (see small map) were plotted, the coolest nearest to northern Europe in climate, the hottest most like the south of Spain or North Africa.

The constant contention of the Enology De-partment has been that the way ahead lies in planting the right grape variety in the right place. It offers definite advice and has led to interest being concentrated on the question of grape varieties. This more than anything started the swing away from 'generic' (e.g. Chablis, Rhine) wine names. Today grape varieties are the key to California wine. It seems that when the wheel has turned full circle some of the best California wine districts will specialize in one grape, and therefore one type of wine, as, after 2,000 years, Burgundy and the Mosel have come to do.

There is a good way to go before the millennium is reached. Some big wineries (on their own admission) put 'Chablis' and 'Rhine wine' labels on wine from the same vat. And the law still only demands that 51% of the grapes in a varietal wine be of the variety named. In this respect the law lags behind the accepted practice of the most important producers.

For the moment most wineries feel it is expected of them to carry a full range of wines, which makes a visit to them a strange experience, like being in Bordeaux, Burgundy, Portugal and Champagne all at the same time.

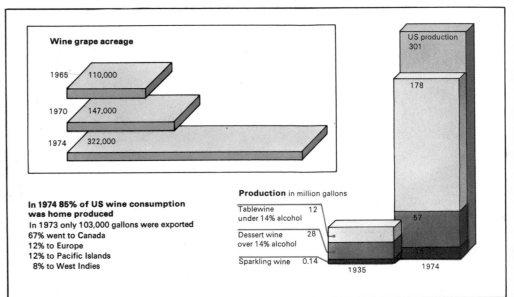

Wine grape acreage

1965 — 110,000
1970 — 147,000
1974 — 322,000

US production 301 / 178

In 1974 85% of US wine consumption was home produced
In 1973 only 103,000 gallons were exported
67% went to Canada
12% to Europe
12% to Pacific Islands
8% to West Indies

Production in million gallons
Tablewine under 14% alcohol — 12
Dessert wine over 14% alcohol — 28
Sparkling wine — 0.14
57 / 1935 / 1974

California Grape Guide

Seventeen of the best varieties are described here, with the climate regions (see opposite) for which they are recommended by the University of California, and the normal yield per acre. One ton of grapes gives about 160 U.S. gallons (606 litres) of wine. So 5 tons/acre = 3030 litres/acre, or approximately 73 hectolitres/hectare. Lower yields usually give higher quality. The 1975 acreage figures for the leading counties for each grape are given last.

Barbera (regions 3–4; 5–8 tons) Dark red wine with good balance of acidity even when grown in very hot conditions. Italian style. Fresno 5,694; Kern 4,313; Madera 3,751

Cabernet Sauvignon (regions 1–2; 4–6 tons) The best red wine: perfumed, fruity, dry, long-lasting. Needs aging at least four years. Monterey 5,634; Napa 5,209; Sonoma 4,164; Santa Barbara 1,889

Chardonnay (regions 1–2; 4–6 tons) The best white wine: dry but full and sappy; perfumed; grape flavour; improved by short time in oak. Lasts well. Monterey 2,929; Napa 2,249; Sonoma 1,808

Chenin Blanc (region 1; 6–10 tons) (sometimes wrongly called White Pinot; is not Pinot Blanc). In hills sometimes makes well-balanced, rich but tart wine. Often not very distinctive. Kern 4,844; Fresno 2,373; Merced 2,377; Monterey 2,092

French Colombard (regions 3–4; 6–10 tons) Rather neutral dry white used for blending; in cooler areas fresh and pleasant unblended. Fresno 5,835; Kern 4,995; Madera 3,365; Merced 2,509

Gamay (also known as Napa Gamay) (regions 1–2; 6–9 tons) In fact the true French Gamay, but only good for pink wine. Monterey 1,218; Napa 1,006; Kern 425; Sonoma 328

Gamay Beaujolais (regions 1–2; 3–4 tons) A form of Pinot Noir; light red wine, not comparable with French Beaujolais. Monterey 1,223; Napa 603; Mendocino 589; San Benito 518

Gewürztraminer (region 1; 4–6 tons) Gentle, often slightly sweet, distinctively spicy white wine. Monterey 795; Sonoma 473; Napa 300

Grenache (region 2; 5–9 tons) Very good for rosé; light-coloured full-bodied red used for blending. Madera 3,967; Kern 3,578; Fresno 3,041

Petite Sirah (also called Shiraz) (region 2; 4–8 tons) Dark red, strong, tannic and long-lasting. Monterey 2,234; Kern 1,887; Fresno 1,358; Sonoma 1,194

Pinot Blanc (region 1; 4–6 tons) Fruity, dry, medium to good quality white. Monterey 670; San Benito 180; Sonoma 74

Pinot Noir (region 1; 3–4 tons) Good lightish red with distinctive grape aroma; rarely absolutely first-rank in California. Monterey 2,590; Napa 2,526; Sonoma 2,523; Santa Barbara 826

Ruby Cabernet (regions 3–4; 6–8 tons) New variety makes good dry table wine in hot areas; useful not great. Kern 4,802; Fresno 4,014; Madera 2,525

Sauvignon Blanc (regions 2–3; 4–7 tons) Good to very good earthy/grapy dry white. Monterey 1,027; Napa 534; Merced 390

Semillon (regions 2–3; 4–6 tons) Medium to sweet golden-white; occasionally excellent. Kern 670; Stanislaus 504; Monterey 519

White Riesling (also called Johannisberg Riesling) (regions 1–2; 4–6 tons) Scented, fruity, ideally tart, but often soft, first-class white. Monterey 2,374; Napa 1,414; Santa Barbara 1,009; Sonoma 814

Zinfandel (region 1; 4–6 tons) 'California's Beaujolais'; raspberryish, spicy and good; also used for blending. San Joaquin 10,927; Sonoma 3,721; San Bernardino 3,303; Monterey 3,194; Napa 1,315

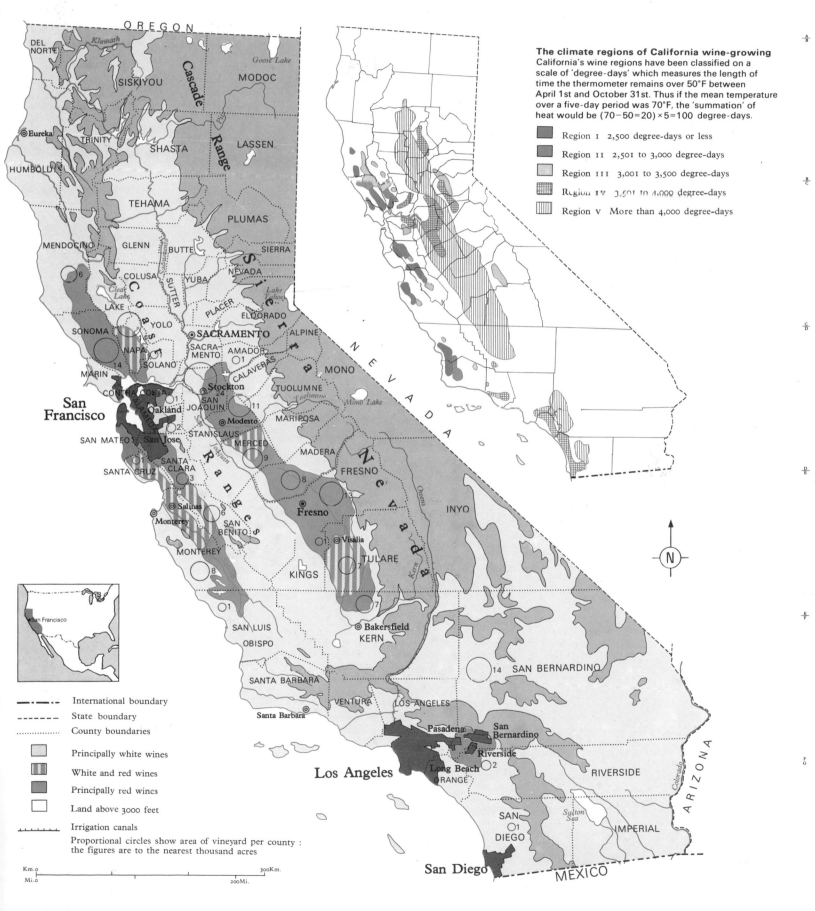

OREGON

DEL
NORTE

SISKIYOU

Klamath

MODOC

Goose Lake

Cascade

◎Eureka

TRINITY

SHASTA

LASSEN

Range

HUMBOLDT

TEHAMA

PLUMAS

MENDOCINO

GLENN

BUTTE

SIERRA

NEVADA

COLUSA

YUBA

Coast

Clear Lake

LAKE

SUTTER

PLACER

ELDORADO

YOLO

SONOMA

6

NAPA

◎SACRAMENTO

SACRA-
MENTO

AMADOR

ALPINE

SOLANO

1

CALAVERAS

MONO

MARIN

Stockton

TUOLUMNE

Lake Tahoe

Ranges

CONTRA COSTA

1

SAN
JOAQUIN

24

11

Tuolumne

Mono Lake

San
Francisco

Oakland

ALAMEDA

Modesto

MARIPOSA

SAN MATEO

San Jose

STANISLAUS

MERCED

MADERA

FRESNO

1

SANTA CRUZ

SANTA
CLARA

3

9

8

13

◎Salinas

6

Monterey

SAN
BENITO

Fresno

INYO

MONTEREY

8

1

◎Visalia

1

KINGS

7

TULARE

1

7

SAN LUIS
OBISPO

Bakersfield

KERN

SANTA BARBARA

14

SAN BERNARDINO

VENTURA

LOS ANGELES

Santa Barbara

Pasadena

San
Bernardino

Los Angeles

Long Beach

Riverside

2

ORANGE

RIVERSIDE

*Salton
Sea*

SAN
DIEGO

1

IMPERIAL

San Diego

MEXICO

ARIZONA

Colorado

San Francisco

The climate regions of California wine-growing

California's wine regions have been classified on a scale of 'degree-days' which measures the length of time the thermometer remains over 50°F between April 1st and October 31st. Thus if the mean temperature over a five-day period was 70°F, the 'summation' of heat would be $(70-50=20) \times 5=100$ degree-days.

Region I   2,500 degree-days or less
Region II   2,501 to 3,000 degree-days
Region III   3,001 to 3,500 degree-days
Region IV   3,501 to 4,000 degree-days
Region V   More than 4,000 degree-days

International boundary
State boundary
County boundaries

Principally white wines
White and red wines
Principally red wines
Land above 3000 feet
Irrigation canals

Proportional circles show area of vineyard per county : the figures are to the nearest thousand acres

Km.0   300Km.
Mi.0   200Mi.

The Napa Valley

Left: the Burgess Cellars vineyard in spring from
inside the owner's modern house
Top: the Heitz family's house is typical of St Helena
Above: the big wood and stone winery of Charles Krug
is one of the central landmarks of the valley

THE NAPA valley has become the symbol as well as the centre of the top-quality wine industry in California. It does not have a monopoly, by any means. But in its wines, its wine-makers and the idyllic Golden Age atmosphere which fills it from one green hillside to another, it captures the imagination and stays in the memory.

The valley runs in an arc north-west from Napa, most of its vineyards lying on its nearly flat floor. It is realistic to consider the vineyards of the old city of Sonoma, the proclaimed capital of the Californian Republic which never was, as part of the same complex, although they lie beyond the ridge of the Mayacamas Mountains: in these mountains are some of the best of the 'Napa' vineyards, and the future is likely to see more planting both in the hills and round the southern, San Francisco Bay end of them, in the area known as Los Carneros.

Sonoma is the site of the most famous winery of the early days of California; the Buena Vista vineyard founded by Colonel Agoston Haraszthy in 1857. It was reopened in 1943 and makes good table wine today, including the Zinfandel, unique to California, which legend says was the Colonel's own contribution to his new country from his native Hungary. It is known as California's Beaujolais.

North of Sonoma the very small, super-high-quality Hanzell winery makes brilliantly rich and intense Chardonnay and Pinot Noir. Sebastiani is a full-blooded Italian family business, whose red Barbera and (white) Green Hungarian are their hallmark; racy wines for dishes made with olive oil and ham and cheese.

The typical Napa valley winery is set beside the valley road in its vines, but has more vines scattered round on the flat and in the hills. Louis Martini, for example, has five vineyards, of which the most famous is Monte Rosso, high above the Sonoma valley. Others, like the Christian Brothers at Mont la Salle, Schramsberg or Mayacamas have their vines around them in an enclave of their own in the hills.

The valley falls into two climate zones. From Napa to Rutherford is Region 1, the coolest. The northern part is in Region 2, a shade warmer. In fact a great deal depends on the altitude of the vineyard: Stony Hill and Chappellet are examples of wineries in the hills whose wines have particular finesse. The Schramsberg which Robert Louis Stevenson loved is another: the top name in California 'champagne'. So good is Napa 'champagne' that Moët & Chandon (of Champagne) are building a new winery at Yountville to make their own.

Going north from Oakville, the modernistic adobe winery of Robert Mondavi is the first essential visit. Mondavi believes passionately in temperature control and has made a study of barrel-oak, with the result that he can make his Chardonnay taste astonishingly like Meursault. Sauvignon (which he calls Fumé) Blanc, Pinot Noir and Gamay rosé are some of his other successes.

Two of the best-known wineries of the valley are next up the road. Beaulieu and Inglenook both now belong to the massive Heublein Corporation, but Beaulieu at least continues in its tradition of making the best kind of Napa wine. Its Cabernet is dark, fat and stylish.

Before St Helena there is a little showplace for the prestigious Heitz Cellars—Joe Heitz's house and cellars are up Spring Mountain Road to the east—and then the big plain hangars which house Louis M. Martini, in some ways the most distinguished winery in California. Martini is remarkable for his best wines (Cabernet and Chardonnay in particular), but also for his amazing 'jug' wines, Mountain Red and White, which must be among the best value for money in the world.

Beyond St Helena are the last two big-scale wineries of the valley; the eminent Charles Krug (with a wide range of good-average varietals) and Beringer, a winery which has changed hands and greatly improved recently.

As the valley narrows the country becomes more and more beautiful. Oaks and pines, streams, darting birds, fruit-trees, sunlit meadows stretch to the little spa of Calistoga and beyond. The wooded hills here are alive with ambitious new ventures. Seven wineries have started in the last five years, and some of their results have been very impressive.

The little Freemark Abbey, which has quickly made an excellent reputation, lies by the road going north. Then comes the famous Larkmead 'champagne' cellars of Hanns Kornell. Finally, as though to bring the whole valley journey to a fitting finish, the new English-owned Sterling winery floats on its mid-valley knoll like a Greek monastery.

Sterling's blend of elegance and showmanship (a chair-lift, and a full peal of bells from a London church) are in the pure San Francisco idiom: folly justified by dazzling quality.

Below: the Napa valley's best wines are Cabernet Sauvignon among reds; Johannisberg Riesling and Chardonnay among whites. 'Champagnes' can be outstandingly good. Kornell (not shown) and Schramsberg are specialists

County boundary

■ MAYACAMAS   Wineries

Vineyards

Woods

Contour intervals: below 100ft every 20ft   above 100ft every 100ft

Russian River

THE GREAT part of Sonoma county's vineyards lie along the Russian River (so-called from a former Russian trading post) and its tributaries, between Santa Rosa, 20 miles north of Sonoma city (see pages 216–217), and Asti, another 30 miles farther on.

The California coastal climate avoids the obvious. North of the Bay it starts cool, then grows steadily warmer. At Santa Rosa it is still Region 1. By Asti it is Region 3: essentially red-wine country.

Traditionally this Russian River territory has been the source of good-quality 'bulk' wine, bought by the big firms of the Central valley for blending. It is still a major source of the excellent Gallo standard wines. Wineries have flourished here (barring the Prohibition period) for a century, but in the main anonymously. The most famous exception is Italian Swiss Colony, founded at Asti in 1881 by the Rossi family, which still produces one of California's widest ranges of wines and which pioneered fruit-flavoured wines as a way of reaching out to a wider market—with results for which the whole industry is grateful. Although I.S.C. now belongs to United Vintners a Rossi still directs the wine-making.

In a more specialized field Korbel also has an old and excellent reputation. Their vineyards are planted among the stumps of an old redwood forest along the winding course of the Russian River as it threads the Coast Range westwards to the ocean. Few, even in California, are as beautiful. Their specialities are 'champagne' and brandy. Korbel Brut is certainly among the best sparkling wines California has to offer—which is high praise.

Otherwise, until the last five years, only the small family wineries of Pedroncelli and Parducci were known outside the area.

The news of the last five years is that the sense of purposeful excitement in the wine industry has spilled north from the Napa valley and flooded the Russian River basin. Already Alexander valley, whose first quality vines are barely ten years old, is an appellation commanding respect. Simi is typical of the sleepy old stone-built wineries which have woken to a new life. Wine technology has made such strides that clean, grapy, new-style wine is within easy reach. What follows is the fascinating part; as wine-makers discover the potential of their new vineyards and vats.

Sonoma (formerly Windsor) Vineyards has already established a sound name in the area. Cambiaso, Foppiano and Nervo are smaller old wineries which are moving with the times. It is still too soon to say which of the half-dozen others now in their infancy will be prominent, or indeed permanent.

One which is breaking new ground to some purpose is Parducci, off the map to the north at Ukiah in Mendocino county. Ukiah is in Region 3, but the Parduccis are planting in neighbouring valleys, in a range of locations and altitudes, to discover the full range of Mendocino's possibilities. Recently they have been joined by Cresta Blanca from Livermore and Weibel from San Jose. The stress the Parduccis and others are putting on local appellations may be another stage in California's self-discovery as a great wine region.

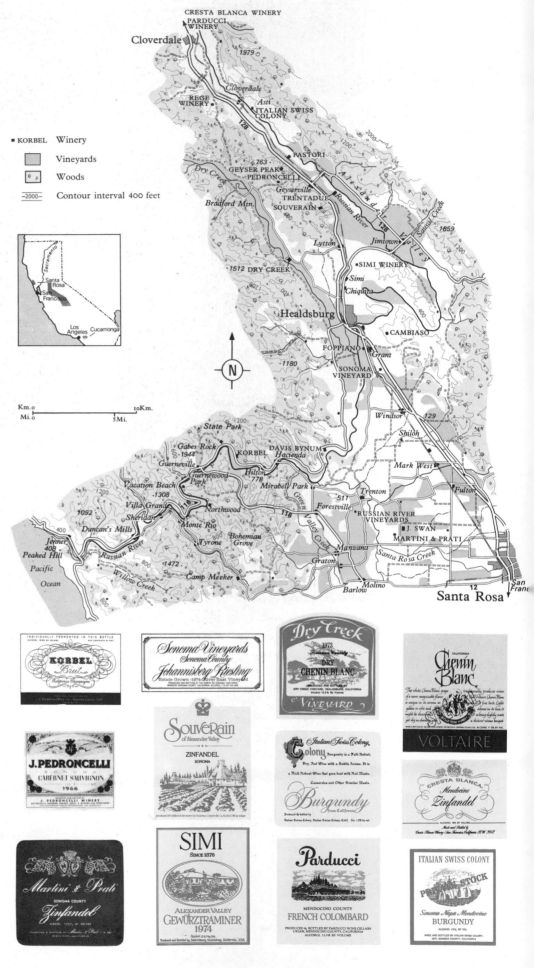

■ KORBEL Winery

Vineyards

Woods

Contour interval 400 feet

The Central Valley

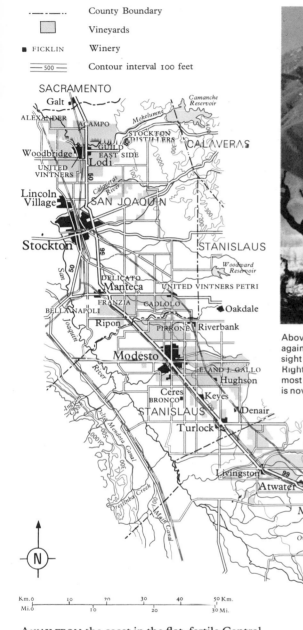

County Boundary

Vineyards

FICKLIN Winery

Contour interval 100 feet

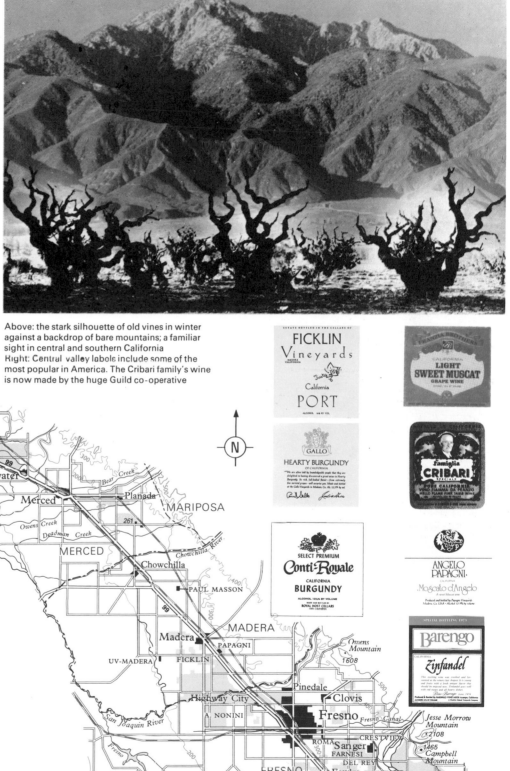

Above: the stark silhouette of old vines in winter against a backdrop of bare mountains; a familiar sight in central and southern California
Right: Central valley labels include some of the most popular in America. The Cribari family's wine is now made by the huge Guild co-operative

AWAY FROM the coast in the flat, fertile Central valley, wine- and table-grape growing are of equal importance. Many farmers grow grapes which will do for either. The climate is comparable with Algeria or Andalucia. Yet the last decade has seen changes here as dramatic as any in the fashionable coastal vineyards.

Fifteen years ago Americans drank 70% high-strength wine, 30% light wine. Today the proportions are reversed. The Central valley has had to adapt to the new demand.

Refrigeration and, above all, total control of the grape's environment from vine to bottle, preventing any oxidation, have been the secret. So have new grape varieties, developed at Davis to keep acidity even in desert heat. Gallo, the world's biggest winery, has been the leading pioneer in the light wine revolution. But as the map shows Gallo is not alone.

South of the Bay

THE AREA just south and east of San Francisco Bay is wine country as old as the Napa valley. Its wineries are fewer, but several of them are among California's most famous names. And recently they have been hit by a typically Californian fate: the swallowing of whole valleys by the exploding conurbation. Subtopia has driven them to look for new vineyards—and hence to make a discovery of enormous importance for the future of California wine.

Climate studies by the University of California at Davis have shown that the valleys sidling to the ocean between the parallel ranges of mountains—Salinas, Gabilan, Santa Cruz, Diablo—are cool-air corridors, benefiting from being near the sea and the Bay, but protected from the smothering Pacific fogs. That Salinas, in fact, though it is 150 miles south of St Helena, is marginally cooler, and could be even more suited to the best table-wine grape varieties. The university oenologists found that Soledad, in the Salinas valley, has the best conditions of all, possibly the best in California. . . .

Almadén winery, whose home ground at Los Gatos was rapidly being overrun by suburbs, was the pioneer in moving south, to Paicines, 1,000 feet up in San Benito county. Their initial 2,000 acres of Cabernet and Chardonnay succeeded superbly.

More recently Paul Masson from Saratoga, Mirassou from San Jose and Wente Brothers from Livermore, all pressed by suburbs, have gone farther south into the Salinas valley. The whole area now has a greater acreage than the Napa valley—and virtually all of it in very good varieties. Some of California's best wine is being made there already.

The traditional centres of wine-growing here do not stretch so far south. They are concentrated in the Livermore valley east of the Bay (gravelly and good for white wine; one of California's few compact areas with a recognizable local character); the western foot-hills of the Diablo range, where Weibel and Mirassou still have their wineries, though most of their grapes come from elsewhere; the towns south of the Bay, now built up, and along the slopes of the Santa Cruz mountains down to a cluster of family wineries round the Hecker Pass.

Their products vary from the extremely high-priced varietals of Martin Ray to very good cheap 'burgundy' from Live Oaks. Paul Masson and Almaden are the classic big two of the area. Almaden, advised by the great Frank Schoonmaker, was the pioneer of varietal labelling in the '50s. Recently Paul Masson has made the running, using the new grape varieties Emerald Riesling and Ruby Cabernet with conspicuous success.

The most startling newcomer is the mammoth Monterey Vineyards winery, the first to be built in the Salinas valley, with no less than 10,000 acres of its own land planted with top varieties. Its first wine, of the 1974 vintage, was very promising.

Perhaps the most encouraging is Chalone, 2,000 feet up in the hills just east of Soledad, where a limestone slope and a cool climate are giving Chardonnay and Pinot Noir as good as any in California, and most in France.

Above: vineyards alternate with typical golden California grassland dotted with dark oaks
Below left: grape-picking machines are a revolutionary innovation for huge vineyards with a small population
Below: some of the best-known wineries of this rapidly developing area of California; the future here lies in concentrating on first-class table wine

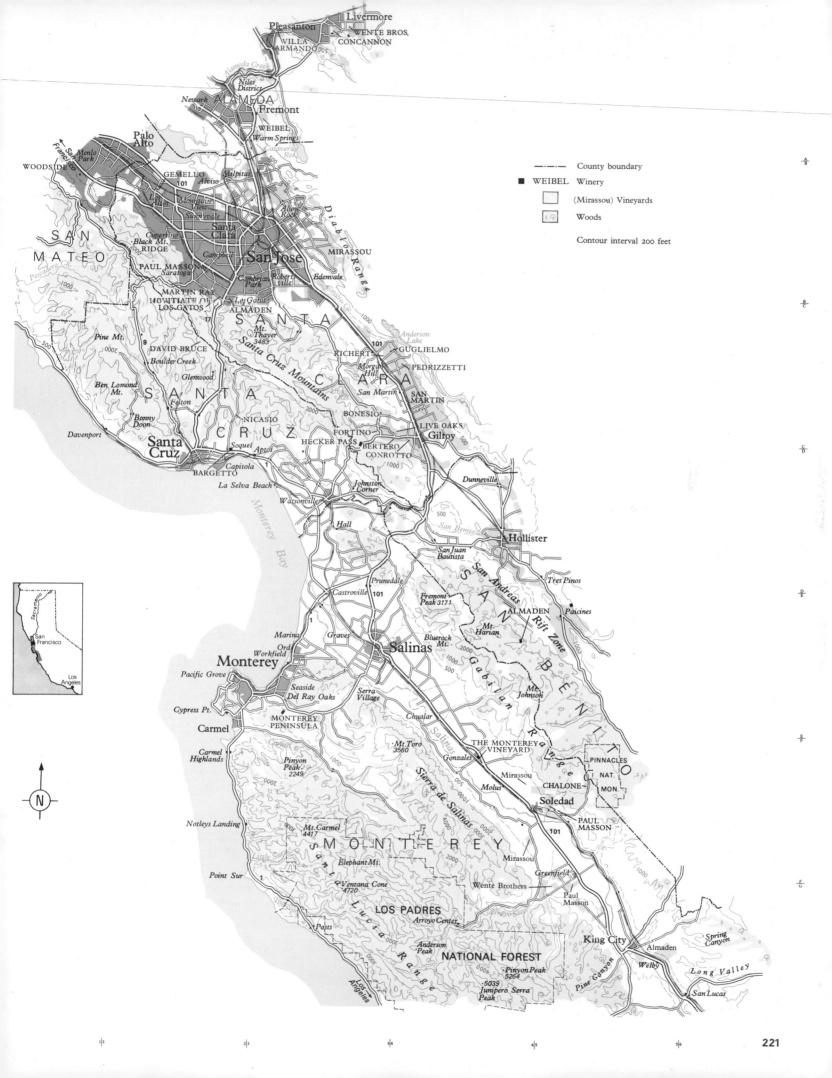

Livermore
Pleasanton
WENTE BROS.
CONCANNON
VILLA
ARMANDO 005

Alameda Creek

Niles
District
Newark
ALAMEDA
Fremont

WEIBEL
Warm Springs

Palo
Alto
Menlo
Park
WOODSIDE
GEMELLO
101
Alviso
Milpitas
Mountain
View
Sunnyvale
Alum
Rock
SAN
Cupertino
Santa
Clara
MATEO
Black Mt.
RIDGE
Campbell
San Jose
MIRASSOU
PAUL MASSON
Saratoga
Cambrian
Park
Roberts-
ville
Edenvale
MARTIN RAY
NOVITIATE OF
LOS GATOS
Los Gatos
ALMADEN

Pine Mt.
9
DAVID BRUCE
SANTA
CLARA
Mt.
Thayer
3483
17
RICHERT
101
GUGLIELMO
Boulder Creek
Glenwood
Santa Cruz Mountains
Morgan
Hill
PEDRIZZETTI
Ben Lomond
Mt.
Felton
San Martin
SAN
MARTIN
Bonny
Doon
NICASIO
BONESIO
LIVE OAKS
Davenport
SANTA
FORTINO
BERTERO
Gilroy
Santa
Cruz
CRUZ
HECKER PASS
CONROTTO
BARGETTO
Soquel
Aptos
Capitola
Johnston
Corner
Dunneville
La Selva Beach
Watsonville
Hall
San Benito
Hollister
San Juan
Bautista
Tres Pinos
SAN
Castroville
101
Fremont
Peak 3171
ALMADEN
Paicines
Prunedale
ANDREAS
Marina
Graves
Mt.
Harlan
RIFT
Ord
Bluerock
Mt.
Mt.
Johnson
BENITO
Workfield
Salinas
ZONE
Monterey
Seaside
Del Ray Oaks
Serra
Village
Pacific Grove
GABILAN
Cypress Pt.
MONTEREY
PENINSULA
Chualar
PINNACLES
Carmel
Mt.Toro
3560
THE MONTEREY
VINEYARD
NAT.
CHALONE
MON.
Carmel
Highlands
Pinyon
Peak
2249
Gonzales
Mirassou
Soledad
Notleys Landing
Mt.Carmel
4417
Molus
PAUL
MASSON
Point Sur
1
MONTEREY
101
Elephant Mt.
Mirassou
Greenfield
Ventana Cone
4720
Paul
Masson
LOS PADRES
Wente Brothers
Arroyo Center
Posts
Anderson
Peak
NATIONAL FOREST
King City
Spring
Canyon
Almaden
Pinyon Peak
5264
Welby
5039
Junipero Serra
Peak
Long Valley
San Lucas

RANGE

Santa Lucia Range

Sierra de Salinas

Salinas

Los Angeles

Monterey Bay

San Francisco Bay

Diablo Range

Pescadero

Anderson
Lake

Calaveras
Res.

San Francisco
Sacramento
San Francisco
Los Angeles

N

--- · --- County boundary
■ WEIBEL Winery
(Mirassou) Vineyards
Woods

Contour interval 200 feet

The Finger Lakes

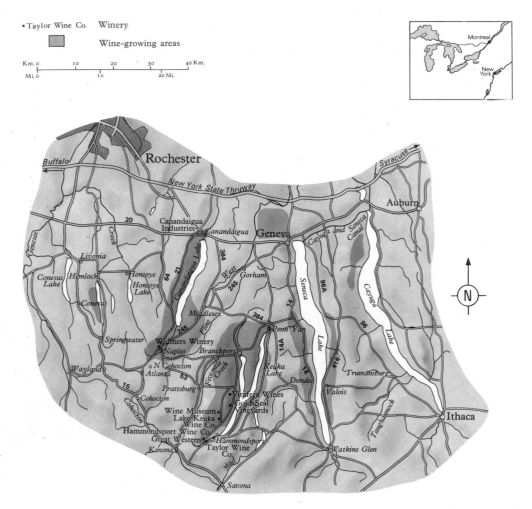

The rambling old stone winery of the Pleasant Valley Wine Co is the most imposing building in the little town of Hammondsport. Its principal brand name is Great Western, best-known for its 'champagne'

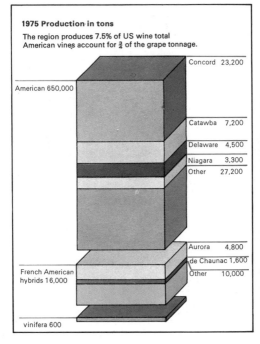

1975 Production in tons
The region produces 7.5% of US wine total
American vines account for ¾ of the grape tonnage.

American 650,000	Concord 23,200
	Catawba 7,200
	Delaware 4,500
	Niagara 3,300
	Other 27,200
French American hybrids 16,000	Aurora 4,800
	de Chaunac 1,600
	Other 10,000
vinifera 600	

THERE ARE two distinct wine-making traditions in the United States—that of the east coast and that of the west. They are much more distinct than, say, Spanish and German wine-making, because they start with a different plant: not merely variety but species of vine. California's tradition is at present by far the more important, both for quality and quantity. But there is no more reason why California should be the only wine-making state in America than there is for Italy to be the only wine country of Europe. A Mediterranean climate like that of California is excellent for vines—but so is the totally different, much colder climate of Champagne or the Moselle.

The east coast tradition has its home in the Finger Lakes area of upper New York State, 200 miles north-west of New York City. The little town of Hammondsport is the St Helena or Bernkastel of the area.

The sight of fields of vines growing comes almost as a shock in these distinctly northern, New England-style surroundings, with low hills around the long blue lakes covered with birch and oak, and one-storey frame houses painted cream and blue and green like any quiet corner of the eastern states.

Conditions are more comparable with those of Germany than any other European wine region. Despite the fact that the Finger Lakes

and the great sheet of Lake Ontario to the north help to moderate the climate it is tough and continental; there is a short, hot growing season and a long and bitterly cold winter.

Vitis vinifera, the wine vine, has often been killed or crippled by the extreme weather of the area. This, and a well-established taste for a different kind of wine, are the reasons why New York State vintners in general plant not wine vines as the rest of the world understands them but varieties of the native American vines, Vitis labrusca, rotundifolia, riparia. They are tough and prolific and their berries make wine with a very distinct and easily recognized taste —a simple, scented taste which drinkers of European wine find rather hard to get used to.

The most famous of the American vines is the Vitis labrusca Concord. It is widely used for making grape juice as a drink and the very popular grape jelly, as well as its particular kind of fruity wine.

The brands of Taylor Wine Co (which embraces Pleasant Valley and Great Western) and Gold Seal Vineyards (which includes Charles Fournier and Henri Marchant) use native American vines for most of their products. Widmer's use them for all. In sparkling wine and 'sherry', processing does something to moderate the 'foxiness'—as the special taste is called—of these wines. Neutral California

wine is also blended in to reduce their obviousness. 'Champagne' is probably the best of the products of this traditional New York industry.

But today most of the young wine-makers are rejecting the theory that Vitis vinifera will always be too tender for their climate. For many years they have been experimenting with planting hybrid vines, crosses between vinifera and American varieties, which French breeders —among others—have developed in the hope of finding an answer to the phylloxera problem.

Although these P.Ds. (producteurs directs, as the French call them, since they are not grafted) are banned in French Appellation areas, some of them, notably Baco 1, Seyval, Chelois and De Chaunac are establishing reputations in the USA for interesting wine of distinct quality. Moreover they are encouraging growers to reconsider their prejudice for native vines, and even to experiment with uncrossed vinifera varieties.

Today there is a growing school of wine-making in the heart of the American-grape country which is dedicated to proving that Rieslings, Chardonnays and even red wine varieties, Cabernet and Pinot Noir, can survive the winters and ripen their grapes in the short summers of the Finger Lakes. The champion of the cause is Dr Konstantin Frank, a Russian-born German. He has had some successes with

Riesling and Pinot Noir, and calls his company, pointedly, Vinifera Wines. A new small winery, Lake Keuka Wine Co, specializes in hybrids but is experimenting with Chardonnay and Riesling. The big firms of Taylor and Gold Seal are also planting experimental patches.

It does not sound like a revolution, but it puts in doubt the survival of the tradition of New York as the one non-vinifera wine area of the world for ever.

It is crystal-gazing to discuss American wine in a much broader context today. Yet there are small beginnings of wine industries in so many places: Oregon, Washington (where the Ste Michelle wine company of Seattle has been very successful with grapes grown in the Yakima valley, particularly Rieslings), Missouri, Ohio (which had big vineyards in the last century), Maryland, Virginia, that seeing the galloping increase in wine-drinking one can confidently predict rapid expansion of whichever sites prove best. Even the Canadian province of Ontario has recently produced some very creditable table wines, particularly from the vinifera hybrid vine Maréchal Foch.

There is room in North America for thousands of new wine-makers. The challenge, technical but at the same time romantic, suits Americans perfectly. The wine-makers are sure to come.

Most New York State wine is still made from American grape varieties. The 'champagnes' are among the best. But the label at bottom right represents a revolution

Grape Guide

Baco Noir Red hybrid from Vitis riparia. Great acidity but good clean dark wine
Catawba One of the earliest developments from V. labrusca and still one of the best. A pale red grape from which white, red or rosé wine can be made. Not too acid
Chelois A hybrid developed by Seibel. Dry red wine, slightly foxy
Concord The dark red small V. labrusca which is most widely planted. Needs sugaring and makes strongly foxy wine.
De Chaunac A good red French American hybrid; dark colour; rich, heavy wine
Delaware A pink grape, only slightly foxy; ripens well and hardly needs sugaring
Duchess White wine; rather neutral
Elvira White wine; now not much planted
French American Several varieties, including the popular Aurora
Isabella Sweetish dark red grape; very foxy
Moore's Diamond For dry white wine; fairly neutral
Niagara For sweet white wine; very foxy
Seyve-Villard Several varieties of white grape. Good but rather neutral

Australia

IF THE FIRST flag to flap over Australian soil in 1770 had been the white and gold of the Bourbons instead of the red, white and blue of King George . . . it is pleasant to speculate what the results would have been.

But even in Anglo-Saxon hands, wine-growing got off to a flying start. The First Fleet of 1788, bringing the first permanent settlers, carried vines among its cargo; the first Governor made wine; the first number of the *Sydney Gazette*, in 1803, carried an article (translated from the French) called 'Method of Preparing a Piece of Land for the Purpose of Forming a Vineyard', and by the 1820s the first of the present-day vineyards in New South Wales was making wine.

Doctors, brewers, seamen, labourers were among the immigrants who put their faith in wine as a way of life and scoured the empty country for suitable places to plant. They went by the natural vegetation, by stands of particular trees (peppermint gum was one, box another) and meadows of certain types of grass to find the kind of land they were looking for. As Max Lake, Hunter Valley wine-grower and author,

Modern machinery for the total control of the wine's environment from picking to bottling helps overcome Australia's climate problems. Here at Gramp's Orlando in the Barossa valley (see page 228) a German filtering plant is part of an up-to-date bottling system

points out, they were remarkably adept at choosing their sites. They sniffed out patches of good vineyard soil miles from anywhere.

All the best sites were chosen first. By the middle of the last century a powerful dynastic system, of families down to the fifth and sixth generation (to date) making wine on the same land, had begun. The majority of Australian wine today is made by people whose parents and grandparents were wine-makers. California has nothing like this continuity.

Australia's good vineyards lie between the 38th and 34th parallels. Melbourne is near the 38th, the same as Cordoba in Spain (and Sicily and San Francisco). Sydney is near the 34th, the same as Rabat, the capital of Morocco. Strong wines full of sugar but tending to lack acidity are what you would expect. Traditionally this is what Australia has produced— dessert wines and 'tonic burgundies'.

But the world-wide change of taste in favour of lighter wines, coinciding with new techniques of temperature-control, is changing the pattern rapidly. All Australia's best wines being made today are table wines.

Wine production

Left: South Australia **4** has by far the greatest production; New South Wales **3** and Victoria **5** follow; Queensland **2**, Western Australia **1** and the island of Tasmania **6** only dabble in wine

Below: nearly half the annual crop of 63m Imperial gallons is distilled: as brandy, for fortifying wine, or (most of it) as industrial alcohol

Right: table wine production grows steadily (left-hand column) while fortified wines (right), traditional for Australia, fluctuate from year to year

1961
1962
1963
1964
1965
1966
1967
1968
1969
1970

Table wines   Dessert wines

Wine   Distilled wine
Brandy
Fortifying spirit

Right: Great Britain, traditionally Australia's best customer, now buys less of her wine than Canada. The American market is new and promising; Japan less so

Canada
Great Britain
Papua/New Guinea
New Zealand
USA
Japan

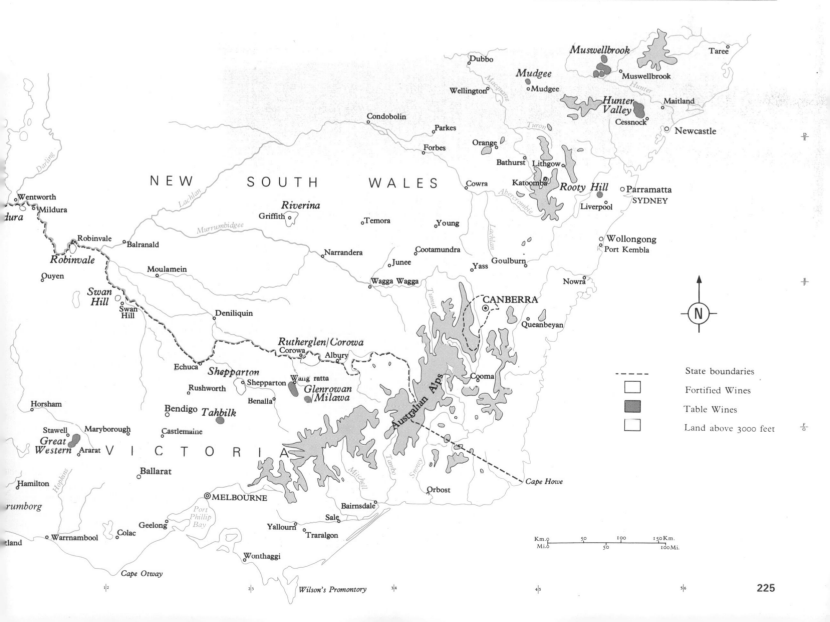

State boundaries

Fortified Wines

Table Wines

Land above 3000 feet

225

New South Wales

NEW SOUTH WALES, the cradle of Australian wine-growing, has long since been overtaken by South Australia as the nucleus of the industry. But there remains one district 100 miles north of Sydney as famous as any in the country; the Hunter river valley round Branxton and Cessnock.

Exceptionally, being so far north, the Hunter area is one of the few in Australia which concentrates entirely on table wines. Its production is small. Vines were planted here (at Dalwood, near the river just east of Branxton) as early as 1828, but the soil which has given the Hunter valley its reputation is found to the south in the foot-hills of the Broken Back Range. Round the east side of the hills there is a strip of weathered basalt, the sign of ancient volcanoes.

McWilliam's Mount Pleasant, Penfolds' HVD, Drayton's Happy Valley and Bellevue, Lindeman's Ben Ean, Tulloch's Glen Elgin, Elliot's Oakvale and Tyrrell's 'Ashman's' wineries lie on the lower slopes and the first flat land under the hills, and Lake's Folly and

Rosehill on another basalt outcrop to the east. Tyrrell, Elliot, Drayton and Lake are all family businesses.

The fame of these wineries is founded chiefly on red wines, made of Cabernet and Shiraz (or Hermitage) and sometimes Pinot grapes. Softness, roundness and a faint earthiness are their special qualities.

The Hunter Valley is the farthest north of Australia's first-class vineyards, and it becomes very hot in February. White wines, before refrigeration, lacked freshness—though to those who liked them they made up what they lacked in body. Varieties which appreciate hot weather; the Ugni Blanc (or white Hermitage), the Blanquette and above all the Semillon are the white specialities of the valley. The Semillon is usually known on labels as the Hunter Valley Riesling, for some wry reason.

Penfolds and Lindeman are the biggest wine firms. McWilliam at Mount Pleasant, with four vineyards close together, totalling about 300 acres (Rosehill and Lovedale are their other

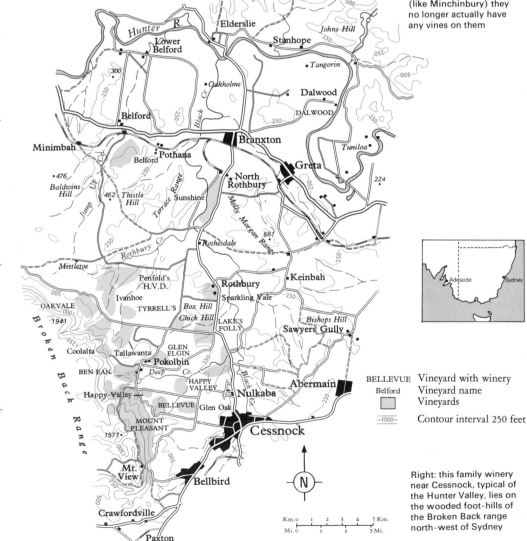

BELLEVUE — Vineyard with winery
Belford — Vineyard name
▨ — Vineyards
—1000— Contour interval 250 feet

Right: this family winery near Cessnock, typical of the Hunter Valley, lies on the wooded foot-hills of the Broken Back range north-west of Sydney

Victoria

well-known ones), is the biggest to be concentrated in New South Wales alone. For Australian wine companies have a habit of owning property in different districts and states, and often blending their wines. Many labels say exactly what is in the blend, but the practice makes it hard to build up a picture of local wine styles.

Lindeman's headquarters in the district is at Ben Ean. Their other well-known vineyard is Sunshine, lower in the valley and on the lighter soil, making it more suitable for white wines. Penfolds have moved the centre of their activities from old Dalwood to a new Dalwood Estate at Wybong, 40-odd miles up-river to the west (not on the map) where they have more than 1,200 acres.

At Corowa, just across the Murray river from Rutherglen in Victoria, some of Australia's best fortified wines are made. The Murrumbidgee Flats (the Riverina), irrigated from the Murrumbidgee river, have 50 times the production of the Hunter Valley; but most of this wine is either fortified or distilled.

AT THE END of the last century Victoria had as many vineyards as New South Wales and South Australia together: 1,200, scattered over the entire state. But phylloxera, which has never reached South Australia, was appallingly destructive here; today there are only 20 or so.

Among them, however, are two of the best small districts in the country, Great Western (remote enough to escape phylloxera) and the single substantial estate of Château Tahbilk. Great Western (see map on page 225) is 110 miles north-west of Melbourne, 1,100 feet up on the westernmost end of the Great Dividing Range. The soil is rich in lime but otherwise unfertile, like that of some of the best vineyards of Europe. Two firms own the vineyards; Seppelt, with 650 acres, and Best, with 20. By far the most famous product is Seppelt's Great Western 'champagne', Australia's best sparkling wine. Good red and white wines are also made. Seppelt give them local place names: Arawatta, Moyston, Chalambar, Rhymney. Best's estate name is Concongella; they also make fortified wines in the Murray valley.

Château Tahbilk is at Tabilk (sic), 76 miles north of Melbourne on the Goulburn river. It belongs to Eric Purbrick, who makes red wines typical of Australia's best style, needing considerable age in the bottle to sort out their strong and complex flavours. His grapes are the usual Shiraz and Cabernet for red wines, and (among others) Marsanne for white.

Apart from a new experimental area at Drumborg, the southernmost in Australia, where cool conditions may well produce exceptional wine, the other Victorian wines all come from further north, round the valley of the river Murray. They are mainly fortified, but such wineries as All Saints at Wahgunyah near Rutherglen and Brown Brothers near Wangaratta make red table wines as well.

Much further down the Murray river at Mildura there is a large vineyard district (also untouched by phylloxera) for fortified wines and brandy. The Chaffey Brothers, who started this region, sell theirs, in the confusing Australian style, under the name Mildara.

Above: the enormous yield of a vintage of the 1930s was collected by teams of horses as well as tractors
Below: Victoria labels. Seppelt's Chalambar is a blend of Hermitage from Great Western, Rutherglen and Barossa

New Zealand

Of 3,000 acres of vineyards, 85% are round Auckland, Hawke's Bay (planted as early as 1865) and Gisborne. Four-fifths of production is fortified wine. Hybrid and vinifera grapes are both grown; the former in the wetter Auckland area. Emphasis is shifting from ordinary to better-quality wine

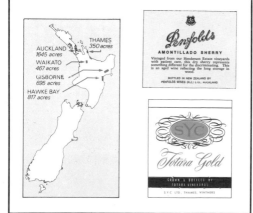

South Australia

ADELAIDE, the capital of South Australia, and hence of Australian wine-growing today, is fittingly ringed about with vineyards. A few still exist within the suburbs of the city. They have spread north to Clare and Watervale and south to Langhorne Creek (see page 224), beside the outpost of South Australian wine-making down at Coonawarra, 200 miles away.

But the most famous of them is undoubtedly the Barossa valley, only 30 miles away to the north-east; a settlement which was originally largely German, and keeps certain German characteristics to this day.

With its 20,000 acres it is Australia's biggest quality wine district. It follows the Para river for about 20 miles, and spreads eastwards into the next valley, from the 750 feet of Lyndoch to twice that height between Keyneton and Springton, where vineyards are scattered among rocky hills.

The Barossa speciality is the Rhine Riesling. At its best, particularly on high ground, it gives wine of remarkable acidity and delicacy for such a hot climate. If the 'breed' of the great German wines is missing, some of these wines have an attractive style of their own.

The most celebrated Rieslings come from Yalumba near Angaston, Hamilton's Springton vineyards, Gramp's Orlando and Henschke's Keyneton. The valley's co-operative at Nuriootpa, which sells its wine under the name Kaiser Stuhl, and Buring's Château Leonay also make good Rieslings, as well as fine reds from Cabernet grapes, which here give big and fruity wine, sometimes less tough than the majority of Australian red wines (and often blended with some Shiraz).

The Barossa Cabernet specialist is Seppeltsfield, the big Seppelt winery down in the valley west of Nuriootpa. Wine from their Great Western winery in Victoria is also bottled here. Penfolds have an estate called Kalimna nearby, north of Greenock.

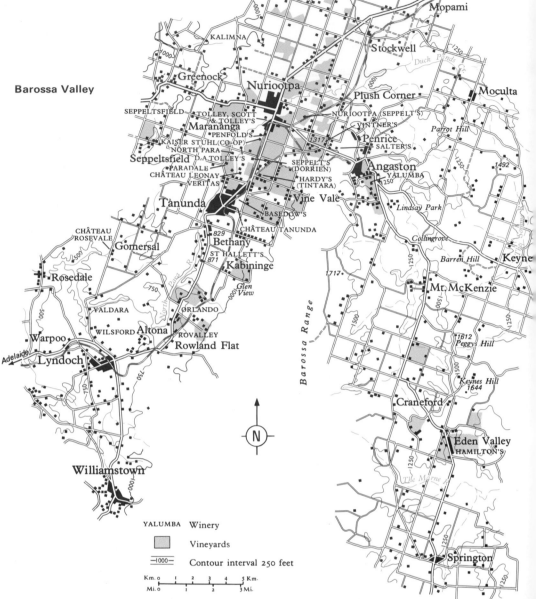

Barossa Valley

YALUMBA — Winery

Vineyards

—1000— Contour interval 250 feet

Above: 19th-century houses with graceful cast iron survive from Barossa's first German settlers, who established the Rhine Riesling as the speciality of the region, Australia's biggest quality wine district
Left: at the Barossa Valley vintage fair in April a grape-treading contest draws crowds
Right: most of the vineyards are on high but comparatively flat land, but experimental plantings of vines in the hills all round them are having good results

THE SOUTHERN VALES district starts almost in the southern outskirts of Adelaide. It is South Australia's oldest: the John Reynell who gave his name to Reynella planted his vines in 1838. Today the company he started has 550 acres round the same site.

Reynella, Seaview and Tintara (Hardy) are the important names among over a score of smaller estates in Southern Vales. Their wines are not unlike those of the Barossa valley, and the same grapes—Rhine Riesling for white wine, Cabernet and Shiraz for red—are grown.

Reynella follows a not uncommon Australian practice of classifying most of its red wine as either claret or burgundy according to the way it turns out. Generally lighter and softer more aromatic wines from Shiraz become burgundies, and tougher and more acidic or tannic Cabernet wines are called claret—but it is the wine itself which decides.

Hardy, the owners of Tintara, also believe in blending wines of one district with another to achieve a consistent house style. Their Old Castle Riesling, St Thomas Burgundy and Cabinet Claret are all good standard blends which aim at staying the same year after year.

COONAWARRA is not mapped here, but many say this small and remote district gives the best red wines in all Australia. It lies between Naracoorte and Millicent (see page 224), and is the southernmost vineyard in South Australia; correspondingly cooler and prone to frosts. What marked out this little plot for vines was its strange red soil, a narrow strip (at its narrowest 200 yards wide), quite different from the surrounding land, poised over limestone and a good supply of water. Wynns, Lindeman ('Rouge-Homme'), Penfolds and Mildara own the vineyards, and the general style of Coonawarra claret is less rich and better balanced than most Australian red wines.

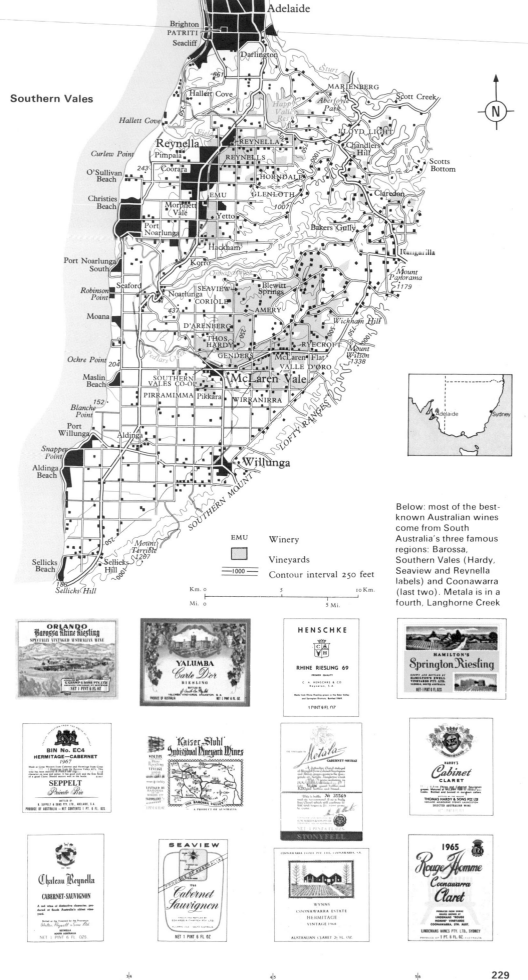

Southern Vales

EMU Winery

Vineyards

1000 Contour interval 250 feet

Km. 0 — 5 — 10 Km.
Mi. 0 — 5 Mi.

Below: most of the best-known Australian wines come from South Australia's three famous regions: Barossa, Southern Vales (Hardy, Seaview and Reynella labels) and Coonawarra (last two). Metala is in a fourth, Langhorne Creek

South Africa

THE SCENERY of Cape Province combines the luxuriant and the stark. Blue-shadowed crags rise from placid green pastures. Smooth rivulets of cultivation run between gaunt walls of rock. An almost perfect climate, with rare summer rain, gives the vine everything it needs.

From these Elysian fields used to come one of the very greatest wines in the world—the legendary Constantia. Constantia was bought by European courts in the early 19th century in preference to Yquem, Tokay, madeira . . . an indication that the Cape is capable of producing wines of the very highest class.

It takes certain social conditions, however, as well as the right climate, to develop an industry in fine wines. They existed briefly with the early Dutch governors—it was the second, de Stel, who planted the Constantia vineyard, as well as giving his name to Stellenbosch. But in more recent times South Africa has been more of a spirit-drinking country, and only very recently has the modern trend towards wine got under way. Still something like half of the grape harvest is distilled, and South Africans drink more brandy than any other nation.

The difficulties experienced by wine farmers in the past have left a useful legacy in the form of a constitutional body to control prices and absorb surplus. This is the KWV, a sort of national co-operative with five wineries and, at Paarl, some of the world's biggest and most modern wine-processing premises.

The South African vineyards fall into two regions; those of the west, near the Cape, subject to Atlantic weather conditions and with a good 25 inches of rain a year, usually falling harmlessly in the winter, and those beyond the mountains in the Little Karoo, which, with only ten inches or so of rain, need irrigation. All the best wines come from the former; the latter can be compared with France's Languedoc, California's Central Valley, or Australia's Murray valley: all with improved grape varieties and processing, but a long way yet from being interesting to international markets.

The heart of the best vineyards of the Cape is mapped overleaf. Of the rest the most interesting districts are the old Constantia vineyards, south of Cape Town, sheltering behind the ridge of Table Mountain from the sea winds, and Tulbagh, 32 miles north of Paarl, where white wines are made.

Château Alphen is the best-known of the Constantia area today. Groot Constantia, de Stel's magnificent old white farmhouse, is still surrounded with vines but no longer operates as a winery. And sadly, sweet wines (Constantia was a muscatel) are no longer made. South African law demands that any wine with more than 2% sugar must be fortified—a relic of days before modern techniques could guarantee stability. Alphen wines are good red and white table wines—but not particularly noteworthy.

Twee Jongegezellen is the name of the best estate at Tulbagh. It makes a range of wines, including South African sherry, but is best known for its good dry Riesling—a rare grape in South Africa—and a local variety, the Steen.

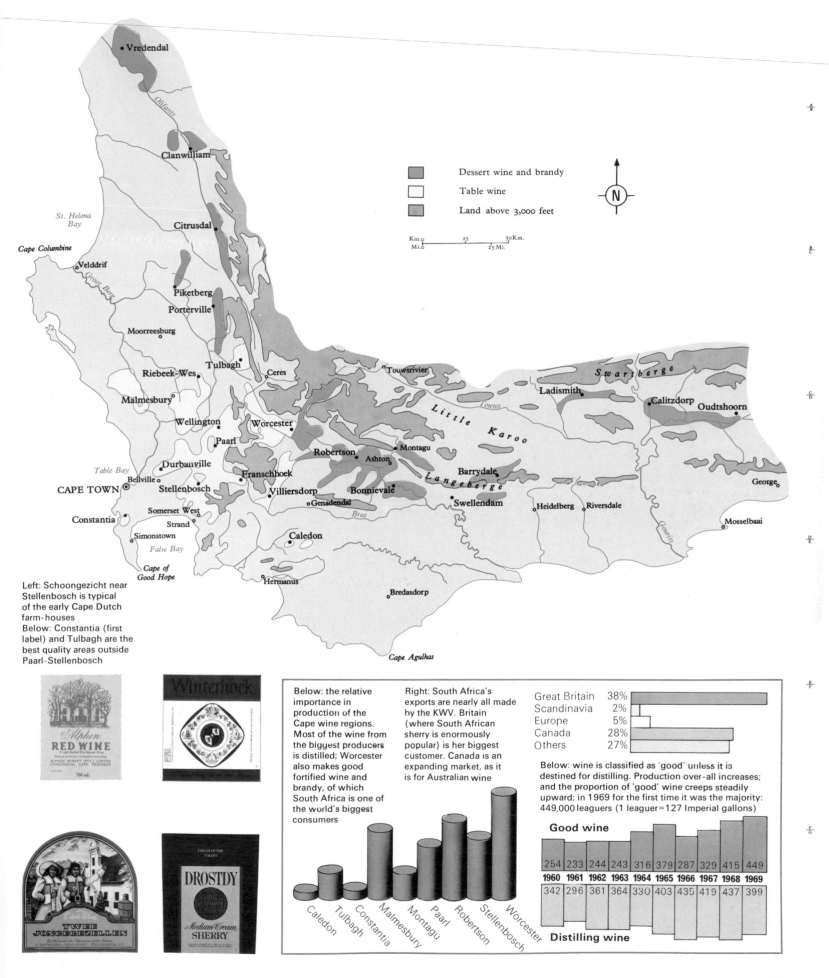

Vredendal

Clanwilliam

Citrusdal

St. Helena Bay

Cape Columbine

Velddrif

Piketberg

Porterville

Moorreesburg

Riebeek-Wes Tulbagh Ceres

Malmesbury

Wellington Worcester

Paarl

Durbanville

Table Bay Bellville

CAPE TOWN Stellenbosch

Constantia Somerset West
Strand

Simonstown

False Bay

Cape of Good Hope

Franschhoek

Villiersdorp Genadendal Bonnievale

Caledon

Hermanus

Bredasdorp

Cape Agulhas

Touwsrivier Swartberge

Ladismith Calitzdorp Oudtshoorn

Little Karoo Loews

Robertson Ashton Montagu

Barrydale Langeberge

Swellendam George

Heidelberg Riversdale

Mosselbaai

Bree Gourits

Olifants Groot Berg

Dessert wine and brandy

Table wine

Land above 3,000 feet

Km.0 25 50Km.
Mi.0 25 Mi.

N

Left: Schoongezicht near Stellenbosch is typical of the early Cape Dutch farm-houses
Below: Constantia (first label) and Tulbagh are the best quality areas outside Paarl-Stellenbosch

Below: the relative importance in production of the Cape wine regions. Most of the wine from the biggest producers is distilled; Worcester also makes good fortified wine and brandy, of which South Africa is one of the world's biggest consumers

Right: South Africa's exports are nearly all made by the KWV. Britain (where South African sherry is enormously popular) is her biggest customer. Canada is an expanding market, as it is for Australian wine

Great Britain	38%
Scandinavia	2%
Europe	5%
Canada	28%
Others	27%

Below: wine is classified as 'good' unless it is destined for distilling. Production over-all increases; and the proportion of 'good' wine creeps steadily upward; in 1969 for the first time it was the majority: 449,000 leaguers (1 leaguer=127 Imperial gallons)

Good wine

254	233	244	243	316	379	287	329	415	449
1960	**1961**	**1962**	**1963**	**1964**	**1965**	**1966**	**1967**	**1968**	**1969**
342	296	361	364	330	403	435	419	437	399

Distilling wine

Caledon Tulbagh Constantia Malmesbury Montagu Paarl Robertson Stellenbosch Worcester

Paarl and Stellenbosch

THE WINE-MAKERS of Paarl do not let you forget that their vineyards lie on almost the same latitude as Jerez. The South African sherry they make, using the Spanish methods, including both the solera system and the flor yeast, has been their fortune since they started it in the 1930s. They do make the best imitation in the world of Spanish sherry—in its middle ranges of sweetness indistinguishable from the original to most people. The chalky soil of Jerez which gives the wine its ultimate finesse is all they lack.

The huge KWV winery at Paarl is also the centre of the South African industry in Tawny, Ruby and Vintage port-style wines—which again, at their best, are truly remarkable.

These are the natural kinds of wine for South Africa, even here in its cooler parts, to make. Table wines have suffered in the past from overweight, and above all from over-rapid fermentation, leading to oxidization, darkening and lack of scent. Now with pressure tanks or refrigerated tanks very good light wines are made. The Hermitage, Gamay and Pinotage (a cross between Hermitage and Pinot Noir made by the KWV) all make round, soft and fruity red wines—sometimes blended with the Cabernet, which still tends to be rather dark and hard here. The Steen is the best of the white grapes, made into totally dry wine or a Late (picked) Vintage slightly sweet one. But Riesling and Clairette Blanche are also good.

On the map, estates which make and sell their own wine are distinguished from those farms which deliver their grapes to a co-operative. Of the former, Nederburg is perhaps the best-known, but Bellingham and the enchanting old farm of Schoongezicht are also famous in South Africa, and gaining a market abroad.

Above: Groot Constantia near Cape Town once made one of the world's great wines. It is a museum today
Below: Paarl Steen, Roodeberg and Mymering are three of the brand names of the KWV, which is based at Paarl. Zonnebloem, Lanzerac and La Gratitude are from the Stellenbosch Farmers' Winery Co-operative, based at Libertas. Nederburg, Bellingham, Schoongezicht (see photograph on page 230) are private estates

Above: the floor of the Hex River Valley looking Westward towards Buffelshoekkloof and the peaks of Hexrievierberge

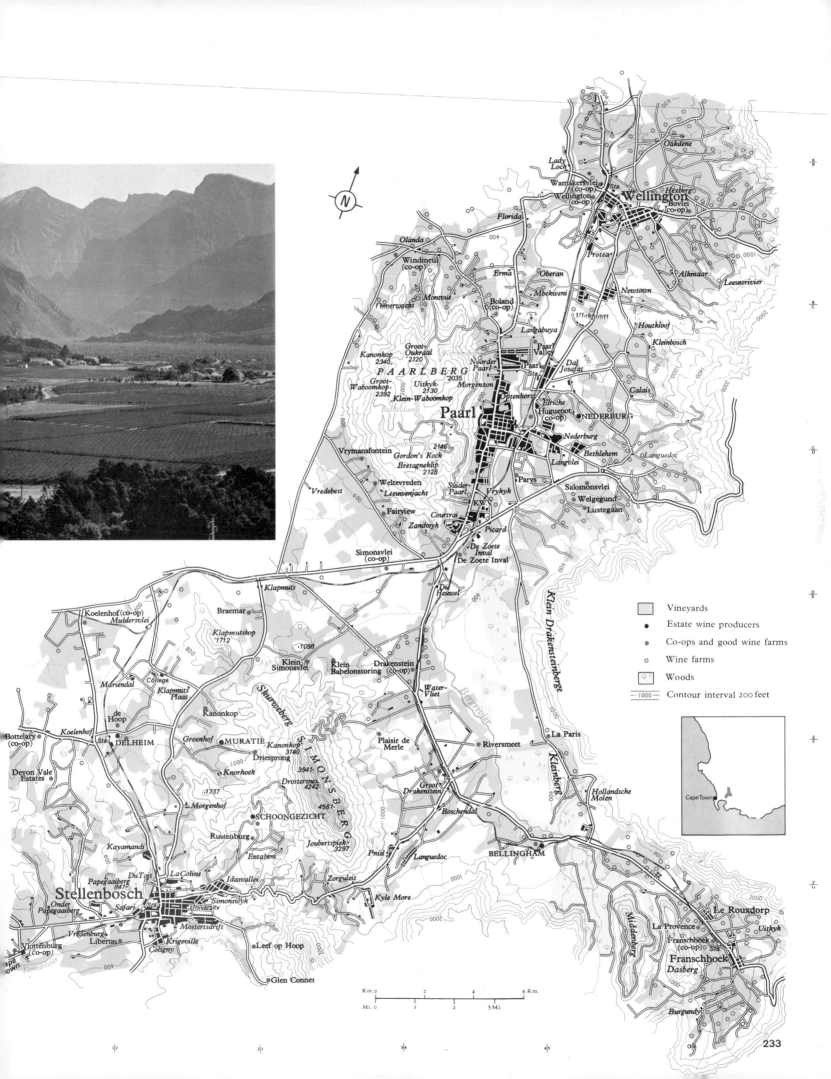

South America

International boundary

▨ Principal wine-producing regions

☐ Other wine growing regions

▨ Land above 3000 metres

Km.0 — 1000 — 2000 Km.
Mi.0 — 500 — 1000 Mi.

Above right: the vineyards of Chile give South America's best wine. Most of them are irrigated, although such foot-hills areas as the bottom picture, Los Perales at Marga-Marga in the south, have enough natural rainfall. Low-paid workers are one reason why Chilean wine is remarkably cheap for its high quality

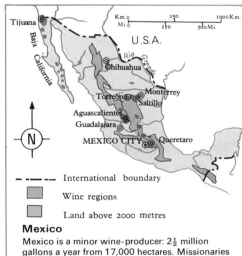

International boundary

▨ Wine regions

▨ Land above 2000 metres

Mexico

Mexico is a minor wine-producer: 2½ million gallons a year from 17,000 hectares. Missionaries planted vines in the 16th century, but the climate is too hot for quality. The best-known bodegas are in Baja California, Chihuahua, Aguascalientes and Torreón. Most wine is poor sherry-type

ALMOST A TENTH of the wine of the world is grown in South America; more than in Germany, Portugal and Algeria combined. Very little is exported. By far the greater part is grown in Argentina, and is the *vino común* of the Argentine daily diet. Seventy per cent of the vineyards of Argentina (or half of those of South America) are in the state of Mendoza, under the Andes and on the same latitude as Morocco.

The climate is arid and the massive flat vineyards are irrigated by canals. Giant wineries with vat capacities which make the mind reel punctuate the featureless landscape. It is not the terrain for great wine; but the equipment of the major wine companies is completely up to date, and they are capable of making very good ordinary wine, comparable to the better (but not the best) table wines of Spain.

The most widely-planted grape is the Malbec, one of the less important red varieties of Bordeaux. Red wines are better than white, which tend towards the oxidized condition of sherry (and are sometimes called Jerez).

On exactly the same latitude barely 150 miles west of Mendoza lies the centre of Chilean wine-growing. But in those 150 miles the Andes climb to 17,000 feet. The highest peak in the Americas, Aconcagua, reaches 23,000 feet just to the north. There is a radical change of climate here, with the arid zone which reaches into northern Chile from the Bolivian plateau crossing the Andes into Argentina. Arica in northern Chile gets one millimetre of rain a year. Santiago gets 370. Concepción, only 250 miles further south, gets 1,320 and Valdivia, another 200 miles to the south, gets 2,540.

Chile grows wine for nearly 2,000 miles out of its total length of 3,000. Her northernmost vineyards have no rain at all; her southernmost are almost swamped (both make poor wine from a native grape called the País; in the north it is distilled into 'pisco'). But in the middle, round Santiago, the climate is ideal for viticulture. The valleys of the Aconcagua, Maipo and Cachapoal rivers are planted with Bordeaux grapes—Cabernet, Sauvignon, Semillon—trained and pruned Bordeaux-fashion. Despite the widespread use of irrigation, the wine of this area is good, and sometimes outstanding.

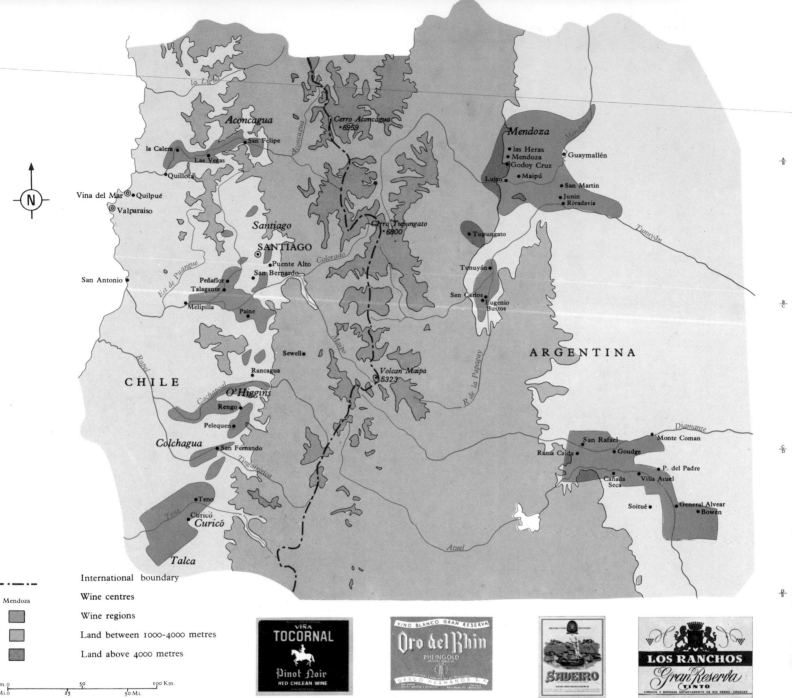

International boundary
Mendoza   Wine centres
Wine regions
Land between 1000-4000 metres
Land above 4000 metres

The Cabernet is fruity, tannic, balanced and long-lived. Treated like a red Bordeaux, bottled after two years and kept for another five or six, it develops into very fine wine. Furthermore it is at present remarkably cheap: perhaps the greatest wine bargain anywhere.

The Sauvignon makes a powerful dry but mellow wine with plenty of character in Chile, as it does in California. The Riesling, which is grown in small quantities, tends to be drier and stronger than the ideal, but can have a fine lingering flavour. All the evidence is that Chile will be a very important wine country.

Brazil and Uruguay both have flourishing wine industries for the home market. Their warm, humid climate is not ideal for the vinifera grape, however, and a large part of their plantation is New York-style, hybrids or non-vinifera varieties (see page 223). The state of Rio Grande do Sul is the centre of the Brazilian industry, South America's third largest.

Right: the left-hand labels come from Chile, which makes South America's best wine; the second column from Argentina; the third from Brazil, and the last from Uruguay

England and Wales

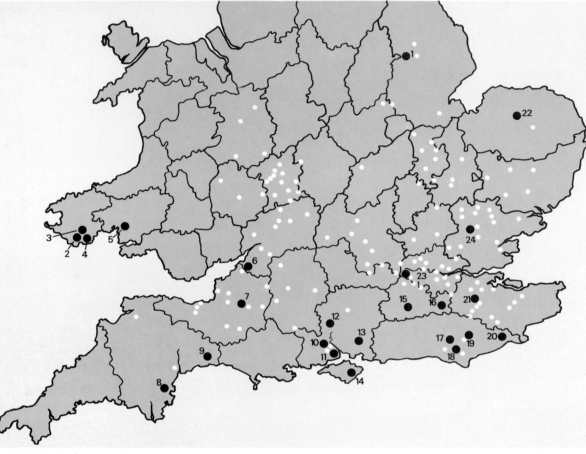

Left: on this map, modern
English and Welsh
vineyards ranging from
¼ acre to 11 acres are
shown in relation to
known mediaeval
vineyard sites (the
white dots)

1 Lincoln, Lincolnshire
2, 3 Pembroke,
Pembrokeshire
4 Lamphey,
Pembrokeshire
5 Trimsaran,
Carmarthenshire
6 Filton, Gloucestershire
7 Pilton, Shepton Mallet,
Somerset
8 Paignton, Devon
9 Colyton, Devon
10, 11 Beaulieu,
Hampshire
12 Stockbridge,
Hampshire
13 Hambledon,
Hampshire
14 Sandown, Isle of
Wight
15 Ockley, Surrey
16 Oxted, Surrey
17 Newick, Sussex
18 Plumpton Green,
Sussex
19 Horam, Sussex
20 Rye, Sussex
21 Wateringbury, Kent
22 Dereham, Norfolk
23 Shepperton. Middlesex
24 Felsted, Essex

THE IDEA of English wine is usually greeted with mockery or disbelief. It is commonly thought that England lies too far north for grapes to ripen—and besides that there is too much rain.

The fact remains, however, that in the early Middle Ages the monastic vineyards of England were extensive and by all accounts successful. Had it not been for England's acquisition (by the marriage of Henry II to Eleanor of Aquitaine in 1152) of Bordeaux—an easily accessible source of better wine—they would probably have continued to this day. But they faded away in the later Middle Ages, and since then only spasmodic attempts at wine-growing in England and Wales were made until recently.

Now there is every sign that a serious revival is afoot; as many as 24 vineyards are making wine. Most are in the south of England. The map compares them with the location of the mediaeval vineyards of which we have a record.

A cross between Riesling and Sylvaner and a hybrid vine produced in France by Seyve-Villard, both white varieties which ripen early and are disease-resisting, are the two most popular at present. The wine normally needs the help of sugar, as it does in Germany and often in Burgundy. But the quality is satisfactory, and it only needs a more helpful attitude by the government, who at present charge duty on English wine as though it were imported, to make possible a small but serious wine industry in England.

Above: almost all modern
English wine is white;
Beaulieu Abbey rosé is the
exception. There is already
an elegant country-house
style of label design: the
Hambledon motif comes
from the first cricket club,
which was at Hambledon

Left: a strange setting
for the vine; Sir Guy
Salisbury-Jones's
vineyard on the South
Downs at Hambledon near
Portsmouth consists of 4½
acres of Seyve-Villard
and Chardonnay vines.
His average crop is
12,000 bottles

A whisky distillery in the austere beauty of the western islands of Scotland: Caol Ila on the island of Islay

The World of Spirits

THE WINE COUNTRIES of the world are limited to the temperate zone, and to places where Mediterranean civilization has set the pattern of life. Spirits have no such climatic or cultural limits. They can be made wherever they are wanted. Distilling is not agriculture, with its roots directly in the ground, but industry. Where water runs and a truck can go you can make whisky, brandy, gin, rum or any other spirit.

But there is an élite among spirits—and for very much the same reasons as there is an élite among wines. Occasionally a complex set of natural conditions adds up to a style and quality of drink which can be imitated—but can never be reproduced. These are the spirits which bear their geographical origins like a coat of arms, and whose production, like wine-making, is partly science, mostly hard work, but also partly a creative art. International trade in spirits consists almost entirely of these superior products, and is limited to the richer nations.

Spirits can be distilled from anything which can be induced to ferment; anything containing sugar which can be turned into alcohol. Mankind has shown real ingenuity in finding fermentable and distillable supplies in the most unlikely places.

The list below shows some of his resources, from wine to milk, hogweed, potatoes and cactus. The maps also show his capacity for drinking (or at least for paying for) spirits, ranging from 14.8 litres a head a year in the Soviet Union to 1.6 in over-taxed Britain.

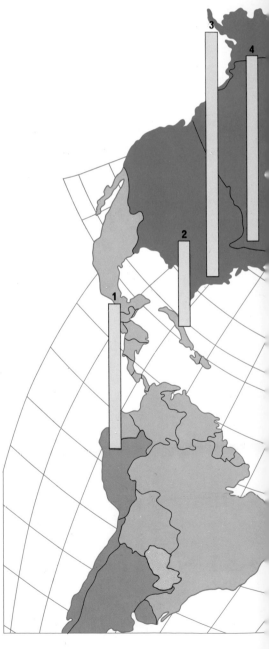

Apples
Applejack	New Jersey, USA
Batzi	Switzerland
Trebern	Austria

Apricots
Barack pálinka	Hungary

Cactus
Pulque	Mexico
Tequila	Mexico

Cherries
Kirsch	Austria, Germany, Switzerland
Kirsebaerlikoer	Denmark

Cider
Calvados	Calvados, France
Eau de vie de cidre	Northern France

Coconuts
Arak, Arrack	East

Dates
Arak, Arrack	Middle East, North Africa
Zibib	Egypt, Middle East

Fruit
Alcools blancs	France
. . . Geist	Germany, Switzerland
. . . Wasser	Germany, Switzerland

Gentian
Enzian	Switzerland

Grain
Akvaviittee	Finland
Akvavit	Norway, Sweden, Denmark
Bourbon whisky	USA
Gin	England, North America
Genever	Holland
Korn	Germany
Poteen	Ireland
Schnapps	Germany
Steinhäger	Germany
Vodka	Russia, Poland
Whiskey	Ireland
Whisky	Scotland, North America

Grape skins
Bagaceira	Portugal
Grappa	Italy
Komovica	Jugoslavia
Marc	France

Hogweed
Bartzch	Northern Asia

Milk
Awein	Tartar Russia
Skhou	Caucasus, Russia

Molasses
Aguardiente	Dominican Republic
Arrack	Indonesia
Basi	Philippines
Pinga	Brazil
Rum	West Indies; Mexico, Central America, and S America; Madagascar; New England; Java; Philippines; Egypt

Plums
Rakia	Bulgaria
Sljivovica, slivovitz,	Bulgaria, Austria
Slivowitz	Jugoslavia
Szilva	Hungary
Tuica	Romania

Potatoes
Akvaviittee	Finland
Akvavit	Norway, Sweden, Denmark
Schnapps	Germany
Vodka	Finland, Sweden

Rice
Arak, arrack	Far East

Sugar-cane
Cane spirit	South Africa
Rum	West Indies

Water-melons
Kislav	Russia

Wine
Aguardente	Portugal
Aguardiente	Spain
Arak, Arrack etc (or dates, rice, coconuts)	Africa; Middle East; Far East
Armagnac	Armagnac, France
Brandy	South Africa; Australia, New Zealand; Middle East; Italy; Germany
Cognac	Cognac, France
Cõnac, Kanjak, Konjak etc	Spain, Portugal; Chile; Eastern Europe, Greece, Turkey; Russia
Mastika	Greece
Ouzo	Greece, Egypt, Middle East
Pisco	Peru
Rajika, Raki, Rakía	Balkans, Turkey, Middle East
Vinjak	Jugoslavia

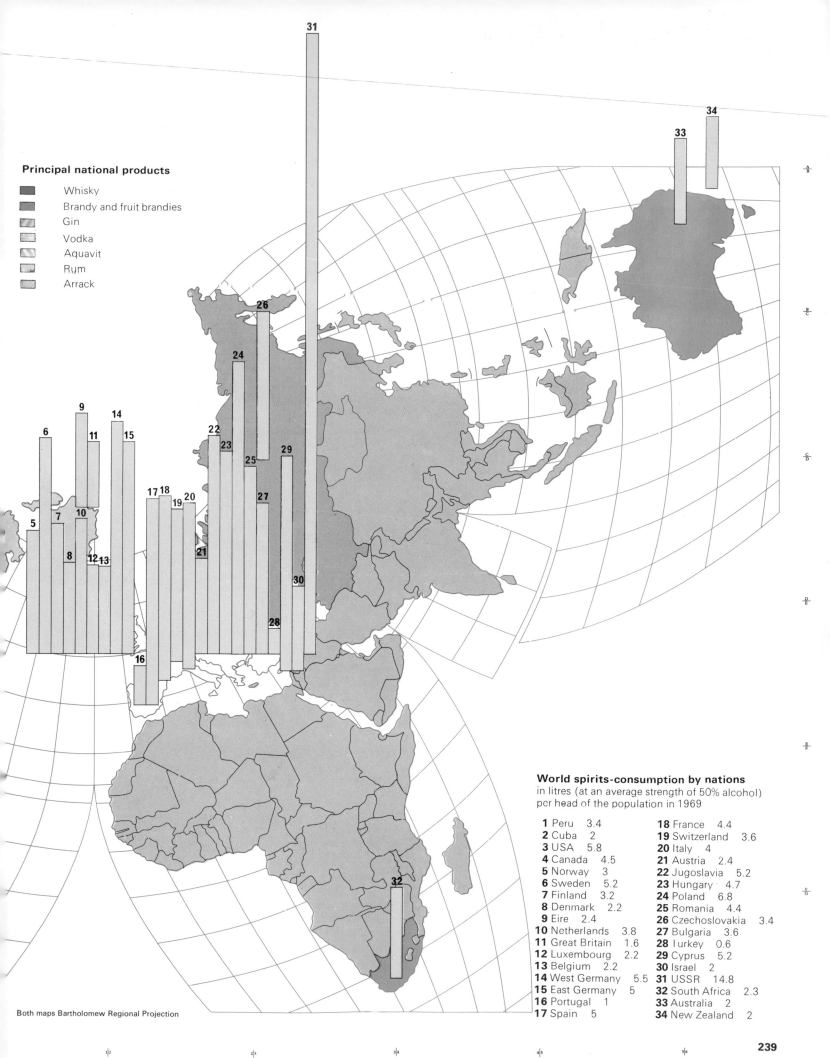

Principal national products

- ▨ Whisky
- ▨ Brandy and fruit brandies
- ▨ Gin
- ▨ Vodka
- ▨ Aquavit
- ▨ Rum
- ▨ Arrack

World spirits-consumption by nations

in litres (at an average strength of 50% alcohol) per head of the population in 1969

1 Peru	3.4	**18** France	4.4
2 Cuba	2	**19** Switzerland	3.6
3 USA	5.8	**20** Italy	4
4 Canada	4.5	**21** Austria	2.4
5 Norway	3	**22** Jugoslavia	5.2
6 Sweden	5.2	**23** Hungary	4.7
7 Finland	3.2	**24** Poland	6.8
8 Denmark	2.2	**25** Romania	4.4
9 Eire	2.4	**26** Czechoslovakia	3.4
10 Netherlands	3.8	**27** Bulgaria	3.6
11 Great Britain	1.6	**28** Turkey	0.6
12 Luxembourg	2.2	**29** Cyprus	5.2
13 Belgium	2.2	**30** Israel	2
14 West Germany	5.5	**31** USSR	14.8
15 East Germany	5	**32** South Africa	2.3
16 Portugal	1	**33** Australia	2
17 Spain	5	**34** New Zealand	2

Both maps Bartholomew Regional Projection

239

How Spirits are Made

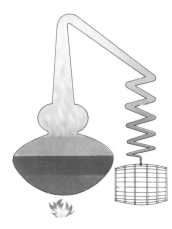
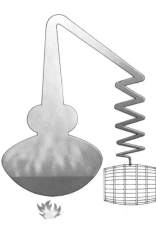

Above: the pot-still or alembic; the original design and still the best. A kettle holding 1200 litres of white wine (in the case of cognac) sits on a fire. Highly volatile elements vaporize first. These are condensed in the copper coil (which is immersed in cold water) and collected in a barrel. They are known as headings (for whisky, foreshots). As it heats further the alcohol vaporizes and is in turn condensed and collected in another barrel. This is 'brouilli' (or in whisky 'low wines'). The less volatile part goes into a third barrel; these tailings (for whisky, feints) and the headings are added to the next kettle of wine to be distilled. Then the same process is repeated, using the brouilli in place of wine. This time the middle third is brandy

Above: brandy flows from the condenser of a pot-still in Cognac. The clear white spirit is running into a brass tray with a funnel into the oak barrel below
Below: one of the few big distilleries of Cognac has six identical pot-stills built over brick furnaces. In the smaller vase-like tanks on top (right) the wine is warmed by the vapour before it goes into the alembic

PUT AT ITS simplest, distilling is a way of concentrating the strength and flavour of any alcoholic drink by removing most of the water. It relies on the fact that alcohol is more volatile than water—which is to say that it boils at a lower temperature. If you boil wine in a saucepan it will lose all its alcohol and most of its aromatic elements into the air long before the pan is dry. So if you collect the steam and condense it you will have the alcohol and very little of the water; you will have, in fact, brandy.

This fact has been known in the East for thousands of years. It entered the western world in the 14th century, via the Arabs, whose words al embic (meaning a still) and al cohol we still use.

The original form of still, the pot-still (illustrated left), is simply a kettle on a fire, with a long spout, usually curled into a worm, in which the vapour condenses. Even now this is the best design, and used for all the highest-quality spirits. Its great advantage is that it gives total control. The distiller can choose precisely what part of the vapour he wants to keep, as containing the desirable proportion

Above: the art of distilling arrived in Europe late in the Middle Ages. This engraving of about 1480 from Salerno is one of the earliest illustrations of a still

of alcohol and flavour. He can eliminate undesirable elements which vaporize sooner than alcohol and 'pass over' first or which are less volatile and 'pass over' later.

The pot-still's disadvantage is that it is slow, it needs a craftsman to operate it, and it needs to be cleaned out and filled up after every operation.

Most modern distilling is done in the patent continuous still, which was invented by an Irish exciseman called Coffey. The picture on the right shows how it uses steam to vaporize the alcohol, letting the waste run away continuously, which makes it faster in operation than the pot-still and much cheaper to run. The only drawback is that you must distil at very high strength in order to get a clean enough spirit to drink; you cannot choose precisely which 'fraction' of the vapour you will keep. Continuous-still spirits therefore normally have less of the congenerics, as the flavouring elements which 'pass over' with the alcohol are called. They have less of the original taste and smell of the raw material; they also need less time in wood to mature.

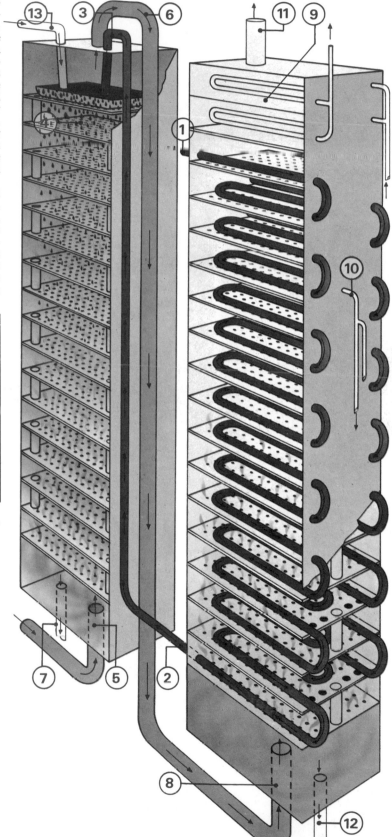

Left: most spirits are made in the continuous still. It takes in a steady stream of 'wash' (which can be wine, beer, or fermented molasses) at one end and emits a stream of spirit at the other: a more efficient and time-saving process than the pot-still on the opposite page. The continuous still consists of two columns as much as 80 feet high. Cold 'wash' goes into the 'rectifier' column at 1 and passing down twisting pipes is heated by mounting hot vapour. At 2 it emerges very hot from the rectifier and is taken to the top of the 'analyser' 3 where it flows into an open trough. The trough overflows, letting the hot wash fall on to perforated plates 4.
Meanwhile very hot steam enters at 5, rises and meets it, causing the volatile elements to boil away immediately. They pass as vapour out of the analyser at 6. Most of the water in the wash continues to fall down the column and is drained away at 7.
At 8 the spirit vapour (from 6) re-enters the rectifier. As it rises in this column, being cooled by the incoming wash pipes, less volatile elements ('feints') condense first and fall back to 12. From there they are pumped to join the fresh wash in the analyser at 13 and go through the process again. The spirit alone reaches the top. A cold-water radiator 9 there finally condenses it and it flows out of the column at 10. Only the most volatile elements (the equivalent of the foreshots of a pot-still) remain as vapour and emerge at 11.
While this method is much less laborious than the old one, there is not the nicety of control; the distiller does not choose an exact moment to separate spirits from foreshots and feints. To be safe he must treat a smaller and stronger fraction of the total as drinkable spirit and reject or redistil the rest. Hence the use of the pot-still for the fine spirits (e.g. cognac and malt whisky) which need to retain more of the congenerics which give flavour

Cognac

The cognac houses

⁂ 1 Martell		● 17 Croizet-Eymard
⁂ 2 Hennessy		● 18 Dist. de Segonzac (M
⁂ 3 Remy Martin		● 19 Dist. de Galienne (Ma
⁂ 4 Otard-Dupuy		● 20 Dist. de St-Martin (M
⁂ 5 Courvoisier		⁂ 21 Moulineuf (Martell)
● 6 Ricard-Bisquit Dubouché		⁂ 22 Hennessy
● 7 Hardy		● 23 Viticulteurs Réunis
⁂ 8 J. G. Monnet		⁂ 24 Coop. de Cognac et
⁂ 9 Camus		Vins Charentais
⁂ 10 Salignac		⁂ 25 Hennessy
⁂ 11 Prince de Polignac		⁂ 26 Hennessy
● 12 Castillon		⁂ 27 Martell
⁂ 13 Larsen		● 28 Hennessy
⁂ 14 Hine		⁂ 29 Hennessy
● 15 Tiffon		● 30 Hennessy
⁂ 16 Frapin		⁂ 31 Delamain

● Distillery ⁂ Warehouse

Canton boundary
Commune boundary
Vineyards
Woods
Contour interval 10 metres

Above: the river Charente among vines near Jarnac
Below: fume-blackened warehouse roofs in Cognac
Bottom: cognac matures at least two years in oak

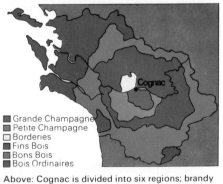

Above: Cognac is divided into six regions; brandy
of the finest quality comes from the central zones
Below: of the five chief consumers of cognac,
Great Britain is the biggest outside France

■ Grande Champagne
□ Petite Champagne
□ Borderies
■ Fins Bois
■ Bons Bois
■ Bois Ordinaires

Great Britain 16%
Germany 14%
France 29%
USA 13%

THERE IS an uncanny fresh-grape sweetness about good cognac, as though the soul of the vine has been etherealized and condensed. It makes you think not just of wine but of great wine—it has the same elusive complexity; the same raciness and excitement.

And yet the wine it comes from is not great at all. The Charente vineyards, now given over exclusively to cognac, were originally the poor pedlars of very inferior stuff to seamen from Britain and the Low Countries coming to buy salt. It was only in the 17th century that some of these immigrants began 'burning' the wine. But once the experiment had been made the word got round. A Mr Martell came from the Channel Islands, a Mr Hennessy from Ireland and a Mr Hine from Dorset. Cognac had found its métier.

The Appellation Contrôlée Cognac covers almost two whole departments just north of the Gironde estuary, the whole sparsely-contoured basin of the river Charente, and even the small islands off-shore in the Bay of Biscay.

Some 70,000 farmers in this area grow white grapes, and as many as one in ten have a still of their own for distilling the wine. The variety they grow—today mainly Ugni Blanc, known locally as St-Emilion—gives wine without

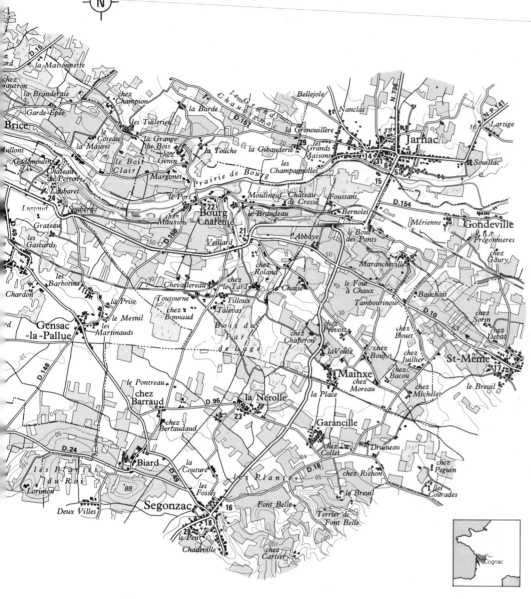

many other possibilities; only about $7\frac{1}{2}\%$ alcohol and with as much as 10 grammes per litre of acidity. Indeed they tend to pick before the grapes are fully ripe to be sure of this acidity, which makes it the perfect wine for distillation. The St-Emilion crops heavily here in the mild coastal climate with high rainfall.

The quality of the resulting brandy depends almost entirely on the soil. At its best, in the heart of the Charente (see the small map) it is as chalky as in Champagne. Hence the similarity of names between the two unrelated regions. Concentric circles of progressively less chalky and (for this purpose at least) inferior soils surround it. From a topsoil of 35% chalk, with 80–90% chalk only 20 centimetres down, to 25%, to 15% is the progression from Grande Champagne to Petite Champagne to Borderies. The corresponding progression in the cognac is from maximum finesse to a more full-bodied and high-flavoured spirit—still excellent in its way. Beyond the small and central Borderies, however, the three Bois—Fins, Bons and Ordinaires—have yellower, richer soil which results in less delicate cognac, with a distinct goût de terroir or earthiness.

Cognac is distilled in the winter months as soon as possible after the wine has stopped fermenting. The pot-still used is shown on page 240. The wine is warmed in a tank beforehand and then boiled away by a steady coal fire. Two distillations are needed to get the fraction with exactly the right amount of alcohol and congenerics: it runs from the still for the second time, white and clear, at about 70% alcohol: one barrel of brandy for every ten of wine which went in.

New cognac is harsh, overstrong, incomplete. Aging in oak is as much part of the process as distillation. The forest of the Limousin, 80 miles to the east, supplies the perfect material; oak with a high porosity and rather low tannin content. Two years in a Limousin barrel is the legal minimum for any cognac; most good ones in practice have three and VSOPs (Very Special Old Pale) have five or more. The airy *chais* where the barrels lie are scattered throughout the region, their roofs blackened with a fungus which lives on the fumes; for the rate of evaporation is daunting: as much cognac is lost into the air every year as is drunk in the whole of France.

Five years is now the maximum age which the law allows a firm to claim on the label for its cognac, however old it may really be. The former practice of keeping unblended vintages has been outlawed as being impossible to control. One kind of certified older cognac, however, is still available; cognac which has been 'early-landed' in a foreign port in barrel and kept in the customs cellar while it matures. The London docks have long been famous for the gentle and exquisite, faintly sweet and faintly watery-tasting, very pale old cognac which has passed 20 or 30 years gradually losing alcohol and gaining finesse in their particularly damp cellars.

Normal commercial cognac is diluted to 40% alcohol with distilled water, and its sweetness and colour are adjusted with sugar and caramel. Each shipper has his house style, which he keeps constant from year to year.

The large map shows the heart of Cognac; the country between Cognac, the prosperous little capital, Jarnac and Segonzac. The area south of the Charente is in Grande Champagne, north is mainly Fins Bois and north-west, facing Cognac, is Borderies. The principal distilleries and warehouses are marked. In the well-tended but rather dull countryside the characteristic building is the *logis*; the old fortified farmhouse, high-walled and gated. Many have stills: the greater part of cognac is made by farmers and matured by shippers.

Armagnac

THE WORLD has only one other brandy which can be compared with cognac—and it too comes from western France, from an area which at its closest point is only 80 miles from the Charente. But armagnac shares only its subtlety and its very high standards with cognac; for the two brandies are poles apart in style, and in the techniques used to make them.

Armagnac is a remote country region, hilly in the south, known as Haut-Armagnac, and almost a plain in the north—Ténarèze and Bas-Armagnac, the areas which give the best-quality brandy. Bas-Armagnac might be called the Grande Champagne of the region, except that in place of chalk it has sandy soil.

Apart from the soil and Armagnac's generally warmer climate the big differences between armagnac and cognac come from the type of still and the local wood. The armagnac still is something between a pot-still and a continuous still, a sort of double boiler in which the wine is distilled once, at a much lower strength than most spirits: 53% as against cognac's 70.

The lower the strength of the distillation the more flavouring elements are left besides the alcohol in the brandy. Thus armagnac starts with a stronger flavour and scent than cognac. To this the local 'black' oak, sappy (so sappy in fact it should be hewn with an adze rather than sawn) and itself full of flavour, adds its character. In black oak brandy ages much faster than in the white Limousin oak in Cognac. At eight years armagnac is well-aged; at 20 simply superb.

Until 1905 armagnac had no real identity. It sold all its good brandy to shippers in the Charente; a large part of the cognac of those days was really armagnac, for the deep blackish colour and seeming extreme age of armagnac helped young cognacs to appear older.

Comparisons of the flavours of armagnac and cognac always class armagnac as 'rustic', with the implication that it is a coarser spirit. It has been compared with hand-woven tweed in contrast with worsted. But tweed is a rough cloth, and it is armagnac's special distinction to be marvellously velvety smooth. At the same time it is dry; sugar is not normally added, as it is to cognac. Armagnac has a great pungent smell, which stays in your mouth or even in an empty glass for a long while. Its spirity, fiery quality is very similar to cognac's. The only great quality of the best cognacs it does not have is the brilliant, champagne-like finesse.

There are no great shippers like Martell and Hennessy in Armagnac. The labels here are those of some of the best of the many small houses; some of which also make liqueurs— the lower-quality brandy of Haut-Armagnac lends itself to this kind of processing and flavouring.

The main centres of the industry are the little market-towns of Auch, Condom and Eauze. As in most of the wine areas of France, a good deal of private buying goes on direct from farmers.

Above left: the Armagnac pattern of still is quite different from those of Cognac and produces lower-strength spirit with more flavour-giving congenerics
Left: the rolling green countryside of Bas-Armagnac in the west of the region produces the best brandy

Above. two small Appellation Contrôlée areas for wine adjoin Armagnac's best area in the south. Madiran is a strong red (which must legally stay three years in cask); Pacherenc du Vic-Bilh is a sweet white . Both are rare

	Limits of A C Madiran and Pacherenc du Vic Bilh
---	Département boundary
▢	Haut-Armagnac
▢	Ténarèze
▢	Bas-Armagnac
•Panjas	Production centres

Km.0   10   20   30   40 Km.
Mi.0   10   20 Mi.

Below: a large number of small producers make Armagnac an interesting subject to explore. Armagnac ages more rapidly than cognac, and at ten years has a dark colour and enormously attractive scent. The traditional bottle is round and squat; labels usually conform to this shape

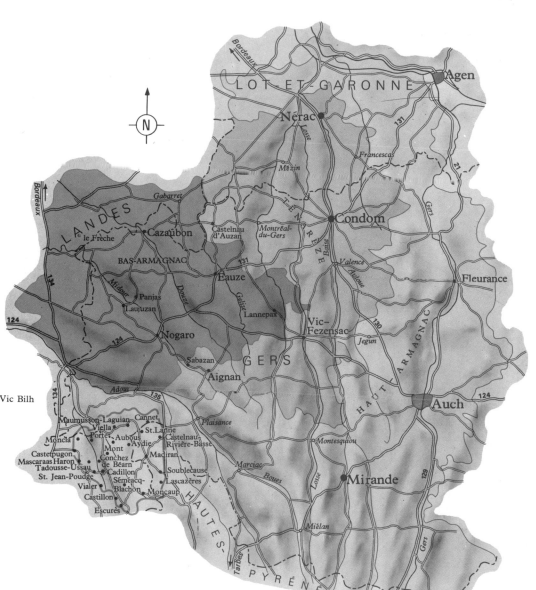

Scotland: the Highland Malts

Above: the fire and water of the Highlands; peat for drying the malt and the silver thread of the river Spey Below: some of their classic products. Less than half the malt distilleries mapped opposite sell their whisky unblended; these are among the most famous

THE 'SINGLE', or unblended, malt whiskies of the Highlands round the river Spey are to Scotch what château-bottled classed growths are to Bordeaux. The highest quality is combined in them with the maximum individuality and distinction. Each of them is superb, recognizable, consistent, and exactly like no other whisky on earth.

Most malt whisky is used to give character to the famous blends which sell all over the world. Only a little is sold 'single'. It has much more body, fragrance, texture and usually sweetness than blended whisky—but no two are alike.

On the next pages the products of the whole of Scotland are mapped. On the facing page is singled out the very heart of the whisky world; the extraordinary concentration of an industry which is also an art, miles from anywhere in barren and beautiful hills beside the Moray Firth in north-eastern Scotland.

A typical Speyside distillery is a quiet place. It seems to have the pace of farm life rather than industry. On a bright cool summer morning or in the almost permanent darkness of a Scottish winter the same simple processes are repeated by quiet men.

One long building covers the malting floor. Painted iron pillars punctuate a sea of barley, knee-deep, raked patiently this way and that while it germinates by men who do not speak.

The pointed building with the little hat contains the drying kiln, where peat from Pitsligo to the south smoulders on the red coke under a smoking hill of the germinated malt.

The next big stone barn is full of tanks and pipes and copper covers and the soothing smell of a brewery. And the next with the strange massive heads of stills, monster kettles squatting on bright points of fire, rumbling like old men who have lost touch with the world.

In this last is the first sight of whisky; a smooth little burn running a short course in a brass-bound glass case. Padlocked. And silent.

There is endless debate about the sources of quality and character in Scotch. The water is one favourite topic. There is general agreement that it should be soft, since soft water is a better solvent than hard, and extracts more proteins from the malted barley. Traditionally the best water is said to come through peat over red granite—as the burns do which flow down from the hills of the treeless deer forests past the distillery doors.

Another factor is the barley. Highland barley is not 'fat', but full of protein, which means more flavour. Another is the peat for the fire on which the barley is dried. Its smoke contributes to the taste. Another is the shape of the still; any alteration will alter its product. Another is the oak barrels in which it is matured —old sherry casks are best.

And most important is the age. Three years is the legal minimum, but at ten years or more a malt reaches its peak. Beyond 15 years or so in oak it is said to go 'slimy'.

The most famous of all the distilleries is the Glenlivet, standing on a bare slope overlooking the little river Livet where it runs down from Glenlivet forest to join the Avon, a tributary of the Spey. It was the first distillery to conform to the licensing laws which in 1823 made the hundreds of small stills of the Highlands illegal. Its fame today rests on its gently sweet, slightly smoky, marvellously delicate whisky.

No fewer than 23 other firms all over Speyside have annexed Glenlivet's name to their own at some time, among them Glen Grant, Macallan, Longmorn, Dufftown and Glenfarclas—all superb in their own right, and all bottled and sold (in small quantities) unblended.

Others in this area which can be bought 'single', each with its own character, are Glenfiddich, Balvenie and Mortlach from Dufftown, and Strathisla from Keith. The rest, with their musical, savage names, find oblivion in the blending vats of the great brands. But without them the Scotch whisky that the world knows would not exist.

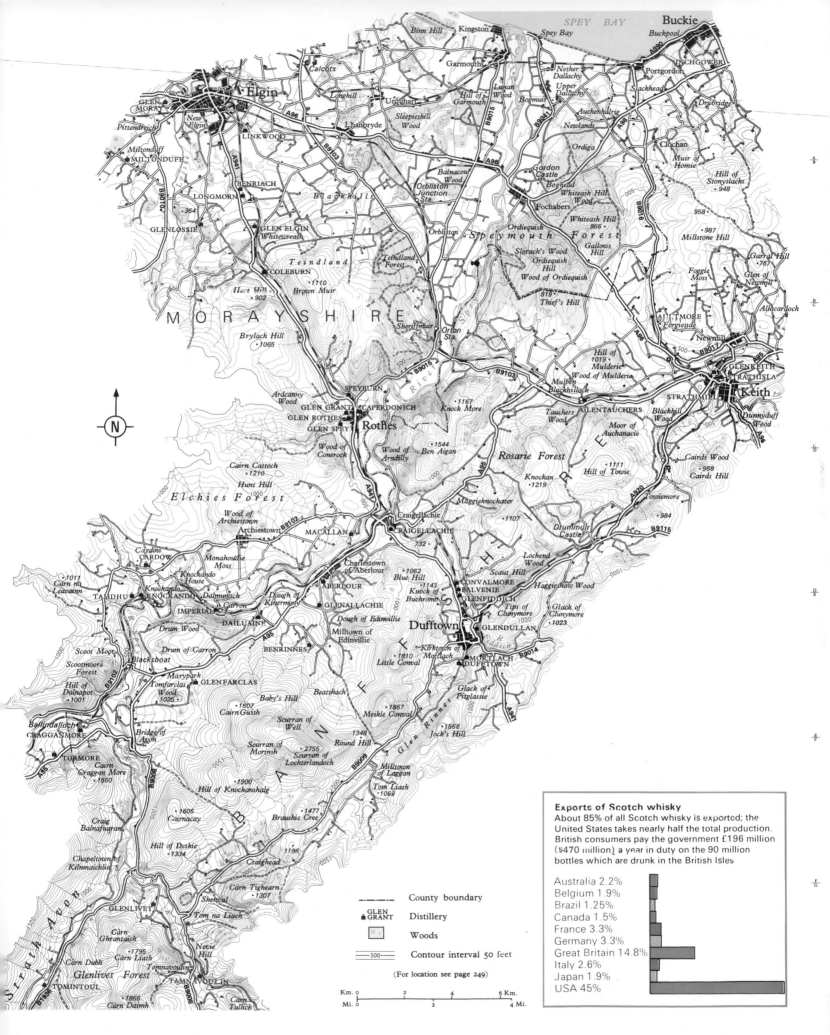

Exports of Scotch whisky

About 85% of all Scotch whisky is exported; the United States takes nearly half the total production. British consumers pay the government £196 million ($470 million) a year in duty on the 90 million bottles which are drunk in the British Isles

Australia 2.2%
Belgium 1.9%
Brazil 1.25%
Canada 1.5%
France 3.3%
Germany 3.3%
Great Britain 14.8%
Italy 2.6%
Japan 1.9%
USA 45%

County boundary

GLEN GRANT Distillery

Woods

—500— Contour interval 50 feet

(For location see page 249)

Km. 0   2   4   6 Km.
Mi. 0   2   4 Mi.

247

Scotch Whisky

ANY WHISKY which is made in Scotland, whether in the Highlands or the Lowlands, whether of barley or corn, whether in a pot-still or a continuous steam still, is Scotch. The vast majority of the Scotch which is sold, in fact, is a mixture of all these different kinds of whisky, adding up to a standard drink with an unmistakable but not too pronounced flavour. There are over 2,000 of such blends. Anybody could devise a new one tomorrow. But of the individual whiskies which go into them there are only about 100, from 100 different distilleries. And of these only about 40 are ever sold 'single', and known by the name of their distilleries: the rest are entirely used in blends.

Very loosely speaking, whisky is distilled beer; beer unflavoured with hops. The distiller's first job is the same as the brewer's; to make malt from barley; to dissolve it in water, and to ferment the resulting 'wash'. The brewer would add hops to the resulting 'worts'; the whisky-maker distils it, twice over. The first and last of the liquid which runs from the condenser the second time goes back to be distilled again. The middle part is whisky.

What sort of whisky it is is determined by where it is done and with what equipment and materials. Five kinds of Scotch are recognized.

The first is grain whisky, distilled from barley and maize in continuous stills—a comparative newcomer but now the bigger part of the industry. Grain whisky has little flavour or colour. Practically none of it is ever drunk unblended. But it is the vehicle for the flavours of all blended Scotch; the cheaper blends have as much as 70% of it; the best about 30%.

Being mild and light it needs less maturing than the more highly-flavoured kinds.

One straight grain whisky, from Cameronbridge distillery, is sold, under the name 'Old Cameron Brig'. It is rare, but for the curious an interesting experience: a smooth, pleasant and rather neutral spirit.

All the other kinds of Scotch are known as malts—being made from malted barley. There are four, because four areas of Scotland make them; and each has its own particular character.

Best and most famous of all are the malts from the district of the river Spey. They are mapped and described on the previous two pages. The malts of northern Scotland come nearest to them. Some are equally fine; often with rather stronger flavours. Of the northern malts Clynelish, Dalmore, Glenmorangie and Balblair are all bottled 'single'. One particularly fragrant and full-flavoured malt from the island of Orkney, Highland Park, is considered in the top rank.

Most distinctive of all are the malts from the western islands Islay, Jura and Skye. They are known by the strong peaty smell and flavour which gives them a slightly medicinal character. One theory is that the island peat consists of ancient deposits of seaweed which contain iodine. Certainly they are the easiest malts to recognize; those who like them will drink nothing else. A little goes a long way in a blend. Islay Mist and Laphroaig, both from the Laphroaig distillery, are the most famous. Another Islay distillery, Lagavulin, sells a little in bottle and is highly thought of. Caol Ila, one of the most beautiful, is shown on page 237.

Just south of the islands on the promontory of Kintyre are two remaining distilleries from what was once a thriving centre; Campbeltown. Only Springbank can be bought unblended.

The rest of the malt distilleries are classed as Lowland and are reckoned to produce rather gentler, less high-flavoured Scotch. All except three, Bladnoch in the west and Rosebank and Littlemill in the centre, sell their entire production for blending.

Of the hundreds of blends of Scotch the most famous are the six classics produced by the giant Distillers Co: John Haig, Johnnie Walker, Black & White, Dewar's White Label, White Horse and Vat 69. All are irreproachable and wholly consistent. Many knowledgeable people think Haig the best of them; Johnnie Walker is the best-seller; White Horse is the maltiest. The Distillers Co owns almost half the malt distilleries in Scotland and accounts for half the exports of Scotch . . . and about 85% of the total is exported.

Their principal rivals include the favourites in America, Cutty Sark and J & B Rare, which are light in colour and flavour, and such brands as Standfast, Teacher's, Bell's, Long John, Ballantine's and Whyte & Mackay's.

Then there are some excellent smaller concerns with such blends as The Antiquary, Catto's, Usher's, McCallum's, Grouse, Queen Anne, Spey Royal.

And finally there are a number of de luxe blends, among them Dimple Haig, Johnnie Walker Black Label and Chivas Regal, which contain more and older malts and are correspondingly more expensive.

Far left: the 'worts' of barley-malt and water ferment briefly and turbulently in the 'wash-back' to reach the strength of strong beer
Left: malt whisky is distilled twice. The wash-still for the first and the spirit-still for the second distillation stand side by side over a coal furnace
Above: from the wash-still the 'safe' receives 'low wines'; then from the spirit-still whisky and finally 'feints'

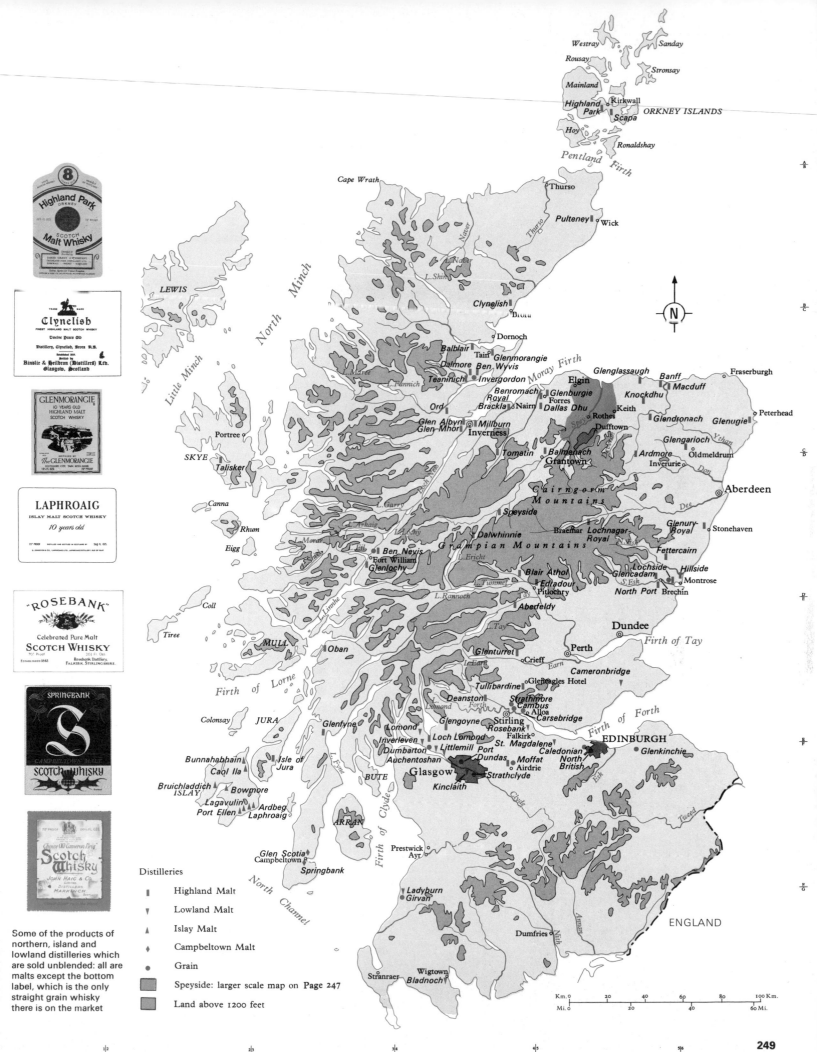

Distilleries

Highland Malt

Lowland Malt

Islay Malt

Campbeltown Malt

Grain

Speyside: larger scale map on **Page 247**

Land above 1200 feet

Some of the products of northern, island and lowland distilleries which are sold unblended: all are malts except the bottom label, which is the only straight grain whisky there is on the market

249

Rum

EVER SINCE the Spaniards in the 16th century took sugar-cane, which had come to Europe from China, to their colony of Santo Domingo, its pungent fiery distilled essence has been the drink of the chain of Caribbean islands which curve like a cutlass from Cuba to Venezuela.

All these islands, British, French, American, Spanish or Dutch, make at least a little rum. Sometimes it is only in a palm-thatched shelter in the cane-gardens, with a decrepit old copper pot-still. In Guyana such moonshine is known as 'Bushie'; in St Kitts 'Hammond'; in St Lucia 'L'Esprit d'Amour'.

The modern rum industry, however, has little to do with such folk-lore. Its big distilleries grow bigger and fewer year by year as rum gets in line as a polite social drink. The map shows where the principal ones are today.

Rum is made of either cane juice, crushed out of fresh cane by roller mills, or molasses, the residue after the juice has been boiled to make sugar. Distillers on the British and American islands, who use molasses almost exclusively, call it by the intimidating name of blackstrap. The French contrast their cane juice rum by calling it 'agricole'.

Either material is first fermented. Then it can be distilled in either of the two kinds of still: pot or continuous. Just as with whisky, the continuous still makes a more neutral but cheaper spirit; the pot-still, operated with skill, can give the perfect fraction, without too much or too little of the flavouring essences. Commercially the same answer has been found for rum as for whisky: most rums on the market are a blend of the two.

Different methods and tastes give different styles to the rums of various islands. Distillers also give credit for the individuality of their products to the yeasts they use, their water, their local variety of cane, the soil it grows on (in about that order). Particular attention is paid to yeasts. Some fresh yeast cultures are perfect for giving a quick clean fermentation with a minimum of flavour. In Guyana natural yeasts found on the canes start the molasses fermenting. But for what in Jamaica is known as Plummer or Wedderburn rum or in Martinique as Grand Arôme, the residue from previous distillations is stored in 'dunder pits' where it ferments slowly and continuously, a black and astonishingly pungent concentration of everything that gives rum its taste and smell. Dunder is used to start the fermentation of fresh batches, just as 'sour mash' is used in Kentucky. The result is a sort of ancestral character continuing from batch to batch.

Rum does not need nearly so much aging as brandy. Six months in oak is enough for good light rum. Five years would be enough for any.

Fashion today is abandoning the sweet, dark, rummy rums in favour of drier and paler sorts which impose their character less forcefully on mixed drinks. Germany and France (where it accounts for 42% of all spirits sold) still like the taste of rum, but the United States is in two minds about it. In fact the best rums today manage to keep the familiar happy pungency but in a lighter and more elegant vehicle.

Cuba, the original home of Bacardi, exports little now, but Cuban rum is apparently excellent and light.

Jamaica is by tradition the home of the heaviest rum. Some (Hampden) is still made hyperflavoured for mixing with neutral spirit to make the German 'Rum Verschnitt', but most are of medium richness today.

Haiti. Fully-flavoured rum, but being double pot-distilled like Scotch or cognac the best have real finesse. Barbancourt is the most famous.

Puerto Rico is the world's biggest producer. All

Left, from top: Bacardi moved from Cuba to Puerto Rico and is now also made in the Bahamas, Mexico and even Spain; Lemon Hart is a Jamaica blend; the three famous French rums are from Martinique; Mount Gay is from Barbados, Caroni from Trinidad and Lamb's from Guyana Right and below: cane gardens and a farm in Guadeloupe

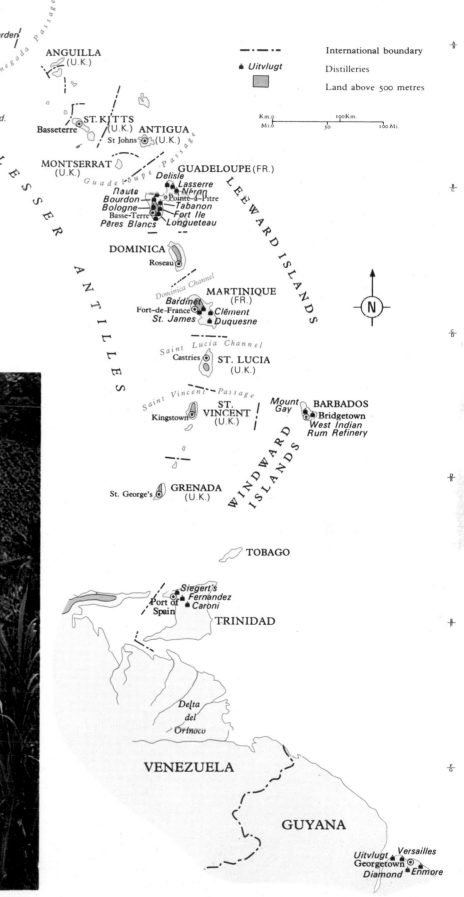

continuous-still, the classical rums are Bacardi Carta Blanca and Carta Oro, respectively white and dry and pale gold and a little richer.
Martinique and Guadeloupe tend to make fine and richly-flavoured rums. Martinique in particular makes some of the best: St James is Jamaica-style, dark and fruity. Clément is very highly regarded.
Barbados uses both kinds of stills to make good quality medium-light rum. Mount Gay is considered one of the best.
Trinidad. Continuous-still rum of good quality rather than great character.
Guyana. Rum and sugar from Guyana are better-known as Demarara. They are not the fruitiest rums, but they have quite a dark colour as well as considerable character. One third of the production is pot-distilled. 'Fruitcured'—which means fruit- and spice-flavoured—rum is the celebrated local drink.

--- International boundary
▲ Uitvlugt Distilleries
▨ Land above 500 metres

Kentucky's Bourbon

BOURBON whisky, or whiskey, is defined in terms of what it is made of and how, rather than where it comes from. Kentucky has no monopoly of its production. Yet history and sentiment identify bourbon with the state where it was first made (in Bourbon County), and even today more than half of America's bourbon distilleries are in Kentucky.

United States law lays down that bourbon must be made from not less than 51% corn grain; be distilled at not over 160 US proof (or 80% alcohol); be reduced with water to 125 proof before maturing; be matured for two years or more in new barrels of white oak, charred on the inside; and be bottled at not less than 70 proof.

In more sensual terms, bourbon is a light brown, fruity-flavoured, often rather sweet whisky, with a penetrating and unforgettable taste composed of charcoal and caramel. In practice it is made of a mixture of corn (maize), rye and barley malt fermented either with fresh yeast or by adding part of a previously fermented batch known as 'sour mash'.

Distillers who use a higher proportion of corn get a lighter whisky. By increasing the proportion of rye they make one with more body and flavour which needs longer aging.

Bourbon has been traced back to the still of Elijah Craig, a Baptist preacher in Georgetown, ten miles north of Lexington. He is reputed to have made the first bourbon in 1789, the year George Washington became first president. How it differed from the produce of all the other stills which had been making whisky up till then is not clear.

It differed from the modern whisky chiefly in being made in a copper pot-still, whereas today gigantic continuous stills are used. Hence the law setting a maximum strength: a continuous still could remove all the flavouring elements and leave pure alcohol.

Bourbon is normally sold 'straight'—either just the produce of one distillery or as 'a blend of straights', the produce of several. If it is mixed with neutral spirit, as in some of the cheaper blends, it is no longer called bourbon but simply 'blended whisky'. If labelled Bottled in Bond it is stronger (50% alcohol as against the normal 43), older (as least four years) and probably fuller-flavoured and better.

There are more than 2,900 brands of bourbon. Sales of them all together make it possibly the biggest-selling spirit in the world.

Geography is not totally irrelevant to bourbon-making. What first made Kentucky a distilling centre was partly the good supply of corn, and the difficulty of moving it to market —a keg of whisky being easier to transport than 11 bushels of grain—and partly the ample supply of limestone spring water for making the mash and cooling the condenser.

Most of the bourbon distilleries outside Kentucky lie in states on the same limestone belt: Virginia makes excellent bourbon; Pennsylvania and Maryland (traditionally the centre for rye whisky) also have bourbon distilleries. And Tennessee makes, in the 'sour mash' Jack Daniels, though it is not technically bourbon, a whisky of similar style which is certainly one of the best in America.

Top: when bourbon was sold to saloons in barrels the labels were barrel-head size. This label shows an early pot-still
Above: beside a distillery, a pond of Kentucky's famous limestone water. Neighbouring states which make bourbon are on the same belt of limestone
Left: bourbon must be matured in new white oak barrels; cooperage is a thriving trade; old barrels are sold to (among others) Scotch distillers to be used again
Right: barrels are set on fire inside; the charring gives flavour and colour to bourbon

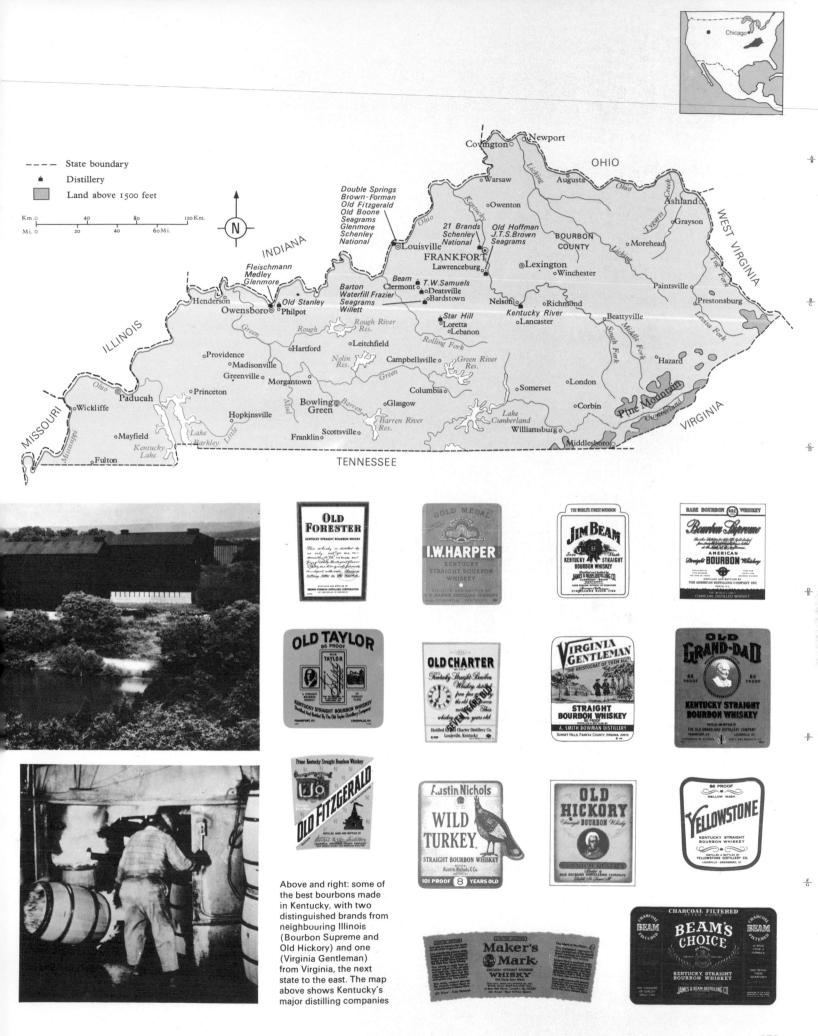

Above and right: some of the best bourbons made in Kentucky, with two distinguished brands from neighbouring Illinois (Bourbon Supreme and Old Hickory) and one (Virginia Gentleman) from Virginia, the next state to the east. The map above shows Kentucky's major distilling companies

The Kirsch Family

Every fruit that grows in the orchards of Switzerland, the Vosges mountains and the Black Forest is distilled to make high-strength clear white spirit of great fragrance. Above right are some of the scores of good producers

DISTILLING nowadays is nearly all big business. There are bootleggers still—probably more than most people suppose—but in most countries the old cottage industry has been taxed out of existence. Only where the results are exceptional does it still flourish. That place, above all, is the stretch of Europe east and south of the Vosges; the Black Forest and the northern half of Switzerland.

The local eau-de-vie is distilled in pot-stills from every edible fruit, and several which are not eaten. Kirsch, made of cherries, is the most common and widespread of these 'alcools blancs'—so-called because they are aged in glass or pottery rather than wood, and thus have no colour. But pears, apricots, blue plums, and more extravagantly raspberries, wild strawberries, and even holly berries (which give a fantastically pungent—and expensive— spirit) are distilled. The soft fruits and small berries are needed in huge quantities; prices for the genuine article are thus very high.

There are comparatively few big firms in the business: names such as Schladerer, Jacobert, Etter are well-known, and Alsace wine-shippers sell alcools, whether they make them or buy them, under their own names. Some of the finest of all come from farm-houses in the Black Forest or the Vosges, with the still in a little room off the kitchen and a vat house no bigger than a one-car garage, lined with little tanks of the essences of the local orchards.

The French tend to distil lightly for maximum flavour; the Swiss distil further and get a more neutral spirit. The Germans distinguish between a 'Wasser', which is a spirit obtained by direct distillation of the fermented fruit, and a 'Geist', which is partly a Wasser, but partly also made by infusing the fruit in alcohol—the method used with soft fruit.

The best fruit brandies are made of pears (called in France Poire William, in Germany Birngeist), raspberries (framboise, Himbeergeist), cherries (Kirsch), apricots (abricot, Aprikosengeist), blue plums (quetsch, Zwetschenwasser), gentian (gentiane, Enzian) and, principally in France, yellow plums (mirabelle), wild strawberries (fraise des bois), bilberries (myrtille), blackberries (mûre sauvage), rowan (alise) and holly (baie de houx).

Calvados

AN ARMADA galleon, *El Calvador*, wrecked on the Normandy coast as it ran from the guns of Drake's flotilla, is supposed to have given its name to the département of Calvados, and hence to the world's most famous apple brandy. Cider is the local wine of this grapeless part of France. And the local brandy is cider 'burnt' in a still. There are records of cider-distilling going back to the 16th century on the Cotentin peninsula, west of Calvados. Now 11 regions, shown on the map above, use the name, followed by their own.

In 1946 one limited area and one method of distilling cider was given an Appellation Contrôlée: Calvados du Pays d'Auge. It must be made of cider from fruit crushed in the traditional fashion and fermented for at least a month (though in a whole month it only reaches about 4% alcohol). It must be distilled twice in a pot-still, in exactly the same way as cognac, and at about the same strength (72% alcohol). It must be sold at between 40 and 50%. It must be aged for at least a year.

Well-made Calvados is quite drinkable, though very fiery, when new, but in practice the best is aged for several years in big oak casks. Before it is sold it is slightly coloured with caramel, but not normally sweetened, so it remains a very dry spirit. In its degree of scent and flavour it is very like brandy. But good Calvados recaptures in an uncanny way the evocative smell of apples. It plays an important part in Norman cooking: terrines, tripes, creamy dishes of chicken or sole are perfumed with it, and often called Pays d'Auge. There is a famous local custom of drinking a glass of Calvados between two courses of a long meal, to make a hole, a 'trou Normand', to fill with yet more delectable dishes.

The other regions which make Calvados are not obliged to use the pot-still, but if they use a continuous still it must have devices for extracting undesirable essences from the column. This less refined Calvados is not Appellation Contrôlée but only Réglementée.

Cheaper apple brandy is permitted to be made in an ordinary continuous still, but is not allowed the name Calvados. It can call itself eau de vie de cidre (or poiré, from pears) de Normandie, Bretagne or Maine.

Acknowledgements

IN ADDITION to the bodies named on page 4, and the hundreds of wine-lovers whose help has been invaluable in making this atlas, the author particularly acknowledges the contributions in information, time and advice of the following:

France
Bureau Interprofessionnel de l'Armagnac, Eauze
Comité Interprofessionnel des Vins de s Côtes de Provence, Les Arcs-sur-Argens
Comité Interprofessionnel des Vins des Côtes du Rhône, Avignon
Comité Interprofessionnel des Vins Doux Naturels et Vins de Liqueur à Appellations Contrôlées, Perpignan
Comité Interprofessionnel du Vin d'Alsace, Colmar
Conseil Interprofessionnel des Vins à Appellation Contrôlée de Touraine, Tours
Conseil Interprofessionnel des Vins de la Région de Bergerac, Bergerac
Conseil Interprofessionnel du Vin de Bordeaux, Bordeaux
Mr Nicolas Barrow, Château Courant, Arcins
M Roger Danglade, Château Rouet, Fronsac
M J. Dargent, Conseil Interprofessionnel du Vin de Champagne, Epernay
M Yves Fourault of Eschenauer, Bordeaux
Fédération Nationale des Vins Délimités de Qualité Superieure, Paris
Fédération Regionale des Vins de Savoie, Bugey, Dauphiné, Chambéry
Food from France, London
Groupement Interproducteurs du cru Banyuls, Port-Vendres
M Jean Latour, Hospices de Beaune, Beaune
M Jean Hugel of F. E. Hugel & Fils, Riquewihr
Institut National des Vins de Consommation Courante, Paris
M Louis-Noël Latour of Beaune
Mlle Liliane Le Roy, Château Fortia, Châteauneuf-du-Pape, Epernay
Mr T. Marshall, Nuits-St-George
Martell & Co, Cognac
M J. C. Berrouet of J-P Moueix & Co, Libourne
Mr Peter Sichel, Château d'Angludet, Cantenac
Syndicat des Distillateurs et Liquoristes d'Alsace et de Lorraine, Mulhouse
Syndicat du cru Corbières, Lézignan
Union Interprofessionnel de la Côte d'Or et de l'Yonne pour les Vins de Bourgogne, Beaune
Union Interprofessionnel des Vins du Beaujolais, Villefranche
Union Viticole Sancerroise, Sancerre

Germany
Dr Hans Ambrosi, Verwaltung der Staatsweingüter im Rheingau, Eltville am Rhein
Dr H. Breider, Bayerische Landesanstalt für Wein-, Obst-und Gartenbau
Herr Paul Bergweiler, Wehlen
Dr Albert Bürklin, Wachenheim/Pfalz
Herr Hermann Herlet of Deinhard's, Koblenz
Deutscher Weinbauverband, Bonn
Dr H. G. Woschek, Deutsche Wein-Information, Mainz
Dr Aichele, Deutscher Wetterdienst, Trier
Herr W. Tyrell, Gutsverwaltung Karthäuserhof, Eitelsbach, Trier-Ruwer
Professor Heinrich Zakosek, Hessisches Landesamt für Bodenforschung, Wiesbaden
Hessische Lehr-und Forschungsanstalt für Wein, Geisenheim am Rhein
Industrie-und Handelskammer, Baden-Baden
Dr Weiss, Industrie-und Handelskammer, Stuttgart
Herr Hoepfener of Karl Heinrich Kraus, Nierstein
Herr Breithaupt, St Nikolaus Hospitien, Kues
Statistisches Landesamt von Rheinlandpfalz
Dr Goedecke, St atliche Weinbaudomänen Niederhäusen-Schlossböckelheim
Bürgermeister Schuh, Neumagen

Bürgermeister Schütz, Enkirch
Verwaltung der Bischöflichen Weingüter, Trier
Herr A. von Schubert, Maximin Grünhaus, Trier
Herr Karl-Felix Wegeler, Oestrich
Dr A. Krayer, Weinbauamt, Eltville
Herr Karl Schnitzius, Weinbauamt, Kröv
Olr. F. Rath, Weinbauschule, Bad Kreuznach

Algeria
Office de Commercialisation des Produits Viti-Vinicoles, Algiers

Argentina
Vinos Argentinos S.A. Exportadora, Buenos Aires

Australia
Mr Stuart Foulds, Australian Wine Centre, London
Barossa Co-operative Winery, Nuriootpa
Federal Wine and Brandy Producers, Adelaide
Hamilton Ewell Vineyard Prop., Adelaide
Thomas Hardy & Sons, Mile End, South Australia
Lonsdale Public Relations, London

Austria
Herr Lorenz Moser, Rohrendorf bei Krems
Winzergenossenschaft Wachau, Dürnstein

Bulgaria
Bulgarian Trade Department, London
Vinimpex, Sofia

Chile
Anglo-Chilean Society, London
Asociación Nacional de Viticultores, Santiago

Corsica
Groupement Interprofessionnel des Vins de l'Ile de Corse

Cyprus
Keo, Limassol
Vine Products Commission SAP, Limassol

Egypt
Commercial Counsellor, London Embassy
Egyptian Vineyards & Distillers Co, Alexandria

Greece
Ministry of Agriculture, Athens

Hungary
Mr I. Toporczy, Commercial Secretary, London Embassy
Monimpex, Budapest
Mr Edward Roche, London

Israel
Israel Wine Institute, Rehovot

Italy
Consorzi di Vini di Asti, di Verona, di Alto Adige
Italian Institute for Foreign Trade, London
Rivista di Viticoltura e di Enologia, Conegliano, Treviso

Japan
Japan Spirits & Liquors Makers Association, Tokyo

Lebanon
Caves de Ksara, Ksara
Vins Musar, Beirut

Luxembourg
Fédération des Associations Viticoles de Luxembourg, Grevenmacher
Station Viticole, Remich

Madeira
Mr A. Jardim of Henriques & Henriques

Morocco
Comité National de Géographie du Maroc, Rabat
Moroccan Office for Commerce and Export, London

New Zealand
Viticultural Advisory Committee, Department of Agriculture, Wellington

Portugal
Casa de Portugal, London
Comissão de Viticultura da Região dos Vinhos Verdes, Porto
Mr Robin Reid of Croft's, Vila Nova de Gaia
Instituto do Vinho do Porto, Porto
Mr Alistair Robertson of Taylor, Fladgate & Yeatman, Vila Nova de Gaia

Romania
Institutul de Cercetari Pentru Viticultura si Vinificatie Romagricola, Bucharest
Romanian Trade Department, London

Scotland
Distillers Co Ltd, London

South Africa
K W V, Cape
South African Wine Farmers Association, London

Spain
Consejo Regulador de Denominación de Origen Panades, Vilafranca del Panadés
Consejo Regulador de Denominación de Origen Priorato, Reus
Consejo Regulador de Denominación de Origen Tarragona
Consejo Regulador de Denominación de Origen Valencia, Valencia
The late L. W. Steer, Rioja Wine Shippers Association, London
Mr John Lockwood of Sandeman Bros, Jerez de la Frontera
Mr Derrick Palengat of Williams & Humbert, London

Switzerland
Office de Propagande des Vins de Neuchâtel, Neuchâtel
Société des Exportateurs de Vins Suisses, Lausanne
Société Suisse des Liquoristes, Berne

Tunisia
Union Centrale des Cooperatives Viticoles, Tunis

Turkey
Turkish State Monopolies, Istanbul

USA
Brother Justin, The Christian Brothers, California
Professor Maynard A. Amerine, Department of Viticulture and Enology, University of California, Davis, California

USSR
Russian Trade Delegation, London
Sojuzplodoimport, Moscow

West Indies
Mr Ben Cross de Chavannes of Booker Brothers McConnell, London
Mr Robert Engelhard, Comité Français du Rhum, Paris
United Rum Merchants, London
West Indies Rum Committee, Barbados

General
Mr Gerald Asher
Mr Ronald Avery of Avery's, Bristol
Mr Michael Broadbent of Christie's, London
Dr Peter Fenwick, Institute of Psychiatry, London University
Dr Peter Hallgarten of S. F. & O. Hallgarten, London
Mr George Bull and Mr James Long of International Distillers & Vintners, London
Mr Anthony Goldthorpe of O. W. Loeb, London
Mr Edmund Penning-Rowsell, London
Mr Peter Reynier of J. B. Reynier, London
Dr James Rose, Birkbeck College, London
The late André L. Simon

Index

Gazetteer

This 7,000 entry gazetteer includes place name references of all vineyards, châteaux, general wine areas and other information appearing on the maps in the Atlas, with the exception of minor place names which appear as background information in italic type. All châteaux are listed under C (e.g. Château Palmer) in the gazetteer. All place names, vineyards etc beginning with le, la or les (e.g. la Perrière) are indexed under L. Names of wine or spirit producers appearing on the maps are also listed.

A

Aarau 185 B3, 254 E4
Aarberg 254 F3
Aare 185 B3, 254 F4
Aargau 185 B3, 254 E4
Abacus 178 E3
Abaújszántó 191 B3
Abbaye de Morgeot 57 F5
Abel, Lepître 101 C5
Aberdeen 249 D6
Aberfeldy 249 E4
Abergement-le-Grand 117 E5
Aberlour 247 D3
Abermain 226 F3
Abîmes 117 D1
Abos 120 E4
Abrantes 175 D4
Abruzzi 160 B2
Abtsleite 145 F5
Abú Hummus 208 G2
Abymes 117 D1
Achern 146 E4
Achkarren 146 F3
Achleiten 188 F6
Aconcagua 234 C1, 235 A3
Acqui 151 D5
Adana 208 D4
Adapazari 208 B3
Adelaide 229 A4, 224 E5
Adelaide Metropolitan 224 E6
Adissan 119 C1
Adorigo 178 G5
Affoltern 254 E5
Afyonkarahisar 208 C3
Agde 118 D6
Agen 51 F2, 245 B6
Aglianico del Vulture 160 C4
Agricoltori del Chianti
   Geografico 159 F4
Agrigento 160 G2
Agritiusberg 129 B5
Agualva 176 F2
Aguascalientes 234 F2
Aguiar de Beira 177 E6
Aguilar 171 G3
Ahrweiler 125 A3
Aigeshat 201 C4
Aigle 183 C1
Aignan 245 D4
Aigrefeuille-sur-Maine
   106 C3, F2
Aiguamurcia 170 B5
Aigues-Mortes 119 D4
Ain 51 D4, 53 F6
Ain-Bessem 207 B3
Airdrie 249 F4
Aisne 51 A3
Aiud 197 E3
Aix-en-Provence 51 F5, 116 B1
Aix-les-Baines 117 C1
Ajaccio 122 C2
Akhaia 203 D2
Akhisar 208 C2
Aksehir 208 C3
Akstafa 201 C6
Alameda 215 D2, 221 A2
Alaminos 204 D3
Alba 149 D3, 151 D3
Albacete 163 C4
Alba Iulia 197 E3
Albana 153 G4
Albana di Romagna 153 G3, 157 A5
Albanello 160 G3
Albas 120 B4
Alberto, Crastan 154 A2
Albi 51 F3, 121 F4
Albiñana 170 C5
Albo 122 A3
Albury 225 F3
Alcalde 165 D2
Alcamo 160 F1
Alcobaça 176 E1
Alcover 170 B4
Aldeanueva 169 C3
Aldinga 229 D3
Aldinga Beach 229 D3
Aleatico 157 C2, D3
à l'Ecu 60 E5
Alegria Velha 179 F4

Aleixar 170 C4
Aleksinac 195 E5
Alella 171 A2, 163 B6
Alençon 51 C1, 255 B2
Alep (Halab) 208 D5
Aleppo (Halab) 208 D5
Aléria 122 C3
Alessandria 149 D4, 151 B6
Alexander 219 B1
Alexandria (Al-Iskandariyah)
   208 G2
Alexandrie (Alessandria) 149 D4,
   151 B6
Alf 125 B4
Alfaraz 165 D2
Alfaro 169 D4
Alforja 170 C3
Algarrobo 164 C4
Algarve 175 G4
Algeciras 163 E2
Alger 207 B2
Algeria (Algérie) 207 B2
Algérie 207 B2
Algueirao 176 E2
Alicante 163 D5
Aligoté 120 A1, B2
Alio 170 B4
Al-Iskandariyah 208 G2
Al-Jumhuriyah Al'Arabiyah
   Al-Muttahidah 208 G3
Al-Lādiqīyah 208 E5
Allaman 182 B5
Allauch 116 C2
Allemagne (Deutschland) 125,
   254 D5
Allier 51 D3
Alloa 249 E4
Al-Lubnan 208 F4
Almada 176 F3
Almadén 221 C2, E4, G5
Al-Magreb 206 C4
Almendralejo 163 C2
Almeria 163 D4
Almocaden 165 C3, C4
Almoçageme 176 F1
Almoster 170 C4
Alos 121 E2
Aloxe-Corton 53 C5, 61 F3
Alpes-Maritimes 51 F6
Alsace 51 B5
Alsenz 125 C5
Alsheim 125 C6
Alstätten 254 E6
Altafulla 170 C5
Altärchen 133 G1
Altdorf 254 F5
Altenahr 125 A3
Altenberg 129 B3, B5, C5, A5,
Altenburg 143 D4
Alto Adige 153 C2, 154
Alto-Alentejo 175 E5
Alto-Douro 175 B5
Altona 228 C4
Al-Urdunn 208 F5
Aluştina 201 B2
Alušta 201 B2
Alvações do Corgo 178 F2
Alzey 125 C6
Amador 215 D2
Amalfi 160 C3
Amarante 177 C5
Amarens 121 E3
Amares 177 B5
Amarquillo 165 C2
Amasya 208 C5
Ambares-et-Lagrave 72 E3
Ambelakia 203 C3
Amboise 107 B2
Ambonnay 99 D5
Amérique du Sud 234
Amery 229 C4
Amiens 51 A3
Amintaion 203 B2
Amman 208 F5
Ammerschwihr 103 B2
Amorgos 203 E5
Amorosa 165 C4
Ampuis 113 B3
Anaferas 165 F3

Anapa 201 B3
Ancenis 51 D1, 106 B3
Ancona 157 C6
Ancône (Ancona) 157 C6
Andalucia 163 D3
Andau 186 D4
Andel 134 G6
Andernos-les-Bains 72 F1
Andillac 121 E3
Andriano 154 D2
Andros 203 D4
Angaston 229 B5
Angers 51 C1, 106 B5
Anglars-Juillac 120 B4
Anglisidhes 204 D4
Anguilla 251 B4
Anhaux 121 C5
Anières 182 C4
Animas 165 D1
Aniña 165 C2
Ankara 208 C3
Annaba 207 B4
Annaberg 143 A4
Annecy 51 D5, 117 B1
Annemasse 117 B2
Ansonica 157 C2
Antakya 208 G4
Antalya 208 D3
Antigua 251 B4
Antinori 159 B2
Antioch (Antakya) 208 D4
Antofagasta 234 C1
Antonius Brunnen 129 E1
Aosta 149 B2
Apetlon 186 D4
Apotheke 133 G1
Appenzell 185 B5, 254 E6
Appiano 154 D2
Appleton 250 A3
Apremont 117 C1
Arad 197 E1, E2
Aradhippou 204 C4
Aragón 163 C1
Arákhova 203 C3
Aranibal 165 E1
Ararat 201 D4
Arbin 117 D1
Arbois 117 E5
Arbos 170 B5
Arbus 120 F4
Arcambal 120 B6
Arcoules 113 F2
Ardbeg 249 F3
Ardèche 51 E4, 112 D5
Ardennes 51 A4
Ardila 165 C3
Ardmore 249 C5
Ardon 183 D3
Arevshat 201 D4
Arezzo 157 B4
Arganil 177 G4
Argentera 170 C3
Argentina 234 C2, 235 C5
Argentine (Argentina) 234 C2
Arges 197 F3
Ariège 51 G3
Arlay 117 E4
Armagnac 245 51 G2, F2
Arm'anskaja 201 C5
Armenia (Arm'anskaja) 201 C5
Armijo 164 C4
Arnedo 169 D3
Arnex 182 C4
Arnozelo 179 G5
Arouca 177 D5
Arrancon 89 E5
Arras 51 A3
Arsac 85 D3, E2
Arsos 204 C4, D2
Artigouleuve 120 F4
Arzie 182 B4
Ascarat 121 C5
Asco 170 C2
Ascoli Piceno 157 D5
Asenovgrad 199 D3
Ashland 253 B6

Ashtarak 201 C4
Ashton 231 D3
Aspiran 119 C1
Asprinto 160 C4
Assmannshausen 125 B5,
   139, E2
As-Sūrīyah 208 E5
Asti 149 D3, 151 C4, 218 A4
Astipalaia 203 E5
Asti Spumante 149 D3
Asturias 163 A2
Aszu 190 A4
Atacama 234 C1
Atalaya 164 B5
Athens (Athinai) 203 D3
Athienou 204 C4
Athinai 203 D3
Attiki 203 D3
Atwater 219 E3
Aube 51 B4
Aubertin 120 F5
Aubonne 182 B5
Aubous 245 D3
Auburn 222 C4
Auch 51 G2, 245 D6
Auchentoshan 249 F4
Au Clos, 'Pouilly' 66 E4
Aude 51 G3, 118 C3
Auersthal 186 C3
Auflangen 144 E4
Auggen 146 G3
Augusta 253 B5
Aultmore 247 C5
Aurillac 51 F3
Aussac 121 F4
Autun 53 D4
Auvernier 254 F3
Auxerre 53 A3, 51 C3
Auxey-Duresses 59 E1, 53 D5
aux Argillats 63 F2
aux Boudots 63 F3
aux Bousselots 63 F2
aux Chaignots 63 F3
aux Champ-Perdrix 63 F3
aux Charmes 65 E3
aux Cheusots 65 E3
aux Clous 61 D1
aux Combottes 64 F5
aux Coucherias 60 E4
aux Cras, Beaune 60 F4
aux Cras, Nuits-St-Georges
   63 F3
aux Crots 63 F1
aux Brûlées 63 F3
aux Damodes 63 F3
aux Fourneaux 61 E2
aux Grands Liards 61 E1-2
aux Gravains 61 D1
aux Guettes 61 D2
aux Malconsorts 63 F4
aux Murgers 63 F3
aux Murs 66 G5
aux Perdrix 62 F5
aux Petits Liards 61 D1
aux Quatre Vents 69 C4
aux Serpentières 61 D1
aux Thorey 63 F2
aux Vergelesses 61 E2
aux Vignes-Rondes 63 F3
Avallon 53 B3
Aveiro 175 C4
Avellino 160 C3
Avelsbach 131 F3
Avenay-Val d'Or 99 D4
Avensan 83 G4
Aveyron 51 F3
Avezzano 157 F4
Avignon 51 F4, 112 G5
Ávila 163 B3
Avinyonet 170 B6
Avise 117 B2
Avusy 182 D3
Ay 99 D3
Aydie 245 D3
Ayent 183 C3

Ayios Evstratios 203 C4
Ayios Nikolaos 203 F5
Ayl 129 D2
Ayr 249 F4
Ayze 117 B2
Azay-le-Rideau 107 C1
Azenhas do Mar 176 E1
Azerbaijan (Azerbajdžanskaja)
   201 C5
Azerbajdžanskaja 201 C5
Azille 118 B4
Azov, Sea of (Azovskoje More)
   201 B3
Azovskoje More 201 B3
Az-Zarga 208 F5

B

Baalbek (Ba'labakk) 208 F5
Bãbeascã neagrã 197 F5
Bacardi 251 A2
Bacãu 197 E4
Badascony 201 C1, 192 G3
Badacsonylábdihegy 192 G2
Badacsonytomaj 192 G3
Badajoz 163 C2
Bad Cannstatt 146 D6
Bad Dürkheim 125 D6, 143 C3
Baden, Österreich 186 D3, 188 F2
Baden, Suisse 185 B3
Baden-Baden 146 D4
Badenweiler 146 G3
Baden-Württemberg 125 D2,
   146 E4
Bad Hönningen 125 A4
Bad Kreuznach 125 C5, 137 E1
Bad Münster 137 F1
Bad Neuenahr 125 A4
Bad Pirawarth 186 C3
Bad Vöslau 186 D3, 188 G2
Baena 171 F4
Bagat 120 C4
Bagno a Ripoli 159 A4
Bagnols-en-Forêt 116 B5
Bagnols-sur-Cèze 112 F4
Bagrina 195 D6
Baia-Mare 197 D3
Baião 177 C6
Baiken 141 E3
Bairrada 175 C4
Bairro 178 F2
Bairnsdale 225 G3
Baixas 118 F3
Baixo-Alentejo 175 F4
Baja 190 C2
Baja California 234 F1
Bakersfield 215 F3
Bakers Gully 229 B5
Baku 201 C5
Ba'labakk 208 F5
Balagne 122 B2
Balaton 190 C2, 192
Balatonbogler 190 C2
Balatonfüred 190 C2, 192 F6
Balatonudvari 192 G6
Balbaina 165 F5
Balbaina Alta 165 D1
Balbaina Baja 165 E1
Balblair 249 C4
Balearija 199
Balikesir 208 B2
Ballaison 117 A2
Ballarat 225 G2
Balmenach 249 C9
Balranald 225 E2
Balvenie 247 D4
Banat 197 F2
Banatski Rizling 195 C5
Bandol 116 C2
Bandol 116 C2
Bañeras 170 B5
Banff 249 C5
Banja Luka 195 C3
Banyuls 118 G3
Banyuls-dels-Aspres 118 F2
Banzão 176 E1
Baraillot 87 A1

Barbacarlo 149 D5
Barbados 251 D5
Barbadillo 164 D6, 165 C4, D1
Barbancourt 250 A5
Barbaresco 149 D3, 151 D3
Barbechat 106 E2
Barbera 195 C1
Barbera d'Asti 149 D3, 151 B4
Barbera del Monferrato 149 D3,
   151 B6
Barcelona 163 B6, 171 B2
Barcelos 175 B4, 177 B4
Bardinet 251 C5
Bardolino 153 E2, 154 B6,
   155 A1, C1
Bardolino Classico 155 B1
Bardonnex 182 D4
Bardstown 253 C4
Bari 160 B5
Bar-le-Duc 51 B4
Barletta 160 B4
Barolo 149 D3, 151 E2
Barone Ricasoli 159 F5
Barossa Valley 224 E6, 228
Barramunda 164 A5
Barros 181 D3
Barrydale 231 D4
Barsac 72 G4, 89 A5, B4
Barsonyos-Császár 190 B2
Barton 253 B3
Bas-Armagnac 245 C3
Bas de Duresses 59 E2
Basedow's 228 B5
Basel 146 G3, 185 B3, 254 E4
Basel-Land 254 E4
Basilicata 160 C4
Basle (Basel) 146 G3, 185 B3,
   254 E4
Bas-Morgon 69 E4
Bas-Rhin 51 B5
Bassano di Grappa 153 D4
Basses-Alpes 51 F5
Basses-Pyrénées 51 G1
Basse-Goulaine 106 E1
Bassens 72 E3
Basse-Terre 251 B4
Basseterre 251 B4
Bastia 122 B3
Bâtard-Montrachet 58 G3
Bathurst 225 E4
Baule 107 A3
Bayern 125 C2
Bayon 96 F2
Bayonne 51 G1
Bayrūt 208 F4
Bayt Laym 208 G4
Beam 253 B4
Beattyville 253 C5
Beaucaire 119 D6
Beaujolais 53 F5, 69
Beaulieu, Hampshire 236 D3
Beaulieau-sur-Layon 106 B5, 108 D4
Beaulieu Vineyard Winery 217 C4
Beaumes 114 C4
Beaumes de Venise 112 F6
Beaumont-en-Véron 109 C3
Beaumont-sur-Vesle 99 B5
Beaune 51 C4, 53 D5, 56, 60 G5
Beaupuy 109 B2
Beauregard 57 F4
Beaurepaire 57 E3
Beauroy 71 C2
Beauvais, Oise 51 B2
Beauvais, Restigné 109 B3
Beauvoisin 119 D5
Beaux Bruns 64 F3
Beaux Monts 119 E5
Beblenheim 103 C3
Beblenheim 103 C3
Bečej 195 C5
Beershiba (Be'er Sheva) 208 G4
Be'er Sheva 208 G4
Begas 171 B1
Begles 72 F3
Begnins 182 B4
Beilstein, Baden-Württemberg
   146 D6
Beilstein, Rheinland-Pfalz 125 B4
Beira-Alta 175 C5
Beira-Baixa 175 D5
Beira-Littoral 175 D4

Beirut (Bayrūt) 208 F4
Beja (Bejaïa) 207 B3
Beja, Portugal 175 F5
Bejaïa 207 B3
Bekaâ 208 F4
Békéscsaba 190 C3
Bel-Air, Chiroubles 69 D3
Bel-Air, Gevrey-Chambertin 64
Bel-Air, Pomerol 91 A3
Bel-Air, Vouvray 110 C3
Belan 195 G6
Bélaye 120 B4
Belford 226 D2
Belfort 51 C5
Belgrade (Beograd) 195 D5
Beli Pinot 195 B3
Bella Napoli 219 D1
Bellbird 226 G2
Bellegarde 51 F4, 119 D5
Bellet 51 F6
Bellevue 226 F2
Belley 51 E5
Bellingham 233 F4
Bellinzona 185 D4
Bellmunt de Ciurana 170 C3
Belluno 153 C4
Bellvey 170 C5
Bellville 231 D2
Berner Alpen 254 G4
Bemposta 176 E3
Benais 109 B3
Benalla 225 F2
Bendigo 225 F2
Ben Ean 226 F1
Benevento 160 B3
Benisanet 170 C2
Ben Nevis 249 D3
Bennwihr 103 C3
Benriach 247 E3
Benromach 249 C4
Bensheimo 146 B5
Ben Wyvis 249 C4
Beograd 195 D5
Bergamo 149 B3
Bergerac 51 F2 97 E5
Bergheim 103 D5
Bergholtz 102 B2
Bergholtzzell 102 A2
Bergrivier 233 E4
Berg Roseneck 139 F3
Berg Rottland 139 F2
Berg Schlossberg 139 F2
Bergstrasse 146 B5
Bergzabern 125 E5
Beringer Bros 217 B3
Bermet 195 C5
Bern 185 C3, 254 F3
Bernac 121 E3
Berner Oberland 185 C3
Bernex 182 D3
Bernkastel 125 B3, C4
Bernkastel-Kues 135 C2
Berri 224 E6
Berson 96 D3
Bertero 221 C3
Bertineau 95 C3
Besançon 51 C5
Besigheim 146 D6
Bessay 69 A4
Besse-sur-Issole 116 C4
Bethany 228 C4
Bethléem (Bayt Laym) 208 G4
Bethlehem (Bayt Laym) 208 G4
Bettelhaus 143 B5
Beugnons 71 E2
Beurig 129 F2
Beychevelle 81 D5, 83 A4
Beyrouth (Bayrūt) 208 F4
Bex 183 C2
Béziers 118 C6
Bianchello 157 C5
Biard 21 D3
Bidarray 121 B5
Biebelhausen 129 D2
Biel 185 B2
Bieler See 254 F3
Biella 149 B3
Bienne (Biel) 185 B2
Biganos 72 F1

Côte d'Or 53 C5
Cortese 149 D4
Cortina d'Ampezzo 153 C4
Corton Charlemagne 61 E3
Corum 208 B4
Corunna (La Corãna) 163
Corvo 160 F2
Cosne-sur-Loire 107 B6
Costalunga 155 C5
Costermano 155 B1
Costières du Gard 119 D5
Cotas 179 E2
Coteaux d'Aix-en-Provence 51 F5, 116
Coteaux d'Ajaccio 122 C2
Coteaux d'Ancenis 51 D1, 106 B3
Coteaux de la Loire 106 B3, B4
Coteaux de l'Aubance 106 B5, 108 C4, E6
Coteaux de Saumur 106 C6
Coteaux des Baux 51 F5
Coteaux du Giennois 51 C3, 107 A5
Coteaux du Jura 185 C2
Coteaux du Layon 106 B5, C5, 108
Coteaux du Loir/Jasnières 107 A1
Côte Blonde 113 B3
Côte Brune 113 B3
Côte de Beaune 53 C5, D5
Côte de Beaune: Beaune 60, 61
Mersault 58, 59
Santenay 57
Côte de Brouilly 69 F3
Côte de Fontenay 71 C3
Côte de Haut Roussillon 118 F2
Côte de Léchet 71 D2
Côte de Nuits C6, 62, 63, 64, 65
Côte d'Or 51 C4
Côte-Rôtie, Chiroubles 69 D3
Côte-Rôtie, Côtes du Rhône 112 A5, 113 B3
Côte-Rôtie, Morey-St-Denis 64 F4
Côtes Canon-Fronsac 72 E4
Côtes d'Agly 118 E2
Côtes de Bordeaux-Saint-Macaire 72 F6
Côtes de Fronsac 72 E4
Côtes de Néac 72 E4
Côtes-du-Nord 50 C6
Côtes-du-Rhone 51 E4, F4, 112
Côtes-Fronsac 94 C5
Cotignac 116 B4
Cotnari 197 F4
Coufouleux 121 G1
Coulée de Serrant 108 B3
Cour-Cheverny 107 B3, 51 C2
Courgis 71 F2
Courmayeur 149 B2
Cours-de-Piles 97 E5
Courvoisier 243 B3
Coutras 72 D5
Covelinhas 178 G4
Covilhã 175 C5
Covington 253 A4
Cowra 225 E4
Cragganmore 247 E1
Craigellachie 247 D4
Craiova 197 G3
Cramant 99 F3
Craneford 228 D5
Crans 182 C4
Crassier 182 C4
Cravant-les-Coteaux 109 E5
Crawfordville 226 G1
Cray 110 D6
Crayssac 120 B5
Creixell 170 C5
Crema 149 C5
Cremona 149 C6, 153 E1
Crémone (Cremona) 153 E1
Crepy 117 A2
Cres 195 C1
Cresta Blanca 221 A3
Crestview 219 G5
Creta 203 F4
Crete (Kriti) 203 F4
Creuse 51 E3
Creux de la Net 61 D3
Creysse 97 E5
Crézancy-en-Sancerre 111 F2
Crieff 249 E4
Crissier 182 A6
Crna Gora (Montenegro) 195 E4
Croft 181 C5
Crouin 242 B5
Croix des Bouquets 250 A6
Croizet-Eymard 243 C4
Crotone 160 E5
Crozes-Hermitage 112 B6, 114 B4
Cru Barjuneau 89 G3
Cru Caplane 89 F4
Cru Commarque 89 G3
Cruet 117 D1
Cru la Clotte 89 B5
Cru Lanère 89 F3
Cru Thibaut 89 F5
Cuba 250 A4
Cubaexport 250 A4
Cubellas 170 C6
Cuenca 163 C4
Cubuk 208 C4
Cucamonga 218 G4
Cucamonga Vineyard Co 218 G4
Cucamonga Winery 218 G5
Cuers 116 C3
Cuidad Real 163 C3
Cuis 99 E3
Cully 182 B6
Cumières 99 D2
Cunèges 97 F4
Cuneo 149 E2
Cunit 170 C6
Cuges-les-Pins 116 C2
Cuqueron 120 F4
Curicó 234 C1, 235 D2
Cussac 83 C4
Cutler 219 G6
Csengöd 190 C2
Csopak 190 C2, 193 F1
Cviček 195 B2
Cyprus (Kipros) 208 E3, 204

D

Dachsberg 140 F3
Dahra 207 B1
Dailuaine 247 E2
Dallas Dhu 249 C5
Dalbuki 133 C4
Dallenberg 145 F5
Dalmatia 195 E3
Dalmore 249 C4
Dalwhinnie 249 D4
Dalwood 226 D3
Damas (Dimashq) 208 F5
Damascus (Dimashq) 208 F5
Damery 99 D2
Dão 175 C4, 177
Dar bel Amri 206 C4
Darbonnay 117 F4
Dardagny 182 D3
D'arenberg 229 C4
Darlington 229 A4
Daub-Haus 144 F6
Daubos 79 E5, 81 A4
Davayé 66 E4
Davos 185 C5
Dealul Mare 197 F4
Deanston 249 E4
Deatsville 253 B4
Debrecen 190 B4
Debroi Hárslevelü 190 B3
de Castellane 101 F5
Dehesilla 164 B4
de Hoop 233 E2
Deidesheim 125 D6, 143 F5
Delaforce 181 C3
Delamain 243 B3
Delgado and Zuleta 164 C5
Delheim 233 G2
Delicato 219 C2
Delisle 251 B4
Dellchen 136 F6
Del Rey 219 G5
Demesticha 203 D2
Denair 219 D2
Denens 182 A5
Denges 182 B6
Denia 163 C5
Deniliquin 225 F2
Denizli 208 D2
Derbent 201 C6
Dereham, Norfolk 236 B5
Derriere-le-Grange 64 F3
Desenzano del Garda 154 C5
Deutschherrenberg 134 C5
Deutschland 125, 254 D5
Deutschkreutz 186 E3
Deutschlandsberg 186 G1
Deutschschutzen 186 F3
Deux-Sèvres 51 D1, 106 C5
Deva 197 F2
de Venoge 101 G5
Devesas 178 G2
Devon Vale Estates 233 F1
Dézaley 182 B6
Dezize 53 D5
De Zoete Inval 233 D4
Dhali 204 C4
Dhoros 204 D2
Dhron 133 D1
Diamond 251 G6
Dienheim 125 C6, 144 G5
Dieppe 255 A2
Diez Hermanos, Jerez 165 C4
Diez Hermanos, Vila Nova de Gaia 181 B3
Digne 51 F5
Dijon 51 C4, 53 C6
Dimashq 208 F5
Dimcha 199 C3
Dimiat 199 B5, D4
Dingač 195 E3
Dinuba 219 G6
Dizy-Magenta 99 D3
Djidjelli 207 B3
Dobrogeia 197 G5
Doctor 135 F2
Dolceacqua Rossese 149 F3
Dolcetto delle Langhe 149 E3
Dolcetto d'Ovada 149 D4
Domaine d'Arche-Pugneau 89 E4
Domaine de Chevalier 87 G2
Domaine de Grandmaison 87 E4
Domaine-de-la-Combe 91 A4
Domaine-de-l'Eglise 91 B5
Domaine la Solitude 87 G5
Domäne 129 E3
Dom Avelsbach 131 E1
Domblans 117 F4
Dominica 251 C4
Dominican Republic 250 A6
Domodossola 149 A4
Domprobst 135 E1
Don 249 D6
Doña Elvira 164 B4
Doña Mencia 171 G4
Donauland 186 D3
Donnazac 121 E3
Donnerskirchen 186 D3
Doosberg 140 F5
Dordogne 51 E2, 72 D6
Dornach 254 E4
Dornoch 249 C4
Dosaiguas 170 C3
Double Springs 252 B2
Doubs 51 C5
Douby 69 D4
Doué-la-Fontaine 106 C5
Douelle 120 B5
Douro (Duero) 163 B2, 175 B5
Douro-Littoral 175 B4
Douvaine 117 A2
Douville 97 D5
Dow 181 D4
Drachenstein 139 F3
Drăgăşani 197 G3
Draguignan 116 B4, 51 F6
Drakenstein (co-op) 233 E4
Drama 203 A4
Driesprong 233 F3
Dhronhofberger 133 D2
Drôme 51 F5, 112 D5
Drumborg 225 G1
Dubbo 225 D4
Dubois 110 C4
Dubravka 195 E6
Dubrovnik 195 E3
Duchroth 125 C5
Düdingen 254 F3
Duero 163 B2
Dufftown 247 E4, 249 C5
Duillier 182 B4
Dulce Nombre 165 C4
Dully 182 B4
Dumbarton 249 F4
Dumfries 249 G5
Dunaujvaros 190 C2
Dundee 249 E5
Duquesne 251 C5
Duravel 120 B3
Durbach 146 E4
Durbanville 231 D2
Dürnstein 186 C1, 189 G1
Durtal 106 A5

E

East Side 219 C1
Eauze 245 C4
Ebernburg 125 C5
Ebersberg 144 F3
Ebersweier 254 C4
Ebro 163 B5
Echandens 182 B5
Echichens 182 B5
Echuca 225 F2
Ecuador 234 B1
Ecublens 182 B5
Ecueil 99 B3
Edelberg 135 B3
Edelmann 140 F4
Eden Valley 228 D6
Edinburgh 249 E5
Edredour 249 D5
Egelsee 189 F3
Eger 190 B3
Eggenburg 186 B2
Eguisheim 102 C5
Ehrenhausen 186 G2
Ehrenstetten 146 F3
Eibelstadt 145 G3
Eibingen 139 F4
Eichberg, Alsace 103 B1
Eichberg, Eltville 141 E1
Eisenberg 186 F3
Eisenstadt 186 D3
Eitelsbach 131 D4
El Alamo 165 C1
Elâzig 208 C6
Elba 157 B1
El Barco 165 C2
El Bizarron 165 E2
El Bonete 165 B4
El Caballo 165 E1
El Carmen 165 C4
El Castillo 165 C4
El Cerro Viejo 165 D3
El Ciego 168 B6
El Condado 163 D2
El Corchvelo 165 D2
El Corvegidor 165 C4
El Corregidor Viejo 165 C4
El Cuco 165 D1
El Cuerno del Oro 165 B3
Elderslie 226 D2
Elgin 247 A2, 249 C5
El Hornillo 164 B5
Elizabeth 224 E5
El Jardinito 165 C4
Ellas 203
Ellergrab 135 C4
Elne 118 F3
Eloro 160 G3
El Paraiso 165 D2
El Parradero 165 C3
El Peral 164 A5
El Pollero 164 D6
El Rancho 165 D2
El Ribiero 163 A2
El Romano 165 C4
El Salvador 165 C4
El Señor 164 B4
Els Monjos 170 B6
Elster 143 E5
El Telegrafo 165 C4
El Toro 165 E1
Eltville 125 B5
Eltville-am-Rhein 141 3G
Elvas 175 E5
Emeringes 69 B3
Emilia-Romagna 149 D5, 153 G2, 157 A4
Emilio Lustau 165 D1, D4
Emme 254 F4
Emmendingen 254 D4
Emu 229 B4
en Cailleret 59 F4
en Caradeux 61 D3
en Chevret 59 F3
Endingen 146 F3
Enfer 149 B2
Engadin 185 D5
Engelgrube 133 E1
en Genêt 60 E6
England and Wales 236
en Guinelay 69 B5
Enkirch 135 B4
en l'Orme 60 E6
en l'Ormeau 59 F4
Enmore 251 G6
Enna 160 F3
en Paulaud 61 F4
en Redrescul 61 E1
Entraygues 51 F3
Entrecasteux 116 B4
Entre-Deux-Mers 72 F4
en Verseuil 59 F4
Épernay 99 E3, 101
Epesses 182 B6
Épinal 51 B5
Epiré 108 B3
Epirus (Ipiros) 203 C2
Episkopi 204 D2
Équateur (Ecuador) 234 B1
Erbach 141 F2
Erbaluce 149 C3
Erdek 208 B2
Erden 134 C6
Erdöbénye 191 B4
Erdöhorváti 191 B4
Ereğli 208 D4
Erlenbach 146 C6
Ervedosa do Douro 179 F2
Escherndorf 145 F4
Escuréo 246 E3
Eskisehir 208 C3
España (Espagne) 163
Espejo 171 F4
Espinho 178 G6
Esposende 177 B4
Essaouira 206 D3
Essertines 182 B4, D3
Essonne 51 B2
Estagel 118 E2
Estaing 51 F3
Est Est Est 157 D3
Estialescq 120 G4
Estoril 176 F2
Estremadura 175 D4
Estremoz 175 E5
Esvres 107 B1
Esztergom 190 B2
Etournelles 65 E1
Etoy 182 B5
Etna 160 F3
Etroyes 67 C6
Euboea (Evvoia) 203 C3
Euchariusberg 129 A5
Eugenio Bustos 235 B4
Euphrates (Firat) 208 D5
Eure 51 B2
Eure-et-Loir 51 B2
Evenos 116 C3
Evionnaz 183 D1
Evora 175 F5
Evorilla 164 A6
Evreux 51 B2
Evvoia 203 C3
Extremadura 163 C2
Eymet 97 G4
Eyrans 96 B2
Eyrenville 97 F5
Eysines 72 E3
Ezerjó 190 B2, C3, 195 B4

F

Fabriano 157 C5
Faconnières 64 F4
Fafe 177 C5
Fahrwangen 254 E4
Fairview 233 D4
Falkenberg 133 C2
Falkenstein 129 A4, 186 B3
Falkirk 249 E4
Falqueyrat 97 G5
Falset 170 C3
Famagusta 204 C5
Fanhões 176 E3
Fara 149 C4
Fargues 89 F6
Farnesi 219 G5
Faro, Italia 160 F4
Faro, Portugal 175 G4
Farques 120 C4
Faugères 51 G3, 118 B6
Favaios 179 D2
Faye-d'Anjou 108 D5
Fayssac 121 E3
Féchy 182 B6
Feherburgundi 190 C2
Fehring 186 G2
Felgueiras 177 C5
Fels 129 B2
Fels 186 C2
Felsenberg 136 G4
Felsen Eck 137 F2
Felsen-Steyer 136 F5
Felsted, England 236 C4
Fénols 121 F3
Feodosija 201 B3
Ferianes 164 C5
Fernandez 251 B2, E5
Fernando A de Terry 165 E1, F3
Fernán Núñez 171 F3
Ferrals-les-Corbières 118 C3
Ferrara 153 F3
Ferreira 181 B3
Ferres 133 C1
Fès 206 C5
Fetească albă 197 D4, E3, E5
Fetească neagră 197 E5
Fetească regală 197 E3, E5, F2, F3, G3
Fetiaska 199 B5
Fetjaska 201 A1
Fettercairn 249 D5
Feydieu 85 F4
Fiano 160 C3
Ficklin 219 F4
Figanières 116 B5
Figari 122 D2
Figline 159 C5
Filippi Winery 218 G5
Filton, Gloucestershire 236 C3
Filzen 129 B2, 133 B4
Findling 144 D4
Finger Lakes 222
Finistère 50 C5
Firat (Euphrates) 208 D5
Firenze 157 A4, 159 A3
Firvida 178 F2
Fitou 118 D3, E3
Fiuggi 157 F4
Fixin 53 C6, 65 E4
Flagey-Echézeaux 63 G5
Flassans-sur-Issole 116 B4
Flaugeac 97 F4
Floujac Poujols 120 C6
Flayosc 116 B4
Flein 146 D6
Fleischmann 253 B3
Fleurance 245 C6
Fleurie 53 F5, 69 C4
Fleury-les-Aubrais 107 A4
Fleys 71 D6
Flohhaxn 189 F1
Floirac 72 E3
Florence (Firenze) 157 A4, 159 A3
Florentin 121 F3
Floressas 120 B4
Fochabers 247 B5
Focsani 197 F5
Fogarina 153 F2
Foggia 160 B4
Foix 51 G3
Folgosa 178 G4
Foligno 157 D4
Fonroque 97 F4
Fonseca 181 B2
Fontalioux 113 F2
Fontana 218 G5
Fontanafredda 151 E3
Fontanelas 176 E1
Fortelo 178 G3
Fontès 119 C1
Fontevrault-L'Abbaye 106 C6
Fontrubi 170 B5
Foppiano 218 C5
Forbes 225 E4
Forcine 109 B1
Forez 113 F2
Forli 153 G4, 157 A5
Fornos de Algodres 177 F6
Forres 249 C5
Forst 125 D6, 137 D1
Forst a. d. Weinstrasse 143 E5
Forsterlay 135 C1
Fort-de-France 251 C4
Forth 249 E4
Fort Ile 251 C4
Fort William 249 D3
Fougueyrolles 97 E3
Foujouin 110 B4
Founex 182 C4
Fourques 118 F2
Fours 96 B2
Fousselottes 64 F2
Fowler 219 G5
Fracia 149 A5
Fraisse 97 D3
France 51
Francesco Bertolli 159 F2
Franciacorta 149 B6, 153 D1
Franconia 145
Frangy 117 B1
Franken 125 C2
Frankenthal 139 E1
Frankfort, Kentucky 253 B4
Frankfurt 125 C2
Franklin 253 C3
Frankovka 195 C4
Franschhoek 231 D2, 233 G6
Franzia 219 D1
Frapin 243 D2
Frascati 157 F3
Fraserburgh 249 C6
Fratenilli 159 E2
Frauenfeld 185 B4
Fraussailles 121 E3
Frecciarossa 149 D5
Freemark Abbey 217 B3
Freiburg 125 D1, 146 F3, 254 D4
Freisa 149 C3
Freixial 176 E3
Fréjus 116 B5
Fremont 221 A3
French Guiana (Guyane Française) 234 B2
Fresno 215 E3, 219 F5
Fréterive 117 C2
Freundstück 143 E4
Fribourg 185 C2, 254 F3
Frickenhausen 145 G4
Friularo 153 E4
Friuli Venezia Giulia 153 C5
Frohnhof 143 C4
Fronsac 72 E4, 94 D6
Frontignan 119 D2
Fronton 51 F2
Frosinone 157 F4, 160 B2
Fruska Gora 195 D4
Fuchs 129 E2
Fuchsberg 139 F5
Fuchsmantel 143 D4
Fuenmayor 168 B6
Fuissé 66 F4
Fully 183 D2
Fulton 253 D1
Fumane 155 B2
Funchal 173 D4
Furmint 190 A4, C2, B2
Furore Divina Costiera 160 C3
Fye 71 C4

G

Gabilan Range 221 E4
Gabrovo 199 C3
Gaeta 160 B2
Gageac-et-Rouillac 97 E4
Gaillac 51 F3, 121 F3
Gainfarn 188 G2
Gaiole in Chianti 159 E5
Galafura 178 F4
Galaţi 197 F5
Galbenă 197 E5
Gallega 165 E1
Gallicia 163 A1
Gallician 119 D4
Gallipoli 160 C6
Gallo-S. California Winery 218 G5
Gallo, W. E. & J. 219 D2
Galt 219 B1
Gamay 58 E3, 195 F5
Gambellara 153 E3, 155 C6
Gamlitz 186 G2
Gampel 183 C5
Gan 120 G5
Gandesa 170 C1
Gap 51 E5
Garanche 69 G3
Garancille 243 D3
Garcia 170 C2
Gard 51 F4, 112 G4, 119 D5
Garda, Lago di 154 B6
Gardone 154 A5
Gardonne 97 E4
Garidells 170 C4
Garmouth 247 A4
Garonne 51 F2
Garvey 164 D6, 165 D1, B3, B4, D3
Gaspar F. Florido Cano 164 C4
Gassin 116 C5
Gattinara 149 B3
Gauriac 96 F2
Gavá 171 B1
Gavi 149 D4
Gawler 224 E5
Gazetiers 65 E2
Gaziantep 208 D5
Gazzah 208 F4
[illegible] 61 D1
Gedersdorf 186 C2
Geelong 225 G2
Gehrn 141 E3
Geisberg 129 E4, 135 D4, 141 E5
Geisböhl 143 G5
Geisenheim 125 B5, 139 G5, 140 G2
Gelida 170 B6
Gelos 120 F5
Gemeaux 64 F6
Gemello 221 B2
Genadendal 231 D3
Genders 229 C4
General Alvear 235 D6
Gengenbach 254 C4
Gênes (Genova) 149 E4
Geneva 51 D5, 117 B2, 182 C4, 185 D1
Genève 51 D5, 117 B2, 182 C4, 185 D1
Genoa (Genova) 149 E4
Genova 149 E4
Gensac-la-Pallue 243 C1
George 231 D6
Georgetown 234 B1, 251 G6
Georgia (Grunzinkaja) 201 C4
Germany (Deutschland) 125
Gerona 163 B6
Gers 51 G2, 245 D4
Gerümpel 143 E4
Gervide 178 F2
Getashan 201 D4
Gevrey-Chambertin 53 C5, 65 E2
Geyserville 218 B5
Ghemme 149 B4
Ghioroc 197 E2
Ghisonaccia 122 C3
Gibraltar 163
Gien 51 C3, 107 A5
Gigondas 112 F6
Gilly 182 B4
Gilly-les-Citeaux 64 G2
Gilroy 221 C4
Gimmeldingen 125 D6
Ginestar 170 C2
Ginestet 97 D4
Giretti 221 C3
Giro 157 G2
Giroussens 121 G2
Gironde 51 F1, 72
Girvan 249 G4
Givry 53 D5, 67 E6
Gizeux 106 B6
Gland 182 B4
Glarus 185 C4
Glasgow, Kentucky 253 C3
Glasgow, Scotland 249 F4
Glen Albyn 240 C4
Glenallachie 247 E3
Glenburgie 249 C5
Glencadam 249 D5
Glen Conner 233 G3
Glendora 218 F3
Glendronach 249 C5
Glendullan 247 E4
Gleneagles Hotel 249 E5
Glen Elgin 226 F2
Glen Elgin 247 B3
Glenfarclas 247 E2
Glenfiddich 247 E4
Glenfyne 249 E3
Glengarioch 249 C5
Glenglassaugh 249 C5
Glengoyne 249 E4

la Maison Blanche 114 C5
la Maladière 57 E3
la Maltroie 58 G1
La Mancha 163 C4
Lamarque 83 D5
la Martellière 109 B2
La Masó 170 C4
Lambrusco 153 F2
la Medoquine 87 A3
La Méjanelle 119 D3
la Meslérie 110 B4
Lamia 203 C3
la Mignotte 60 F4
la Milletière 110 D5
la Môle 116 C5
Lamonzie-St-Martin 97 E4
La Morera de Montsant 170 B3
la Morra 151 E2
Lamothe 89 C4
Lamothe-Montravel 97 E2
la Motte 116 B5
la Mouline 85 E2
Lamphey, Wales 236 C2
la Mure 66 E4
Lana 154 B1
La Nava 163 B3
Lancaster 253 C4
Lancellotta 153 F2
Lancié 69 D5
Landau 125 E6
Landes 51 F1, 245 C3
Landskrone 125 C6
la Nérolle 243 D3
Langeais 106 B6
Langenberg 141 E3, E5, F5
Langenlois 186 C2
Langenlonsheim 125 C5
Langen-Morgen 143 F4
Langenstück 141 F4
Langhorne Creek 224 F6
Langlade 119 C5
Langnau 254 F4
Langon 72 G4
Languedoc 51 G3, G4
Lania 204 D2
Lannepax 245 C4
la Noblaie 109 F3
La Nou de Gaya 170 C5
La Norieta 165 C4
Lanquais 97 E6
Lansac 96 F4
Lanson 101 A5, C4
Laon 51 A3
La Pagliaia 159 F5
la Paillère 87 B2
La Palma 165 C2
Lapalme 118 D4
La Pampa 234 C2
La Panamena 165 C2
La Paris 233 E5
La Pastranilla 164 C5
La Paz 234 C1
la Perrière, Fixin 65 E3
la Perrière, Gevrey Chambertin 65 F1
la Pierrière, Nuits-St-Georges 62 F6
la Perrière, Sancerre 111 E3
La Pesanella 159 D4
Laphroaig 249 F3
la Pièce-sous-le Bois 58 F5
la Pierelle 114 C5
la Pierre 69 C5
la Pinesse 89 C4
la Platerie 109 B3
la Pommeraye 106 B4
la Possonnière 108 B2
La Provence 233 G5
L'Aquila 157 E5
La Racha 165 C2
La Rambla 171 F3
Laredorte 118 B3
la Refène 60 F1, 59 F6
la Regrippière 106 F3
La Réole 72 G5
la Richemone 63 F3
La Riera 170 C4
la Riotte 64 F4
Larisa 203 C3
La Rioja 234 C2
Larnaca 204 C4
la Roche 113 B3
la Roche aux Moines 108 D3
la Roche-sur-Yon 51 D1
la Rochelle, Charente-Maritime 51 E1
la Rochelle, Chinon 109 E3
la Rochelle, Moulin-à-Vent 69 C4
la Rochère 110 C5
la Roilette 69 C4
Laroin 120 F5
la Romanée 63 F4
la Romanée 57 F5
la Romanée-Conti 63 F4
la Roncière 62 F6
Larroque 121 E1
Larsen 242 B5
la Salpetrière 109 B2
Lascazères 245 E4
la Secuita 170 C4
La Selva 170 C4
la Seyne-sur-Mer 116 D3
Lasgraisses 121 G3
las Heras 235 A5
Las Irlas 170 C3
Laski Rizling 195 A3
la Solitude 115 C5
La Spezia 149 E5
Lasserre 251 B4
Lasseube 120 G4
Lasseubetat 120 G5
Lastra 159 A1
Las Vegas (Chile) 235 A2
la Tâche 63 F4
La Taconera 165 F3
Latakia (Al-Lādiqīyah) 208 E5
Latakie (Al-Lādiqīyah) 208 E5
la Thierrière 110 C4
Latina 157 F3, 160 B1
La Torre Alta 164 D6
la Tour du Bief 69 B5
Latour-de-France 118 E2
la Tour de Peitz 183 B1
Latricières 64 F5
La Trinidad 165 D2
la Tuilerie 89 F5
La Tula 165 E1
l'Auberdière 110 C3
Laudamusberg 133 E1
Laudun 112 G5
Lauffern 146 D6
Laujuzan 245 C3
Laure-Minervois 118 B3
Laurentiusberg 133 F1
Laurentiuslay 133 F1
Lauria 160 D4
Lausanne 182 B6, 185 C2, 254 G3
Laval 51 C1
la Valette-du-Var 116 C3
la Vallée 111 E2
la Vallée Chartier 110 C4
la Vallée Coquette 110 C2
la Vallée de Nouy 110 C3
la Vallée de Vaux 110 B5
la Varogne 114 C3
Lavaux, Suisse 183 A1, 185 C2
Lavaux, Gevrey-Chambertin 65 E1
La Verne 218 G3
Lavey Morcles 183 D2
la Vigne au Saint 61 E3
Lavigny, Jura 117 G4
Lavigny, Suisse 182 B5
la Villatte 109 B2
Lavilledieu 51 F4
la Voirosse 61 E3
la Voulte-sur-Rhône 112 D5
Lawrenceburg 253 B4
Lay 135 F2
La Zarzuela 165 D2
Lazio 157 E3, 160 B2
Lazise 154 C6
Leányka 190 A3, C3
le Bais Clair 243 B2
Lebanon (Al-Lubnan) 208 F4
Lebanon, Kentucky 253 C4
le Beausset 116 C3
le Bois Rideau 110 C3
le Boucou 115 C5
Le Boulay 107 B1
le Boulvé 120 C4
le Bouscat 72 E3
le Bouscaut 87 E5
le Breynets 69 C5
le Cailleret 58 G3
le Cannet-des-Maures 116 B5
le Carquelin 69 C5
le Cassereau 110 B4
le Castellet 116 C2
Lecce 160 C6
le Champ-Canet 58 F5
le Champ de Cours 69 C5
le Champ-sur-Layon 108 E4
le Clos, Châteauneuf du Pape 115 C4
le Clos, Pouilly-Fuissé 66 F4
le Clos, Vernou-sur-Brenne 110 C4
le Clos Baulet 64 F4
le Clos des Chênes 59 F3
le Clos des Réas 63 F4
Le Corti 159 C2
le Corton 61 E4
Le Creusot 53 D4, 51 D4
le Désert 87 E4
Leef op Hoop 233 G3
Leeward Islands 251
le Fleix 97 E3
le Fougeray 110 B4
le Frèche 245 C3
le Frérie 66 F4
le Grand Carretey 89 A4
le Haut Cousse 110 B4
le Haut Lieu 110 C3
Le Havre 51 B1, 255 B2
Leibnitz 186 G1
Leimen 146 C5
Leinhöhle 143 F4
Leininger Haardt 125 D6
Leistadt 143 A4
Leiste, Würzburg 145 E5
Leitchfield 253 C3
Leiweu 132 G6
le Landreau 106 E2
le Loroux-Bottereau 106 C3, E2
le Luc, Var 116 B4
le Luc, Cissac-Médoc 77 G2
Léman, lac 51 D5, 182 B6, 185 C2 254 G3
le Mans 51 C1
le Mayors 116 C4
Lembras 97 E5
le Méal 114 C4
Le Mesnil-sur-Oger 99 F3
le Mont 110 C3
le Montrachet 58 G3
le Moulin 69 C4
le Moulin-à-Vent 69 C5
Le Muy 116 B5
Lenchen 140 F4
Lengenfeld 186 C1
Lens 183 C3
Léognan 72 F3, 87 F3
Léon 163 A2
Leopoldsberg 188 B3
l'Epaisse 109 B2
le Pallet 106 F2
le Paradis 111 F3
le Passe-Temps 57 F3
le Pave 69 F3
le Pellerin 106 C2
le Petit Mont 110 C2
le Petit-Pujeaux 83 G3
Le Pian-Médoc 85 G4
Le Piazze 159 F3
Le Pile e Lamole 159 D4
le Pin, Huismes 109 D3
le Pin, Jura 117 G4
le Plâtre 69 D4
le Point du Jour 69 C4
le Pontet 112 G5
le Port 113 C3
le Poruzot 58 F6
le Poruzot dessus 58 F6
le Pouyalet 79 B5
le Pradet 116 D3
le Pressoir 109 E5
le Puch 89 C5
le Puizac 111 F5
le Puy 51 E4
Legé 106 D3
le Royal-Canadel 116 C5
le Richebourg 63 F4
Lérida 163 B5
le Rognet-Corton 61 F5
Le Rouxdorp 233 G6
les Aigrots 60 E3
les Amoureuses 64 F2
les Angles 59 F4
les Arcs 51 F6, 116 B5
les Argillats 63 E2
les Argillières 60 F1
les Armusèries 110 B2
les Arsures 117 E5
les Arvelets 59 E6, 60 E1, 65 E4
les Aubuis 109 E3
les Aussy 59 F4
les Avaux 60 F3
les Baraques de Gevrey Chambertin 65 F1
les Barguins 110 C3
les Bas-des-Teurous 60 F4
les Basses Vergelesses 61 E2
les Baudes 64 F3
les Baux 51 F5
les Belletins 111 F3
les Berthiers 111 F4
les Bertins 59 F5
les Bessards 114 C4
les Bidaudières 110 C4
les Bienvenues 58 G3
les Billaux 95 C1
les Blottières 109 B4
les Bonnes Mares 64 F3
les Borniques 64 F2
les Bouchères 58 F6
les Boucherottes 60 F2
les Bouchots 64 E4
les Bouthières 66 E5
les Bressandes 60 E5, 61 F4
les Breuillards 111 E4
les Brussolles 57 F5
les Bruyères 69 E3
les Cabannes 121 D3
les Caillerets 59 F3
les Cailles 62 F6
les Calinottes 83 F5
les Capitans 69 A5
Les Carmes-Haut-Brion 87 A2
les Cassiers 111 F4
les Cent-Vignes 60 E5
les Chaboeufs 62 F6
les Chaillots 61 F4
les Chalumeaux 58 F4
les Champeaux 65 E2
les Champlains 67 D6
les Champonnets 65 E1
les Champs Fulliot 59 F3
les Champs' Gain 57 F6, 58 G1
les Champs Grilles 69 A5
les Chanlin 59 E5
les Chanlins Bas 59 E5
les Chanoriers 69 A4
les Chaponières 59 F5
les Charmes 64 F2
les Charmes dessous 58 G5
les Charmes dessus 58 G5
les Charmots 60 E1
les Charnières 61 D2
les Chassaignes 111 E2
Les Chatelots 64 F2
les Chaumes, Côte de Beaune 61 E3
les Chaumes, Côte Chalonnais 67 D5
les Chênes 69 D4
les Chenevottes 58 F2
les Chers 69 A4
les Chétives Maisons 111 F5
les Chouacheux 60 F3
les Claveries 89 G5
les Clos 71 D4
les-Clos-des-Mouches 60 E2
les Clos du Roi 61 F4
les Closeaux 109 E4
les Combes-dessus 59 F5
les Combettes 58 G4
les Corbeaux 65 F1
les Corvées Pagets 62 F4
les Cras, Côte de Beaune 59 F3
les Cras, Côte de Nuits 64 F2
les Crays 66 E4
les Criots 58 G2
les Croix-Noires 59 F5
les Deduits 69 C4
les Diognières 114 C5
les Duresses 59 E2
les Echézeaux 63 F5
les Echoppes 87 A2
les Epenots 60 F1
les Epenottes 60 F2
les Epinottes 71 D3
les Evois 109 B3
les Fèves 60 E5
les Fiètres 61 F3
les Fichots 61 E3
les Folatières 58 F4
les Fondis 109 B1
les Fontenys 65 E1
les Forêts 71 E3
les Fourneaux 71 D6
les Fournières 61 F3
les Fremières 64 F4
les Fremiers 59 F5
les Froichots 64 F4
les Fuées 64 F3
les Galuches 109 B2
les Garrants 69 C4
les Gaudets 69 D4
les Genevrières 64 E4
les Genevrières dessous 58 G6
les Genevrières dessus 58 F6
les Gimarets 69 C5
les Girardières 110 C4
les Girarmes 111 F4
les Goulots 65 E2
les Grandes Bastes 110 B5
les Grands Champs 59 E2
les Grands Cras 69 E4
les Grands Echézeaux 63 F5
les Gravières 57 F4
les Grettieux 114 C4
les Grèves 61 F4, 60 F5
Les Groseilles 64 F3
les Gruenchers 64 F4
les Guerets 61 E3
les Gués d'Amant 110 C2
les Guillattes 69 C5
les Hauts Champs 109 B3
les Hauts Jarrons 61 E1
les Hauts-Marconnets 60 E6
les Hauts-Pruliers 62 F6
les Hervelets 65 E4
Les Jarollières 59 F5
Leskovac 195 E5
les Languettes 61 E4
Les Larreys 64 F4
les Lavières 61 E2
les Lavrottes 64 F3
les Lèches 97 D4
les Lignes 109 D1
les Loges 111 F4
les Lurets 59 F4
les Lys 71 D3
les Macherelles 58 F2
les Madères 110 C5
les Marconnets 60 E6
les Maréchaude 61 F4
les Mayons 116 C4
les Meix 61 F3
les Ménétrières 66 F5
Les Mesneux 99 A3
les Millandes 64 F4
les Mitaus 59 F4
les Montremenots 60 E2
les Monts Damnés 111 F2
les Moriers 69 C4
les Murets 114 C5
les Musigny 63 F6, 64 F1
les Narbantons 61 E1
les Noirots 64 F3
les Noizons 60 E2
Lesparre-Médoc 72 C2
les Perrières 58 F5
les Perrières 60 E6, 61 F4
les Petites Bruyères 111 E4
les Petits Epenots 60 F2
les Petits-Monts 63 E4
les Petits Musigny 63 F6, 64 F1
les Petures 59 F3
les Peuillets 60 E6
les Pezerolles 60 F2
les Picasses 109 D3
les Pinchons 69 B5
les Pineaux 109 D3
les Pins 109 B2
les Pitures dessus 59 E5
les Planches-près-Arbois 117 E5
les Planchots 61 F3
les Plantes 64 F2
les Plessis 66 G5
les Porets 62 F6
les Pougets 61 E3
les Poulettes 62 F6
les Poutures 59 F5
les Preuses 71 C4
les Procès 63 F1
les Pruliers 62 F6
les Pucelles 58 G3
les Quarts 66 F5
les Raguenières 109 B3
les Referts 58 G4
les Reignots 63 F5
les Renardes 61 F4
les Réversées 60 F4
les Roches 110 C2
les Rocoules 114 C5
les Rosettes 109 F3
les Rouvrettes 61 E1
les Rugiens-Bas 59 F5
les Rugiens-Hauts 59 E5
les Ruchots 64 F3
les Sablons 109 B2
les Saint-Georges 62 F5
les Santenots Blancs 59 F3
les Santenots du Milieu 59 F3
les Saucilles 60 E2
les Saunières 57 D2
les Sentiers 64 F3
Lesser Antilles 251
les Seurey 60 F4
les Sicots 110 D4
les Sizies 60 F3
Lessona 149 B3
les Sorbés 64 F4
les Suchots 63 F4
les Talmettes 61 D2
les Teurons 60 F4
les Thorins 69 C5
les Toussaints 60 E5
les Vallerots 62 F6
les Valozières 61 F4
les Vaucrains 62 F5
les Verchers-sur-Layon 106 C5
les Vercots 61 E3
les Vergennes 61 F5
les Vergers 58 F2
les Véroilles 65 D1
les Verrillats 69 B5
les Vignes 111 E2
les Vignes Dessus 66 D4
les Vignes-Franches 60 F2
Lesvos 203 C5
le Teil 112 E5
le Tholonet 116 B2
le Thoronet 116 B4
l'Etoile, Vernou-sur-Brenne 110 C4
l'Étoile, Jura 117 G4
le Tris 83 E1
Letten 143 E5
Letterlay 135 B3
Leucate 118 E4
Leuk 183 C4
Leutesdorf 125 A4
Leutschach 186 G1
le Vau Breton 109 F4
le Velay 113 F2
le Verdier 121 E2
le Vernois 117 G4
le Vieux Télégraphe 115 C5
le Vivier 69 C5
Levkas 203 C2
Lexington 253 B4
Leynes 66 F4
Leyssac 77 F4
Leytron 183 D2
Lézignan-Corbières 51 G3, 118 C4
Lhanbryde 247 A3
l'Hermite 114 C4
l'Homme, Hermitage 114 C5
l'Homme, Sarthe 107 A1
l'Homme Mort 71 B3
Liban (Al-Lubnan) 208 F4
Libertas 233 G2
Liberty 219 B1
Libourne 51 F1, 72 E4, 91 D1, 95 D1
Lieser 134 F6
Liesing 188 D3
Liestal 254 E4
Ligist 186 F1
Ligné 106 B3
Ligré 109 F4
Liguria 149 E4
l'Ile Bouchard 109 F6
l'Ile Rousse 122 B2
Lille 51 A3
Lilliano 159 F3
Lima 234 B1
Limassol 204 D2
Limmattal 185 B4
Limnos 203 B4
Limoges 51 E2
Limony 113 F2
Limoux 118 B2
Linares 234 C1
Lincoln, England 236 B4, 1
Lincoln Village 219 C1
Lindos 203 E6
Linkwood 247 A3
Linsenbusch 143 G5
Linz 125 A4
Lipnita 197 G5
Lirac 112 G5
Lisboa 175 E3, 176 F3
Lisbon (Lisboa) 175 F3, 176 F3
Lisbonne (Lisboa) 175 E3, 176 F3
Lisle-sur-Tarn 121 F2
Listrac-Médoc 83 F2
Lithgow 225 E5
Little Karoo 231 D4
Littlemill 249 E4
Live Oaks 221 C4
Livermore 221 A3
Liverpool, Australia 225 E5
Livers-Cazelles 121 E3
Livingston 219 E2
Livorno 157 A2
Livron-sur-Drôme 112 D5
Ljubljana 195 B2
Ljutomer 195 B3
Lloa 170 C2
Llorens del Panadés 170 B5
Lloyd Light 229 B5
Locarno 185 D4
Loché 66 F5
Lochnagar-Royal 249 D5
Lochside 249 D5
Lockeford 219 B2
Locorotondo 160 C5
Lodi 219 C1
Lofty Ranges 229 D5
Logroño 163 A4
Logroño 168 B6
Loiben 186 C2
Loibenberg 189 G2
Loire 51 E4, 112 A5
Loire-Atlantique 50 C6, 106 B2
Loiret 51 C3, 107 A4
Loir-et-Cher 51 C2, 107 B3
Loire Valley 51 D1, D2, C2
l'Olivier 110 C1
Lombardia 149 B5
Lomond 249 E4
Lonay 182 B5
London (Kentucky) 253 C5
Long Beach 215 G4
Longmorn 247 B2
Long Pond 250 A3
Longueteau 251 C4
Lons-le-Saunier 51 D5, 117 G4
Lorch 125 B5
Lorenzhöfer 131 E4
Loretta 253 C4
Lormont 72 E3
Lorques 116 B4
Lörrach 146 G3
Los Angeles 215 G3
Los Angeles Co. 218 F3
Los Barrios 165 F2
Los Cuadrados 165 D1
Los Esteves 165 C4
Los Gatos 221 C2
Lösnich 134 C6
Los Tercios 165 E1
Lot 51 F2
Lot-et-Garonne 51 F2, 72 G6, 245 B4
Loubers 121 E3
Louis M. Martini 217 B4
Louisville 253 B3
Loupiac 72 F4, 121 G2
Loureiro 178 F1
Lousa 176 E3
Lousada 177 C5
Louvois 99 C5
Louroujina 204 C4
Lovech 199 C3
Lower Belford 226 D2
Lozère 51 F4
Lo Zucco 160 F2
Lucca 157 A3
Lucena 171 G4
Lucq-de-Béarn 120 F3
Lucques (Lucca) 157 A3
Ludon-Médoc 85 F6
Ludwigsburg 146 D6
Ludwigshafen 125 D6
Luginsland 143 D5
Lugana 153 E2
Lugano 185 D4
Lugo 163 A2
Luins 182 B4
Lujan 235 B4
Lully 182 D3, 182 B5
Lunas 97 D4
Lunel 119 D4
Luqa 204 G2
Lussac 95 C5
Lussault-sur-Loire 110 D6
Lussy 182 B5
Lustegaan 233 D5
Lutomer (Ljutomer) 195 B3
Lutry 182 B2
Luttenbach 103 D6
Lutzmannsburg 186 E3
Luzech 120 B4
Luzern 185 C3, 254 F5
Lyaskovets 199 C4
Lyndoch 229 C3
Lyon 51 E4, 53 G5

M

Macallan 247 D3
Macau 85 D6
Macduff 249 C5
Macedonia (Makedonia) 203 B3
Macerata 157 D6
Machackala 201 B5
Macharnudo 165 F5
Macharnudo Alto 165 C3
Macharnudo Bajo 165 C3
Machico 173 C6
Mackenzie 181 D4
Mâcon 51 D4, 53 F5
Mâconnais 53 F5, 66
Mád 191 C3
Madeira 173
Madera 215 D3, 219 F4
Madiran 51 G2, 245 D4
Madisonville 253 C2
Madrid 163 B3
Magdalenenkreuz 139 F5
Maggiore, Lago di 185 D4
Magre al'Adige 154 F2
Magyarorszag 190
Maia 177 C4
Mailberg 186 B3
Mailloréns 170 B5
Mailly 99 B5
Maina 164 B5
Maine-et-Loire 51 D1, 106 C5
Mainxe 243 C3
Mainz 125 B6
Maipú 235 B5
Maisdon-sur-Sèvre 106 F2
Maison-Brûlée 64 F4
Makedonia 203 B3
Makedonija (Macedonia) 195 G5
Málaga 163 E3
Malatya 208 C5
Malleval 113 E1
Mallia 204 D2
Malmesbury 231 C2
Malta 204 F2
Malvasia 160 C5, 157 F2, 157 F4, 203 E6, 203 F4
Malvasia del Vulture 160 C4
Malvazija 195 C1
Malveira 176 F1
Mambourg 103 C2
Mamede de Riba Tua 179 D3
Mamertino 160 F3
Manche 50 B6
Mandacou 97 F5
Mandelgarten 143 C5
Mandement 182 C3, 185 D1
Manduria 160 C5
Manèque 250 A5
Mangualde 177 F5
Mannberg 141 F1
Mannheim 125 C2, 146 B5
Manteca 219 C2
Mantinia 203 D3
Mantoue (Mantova) 153 E2

Parisot 121 G2
Parkes 225 D4
Parlier 219 G5
Parma 153 F2
Parme (Parma) 153 F2
Parnac 120 B5
Paros 203 E4
Parpalana 165 F3
Parramatta 225 E5
Parsac 95 D5
Parys 233 D4
Pasadena 215 F4
Pas-de-Calais 51 A2
Passa 118 F2
Passenans 117 F4
Pastrengo 155 C1
Paterhof 144 G6
Paterno 160 F3
Patrai 203 D2
Patras (Patrai) 203 D2
Patrimonio 122 B2
Patriti 229 A4
Pau 51 G1, 120 F5
Paulhan 119 C1
Paulinsberg 131 F4, 133 C3
Paulinshofberg 133 B3
Paul Masson 221 B2, 221 F5, G5
Paul Robert 207 B2
Paulsberg 134 E5, E6
Pauillac 72 C2, 77 G5, 79 C5
Pavia 149 C5
Pavlikeni 199 C3
Paxton 226 G2
Pazardzhik 199 D3
Paziols 118 D3
Peć 195 F4
Pechstein 143 E4
Pécs 190 C2
Pedrizetti 221 C4
Pedro Domecq 165 D2, C3
Pedroncelli 218 B4
Peissy 182 D3
Pekre 195 B2
Pelequen 235 C2
Pelješac 195 E3
Pellaro 160 F4
Peloponnese (Peloponnisos) 203 D2
Peloponnisos 203 D2
Pembroke, Pembrokeshire 236 C2
Penafiel 175 B4, 177 C5
Peñaflor 235 B2
Penalva do Castelo 177 E5
Peney 182 D3
Penfold's 228 B4
Penfold's H.V.D. 226 F2
Penrice 229 B5
Pépieux 118 B4
Peplina Stepu 201 A2
Perafort 170 C4
Perchtoldsdorf 186 D3, 188 D3
Pères Blancs 251 C4
Péret 119 B1
Périgueux 51 E2
Pernand-Vergelesses 61 D4
Pernand-Vergelesses 53 C5
Pernik 199 C2
Pérou (Péru) 234 B1
Pérouse (Perugia) 157 C4
Perpignan 51 G3, 118 E3
Perrière Noblet 63 E3
Perrier-Jouet 101 F4
Perrin 113 E1
Perroy 182 B5
Perth 249 E5
Pertuisots 60 F3
Peru 234 B1
Perugia 157 C4
Perushtica 199 D3
Pesaro 157 B6
Pescadoires 120 B4
Pescantina 155 C2
Pescara 157 F6
Peschiera del Garda 154 C6
Peso da Regua 178 G2
Pessac 72 F2, 87 A2
Pessione 151 B2
Peterborough 224 D5
Peterhead 249 C6
Petit Bois 87 A4
Petite Chapelle 64 F6
Petit Favray 111 E5
Petit Figeac 93 B2
Petit Soumard 111 F4
Petits Godeaux 61 D2
Petits Vougeots 63 F6, 64 F1
Pettenthal 144 C5
Peynier 116 B2
Peyriac-Minervois 118 B3
Peyrole 121 G2
Pez 77 E4
Peza 203 F4
Pézenas 119 C1
Pfaffenberg 189 F3
Pfaffenheim 102 C4
Pfaffenstein 136 G5
Pfaffstätten 188 F2
Pfingstweide 136 F5
Pforzheim 146 D5
Phillippeville (Skikda) 207 B4
Philpot 253 C3
Piacenza 149 D5
Pian d'Albola 159 D4
Piazza Armerina 160 F3
Piccolit 153 C5
Pichetti 221 B2
Picpoul de Pinet 119 C1
Pic-St-Loup 51 F4, 119 B3
Pied d'Aloup 71 D5
Piemonte 150
Piemonte 149 C2
Pierrefeu-du-Var 116 C4
Pierreux 69 G5
Pierrevert 51 F5
Pierry 99 E2
Piesport 133 C2, 125 C3
Pignans 116 C4
Pignerol (Pinerolo) 149 D2
Piketberg 231 C2
Pikkara 229 D4
Pilos 203 E2
Pimpala 229 B4
Pineau-Gris Ai Danil 201 C2
Pinedale 219 F5
Pinell de Bray 170 D1
Pinerolo 149 D2
Pinet 51 G4, 119 C1
Pinhao 178 F6
Pinhel 175 C5
Pinot 153 C3
Pinot Bijeli 195 C1
Pinot gris 197 E3, F5, G5
Pinot Noir 197 F5, G3, G5
Pintéus 176 E3
Pintray 110 D6
Piper, Delbeck & Co. 101 C5
Pirgos 203 D2
Pirin Planina 199 D2
Pirramimma 229 D4
Pirrone 219 D2
Pisa 157 A2
Pissouri 204 D2
Pistoia 157 A3
Pitești 197 F3
Pitigliano 157 C3
Pitlochry 249 D5
Pitsilia 204 C2
Pizay 69 E4
Plaisance (Piacenza) 149 D5
Plaisir de Merle 233 E3
Planada 219 E4
Planá del Panadés 170 B6
Plan-de-la-Tour 116 C5
Planèzes 118 E2
Planoiseau 117 G4
Plantes 64 F2
Plassac 96 D1
Plavac 195 D2, E3
Plavina 195 D2, E2
Plavka 195 F4
Pleasanton 221 A3
Plemenka 195 C5, F5
Plemenka Ružica 195 C3
Pleven 199 B3
Ploești 197 F4
Plovdina 195 E5, G4
Plovdiv 199 D3
Plume la Poule 87 B4
Plumpton Green, Sussex 236 D4
Plush Corner 229 B5
Pobla de Mafumet 170 C4
Pobla de Montornes 170 C5
Poboleda 170 B3
Podersdorf 186 D4
Poggibonsi 159 E2
Poiares 178 F3
Poinchy 71 D3
Pointe-à-Pitre 261 C4
Pointes-d'Angles 59 F5
Poissenot 65 E1
Poitiers 51 D2
Pokolbin 226 F2
Polcevera 149 E4
Poligny 117 F5
Pollestres 118 F2
Pollino 160 D4
Pol Roger 101 G5
Pomerol 72 E4, 93 A1, 95 C2
Pommard 53 D5, 59 F5, 60 E1
Pommery et Greno 101 C6
Pomona 218 G3
Pomorie 199 C6
Pomport 97 F4
Ponce 251 B2
Ponce, Jerez 165 C3
Poncey 67 E5
Ponchapt 97 E3
Pontac 87 C4
Pontcirq 120 B4
Ponte da Barca 177 B5
Ponte de Lima 177 B4
Ponteilla 118 F2
Ponte-Leccia 122 B2
Pontevedra 163 A1
Pontóns 170 B5
Pontremoli 149 E5
Pont-St-Esprit 112 F5
Pordenone 153 D5
Poreč 195 B1
Poros 203 D3
Porrera 170 C3
Portacomaro 151 B4
Port Adelaide 224 E5
Portalegre 175 E5
Port Augusta 224 D5
Port-au-Prince 250 A5
Port Dundas 249 F4
Port Ellen 249 F2
Porterville 231 C2
Portet 245 D3
Portgordon 247 A5
Port Guyet 109 B1
Port Kembla 225 E5
Portland 225 G1
Port Noarlunga 229 C4
Port Noarlunga South 229 C3
Porto 175 B4, 177 C4
Porto Alegre 234 C2
Porto da Cruz 173 C5
Port of Spain 251 E4
Porto Moniz 173 A1
Porto Tolle 153 F4
Porto Vecchio 122 D3
Port Pirie 224 D5
Portree 249 C2
Port Said (Būr Sa'id) 208 G3
Port-Ste-Foy-et-Ponchapt 97 E3
Portugal 175
Portugizac 195 B2
Port Valais 183 C1
Port Vendres 118 G3
Port Willunga 229 D3
Pošip 195 E2
Postup 195 E3
Potenza 160 C4
Pothana 226 E2
Pouilly 66 E6
Pouilly-Fuissé 66 E4
Pouilly-Loché 66 F5
Pouilly-sur-Loire 107 B6, 111 G4
Pouilly-Vinzelles 66 F6
Pourcleux 116 B3
Pourrières 116 B2
Pouvray 110 B4
Pouzols-Minervois 118 C4
Póvoa de Varzim 177 C4
Poysdorf 186 B3
Pradell 170 C3
Pradines 120 B5
Praia da Adraga 176 E1
Praia das Maças 176 E1
Prangins 182 B4
Prat de Llobregat 171 B1
Pratdip 170 C3
Pratteln 254 E4
Prayssac 120 B4
Preignac 89 C6, D4, D5
Prellenkirchen 186 D4
Prémeaux 62 F4
Premiá de Mar 171 A2
Premières Côtes de Bordeaux 72 F4
Presinge 182 D4
Preslav 199 C5
Prestonsburg 253 C6
Prestwick 249 F4
Préverenges 182 B5
Prignac-et-Cazelles 96 G5
Prigonrieux 97 E4
Prilep 195 G5
Primativo 160 C5
Prince de Polignac 242 A5
Princeton 253 C2
Priorato 163 B5, 170 C2
Prissé 66 D4
Prissé 66 D4
Priština 195 F5
Privas 51 F4
Prizren 195 F5
Procanico 157 B1
Prokupac 195 D6, E5, F6, G4
Prokupac Ružica 195 D5
Prosecco 153 D4
Prošek 195 D2
Provence 51 G5
Provesende 178 E6
Providence 253 C2
Provitaro 160 F4
Pruzilly 69 A4
Psara 203 C4
Ptuj 195 B3
Puente Alto 235 B2
Puente Genil 171 G3
Puerto de Santa Maria 165 F4
Puerto Rico 251 A2
Puerto Rico Distillers 251 A2
Puget-sur-Argens 116 B5
Puget-Ville 116 C4
Puglia 160 C4
Puigpelat 170 B4
Puisieux 99 B4
Puisseguin 95 D5
Pujols 72 F5
Puligny-Montrachet 53 D5, 58 G3
Pulkau 186 B2
Pully 182 B6
Pulteney 249 B5
Pupillin 117 E5
Purbach 186 D3
Puycelci 121 E1
Puy-de-Dôme 51 E3
Puyguilhem 97 F4
Puy-l'Evêque 120 B3
Puyloubier 116 B2
Puyoô 51 G1
Puy Rigaud 109 D2
Pyrenées Orientales 51 G3, 118 F2

Q

Quarts de Chaume 108 D3
Quatourze 118 C4
Queanbeyan 225 F5
Querceto e Santa Lucia 159 C3
Queretaro 234 F2
Queyssac 97 D5
Quillan 118 C1
Quillota 235 B2
Quilpué 235 B2
Quimper 50 C5
Quincy 107 C4
Quinta Amarela 179 F1
Quinta da Alegria 179 F4
Quinta da Baleira 179 G4
Quinta da Boa Vista 178 F3
Quinta da Cabana 178 F3
Quinta da Cachucha 178 F6
Quinta da Carvalheira 179 F2
Quinta da Costa 179 D1
Quinta da Costa de Bo 178 F5
Quinta da Ferrad 178 G4
Quinta da Ferradosa 179 G4
Quinta da Foz 178 F6, 178 G3
Quinta da Foz de Temjlobos 178 G3
Quinta da Lagoa Alta 178 F5
Quinta da Pacheca 178 G2
Quinta da Passadoura 179 E1
Quinta da Pilarrela 178 E2
Quinta da Poca 178 F6
Quinta da Portela 178 G4
Quinta da Ribeira 178 D6
Quinta da Sapa de B. 178 F6
Quintas das Baratas 179 F1
Quinta das Carvalhas 179 F1
Quinta da Senhora da Ribeira 179 G6
Quinta da serra 179 F1
Quinta das Lajes 179 G1
Quinta das Manuelas 179 D1
Quinta das Teixeira 179 F1
Quinta da Torre 178 G3
Quinta da Vacaria 178 G2
Quinta de Bagauste 178 G3
Quinta de Campanha 178 F2
Quinta de Napoles 178 G5
Quinta de Roeda 179 F1
Quinta de Romarigo 178 F2
Quinta de Santa Barbara 178 G2
Quinta de São Martinho 179 F3
Quinta de Tourais 178 G2
Quinta de Ventozelo 179 F1
Quinta do Arnozelo 179 G5
Quinta do Barrilario 178 G4
Quinta do Bom Dia 178 F5
Quinta do Bom Retiro 179 F1
Quinta do Bonfim 179 F1
Quinta do Bragão 179 E1
Quinta do Canal 178 G3
Quinta do Carneiro 178 G2
Quinta do Castelinho 179 F3
Quinta do Castello Borges 178 G5
Quinta do Charondo 179 G1
Quinta do Cibio 179 E2
Quinta do Cipreste 179 E3
Quinta do Crasto 178 F5
Quinta do Dr. Christiano 179 G2
Quinta do Eiravelha 178 F6
Quinta do Fojo 179 D1
Quinta do Garcia 178 G2
Quinta do Junco 178 E6
Quinta do Lelo 179 F1
Quinta do Merouco 179 E2
Quinta do Mourão 178 G2
Quinta do Noval 179 E1
Quinta do Panascal 178 G6
Quinta do Pedrogão 179 G2
Quinta do Pego 178 G6
Quinta do Peso 178 F3
Quinta do Roriz 179 F2
Quinta do Sagrado 178 F6
Quinta dos Canais 179 G5
Quinta dos Currais 178 G2
Quinta do Seino 178 F6
Quinta dos Frades 178 G4
Quinta do Silval 179 E1
Quinta dos Lagares 179 D1, 178 F2
Quinta dos Malvedos 179 E2
Quinta do Sol 178 G3
Quinta do Tedo 178 G5
Quinta do Vale de Figuira 178 F6
Quinta do Vale de Sapos 178 G2
Quinta do Vargelas 179 G5
Quinta do Vesúvio 179 G6
Quinta do zambujal 178 G3
Quinta do zimbro 179 G6
Quinta Milieu 179 E3
Quinta Nova do Roncão 179 E1
Quinta Velha 178 G2
Quintigny 117 G4
Quorn 224 D5

R

Rabastens 121 G1
Rabat 204 G2, 206 C4
Rabelais 207 B2
Rablay-sur-Layon 108 D4
Raboatun 165 D4
Raboso Piave 153 D4
Radda in Chianti 159 E4
Radgonska Ranina (Tigrovo Mleko) 195 B3
Ragusa 160 G3
Raiding 186 E3
Rainha Santa 181 C4
Rama Caida 235 D5
Ram Allah 208 F4
Ramatuelle 116 C5
Ramos Pinto 181 C4, B4
Rancagua 235 C3
Randersacker 145 G3, F6
Randogne 183 C4
Rapsani 203 C3
Raron 183 C5
Rasquera 170 D2
Rastatt 146 D4
Rasteau 112 F6
Rátka 191 C3
Rauenthal 125 B5, 141 D4
Rausch 129 E2
Ravello 160 C3
Ravenna 157 A5, 153 G4
Ravenne (Ravenna) 153 G4, 157 A5
Ray, Martin 221 B2
Razac-de-Saussignac 97 E3
Razac d'Eymet 97 F4
Razgrad 199 B4
Rcatzitelli 199 B5, D5, D1
Rebeninha 179 E1
Rebula 195 B1
Rech-Bächel 143 D4
Rechnitz 186 F3
Recioto 153 D2
Reedley 219 G6
Refosko 195 B1
Refosco 153 D5
Rege Winery 218 A4
Reggio di Calabria 160 F4
Reggio Emilia 153 F2
Regina Grape Products 218 F5
Régua 175 B5
Reigny 111 F2
Reims 51 B4, 99 A3, 101
Reinsport 133 D2
Reiterpfad 143 F4
Rekord 195 E6
Remigny 57 G4
Remy Martin 242 B5
Renau 170 C4
Renault 207 B1
Renchen 254 C4
Rengo 235 C2
Renmark 224 E6
Rennes 50 C6
Renski Rizling 195 A3
Requeña y Utiel 163 C4
Resende 177 D6
Restigné 109 B3
Retsina 203 D3
Retz 186 B2
Reugne 59 E2
Reuilly 107 C4
Reus 170 C3
Reynella 229 B4
Reynells 229 B4
Rezé 106 C3, F1
Rhein 185 B3, 254 C4
Rheinburgengau 125 A4, 125 B5
Rheinfelden 254 E4
Rheingau 125 B5, 139, 140, 141
Rheinhessen 144
Rheinland-Pfalz 125 B4, C1
Rheinpfalz 142
Rheintal 185 B5
Rhinau 254 D4
Rhône 51 D4, 53 G5, 185 D2
Rialto 218 G6
Ribagnac 97 F5
Ribalonga 179 E3
Ribatejo 175 E4
Ribaudy 113 E1
Ribeauvillé 254 D3, 103 C4
Ribeira Brava 173 D2
Ribeira de Penha 177 B6
Ricard-Bisquit Dubouché 243 B3
Richert 221 C3
Richmond 253 C4
Richon-le-Zion 208 F4
Riddes 183 D3
Riebeek-Wes 231 C2
Riegersburg 186 F3
Riesling 153 C3, D6, 197 E2, E3, E5, F3, F5, G3, G5, 199 B5, D1, 201 B2, B3
Rieti 157 E4
Rieux-Minervois 118 B3
Riex 182 B6
Rijeka 195 B2
Rilly 99 B4
Rimini 157 B5
Rio Bom 178 G1
Rio de Janeiro 234 C2
Rio Ebro 168-9
Rio Grande do Sul 234 C2
Rioja 168
Rioja Alavesa 168 B5, B6
Rioja Alta 163 A4, 168 B5
Rioja Baja 163 A4, 169 C2
Rioja Valley 169
Rio Minho 177 A5
Rio Negro 234 C2
Ripaille 117 A2
Ripon 219 D1
Riquewihr 103 C3
Rittergarten 143 B4
Ritterpfad 129 C2
Ritzling 188 G5
Riudecols 170 C3
Riudoms 170 C3
Riva 153 D2
Rivadavia 235 B5
Riverbank 219 D2
Riverina 225 E3
Riversdale 231 D5
Riverside 215 F4, G5
Riversmeet 233 E4
Riversaltes 118 E3
Riviera del Garda 153 D2
Rivières 121 F3
Rivoli Veronese 155 B1
Rizling 195 G6
Rizling Rajnski 195 B2
Roanne 51 D4
Roa y Penafiel 163 B3
Robardelle 59 F3
Robert Lasdin 218 D5
Robert Mondavi Winery 217 C4
Robertson 231 D3
Robinvale 225 E1
Rocfort 110 C5
Roche 183 C1
Rochecorbon 110 C1
Rochefort-sur-Loire 108 C3, 106 B5
Rochegrés 69 B4
Rochester 222 B2
Rochesvière 106 C3
Rochette-St-Jean 109 D4
Roda de Bara 170 C5
Rödelsee 145 G4
Rodern 103 D5
Rodez 51 F3
Rodhos 203 E6
Rodo 178 F2
Rodoña 170 B5
Roederer, Louis 101 A5
Rogliano 122 A3
Rohrendorf 186 C2
Rolle 182 B5
Roma 157 E3, 219 G5
Romanèche-Thorins 69 C5
Romanée-St-Vivant 63 F4
Romanel 182 A5
Romanesti 201 A1
Romania 197
Rombola 203 D1
Rome (Roma) 157 E3
Romorantin-Lanthenay 107 B3
Ronaldshay 249 A5
Ronco 155 C6
Roncé 109 E6
Ronceret 59 F4
Rontignon 120 F6
Rooty Hill 225 E5
Ropa 203 C1
Roquebrune-sur-Argens 116 B5
Roquefort-la-Bédoule 116 C2
Rorschwihr 103 D5
Rosato del Salento 160 C6
Röschitz 186 B2
Roseau 251 C4
Rosebank 249 E4
Rosenberg, Mosel 133 D3, 134 F5, 135 C1, F1
Rosenberg, Nahe 136 F5
Rosenberg, Rheinhessen 144 C4
Rosenberg, Saar 129 B4, C4
Rosedale 228 C3
Rosengarten 137 D1
Rosengarten 125 C5
Rosengartchen 133 F1
Rosenheck 136 G5
Rosey 67 F5
Rosheim 254 C4
Rosmarineira 179 E1
Rossano 160 D4
Rossatz 189 G1
Rosso Conero 157 C6
Rosso Delle 157 A3
Rossiskaja 201 B4
Rosso Montesanto 157 B5
Rosso Piceno 157 C6, D6
Rosso Piceno Superiore 157 D6
Rostov 201 A3
Rotenfelser Bastel 137 F1
Rotenfels 136 F6
Roterd 133 D1, E2
Rothbury 226 F2
Rothenberg, Dürnstein 189 G2
Rothenberg, Rheingau 139 F6 140 G1, 141 E4
Rothenberg, Rheinhessen 144 B5
Rothenburg Suisse 254 F4
Rothes 249 C5, 247 C3
Rotlei 131 F2
Rouen 255 B2, 51 B2
Rouffach 102 C3
Rouffignac-de-Sigoules 97 F4
Rouftîac 121 F4
Rougeot 59 E3
Roumanie (Romania) **197**
Rouquette 97 G4
Rourell 170 C4
Rousset 116 B2
Roussillon dels Aspres 51 G3, 118 F2
Roussillon 112 A5
Routa 251 C4
Rovalley 228 C4
Rovereto 153 D3
Rovigo 153 E4
Rowland Flat 228 C4
Royal Brackla 249 C4
Rozés 181 C4
Rubbina di Cantavenna 149 C3
Ruchottes-Chambertin 64 F6
Rüdesheim 125 B5, 139 F3
Rudesheimer Borg 139 E2
Rudežuša 195 E3
Rueda 163 B3
Rue-de-Chaux 63 F1
Rufina 157 A4
Ruffey-sur-Seille 117 F4
Ruffieux 117 C1
Rui Diaz 165 D2
Ruinart Père et Fils 101 C6
Rully 67 B6, 53 D5
Rumania (Romania) 197
Rumeni Muškat 195 B3
Ruppertsberg 125 D6, 143 F5
Ruse 199 B4
Rushworth 225 F2
Russia (Rossiskaja) 201 B4
Russian River 218 E3
Russilly 67 E5
Russin 182 D3
Rust 186 D3
Russtenburg 233 F2
Rust-Neusiedler See 186
Rutherglen/Corowa 225 F3
Ruwer 131 C3
Ružica 195 C4, 195 G4, 195 F6
Ryecroft 229 C5
Rye, Sussex 236 D5

S

Saar 125 C1
Saarbrücken 125 C1, E3
Saarburg 125 D3, 129 E2
Saarland 125 D3
Sabazan 245 D4
Sables St-Emilion 95 E1
Sabugo 176 E2
Sack-Träger 144 F6
Sacramento 215 D2, 219 B1
Sadillac 97 F5
Sadilly 201 C6
Sadova 197 G3
Safi 206 C3
Saillans 94 B6
Saillon 183 D2
St-Aignan 94 C6
St-Aigne 97 E6
St-Aldegund 125 B4
St-Amour 53 F5, 69 A5
St-Amour-Bellevue 66 G4, 69 A5
St-Andelain 111 F4
St-André-de-Cubzac 72 E3
St-André-de-Roquelonque 118 C4
St-Androny 96 B2
St Anna 186 G2
St-Antoine-du-Breuilh 97 E?
St-Aubin 58 D2
St-Aubin-de-Cadelech 97 F5
St-Aubin-de-Lanquais 97 E5
St-Aubin de Luigné 108 D2
St-Barthélémy-d'Anjou 106 B5
St-Beauzile 121 E2

St-Bouize 111 F3
St-Brice 243 B1
St-Brieuc 50 C6
St-Capraise-d'Eymet 97 F5
St-Cernin-de-Labarde 97 F5
St-Christophe 93 D6
St-Chinian 51 G3, 118 B5
St-Christol 51 F4, 119 C4
St-Christoly-Médoc 72 C2
St-Christophe-des-Bardes 95 E4
St-Ciers-de-Canesse 96 E2
St-Clément-de-la-Place 106 B4
St-Corbian 77 D3
St-Crespin-sur-Moine 106 F3
St. Croix 251 B3
St-Cyr-sur-Mer 116 C2
St-Cyr-sur-le-Rhône 113 A4
St. Denis 64 F4
St-Désert 67 F5
St-Didier 117 G4
St-Drézéry 51 F4, 119 C3
St-Emilion 72 E4, 91 D6, 93 D4, 95 E3
St-Erhard 254 E4
St-Estèphe 72 C2, 77 D5
St-Étienne 51 E4
St-Etienne-de-Baïgorry 51 G1, 121 B5
St-Etienne-de-Lisse 95 E5
St-Faust 120 F5
St-Fiacre-sur-Maine 106 F1
St-Florent 106 C5
St-Florent-le-Vieil 106 B4
St-Foy-la-Grande 72 E6
St-Genes-de-Blaye 96 C2
St. Georgen 186 D3
St. George's 251 E4
St-Georges 93 A5, 95 D4
St-Georges-d'Orques 51 G4, 19 C2
St-Georges-sur-Loire 106 B4
St-Géraud-de-Corps 97 D3
St-Germain-et-Mons 97 E5
St-Géry 97 D4
St-Gilles 119 D5
St-Goar 125 B5
St. Goarshausen 125 B5
St. Hallett's 228 C4
St. Helena 217 B3
St. Helena Highway 217 E5
St-Herblain Couëron 106 C2
St-Hilaire, Maine-et-Loire 106 B5
St-Hilaire, Aude 118 B2
St-Hippolyte, Indres-et-Loire 107 C2
St-Hippolyte, Gironde 95 E4
St-Hippolyte, Alsace 103 D6
St. James 251 C5
St-Jean-de-Braye 107 A4
St-Jean-de-la-Blaquière 119 B2
St-Jean-de-la-Porte 117 D2
St-Jean-de-Minervois 118 B5
St-Jean-de-Vaux 67 D5
St-Jean-Poudge 245 D3
St. Johns 251 B4
St-Joseph 112 B5, 114 C3
St-Julien-Beychevelle 72 D2, 81 B5
St-Julien-de-Concelles 106 E2
St-Julien-d'Eymet 97 F4
St. Kitts 251 B4
St-Lager 69 F3
St-Lamain 117 F4
St-Lambert 79 E5
St-Lambert-du-Lattay 108 D3
St-Lanne 245 D4
St-Laurent, Médoc 83 B2
St-Laurent, Nievre 111 E5
St-Laurent, St. Emilion 93 D5
St-Laurent-de-la-Cabrerisse 118 C3
St-Laurent-des-Combes 95 E4
St-Laurent-des-Vignes 97 E4
St-Laurent-et-Benon 81 D1
St-Légier 183 B1
St-Leonard 183 C3
St-Livres 182 B5
St. Lô 51 B1, 255 B1
St-Lothain 117 F5
St-Louand 109 E3
St-Loubès 72 E3
St-Louis, Gard 115 C6
St-Louis Haut-rhin 254 E4
St. Lucia 251 D5
St-Lumine-de-Clisson 106 F2
St-Macaire 72 G4
St. Magdalene 249 E4
St-Mard-de-Vaux 67 D5
St. Margarethen 186 D3
St. Martin 137 C2
St-Martin-d'Arrossa 121 B5
St-Martin-de-Gurçon 97 D2
St-Martin-Lacaussade 96 C2
St-Martin-le-Beau 110 F6
St-Martin-sous-Montaigu 67 D5
St-Martin-sur-Nohain 111 E5
St-Matré 120 C4
St-Maurice 183 D1
St-Maxime 116 C5
St-Méard-de-Gurçon 97 D3
St-Médard 120 B5
St-Médard-en-Jalles 72 E2
St-Même 243 C4
St-Michel-de-Fronsac 94 C5
St-Michel-de-Montaigne 97 E2
St-Michel-sur-Rhône 113 C2
St-Naixent 97 E5
St-Nazaire 106 B2
St-Nicolas-de-Bourgueil 109 B2, 106 B6
St-Paul, Gironde 96 C2
St-Paul, Indres-et-Loire 109 F4
St-Paul-de-Fenouillet 118 D2
St-Paul-en-Lorêt 116 B5
St-Péray 112 C5
St-Perdoux 97 F5
St-Pey d'Armens 95 F4
St-Philbert-de-Gd-Lieu 106 C3
St-Pierre-de-Boeuf 113 E2
St-Pierre-de-Clages 183 D3
St-Pierre-des-Corps 107 B1
St-Pierre-d'Eyraud 97 E4
St. Pölten 186 C2
St-Pourcain-sur-Sioule 51 D3
St-Prex 182 B5
St-Raphaël 116 B6
Saint-Remèze 51 F4
St-Rémy 97 D3
St-Saphorin 182 B6
St-Satur 111 F3
St-Saturnin 51 F4, 119 B2
St-Sauveur 79 C2, C3, 97 E5
St-Sébastien-sur-Loire 106 E1, 106 C3
St-Seurin 77 B4
St-Seurin-de-Bourg 96 F3
St-Seurin-de-Cadourne 72 C2, 77 C4
St-Seurin-de-Cursac 96 B2
St-Sigismond 106 B4
St. Stefan 186 G1
St-Sulpice, France 121 G1
St-Sulpice, Suizze 182 B6
St-Sulpice-d'Eymet 97 G4
St-Sulpice-de-Faleyrens 95 F2
St-Symphorien, Indres-et-Loire 107 B1
St-Symphorien, Nuits-St-George 63 F1
St-Symphorien, Nuit-St-George 63 F1
St. Thomas 251 B3
St-Trojan 242 A6
St-Tropez 116 C5
St-Veran 66 F4, G4, G5
St-Vérand 66 G4
St. Vincent 251 D5
St-Vincent-Rive-d'Olt 120 B5
St-Vivien 97 D2
St-Yzans 77 A4
Ste-Cécile-du-Cayrou 121 E2
Ste-Croix 121 E4
Ste-Croix-du-Mont 72 G4
Ste-Eulalie-d'Eymet 97 F4
Ste-Innocence 97 F4
Ste-Marie d'Alloix 117 D1
Ste-Maure-de-Touraine 107 C1
Ste-Seurin-de-Prats 97 E2
Salamanca 163
Sale 225 G3
Salerno 160 C3
Salgesch 183 C4
Salgotarjan 190 B3
Salignac 242 A5
Salinas 215 E2, 221 E4
Salins 183 D3
Salins d'Hyères 116 D4
Salò 154 A5
Salomo 170 C5
Salomonsvlei 233 D5
Salonica (Thessaloniki) 203 B3
Salqueiral 178 G1
Salses 118 E3
Salta 234 C2
Salter's 228 B5
Saltillo 234 F2
Salto Grillo 164 A5
Saluzzo 149 D2
Salvador 217 E5
Salvagnac 121 F1
Samonac 96 E3
Samorodno 195 C5
Samos 203 D5
Samothraki 203 B4
Samotok 195 G6
Sampigny 53 D5
Samsun 208 B5
Samuels (T.W.) 253 B4
San Adrian 169 C3
S. Ambrogio di Valpolicella 155 B2
San Antonio 235 B2
San Antonio, Jerez 165 C3
Sanary-sur-Mer 116 D2
San Baudilio de Llobregat 171 B1
San Benito 215 E2, 221 E5
San Bernardo 235 B3
San Bernardino 215 F4, 218 G5
S. Bonifacio 155 D6
San Borondon 164 C4
San Carlos 235 B4
San Casciano 159 C2
Sancerre 107 B5, 111 F3
Sanchez Romate 165 D2
San Cugat del Valles 171 A1
Sandeman, Portugal 181 C4, B5
Sandeman, Spain 165 C4, D3, F3, C2
Sandgrub 141 E3
San Diego 215 G4
Sandown, Isle of Wight 236 D3
San Fausto de Campcentellas 171 A1
San Felice 159 F5
S. Felice del Benacò 154 A5
San Felipe 235 A3
San Feliú de Llobregat 171 B1
San Fernando 235 C3
San Francisco 215 D1
Sanger 219 G5
San Gimignano 159 D5
San Ginés de Vilasar 171 A2
San Giovanni 159 E1
S. Giovanni Ilarione 155 B5
Sangiovese di Romagna 153 G4, 157 B5
S. Giustina 153 B3
Sangue di Giuda 149 D5
San Isidro 165 C4
Sanitarium 217 A3
San Jaime del Domenys 170 B5
San Joaquin 215 D2, 219 C2
San Jose 215 D2, 221 B3
San Jose, Uruguay 234 C2
San Juan, Argentina 234 C1
San Juan, Puerto Rico 251 A2
San Juan, Spain 165 D2
San Juan Bautista 221 D4
San Julian 165 D2
Sankt Gallen 185 B5
Sankt Nikolaus 140 F4
Sanlúcar de Barrameda 163 D2, 164 A4, 165 F5
San Luis 234 C2
San Luis Obispo 215 F3
San Marino 157 B5
San Martin, Argentina 235 B5
San Martin, California 221 C4
San Martin de Valdeiglesias 163 C3
S. Martino Buonalbergo 155 D4
San Martino de Castra 153 C3
San Martin Sarroca 170 B5
San Mateo, California 221 B1
San Mateo, Spain 163 B5
San Miguel 165 C4
San Pawh il Bahar 204 F2
San Pedro de Premiá 171 A2
San Pedro de Ribas 170 B6
San Pedro de Riudevitlles 170 B6
S. Pietro in Cariano 155 C2
San Quintin de Mediona 170 A6
San Rafael, Spain 165 C4
San Rafaél, Argentina 235 C5
San Remo 149 F3
San Sadurni de Noya 170 B6
S. Salvatore Monferrato 151 B6
San Sebastián 163 A4
Sansevero 160 B3
Santa Barbara 215 F3
Santa Catarina 234 C2
Santa Clara 215 D2, 221 B2, 221 C3
Santa Comba Dão 177 F4
Santa Cruz, California 215 E2, 221 C2
Santa Cruz, Madeira 173 D6
Santa Cruz, Spain 165 E1
Santaella 171 G3
Santa Emilia 165 C2
Sante Fe 234 C2
Santa Fe del Panadés 170 B6
Santa Honorata 165 D2
Santa Isabel 165 B3
Santa Maddalena 154 D3, 153 B3
Santa Maria de Martorellas 171 A2
Santa Marta de Penaguirão 178 E2
Santana 173 B5
Santander 163 A3
Santa Olivia 170 B5
Santarem 175 E4
Santa Rosa 218 E6
Santa Rosa and Cucamonga 218
Santa Teresa 165 C2
Santa Teresa de Jesus 165 D1
Santedame 159 E3
Santenay 53 D5, 57 F3
Santiago, Chile 234 C1, 235 B3
Santiago, Dominica Republic 250 A6
Santiago de Cuba 250 A4
Santiago del Estero 234 C2
Santillana 164 A4
Santo Domingo, Spain 165 C2
Santo Domingo, Dominican Republic 250 A6
Santorin 203 E4
Santo Stefano 160 B4
Santo Tirso 177 C5
San Vicente dels Horts 171 B1
San Vito di Negrar 155 B2
Sao Cristovão do Douro 178 E6
Sao Domingos de Rana 176 F2
Saône 51 D4
Saône-et-Loire 53 E4, 51 D4
Sao João da Pesqueira 179 G3
Sao Paolo 234 C2
Sao Vicente 173 B2
Sao Xisto 179 G5
Saperavi 201 C4
Sarajevo 195 D4
Saratoga 221 B2
Sarazsadány 191 B5
Sarcignan 87 C4
Sardaigne (Sardegna) 157
Sardanyola 171 A1
Sardegna 157
Sardine 87 B2
Sardinia (Sardegna) 157
Sarnen 254 F4
Sárospatak 190 B4, 191 B6
Sartènais 122 D2
Sartène 122 D2
Sarthe 51 C1, 106 A6
Sarzedinho 179 G1
Sassari 157 F2
Sassella 149 A5
Sátão 177 E5
Satigny 182 D3
Salò 154 A5
Satoraljaujhely 190 B4, 191 A6
Saulieu 53 C4
Saumur 106 C5
Saussignac 97 E4
Saute aux Loups 109 F4
Sauternes 72 G4, 89 F3
Sauveterre-de-Guyenne 72 F5
Sauvignon 153 D6, 195 A3, C4, 197 E3
Sauzet 120 C4
Savennières 106 B5, 108 B2
Savièse 183 C3
Savigny 53 C5
Savigny-les-Beaune 61 D1
Savoie 51 E5
Savona 149 E4
Savuto 160 E4
Sawyer's Gully 226 F3
Saxon 183 D2
Scandiano 153 F2
Scapa 249 A5
Sciacca 160 G2
Sciez 117 A2
Scott Creek 229 B5
Scotts Bottom 229 B6
Schaffhausen 146 G4, 185 B4, 254 E5
Schaffhouse (Schaffhausen) 146 G4
Schlangengraben 129 B3
Scharz Berg 129 C4
Scharzhofberg 129 C4
Schatzgraben 135 B3
Scheidterberg 129 D1
Schenley 253 B3, B4
Schliengen 146 G3
Schönberg 186 C2
Schloss 144 G5, F5
Schlossberg, Haut-Rhin 103 B3
Schlossberg, Mosel 134 D6, F6
Schlossberg, Pfalz 143 D4, 135 F2, 135 E3
Schlossberg, Rheingau 140 F3
Schlossberg, Rheinhessen 144 F5
Schlossberg, Saar 129 F2, 129 C3
Schlossberg, Würzburg 145 E5
Schlossböckelheim 125 C5
Schlossböckelheim 136 G3
Schloss Eltz 141 G3
Schloss, Johannisberg 140 F2
Schloss, Kauzenberg 137 E2
Schloss, Reinhartshausen 141 G2
Schloss Saarfels 129 G3
Schloss Schwabsburg 144 E3
Schloss Staufenberg 146 E4
Schloss Vollrads 140 E3
Schnait 146 D6
Schoden 129 D3
Schoenenbourg 103 C4
Schönhell 140 E5
Schoongezicht 233 F3
Schossgut Hohenrechen 144 E3
Schramsberg Champagne Cellars 217 A2
Schriesheim 146 C5
Schütten 186 D3
Schützenhaus 140 F6
Schwabsburg 144 F3
Schwaigern 146 C6
Schwarzwald 146 F4, 254 D4
Schweich 125 C3
Schweigen 125 E6
Schweiz 185
Schwenningen 146 F5
Schwyz 254 F5
Scottsville 253 C3
Seacliff 229 A4
Seaford 229 C3
Seagrams 253 B3, B4, C3
Seaview 229 C4
Sebastiani 217 F3
Sèché 71 E3
Seeberg 254 F4
Segarcea 197 G3
Segonzac 245 D2
Segovia 163
Seia 177 F5
Seiberer 188 F5
Seillans 116 A5
Seine-et-Marne 51 B3
Seine Maritime 51 A2
Seine-St-Denis 51 D3
Seixal 173 B2
Sellicks Hill 229 E3
Sellicks Beach 229 E3
Selma 219 G5
Semblancay 107 B1
Sembrancher 183 D2
Séméacq-Blachon 245 E3
Semillon 195 C4
Semillon Sauvignon 195 C5
Semons 113 C3
Seneca Lake 222 C3
Senhor do Carmo 178 F5
Senouillac 121 F3
Seppelt's (Dorrien) 228 B5
Seppeltsfield 228 B4
Serifos 203 E4
Sérignac 120 B3
Sernhac 119 C6
Serra da Carrequeira 176 E3
Serra da Estrela 175 C5
Serra do Marão 175 C5
Serrai 203 B3
Serrallez 251 B2
Serralunga 151 E3
Serres-et-Montguyard 97 G4
Serrières 66 D3
Serrig 125 D3, 129 G3
Serviès-en-Val 118 C3
Sestriere 149 C2
Sète 119 D2
Setúbal 175 F4
Sevilla 163
Sewell 235 C3
Seyssel 117 B1
Shemakha 201 C6
Shepparton 225 F3
Shepton Mallet, Somerset 236 D3
Sibenik 195 D2
Sicilia 160
Sicily 160
Sidi-bel-Abbès 207 B1
Sidi Larbi 206 C4
Siegelsberg 141 F1
Siegendorf 186 D3
Siegert's 251 E5
Siena 157 B3, 159 G4, 159 E4
Sienne (Sienna) 157 B3
Sierra de Cantabria 168 A5
Sierra de San Cristobal 165 F3
Sierra Nevada 215
Sierre 183 C4, 185 D3, 254 G4
Sievering 188 B3
Sifnos 203 E4
Siggiewi 204 G2
Sigoulès 97 F4
Signy-Avenex 182 B4
Siklós 190 C2
Silberberg 139 E1
Silikou 204 D2
Silistra 199 B5
Sillery 99 B5
Silvaner 199 B5
Silvaner Feodosiisky 201 B2
Silverado Trail 217 D6
Simferopol 201 B2
Simiane-Collongue 116 B1
Simi Winery 218 C5
Simonsberg 233 F3
Simonstown 231 D2
Simonsvlei (Co-op) 233 D3
Simonsvlei, Klein 233 E3
Singen 146 G5
Singleyrac 97 F5
Sintra 176 F2, 175 E3
Sion 185 D3, 183 C3, 254 G4
Sipon 195 B3
Siracusa 160 G4
Siria 197 E2
Sirmione 154 C6
Siros 203 D4
Sitges 163, 170 C6
Sitzendorf 186 B2
Sivas 208 C5
Six-Fours-la-Plage 116 D2
Sizzano 149 B4
Skikda 207 B4
Skiros 203 C4
Skopje 195 F5
Skye 249 D2
Slavjanci 199 C5
Slavonski Brod 195 C4
Sliema 204 G2
Sliven 199 C4
Slovenija 195 B1-2
Smederevka 195 G6, 195 D5
Smederevo 195 D5
Smolyan 199 E3
Smyrna (Izmir) 208 C1
Soave 153 E3, 155 C4, 155 C5, 155 D5
Soave Classico 155 C5
Societa Esportazione Vini Affini 159 C4
Sofia 199 C2
Soïtue 235 D5
Soke 208 C1
Solano 215 D2
Soledad 221 F5
Solis 221 C3
Solliès-Pont 116 C3
Solnechnaya Dolina 201 B2
Solopaca 160 B3
Solothurn 185 B3, 254 E4
Solotoje polje 201 A2
Soltvadkert 190 C3
Solutré-Pouilly 66 E4
Sombernon 53 C5
Somerset 253 C4
Somerset West 231 D2
Somló 190 B1
Somlóire 106 C5
Somme 51 A2
Sommerach 145 F4
Sommerhausen 145 G3
Somontano 163 A5
Sonnay 109 E5
Sonnenberg 129 A5, 129 C3, 129 E3
Sonnenberg, Ruwer 131 D4
Sonnenberg Nahe 136 F6
Sonnenberg Rheingan 141 F4
Sonnenglanz 103 C3
Sonnenlay 134 G6, 135 C3
Sonnenuhr 135 D1
Sonoma 215 D1, 217 F4
Sooss 188 G2
Sopron 186 E3, 190 B1
Soral 182 D3
Sorbara 153 F2
Sorgues 112 G5
Soria 163 D4
Soriano 234 C2
Sorni 153 C2
Sottocenerri 185 D4
Sotteceneri 185 D4
Soturac 120 B3
Soublecause 245 D4
Souel 121 E3
Soultzmatt 102 B3
Sous le Dos d'Ane 58 F5
Sous-le-Puits 58 F4
Soussans 83 G6, 85 A2
Sousse 207 B6
Soutelo do Douro 179 F2
South Africa 231
South America 234
South Australia 224, 228–9
Southern Mount 229 D4
Southern Vales 224 E5, 229 A3
Southern Vales Co-op 229 D4
South Esk 249 D5
Souverain Cellars 217 A3
Spain (España) 163
Spannberg 186 C3
Sparkling Vale 226 F2
Sparti 203 E3
Spey 247 C4, 249 C5
Spey Bay 247 A5
Speyburn 247 C3
Speyer 125 D6
Speyside 249 D4
Spielberg 143 B4
Spielfeld 186 G2
Spitz 186 C1
Split 195 D2
Spoleto 157 D4
Sporen 103 C3
Springbank 249 F3
Springton 228 E6
Squinzano 160 C6
Srbija (Serbia) 195 E4
Stainz 186 G1
Stalden 183 C6
Stanhope 226 D3
Stanislaus 219 C2, D2, 215 D2
Stara Planina 199 C1, C2, C3, C4
Stara Zagora 199 D4
Star Hill 253 C4
Starkenburg 135 D4
Staufen 146 F3, 254 D4
Stawell 225 F1
Stefanesti 197 F4
Steige 254 D3
Steiger Dell 137 F1
Steinacker 143 A4
Stein a.d. Donau 189 F3
Steinbach 146 D4
Steinberg, Saar 129 B2
Steinberg, Nahe 136 G4
Steinberg, Rheingau 140 E6
Steinberg Rheinpfalz 143 B4
Steinen 254 E4, F5
Steinmorgen 141 F2
Steinwingert 136 G5
Stein, Würzburg 145 D4, D5
Steffensberg 135 B2, 135 B4
Stellenbosch 231 D2, 233 F2
Stenfanslay 133 C4
Sterea Ellas 203 C3
Sterling Winery 217 A2
Stetten 146 D6, 254 E4
Stift 143 E5
Stirling 249 F4
Stockbridge, Hampshire 236 D3
Stockton 215 D2, 219 C1
Stockwell 228 A5
Stonehaven 249 D6
Stony Hill Winery 217 A2
Straden 186 G2
Strand 231 D2
Stranraer 249 G3
Strasbourg 51 B5, 254 C4
Strass 186 C2
Strathclyde 249 F4
Strathisla 247 C6
Strathmill 247 C6
Strathmore Cambus 249 E4
Strem 186 F3
Stuttgart 125 D2, 146 D5
Subirats 170 B6
Subotica 195 C5
Suceava 197 D4
Südliche Weinstrasse 125 E6
Südsteiermark 186
Suisse 185
Suisse (Schweiz) 254
Sukhindol 199 C3
Sulmona 160 B2
Sulzfeld 145 G4
Sumen 199 B5
Sungurlare 199 C5
Sunny St Helena Winery 217 B4
Sunshine 226 E2
Surinam (Suriname) 234 B2
Suriname 234 B2
Sur Lavelle 59 E3
Sur-les-Grèves 60 E4
Sursee 254 E4
Sury-en-Vaux 111 E2
Süsskopf 143 E5
Sutter Home Winery 217 B3
Suzon 87 A4
Svetozarevo 195 E5
Svishtov 199 B3
Swan Hill 225 F1, 225 F2
Swellendam 231 D4
Switzerland 184, 185
Switzerland (Schweiz) 185, 254
Switzerland-Valais and Vaud 182
Sydney 225 E5
Sylvaner 153 D4
Sympérieux 113 C2
Syracuse, Sicily 160 G4
Syria (As-Sūrīyah) 208 E5
Syrie (As-Sūrīyah) 208 E5
Szamorodni 190 A4
Szarvas 190 C3
Szeged 190 C3
Szegilong 191 C4
Szekszárd 190 C2
Szerencs 191 C3
Szigliget 192 F2
Szilvâni 190 C3
Szolnok 190 B3
Szombathely 190 B1
Szürkebarát 190 C2

T

Tabajete, Caserio 165 B2
Tabanon 251 C4
Tábua 177 G4
Tacna 234 C1
Tadousse-Ussau 245 E3
Tagus (Tajo) 163 C2
Tahbilk 225 F3
Taille-Pieds 59 F4
Tain 249 C4
Tain-l'Hermitage 112 B6, 114 C3
Taittinger 101 C5
Tajo 163 C2
Talagante 235 B2
Talca 234 C1, 235 D2
Talence 72 F3
Talence 87 B3

Gazetteer (additional)

Index (additional)

Map Director: Harold Fullard
Art Director: Peter Kindersley
Editorial Director: Christopher Dorling
Assistant Designer: Roger Bristow
Chief Cartographer: Jack Briggs
Text Editor: Ann Barr
Map Editor: Averil Macintyre

Illustrators

Roger Bristow
David Cook
David Fryer
Gilchrist Studios
Patrick Leeson
Michael McGuinness
Vernon Mills

Shirley Parfitt
Charles Pickard
Quad
Colin Rose
Diagram
Rodney Shackell

Photographs

Sequence, left to right, top to bottom from A

6 Royal Botanical Gardens, Kew
9 National Gallery, London
12 B Michael Holford Library
13 A BPC Library; B,C Reading Museum
14 A Bodleian Library; C John Rylands Library; E Michael Holford Library
15 C Photographie Giraudon, Paris
16 A André Simon collection; B Richard Winslade
18 B,C,D,E,I Pierre Mackiewicz
28 A Harry Cullum; B,C Pierre Mackiewicz
30 A Photographie Giraudon
31 B Historisches Museum der Pfalz
33 A Richard Winslade
35 French National Tourist Office
36 John Hedgecoe; Bacchus model by Alistair Bowtell
37 Photographs of Michael Broadbent, wine director of Christie's, by John Hedgecoe
38 A,B,C,D Richard Winslade
39 A John Hedgecoe; B Richard Winslade
40–41 John Hedgecoe, photographs of lockets by Michael Busselle
42–43 John Hedgecoe; punch bowl, N. Bloom & Son, London; decanter labels, Wyard Druitt & Co, London
49 Hugh Johnson
50 John Bulmer
52 Jean Michot
56 B,E Jean Michot; C,D,F Guy Gravett
58 A,B,D,E Hugh Johnson; C Guy Gravett
61 Hugh Johnson
62 Guy Gravett
63 Hugh Johnson
65 Guy Gravett
66–67 A Guy Gravett; B Hugh Johnson
68 A,B Picturepoint
70 Guy Gravett
73 Guy Gravett
76 A Guy Gravett; B International Distillers & Vintners, London
78 Guy Gravett
80 B Marc Riboud
82 Les Éditions des Deux Coqs d'Or
86 A Grants of St James's; B Guy Gravett
88 Guy Gravett
90 A,B,C Guy Gravett
92 A Marc Riboud; B Guy Gravett
94 Guy Gravett
97 Aerofilms
98 Daily Telegraph Magazine
100 B Comité Interprofessionnel du Vin de Champagne
102–103 A Ian Yeomans; B,C,D Comité Interprofessionnel du Vin d'Alsace
107 Guy Gravett
108 Guy Gravett
111 French National Tourist Office
113 Editions J. Cellard

114–115 A Editions des Deux Coqs d'Or; B Guy Gravett; C Conseil Interprofessionnel des vins des Côtes du Rhône
116 French National Tourist Office
122 Colorific
123 Picturepoint
128 Bavaria-Verlag
130 Bavaria-Verlag
132 A Hugh Johnson; B Adam Woolfitt
133 Toni Schneiders
134–135 Deinhard & Co
136 Staatlichen Weinbaudomönen Niederhäusen-Schlossböckelheim
137 Picturepoint
138 A Peter Hallgarten; B,C Editions des Deux Coqs d'Or
139 Peter Hallgarten
142 A Editions des Deux Coqs d'Or; B,C,D Urbanus-Fotopress
144 Adam Woolfitt
145 Georg Christ
147 Hugh Johnson
150 Guy Gravett
152 Italian State Tourist Department
155 Camera Press
156 Paul Popper Ltd
158 Hugh Johnson
161 Camera Press
162 Guy Gravett
164 A Guy Gravett
166 Guy Gravett
168 Picturepoint
170 Michael Holford Library
171 Western Licence Suppliers
173 Picturepoint
174 Guy Gravett
176 A Hugh Johnson; B Guy Gravett
178–179 Guy Gravett
180–181 Guy Gravett
182–183 Camera Press
184 A,B Swiss National Tourist Office
187 A,B Austrian State Tourist Department
189 Radio Times Hulton Picture Library
191 Editions des Deux Coqs d'Or
192–193 A,C Monimpex
194 A David Ross; B Guy Gravett
197 A Romanian Press Office; B Camera Press
198 A D. C. Williamson; B Camera Press
200 Novosti Press Agency
201 Peter Keen
202 A Guy Gravett; B Greek National Tourist Office
205 Guy Gravett
206 B Paul Almasy
209 M. E. Archive
210 British Museum
211 Wine Institute
213 Wine Institute
214 Wine Institute
216 Hugh Johnson
219 Wine Institute
220 A Wine Institute
223 Taylor Wine Co
224 Gramp's Orlando
226 New South Wales Government Office
227 George Rainbird
228–229 John Hedgecoe
230 KWV
232 KWV
234 A Anglo-Chilean Society; B Picturepoint; C Evans Brothers
236 Guy Gravett
237 Scotch Whisky Association
242 A Hugh Johnson; B,C Martell
244 BNIA André Canal
246 A Scotch Whisky Association; B Hugh Johnson
248 A,B,C Distillers Co Ltd
250–251 Photo Yves Alexandre, Paris
252–253 Bourbon Institute
254 Swiss National Tourist Office
255 Guy Gravett